Perfektionismus der Autonomie

HegelForum
Studien

Herausgegeben von

Annemarie Gethmann-Siefert
Alain Patrick Olivier
Michael Quante
Elisabeth Weisser-Lohmann

Wissenschaftlicher Beirat

Paul Cobben
Paolo D'Angelo
Axel Honneth
Jussi Kotkarvirta
Jeong-Im Kwon
Herta Nagl-Docekal
Robert B. Pippin
Erzsébet Rózsa
Norbert Waszek

Douglas Moggach, Nadine Mooren,
Michael Quante (Hg.)

Perfektionismus der Autonomie

Wilhelm Fink

Bibliografische Information der Deutschen Nationalbibliothek

Die Deutsche Nationalbibliothek verzeichnet diese Publikation in der Deutschen Nationalbibliografie; detaillierte bibliografische Daten sind im Internet über http://dnb.d-nb.de abrufbar.

Alle Rechte vorbehalten. Dieses Werk sowie einzelne Teile desselben sind urheberrechtlich geschützt. Jede Verwertung in anderen als den gesetzlich zugelassenen Fällen ist ohne vorherige schriftliche Zustimmung des Verlags nicht zulässig.

© 2020 Wilhelm Fink Verlag, ein Imprint der Brill-Gruppe
(Koninklijke Brill NV, Leiden, Niederlande; Brill USA Inc., Boston MA, USA; Brill Asia Pte Ltd, Singapore; Brill Deutschland GmbH, Paderborn, Deutschland)

Internet: www.fink.de

Einbandgestaltung: Evelyn Ziegler, München
Herstellung: Brill Deutschland GmbH, Paderborn

ISBN 978-3-7705-6284-8 (hardback)
ISBN 978-3-8467-6284-4 (e-book)

Inhalt

1. Spontaneity, Autonomy, and Perfection. Historical and Systematic Considerations 1
   Douglas Moggach

2. Rights-Perfectionism, from Kant's *Grundlegung* to Politics. Kantian Debates 29
   Maximiliano Hernández Marcos

3. Teleology and Perfection. Law, Freedom and the Search for Unity, from Kant to the Post-Kantians 69
   Luca Fonnesu

4. Herder. Perfectibility, Plasticity, and Pluralism 89
   Stefanie Buchenau & Douglas Moggach

5. Schiller, das Gute am Schönen oder warum wir uns auf zweifache Weise verfehlen können 117
   Eva Schürmann

6. The Reciprocal Cultivation of Self and State. Fichte's Civic Perfectionism 139
   Dean Moyar

7. Hegelian Perfectionism and Freedom 163
   Loughlin Gleeson & Heikki Ikäheimo

8. Ergänzung und Überschreiten von Hegels politischer Philosophie durch Eduard Gans 183
   Norbert Waszek

9. 'The Republic of Self-Consciousness'. Bruno Bauer's Post-Kantian Perfectionism 203
   Michael Kuur Sørensen & Douglas Moggach

10. Perfektionistische Gehalte der Rugeschen Geschichtsphilosophie? Historische Zuordnungsfrage und systematische Herausforderung 227
    Tim Rojek

| 11. | Karl Marx – ein postkantischer Perfektionist? 245
Michael Quante |

| 12. | The Non-Essentialist Perfectionism of Max Stirner 269
David Leopold |

| 13. | Søren Kierkegaard's Critique of Eudaimonism
and Autonomy 291
Roe Fremstedal |

| 14. | Antipaternalismus und Perfektionismus in
Mills Axiologie der Selbstentwicklung 309
Simon Derpmann |

| 15. | Becoming Artists of One's Own Life. Perfectionist Thinking
in Friedrich Nietzsche 331
Maria Cristina Fornari |

| 16. | Neukantianische Autonomie. Hermann Cohens Beitrag 351
Myriam Bienenstock |

| 17. | Theodor W. Adorno. Education for Autonomy 371
Samir Gandesha |

| 18. | Systematischer Ausblick 399
Nadine Mooren & Michael Quante |

Zu den Autorinnen und Autoren 405

Personenregister 411

Spontaneity, Autonomy, and Perfection
Historical and Systematic Considerations

Douglas Moggach

German Idealism from Kant onwards achieves a revolution in ethical and social thought, introducing new concepts of freedom and personhood,[1] and reconfiguring the domain of political debate; but this revolution has deep historical roots. In the German territories, political theories of Kantian inspiration emerge in the eighteenth century through a long process of engagement with the heritage of Leibniz, represented especially by Christian Wolff and his school. These debates are framed by the opposition between the contending political aims of perfection and freedom. The decisive question is the extent to which the state ought authoritatively to prescribe, and impose, a substantive vision of the good life for its subjects. Wolff's theory of political perfection is broadly inspired by Leibniz, and is reminiscent of Aristotle's doctrine of *eudaimonia*,[2] or happiness as fulfilment of natural capabilities. On this account, the state must actively promote the felicity or thriving of its members, including their material needs, and also their higher intellectual and spiritual aspirations. The Kantian criticism of Wolff rejects the paternalistic state and its theoretical basis in the ethics of perfection, in favour of spontaneous, self-determining activity; and it derives the idea of a juridical order which upholds the principle of free, rightful interaction. Kant's strictures constitute a decisive repudiation of the previous tradition, and the effect of this shift in orientation is to disempower political perfectionism of the Wolffian kind.

As this volume illustrates, political thought in the Germanic lands pursued this critical path throughout the 1780's and 1790's, and well beyond. And yet in the process of distancing from the older perfectionism, a renewal and transformation of perfectionist ethics occurs, and it occurs among Kantians themselves. What is at stake is the development of a new approach, which focuses not on the substantive goods toward which human nature putatively tends, but rather on the perfection of autonomy itself. Its starting point is the new concept of rational self-legislation which the Kantian account of practical reason

---

* The author gratefully acknowledges the support of the Social Sciences and Humanities Research Council of Canada for this project.
1 Jaeschke (1990), 2.
2 Cf. Aristotle, *Nicomachean Ethics*, Book I; Kenny (1977), 25-32.

had revealed, and new interrogations of its possible field of application: it is the enhancement of the capacity for free, rational self-determination, and not any given substantial end, that defines the objective of this perfectionism after Kant. Accompanying this change are close explorations of the objective, institutional, and intersubjective conditions for the practice of freedom, and demands for the reform, extension, and consolidation of these conditions. It is in this broad sense that we employ the concept of autonomy-perfectionism here. We depart from the strict Kantian usage of autonomy as moral self-legislation, but broaden the concept to include capacities for rational agency in general, and particularly the transformation of the political and social sphere, in the name of freedom.

Some of these motifs are to be found in Kant's later work itself.[3] Strains of the new perfectionism can already be detected among early adherents of Kantian philosophy, notably Wilhelm von Humboldt, whose work is addressed briefly in the present chapter. These ideas achieve explicit formulation in the works of Schiller and Fichte in the 1790's,[4] and persist in Hegel[5] and the Hegelian School and far beyond, into Marx, neo-Kantianism, and twentieth-century critical theory.[6] The tradition is not limited to the German territories. John Stuart Mill is included here as an example of its articulation elsewhere, though in this case its origin is not independent, since Mill expressly acknowledges his debt to Humboldt in shaping his views on individuality and liberty.[7] In these versions, with elaborations, exceptions, and complications that form the subject of this book, the central idea is that of spontaneous, inner-directed activity, and the context for its effective exercise. This idea imparts a measure of unity to the diverse thinkers considered here. The young Marx, for example, conceives labour as spontaneous action linked both to freedom and to need-satisfaction; the solution to alienated labour lies not merely in a more just distribution of products, but in the transformation of the ways in which labour is performed.[8] Kierkegaard seeks an authentic expression of interior selfhood

---

3 Fonnesu (2004), 49-61; and Maximiliano Hernández Marcos, "Rights-Perfectionism, From Kant's *Grundlegung* to Politics. Kantian Debates", in this volume.
4 See, in this volume, Luca Fonnesu, "Teleology and Perfection. Law, Freedom and the Search for Unity, from Kant to the Post-Kantians"; Dean Moyar, "The Reciprocal Cultivation of Self and State. Fichte's Civic Perfectionism"; Eva Schürmann, „Schiller, das Gute am Schönen oder warum wir uns auf zweifache Weise verfehlen können".
5 Loughlin Gleeson and Heikki Ikäheimo, "Hegelian Perfectionism and Freedom", in this volume.
6 Samir Gandesha, "Theodor W. Adorno: Education for Autonomy", in this volume.
7 Mill (1991 [1859]), 64; Simon Derpmann, „Antipaternalismus und Perfektionismus in Mills Axiologie der Selbstentwicklung", in this volume.
8 Michael Quante, „Karl Marx – ein postkantischer Perfektionist?", in this volume.

and the proper grounds for norms that might bind its activity.[9] Nietzsche in contrast divorces spontaneous self-determination from notions of rational autonomy,[10] while the neo-Kantian Hermann Cohen rigorously reunites these terms.[11] Typically, in this approach, too, the proper role for political and social institutions is to maintain and consolidate the conditions for free agency itself, extending and reforming the juridical order (or transforming economic relations) as the forum in which the spontaneous activities of its members occur. In these reformulations, the harmonisation of diverse and possibly conflicting interests is conceived as a work of practical reason, or an end to be achieved, and not (in contrast to the Leibnizian tradition) as a theoretical or metaphysical presupposition. This practical task involves the rational critique of existing political, economic, and social relations, and the test of their conformity with standards of rightful interaction. These evaluative standards are not fixed, but they also evolve historically, and the process of history can be understood as the ongoing approximation of objective social and political relations to new and richer conceptions of freedom and right.

1. Leibniz

In his lucid histories of modern philosophy, Ernst Cassirer stressed Leibniz's role as the genuine initiator of the traditions of German Idealism.[12] Through his ideas of self-determining activity and its rights, Leibniz provided the theoretical impulse which is articulated and systematised in Kant and in subsequent idealist thought.[13] For Cassirer, the fruitfulness of the Leibnizian conceptions of activity, and their ethical implications, are only fully grasped by Kant, rather than by Leibniz's immediate successors like Christian Wolff. Leibniz's reception history in the eighteenth century is marked by close critical engagement, wherein the basic concepts are not discarded, but transformed. Kant characterises his own work as the true apology for Leibniz, reclaiming its most vital elements, while according these a new systematic context and meaning.[14] At the root of German debates about perfection and freedom lies the Leibnizian

---

9   Roe Fremstedal, "Søren Kierkegaard's Critique of Eudaimonism and Autonomy", in this volume.
10 Maria Cristina Fornari, "Becoming Artists of One's Own Life. Perfectionist Thinking in Friedrich Nietzsche", in this volume.
11 Myriam Bienenstock „Neukantianische Autonomie: Hermann Cohens Beitrag", in this volume.
12 Cassirer (1962 [1902]), 457f.
13 Cassirer (2001 [1917]).
14 Kant (1923 [1793]), Ak. 8, 250; Allison (2012), 189-200.

concept of spontaneity, which is subject to intense scrutiny and reformulation by Kant and the post-Kantians. The new perfectionism arises in this encounter.

Leibniz had developed a dynamic account of the individual (or monad, in his later designation) as the source of self-directed change, in constant transition through states of awareness and perception, whereby its inner content is progressively revealed. This sequence is governed by a unique internal law of development, distinct for every self.[15] Spontaneity is the capacity of subjects to be the self-initiating cause of change, enacting inner imperatives, and not simply determined by external natural causality, as Enlightenment materialism holds; we will return to this question more systematically below. The perfection of the systemic order in which the activity of monads occurs is constituted by this ceaseless exposition of implicit properties, and by the irreplicable character and uniqueness of each agent, making a specific contribution to the universe of striving.

Leibniz defines perfection in two distinct ways: first, as the full realisation and exposition of implicit content, or the complete concept;[16] and secondly as the unity of unity and multiplicity.[17] Such an articulated unity occurs when each constitutive element achieves its thorough and individualised expression, while being harmonised and balanced by a singular directive principle, which endows the whole with unity, form, and coherence. In subsequent thinking, the two dimensions of Leibnizian perfection come to be distinguished more clearly, an absolute notion as the achievement of potentiality, and a relative notion of unifying difference.[18] Each of these conceptions will play a role in the development of perfectionism after Kant.

Leibniz further contends that the community of monads subsists in pre-established harmony, on the perfectionist metaphysical premise that only the system of monads which exhibits the highest degree of mutual compatibility, or the unity of unity and multiplicity, has been actualised, but these monads co-exist without effective reciprocal interdetermination, since Leibniz's particular notion of spontaneity precludes the admissibility of external causes. While Leibnizian monads are said to be constantly adjusting to each other, the dynamics of these adjustments and relations remains obscure. Kant's own redefinition of spontaneity will allow for real interaction, on the basis of which

---

15   *Leibniz-Thomasius, Correspondance* (1993), 55-117; Leibniz (1991 [1720]), esp. Section 11-13; Rutherford (2005), 156-180.
16   Leibniz (1969), 167: "By perfection I mean every simple quality which is positive and absolute, or which expresses whatever it expresses without any limits."
17   Leibniz to Wolff, May 18, 1715, cited and translated in Beiser (2009), 35, n. 16: "Perfection is the harmony of things, that is, the state of agreement or identity in variety."
18   Hernández Marcos, "Rights-Perfectionism", in this volume.

the reciprocal relations of the sphere of right become possible. In the Kantian re-ordering, the co-existence and compatibility of interests become central concerns of practical reason.

2. Christian Wolff: Political Perfectionism

The autonomy-perfectionism deriving from Kant emerges in polemical encounters with a particular elaboration of Leibniz developed by Christian Wolff and his school, predominant in the German territories for much of the eighteenth century. Wolff's own complex relations with Leibniz cannot be addressed here.[19] It suffices for our purposes to note that for Wolff the ethical and political question is to determine the conditions under which an essentially Leibnizian concept of spontaneity can be both activated and directed toward the goal of perfection. Wolff is exemplary of the older perfectionism, which has *eudaimonia* or thriving as its object.

In Wolff's theory of enlightened absolutism, the goal of the state is the happiness of its subjects.[20] In common with other early-modern natural law theories, Wolff holds that there is an original state of nature, prior to the establishment of political institutions or private property. The distinctive claim of the Wolffian school, however, is that this natural condition is not primarily characterised by the permanent threat of conflict and violent death, as in Thomas Hobbes,[21] but by mental and physical stagnation. It is precisely this inability to cultivate latent capacities for self-improvement and for co-operation[22] that imposes an obligation on individuals to leave behind their torpid natural existence, and to submit to political authority. Formed through a social compact, the state is authorised to promote the felicity of its members. This end is understood broadly, not only as the satisfaction of basic needs, but as educational and moral growth.[23] Thus, like Aristotelian *eudaimonia*,[24] perfection for Wolff has physical, intellectual, and spiritual aspects. Like Aristotle, Wolff defines a natural end toward which human beings tend, and invests that end with substantive content. He takes perfection primarily in its absolute sense, as the realisation of implicit content or of latent potentiality; in this respect too he resembles Aristotle. The relative sense of perfection, the unification of

---

19   See, for example, Corr, (1975), 241-262. See also Dreitzel (1992); and Klippel (1976).
20   Wolff (1969 [1754]), 43, 106-108; Wolff (1988 [1758]), 16, 41.
21   Hobbes (2012 [1651]), Part I, ch. 13.
22   Wolff (1969 [1754]), 972.
23   Wolff (1969 [1754]), 186-189; Wolff (1988 [1758]), 88-89.
24   See above, note 2.

the diverse, is less central to him. Yet, unlike Aristotle, a contract is necessary to effect the passage to the state from simpler forms of association, pre-existent in the state of nature, such as households. Wolff thus strives to accommodate Aristotle within modern natural law theory.

In its physical aspects, Wolffian perfection involves the duty to labour, and to contribute productively to society; but in order for this duty to be operative, the state must undertake to provide its subjects with adequate food, housing, and living conditions, including clean air and water.[25] Physical perfection as Wolff describes it has affinities with a particular current of political economy known as cameralism, which was also widely disseminated in Prussia and elsewhere at this time.[26] In contrast to mercantilist policies pursued by England and France at the time, which were based on access to colonies for raw materials and markets,[27] cameralism stressed the development of the local productive forces, mobilising available natural resources, and fostering and retaining a skilled workforce. The Wolffian programme of enlightened absolutism accords with these priorities, and perfection has a marked economic and demographic component.[28] Moreover, material wellbeing is partly dependent on education and training, which, as intellectual perfection, are also the purview of the enlightened state. Spiritual wellbeing too is central for Wolff, though here the role he ascribes to the state appears less clearly defined, and his early defence of the possibility of a purely rationalistic ethic led to a serious controversy with German Pietists, ending in his temporary exile from Prussia, before his recall and ennoblement by Frederick the Great.[29]

The Wolffian tutelary state, with its highly interventionist policies, nonetheless has certain recognised limits. These arise not because of an idea of individual natural rights that are retained against the state,[30] as in John Locke,[31] for example, but because of fiscal considerations and questions of efficiency. The local redress of social problems (such as indigence) is to be favoured, when possible, over standardised, central interventions,[32] because the former is more flexible, and better attuned to specific situations. Wolff thus heralds developments that have come into European practice as the principle of

---

25 Wolff (1969 [1754]), 112-116; Wolff (1988 [1758]), 32, 36-39. See also Wolff (1971 [1721]), 224.
26 Seppel/ Tribe (2017).
27 Tribe (1988); Backhaus (1998).
28 In contrast, this programme has been described as an antimodernising resacralisation of politics: Hunter (2001).
29 Schneewind (1998), 442-444.
30 Klippel (1998), 81.
31 Locke (1980 [1690]), esp. ch. 2, 3, 8.
32 Wolff (1971 [1721]), 383-385.

subsidiarity,³³ the proximity of administrative agencies to the sources of the problem addressed. Wolff frames the issue as a pragmatic restriction on political authority,³⁴ and not as a matter of fundamental right; thus, he differs fundamentally from later Kantian approaches.

In his account of state-induced perfection, Wolff does not repudiate the central Leibnizian idea of spontaneity, since subjects' activities are still governed by teleological principles and ideas of goods to be achieved, and are not merely determined by mechanistic laws. He insists, however, that such spontaneity must be stimulated, harmonised, and directed by an external cause, namely the enlightened ruler and his agents, in order to attain a social order of maximal individual and collective happiness.³⁵ The Wolffian tutelary state becomes the target of Kantian denunciations as a debilitating despotism.³⁶ In Kant's critique, the idea of right is fundamental. The vindication of right is part of his profound reconfiguration of the field of practical reason.

3. Kantian Critiques

In his 1785 text, *Groundwork of the Metaphysics of Morals*, Kant outlines a critique of Leibniz's and Wolff's perfectionist ethical systems. He describes them as forms of rational heteronomy,³⁷ because they posit a given, metaphysically-determined order of perfection to which the moral wills of subjects must conform. The defect of such systems is that they consider the will as determining itself teleologically in order to attain an external end, rather than deontologically, through self-given laws of unconditional validity. It is the externality of the end that characterises all heteronomous systems. Kant distinguishes rational heteronomy from the empirical heteronomy of Hobbes, for example, because the former is not based on gratifying sensuous impulses, but on an idea of perfection, taken as an external determinant of the will. But Kant further distinguishes Leibniz's system from his own deontological position because Leibnizian ethics orients itself to the production of an extrinsic state of affairs, rather than to the intrinsic quality of the moral will.³⁸ The ethical worth of an act is not to be measured by its results, even its contribution to the perfection

---

33 Backhaus (1999).
34 Schneewind (1998), 432-444.
35 Wolff (1971 [1721]), 264.
36 Kant (1923 [1793]), Ak. 8: 290-91. On the Kant-Wolff relation, see Grapotte and Prunea-Bretonnet (2011). See also Jauernig (2011), 289-309.
37 Kant (1908 [1788]), Ak. 5: 32-41 and Kant (1903 [1785]), Ak. 4: 441-443.
38 Kant (1903 [1785]), Ak. 4: 441-443.

of the social or the cosmological order, but depends instead on its underlying maxim, and its enactment of the categorical imperative to treat all individuals as ends in themselves. In his text of 1793, "Theory and Practice," Kant draws explicit political consequences from this imperative. The state may not rightfully determine the ends of its subjects in their quest for happiness, as long as the pursuit of these ends does not impede the freedom of others. He decries the Wolffian paternalistic state as a reprehensible form of despotic rule, which reduces its subjects to the condition of incompetents or minors, rather than acknowledging their status as rational, autonomous agents.[39]

Kant's repudiation of ethical and political perfectionism raised the vital question of the ends and limits of state authority. It is not that the legitimacy of the state itself was called into question among the early Kantians, but rather that the range and contents of permissible political activity had to be thought anew. In the long interim between the publication of the *Groundwork* in 1785 and the definitive formulation that Kant offered in his *Metaphysics of Morals* of 1797, his adherents explored various combinations of spontaneity and perfection, producing different configurations of Kantian and Leibnizian principles.[40] These theoretical moves can be considered as shaping the contours of post-Kantian perfectionism. Among the first to intervene, already in 1785, Gottlieb Hufeland (1760-1817) identifies the difficulty which Kant's *Groundwork* poses for any potential theory of right: if there exists a categorical imperative to treat individuals always as ends in themselves, on what basis can the coercion of rational beings, and therewith the possibility of a political order, be justified?[41] Hufeland proposes a Leibnizian solution to this Kantian problem. He derives the right of coercion from the moral law of perfectibility: constraint is legitimate only to the extent that it reduces external obstacles to systemic perfection and thriving, and thus achieves a higher moral good. Thus, juridical constraint may contribute to collective perfection, in its first, absolute sense, as fulfilment of potentiality, by fostering the maximal development of all the members of the political community.[42] In framing his response, Hufeland is possibly influenced by J.G. Feder, his professor at Göttingen, who had earlier advanced a consequentialist defence of coercion through its contribution to perfection,[43] but without Hufeland's Kantian interrogation of its permissibility.

---

39 Kant (1923 [1793]), Ak. 8: 290-291.
40 For a discussion of the polemics of this period, see Hernández Marcos (1995), 243-280.
41 Kersting (1984).
42 Hufeland (1785).
43 Feder (1773); Cesa (2000), 24-25.

Hufeland's first book, as well as his second of 1790,[44] opened a lively debate within the Kantian school. Contemporary critics like K.L. Reinhold (1757-1823) contested Hufeland's conclusion, on the grounds that his perfectionist arguments were incompatible with Kantian ideas.[45] Reinhold distinguished material and formal principles of right, and argued that in a Kantian juridical order, the only possible justification of political coercion would be its elimination of obstacles to the *freedom* of the self and others, not its enhancement of their moral capacities or material satisfactions.[46] Here the premise of post-Kantian perfectionism is clearly introduced. In Kant's own initial contribution to the debate,[47] he contended that Hufeland conflated rights and duties, so that the possession of a right would imply its obligatory exercise. In his review, Kant rejects this conception of right, anticipating a distinction between right and morality that will be fully elaborated only a decade later in the *Metaphysics of Morals*.[48]

Profoundly immersed in Kant's *Critique of Judgement*, published in 1790, Friedrich Schiller approaches the issue of the ends of the state from an aesthetic perspective. He takes the Wolffian tutelary state as a form of imposed unity, which is brittle and lifeless, because it is not animated by an internal energy.[49] By seeking to secure perfection through constraint rather than consent, Wolff cuts perfection off from its sources in freedom. Schiller distinguishes the perfect from the beautiful: perfection means the achievement of the complete concept, or the objective realisation of implicit content, but in beauty, external form is determined by inner essence. "The perfect, represented with freedom, is transformed directly into the beautiful."[50] The perfection of the political community must arise from an internal source, manifesting the freedom of subjects who in their interactions seek harmony and mutual recognition; and such perfection must take seriously the second, relative meaning of the term, the preservation of diversity within unity, which theories like Wolff's had insufficiently acknowledged. The proper accommodation of social diversity is for Schiller among the central tasks of the modern state.[51]

Wilhelm von Humboldt's approach to politics shares with Schiller this endorsement of diversity; and like Reinhold, he holds that coercion is justified

---

44 Hufeland (1790); second edition (1795).
45 Rohls (2004), 41 n. 121; 49.
46 Reinhold (1792), 445-460.
47 Kant (1923 [1786]), Ak. 8: 127-130.
48 Kant (1907 [1797]), Ak 8: 205-213.
49 Schiller (1967 [1795]), letter XVI.
50 http://www.wissen-im-netz.info/literatur/schiller/briefe/vSchiller/1793/179302231.htm
51 See Schürmann on Schiller in this volume.

only to the extent that it contributes to freedom, not to perfection. The entire project of his early text, *Ideen zu einem Versuch, die Grenzen der Wirksamkeit des Staates zu bestimmen* [*The Limits of State Action*], is to maintain maximal variety and energy in civil society, and to resist tendencies toward standardisation and uniformity. The unity afforded by the state must be so constructed that it maintains and protects the conditions for individual agency, while interfering as little as possible in personal quests for happiness.[52] Humboldt's originality lies in his radical anti-interventionism, which has both Kantian and Leibnizian aspects. What he derives from Leibniz is profoundly different from Wolff, but equally determinant.

Humboldt reads Kant's critique of perfectionism in the *Groundwork* as implying a categorical prohibition of state intervention in the activities of its members, except to protect individual rights and property. The happiness of its citizens is not the proper object of the state, whether in its physical, intellectual, or spiritual dimensions. For Humboldt, individuals ought to experience minimal constraint within their own designated spheres of activity, and in pursuit of their own private conceptions of the good. Their choices ought not to be coerced or homogenised by the state, which is to uphold the juridical order, but not to intrude into it. Persons are ends in themselves, and must never be treated as means for the satisfaction of others, even in the interest of a collective benefit, as in the Wolffian tutelary state (or, indeed, in Hufeland's account).[53] Humboldt imports the Kantian moral imperative into the political arena, and interprets it in a most restrictive manner. Other Kantians, and Kant himself, will offer alternative readings, as we shall see.

If the Kantian categorical imperative underlies Humboldt's political reflections, his idea of what is involved in spontaneous freedom remains closer to Leibniz's: each individual enacts a unique, personal law of development that must not be hindered by external impediments, and that is, in principle, compatible with the free development of others, or at least capable of mutual attunement.[54] The constant changes and adaptations that constitute the life-activity of the self ought not to be imposed from without, but to be expressive of inner motivations and insights. In adopting this fundamentally Leibnizian view of spontaneous action, Humboldt resists the interpretation that Wolff had imparted, the need for external stimulus and co-ordination. Humboldt maintains further that if unconstrained, the social sphere will exhibit maximal variety, as each person pursues an independent path toward the development of

---

52   Humboldt (1969), 32.
53   Humboldt (1969), 32.
54   Leibniz (1991 [1720]), sections 10-22, 49, 50.

capacities. He thus repudiates the Wolffian interventionist system in the name of a dynamic, spontaneous order. In opposing paternalistic provision by the state, Humboldt draws on Leibniz' sense of the self-determining monad, and on the idea of relative perfection, the unity of unity and multiplicity. He places these under the Kantian categorical imperative, narrowly interpreted as prohibiting welfare measures, state economic initiatives, and public schooling.[55]

The conclusions that Humboldt draws from Kant are not, however, undisputed, even by Kant himself. While the distinction that he makes in "Theory and Practice" between political and economic equality might seem to align him with Humboldt,[56] Kant authorises a broader range of legitimate political functions. In the same text of 1793, he admits state interventions in education (which Humboldt had expressly precluded), and advocates the prudent introduction of welfare measures to secure the loyalty of the population in a world of international rivalries.[57] Most importantly, he promotes ongoing legal reforms, as gradual approximations to the ideal of reason.[58] The state is not only to uphold the sphere of right, but to perfect it. Kant's position in this regard represents neither the sacralisation of politics, nor a reversion to Wolffian consequentialism, but progress in freedom. It can be taken to contain many of the features of autonomy-perfectionism, outlined more systematically in what follows. It is in this spirit, too, that Fichte's political reflections can be seen. Among the lessons that Fichte draws from Kant in the 1790's is the necessity for processes of social creation,[59] or transformation, which consolidate and perfect the domain of rightful interactions. For Fichte, the justification of a system of wide-ranging political intervention is not that it makes its subjects happy or moral, but that it makes freedom accessible to all.[60]

Freedom for Fichte is the independent causality that each subject exerts in the sense-world, modifying it in light of ideas and needs, and thus securing a closer accord between the demands of reason and its objective realisations.[61] The goals pursued by subjects must be self-determined, and, in this sense, spontaneous. In order for their purposes to be effectively accomplished, all subjects must have access, by right, to the necessary material and instrumental means to effect changes in the world of objectivity. Fichte defines the right to labour,

---

55   Humboldt later revises his views substantially. Beiser (2011), 167-213, describes him as a "German Proteus".
56   Kant (1923 [1793]), *Ak.* 8: 290-293.
57   Kant (1923 [1793]), *Ak.* 8: 298-300; Kaufman (1999), 28-30.
58   Hernandez Marcos, "Rights-Perfectionism", in this volume.
59   Maesschalck (1996).
60   Fichte (1988), 37-141.
61   Fichte (1971), 9.

and to live from the fruits of one's labour, as *the* fundamental right. Such a right is thoroughly egalitarian: none may rightfully live in luxury or idleness while others live in penury, denied the essential conditions for their own self-activity. Fichte thus connects labour to freedom as well as to need-satisfaction, anticipating the thematic of alienated labour in Karl Marx.[62] Fichte envisages the state as the promoter of freedom in this sense: its task is not merely to defend the existing distribution of property, as on Humboldt's account, but to secure justice through economic reform, guaranteeing to each citizen the conditions for the effective exercise of right. The detailed system of political oversight and regulation that Fichte describes in his *Closed Commercial State* of 1800 is not intended, as in Wolff, to foster happiness or maximise production, but to sustain the practice of individual rights by all citizens. Fichte thus partakes in the Kantian reorientation of political thought, but differs from Humboldt in his concern for equal access to the material conditions of freedom. Fichte acknowledges that Humboldt's emphasis on freedom and self-development is correct,[63] but he holds that a strictly non-interventionist political system would only be legitimate if the underlying distribution of property itself met the critical standards of distributive justice. Where there is extreme concentration of wealth, dire poverty and unemployment, the social system stands condemned, and there exists an ethical imperative to change it. Nor, as Fichte informs us elsewhere, can irrational institutions such as serfdom and the enforced subordination of labour be justified simply in virtue of their longevity, as the contemporary Historical School of Law was attempting to do.[64] Despite its intrusive and coercive features, Fichte's *Closed Commercial State* is not a reversion to Wolff, but a defence of the institutions that Fichte thinks are required to enable the universal practice of freedom. Its pervading spirit is that of Kant, and its execution represents an early, full statement of post-Kantian perfectionism.

In subsequent elaborations, history for German idealism is the progressive expression of practical reason, as the ongoing process of securing the accord of subjectivity and objectivity. In the historical process, ideas of freedom and personality, and the institutional and relational exigencies they impose, are themselves modified and perfected. For Hegel the standards of rational willing too are inscribed in a developmental history of reason; the *Phenomenology of Spirit*[65] traces such a path, and the *Philosophy of Right* seeks to articulate

---

62 Moggach (2013), 82-107; Quante (2009), 209-31.
63 Fichte (1971), 39.
64 Fichte (1845 [1794]), 313.
65 Hegel (2008 [1807]).

the rational institutional requirements of the modern age, along with its unresolved inner tensions.[66] The dialectic of the will in the latter text (§5-§7) expounds Hegel's conception of spontaneity as the capacity, first, to abstract from externality, and then to re-engage in it in a transformative manner, such that both the self and the object assume new properties and configurations. The will and ideas of freedom are enriched by the passage through the domains of formal right, inward morality, and ethical life (*Sittlichkeit*), within whose practices, institutions, and relations Kantian autonomy becomes concrete.[67] Hegel's conception of history can be viewed as a process of perfection, now understood as the history of freedom and of reason itself, propelled by the dialectical unfolding of spontaneity. A fundamental consideration is also the repudiation of naturalism, which, though raising issues of far broader scope, can be taken here in a relevant sense to mean the idea of a (relatively) fixed human nature,[68] or else the assimilation of human action to natural-scientific explanatory paradigm, such as early-modern mechanism.[69] A repudiation of naturalism in these senses is also emblematic of much of the new perfectionist approach, and is not specific to Hegel (Herder forms an exception in the present volume; he appears here as representative of the older, but much revised perfectionism, but his work points up important aspects of the new).[70] Hegel distinguishes process in the natural world, which simply effects the gradual unfolding of a given, implicit content, from the conscious and reflective activity of thought, or spirit: spirit is propelled by negativity and contradiction, and not by mere expression. It works through inner and outer conflicts with itself, and through alienation or loss of self. Self-consciousness as the knowledge of freedom is not immediate, but emerges in struggle, before it can recover its unity at a higher level. The result is "Spirit in its *completeness*, in its essential nature, *i.e.*, Freedom. This is the fundamental object, and therefore also the leading principle of the development (...). Universal History exhibits the *gradation* in the development of that principle whose substantial *purport* is the consciousness of Freedom."[71] In Hegel the thematic of autonomy-perfectionism is clearly on display: the progress of freedom itself, its rational

66 Hegel (2009 [1821]).
67 Yeomans (2015), 163-187.
68 See above, note 2.
69 Gaukroger (2010), 58-64, 148-49.
70 Stefanie Buchenau and Douglas Moggach, "Herder: Perfectibility, Plasticity, and Pluralism", in this volume.
71 Hegel (2007), §61-63, pp. 55-56. While these posthumous lecture series are not entirely reliable sources, this passage gives cogent expression to ideas exhibited in Hegel's own publications.

comprehension, and the changing forms of its objective exercise comprise the substance of history.

The intense mutual polemics among members of the Hegelian School of the 1830's and 1840's illustrate a wide range of metaethical and normative options opened by the new perfectionism. We can distinguish, for example, the more naturalistic position of Karl Marx, combining pre- and post-Kantian elements, from the rigorous Kantianism of Bruno Bauer.[72] The specificities and limits of their contributions, along with those of other Hegelians like Arnold Ruge[73] and Eduard Gans,[74] can be better understood in this context. The explicit anti-perfectionism of Max Stirner can also be elucidated with reference to these debates.[75] The internal divisions of the School and the intellectual trajectories of its proponents can thus be presented more methodically and comprehensively, as we begin to undertake here.

4. Systematic Considerations

In reconstructing the systematics of autonomy-perfectionism, it is important to note an initial distinction from other current approaches to Kantian ethics. Recent authors have stressed the importance of perfectionist elements in Kant's own work, or the presence of teleological considerations within his deontological theory.[76] The distinction between Kant and Wolff is elaborated through the former's rejection of all substantive ideas of happiness or *eudaimonia* as the foundation of ethics, in favour of the perfection of the moral will itself.[77] The ethical perfectionism that authors like Paul Guyer identify in Kant precisely seeks to strengthen the will, and to foster virtuous attitudes, i.e. it deals with the acquisition of the capacity for *moral* autonomy; and its domain is the Kantian sphere of virtue, not of right. On the contrary, post-Kantian perfectionism, or autonomy-perfectionism in the sense proposed in the present volume, aims not so much at the acquisition of virtue, but rather at the enhancement of the capacity for rational agency in general. Its end is securing

---

72 Michael Kuur Sørensen and Douglas Moggach, "'The Republic of Self-Consciousness': Bruno Bauer's Post-Kantian Perfectionism", in this volume; Quante (2019).
73 Tim Rojek, „Perfektionistische Gehalte der Rugeschen Geschichtsphilosophie? Historische Zuordnungsfrage und systematische Herausforderung", in this volume.
74 Norbert Waszek, „Ergänzung und Überschreiten von Hegels politischer Philosophie durch Eduard Gans", in this volume.
75 David Leopold, "The Non-Essentialist Perfectionism of Max Stirner", in this volume.
76 Guyer (2004), 27-47. See also Sherman (1997), 331-361.
77 Guyer (2011), 194-213.

political and social freedom, and the conditions for its exercise. It seeks to consolidate the sphere of right, to expand the scope of rightful interactions in the objective world, and to make available the necessary means for effective action in pursuit of spontaneous, self-given ends. We will approach the sphere of right first through concepts of spontaneity, and then through the Kantian architectonic of practical reason. We can distinguish three relevant senses of spontaneity, deriving respectively from Leibniz, Kant, and Fichte.

If Kant criticises Leibniz for upholding a rationally heteronomous system, he does not reject this system outright, since it contains valuable conceptual resources that must be retained and utilised in new ways. Fundamental to this enterprise is Kant's revised concept of spontaneity. Kantian spontaneity is not a process of externalising a unique content, as in Leibniz, but, as it is conceived in the *Critique of Practical Reason*, it refers to negative freedom in a precise sense, namely, the indetermination of the will by any cause external to it. Fichte then elaborates the Kantian meaning, enquiring into the prerequisites of *effective* spontaneous action.

In Leibniz, spontaneity means processes of internally-generated, self-caused change, where activity never derives from an outside cause, but always from the subject's own inner resources and potentialities. The expression or manifestation of this implicit content characterises the subject's perfection. From his earliest reflections onwards, Leibniz is tireless in his opposition to emergent theories of mechanistic materialism such as that of Thomas Hobbes, where movement is induced from without, through the attraction and repulsion which external objects exert upon subjects.[78] Leibniz views such theories not as absolutely erroneous, but as overreaching their appropriate limits. He acknowledges a field of mechanistic interactions among phenomena or what he designates as derivative forces; here the principles of efficient causality apply, but they do not apply to rational agency itself. He locates a productive, primary domain from which these phenomena originate, and in which predominate teleological considerations, final causes or goods to be attained.[79] He thus seeks to reconcile elements of Aristotle with modern natural science. In describing the primary forces deployed in teleological action, Leibniz attributes to subjects, or monads, an individual law of development, governing from within the sequence of their actions, their acquisition of new properties, and their attainment of perfection in the relative and absolute sense: respectively, as the harmonious display of a many-sided development, the unity of unity and multiplicity; and (like Aristotle) as a teleological process of

---

78 *Leibniz-Thomasius. Correspondance*, 55 ff.
79 See, for example, Phemister (2005), 187-207.

rendering explicit an implicit content, or realising a potential. This internally-generated, dynamic unfolding of possibilities defines Leibnizian spontaneity.

Kant retains a concept of spontaneity while transforming its meaning and register.[80] In his critical appropriation of the Leibnizian notion, Kant shifts the emphasis from the metaphysics of (monadic) causality and its intrinsic laws of motion, to the practical use of reason. In this new conception, subjects are not metaphysically impervious to outside influences, but are able critically to distance themselves from causes that might determine their actions and that lie outside the rational will, whether as external objects or as unexamined inner drives and inclinations. In exercising practical reason, subjects reflectively assess the admissibility of these causes, and their correspondence to the requirements of rational agency in general, of which moral agency is a special case.[81] Kant defines this self-determining capacity of the will as negative liberty, the ability to abstract from external causes that impinge on the will, and to admit them selectively, insofar as they satisfy rational criteria.[82] As one commentator puts it, for Kant, human beings as imperfectly rational creatures are sensibly *affected*, but not, as in materialist doctrines, sensibly *determined*.[83] This evaluative process differs in Kant's account from an inner monadic law of development, prescribing a sequence of states of being and perceptions, as Kant reads Leibniz to assert; but it retains the core meaning of spontaneity as self-defining activity. Our spontaneity consists in our ability freely to set goals for ourselves. In terms set by current research, Kant thus endorses a version of agent-spontaneity, while retaining a notion of monadic spontaneity in that all judgements of apparent goods are related to a singular evaluative source in personhood, the transcendental unity of self-conscious reason.[84]

Through pure practical reason, spontaneous processes of self-determination are not immediately governed by inclination or arbitrary will, but by rational critical assessment. Such processes of evaluation characterise rational action in general, on Kant's account. Specifically moral agency follows this pattern, but with additional requirements. In testing their maxims for validity and universalisability, and acting from the consciousness of duty rather than inclination, wherever these conflict, subjects practise autonomy in its strict ethical sense, enacting categorical imperatives,[85] or moral rules valid for their own sake, not for any ulterior ends. Spontaneity now assumes the form of self-legislation, in

---

80   See Sgarbi (2012), 61-78, 102-16.
81   Allison (1990), 5-6, 39-40, 60-61, 191-98.
82   Kant (1908 [1788]), *Ak.* 5: 33.
83   Allison (1990), 60.
84   Rutherford (2005), 156-80.
85   Kant, (1903 [1785]), Ak. 4: 440-441.

which subjects prescribe the moral law to themselves, and do not rely on external authority to dictate their conclusions. The source of normativity lies in the rational faculties, and not in any external standards.[86] This recognition marks the emergence from self-imposed tutelage in a moral sense, and the dawning of genuine enlightenment.

Even in cases of empirical heteronomy, where violations of autonomy arise by following sensuous inclination in opposition to duty, (Kantian) spontaneity is still at work, in that subjects direct *themselves* in conformity with a desire; the desire does simply determine the subjective will, as it does for materialists like Hobbes. Rather, in these cases, the will retains but misuses its agency, accepting the illicit desire as a valid end, and thus colluding in its determination from without. For Kant, the empirical pursuit of happiness is an essential aspect of our constitutive imperfect rationality, our combination of sensuous and intelligible character, and it becomes morally problematic only when it conflicts with the demands of duty.[87] But an ethical system may not be based on the quest for happiness, and still less can a political order enforce it coercively.

The Kantian meaning of spontaneity is given a further theoretical extension in the work of Fichte, for whom it refers to the capacity of subjects to exert causality in the objective order,[88] and to transform it in light of their own evolving self-consciousness and of their needs. Fichte thus lays stress on the effectiveness of action,[89] in two respects: as the production of a beneficial effect, and also as a manifestation of freedom, in the successful translation of a subjective idea into objective reality.[90] For Fichte, as later for the young Marx, mental and physical labour is a vehicle of spontaneous freedom, transforming external nature in accord with a concept or a self-given end. It is this third meaning of spontaneity which is most closely aligned with the theoretical programme of post-Kantian perfectionism, aiming at the development of the conditions of free agency in its broadest sense, and not exclusively at moral agency or virtue, as in readings of a strictly Kantian perfectionism. Rather, it consists in the promotion of freedom, the capacity to be self-fashioning, and to determine the objective conditions for realising this freedom, political, social, and economic. Thus, while Kant in many ways participates in the shift toward

---

86 This is expressly contested by Kierkegaard. See Fremstedal on Kierkegaard, in this volume.
87 Kant (1908 [1788]), Ak. 5: 25; see Fremstedal on Kierkegaard in this volume on anti-eudaimonism.
88 Fichte (1971), 9.
89 Yeomans, (2015), 60-68.
90 As we will see below, these two aspects correspond respectively to empirical and pure practical reason.

a juridical perfectionism, as Hernández Marcos demonstrates in this volume,[91] the extended meaning of spontaneity developed by Fichte and others provides a solid conceptual foundation for the fuller elaboration of this approach.

The primary reference for such elaboration is to the Kantian domain of right, of compatible free actions in their external aspect, and not primarily of virtue, or the internal adjudication of ends. The sphere of right is the arena of spontaneous and compatible actions, established through mutual limitation among juridical subjects, where the free goal-setting of each individual in its external aspect is acknowledged and harmonised. In the juridical sphere, subjects exert a reciprocal causality upon one another, determining the appropriate limits for their individual, spontaneous goal-setting in pursuit of happiness. This idea is that of a genuine intersubjective causality that is compatible with individual spontaneity, while circumscribing it within appropriate limits, so that none is precluded from the possibility of self-determination. This is a significant addendum in the Kantian account of spontaneity, which opens onto more comprehensive theories of intersubjectivity in Fichte and Hegel.[92]

In *The Metaphysics of Morals*,[93] Kant distinguishes empirical practical reason (whose domain is *das Wohl*, the quest for individual happiness or need-satisfaction) from pure practical reason, as the capacity for freedom and autonomy. Pure practical reason is itself further distinguished, as underlying two related but separate spheres of activity: the sphere of morality, or *das Gute*, the domain of full autonomy as moral self-legislation; and the sphere of *right* (*das Recht*, or conformity to the conditions of free agency for all subjects). In positing three distinct but interrelated spheres of practical reason, Kant effectively divides Wolffian perfection into its components, material well-being on the one hand, and the intellectual and moral virtues on the other. He holds that the latter are not subject to coercion, but are matters of individual self-cultivation, or duties to self, whose moral worth is only enhanced by their self-given character. Kant is far from renouncing perfection as a moral end, but he places it outside the purview of the state.

Kant takes right, too, in a sense distinct from Wolff, for whom the primitive rights enjoyed in the state of nature are to be renounced in the name of systemic and personal perfection. Right for Kant is an aspect of pure and not empirical practical reason: it is the field in which the principles limiting individuals in the pursuit of their particular goods (their own spontaneous, self-defined *Wohl*) are worked out, in such a way that these quests become

---

91 Hernández Marcos on "Rights-Perfectionism", in this volume.
92 Moggach (2000), 201-209.
93 Kant (1907 [1797]), Ak. 6: 211-215.

maximally compatible. Right is not based on utility or happiness, but in the dignity of freedom, and cannot be overridden by appeals to welfare, which are always provisional and empirical. Any legitimate restrictions on right must lie in considerations of freedom and its reciprocal exercise, and not in happiness: hence Kant's repudiation of Wolffian paternalism.

Yet in Kant's formulation, if right is differentiated from welfare, it also remains distinct from virtue or the good, because right concerns only the external aspects of action, not its maxim or principle. It explicitly leaves the motivations of actions out of account. Kantian juridical subjects may legitimately act from prudential calculation.[35] While enjoining at least outward compliance with the independence and spontaneity of others, right cannot compel motives for this respect, which may be entirely self-regarding. On the other hand, right further differs from morality in being coercible in its external aspects; outward compliance, but not inward, may be enforced. The legal order exists to prevent subjects from encroaching on the capacity of others to exert their own free agency; though Kant is explicit that the state ought not paternalistically to dictate the means or the substance of its citizens' happiness. As we have seen, however, these Kantian reflections are open to widely diverging assessments of the proper scope of political activity. Humboldt and Fichte share this starting point in the Kantian conception of right, but arrive at vastly different models of politics. Humboldt upholds the minimal state on the grounds of spontaneity, while Fichte authorises a broad range of social and economic interventions because the state, as an order of right, has a duty to hold open, for all, the possibility of freedom and the quest for happiness. This imperative to extend and reform the practices and relations of right is a hallmark of the new perfectionism. Its Kantian roots are deep.

Right differs from morality not only in its externality and its coercible character, but in another important respect, already noted by Kant in his review of Hufeland.[94] Unlike a duty, the possession of a right does not imply its obligatory enactment. The application of any particular right is conditional upon concrete circumstances and the exercise of prudential judgement. On Kantian grounds the principle of right may not be trumped by appeals to happiness, but this does not imply the rigorous enforcement of specific rights in all instances, since the bearers of rights may forego their stringent enforcement, without calling the concept of right itself into question. It may be that this more flexible interpretation of particular rights underlies Schiller's distinction

---

94   Kant (1923 [1786]), Ak. 8: 127-130.

between the litigious mechanical state and the harmonising aesthetic state, in which rights bearers seek mutual adjustment of interests.[95]

If no particular right has an absolute, peremptory status, it is nevertheless morally necessary for Kant that a sphere of right exist, as a requirement of pure practical reason: 'e statu naturae exeundum'[96]. The passage from the state of nature to the civil condition is a rational requirement whose categorical force does not repose on calculations of advantage, but expresses a practical imperative, to create a situation in which rights can be practiced at all. If the civil condition is to be instituted and maintained, it may also be concluded that its preservation entails regular adaptation and extension. As this volume demonstrates, Kant's own thought displays a commitment to a process of ongoing political reforms, as gradual approximations to the ideal of reason.[97] The juridical *ought* that underlies the new perfectionism originates here, and is extended and concretised through further reflections on the requisites of spontaneous action in its formative aspects, in its dynamic relations with the objective and social worlds. The rationalisation of those worlds, and the liberation of the spontaneous energies that generate them, become the demands of the new perfectionism after Kant.

In this process we witness what has been described as the expansion of autonomy.[98] If Kant himself reserves the concept exclusively for the sphere of moral action, his followers extend its range to encompass relations of right. The Fichtean stress on the material and institutional prerequisites of free activity is a step in this direction, and Hegel's idea of *Wirklichkeit*, the effective reality of reason, achieves its concrete expression in the structures of the modern state and civil society. In the Left-Hegelians, Ruge, Bauer, and the early Marx, autonomy is further radicalised as a doctrine of popular sovereignty, repudiating tutelage and domination in favour of free self-determination. The need to reform political, social, and economic institutions to assure their conformity with justice is taken as an imperative governing the political activities of a self-constituting republican citizenry. The Hegelian Left repudiates Kant's own version of juridical perfectionism,[99] his advocacy of gradual reform from above. For these revolutionaries, autonomy demands that change be initiated and sustained by the popular will, and not by the arbitrary favour

---

95 Schiller (1967 [1795]), Letter XXVII.
96 Kant (1907 [1797]), Ak. 6: 256, 267.
97 Hernandez Marcos, "Rights-Perfectionism", in this volume.
98 Yeomans (2015).
99 Hernandez Marcos "Rights-Perfectionism", in this volume.

of rulers.[100] In such cases, the politicisation of autonomy supports a doctrine of popular sovereignty.

In all such accounts, from Kant onward, the concept of spontaneity is also rethought in conjunction with a reformulation of the Leibnizian postulate of pre-established harmony. In modern civil society, the mutual compatibility of interests cannot be presupposed, but is always a problematic and provisional result; not a metaphysical postulate, but an achievement of practical reason. The unity of unity and multiplicity is thus problematised further, as a matter of political resolution in ways compatible with subjective liberty. This relative concept of perfection, and its connection with political freedom, is an essential question for Schiller and Humboldt.

Here two sets of further considerations emerge, historical and systematic: First, from a historical perspective, for Kant and Schiller, interactions in the juridical sphere are mutually limiting, but potentially reconcilable; civil society does not appear to generate irreconcilable interests, but rather interests capable of intelligent mutual accommodation. Kant envisages juridical space as a system of limits, within which each subject is authorised to pursue his or her own particular ends. The maximal compatibility of these ends is assured precisely by means of mutual demarcation of arenas of private effort. Schiller further problematises this compatibility; his aesthetic state is a model of voluntary, self-conscious adaptation of diverging interests, in contrast to their rigid and conflictual affirmation. With Fichte, the problem is more radicalised, since he perceives that the ways in which the pursuit of happiness is organised, and sanctioned by existing codes of right, might themselves be sources of constraint, by disabling the spontaneous self-expression of all: that is, some members of civil society are unable to participate in this pursuit because of an unjust distribution of resources. Here his redefinition of spontaneity as *effective* action is most pertinent. Effectiveness requires access to appropriate objective means, and the perfectionist mission of the state is to assure the availability of these means to all. These considerations assume even greater saliency with the emergence of the social question in the nineteenth century as a major issue of political debate,[101] and the growth of the modern class economy. In light of these social changes, interests are taken to be not only divergent, but diametrically opposed, locked in a conflict which both threatens and perhaps accelerates social progress. The need to address the issue of the new division of labour and the causes of urban poverty leads to a fundamental reappraisal of the relations among the spheres of practical reason. This reassessment, though already

---

100   Moggach (2018), 216-235.
101   Langewiesche (1980), 529-547.

prefigured to some extent in Herder,[102] is undertaken rigorously by Fichte, and continues into Hegel's reflections on the crisis-laden dynamics of civil society, and into the works of Eduard Gans, Bruno Bauer, Karl Marx, and twentieth century critical theory. From the perspective of political and social autonomy, to the extent that authorised practices and institutions no longer satisfy the emancipatory demands of the critical consciousness, such practices must be reformed, with the aim of infusing all relations with justice, as Bauer puts it.[103] Thus, for many practitioners of the new perfectionism, the social question becomes a central concern, imparting a special urgency to the redress of social ills. For Gans, Marx, Bauer, and arguably Hegel himself, the resolution of this burning question of economic and social exclusion and disempowerment is the determinate negation at the heart of the present, the vital issue that must be addressed if further progress in freedom is to be achieved. In many of the instances we examine here, the ongoing reform of the juridical order, as the task of the new perfectionism, has not only political, but also economic and social dimensions.

The second set of considerations is more systematic in nature. If the relation between perfection and freedom is the defining issue of the entire post-Kantian tradition examined here, it is possible to identify at least two patterns of interrelationship between these concepts. In some instances, spontaneity is the essential precondition for perfection. In Humboldt, for example, perfection as the unity of unity and multiplicity, and as realisation of subjective potential, remains the end of ethical action, but he holds that freedom is the necessary condition for individuals and societies to approximate that goal. The aim is still individual self-cultivation, but political freedom is its precondition, and such freedom is best assured when diversity prevails in civil society, and when the state remains largely passive. Here a type of Kantian juridical order secures the possibility for free self-determination by an essentially Leibnizian self, equipped with its own specific set of developmental possibilities. This approach has some affinities with Guyer's account of Kantian perfectionism, noted above, but differs through its stress on the role of the juridical order as the context for effective moral growth. Without the reform and perfecting of the political sphere, no sustained ethical and intellectual advance is possible. Conversely, in Nietzsche, self-emancipation from the stultifying grip of such an order is an essential step toward affirmative freedom and self-perfection. We could describe this approach as holding an instrumental view of the juridical

---

102   Buchenau and Moggach on Herder, in this volume.
103   Bauer (1972), 526-529.

order, whether positively or negatively. In other approaches, the goal is less the attainment of individual moral perfection than the reform or transformation of political and social relations themselves. Here the juridical order and its sustaining social institutions are themselves the site of a historical process of perfecting. Bruno Bauer and Arnold Ruge exemplify such a stance, one that could be designated as constitutive rather than instrumental. In both versions, freedom and perfection, though in tension with each other, are not mutually exclusive. If the specific concept of spontaneity varies, the common core is an idea of self-causing, self-determined action, and the conditions for its exercise. It is, in different ways, the perfection of these conditions, and the full and objective expression of spontaneity itself, that constitute the subject matter of autonomy-perfectionism, and that endow these approaches with a relative unity, however much specific normative conclusions may vary.

The treatment offered in this volume is intended as exploratory, and is far from comprehensive. Humboldt merits a much more detailed exposition. Other proponents of the tradition outside the German territories, such as the British idealists F.H. Bradley and Bernard Bosanquet, should also be included.[104] Among the authors considered below whose normative stance differs widely from a juridical perfectionism, such as Kierkegaard, Nietzsche, and Marx, it is important to stress affinities at the meta-ethical level, namely in specific concepts of spontaneity and the conditions for its exercise. It would be informative, further, to compare autonomy-perfectionism, with its Kantian roots, to current versions of perfectionist ethics deriving from other sources, such as that developed by Joseph Raz,[105] or the capabilities approach espoused by Amartya Sen.[106] Additional differentiations and refinements within the autonomy tradition could be investigated: do these theories invite a reconsideration of the conventional split between deontological and consequential ethics, insofar as the end to be promoted is itself the idea of free self-determination? Is it possible to distinguish among our theorists themselves a justificatory orientation from a results orientation;[107] that is, whether they lay greater stress on the imperative to reform the social order, or on the progressive and emancipatory effects of an action? More concretely, what are the implications of autonomy-perfectionism for current political, economic, and ecological concerns? How can we conceive the role of the contemporary state, and its

---

104   See Sweet (2009).
105   Raz et al. (2003).
106   Sen (1999).
107   Düber (2016), 103.

relations with globalising civil society, in light of this approach? How might this thinking contribute to the reconceptualisation of the modern welfare-state as a promoter of freedom rather than happiness? These are some desiderata for future research.

The shift from the old to the new perfectionism can be summarised as the transition from the primacy of happiness to freedom; and from the intrinsic harmony of particular interests to their divergence and opposition, setting the political task of effecting their possible reconciliation. The account of perfection and its obstacles is historical and practical, not metaphysical or naturalistic. The approach is committed to the thoroughgoing critique of social relations and to the task of their progressive reform. It aims to bring about, not the best of all possible worlds, but the world at its possible best, as good as we can make it. The emergence of autonomy-perfectionism is not a radical rupture in the history of ethics, but a series of complex syntheses and gradations, in which the new appears imbricated with earlier forms. We offer here a selective examination of some of these formulations, from their initial appearance in the eighteenth century, onward into the twentieth. The intent is to retrieve valuable resources for understanding, and for defending, the programme of rational autonomy that is definitive of this tradition, and of the German idealism at its heart.

Bibliography

Allison, Henry E., *Kant's Theory of Freedom*, Cambridge, 1990.
– *Essays on Kant*, Oxford, 2012.
Aristotle, *Nicomachean Ethics*, ed. and transl. by Roger Crisp, Cambridge, 2000.
Backhaus, Jürgen (ed.), *Christian Wolff and Law and Economics*, Hildesheim: Olms, 1998.
– "Subsidiarity as a Constitutional Principle in Environmental Policy", Research Memorandum 005, Maastricht University, Maastricht Research School of Economics of Technology and Organization (METEOR), 1999.
Bauer, Bruno, „Erste Wahlrede von 1848", in: Ernst Barnikol, *Bruno Bauer, Studien und Materialien*, ed. by P. Riemer und H.-M. Sass, Assen, 1972, pp. 526-529.
Beiser, Frederick, *Diotima's Children, German Aesthetic Rationalism from Leibniz to Lessing*, Oxford, 2009.
– *The German Historicist Tradition*, Oxford, 2011.
Cassirer, Ernst, *Leibniz' System in seinen wissenschaftlichen Grundlagen*, Hildesheim, 1962 [1902].
– *Freiheit und Form. Studien zur deutschen Geistesgeschichte*, Hamburg, 2001 [1917].

Cesa, Claudio, „Introduzione. Diritto naturale e filosofia classica tedesca", in: *Diritto naturale e filosofia classica tedesca*, ed. by Luca Fonnesu and Barbara Henry, Pisa, 2000, pp. 9-38.

Corr, Charles, "Christian Wolff and Leibniz", in: *Journal of the History of Ideas*, 36 (2), 1975, pp. 241-262.

Dreitzel, Horst, *Absolutismus und ständische Verfassung in Deutschland*, Mainz, 1992.

Düber, Dominik, *Selbstbestimmung und das gute Leben im demokratischen Staat. Der Paternalismus-Einwand gegen den Perfektionismus*, Münster, 2016.

Feder, J.G., *Lehrbuch der praktischen Philosophie*, Göttingen, 1773.

Fichte, J.G., *Grundlage des Naturrechts nach Prinzipien der Wissenschaftslehre, Werke* vol. 3, Berlin, 1971 [1796].

– *System der Sittenlehre, Werke*, vol. 4, Berlin, 1971.

– *Einige Vorlesungen über die Bestimmung des Gelehrten, Sämtliche Werke*, vol. 6, Berlin, 1845 [1794], pp. 291-346.

– *Der geschloßne Handelsstaat, Werke*, vol. 3, Berlin, 1971 [1800], pp. 388-513.

Fonnesu, Luca, „Kants praktische Philosophie und die Verwirklichung der Moral", in: *Recht-Geschichte-Religion. Die Bedeutung Kants für die Gegenwart*, ed. by Herta Nagl-Docekal and Rudolf Langthaler, Berlin, 2004, pp. 49-61.

Gaukroger, Stephen, *The Collapse of Mechanism and the Rise of Sensibility*, Oxford: Oxford University Press, 2010.

Grapotte, Sophie/Tinca Prunea-Bretonnet (eds.), *Kant et Wolff. Héritages et ruptures*, Paris, 2011.

Guyer, Paul, "Civic Responsibility and the Kantian Social Contract", in: *Die Bedeutung Kants für die Gegenwart*, ed. by Herta Nagl-Docekal and Rudolf Langthaler, Berlin, 2004, pp. 27-47.

– "Kantian Perfectionism", in: *Perfecting Virtue. New Essays on Kantian Ethics and Virtue Ethic*s, ed. by Lawrence Jost and Julian Wuerth, Cambridge, 2011, pp. 194-213.

Hegel, G.W.F., *Grundlinien der Philosophie des Rechts, Gesammelte Werke*, Bd. 14/1, Hamburg, 2009 [1821].

– *Phenomenologie des Geistes. Gesammelte Werke*, Bd. 8, Hamburg, 2008 [1807].

– *The Philosophy of History*, transl. by J. Sibree, New York, 2007.

Hernández Marcos, Maximiliano, „La formación del criticismo jurídico de Kant", in: *Revista de Estudios politicos*, 89 (1995), pp. 243-280.

Hobbes, Thomas, *Leviathan*, Critical Edition in 3 volumes, ed. by Noel Malcolm, Oxford, 2012 [1651].

Hufeland, Gottlieb, *Versuch über den Grundsatz des Naturrechts*, Leipzig, 1785.

– *Lehrsätze des Naturrechts*, Jena, 1790; second edition Frankfurt and Leipzig, 1795.

Humboldt, Wilhelm von, *Ideen zu einem Versuch die Grenzen der Wirksamkeit des Staates zu bestimmen. Gesammelte Schriften* Bd. 1, Berlin, 1903 [1792]; *The Limits of State Action*, ed. by J.W. Burrow, Cambridge, 1969.

Hunter, Ian, *Rival Enlightenments. Civil and Metaphysical Philosophy in Early Modern Germany*, Cambridge, 2001.

Jaeschke, Walter, „Ästhetische Revolution: Stichworte zur Einführung", in: *Früher Idealismus und Frühromantik. Der Streit um die Grundlagen der Ästhetik (1795-1805)*, ed. by Walter Jaeschke and Helmut Holzhey, Hamburg, 1990.

Jauernig, Anja, „Kant, the Leibnizians, and Leibniz", in: *Bloomsbury Companion to Leibniz*, ed. by Brandon Look, London, 2011, pp. 289-309.

Kant, Immanuel, *Grundlegung zur Metaphysik der Sitten, Immanuel Kants Gesammelte Schriften*, Akademie edition, vol. 4, Berlin, 1903 [1785], pp. 387-463.

– *Kritik der praktischen Vernunft*, Akademie edition, vol. 5, 1908 [1788], 3-163.

– *Metaphysik der Sitten, Immanuel Kants Gesammelte Schriften*, Akademie edition, vol. 6, 1907 [1797], pp. 205-493.

– „Über den Gemeinspruch: ,Das mag in der Theorie richtig sein, taugt aber nicht für die Praxis'", Akademie edition, vol. 8, 1923 [1793], pp. 273-313.

– „Rezension zu Gottlieb Hufeland, Versuch über den Grundsatz des Naturrechts", Akademie edition, vol. 8, 1923 [1786], pp. 127-130.

Kaufman, Alexander, *Welfare in the Kantian State*, Oxford, 1999.

Kenny, Anthony, "Aristotle on Happiness", in: *Articles on Aristotle*, vol. 2, Ethics and Politics, ed. by J. Barnes, M. Schofield and R. Sorabji, London, 1977, pp. 25-32.

Kersting, Wolfgang, *Wohlgeordnete Freiheit. Immanuel Kants Rechts- und Staatsphilosophie*, Berlin, 1984.

Klippel, Diethelm, „Der liberale Interventionsstaat. Staatszweck und Staatstätigkeit in der deutschen politischen Theorie des 18. und der ersten Hälfte des 19. Jahrhunderts", in: *Recht und Rechtswissenschaft im mitteldeutschen Raum*, ed. by Heiner Lück, Köln, 1998, pp. 77-103.

– *Politische Freiheit und Freiheitsrechte im deutschen Naturrecht des 18. Jahrhunderts*, Paderborn, 1976.

Langewiesche, Dieter, „Republik, konstitutionelle Monarchie und ,soziale Frage': Grundprobleme der deutschen Revolution von 1848/49", in: *Historische Zeitschrift*, Bd. 230, Nr. 3 (1980), pp. 529-547.

Leibniz, G.W., *Die philosophischen Schriften von Gottfried Wilhelm Leibniz*, Bd. III, ed. by C.I. Gerhardt, Berlin, 1887.

– *Textes inédits, d'après les manuscrits de la Bibliothèque provinciale de Hanovre*, publiés et annotés par Gaston Grua, Paris, 1948.

– "Two Notions for Discussion with Spinoza", in: *Leibniz Philosophical Papers and Letters*, ed. by L. Loemker, Dordrecht: Reidel, 1969.

– *Philosophical Essays*. transl. and ed. by Roger Ariew and Daniel Garber, Indianapolis, 1989.

– *Monadology*, ed. by Nicholas Rescher, Pittsburgh, 1991 [1720].

– *Leibniz-Thomasius. Correspondance (1663-1672)*, ed. by Richard Bodéus, Paris, 1993.

Locke, John, *Second Treatise of Government*, ed. by C.B. Macpherson, Indianapolis, 1980 [1690].

Maesschalck, Marc, *Droit et création sociale chez Fichte: une philosophie moderne de l'action politique*, Louvain, 1996.

Mill, John Stuart, *On Liberty and Other Essays*, Oxford, 1991 [1859].

Moggach, Douglas, "The Construction of Juridical Space: Kant's Analogy of Relation in *The Metaphysics of Morals*", in: *Proceedings of the Twentieth World Congress of Philosophy*, Vol.7, *Modern Philosophy*, ed. by Mark Gedney, Bowling Green, OH, 2000, pp. 201-209.

– "German Idealism and Marx", in: *The Impact of Idealism – the Legacy of Post-Kantian German Thought*, ed. by Nicholas Boyle and John Walker, vol. 2, Cambridge, 2013, pp. 82-107.

– "German Republicans and Socialists in the Prelude to 1848", in: *The 1848 Revolutions and European Political Thought*, ed. by Douglas Moggach and Gareth Stedman Jones, Cambridge, 2018, pp. 216-235.

Phemister, Pauline, *Leibniz and the Natural World*, Dordrecht, 2005.

Quante, Michael, „Auf dem Weg zur materialistischen Geschichtsauffassung? Die Bedeutung des Streits mit Bruno Bauer für die Geschichtsphilosophie von Karl Marx", in: *Die Gestaltbarkeit der Geschichte*, ed. by Kurt Bayertz und Matthias Hoesch, Hamburg, 2019, pp. 117-136.

– „Kommentar", in: Karl Marx, *Ökonomisch-philosophische Manuskripte*, Frankfurt am Main, 2009, pp. 209-390.

Raz, Joseph, et al., *The Practice of Value*, ed. by R. Jay Wallace, Oxford, 2003.

Reinhold, K.L., *Briefe über die Kantische Philosophie*, 2nd edition, Jena, 1792.

Rohls, Michael, *Kantisches Naturrecht und historisches Zivilrecht. Wissenschaft und bürgerliche Freiheit bei Gottlieb Hufeland (1760-1817)*, Baden-Baden, 2004.

Rutherford, Donald. 2005, „Leibniz on Spontaneity", in: *Leibniz. Nature and Freedom*, ed. by D. Rutherford and J.A. Cover, Oxford, 2005, pp. 156-180.

Schiller, Friedrich, „Brief an Gottfried Körner" (letter of 23 February, 1793), http://www.wissen-im-netz.info/literatur/schiller/briefe/vSchiller/1793/179302231.htm.

– *On the Aesthetic Education of Man in a Series of Letters*, bilingual edition, ed. by Elizabeth Wilkinson and L.A. Willoughby, Oxford, 1967 [1795].

Schneewind, J.B., *The Invention of Autonomy*, Cambridge, 1998.

Sen, Amartya, *Development as Freedom*, New York, 1999.

Seppel, Martin/Keith Tribe (eds.), *Cameralism in Practice. State Administration and Economy in Early Modern Europe*, Martlesham, UK, 2017.

Sgarbi, Marco, *Kant on Spontaneity*, London, 2012.

Sherman, Nancy, *Making a Necessity of Virtue. Aristotle and Kant on Virtue*, Cambridge, 1997.
Stipperger, Emanuel, *Freiheit und Institution bei Christian Wolff (1679-1754)*, Frankfurt, 1984.
Sweet, William (ed.), *The Moral, Social, and Political Philosophy of the British Idealists*, Exeter, 2009.
Tribe, Keith, *Governing Economy. The Reformation of German Economic Discourse, 1750-1840*, Cambridge: Cambridge University Press, 1988.
Wolff, Christian, *Institutiones juris naturae et gentium. Gesammelte Werke*, Bd. 26, ed. by M. Thomann, Hildesheim: Olms, 1969 [1754].
– *Principes du droit de la nature et des gens, extrait du grand ouvrage latin*, par Jean-Henri-Samuel Formey, tome premier, Caen, 1988 [1758].
– *Vernünftige Gedanken von dem gesellschaftlichen Leben der Menschen und insonderheit dem gemeinen Wesen*, Frankfurt am Main, 1971 [1721].
Yeomans, Christopher, *The Expansion of Autonomy. Hegel's Pluralistic Philosophy of Action*, Oxford, 2015.

Rights-Perfectionism, from Kant's *Grundlegung* to Politics. Kantian Debates

Maximiliano Hernández Marcos

The objective of this paper is to examine the question of perfectionism in the political debates among Kant and his contemporaries in the context of the French Revolution. The clash between 'rationalism' and 'empiricism' on matters of state, occasioned in Germany by events in France, directly involves Kantian criticism and its Enlightenment project of moral autonomy, which, in opting for a public practice of juridical perfection tending toward a democratic republicanisation of existing states, now acquires a clear political dimension. This is precisely what the empiricists oppose in the name of preservation of the *ancien régime*; they are partisans, at most, of unpolitical and non-juridical forms of perfectionism, or of minor improvements to its civic order. The dispute with empiricism in matters of state is thus converted, for Kant, into a historical necessity, for what is at stake here is the present and future of the general project of an autonomous human life contained in his pure practical rationalism. The political debate constitutes a certain prolongation of the moral debate that he promoted from 1784-85 onwards, following the German translation of Cicero's *De Officiis* by the eclectic empiricist Christian Garve, which remains a polemical reference in the ensuing political discussion. It was the historical urgency of struggling against empiricism in practical issues, as promoted by Garve, that impelled Kant to elaborate and make public, first, in the 1780's, his moral criticism in response to Garve's reading of the Ciceronian text, and then, in the 1790's, his political criticism.

We will therefore examine here the Kantian controversy on politics in view of this historical trajectory that extends for approximately a decade, from the *Grundlegung zur Metaphysik der Sitten* (1785), the first foundational text of critical ethics as a doctrine of autonomy, to *Zum ewigen Frieden* (1795), the work in which Kant formulates his political criticism as a definitive response to Garve and to the German empiricist followers of Burke. To this end we will trace first the theoretical bases of Kant's juridical perfectionism in his anthropology and philosophy of history, and then proceed to a direct analysis of the political debates of the 1790's.

1. The Theoretical Presuppositions. Approach and Horizon of Juridical Perfectionism

1.1 *The Anthropological Point of Departure: Perfection as the Destiny of Man*

The idea of perfection, though precluded as a foundational moral principle, occupies a central place in Kant's practical philosophy. It constitutes a notion whose only valid use lies in the practical ambit of reason, with a primarily moral signification. This strictly practical orientation has as its historical basis the abandonment of the ontological-naturalistic conception of Christian Wolff, which Kant undertook already around 1762-63, and its replacement by an anthropological approach, clearly perceptible in the *Vorlesungen zur Anthropologie* from 1775-76 onwards. Here perfection becomes a matter exclusively of freedom and the rational will of man, completely divorced from the objective order of nature.

In Kant's new anthropological vision of perfection, two currents of ideas converge, characteristic of the Late Enlightenment, after 1750: on the one hand, the idea of *perfectibilité* as the distinctive trait of the human being as opposed to other animals, which Kant was able to read in J.-J. Rousseau's *Discours sur l'origine et les fondements de l'inégalité parmi les hommes* (1755); and on the other, the parallel idea of the end (*finale Bestimmung*) of man, made current by the theologian J.J. Spalding in his short text *Betrachtung über die Bestimmung des Menschen* (1748), and, in the second half of the eighteenth century in Germany, converted into a fundamental theme of philosophical debate and self-understanding of the age.[1] The Rousseauean notion implies a rupture in the cosmological continuum of creatures, which the thought of Leibniz and Wolff had defended in accord with the Aristotelian-scholastic tradition. It opens in its place an 'infinite abyss' between man and the rest of nature.[2] At the same time, the question of the teleological vocation of the human being implied a displacement of the object of philosophical reflection, announcing the new historical course of society: the speculative disquisitions on the nature of things which preoccupied German rationalist metaphysics, and which were of interest only to the learned in the closed circle of the universities, were displaced by a concern for the concrete existence of men, their role and their task in this world and their future on earth. Both these questions

---

1 See Macor (2013), and, on the importance of the theme in Kant, Brandt (2007). All citations of Kant in this text follow the Akademie edition (*AA*). [All cited passages translated from German by Douglas Moggach]
2 Brandt (2007), 161.

channeled an incipient consciousness of an epochal historic change, which affected the form of the social organisation under the *ancien régime*, the very idea of Enlightenment, and also the function of philosophy, which ceased to be understood as logical-ontological thought, centred on the contemplation of the rationality of the cosmic order of nature and of the monarchical-estate order of society. Instead, philosophy presented itself as a reflection on praxis, whose task consisted in orienting man in his doings as a citizen of this world. In accordance with the German terminology of the time, what occurred was a transition from *Schulphilosophie* to *Weltphilosophie*, developed in large measure as *Popularphilosophie* in the last third of the eighteenth century.

Kant not only adheres to this tendency to displace the focus of Enlightenment "from theoretical to practical reason, from the knowledge (of a few) to the willing (of all)"[3]. In a sense he even radicalizes it in taking up Enlightenment ideas from Britain and France, which he nonetheless articulates into his system through a rigorous critical dialogue with the metaphysical heritage of the Wolffian School. This practical radicalization consists in connecting and re-elaborating the received ideas of *perfectibilité* and the vocation of man by equating (moral) autonomy precisely with perfection, and with the final end or authentic historical mission of the human being. The key to this conceptual operation lies in a redefinition of perfectibility in relation to the notion of human destiny, through the introduction of teleology as a connecting thread between both, and of history as the horizon of realisation.

This initial conceptual mutation implies that the lack of instinctual determination of the human animal which is at the base of its capacity for self-perfection is not to be conceived, as in Rousseau, as mere indeterminacy and possible variability of forms of being, but, in conformity with the Stoic-biological model of the time, as 'seeds' and 'natural dispositions' which are to be developed in a determinate direction, 'according to an end'[4]; it thus remains linked to a teleology of nature. Hence perfectibility is understood, positively, as a teleological power specific to man as rational being: it is the capacity to give oneself one's own ends thanks to one's freedom,[5] through which man emerges as that unique 'end of nature' harbouring the legitimate claim to transform himself into an 'end in himself'[6]. Perfectibility thus certainly entails human emancipation from nature, but this now implies that the human being has a mission, a pre-established task: 'to make himself, as an animal

---

3 Brandt (2007), 62.
4 *AA* VIII, 18.
5 Cf. Brandt (1990), 469; Fonnesu (2004), 56-57.
6 *AA* VIII, p. 114.

endowed with the capacity for reason (*animal rationabile*), into a rational animal (*animal rationale*)'[7]. That is, he is to transform his perfectibility into (moral) perfection, through free action.

Now this teleological-practical orientation of the capacity for self-perfection follows from the new conception of the destiny of man diffused by Spalding and taken up by Kant, the meaning of which is *destinatio*, being determined *for* an end[8], and not logical or causal *determinatio*. That the human being possesses such a final *Bestimmung* means then that he is not in the world to make of himself anything he wants, or to adopt any form of life whatsoever, but to realise an end which has been prescribed to him and which he is called necessarily to effect. "This paradoxical self-realisation out of an inherently purposive natural foundation is the destiny"[9]. It is not thus a question of a fatality, blind and ineluctable, dictated from without by a power alien to man; it is a practical question, the proclamation of the intrinsic necessity of action for the human being. Such action has its correct direction demarcated, its objective fixed. This aim is in principle double: on the one hand, it is the fulfilment of our natural destiny (*Naturbestimmung*) as living beings – animals – through the adequate and complete development of all natural dispositions, making use simply of our free will (*Willkür*); on the other, it is the realisation of our specific destiny as rational beings (*Vernunftbestimmung*), situated above the other creatures, through an activity governed by the law of our own freedom, instead of by natural laws. It is by this means that is established an alternative realm to that of nature itself: the realm of morality. Thus, *Bestimmung* is above all *Selbstbestimmung*, but the highest form of this self-determination is moral autonomy (both juridical and ethical), the conquest of which constitutes in the strict sense the destiny of man.

In respect to the second conceptual change effected in the notion of the human destiny through the idea of perfectibility, another innovation appears in the Kantian doctrine as to how it is possible to reach this end. Because of the abyss opened between nature and culture through the idea that Kant takes up as a reader of Rousseau, the fate of man can only be realised by the entire species, not by the single individual. "In all the other animal species left to themselves," we read in the *Anthropologie in pragmatischer Hinsicht*, "each individual fulfils its entire destiny, but in men, in any case, only the species"[10]. With this displacement of the subject of its realisation, the problematic of the

---

[7] AA VII, 321.
[8] Brandt (2001), 211.
[9] Brandt (2007), 17.
[10] AA VII, 324; AA VIII, 18-19.

destiny of man is transposed from anthropology to the collective history of humanity as a whole. Therewith the resolution of the conflict between nature and culture is lost indefinitely in the expectant obscurity of the future, while the historical achievement of the end demands paradoxically the work and constant sacrifice of every generation – its instrumentalisation- in the name of happiness, always postponed, of future generations.[11] It is the idea of perfectibility which makes possible this historical dynamic, and which opens the horizon of a history of humanity separate from the repetitive and predetermined rhythms of the universal history of nature.[12]

From this anthropological connection between the ideas of perfection and of the destiny of man, there derive some conclusions about Kant's practical perfectionism. The first concerns the preservation of the old notion of perfection (*Vollkommenheit, perfectio*), which was rehabilitated by the tradition of Leibniz and Wolff, but which now undergoes a reformulation that restricts its meaning. Reduced to a practical issue for man, perfection is conceived as the supreme task of his destiny in the world and is distinguished by its strictly moral meaning. Kant writes in the *Metaphysics of Morals* that perfection must be seen as a result of human action, and not simply as a gift of nature.[13] Perfection thus constitutes a duty of virtue for each individual as such, because it is linked to the accomplishment of the objective ends of his destiny.[14]

The second conclusion refers to a linguistic-conceptual innovation introduced by Kant through the neologism 'perfecting' (*Perfektionierung*)[15], which implies historically rendering dynamic a traditionally static concept. Its introduction by Kant results, doubtless, from the general historicising of the realisation of anthropological destiny as a task and object specific to humanity. But what is peculiar in this new idea of perfecting is its character as a 'concept of movement' (*Bewegungsbegriff*),[16] whose content consists in projecting an always-renewed horizon of expectations for a better possible (indefinite) historical future, which functions as a constant mobilising factor for action. Perfecting implies a permanent dilation in time of the *telos* of history, of the final end of human destiny, and at the same time an unstoppable dynamisation of praxis, of human collective life, spurred on by the duty to approximate a factually unattainable goal. Kant succeeded in giving a more concrete

11 *AA* VIII, 20.
12 Cf. Brandt 2007, 180, 182.
13 *AA* VI, 386.
14 Cf. *AA* VI, 387, 391-392; Brandt (2007), 188.
15 This neologism already appears in Reflexion 1468 (*AA* XV2, 648), dated from the late 1780's.
16 Cf. Koselleck (1989), 339-340.

content to this general imperative of perfecting, making use of three other concepts of movement with which he tried to indicate the many directions of cultural development of the human species' potentialities and dispositions: *Kultivierung, Zivilisierung*, and *Moralisierung*. But above all he made very clear what was or should be the specific mode of perfecting of the human species, namely, the rhythm of its praxis and the temporal direction of its historical movement: "progress (from worse) to better"[17], or "the perfecting of mankind through progressive culture"[18].

1.2   *Historical Optimism: Perfecting as Progress toward the Better*

Thus, the question of human destiny leads from anthropology to history. In the structure of the *Vorlesungen zur Anthropologie*, from the mid-1770's, Kant reserved the final section, entitled "Von dem Charakter der Menschengattung," which dealt with the moral end of humanity, for his philosophical reflections on history, whose principal results he published in his two well-known articles in the *Berlinische Monatsschrift* in 1784 and 1786. The so-called Kantian 'philosophy of history' emerges as a continuation- almost as an epilogue- of anthropological reflection, or better, as the culmination of pragmatic anthropology. But what makes this transition necessary is the idea that the destiny of man can only be realised in the species, through an infinite process of perfecting whose temporal structure is progress toward the better.

This last thesis, the key to the Kantian conception of history, must now retain our attention, because only on this basis can we understand how and why constant perfecting comes to be for Kant not only a matter of human praxis in general, but above all a task – the task – of politics. Since the vision of history constitutes the horizon of expectations from which the normative tasks of political action are defined and justified, we will examine here the perfectionist thesis of progress toward the better, attempting first to unravel its significance as a new, practically-oriented optimism, which as such enters into polemics with other ways of understanding human history. Next, we will discuss the basis and the subject of the viability of progress, which endorse the optimism thesis. Kant's positions in these matters were not always completely unequivocal. In general, an evolution occurs, sometimes even a relevant change of position, between the writings on philosophy of history from the 1780's, and those which discuss the same theme from 1793 onwards. This revision of the initial position seems inseparable from the course of political events in France in the 1790's, and likewise from the parallel Kantian conviction of the central role of

---

17   *AA* VIII, 322; cf. 323.
18   *AA* VII, 322.

political practice in the direction of progress and its express normative definition, which was occasioned by the political debate launched in the German lands in the wake of the French Revolution.

Before embarking on these questions, it is essential to define the nature of progress toward the better and its historic goal. In this regard Kant always maintained that perfecting, as a work of culture, ought to consist above all in the perfecting of autonomy, in moral progress, consistent with man's specific rational destiny, and that the historical aim that the human species can and ought to propose for itself collectively in this respect is not ethical autonomy, the inner self-legislation of freedom, but juridical autonomy, or the perfect external (self)legislation of the free will (*Willkür*). *Moralisierung* in the intramundane context of the collective history of humankind as finite beings thus is equivalent to *juridical* progress. Kant firmly declares in his first writing in philosophy of history that the great objective, but also the greatest problem of the human race, is the "attainment of a civil society which universally administers right"[19], implying the necessity of transition to a cosmopolitan condition of international peace.

Kant changed his position in respect to the concrete political form of this international order, and the way it is to be configured. Up to 1793, including the short text *Über den Gemeinspruch*, Kant attributed pre-eminence to the right of peoples (*Völkerrecht*). In this construction, the existence of a legitimate civil constitution in each particular state was made to depend on the foundation of a legal condition among all states, endowed with its own political constitution. After 1793, Kant modifies and even inverts this schema, because the weight of the construction and political form of international peace "shifts away from the right of peoples, toward political right"[20], in light of the attractive prospects offered by the political evolution of France: the problem of world peace now depends essentially – already in *Zum ewigen Frieden* (1795) – on individual states endowing themselves with republican constitutions, or at least governing themselves in the spirit of republicanism. The structure of the new international order ceases to be that of a world state articulated on its own public constitution but adopts instead the open and pluralist figure of a 'free federalism', spreading out from an initial nucleus of republican states. With this, the historical task of juridical-pacific perfectionism becomes more dynamic: it consists in a process of internal republicanisation in each state, and in a movement of free and expansive federative association among the various states.

---

19 *AA*, VIII, 22.
20 Brandt 2007, 213-214.

1.2.1   A Principle of Hope for Practical Reason. The Debate on History

In considering the meaning of the general idea of progress toward the better, there is no doubt, first, that it proposes to define a direction of history in accordance with the moral destiny of the human race, and that its epistemic status is reduced to being a principle of hope or, in Kantian terms, a practical postulate of rational faith (*Vernunftglaube*) which provides us with "certainty sufficient for praxis"[21] and inspires "the ardent desire to contribute to the general good"[22]. The idea of progress toward the better thus offers "a consoling perspective on the future", eschewing despondency from a practical point of view[23]. But such a promising perspective on history is determined *a priori* by the practical interest of pure reason itself, and its demand to fulfil the moral destiny of humankind. To find in the real succession of past events the guiding thread of juridical progress, it is necessary to regard history not from the point of view of what men have done, which produces indignation, but from the point of view of what they ought or are called to do. It is thus imperative to change the habitual standpoint on history, to leave the realm of experience and to adopt the Copernican perspective of pure practical reason,[24] in order not to fall into despair about the future of humanity. If the sole hope that can move men to work toward the perfecting of society is that consoling perspective offered by pure practical rationalism, it can be understood why Kant exerts all his theoretical efforts to struggle against historical empiricism, which deprives of their meaning all action and will for moral betterment.

The idea of progress toward the better, as a postulate of practical reason regarding the future, constitutes, secondly, a thesis of historical optimism in general. This new form of Kantian optimism rises above the ruins of the cosmological optimism of Leibniz and Wolff,[25] and as a point of departure for the philosophy of history, it rejects precisely the *Theodicy*'s supposition of the insuperability of the real world, qualified as the "best of all possible". Thanks to this shift, man assumes the role of protagonist "in bringing about a better world" through action[26]. Psychologically, this implies the disappearance of the static satisfaction with an ontologically good order, which could be enjoyed, in the first half of the eighteenth century, in light of the Leibnizian theodicy. In its

---

21   Brandt 2007, 218.
22   *AA* VIII, 309.
23   *AA* VIII, 29-30.
24   *AA* VIII, 30.
25   On the crisis of Leibnizian theodicy, see Marquard (1973) and (1981).
26   Blumenberg (1988), 64-65.

place there opens a preoccupation with evil, derived from "the abandonment of the womb of nature", and with the responsibility to pursue good, departing from evil, through one's own free action in the world[27]. The new optimism does not celebrate the real world and the society that we inhabit, because these have ceased to be seen as a rich and complex order of natural perfections that merit contemplation and revelation. Instead, it refers solely to human action, and in order to impel such action, it looks to the future as a horizon of the good, since the perfect order is yet to come, as the moral world on earth,[28] which can only be attained through an infinite process of perfecting, through constant praxis.

Thus, the first front on which the Kantian philosophy of history engages is the Leibnizian cosmological idea of a natural scale of creatures, constituted by diverse and increasing levels of perfection, as exposed by J.G. Herder in his *Ideen zur Philosophie der Geschichte der Menschheit* (1784-1785). For Kant, one cannot pass from matter to spirit, nor from the organic world to properly human history, without a qualitative leap or a radical rupture in the cosmic chain of cumulative gradients of complexity, in the levels of perfection in the universe. As the history of humanity is the history of freedom, it cannot be understood from the vantage point of a cosmological continuum-optimism, nor of a natural physiological system, but only from that of an anthropology of perfectibility and its corresponding practical-moral optimism.

However, the authentic rival to Kantian historical optimism, its threatening nightmare, was not the naturalistic-organic conception of history deriving from the cosmological optimism of Leibniz and Wolff, but rather empiricism, which occupied the same terrain as Kant's, namely, that of human actions and collective becoming, and not of nature or the metaphysical structure of the universe. What empiricism implied, however, was a practical skepticism toward all hopes for improvement. In his texts on philosophy of history, Kant's polemical gaze was fixed throughout the 1790's on the empiricist vision of the course of human affairs, because what is at stake in this debate between historical optimism and empiricism is, at root, the question whether a politics of pure practical reason is at all possible and has meaning, or whether, on the contrary, there can only be a politics of power that consecrates the given. Without the guiding thread of right, the point of view of experience shows what the historical practices of unjust violence and treachery have made of men, namely, "obstinate and rebellious creatures"; it thereby justifies a skeptical view of the future and, with it, the euthanasia of political reason, as a mere

---

27   *AA* VIII, 120-121, 114-115.
28   Kant transforms Wolffian cosmology into a moral philosophy of history. The best world is not the existing physical world but the juridical-moral order of cosmopolitan peace.

"fantasy of an overexcited head". It supports instead only a *Realpolitik* of force and repression.[29] In *Der Streit der Fakultäten*, Kant criticises the empiricist perspective, with its skepticism about the future, designating it as abderitism[30], a belief in "the perpetual standstill" of the human species in respect to its moral worth, locked in a continuous present, "the eternal rotation around the same point"[31]. In *Über den Gemeinspruch* (1793), in the name of the perfection of humanity, Kant also criticises Moses Mendelssohn's usage of this conception of the absurd and Sisyphus-like course of history, reduced to a simple natural history.

1.2.2 The Viability of Progress: From Natural History to the History of Freedom

If Kantian optimism cannot invoke historical experience *tout court*, is it reduced to a mere manifestation of a blind practical fideism seeking to evade desperation? Can it not escape the empiricist reproach of being an impossible chimera, or can it instead rely on some foundation that might guarantee its rationality, aside from the mere idea of man's moral destiny? This is the crucial problem of the viability or credibility of progress toward the better, the veritable sword of Damocles over Kant's philosophy of history and of his theory of political praxis. The question is whether progress corresponds in some way to the effective course of evolution of humankind as a whole, if such a supposition can be accredited through the passage of historical events, or at least through some unique occurrences. This problem involves the question of a warrant that juridical-moral perfecting actually occurs in the historical world, but also, inseparably, the question of the subject charged with carrying it out. If such a warrant is lacking, practical hope can scarcely maintain itself without falling into the fanaticism of delirious faith; and without a subject responsible for impelling moral progress, belief in progress and confidence in good works would be dissipated. On the question of the historical realisability of progress toward the better thus depends the practical efficacy of Kantian optimism and the corresponding moral politics that it promotes.

When in the *Vorarbeiten zum Streit der Fakultäten* Kant presents the idea of progress of the human race in accordance with the categories of modality (possibility, reality, and necessity), he suggests that the key to the solution of this issue is to consider the effective reality (*Wirklichkeit*) of progress as the

---

29 *AA* VII, 80, 92.
30 *AA* VII, 81ff. On abderitism as a conservative sceptical-empiricist theory of human nature, see AA XXIII, 458-459.
31 *AA* VII, 81.

necessary effect of the two causes that contribute to the future moral success of humanity: "in part morally-influencing inner causes, in part physically compelling external causes"[32]. The practical realisation of perfecting toward the better thus depends on the existence of a moral subject in history who works guided by the idea of a juridical order of international peace, as well as by the anthropological mechanism of discord or social antagonism, which also leads to the establishment of such an order. The former constitutes the free and genuinely practical cause; the latter, instead, represents the coercive, dialectical, and tragic cause of human nature. The former impels progress by means of the very autonomy of willing; the latter presupposes the heteronomy of the course of perfecting of the species. Both causes fulfil distinct functions. To promote progress by working voluntarily for the establishment of world peace is the juridical-moral task of political praxis, and is the unconditional duty of governors and statesmen, the major protagonists of history. The antagonism of natural inclinations operates, on the other hand, as the guarantee of progress in case governments do not act as they ought in following juridical principles: thus, in cases where a good politics is lacking. This guarantee permits us to maintain a sensible practical hope, without blind fanaticism or mere voluntarism, to the degree that it assures the efficacy or the success of good works in providing certainty of acting in the same direction as the sensuous nature of the human being. In sum: politics and nature, the one as the collective praxis of human freedom, the other as the obscure mechanism of necessity, seem to co-operate in favour of historical progress, but natural teleology as the 'physical' cause of perfection is here only ancillary to the 'moral cause', which holds unconditional primacy or practical initiative, and does not supplant it.

This scheme of the viability of optimism, which we can consider to be Kant's genuine critical position on the matter, is present with clarity in his philosophy of history only after 1793, exactly when the idea of progress toward the better was confronted with the harsh attack of historical empiricism, and the necessity to overcome the obstacle of its presumedly chimerical character became more acute. In his writings of the 1780's, Kant had attributed primacy to the antagonism of egoistic inclinations – the 'physical cause' – to the detriment of the 'moral cause', so that both the viability of progress and the practical hope that it elicits come to depend on the hidden plan of nature, the blind mechanism of necessity. There is every indication that this operates not only as the guarantee but also as the real subject of perfecting. "The history of the human species as a whole can be considered as the execution of a hidden plan of nature", Kant

---

32   AA XXIII, 458.

declares in 1784[33]. Such a plan certainly includes the 'natural purpose' of developing completely all natural dispositions in a juridical order of world peace, but it also contains the medium of its realisation: Unsocial sociability, "'which is finally converted into the cause of a legal order of these dispositions"[34]. This restriction of the viability of progress to its 'physical cause' not only supposes the insertion of the history of humanity into the universal domain of the history of nature, but also explains history almost exclusively from nature, with the consequent paradox that the historical process of perfecting the human species remains at the mercy of the blind and heteronomous mechanism of natural necessity. This naturalist vision of history then enters into collision with Kantian ethical criticism, and with the very idea of the moral destiny of man: against what it claims, Kant's moral project becomes chimerical, as his empiricist adversaries object. First, it promotes an optimism without praxis, similar in its effects to the Leibnizian theodicy from which Kant had distanced himself since the late 1750's, though now inspired by the neo-Stoic and liberal 'invisible hand' of Adam Smith. Secondly, it leads to the irrelevance of moral action, and to the naturalistic instrumentalisation of individuals in the historical becoming of the species.

The optimistic determinism and practical immobilism implied in this recourse to natural teleology as the decisive factor in historical progress is not attenuated in *Idee zu einer allgemeinen Geschichte in weltbürgerlicher Absicht* by the recognition, there, of a certain 'moral cause' which operates in some fashion in support of the hidden plan of nature, leaving behind "weak traces of approximation" to the goal which permit us to cherish a hope of improvement. These traces are to be found in the advances discernible in "internal culture" (religious freedom) and in "civil freedom" (economic liberty) that states themselves, in competition with one another, favour through their own interest in power and glory; but they also imply a gradual unfolding of Enlightenment as that "great good" of the human race which "must gradually rise as far as thrones, and even influence their principles of governing"[35]. It is from this

---

33 *AA* VIII, 27.
34 *AA* VIII, 20. In *Idee* Kant concretises unsocial sociability in three known impulses: *Ehrsucht, Herrsucht, Habsucht*, and he considers them as causal factors in the transition from barbarism to culture, because they contribute to the cultivation of taste and social refinement, but also impel the establishment of civil society, even if not yet perfected (*AA* VIII, 21). In *Zum ewigen Frieden*, in contrast, the providential mechanism of nature (now concretised as wars and economic interests), is not understood as the efficient cause of the juridical-civil order, but as a teleological principle of the accord of the empirical behaviour of human beings with the moral end of the species.
35 *AA* VIII, 28.

liberal Enlightenment, as a movement of expanding private freedoms of conscience and the market, in conjunctural alliance with the megalomania and ambitions of the European princes, that Kant anticipates the moralising force that will oblige statesmen to introduce political transformations, internal and external, leading ultimately to the universal cosmopolitan order of peace.

We can conclude that for Kant in the 1780's, the historical perfecting of the human race passes *through* politics but does not originate *out of* politics itself, but rather from instances alien to it. These operate indirectly on it, forcing it to act in the direction of progress toward the better. Both the antagonistic impulses of human nature, and the expansive moral forces of freedom of thought and the market, appear to function in the same way: as indirect, anonymous, secret agents, which ultimately impose their hidden ends through a teleological necessity of things. There is no properly political subject, there is no free and direct protagonist, responsible for the collective course of history. Confronted with the discouraging experience of power politics conducted by the absolute princes and monarchs of the time,[36] Kant, with an eye above all to British liberal thought, places a trust in the social powers of nature and of the human spirit so abstract and even deterministic that in these years it allows him, paradoxically, to nourish a euphoric, almost pre-revolutionary optimism about the future of humanity.

Very different is the schema from the middle years of the 1790's. In consonance with his ethical criticism, Kant now makes clear the primacy of the 'moral cause' over the 'physical cause' in the historical perfecting of the species, and he converts progress toward the better into the unconditional task of politics. Governors are subject to the moral duty to work tirelessly for an international order of peace through the internal republicanisation of their states or at least of its forms of governance. *Zum ewigen Frieden* (1795) contains the precise elaboration of this turn, which implies both the formulation of a critical theory of political praxis integrated into the moral philosophy of pure reason, and also the subsequent establishment of this same politics as the specific moral subject of the history of humanity. The 'moral politics' defended there, based on juridical principles, will succeed in making perpetual peace real, "even if only as an infinitely progressive approximation"[37]. In this historical process, providential nature now concurs only as a 'clause of guarantee' of the duty of politicians.

---

36   On Kant's disenchanted views of rulers in the 1780's, where they appear more as an obstacle than as the motor of moral progress, see *AA* IX, 448-449.
37   *AA* VIII, 386.

The triggering motive for this turn appears to be found in the moral significance of the viability of progress that Kant discovers in the popular republican evolution of the French Revolution since 1793. The enthusiastic and disinterested sympathy of spectators with the just cause of an entire people struggling for its right to give itself a civil constitution of republican stamp is the "historical sign" or singular occurrence of a "moral character" of the human race, or at least a disposition, "which not only permits hope of progress toward the better, but already constitutes it, as far as the capacity currently allows"[38]. The confirmation of this effective moral disposition in the human species means that collective perfecting is no longer due to the mechanical necessity of an external, heteronomous cause, such as the nature of antagonistic forces, but rather depends entirely on the freedom of man and his moral causality, his conscience and feeling for right and justice, attested empirically once and for all by public enthusiasm for the French Revolution.

Conviction about this moral disposition also has repercussions for the scope and meaning of Kantian historical optimism, which now is detached from its perilous linkage with theodicy and liberalism that it had assumed in the 1780's, to acquire its properly critical and political form, since it is now wholly based on the development of this solid subjective tendency toward the good through free activity in the public space of state and governance, and not on the teleological effects of natural necessity. Thus, the existence of this moral disposition permits us to maintain the hope, indeed to predict, that one day an order of cosmopolitan peace will prevail. It assures us that "from this moment on," no regressions in progress toward the better will occur,[39] and that this progress, "even if occasionally interrupted, will never be broken"[40]. But at the same time, together with its clear practical basis and orientation, this optimism becomes more moderate and cautious because of uncertainty about the concrete course of the free action undertaken by men as finite beings, disposed to evil. This means that it is necessary to regard progress toward the better in the open horizon of an "indefinite time"[41], and that we cannot foresee when or how the ideal juridical goal will be attained. Moreover, this (moral-)juridical progress can only be assured in a "negative manner," through the diminution of evil actions, that is, at the political level, through the disappearance of wars, above all of offensive wars,[42] which will lead to a reduction of violent and conflictual conduct in civil society. This moderate and negative optimism is adjusted to

---

38   *AA* VII, 85.
39   *AA* VII, 88.
40   *AA* VIII, 309.
41   *AA* VII, 89.
42   *AA* VII, 85-86, 93.

the sensible limits of the human being, whose finite moral base does not permit him "to exceed a certain measure, above which he could elevate himself, and thus always progress toward something still better"[43], as would be the case with a pure, innately good, rational being.

2.   Politics as the Praxis of Perfecting? The Debate in Light of the French Revolution

Thus, in Kantian thought history and politics are united, and both are inseparable from the moral theory. But the latter does not acquire its properly critical shape or its public dissemination prior to 1788, with the publication of the *Kritik der praktischen Vernunft*. The critical moral theory elaborated and exposed between 1785 and 1788 offers a grounding and an exhaustive analysis of the principle of morality and its ethical implications but contains nothing on its possible application to the field of right and politics. The reader of the *Grundlegung zur Metaphysik der Sitten* and of the *Second Critique* would know with clarity in what the morality of an act consists, and how to be virtuous in one's individual life, but not what type of common juridical legislation follows from the moral principle, and even less what political praxis, if any, one may expect. Ought the moral law of reason to have an immediate application to the contemporary social structure and its mode of governance, in the same way that it applies to each individual, or are certain mediations ineluctable? Or, on the contrary, ought it to remain at the margins of the political realm, restricted in its scope of application only to private life? This series of questions relative to the possible juridical and political extension of moral criticism requires a response, because it was presented by Kant as a worldly ethic, aspiring to produce in the sense-world an effective copy (*natura ectypa*) of the pure intelligible world of morality (*natura archetypa*).[44]

As is well known, Kant's silence in this regard led some of his disciples to take the additional step of proposing theories of natural law or of general political right according to supposedly Kantian principles, or to debate the meaning and specific task of politics, especially when these themes acquired burning actuality in the French Revolution and its unfolding. It was then that Kant, summoned by historic circumstances, invoked by both followers and adversaries in the discussion launched in Germany by the revolutionary process in the neighbouring country, and thus obliged to intervene, pronounced himself publicly for the first time on the themes of right, and began to refine and

---
43   *AA* VII, 82.
44   *AA* V, 43.

diffuse his juridical thought, especially on public right. He succeeded in elaborating a critical theory of political praxis, expressed distinctly in the Appendix to *Zum ewigen Frieden* (1795). Between 1793 and 1795, in the course of the debate with his contemporaries, Kant formulated the conception of political action adequate to his moral criticism. This new political criticism expresses the conviction, facilitated by the recent democratic republicanisation of France, that politics constitutes the genuine praxis of juridical-moral perfection of the human species, and that, therefore progress toward the better can only be produced "from the top down," as an imperative task of governing, and not by way of education in the family and the school[45]. Nor could it arise from a liberal Enlightenment in conjunctural alliance with the megalomaniacal egoism of absolute monarchs, as the *Idee zu einer allgemeinen Geschichte in weltbürgerlicher Absicht* (1784), had maintained. At that time Kant still lacked a theory of political action adequate to his moral criticism.

In the formation of this political criticism, the same polemical catalyst was at work as had motivated Kant to elaborate his critical ethics: empiricism. If what impelled him to write *Grundlegung zur Metaphysik der Sitten* was the awareness of the danger posed for his project of moral enlightenment by Christian Garve's rehabilitation of empiricist-utilitarian eudaimonism in his 1783 German translation and edition of Cicero's *De Officiis*,[46] now in the 1790's the empiricist phantom re-appeared in force, not on the ethical terrain, but on that of politics. It was emergent German Burkeanism that now threatened juridical-moral progress at the very moment when, thanks to the French Revolution, a reasonable historical optimism had gained respect.

To conjure away this danger and to salvage the collective practical hope inspired by republican developments in France, Kant hastens to secure politics as the authentic praxis of the juridical perfecting of humanity, intervening on the debate with two essays that we can interpret retrospectively as the subtle unfolding of a single intellectual operation in two complementary phases. The first of these, *Über den Gemeinspruch* (1793), attempts to defend rationalism as normative for political activity against its empiricist impugnment, which blocked all possibility of a genuine perfectionist praxis in this field. To this end Kant argues against the commonplace, invoked by the empiricists, on the practical invalidity of any theory of reason as merely speculative, or even chimerical. Kant stresses that the distinctive trait of politics, as of all true moral praxis, is to be a practice intrinsically charged with theory. The second of the essays,

---

45 *AA* VII, 92-93; VIII, 313.
46 Garve's work was first published in Breslau in 1783, as a translation of Cicero with a three-volume commentary. New editions appeared in 1784, 1787, and 1792.

Zum ewigen Frieden, (1795) which constitutes a fuller treatment of his political thought, takes account of some of the insufficiencies of the previous text that had been signalled by his adversaries. It constructs a theory of political praxis which critically integrates the realist doctrine of prudence within a normative rationalism. If *Über den Gemeinspruch* presents itself as a forceful plea against political empiricism, the Appendix to *Zum ewigen Frieden* renders partial justice to the adversary through a realist repudiation of revolution in favour of progressive reform as the only valid political practice.

The following discussion presents political empiricism in its two variants: Garve's pre-revolutionary version, and the counter-revolutionary position of Gentz and Rehberg, along with Kant's refutations of a practice of power devoid of juridical-political perfectionism. Thereafter we undertake to reconstruct the Kantian vision of politics as a reforming practice, which results from his incorporating within his juridical rationalism a realist component extracted from his empiricist interlocutors.

2.1 Resistance to a Theory of Normative Juridical Perfection. The Faces of Political Empiricism and the Kantian Critique

The German debate on politics in the context of the French Revolution is posed as a problem of the relation of theory and practice. As the *Vorarbeiten zu Über den Gemeinspruch* attest, this relation could be interpreted in the sense that any metaphysics of reason "is the cause of political revolutions"[47], the idea of a direct connection between rationalist moral theories and revolutionary praxis. This affected Kantian criticism directly, as it had been associated in Germany, by partisans as well as by detractors, with the French Revolution. The essay *Über den Gemeinspruch* certainly disavows this presumed linkage between critical philosophy and events in France, celebrated by German Jacobinism and denounced by counter-revolutionary Burkeanism. To general surprise, Kant's text denied a right of resistance to the people, on the argument of its formal impossibility according to the juridical logic of the social contract. But the basic purpose of the text was to refute political empiricism by denying the commonplace which, in its repudiation of moral rationalism in matters of state, had been disseminated against Kant and against the French Revolution: 'what is correct in theory is not valid in practice'.[48]

---

47 *AA* XXIII, 127.
48 See Kant's letter to J.E. Biester (July 30, 1792), AA XI, 349-350; Henrich (1967), 14. See also Wittichen (1904); Dietrich (1989), 128ff; and Oncina (1991), 160.

This commonplace, which underlined the distance between professional activities and the scientific doctrine taught in the universities (in the Higher Faculties, or some branches of the Faculty of Philosophy)[49], was employed by German Burkeans in the revolutionary context of the 1790's against Enlightenment rationalism in general, and concretely applied to rationalist natural-rights systems (above all, the Physiocrats and Rousseau), supposedly responsible for the collapse of the *ancien régime*; by extension, Kant was also targeted. The intent was to expand the logical-methodological difference between theory and practice into an unbridgeable dualism in collective life, which would delegitimate the applicability of enlightened juridical and moral ideas to the socio-political organisation of the state. Thus, from the perspective of the German Burkeans, any rationalist doctrine of liberty and equality among human beings was simply metaphysics or vain speculation that should be permanently secluded "in university classrooms as mere pedantry"[50].

This dualism covered over another earlier dualism, opened in Germany in the 1780's, the distinction in social life between the private and the public sphere, which had sustained monarchical absolutism since the end of the seventeenth century. The separation between morality and politics was propounded by Christian Garve as a clear apology for the Prussian regime and its expansionist international policies under Friedrich II, first in his essay "Einige zerstreute Betrachtungen über die Moral der Politik" (1783), appended to his German translation of Cicero's *De Officiis*, and then in an expanded and revised edition, published separately as *Abhandlung über die Verbindung der Moral mit der Politik* (1788), a work that provoked a wide-ranging polemic in German intellectual circles.[51] In the name of a utilitarian empiricism, and in the service of an extreme political eudaimonism, Garve called into question the normative rules of rationalist natural law which, in the Wolffian tradition, had placed juridical or simply moral limits on the power of the sovereign. For Garve, historical experience taught that such rules, formulated by an abstract and speculative philosophy alien to reality and its changing circumstances, constituted demands that were impossible for statesmen to fulfil. "The importance of a nation and its welfare," explains, according to Garve, "why politics sometime permits that which morality prohibits to the private man"[52]. The theoretically correct moral position was not always valid in the political realm, where the

---

49   Henrich (1967), 14.
50   AA XXIII, 127.
51   On this polemic see Stolleis (1972).
52   Garve (1788), 47.

"law of general utility" prevails, as the "primary ground of all justice"[53]. Garve thus posited a double morality, one private, for subjects, the other public, for rulers.[54] Any morality with pretensions to universal and unconditional validity and application, irrespective of the diversity of empirical situations, could thus only represent chimerical and vain speculation.

This attack by Garvean empiricism on Wolffian rationalist natural law and its proponents prepared the way for the reception, at the beginning of the 1790's, of the Kantian ethic of pure reason and its categorical imperative as a new metaphysic of enlightenment reason, so abstract and ideal that it could not move the heart of man. Garve suggested this in a critical observation in his essay "Über den Geduld"[55]. But in the context of the French Revolution, what already appeared objectionable in the Kantian moral principle, in respect to practical life in general, acquired a new saliency and importance in relation to political activity. The independence of politics from morality could now be affirmed, no longer in order to justify monarchic absolutism, but to denounce as illegitimate any revolutionary change in the state that might call into question or eliminate the historical order of rights acquired from antiquity. German Burkeanism thus disavowed any possible extension of pure practical reason into the realm of politics and state action, rejecting such criticism as a speculative theory without validity in practice. This anti-Enlightenment operation was certainly the provocation, in 1793, for Kant's pronouncement on the political applicability of his moral criticism, to which corresponded a doctrine of the constitution of the state, a *Staatsrecht*. It also occasioned his response both to Garve and to the Burkeans in the Appendix to *Zum ewigen Frieden*, highlighting the common split between morality and politics in these positions. We can now proceed to a closer examination of these two principal variants, Garve and the German Burkeans, and their respective views on practical perfectionism.

2.1.1   Christian Garve or the Absolute Perfection of Life and the Moral Perfecting of Man

With his broad-ranging eclecticism, Christian Garve (1742-1798), one of the principal writers of so-called *Popularphilosophie*, defined the dominant intellectual line of the Berlin Enlightenment of the 1780's. Through his proximity in education and convictions to the leading circle of bureaucrats, of Silesian origin like himself (von Carmer, E.F. Klein, C.G. Svarez), who assumed administration of the Frederician state after 1779, he can be considered as one of

---

53   Ibid., 68, 34-35, 56.
54   Stolleis (1972), 11.
55   Garve (1792), 112.

the most representative authors of pre-revolutionary political thought in Prussia. This is attested by his defence of the society of estates as a natural, divinely-ordained order,[56] and by his fidelity to enlightened absolutism, of which he offered an empirical-realist legitimation, undermining the natural-law foundations of the recent, official, Prussian tradition (Wolff, Darjes, Achenwall, etc.). Perhaps his most original contribution was the eclectic purging of rationalist elements from Germanic natural law with the help of British empiricism, which he introduced into Germany as the translator and follower of the Scottish philosophers of 'common sense' (Smith, Ferguson, Payley, Hume, Reid, etc.).

It is precisely this application of British empiricism, initiated by the translation and eudaemonist-utilitarian reinterpretation of Cicero's *De Officiis* in 1783, that launched the lengthy dispute with Kant, who immediately detected in this new ethical eudaimonism and its corresponding political paternalism the principal threats to his Enlightenment project of moral autonomy and the republican state of right. The central point of disagreement lay in the negation by Garve of a pure practical reason, with unconditional normative force, and distinct from theoretical reason. For Garve the practical role of reason is relegated to the co-ordination and ordering of human action, "an application of the understanding"[57]; but this intellectual regulation of existence is far removed from moral autonomy or *a priori* self-legislation of reason itself. It is rather the expression of applied theoretical reason, or reason reduced to its strictly logical use (in Kant's sense), because moral rules are derived from experience and acquired knowledge.[58]

In his eclectic borrowings, Garve combines this moral and cognitive empiricism, of British origin, with a dynamic, teleological naturalism derived from the Leibnizian tradition, with marked scholastic-Christian inflections. He introduces the idea of a gradated, hierarchical scale of being that extends beyond the anthropological sphere to encompass all of nature, at least living nature, including the history of the human species. His theory of perfection, still inscribed in an optimistic theodicy, discards the Leibnizian-Wolffian idea of relative perfection (the concordance of the diverse in unity), while retaining the absolute concept (the degree of reality or internal value of a thing), restricted however to the organic sphere (vegetable, animal, human). Perfection is predicated of determinate natural beings in function of their essence, but "man is the criterion of perfection" because "he creates the concept first out

---

56   Stolleis (1972), 47.
57   Garve (1798), 90.
58   Ibid., 4.

of himself" and then projects it comparatively into similar things[59]. This similarity or commonality is organic life, characterised by two traits: "self-activity or self-movement" and "sensation, first manifest through feeling of pleasure and displeasure, and finally transforming itself into representations", and consciousness[60]. Thus, the anthropological model of absolute perfection does not imply, as in Kant, a rupture in the natural order, but simply its culmination, in accord with the old eschatological Christian cosmology. Nonetheless, the human being does introduce a specific difference into the dynamic, teleological scale of life: that of the highest degree of self-activity and sensibility that represent freedom and thought respectively. Thanks to these, man can aspire to the ideal of supreme perfection that corresponds to him by nature: virtue. Moral good thus assures his superiority in respect to the entire universe.

And yet the perfecting of mankind is immersed in the general dynamics of organic life. In conceiving perfecting as the mere unfolding of the forces or capacities intrinsic to a living being through its own (self-)activity, Garve deprives the concept of any normative dimension. It is not based in pure practical reason but is simply the evolving manifestation of a dynamic essence that is (or appears to be) self-determination, and thus it follows the path predetermined by its nature. And thus, it is too in morality. For Garve, virtue as the essence of man implies the complete and harmonious development of all the cognitive faculties and the formation, under the rule of reason, of the capacity for freedom, understood in a Leibnizian manner as complete self-activity;[61] virtue is a consequence of properly-formed theoretical reason.

The historical agent of such perfecting is the socio-cultural movement of the Enlightenment as a whole, understood as the progressive conquest of the truths of reason through scientific and philosophical discovery. In this respect Garve is the clear exponent of the predominant vision of enlightened intellectuals in pre-Revolutionary Prussia, sharing a vision (and a Wolffian education) in common with his Silesian contemporaries C.G. Svarez (1746-1798) and E.F. Klein (1744-1810). For all these figures, the scope of Enlightenment and perfection is reduced solely to its function in the moral formation of man, without extension to the political sphere of the citizen – and even less of the subject – except insofar as it can serve to guarantee precisely his obedience.[62] Particularly with Klein and Svarez the confinement of enlightenment to the private sphere responds to a pre-liberal motive linked with the goal of individual happiness.

---

59 Ibid., 65-66.
60 Ibid., 61-62.
61 Ibid., 97.
62 Hernández Marcos (2017), 47-48.

For Klein, the highest good of existence in the state is the civil liberty (*bürgerliche Freyheit*) of all subjects, with political liberty (*politische Freyheit*) serving only as a possible and circumstantial support.[63]

In a similar vein, Garve does not contemplate a process of juridical-political perfecting involving the constant reform of state institutions to approximate the ideal model of the public constitution. His empiricism and providentialist naturalism underlie his conservatism and practical immobilism: the first, to disavow as chimerical any political reform project based on the alleged daydreams of a normative reason; the second, to condemn any act of rebellion against state power as an assault on the divine order, and as a "religious crime"[64]. Political absolutism and the estate order of the *ancien régime* are for Garve essentially untouchable.

Unlike his Aristotelian filiation, the political community is not for Garve the site for the realisation of the good life or human flourishing, but serves only as the most efficient means to promote the end of individual happiness.[65] Garve is far from absolutising the idea of the state,[66] since what is essential is the moral perfection of the individual, not the best constitution of the state, whose task is to secure the conditions for the greatest possible happiness. Perfection is a private and interior matter, and not a public question of the organisation of power, or a juridical duty. The absolute sovereign is free from any juridical or moral tethers precisely in the name of general happiness and welfare.

Like Klein and Svarez, Garve too considers Enlightenment to be the best antidote to revolution, since it civilises the subjects and contributes to the rational governing of society by the absolute sovereign, without the necessity for changing the monarchical form of the state. Garve professes an almost rationalistic historical optimism, but based on his radical empiricism, because he considers history as having a necessary and irreversible course, characterised by uninterrupted progress of Enlightenment that guarantees the triumph of the healthiest and most rational ideas, best adapted "to the thought-system of

---

63   Cf. Klein (1790), 164; cf. 117-118. By 'civil liberty', the natural rights tradition of the time understood the private sphere (rights of property and conscience) as the supposed residue of 'natural freedom', which was not subject to state intervention, and in which the individual could seek welfare and happiness. 'Political liberty' refers instead to the capacity of all citizens to participate in public legislation, which is only possible in a democratic-republican order such as that proposed by Kant.
64   Stolleis (1972), 54.
65   This is not to be seen as a proclamation of modern liberalism, since happiness for Garve is primarily moral or interior, and in respect to its material conditions, it cannot be dislodged from the hierarchical structure of inequality in estate society.
66   Stolleis (1972), 56.

men at every moment"[67]. This philosophy of the rationality of historical success, almost a precursor to Hegel's, is for Garve the coherent result of his organic, teleological model of human perfection, and of the inexorable necessity of its evolution, which leads him to understand the history of humanity as a simple, if culminating, episode in natural history.

2.1.2   German Burkeans. Gentz and Rehberg

If Garve's empiricism, with its eudaimonistic ethic and its providentialist defence of enlightened absolutism, constitutes the great pre-revolutionary adversary of Kantian moral critique, the German Burkeanism of the 1790's represented a new threat, counter-revolutionary and anti-Enlightenment, especially to Kant's political criticism. Based on a new, historicist, empiricism, its specificity consists in viewing the historical past not, as in Garve, as a mere empirical source of political and anthropological examples, but as a constitutive fact of the immutable normativity of traditional society and state; the best socio-political organisation of human life was resolved into what each people had tacitly agreed *ab initio* as the foundational act of its concrete collective life. This regression to the past, at the precise moment when the French Revolution was putting an end to the *ancien régime*, represented the major danger of de-activating the critical and practical potential of Kantian rational morality in the public sphere, even to the extent of producing its conservative inversion by some of the disciples of Kant who, while adopting his ethics, nevertheless turned against him in political theory. This was the case of the civil servants August Wilhelm Rehberg (1757-1836), in the service of the Anglophile Elector of Hanover, and of Friedrich von Gentz (1764-1832), secretary to the *Generaldirektorium* in Berlin. German Burkeanism was thus not a movement completely foreign to Kantianism. On the contrary, it appeared like a tumour within it, one that could precipitate the death of political criticism before its public delivery by Kant himself. Here we must limit ourselves to the empiricist separation of politics and morality, and the question of perfection, as addressed by these two Kantian authors who responded immediately to Kant's essay *Über den Gemeinspruch*. The Burkean traditionalism of Rehberg, influenced by Justus Möser and Ernst Brandes, is to be distinguished from the pre-liberal Burkeanism of Gentz, closer to the Silesian circle in Berlin, and indebted to the Aristotelianism of his friend Garve. First, we must explain briefly the meaning of historicist empiricism in German Burkeanism.

---

67   Garve (1786), 11.

This historicism repudiates the normative idea of human nature in modern natural right, in favour of a conventionalist thesis, derived from Burke[68], on the forms of social life and political institutions. The origin of the state lies in a contract, interpreted empirically as a tacit or real pact agreed to in antiquity, which sanctions the civil arrangements concluded ancestrally with a mystical aura, eternal and superior to the will of concrete individuals.[69] History becomes (in Weberian terms) a source of patrimonial legitimacy, based on the unaltered transmission of the legacy of the first participants in the alleged original founding contract of civil society. What is transmitted, and what maintains its continuity from generation to generation in an unalterable chain, is the structure of inequality, not only economic but civil, determined by relations to property in the soil, as the basis of all political participation and common association.

In response to the French Revolution, the principal ideologist of German traditionalist historicism, Justus Möser, initiated a debate in the *Berlinische Monatsschrift* on the right of a nation to change its constitution, adducing the binding character for posterity of the original contract made by the first possessors of the land, whose privileged descendants were the hereditary nobility.[70] Rehberg advanced the same patrimonialist argument, justifying civil inequality through the fixed distinction between landholding proprietors, the only citizens endowed with political rights in virtue of the initial contract, and the other members of the community, designated as "protected relatives" by the laws of civil society.[71]

It is precisely against this historical interpretation of the original contract, legitimating civil inequality, that Kant protests in *Über den Gemeinspruch*, denying that such a *pactum sociale* could be identified with a factual event that might at one time really have occurred, as if such an act were necessary for a people to "consider itself bound by a civil constitution"[72]. Against this empiricist devaluation and immobilism, Kant recalls the critical potential of right as a "simple idea of reason", whose practical efficacy consists in serving as a normative criterion for "the legitimacy of all public law"[73].

---

68   Burke (1950), 64.
69   Rehberg (1793), 62.
70   See Möser (1790) and (1791), as well as his response to a perfectionist critic, in Möser (1792), 514-527.
71   Rehberg (1793), 46.
72   *AA* VIII, 297; cf. *AA* VI, 308-310.
73   *AA* VIII, 297, 303.

2.1.2a 'Morality is not valid for politics'. The Necessity of a Theory
from Experience

The relation of theory and practice is addressed in two responses to Kant's *Über den Gemeinspruch*, also published in the *Berlinische Monatsschrift*: Gentz's "Nachtrag zu dem Räsonnement des Herrn Professor Kant über das Verhältnis zwischen Theorie und Praxis" (Dec 1793); and Rehberg's „Über das Verhältnis der Theorie zur Praxis" (Feb. 1794). Both texts stress the inapplicability of rationalist moral theory to political practice, and the necessity instead for a theory derived from experience. Both texts take aim at political rationalism, held responsible by the Burkeans for the French Revolution. By this they meant the belief in the validity and direct application of abstract ideas, forged in the minds of philosophers, to civil society and the state. For Gentz and Rehberg, such a belief, and the idea that reason ought to rule the world, generated a terrible, destructive pathology. The best cure consisted in the recovery of a realist and historical sense in political discourse, which recognises its unbridgeable limits, and which therefore either proclaims the indifferentism of reason before the empirical diversity of constitutional forms,[74] or else directly decrees the silence of reason in the field of civil relations, where only reflection on expediency, and will (*Willkür*), should prevail.[75]

Behind the problem of the questionable applicability of reason lay another issue, the relation of theory and practice understood in this historical context as the relation of morality and politics. Did a rational moral theory (including natural-law ideas of human rights) contain a corresponding theory of the state, and if so, is this theory applicable? The problem has two aspects that were not yet clearly distinguished, the extension and the political application of a rationalist morality. The former aspect was soon to acquire an independent development in the German territories, as *ius publicum universale*, of normative character, whose foundation could be traced back to Rousseau, and of which Kant offers the prototypical scheme in *Über den Gemeinspruch*.[76]

It is precisely here that a notable difference arises between the two Burkean disciples of ethical criticism: while Gentz admits a pure political right based on the rights of man, such that no civil constitution can ever contradict "this theory founded wholly on the concept of duty and its pure product, the original

---

74 Gentz (1837), 26-29.
75 Rehberg (1793), 44.
76 Cf. the essay by the Kantian Heydenreich (1794), 41ff, 50ff, which juxtaposes an ideal *allgemeines Staatsrecht* to an empirical anthropological component, of Hobbesian orientation (pp. 26ff), as a development of the 'introductory metapolitics' proposed by Hufeland (1785), 21; (1790), 351ff.

contract"[77], Rehberg rejects it as an illicit intrusion of reason into alien territory. Even if such a theory could be formulated, it would be "adequate only to a republic of gods, or of perfect, metaphysically free beings, who in any case would have no need for a civil constitution"[78]. Gentz's admission of pre-political rights[79] distances him from Germanic traditionalism and aligns him with the pre-liberal Silesian circle in Berlin; whereas Rehberg follows Justus Möser in insisting on the contingent, conventional origin of all political institutions, and denying that any state has been or could be founded on the universal rights of man.[80] In the civil sphere, only determination by the arbitrary will, and the restrictions and transfers concluded by civil contracts, prevail. In this case, a theory from experience is substituted completely for pure political right.

In Gentz, in contrast, this theory from experience is not the substitution for a rational theory, but its complement, supplying its deficiencies in practical execution. Political practice interprets theory experimentally, according to realist rules, extracted from a knowledge of the historical and natural conditions of a society. Since the problem is not the invalidity but the insufficiency of the theory of political right, Gentz corrects the well-known commonplace as follows: "What you teach is indeed correct in theory, but is *not yet* valid in practice"[81]. Theory also manifests its inadequacy in its impotence to offer real guidance to the activity of the statesman. Gentz reverts to a Wolffian position in conceiving the relation between theory and practice in the civil sphere as logical and cognitive, but not, like Kant, as normative; hence theory appears as a rational *emendatio* of the existing world. Moral theory is the foundation for political practice, as the guiding star of the ruler's decisions[82] insofar as it contains the primary basis of the being and knowledge of the real state itself, but not because it decrees what ought to be, and the corresponding action of the statesman. Gentz thus reduces the pure theory of right to a mere speculative metaphysic with which philosophers understand and explain, in abstract ideas, the reigning social order. To mix these theoretical levels would be not only to commit a logical error of transgressing the border between the ideal system of the science of right, reserved exclusively for thinkers, and the realist art of governing, which depends on empirical knowledge. It would also be an extremely dangerous practical error, which has already led to political anar-

---

77 Gentz (1967), 101.
78 Rehberg (1967) 123, 127.
79 Gentz (1791), 386, 391-392.
80 Rehberg (1793), 44; cf. 45, 50, 62.
81 Gentz (1967), 110.
82 Ibid., 101.

chy, as in the French Revolution with its declaration of the rights of man and citizen.

It is this same revolutionary danger that Gentz detects in the three principles of pure political right (liberty, equality, independence) in *Über den Gemeinspruch*. In the Kantian text the treatment of the state is limited to the pure doctrine of right, without any specification of the effective means of application to historical reality. At the same time, the emphasis on the normative, practical force of this rational theory induces a belief in the urgency of immediate execution of these juridical principles, and in revolution as the only adequate practice for the philosophy of reason, a view widely held in Germany at that time. To dispel this danger of instability in the Germanic lands posed by criticism, Gentz seeks to de-activate the normative potential of the pure theory of political right, not only through conservative limitations on the three juridical principles which deprive them of their emancipatory value, but also by reducing the scope of theory itself to a mere speculative doctrine, necessary as preliminary knowledge but impotent for real practice, and promoting in its place an empiricist theory that sanctioned monarchical power and the traditional order of unequal estates.

Gentz and Rehberg interpret differently the scope and meaning of the new empirical science of politics. For the latter the science is at the service of "the expedient"[83], whose object is to maintain what had been ancestrally concluded *ab origine* and to transmit the inherited culture, customs, institutions and social order.[84] For Gentz, in contrast, the practical science of experience, which is to complement the pure theory of political right as the means of its realisation in a determinate state, must be understood as a doctrine of power and must be concretised in a theory of the good political constitution, the adequate organisation of public authority, which was lacking in Kant's exposition in *Über den Gemeinspruch*. Innovative in this proposal is the stress on the proper organisation of state power as the best form of preserving the maximum civil or political freedom[85] possible for all individuals. This is the end of the state, avoiding the extremes both of repressive despotism and of destructive chaos and anarchy, the worst of political evils.

---

83   Rehberg (1967), 127; (1793), 15.
84   In Rehberg, the modern distinction of public and private does not appear, but rather the ontological division between spiritual inwardness and worldly externality, a separation compatible with estate society.
85   Further on Gentz and Kant, see Hernández Marcos (2000), 230ff.

2.1.2b Rehberg's Political Immobilism, Gentz's Prudent Perfectionism

Another notable difference exists between Rehberg and Gentz on the question of a practical perfectionism, concretely, on the possibility of a perfectionist political practice. The Germanic traditionalism of the former implies a naturalistic vision of the history of peoples as organic wholes constituted from ancient times, which blocks any prospects for perfecting through human action, and any change proceeding from within the social organism. Social changes occur only through gradual evolution, or through hazardous and contingent external circumstances such as war[86]. But even such changes are not inserted into a qualitative or gradated scale of progress, but entail the reproduction of similar structures, based on landed property and the civil differences it generates. This cyclical essentialism does not, however, discount anthropological pluralism, the concrete variety of distinct peoples and forms of social life, resulting from different natural, geographic, and cultural-historical factors.

This constitutive plurality, together with the organic character of each civil society, explains the impossibility for Rehberg of a perfectionist political practice. If every civil constitution is the reflection of the specific life-circumstances of each people, a practice of governance oriented to its reform or improvement based on a given normative model would lack all sense, since it would require a complete change in the nature of the people and its history. Rehberg denies the ideal of a perfect political constitution, to which all peoples must conform, and he considers as vain and useless its employment as a criterion to compare and judge the degree of development or legitimacy of existing constitutions, which are valid only though their own historical facticity as the autochthonous expression of each community.[87] Political immobilism, as conservation without rupture of the inheritance transmitted from the past, constitutes the only possible collective practice for this traditionalist anthropological vision, in which history appears as natural history, impelled only by inertial forces of continuity with the ancestors, and devoid of any internal dynamic.

In Gentz, in contrast, the desire to escape from both traditionalist immobilism and the anarchic and diabolical perversion of revolution, and to promote a political reformism of Burkean inspiration, forces him into a juggling exercise. He attempts to connect philosophically the organic, anthropological relativism of his empiricist conception of the political constitution, as reflective of the historical and cultural situation of each people, with the rationalist perfectionism of his Enlightenment conception of universal history as the progress of the human race and of the corresponding political ideal of the good form

---

86   Rehberg (1793), 56, 58, 53.
87   Rehberg (1793), 54.

of state. The organic dependency of the political system upon the concrete natural and cultural life circumstances of each nation diminishes the possibility of a perfectionist practice for the governors. Moreover, in a despotic regime a reform tending to augment the freedom of the subjects would not even be desirable, since the existence of bad constitutions attests to the incapacity of their subjects to discover better ones.[88] Gentz opposes any attempt to translate the constitutional form from one country to another without first investigating "whether the circumstances of the latter allow for imitation"[89].

The organic irreducibility of the political constitution of each country does not however imply immobilism, because Gentz links it with an Enlightenment vision of the rational perfecting of the human race, including its political tasks, which enables him to insert the heterogeneous plurality of empirical forms of social life into a single universal scale of progress, and to interpret it as a diversity of levels or degrees of development in the infinite historical process of the perfecting of mankind. This is the tenor of the long article published in the *Neue deutsche Monatsschrift* in 1795, in which Gentz manifests an exaggerated historical optimism, of naturalist inclination. Here his defence of the "permanent perfectibility of the human species" as "a necessary idea of reason" is underpinned by the deterministic conviction of slow, inexorable historical progress in the perfection of humanity.[90] It is a question of social perfection, which includes both economic progress (the increase in wealth and welfare), and cultural progress (the spread of Enlightenment, the civilisation of customs, the intellectual cultivation of the spirit). These are respectively the results of the unfolding of external and internal human force or activity by means of the increasing sociability among individuals and peoples. This development of natural dispositions displays continuity between work, production, and exchange, on the one hand, and intellectual flowering and the refinement of social relations, on the other, as mutually reinforcing, connected parts of an organic whole. Gentz emphasises, too, that the combined effect of this increase in wealth and advance of Enlightenment is a process of political perfection in Europe, understood as the guarantee of the civil freedom of individuals thanks to equality before the law; as the parallel approximation to the good state constitution thanks to the passage from feudalism to the monarchical regime; and finally, as the humanisation of the governors themselves, who become "more attentive to the rights of the subjects and more inclined

---

88 Gentz (1837), 20.
89 Ibid., 17.
90 Gentz (1838), 211.

to their freedom"[91]. Improvement in the juridical-civil order is thus presented as a necessary consequence of improvements within the socio-cultural fabric of the nation as a whole. Gentz thus maintains his organic, anthropological conception of the form of rule, but now rendered more dynamic from the perspective of an Enlightenment philosophy of progress and its world-historical temporalisation of civil society.

In light of this conception, we must ask, finally, what is the concrete meaning of political perfectionism in Gentz? We have seen that he holds as unreachable the goal of achieving a perfect state constitution, which has to satisfy two conditions: first, the unity of sovereign power (as opposed to the diversity of feudal jurisdictions), and secondly an adequate distribution in the exercise of power to avoid tyrannical abuse. Gentz considers this latter aspect to be the decisive political challenge of his age, since modern monarchical absolutism has already resolved the former problem. He understands the proper constitution or organisation of state power as an empirical ideal (a factual balance in the exercise of powers), but not as a normative, juridical idea of reason, since this organisation is a matter which cannot be explained by the pure theory of rights, but only by a theory based on experience.[92] The ultimate reason for the absence of juridical-political perfectionism in Gentz lies in his view that human destiny does not pass through the state or an international institutional order, but through the civil freedom of individuals in a social community which enables maximal material and spiritual exchange among all its members. Gentz's pre-liberalism is here inseparable from an instrumental vision, one that reduces politics to the adequate regulation of power in the name of the primacy of society over the state (even of a society divided into estates), and of the liberties enjoyed within it.

But, as an empirical ideal, the good state constitution does not require a normative political practice, tending to its unconditional realisation, but rather a practice adjusted to the empirical knowledge of the global situation of a people, of its specific geographic and cultural circumstances and its historical rhythm of social perfection. Reformist practice is thus a question of political prudence, and the prudence of the good ruler is attested by his capacity to undertake reforms at the opportune moment, without exceeding or falling short of the point of maturation of a nation. Gentz designates as a 'genius' the prudent statesman who can detect such a point of maturity in the governed material.[93] Genius and wisdom consist simply in being the faithful echo of the

---

91 Ibid., 207.
92 Gentz (1967), 103.
93 Gentz (1837), 23.

society and the time in which one lives, neither anticipating nor accelerating the future. Political perfection merely follows the powerful current of social perfection, its inexorable natural history.

2.1.3 Kant's Criticism: 'Political Moralism', A Dialectical Illusion of Political Practice

The Kantian critique of political empiricism is initiated in *Über den Gemeinspruch* (1793) and completed in *Zum ewigen Frieden* (1795). The former extensive article poses the issue indirectly, by defending the thesis of the mutual and necessary implication of theory and practice in moral questions in general, disputing the empiricist separation of the two. In the second essay, the attack is direct, stressing the dialectical illusion of politics that affects the empiricists in principles of the state, which Kant denounces under the figure of the 'political moralist'. Let us examine each moment of the critique.

As is well known, the objective of the 1793 text was to demonstrate, especially against German Burkeanism, the practical efficacy of rational theories of freedom, making clear that the corresponding practice, whether ethical or political, cannot be understood without that theory, whose realisation it is. In this respect Kant maintained that political practice is certainly the application of a theory and of a set of universal principles, "abstracted from the multitude of conditions that necessarily influence its execution"[94]. But it is not a cognitive theory of nature (empirical sciences), but a normative theory of freedom, a moral theory, which, as such, constitutes a doctrine of duty and so is practical in itself, that is, it intrinsically contains its feasibility (*Thunlichkeit*) or the possibility of its realisation.[95] It is in this sense that we must understand the definition of politics as an "applied doctrine of right"[96]. This indicates that politics is practice in the strict sense, and not simply technique, owing precisely to the moral theory of which it is the effective execution, and not merely a refracting interpretation (Gentz). Hence in *Über den Gemeinspruch* Kant focuses on the synthetic exposition of the theory of pure practical reason which ought to govern the action of the statesman, that is, the *a priori* principles of pure *Staatsrecht* and the idea of the original contract as the normative criterion of judgement in all concrete measures of legislation and government.

In emphasising against the empiricists that there is a rational theory of normative perfection for the work of the rulers, Kant ignores any explicit clarification of the specific ways and means of its practical effectuation. He thus

---

94   *AA* VIII, 275.
95   Cf. *AA* VIII, 276-277, 370; *AA* XXIII, 131.
96   *AA* VIII, 370.

exposed himself to a justified objection, by both Gentz and Rehberg, about the inadequate treatment of politics in the 1793 text, that says nothing about the mediations between pure theory and real practice, for which they instead advocated a theory based in experience. Nonetheless Kant was already conscious of such mediations, and, in particular, was aware that experience is essential in determining adequate means for the proper realisation of moral theory,[97] even though he did not yet succeed in developing a doctrine in this respect. Thus, in the *Vorarbeiten* he distinguished the modes of realisation of pure practical theory in ethics and in politics: whereas in the former the realisation is immediate, because there the mere consciousness of duty directly implies the necessity for action, in politics the method of correct application does not follow with certainty from the theoretical fixing of pure juridical principles.[98] By denying immediacy in the application of the rational theory of public right, Kant was certainly disavowing the Jacobin revolutionary path of some of his disciples, but at the same time he was implicitly recognising that his treatment of politics in *Über den Gemeinspruch* only dealt with one side of the problem, that of pure theory or *principia diiudicandi*; it was still necessary to elaborate the other side, the theory of intermediate principles or *principia executionis*, as the indispensable complement of the philosophy of reason, and to insert it properly into a complete theory of political criticism. This will be the task of *Zum ewigen Frieden*.

This work of 1795 developed a direct critique of the 'empiricists in principles of state' that was more exhaustive and rigorous than that suggested in a more occasional manner in passages of the *Gemeinspruch*. In this text Kant denounced above all the conservative political effects of "a practice docile to experience" which, without a theory of rational juridical principles, renounced the "demands for a good political constitution", precisely because it gradually accustomed the people to content themselves with a passive situation regarding their rights and welfare, accepting things as they have always been, instead of seeking something better. Kant simultaneously warned of the dangers of popular subversion. Such dangers threaten all authoritarian governments which obstinately defend an order "solely according to the rules of prudence" or paternalistic benevolence, but without respect for the rights and juridical claims of human beings.[99] The end of the Introduction states the fundamental objection, from a critical perspective, to all political empiricism: by claiming "to reform reason by means of experience" the empiricists end up surreptitiously

---

97   Cf. *AA* VIII, 289; AA XXIII, 135-136.
98   *AA* XXIII, 131.
99   *AA* VIII, 305-306.

transforming the "empirical conditions and contingencies of the execution of the law" into "conditions of the law itself"[100]. Deepening the critical argument, the Appendix to *Zum ewigen Frieden* presents as the great sophistical confusion or dialectical illusion of politics this empiricist supplanting of genuine morality or of pure right by a doctrine of prudence alone, which elevates the mere means of realisation of juridical principles into an end in itself, into an independent and absolute criterion of state action. Kant even coins the new expression 'politischer Moralist' to designate someone who defends or shares this transcendental illusion of politics. The 'political moralism' of empiricists like Garve or the German Burkeans consists in replacing right in public affairs with an ad hoc morality which advantages the statesman.[101] Kant lists some of the rules of prudence which, taken separately as exclusive, directive principles of government action, turn out to be mere rules of cunning, 'sophistical maxims': 'Fac et excusa', 'Si fecisti nega', 'Divide et impera'[102]. Since there is no pure theory of duty or of freedom that can be realised through the effective use of this series of rules, all of which are based solely on empirical knowledge of the natural mechanism of human actions and aspire to manipulate this mechanism, Kant denies to this empiricist vision of politics the character of 'practice' (*Praxis*) in the strict sense. He refers to it instead as an assemblage of 'practices' (*Praktiken*),[103] such that the political art cannot be differentiated from any other art or technique (of doctors, builders, jurists, etc.). Based solely on the knowledge provided by the correlative empirical sciences, it therefore constitutes a false politics (*Afterpolitik*).

The falseness of this merely technical conception of politics rests upon another, more basic sophistry, inherent in moral empiricism and its eudaemonist and utilitarian principle, already denounced by Kant as a dialectical illusion of practical reason, and now projected into the realm of state action. The political moralist commits the error of deriving the principles or maxims of government from material ends, previously given and converted into an object of the statesman's will: general welfare, public order, increase in power, etc., instead of deriving these ends from the formal principle of right (the possible co-existence of the external freedom of all under universal laws). In this way, the primacy of right over power, the basis of 'true politics', is inverted. Where neither moral law nor liberty holds sway in civil relations, but only what occurs, or can occur, according to the mechanism of human nature and

---

100 *AA* VIII, 277.
101 *AA* VIII, 374-375.
102 Ibid.
103 Ibid., 373-374.

historical experience, the art of governing, no matter what concrete ends it proposes, turns into power politics. It is supported in turn by a pessimistic vision of the factual evil of human beings, whose particular wills can only be united by the violence of an irresistible power, erected into a common will. In this way, the analysis of the empiricist figure of the political moralist or the moralising politician enables Kant to denounce the technicising of politics as a falsification of its moral task, a substitution of the sanction of power for the defence of right.

2.2 *Political Perfecting in Kant: The Practice of Progressive Reform*

With the exception of the traditionalist programme of Rehberg, two basic forms of practical perfectionism have been detected in political empiricism, corresponding more closely to the model of a natural history of the human race than to a history of liberty as progress in autonomy: on the one hand, the moral perfection of the individual as a private person (Garve), and on the other, the economic and cultural perfecting of civil society (Gentz), with improvements in private rights and forms of governance. In neither case is political perfection viewed as an agent, protagonist, or directive cause of progress, but only as an effect or patient reflex of other instances: the socio-cultural process of Enlightenment as a factor in moral education (Garve), or the growing civilisation of society as a whole, as a circumstance propitious for prudent improvement in the organisation of state power (Gentz). But not even in this latter case, in which the reform of the governance structure is justified in the name of the protection and increase of civil liberty and individual rights, is political perfecting understood as the juridical perfecting of the constitution of the state itself. Nor are the state and international society conceived as a juridical-institutional community in which the destiny of the human race is played out, nor therefore as a duty, but only as a necessary instrument of order and co-existence to facilitate the attainment of a human destiny that is either ethical or socio-cultural, but not political. Hence it does not require the prior organisation of state life itself in conformity with rational principles of external freedom. Kant defends, on the contrary, a juridical-political perfectionism which implies the institutional ordering of the state and international community according to principles of autonomy, and a political practice of perfecting oriented toward this end. At the basis of the political debate between empiricism and Kantian rationalism, what is at stake is an alternative clearly distinguished by Kant himself: either the state of power, or the state of right.

Now we will briefly present the Kantian conception of public practice that is linked to his juridical-normative rationalism and adapted to his critical philosophy, that is, his political criticism. This project finds its first formulation in *Zum ewigen Frieden*, particularly in the Appendix. It is the result of refinement and completion of the theory of principles of state right, presented in *Über den Gemeinspruch*, through a theory of the means of its practical execution, whose absence had been noted by Gentz and Rehberg in their respective reviews of that essay. Attending to the objections of his empiricist adversaries, Kant systematically integrates them within his critical conception of political practice, assigning them to their appropriate place and function. This new vision implies opting for progressive reformism (by state power) of defective prevailing institutions as the only valid political practice within the limits of critical rationality, and thus as the way to carry out juridical-political perfecting. Thus Kant reinforces his repudiation of revolution and of popular resistance, now adding a properly political argument to the formalistic juridical argument affirmed in 1793: "It is contrary to political prudence, which in this concords with morality", violently to break the civil union, with the sole aim of eradicating some defects of the existing constitution "before a better constitution is ready to appear in its place". Neither popular revolution from below, nor precipitous reforms from above, but only "reforms adequate to the ideal of public right" define a legitimate and prudent practice, and these are the exclusive duty of the governors, or better, of the representatives of the people, but they are not in the competence of subjects[104].

The critical theory of politics that underlies this state practice of progressive reform can be condensed into three basic ideas that Kant formulates in *Zum ewigen Frieden*, re-elaborating suggestions and objections offered in critical dialogue with his contemporaries, and especially with the German Burkeans: the thesis of the republican civil constitution, which concretises the pure doctrine of political right proposed in *Über den Gemeinspruch*; the notion of political wisdom (*Staatsweisheit*) as a new critical conception of public practice; and the innovative concept of permissive law as the form of synthetic integration into juridical logic itself of the historical conditions of execution of the pure rational norm, rendering visible the temporal rhythm of reformist politics. We will briefly examine each in turn.

---

104 *AA* VIII, 373; cf. *AA* VI, 322. For historical referents of the text, see Hernández Marcos (1999), 376-377; and Brandt (1982), 252-253.

The doctrine of the republican civil constitution, presented as the first definitive article of perpetual peace, is clearly Kant's response to Gentz's critical observation on the absence, in *Uber den Gemeinspruch*, of a theory of the good constitution of state power; but this reply in only a partial amendment to the Burkean proposal.[105] On the one hand, the good constitution of the state is not a balanced organisation of the exercise of sovereignty, as political prudence based solely on a theory of historical experience would recommend, because this same historical experience shows that the only known example, Gentz's prototype, is the 'limited monarchy' in England; but this is in fact a concealed form of despotism, in which the absolute monarch imposes his will on a few representatives of the people who are always willing to be suborned by him.[106] The sole guarantee against tyranny must be juridical-coercive, and not empirical-prudential, and it is to be found in an institutional structure of division of powers, complemented by a system genuinely representative of the people.[107] Now, on the other hand, as the perfect republican constitution, as a form of state (*forma imperii*)[108], is a Platonic idea of pure political right which ought to be aspired to, but which is far removed from any existing state, a political practice according to the spirit of the ideal republic is both legitimate and prudent in any given form of state, for example, in an absolute monarchy, so that it might, little by little, approximate that end. Kant thus proposed republicanism as a form of government (*forma regiminis*), that is, as a normative political practice for the monarchs of his age which would permit the gradual approximation of an order of international peace. Thus while presenting the republican constitution as the juridical principle of the division of powers, Kant acknowledged to Gentz that the key to political practice resided in the exercise or form of government, more than in the form of state, but with the full knowledge that governing in a republican manner in monarchical states was a 'provisional duty' borne and endorsed in prevailing defective constitutions by progressive reformism, with a view to attaining, some day, the true republic.[109]

---

105 Kant is also replying to J.E. Biester, who asks him to relate the a priori principles of right to the establishment and maintenance of a good constitution (cf. *AA* XI, 491).
106 Kant makes this criticism of the English model of mixed constitution proposed by Gentz in the *Metaphysik der Sitten* (1797) (*AA* VI, 320), and in *Der Streit der Fakultäten* (1798) (*AA* VII, 90).
107 *AA* VIII, 352.
108 The republican constitution as the ideal of the state is based not only on the division of powers and a system of popular representation, but also on the three a priori principles or juridical attributes of citizenship defined in the *Metaphysik der Sitten*: freedom, civil equality, and independence (*AA* VI, 314; cf. *AA* VIII, 290ff, 350-351).
109 Cf. *AA* VI, 340-341; *AA* VII, 91.

The doctrinal covering of this reformist practice in the spirit of republicanism was provided by the new concept of political wisdom, as a key component of Kantian political criticism. Through this notion Kant was able to link the juridical idealism of his pure theory of the state of right and the international community of peace, with the political realism of the ruler's actual practice, conditioned by the empirical situation of each concrete society.[110] Gentz and Rehberg had demanded theory derived from experience as the exclusive guide for political action, and they understood this theory as a doctrine of expediency according to historical tradition, or of prudence alert to circumstance and the degree of maturity of each people. Kant took up this challenge, but only as a genuine complement to the rational theory of political right, and he situated it in its precise place: on the subordinate plane of the execution of that pure theory, where it is necessary to weigh the appropriate manner and means of its effective application to the real world, thereby asserting political prudence. The Appendix to *Zum ewigen Frieden* concretises this idea of political wisdom in the figure of the moral politician. In contrast to the political moralist, this figure is characterised as a statesman who "takes the principles of political prudence in such a way that they can co-exist with morality."[111]. In this harmonious convergence of moral theory and prudent practice, the normative principle of political action, and its ultimate end, are right and justice in conformity with the idea of the republican constitution and international peace; but the means of realising them requires prudence, taking into account the empirical circumstances and historical specificity of the society in which they are to be applied. It is precisely this prudential consideration of the subjective, contingent conditions for the application of juridical principles which are themselves objective and unconditioned, that validates the progressive reform of (imperfect) existing institutions as the only wise political practice.

But to justify this practical articulation of reason and experience, normative ideality and realist prudence, and make it systematically visible in its reformist dynamic, Kant introduces, also for the first time in *Zum ewigen Frieden*, the previously unknown concept of permissive law (*lex permissiva, Erlaubnisgesetz*), in the elaboration of which the Prussian jurist E.F. Klein would play the relevant role. In one of his letters Klein had raised the problem of *iura quaesita* as a heritage from the past that necessarily limited the will of the legislator.[112]

---

110 On the relation between juridical and transcendental idealism on the one hand, and political and empirical realism on the other, see Hernández Marcos (2007), 66-74.
111 *AA* VIII, 372.
112 On Klein's role in the formulation of the *lex permissiva* and its political significance, see Hernández Marcos (1999), 372-374; Brandt (1982), 279, 243ff.

The pertinence of this concept lies in specifying the historical-temporal form of execution of juridical principles as the criterion of prudence in reformist political practice, and incorporating the rhythm of realisation of right synthetically into juridical logic itself. Permissive laws are, in reality, broad prohibitive laws, which command the maintenance of a juridical situation prohibited in itself and objectively unjust, but only in a provisional manner, until historical circumstances arise that are adequate to the effective carrying out of the prohibition.[113] Thus, far from deactivating reason's objective juridical prohibition, the permission simply imposes a subjective restriction on its application, or postpones the moment of its strict realisation. Thus, the objective duty to establish a republican constitution, which implies the normative prohibition of all existing forms of state, can nonetheless admit a provisional deferral in its execution until a more favourable moment, if the empirical conjuncture (for example, the existence of a monarchical state) is not yet propitious.

It is clear that Kant's permissive laws refer to acquired rights, to a 'state of possession' achieved legitimately in the past, but not to innate or fundamental rights (liberty, equality, personal safety), which are not subject to historical time, and which imply undeferrable juridical duties. This form of safeguarding the historical reality of right, as only provisionally valid juridical acquisitions from the past, constitutive of the civil body of a concrete society, is perhaps the way in which Kant incorporates into his juridical and political criticism the only rational point contained in Rehberg's traditionalism: history as a source of merely temporary legitimacy of what has been acquired.

Translated from Spanish by Douglas Moggach

Bibliography

Blumenberg, Hans, *Die Legitimität der Neuzeit*, Frankfurt/M., 1988.
Brandt, Reinhard, „Das Erlaubnisgesetz, oder: Vernunft und Geschichte in Kants Rechtslehre", in: *Rechtsphilosophie der Aufklärung*, ed. by. Reinhard Brandt, Berlin/New York, 1982, pp. 233-285.
– *Kritischer Kommentar zu Kants Anthropologie in pragmatischer Hinsicht*, Hamburg, 1999.
– *Immanuel Kant: Política, Derecho y Antropología*, México, 2001.
– *Die Bestimmung des Menschen bei Kant*, Hamburg, 2007.

---

113 AA VIII, 347-348.

Burke, Edmund, *Reflections on the revolution in France and other writings*, London/ New York/Toronto, 1950.

Dietrich, Therese, „Kant's Polemik mit dem absprechenden Ehrenmann Friedrich Gentz", in: *Dialektik* 17 (1989), pp. 128-136.

Fonnesu, Luca, „Kants praktische Philosophie und die Verwirklichung der Moral", in: *Recht – Geschichte – Religion. Die Bedeutung Kants für die Gegenwart*, ed. by Herta Nagl-Docekal a. Rudolf Langthaler, Berlin: Akademie Verlag, 2004, pp. 49-61.

Garve, Christian, *Schreiben an Herrn Friedrich Nicolai von Christian Garve, über einige Aeusserungen des erstern, in seiner Schrift, betitelt: Untersuchung der Beschuldigungen des P*[*rofessor*] *G*[*arve*] *gegen meine Reisebeschreibung*, Breslau, 1786 (digital edition: http://digital.slub-dresden.de/werkansicht/dlf/113024/14/).

– *Abhandlung über die Verbindung der Moral mit der Politik, oder einige Betrachtungen über die Frage, in wiefern es möglich sey, die Moral des Privatlebens bey der Regierung der Staaten zu beobachten*, Breslau: Wilhelm Gottlieb Korn, 1788 (facsimile: *Gesammelte Werke*, ed. by Kurt Wölfel, I/4, Hildesheim: Georg Olms, 1987).

– *Versuche über verschiedene Gegenstände aus der Moral, Literatur und dem gesellschaftlichen Leben*, Erster Teil, Breslau: Wilhelm Gottlieb Korn, 1792 (facsimile: *Gesammelte Werke*, ed. by Kurt Wölfel, I/1, Hildesheim: Georg Olms, 1985).

– *Eigene Betrachtungen über die allgemeinsten Grundsätze der Sittenlehre. Ein Anhang zu der Uebersicht der verschiednen Moralsysteme*, Breslau: Wilhelm Gottlieb Korn, 1798 (facsimile: *Gesammelte Werke*, ed. by Kurt Wölfel, II/8, Hildesheim: Georg Olms, 1986).

Gentz, Friedrich von, *Ausgewählte Schriften*, ed. by Wilderich Weick, Zweiter Band: Politische Abhandlungen, Stuttgart & Leipzig, 1837.

– „Ueber den Einfluss der Entdeckung von Amerika auf den Wohlstand und die Kultur des menschlichen Geschlechts" (1795), in: *Ausgewählte Schriften*, ed. by Wilderich Weick, Fünfter Band: Politische Aufsätze, Stuttgart & Leipzig, 1838, pp. 173-216.

– „Ueber den Ursprung und die obersten Prinzipien des Rechts", *Berlinische Monatsschrift* 17 (April 1791), pp. 370-396.

– „Nachtrag zu dem Räsonnement des Herrn Professor Kant über das Verhältnis zwischen Theorie und Praxis", in: *Kant- Gentz – Rehberg. Über Theorie und Praxis*, ed. by Dieter Henrich, Frankfurt/M., 1967, pp. 89-111.

Heydenreich, Karl Heinrich, *Versuch über die Heiligkeit des Staats und die Moralität der Revolutionen*, Leipzig, 1794.

Henrich, Dieter, „Über den Sinn vernünftigen Handelns im Staat", in: *Kant – Gentz – Rehberg. Über Theorie und Praxis*, ed. by Dieter Henrich, Frankfurt am Main, 1967, pp. 7-36.

Hernández Marcos, Maximiliano, *Tras la luz de la ley: legislación y justicia en Prusia a finales del siglo XVIII. Un modelo de Ilustración jurídica*, Madrid: Dykinson, 2017 [digital edition: http://hdl.handle.net/10016/24488].

- „Política y Antropología en Kant", in: *Filosofia Kantiana do Direito e da Política*, ed. by Leonel Riberio dos Santos a. José Gomes André, Lisboa: Centro de Filosofia da Universidade de Lisboa, 2007, pp. 65-100.
- „Gentz, divergencia e insuficiencia del criticismo político de Kant. Presentación de F. von Gentz", in: *Observaciones complementarias al razonamiento del Sr. Profesor Kant sobre la relación entre teoría y praxis*", Res Publica 6 (2000), pp. 227-261.
- „Política y ley permisiva en Kant", in: *Moral, Derecho y Política en Immanuel Kant*, coord. by Julián Carvajal Cordón, Cuenca, 1999, pp. 365-380.

Hufeland, Gottlieb, *Lehrsätze des Naturrechts und der damit verbundenen Wissenschaften*, Jena 1790 (reproduction: Glashütten im Taunus: Detlev Auvermann KG, 1973).
- *Versuch über den Grundsatz des Naturrechts nebst einem Anhange*, Leipzig, 1785 (online: http://reader.digitale-sammlungen.de/resolve/display/bsb10040909.html).

Kant, Immanuel, *Gesammelte Schriften*, ed. by Königlich Preussische Akademie der Wissenschaften (Akademie-Ausgabe), Berlin u.a., 1900 ff. (*AA*)

[Klein, Ernst Ferdinand], *Freyheit und Eigenthum, abgehandelt in acht Gesprächen über die Beschlüsse der Französischen Nationalversammlung*, Berlin und Stettin, 1790.

Koselleck, Reinhart, *Vergangene Zukunft. Zur Semantik geschichtlicher Zeiten*, Frankfurt/M., 1989.

Macor, Laura Anna, *Die Bestimmung des Menschen (1748-1800). Eine Begriffsgeschichte*, Stuttgart-Bad Cannstatt, 2013.

Marquard, Odo, *Schwierigkeiten mit der Geschichtsphilosophie*, Frankfurt/M., 1973.
- *Abschied vom Prinzipiellen*, Stuttgart, 1981.

Möser, Justus, „Ueber das Recht der Menschheit, als den Grund der neuen Französischen Konstitution", in: *Berlinische Monatsschrift* 15 (Jun. 1790), pp. 499-506.
- „Wie und wann mag eine Nazion ihre Konstitution verändern?", in: *Berlinische Monatsschrift* 18 (Nov. 1791), pp. 396-401.

Oncina Coves, Faustino, „La Revolución americana contra la Revolución francesa: un argumento del burkianismo contra el kantismo", in: *Filosofía y Revolución. Estudios sobre la Revolución Francesa y su recepción filosófica*, ed. by Eduardo Bello, Murcia, 1991, pp. 157-196.

Rehberg, August Wilhelm, *Untersuchungen über die Französische Revolution nebst kritischen Nachrichten von den merkwürdigsten Schriften welche darüber in Frankreich erschienen sind*, Erster Theil, Hannover und Osnabrück, 1793 (digital edition: http://reader.digitale-sammlungen.de/de/fs1/object/display/bsb10424086_00001.html).
- „Über das Verhältnis der Theorie zur Praxis", in: *Kant- Gentz – Rehberg. Über Theorie und Praxis*, ed. by Dieter Henrich, Frankfurt am Main, 1967, pp. 113-130.

Stolleis, Michael, *Staatsraison, Recht und Moral in philosophischen Texten des späten 18. Jahrhunderts*, Meisenheim am Glan, 1972.

Wittichen, Paul, „Kant und Burke", in: *Historische Zeitschrift* 93:2 (1904), pp. 253-255.

Teleology and Perfection
Law, Freedom and the Search for Unity, from Kant to the Post-Kantians

Luca Fonnesu

Laws and Laws of Freedom

Kant's philosophical world is dominated by the idea of rules and laws that organize different spheres of reality, from nature up to the rational and human universe. He is probably the most important representative of a tradition which has as its central features the description of the natural world produced by the scientific revolution on the one hand, and the corresponding analysis of the laws of the human world on the other. Already at the end of the seventeenth century, the very notion of *law* – which did in fact have a political origin – becomes the common element of both nature and reason[1]. No more opposition exists, then, between *physis* and *nomos*, but rather analogy. Laws are the common element because they explain the functioning of different worlds, that of nature and that of reason. From this perspective must be read one of the most quoted texts by Kant, even outside of the community of philosophers and Kantian scholars:

> Zwei Dinge erfüllen das Gemüt mit immer neuer und zunehmenden Bewunderung und Ehrfurcht, je öfter und anhaltender sich das Nachdenken damit beschäftigt: Der bestirnte Himmel über mir, und das moralische Gesetz in mir.[2]

The deepest meaning of Kant's words goes far beyond their evocative, rhetorical force. This same position can be found – in a philosophically more elaborated form – in other works. The following passage occurs in his first book on morality, the *Grundlegung zur Metaphysik der Sitten*:

---

* This contribution is written in the framework of the research project FFI2017-82195-P of the AEI/FEDER, UE. It does share some common ground with my article "Die Kritik der Kantischen Gesetzesethik bei Fichte und Hegel", recently published in a book edited by Antonino Falduto and Heiner Klemme (2018). Quotations of Kant are from the *Akademie-Ausgabe* (*AA*), with the usual exception of the first *Critique* (*A/B*); of Fichte from the *Gesamtausgabe der Bayerischen Akademie der Wissenschaften* (*GA*).
1 Cf. Milton (1998).
2 *AA* V, 161.

> Ein jedes Ding der Natur wirkt nach Gesetzen. Nur ein vernünftiges Wesen hat das Vermögen, *nach der Vorstellung* der Gesetze, d.i. nach Prinzipien, zu handeln, oder einen *Willen*.[3]

In the *two* cited passages Kant expresses the thesis that runs all through his intellectual development and that characterizes his philosophical attitude both in the metaphysical and in the practical domain: there are different *orders*, and all depend on rules, laws or norms. The orders of nature and of reason stand confronting each other, each offering its own special, particular features and at the same time its analogy with the other. In the *Critique of Practical Reason*, the starry heaven represents the order of nature and its laws, corresponding to another lawful realm, that of moral law within me. In the passage from the *Grundlegung*, the analogy is accompanied by the emphasis on the distinction. On the one hand, there is nature with its laws; on the other, there are rational beings who do not merely follow laws, but act through the rational representation of laws, i.e. principles. The analogy grounded on laws even explains the idealisation of nature, although morality and freedom are (of course) axiologically superior to the former. Nature can be seen as a model because in nature there is no possibility that the law will not be followed.

The possibility *not to follow the law* is a special feature of rational beings, who *can* will – and in fact often do will – *against* their own laws as rational beings, i.e. against rational principles. This peculiarity of rational beings implies that the human world is not only a realm of laws, but also a realm of *freedom*, a concept closely connected – in Kant's view – with that of law, and essential to morality: without freedom, no responsibility is possible. The very necessity of freedom for Kant concerns the possibility of responsibility because the former is the condition for the latter and the latter is the condition for morality itself[4].

Even the old question of the *proof* of human freedom can be answered through its connection with the law. In this way Kant gives his own solution to the objection raised by Spinoza against Descartes, who in the *Principles of Philosophy* had argued that freedom of the will is one of the first and most common innate notions in us (Part I, § 39). Spinoza's objection will become the highly disturbing question of the following century: the alleged consciousness of freedom is just ignorance of the determining causes of the will (*Ethica, I*, Scholium). Kant's answer is that it is true that we cannot be directly conscious of our freedom, but we are directly conscious of our moral nature, i.e.

---

3   *AA* IV, 412.
4   Cf. *KrV*, A448/B476.

of the moral law, and through this consciousness we are indirectly conscious of freedom too. If the third antinomy of the *Critique of Pure Reason* shows the possibility of freedom as independence from natural causation, the second *Critique* shows its reality[5].

But there is another and equally important aspect of the relation of freedom and law. The independence from causal determination is the first, essential feature of freedom, but Kant thinks that a *positive* meaning of freedom can establish a still closer connection between freedom and law. To this end, Kant takes up again a Greek concept that acquires only through him the philosophical importance which it maintains up to our days, the concept of *autonomy*[6]. Freedom is then self-legislation, and self-legislation is freedom.

Morality and Perfection

From the systematic point of view, the attaining of the fundamental law of pure practical reason at § 7 of the *Critique of Practical Reason* is the turning point of Kant's argument, and offers him the possibility of declaring proudly his own role in the history of ethics, presenting the principle of autonomy as the special and exclusive feature of an ethics grounded upon a *formal* principle (§ 8). The first consequence is that all *material ethics* of the preceding tradition (ancient and modern) are necessarily *heteronomous*. Although different in other respects, all material ethics – as Kant shows at §§ 2 and 3 – are *as such* empirical and reducible to the principle of self-love or happiness *independently* from the nature of the content or material of the principle[7]. What has been proven during the search for a (formal) principle of morality (§§ 2-6) is

---

5 „Damit man hier nicht Inkonsequenzen anzutreffen wähne, wenn ich jetzt die Freiheit die Bedingung des moralischen Gesetzes nenne, und in der Abhandlung nachher behaupte, daß das moralische Gesetz die Bedingung sei, unter der wir uns allererst der Freiheit bewußt werden können, so will ich nur erinnern, daß die Freiheit allerdings die ratio essendi des moralischen Gesetzes, das moralische Gesetz aber die ratio cognoscendi der Freiheit sei. Denn, wäre nicht das moralische Gesetz in unserer Vernunft eher deutlich gedacht, so würden wir uns niemals berechtigt halten, so etwas, als Freiheit ist (ob diese gleich sich nicht widerspricht), anzunehmen. Wäre aber keine Freiheit, so würde das moralische Gesetz in uns gar nicht anzutreffen sein" (*AA* V, 4f).
6 Most recent contributions: *Kant on Moral Autonomy*, Sensen (2009); *The Emergence of Moral Autonomy in Kant's Moral Philosophy*, Bacin/Sensen (2019).
7 It has to be noted that with the principle of happiness Kant does not mean generally eudaimonism but a proper hedonism, because he denies – as in the same years Jeremy Bentham, with opposite aims, does too – the possibility of a qualitative distinction between different pleasures (*AA* V, 22-23).

now related to the discussion of the opposition autonomy/heteronomy (§ 8), offering at the same time the taxonomy of material, i.e. heteronomous ethical theories.[8] They are *all* empirical, even when their claim – as in the case of the ethics of perfection in Wolff and the Stoics – is exactly not to be that:

> Wenn nun also uns Zwecke vorher gegeben werden müssen, in Beziehung auf welche der Begriff der *Vollkommenheit* (einer inneren, an uns selbst, oder einer äußeren, an Gott) allein Bestimmungsgrund des Willens werden kann, ein Zweck aber, als *Objekt*, welches vor der Willensbestimmung durch eine praktische Regel vorhergehen und den Grund der Möglichkeit einer solchen enthalten muß, mithin die *Materie* des Willens, als Bestimmungsgrund desselben genommen, jederzeit empirisch ist, mithin zum *Epikurischen* Prinzip der Glückseligkeitslehre, niemals aber zum reinen Vernunftprinzip der Sittenlehre und der Pflicht dienen kann.[9]

The end of perfection cannot therefore, as every other material principle, ground morality. The central role of a formal law, and Kant's polemical attitude towards all material foundations of ethics, do not imply that he pays no attention to perfection, to its conceptual constellation and to its role in the moral domain. It is not impossible to think of a form of Kantian "moral" perfectionism[10]. Here we want to determine the space of perfection in its relationship with teleology.

From the moral point of view, the idea of perfection refers to the figure that always plays a salient role in Kant's thought beyond its strictly religious meaning, i.e. the idea of God as a rational being with a perfectly rational will in a moral sense, i.e. a *holy* will.[11]

Moral perfection contrasted with an imperfect and finite will (such as the human) does play a role in Kant's texts, both in a synchronic and in a temporal sense, i.e. on the one hand, in view of the understanding of the nature of moral law as a prescription; on the other, as the end of a process of self-improvement which should imply a corresponding recompense, happiness. The synchronic sense introduces imperatives; the latter will form, together with holiness, the *highest good* (which is another form of perfection), the good *vollendet, consummatum, perfectissimum*.[12]

In the *Grundlegung*, introducing the very notion of "imperative," Kant stresses the distance between a perfect and an imperfect will:

---

8   *AA* V, 39-41.
9   *AA* V, 41.
10 Cf. Guyer (2016).
11 *AA* IV, 414, 439.
12 *AA* V, 110.

> Wenn die Vernunft den Willen unausbleiblich bestimmt, so sind die Handlungen eines solchen Wesens, die als objektiv notwendig erkannt werden, auch subjektiv notwendig, d.i. der Wille ist ein Vermögen, *nur dasjenige* zu wählen, was die Vernunft, unabhängig von der Neigung, als praktisch notwendig, d.i. als gut erkennt. Bestimmt aber die Vernunft für sich allein den Willen nicht hinlänglich, ist dieser noch subjektiven Bedingungen (gewissen Triebfedern) unterworfen, die nicht immer mit den objektiven übereinstimmen; mit einem Worte, ist der Wille nicht *an sich* völlig der Vernunft gemäß (wie es bei Menschen wirklich ist): so sind die Handlungen, die objektiv als notwendig erkannt werden, subjektiv zufällig, und die Bestimmung eines solchen Willens, objektiven Gesetzen gemäß, ist *Nötigung*; d.i. das Verhältnis der objektiven Gesetze zu einem nicht durchaus guten Willen wird vorgestellt als die Bestimmung des Willens eines vernünftigen Wesens zwar durch Gründe der Vernunft, denen aber dieser Wille seiner Natur nach nicht notwendig folgsam ist. Die Vorstellung eines objektiven Prinzips, sofern es für einen Willen nötigend ist, heißt ein Gebot (der Vernunft) und die Formel des Gebots heißt *Imperativ*.[13]

The imperfection of human will implies the prescriptive character of the law as a command or imperative. The very question of the relationship between perfect and imperfect will has a further dimension, the temporal one, which emerges clearly in the second *Critique* when Kant faces the problem of the justification of the postulate of the immortality of the soul, another condition (along with the existence of God) for the realisation of the highest good[14]:

> Die völlige Angemessenheit des Willens aber zum moralischen Gesetze ist *Heiligkeit*, eine Vollkommenheit, deren kein vernünftiges Wesen der Sinnenwelt in keinem Zeitpuncte seines Daseins fähig ist. Da sie indessen gleichwohl als praktisch nothwendig gefordert wird, so kann sie nur in einem ins *Unendliche* gehenden *Progressus* zu jener völligen Angemessenheit angetroffen werden.[15]

Only immortality makes possible an infinite improvement and an infinite process of rapprochement to the end of holiness. It is not possible here to follow all the aspects of Kant's idea of perfecting and of development. By dealing with these concepts, Kant engages with the most important philosophers of the *Spätaufklärung*, such as Lessing or Mendelssohn.

It has to be said that a peculiar attention to a perfectionist position oriented to the realisation of morality *in the human world* becomes especially important in Kant's thought after the *Critique of Judgment* with its reflection on teleology in its different aspects. It is not by chance that the greater part of Kant's writings

---

13   AA IV, 412-13.
14   I do not deal here with the highly problematic notion of the highest good. The literature on the question is vast. I refer only to Kleingeld (1995); Tafani (2006).
15   AA V, 122.

in the last decade of his life are dedicated to questions of law, politics and history. It is the question of the realisation of morality which becomes more and more important, and this was not so apparent in the *Grundlegungsschriften*[16].

Finally, in this framework of the worldly realisation of morality the very idea of a moral *improvement* already involved in the postulate of immortality does play a great role in the last important Kantian work concerning morality, i.e. the *Metaphysics of Morals*. We have moral duties only towards human beings, not towards God, i.e. towards ourselves and towards the others. The general class of the duties toward ourselves is exactly the duty to promote our morality, i.e. the duty of moral self-improvement.

The Kantian project of a realisation of morality was neglected by most of his readers, critics and followers alike. Notwithstanding, many of them oriented their thoughts in the very same direction.[17]

Morality and the ‚Aetas kantiana'

Kant's philosophy did not achieve the immediate impact and success that we might today anticipate it would have had. A proper discussion took place only after the publication of a "Kantian" Journal – the *Allgemeine Literaturzeitung*, 1785 – and Reinhold's *Briefe über die Kantische Philosophie* (1786-87, 1790-92, published as a book). Reinhold, who arrived in Jena in 1787, wants to convince the public that Kant's thought is not simply an obscure and abstruse metaphysics, but that it deals with important questions of morality and religion.

From the moral point of view, law and freedom seem to be the fundamental concepts of Kantian morality. Kant holds them together, but the main role is in fact played by the law. The discussion of Kant's philosophy displays on the contrary a polemical attitude towards his stress on the law as the only possible foundation of normativity. Different forms of perfectionism will be the consequence of this criticism. The philosophers that present themselves as the best interpreters of Kant's revolution in philosophy do in fact underline the grounding role of freedom, not of law. This is so true, that the meaning itself of "freedom" is subject to manifold interpretations which go far beyond its merely practical, i.e. moral meaning. Even the question of moral responsibility becomes less important. The very idea of rational spontaneity of Leibnizian origin, which in Kant's thought receives a new interpretation[18], finds a

---

16   Cf. Fonnesu (2004); Id., (2013).
17   Cf. Moggach (2011).
18   Cf. on the question: Moggach (2018).

further extension in the direction of a metaphysical meaning. Kant himself – after all – stressed the meaning of freedom as a power "einen Zustand *von selbst* anzufangen"[19] and spoke of a *Spontaneität der Begriffe* in a cognitive sense.[20] Many Kantian philosophers think that they have to develop these suggestions and leave the – for Kant essential – idea of a law in the background. Even when it retains some role, the law becomes a form of manifestation of freedom in its development, a mere stage of the process of self-determination of reason. And it has to be recalled also that autonomy (*Autonomie*) is understood, or even "translated", as the self-sufficiency (*Selbständigkeit*) of reason, more than its self-legislation, which was on the contrary Kant's peculiar feature, when he made autonomy a central concept of philosophical language[21]. On the one hand, many Kantians after 1790 come to think of freedom as the deepest and most pervasive character of reason in all its expressions, from knowledge to ethics and politics; on the other, it is necessary to show how this original freedom of reason effects its realisation through different stages, building a new man and a new world. The essential feature is now thought to be freedom as spontaneity, as a power to take action in the world, and to exercise actual causality in the world as a capacity to modify it. The meaning of freedom goes far beyond Kant's original position, although deriving from him[22].

For Kant's critical followers who are not satisfied with his results, the critique of the centrality of the law is closely connected with other questionable aspects of his thought. The central role of the law – for example – is thought to imply the formal character of morality and the opposition between reason and nature, while they should be held as complementary.

---

19   *KrV*, A533/B561.
20   *KrV*, A50/B74.
21   Criticism will in some cases move in the opposite direction, considering the development of the autonomy of the whole of reason from moral autonomy to be a clear sign of the arrogance of human reason against superior powers. This is e.g. the later position of Reinhold, when he abandons the Kantian position which he had held during his time in Jena, and declares instead his concern about the irreligious self-sufficiency of reason, which is contrary to the only absolute from which everyrthing derives and to which everything has to revert, i.e. God. In his *Ueber die Autonomie als Princip der praktischen Philosophie der Kantischen – und der gesammten Philosophie der Fichtisch-Schellingschen Schule* (1801) Reinhold attributes to Schelling the responsibility for this dangerous extension of the concept of autonomy to the whole of philosophy. Analogous worries will later be expressed by Franz von Baader (cf. Feil (1987), 85). Reinhold's identification of Fichte and Schelling will provoke the famous Hegelian *Differenzschrift*, where Hegel criticises Fichte from the point of view of Schelling, maintaining a great difference between the two philosophers. For the development of the concept of "autonomy" between Kant and Hegel see: Fonnesu (2004).
22   Cf. Cesa (2013).

The programme of deepening and developing Kant's most important intuitions takes place with reference to perfectionist arguments that stress the teleological aspects of human existence and knowledge, recalling their seminal but insufficient presence in Kant's thought on the one hand, and themes of pre-Kantian philosophy on the other. In this direction, a leading role is played by suggestions which came to assume the utmost importance in eighteenth-century Germany, such as the birth of an *anthropology*, and the connected notion of an endless improvement of man, an idea that is also present in Kant's own thought. Anthropological considerations, also grounded upon Leibnizian and Wolffian arguments, had great importance in the discussion of the *Aufklärung*, and find their most fruitful expression in the teleological, perfectionist idea of a *Bestimmung des Menschen*, a very *Grundidee* of German Enlightenment which exerts an enormous influence on German philosophy and theology up to Fichte.[23]

At the origin of this grounding idea is the small book published in 1748 by the theologian Johann Joachim Spalding – *Betrachtung über die Bestimmung des Menschen* – which will have eleven (official) editions between 1748 and 1794[24]. It is, as far as I know, the first *history of consciousness* in the German language, a form of philosophical exposition which will become famous with Fichte, Schelling and Hegel's *Phenomenology*. But the teleological process of the self-understanding of consciousness is not the only important feature. This self-understanding is at the same time the phenomenological description of a perfectionist attitude which will exert utmost influence in the discussion of the *Spätaufklärung* and later. The *Bestimmung des Menschen* will be one central task of philosophical reflection for Mendelssohn, Abbt, Herder, Fichte and Schiller.[25]

In Spalding's "history" the subject moves forward through a teleological development which is the consequence of self-understanding. This process even has an existential feature, going through different stages from sensibility to immortality. The forms of self-understanding are ways of life with a dominant

---

23 For this expression, cf. Hinske (1990); the special number of the journal *Aufklärung* (11/1, 1996), *Die Bestimmung des Menschen*, 1996. The most recent and informative work is the book of Laura Anna Macor (2013) *Die Bestimmung des Menschen (1748-1800). Eine Begriffsgeschichte*.

24 See the critical edition: Spalding (2007).

25 See the already mentioned book by Maria Anna Macor, although she underestimates in my opinion the importance of the concept and of the underlying teleological attitude in the last decade of the century, e.g. in Fichte and Schiller. For Kant cf. Brandt (2007). The last edition during Spalding's life – 1794 – integrates Kantian themes such as the idea of a law with universal validity (Macor (2013), 306-310).

value – *Sinnlichkeit, Vergnügen des Geistes, Tugend, Religion, Unsterblichkeit* – which has to be overcome through self-improvement.

The German discussion of the *Bestimmung* was closely connected with the discussion of Rousseau's philosophy and his critical attitude towards the very idea of progress and of human improvement. It is not by chance that Moses Mendelssohn, one of the participants to the discussion on the *Bestimmung des Menschen*, was also the translator of the second *Discourse*. Rousseau introduces a neologism – *perfectibilité* – attributing to the word a critical, negative sense – *la source de tous les malheurs de l'homme* – but the German version of the *Perfektibilität* will on the contrary assume a positive meaning in the direction of the possibility of progress and of a perfectionist perspective[26].

The philosophers of the last decade of the eighteenth century, of course, do not have to pay attention only to Kant's philosophical revolution and to its many unsolved questions. The revolution in France arouses European public opinion, and soon the two revolutions will be understood as the philosophical and historical sign of a new era, hence a sort of *eschatologische Stimmung*. And even this is not the end of the story. Profound social and economic changes are also occurring, and keen observers understand that a new world is emerging, a social and economic structure which Karl Marx will call the *capitalist mode of production*.

Teleology as Rationalisation

It is difficult not to see in Fichte the most representative figure of post-Kantian philosophy in the last years of the eighteenth century. Writings such as *Über den Begriff der Wissenschaftslehre* (1794) or the so called *Erste Einleitung zur Wissenschaftslehre* (1797) do in fact have the character of a programme which can be communicated to a philosophically informed public opinion. The *Erste Einleitung* is sometimes still considered as the programme which the entire philosophical movement of German Idealism aims to realise,[27] and it is true that the reaction of philosophers such as Schelling, Hölderlin or Reinhold to the first writings of Fichte was that of an unconditional enthusiasm.[28] The great success of public series of lectures such as those dedicated to the duties of scholars – *de officiis eruditorum* –, held at the University of Jena, is well

---

26 Cf. Hornig (1980).
27 Cf. Hösle (1988), 22 ff.
28 For Fichte's influence on his time see the excellent collection edited by Erich Fuchs (1978-2012).

known²⁹. But there is something more, which has to do with the proper philosophical content of Fichte's thought and with the great influence which he exerts on his contemporaries. A general opinion holds him for the philosopher who can realise the Kantian system of philosophy, and the main concept for the construction of this system is freedom as spontaneity, the activity of reason through different forms and figures. The true system of philosophy is a system of freedom. It has to describe the development of an original activity through its forms: freedom as a practical quality of the will is just a further development of freedom as a theoretical, i.e. metaphysical principle.³⁰ It is this at the same time radical and dynamic character of Fichte's methodology which will influence most of his contemporaries just as they also begin to make explicit their doubts. Everything occurs in a matter of a few years, beginning with Fichte's arrival in Jena – in 1794 – up to the dispute concerning his atheism at the end of 1798. Less than a year later (7. August 1799), another significant fact is to be noted: Kant's public declaration considering Fichte's philosophy "ein gänzlich unhaltbares System"³¹.

Fichte's teleological, perfectionist approach³² is systematically formulated in the *System of Ethics* (1798), but an outline can be found already in the lectures on *de officiis eruditorum*. These lectures are probably the first influential attempt to offer an alternative to Kant's ethics of the law through a teleological approach grounded upon the idea of the *Bestimmung*³³.

Already the discussion in the *Spätaufklärung* of the *Bestimmung des Menschen* had raised the question of the many possible meanings of *bestimmen* and *Bestimmung*: to be *bestimmt* can mean to be called (*berufen*), or teleologically destined or intended (*bestimmt* in the proper sense). But the term *Bestimmung* not only has the teleological meaning of *destination* or *vocation*, but also the "ontological" one of *determination*, in Latin *determinatio*, a central term of the philosophical tradition that plays a crucial role in German classical philosophy. *Bestimmung* implies therefore at the same time a teleologically oriented process of the subject of the *Bestimmung*, and the *individual* determination of the process, as e.g. Mendelssohn argues:

> Die Zweydeutigkeit liegt hier in der Sprache. Das Wort Bestimmung bedeutet sowohl die Festsetzung eines Prädikats, unter mancherley derselben, die dem

---

29 See on this question the excellent introduction of Reinhard Lauth (1976) to his edition of the *Philosophische Bibliothek*, pp. VII-LXVI.
30 GA I 5, 77.
31 AA XII, 370.
32 See Fonnesu (2004). Recently: Ware (2018).
33 See Fonnesu (1993).

> Subjekte zukommen können, Determination; als die Festsetzung des Endzwecks zu welchem etwas als Mittel gebraucht werden soll, Destination ... Die Bestimmung des Menschen kann sowohl Determination; als Destination des Menschen bedeuten.[34]

And the individual determination implies certain ethical tasks[35]. Furthermore, Mendelssohn himself stresses the twofold character of this individual determination: it can be ontological-natural, or social, or both. Human beings are not only abstract human beings: they are human beings that have a certain natural constitution and a certain social role.[36]

Already Fichte's expression *Bestimmung ‚des Gelehrten'* echoes that discussion. The *Bestimmung* of every human being derives from his twofold individual determination; on the one hand the natural, on the other the social, the particular position occupied by the person within the social whole. The teleological structure of individuality is the principle which grounds its moral task, and the individual determination enables Fichte to propose a principle of morality which is universal *but* not formal, because its content is exactly individuality in its development: „Handle so, dass du die Maxime deines Willens als ewiges Gesetz für dich denken könntest"[37]. This command is teleologically justified because its aim is an absolute unity, identity, agreement (*Einigkeit, Identität, Uebereinstimmung*) of the rational being with himself, i.e. of reason with itself. This is possible only by pursuing the agreement of the sensible world inside and outside us with reason, i.e. through the *rationalisation* of nature thanks to our activity. A main feature of Fichte's ethical thought is this "Baconian" attitude toward rational activity and the modification of nature: „Alles vernunftlose sich zu entwerfen, frei und nach seinem eignen Gesetze es zu beherrschen, ist letzter Endzweck des Menschen"[38]. It is of course an infinite process, because otherwise man would cease to be a man and become God, exactly in the same way as the Kantian holy will, although Fichte's rationalisation has different traits: the question is much more that of action in the world and on nature than the improvement of a good will in a moral sense.

The *Bestimmung*, the destination, the task, cannot consist in the perfection of the absolute identity of reason with itself, but in the infinite approximation to this identity. The close connection between perfection as the rational end and perfecting as the process is thus explicit:

---

34 *GS* 5, 35.
35 Ibid., 35-36.
36 Ibid., 116.
37 *GA* I 3, 30.
38 *GA* I 3, 32.

> Nennt man nun jene völlige Uebereinstimmung mit sich selbst Vollkommenheit in der höchsten Bedeutung des Worts, wie man sie allerdings nennen kann: so ist *Vollkommenheit* das höchste unerreichbare Ziel des Menschen; *Vervollkommnung ins unendliche* aber seine Bestimmung.[39]

Fichte insists against Kant that the task has to do not only with the will, but – since the question is concrete action in the world – with the whole man, with all his forces and faculties: all should „zu vollkommener Identität übereinstimmen, und unter sich zusammenstimmen"[40]. This is what he calls *Kultur*: „Die Sinnlichkeit soll kultiviert werden"[41]. The process of control and rationalisation of our own and of external nature is therefore the *Bestimmung* of every individuality from its particular position and point of view. It is a process of *Disziplinierung* of sensibility, a *Zivilisierung* which receives now an ethical meaning, while Kant had stressed the difference between it and *Moralisierung* already in the *Idee zu einer allgemeinen Geschichte in weltbürgerlicher Absicht* (1784), where he explicitly follows Rousseau's suggestions[42]. Fichte's argument looks on the contrary for a justification of his idea of progress, developed in the fifth, last lecture, which is dedicated, not by chance, to the criticism of Rousseau himself.

The proper systematisation of Fichte's perfectionism is the *Sittenlehre*. The foundation of a proper system of duties takes place here through two passages, the first concerning the teleological justification of duty, the second concerning the widening of the perfectionist horizon in the social, collective dimension, which is for Fichte, after the teleology of individuality, the second essential moment of a real, concrete ethics.

First of all, Fichte justifies the very idea of an "applicable" duty through a series of actions of the individual, which is called his *Bestimmung*, i.e. the progress towards the absolute independence from nature, the *Selbständigkeit*,

---

39 *GA* I 3, 32.
40 *GA* I 3, 30.
41 *GA* I 3, 31.
42 „Rousseau hatte so Unrecht nicht, wenn er den Zustand der Wilden vorzog, so bald man nämlich diese letzte Stufe, die unsere Gattung noch zu ersteigen hat, wegläßt. Wir sind im hohen Grade durch Kunst und Wissenschaft *cultivirt*. Wir sind *civilisirt* bis zum Überlästigen zu allerlei gesellschaftlicher Artigkeit und Anständigkeit. Aber uns schon für *moralisirt* zu halten, daran fehlt noch sehr viel. Denn die Idee der Moralität gehört noch zur Cultur; der Gebrauch dieser Idee aber, welcher nur auf das Sittenähnliche in der Ehrliebe und der äußeren Anständigkeit hinausläuft, macht blos die Civilisirung aus" (*AA* VIII, 26). It seems that Kant at least partially accepts Rousseau's criticism of civilisation, maintaining that civilisation does not imply in itself moralisation.

self-sufficiency of reason[43]. The actions that constitute this series are *duties*, although they do not seem to belong to a law, but to the temporal development of the individuality which forms the *Bestimmung*. The principle of ethics is therefore, writes Fichte, *Erfülle jedesmal deine Bestimmung*.[44]

The strategy consists in a shift from the search for a synthesis of reason and sensibility (the pure and the natural drive, *Trieb*) to its teleological solution in a temporal perspective, the *Bestimmung*. Both in the lectures of 1794 and in the *Sittenlehre*, Fichte stresses the importance of nature and sensibility which – in his opinion and in that of many contemporaries – had been neglected by Kant: „Sieht man nur auf das höhere Begehrungsvermögen, so erhält man blos *Metaphysik der Sitten*, welche formal und leer ist. Nur durch synthetische Vereinigung mit desselben mit dem niederen erhält man eine *Sittenlehre*, welche reel sein muss"[45]. Nonetheless, Fichte does insist on the fact that through this indispensable consideration of the sensible part of the human being – without which action itself would be impossible and freedom would be only „Unterlassung", not an actual *causality* of freedom on the world – the end of reason is the *rationalisation* of nature and reality, reducing them, in an infinite process, to reason itself, to its self-sufficiency (*Selbständigkeit*). It seems that sensibility is important mainly as an instrument to pursue its progressive reduction to reason. Teleology and progress consist in the process of rationalisation of reality.

The second essential shift of the *Sittenlehre* implies a passage from the individual *Bestimmung* to its inclusion in a collective, social dimension. The proper subject of morality – we discover suddenly – is not an individual reason, but reason as a whole, reason as it is represented (*dargestellt*) in human society: „Die Selbständigkeit aller Vernunft, als solcher, ist unser letztes Ziel: mithin nicht die Selbständigkeit Einer Vernunft, inwiefern sie individuelle Vernunft ist"[46]. This widening of the horizon is of the utmost importance because the organisation of society, including labour as a central element of the rationalisation of nature, becomes in this way an ethical task, i.e. the organisation of the *Darstellung* of reason and of its activity in the world. The doctrine of duties, teleologically grounded, is at the same time socially determined, deriving the social role of each human being from the division of labour as the essential element in the distribution of tasks among individuals and ranks (*Stände*), i.e.

---

43   *GA* I 5, 141: „Wir können diese Reihe nennen die sittliche Bestimmung des endlichen Vernunftwesens".
44   *GA* I 5, 141.
45   *GA* I 5, 126.
46   *GA* I 5, 209.

in the distribution of duties. At the end of the book Fichte presents a doctrine of duties, which is a curious reformulation of the traditional doctrine of duties in a framework completely different from the latter.[47] Fichte's explicit defence and justification of the division of labour with the formation of different ranks (*Stände*) was announced in 1794 even in the title of the third lecture: *Über die Verschiedenheit der Stände in der Gesellschaft*[48]. The doctrine of duties at the end of the *Sittenlehre* derives from the social, transindividual perspective outlined in 1794 and systematically justified in the *Sittenlehre*. This teleologically grounded doctrine is the consequence of the new approach to the value and role of individuals. The Kantian thesis of the rational being as an end in itself is overthrown, and the individual is now a *means* of reason as a whole. The individual „ist Zweck, als *Mittel*, die Vernunft zu realisiren ... Jedem allein wird vor seinem Selbstbewusstsein die Erreichung des Gesammtzwecks der Vernunft aufgetragen"[49].

The Search for Unity

Between 1794 and 1798, most important German writers and philosophers are under Fichte's influence. In a few years the situation will be completely different: even the most convinced supporters of the philosopher of the *Doctrine of Science* will become his critics. In this very brief space of time, a first signal of the direction in which German thought is moving can be found in the *Briefe über die ästhetische Erziehung des Menschen*, published by Schiller in 1795, one year after Fichte's lectures on the destination/vocation of the scholar[50].

For some years Fichte's philosophy was considered to offer the solution to Kant's difficulties, primarily for his capacity to go beyond Kant's dualism, but soon he too would be criticised for similar reasons: Fichte himself has not been radical enough, and although he has glimpsed new solutions, his philosophy suffers from analogous limits. The kind of criticism which Schiller expresses against Kant in *Über Anmut und Würde* recurs in the writings of the German poet, and in those of others, in the discussion of Fichte's philosophy.

Schiller cannot accept the relation between reason and nature which he finds *both* in Kant and Fichte. His anthropology seeks other solutions, being

---

47   The theory of the *Sittlichkeit* in Hegel's *Philosophy of Right* will mean the end of moral philosophy as a doctrine of duties of the seventeenth and eighteenth centuries. See my "Pflicht und Pflichtenlehre" mentioned above, n. 21.
48   *GA* I 3, 40.
49   *GA* I 5, 230.
50   The best work on Schiller's philosophy is that of Beiser (2005).

much more concerned with a genuine *unity* of man in the form of harmony, and not with the supervenience of reason upon nature. Schiller's criticism in *Über Anmut und Würde* concerns Kant:

> In der Kantischen Moralphilosophie ist die Idee der *Pflicht* mit einer Härte vorgetragen worden, die alle Grazien davon zurückschreckt und einen schwachen Verstand leicht versuchen könnte, auf dem Wege einer finstern und mönchischen Aszetik die moralische Vollkommenheit zu suchen.[51]

Fichte too tries to overcome Kant's dualism both from the metaphysical and from the ethical-anthropological point of view. Even the Fichtean use of the terminology of the anthropology of the *Aufklärung* – for example the use of the word *Trieb* – goes in this direction. Fichte's perspective is notwithstanding characterised by the idea of an original unity of reason and nature, which has to be restored through the domination of reason over nature, a rationalisation as *Disziplinierung*[52]. Fichte's attitude is itself grounded – in Schiller's opinion – upon an opposition of reason and nature which can produce only uniformity between the former and the latter, but not harmony.

This is why Schiller, in the *Briefe*, denounces the opposite risks of deviations (*Abweichungen*) which could have the consequence of "missing" the real *Bestimmung des Menschen*[53]. The unity of man can be endangered not only by inclinations, but also by the arrogance of rational principles: the "deviation" can therefore produce a savage or a barbarian:

> Der Mensch kann sich [...] auf eine doppelte Weise entgegengesetzt sein: Entweder als Wilder, wenn seine Gefühle über seine Grundsätze herrschen; oder als Barbar, wenn seine Grundsätze seine Gefühle zerstören.[54]

The Kantian opposition of reason to nature can still be found in Fichte's thought, which represents only the *letter* of Kant's philosophy, but not its deepest *spirit*. In other words, Fichte remains on the ground of Kant's dualism:

> In einer Transzendental-Philosophie, wo alles darauf ankommt, die Form von dem Inhalt zu befreien und das Notwendige von allem Zufälligen rein zu erhalten, gewöhnt man sich gar leicht, das Materielle sich bloß als Hindernis zu denken und die Sinnlichkeit, weil sie gerade bei *diesem* Geschäft im Wege steht, in einem notwendigen Widerspruch mit der Vernunft vorzustellen. Eine solche

---

51 *WDB* II, 406.
52 See the remarks of Hogrebe (1984), 278.
53 *WDB* II, 506f. (24. Brief).
54 *WDB* II, 4. Brief.

Vorstellungsart liegt zwar auf keine Weise im *Geist* des Kantischen Systems, aber im *Buchstaben* desselben könnte sie gar wohl liegen.[55]

Schiller's search for a "harmony" between reason and sensibility is the main motive for the success of the *Briefe* among philosophers who admired Fichte's project, but who were more and more disappointed with its actual realisation. The necessity of a new philosophical attitude which would go beyond Kant's dualism is also defended by Fichte, but both his metaphysics and his anthropology – in Schiller's opinion, and soon in that of his contemporaries – cannot do that[56]. Fichte is in fact still respected as the most important Kantian philosopher, but the discussion between Schiller and Fichte is the first sign, for some time not generally known, of the perplexities that his thought raised. The German philosophical world looks for new forms of *unity* because Fichte does not solve the problems left by Kant's philosophical dualism.

In their search for unity, thinkers such as Schiller or Humboldt, Hölderlin or Hegel pay great attention to a model which does not play a salient role for Fichte, i.e. the "unity" and harmony of the Greek, classical man that is mentioned by Schiller in his sixth Brief[57]. The Greek man did not have any experience of division, of *Zwiespalt*, and his unity contrasts with the fragmented life of modern man, the result of modern life and of the modern division of labour. In this respect one can find another difference between Fichte and Schiller: both accept the necessity of the division of labour, but Fichte celebrates it, while Schiller cannot refrain from partial regret. In modern times – writes Schiller – one has „von Individuum zum Individuum herumfragen ..., um die Totalität der Gattung zusammenzulesen ... wir sehen nicht bloß einzelne Subjekte, sondern ganze Klassen von Menschen nur einen Teil ihrer Anlagen

---

55   *WDB* II, 473f.
56   Schiller's mention of the difference between spirit and letter of Kant's philosophy provokes Fichte's reaction in an article entitled *Über Geist und Buchstab in der Philosophie* presented for the *Horen* and – not by chance – rejected by Schiller, where Fichte defends his own theory of *Triebe*. Fichte will publish the article only in 1800 in the "Philosophisches Journal" (cf. R. Lauth, *Einleitung*, L). In the meanwhile, Schiller replies to Fichte's paper with the article *Über die notwendigen Grenzen beim Gebrauch schöner Formen*, published 1795 in the "Horen". Even Fichte's theory of drives of the *Sittenlehre* – with its attempt of a synthesis between pure (i.e. rational) and natural drive which leads to the notion of *Bestimmung* as peculiar, i.e. temporal, solution of the problem of causality of freedom – can be read as a further development of the discussion with Schiller.
57   Humboldt sent to Schiller in January 1793 his paper *Über das Studium des Altertums und des Griechen insbesondere*. On the importance of the Greek model for authors such as Kant, Schiller and Hegel see: Taminiaux (1967).

entfalten."⁵⁸ Schiller does not want to go back to ancient times – whence his criticism, following Fichte, of Rousseau⁵⁹ – because human progress was possible only in this way: „Einseitigkeit in Übung der Kräfte führt zwar das Individuum unausbleiblich zum Irrtum, aber die Gattung zur Wahrheit"⁶⁰. One has the impression of regret for the destiny of individuals, although linked with the awareness of the progress of humankind.

What matters here is neither Schiller's *aesthetic* solution for modern man nor his utopian picture of an aesthetic State⁶¹, but the fact that his search for harmony and unity is of the utmost importance for most German philosophers of this time, whence the decisive importance of Schiller's *Briefe* for Schelling, Hölderlin and Hegel⁶². In this respect it is sufficient to think of the so called *Ältestes Systemprogramm des Deutschen Idealismus*. It is still under discussion who of the three friends is – around 1797 – its real author. What seems certain is that it is written by Hegel, but also that it shows the strong influence of Schiller. Exactly the idea of beauty is here the idea which *unifies (vereinigt)* all the ideas: „Ich bin nun überzeugt, daß der höchste Akt der Vernunft, der, indem sie alle Ideen umfast, ein ästhetischer Akt ist, und daß Wahrheit und Güte, nur in der Schönheit verschwistert sind"⁶³.

In Kant's thought, aesthetics plays the role of the unification of freedom and nature, or at least means the search for a mediation between them, and it is well known how much the philosophers of the subsequent generation admired the third *Critique*. But aesthetics is not the only way towards the overcoming of opposite terms, and the search for unity has manifold aspects. From the metaphysical point of view, Fichte's philosophy raises many questions that have to do with this general problem, such as the opposition between subjectivity and objectivity, or the relation between the individual Self and the transindividual reason, the "world of spirits", as Fichte himself writes (*Geisterwelt*)⁶⁴. Aesthetics and metaphysics each suggest a resolution: while Schiller publishes his *Briefe*, Hölderlin writes the fragment *Seyn, Urteil ...*⁶⁵, a genuine metaphysical criticism of Fichte's doctrine of the Self which can be considered a programme of Hölderlin's *Vereinigungsphilosophie*.

---

58   *WDB* II, 454.
59   Hogrebe (1984), 277.
60   *WDB* II, 458.
61   See *WDB* II, 27. Brief.
62   Cf. Pott (1984), 290-313 and Rohrmoser (1984), 314-333. Interesting remarks in: Gerardi (2012).
63   Cf. Jamme/Schneider (1984), 12.
64   See the letter of Fichte to Schelling on 31st May 1801.
65   See Hölderlin (1998), 7.

Analogous questions arise in the practical domain itself, where the limits of morality, in the sense of an *individual* morality and of a "moral point of view", become the object of further criticism. Fichte himself tries already in his Jena period to go beyond the limits of Kant's position: he pays more attention to sensibility, he grants no centrality of the idea of "law", he develops a teleological perfectionism also through a deeper understanding of the social constitution of human beings. In the *Sittenlehre*, he presents a first attempt to go beyond individual morality, and he offers a first sketch of a doctrine of ethical life – *Sittlichkeit* – which only with Hegel receives a proper theory. The time of morality as a mainly individual project seems to be over, and even morality as such – for the later Fichte or for Schelling – comes to seek for the solutions to its problems in the direction of religion.

The external sign of a change of atmosphere is given at the beginning of the new century, when Hegel strikes a critical balance of the moral discussion which was so important in the preceding decade, following the Kantian revolution in philosophy and ethics. In the article *Ueber die wissenschaftlichen Behandlungsarten des Naturrechts* (1802-3) Hegel faces the modern tradition of practical philosophy (Hobbes) and its most recent and for him most important thinkers (Kant and Fichte). In this article we find the first explicit formulation of the distinction between *Moralität* and *Sittlichkeit*, with a first attempt to understand its historical meaning. A new chapter in the history of moral philosophy is about to begin.

Bibliography

Sources

Fichte, Johann Gottlieb, *Von den Pflichten des Gelehrten. Jenaer Vorlesungen 1794/95*, ed. by Reinhard Lauth, Hans Jacob and Peter K. Schneider, Hamburg, 1976.

– *Gesamtausgabe der Bayerischen Akademie der Wissenschaften*, ed. by R. Lauth et alii, Stuttgart-Bad Cannstatt 1962-2012. (*GA*)

– *Fichte im Gespräch*, ed. by Erich Fuchs, 7 vols., Stuttgart-Bad Cannstatt, 1978-2012.

Hölderlin, Johann Christian Friedrich, *Theoretische Schriften*, ed. by Johann Kreuzer, Hamburg, 1998.

Kant, Immanuel, *Gesammelte Schriften*, ed. by Königlich Preussische Akademie der Wissenschaften (Akademie-Ausgabe), Berlin u.a., 1900 ff. (*AA*)

Mendelssohn, Moses, *Gesammelte Schriften. Jubiluämsausgabe*, ed. by Alexander Altmann et alii, Stuttgart-Bad Cannstatt, 1972 ff. (*GS*)

Schiller, Friedrich, *Werke in drei Bänden*, ed. by Gerhard Fricke and Herbert G. Göpfert, 3 vols., München, 1976. (*WDB*)

Spalding, Johann Joachim, *Die Bestimmung des Menschen*, ed. by Albrecht Beutel, Tübingen, 2007.

Literature

Bacin Stefano/Sensen, Oliver (ed.), *Emergence of Moral Autonomy in Kant's Moral Philosophy*, Cambridge, 2019.

Beiser, Frederick, *Schiller as Philosopher. A Re-Examination*, Oxford, 2005.

Brandt, Reinhard, *Die Bestimmung des Menschen bei Kant*, Hamburg, 2007.

Cesa, Claudio, „Libertà e libertà politica nella filosofia classica tedesca", in: Id., *Verso l'eticità. Saggi di storia della filosofia*, Pisa, 2013, pp. 93-112.

Feil, Ernst, *Antithetik neuzeitlicher Vernunft*, Göttingen, 1987.

Fonnesu, Luca, *Antropologia e idealismo. La destinazione dell'uomo nell'etica di Fichte*, Roma/Bari, 1993.

– „Kants praktische Philosophie und die Verwirklichung der Moral", in: *Recht – Geschichte – Religion. Die Bedeutung Kants für die Gegenwart*, ed. by Herta Nagl-Docekal and Rudolf Langthaler, Berlin, 2004, pp. 49-61.

– „Entwicklung und Erweiterung der praktischen Absicht", in: *Kant und die Philosophie in weltbürgerlicher Absicht. Akten des XI. Internationalen Kant-Kongress*, ed. by Stefano Bacin, Alfredo Ferrarin, Claudio La Rocca and Margit Ruffing, Berlin, 2013, vol. 3, pp. 173-184.

– „Pflicht und Pflichtenlehre. Fichtes Auseinandersetzung mit der Aufklärung und mit Kant", in: *Fichte und die Aufklärung*, ed. by Carla De Pascale, Erich Fuchs, Marco Ivaldo and Günter Zöller, Hildesheim/New York, 2004, pp. 133-146.

– „Il ritorno dell'autonomia. Kant e la filosofia classica tedesca", in: *Quaderni fiorentini per la storia del pensiero giuridico moderno*, 43, 2014, pp. 25-61.

Gerardi, Gioavanni, *La nozione di Bildung nel primo Hegel*, Milano, 2012.

Guyer, Paul, "Kantian Perfectionism" in: Id., *The Virtues of Freedom: Selected Essays on Kant*, Oxford/New York, 2016, pp. 70-86.

Hinske, Norbert, „Die tragenden Grundideen der deutschen Aufklärung. Versuch einer Typologie", in: *Die Philosophie der deutschen Aufklärung. Texte und Darstellung*, ed. by Raffaele Ciafardone, Norbert Hinske and Rainer Specht, Stuttgart, 1990, pp. 407-458.

– (ed.), „Die Bestimmung des Menschen", in: *Aufklärung* (11/1, 1996), Hamburg, 1996.

Hogrebe, Wolfram, *Schiller und Fichte. Eine Skizze*, in: *Schillers Briefe über die ästhetische Erziehung des Menschen*, ed. by. Jürgen Bolten, Frankfurt a.M., 1984, pp. 276-289.

Hösle, Vittorio, *Hegels System. Der Idealismus der Subjektivität und das Problem der Intersubjektivität*, Hamburg, 1988.

Jamme, Christoph/Schneider, Helmut (ed.), *Mythologie der Vernunft. Hegels ältestes Systemprogramm des deutschen Idealismus*, Frankfurt a. M., 1984.

Kleingeld, Pauline, *Fortschritt und Vernunft. Zur Geschichtsphilosophie Kants*, Würzburg, 1995.

Macor, Laura Anna, *Die Bestimmung des Menschen (1748-1800). Eine Begriffsgeschichte*, Stuttgart-Bad Cannstatt, 2013.

Milton, John R., "Laws of Nature", in: *The Cambridge History of Seventeenth-Century Philosophy*, ed. by Daniel Garber and Michael Ayers, Cambridge, 1998, pp. 680-701.

Moggach, Douglas, "Post-Kantian Perfectionism", in *Politics, Religion and Art. Hegelian Debates*, ed. by Douglas Moggach, Evanston ILL, 2011, pp. 179-200.

– "Contextualising Fichte: Leibniz, Kant, and Perfectionist Ethics", in: *Fichte-Studien*, 45, 2018, pp. 133-153.

Pott, Hans-Georg, „Schiller und Hölderlin. Die neuen Briefe über die ästhetische Erziehung des Menschen", In: *Schillers Briefe über die ästhetische Erziehung des Menschen*, ed. by Jürgen Bolten, Frankfurt a. M., 1984, pp. 290-313.

Rohrmoser, Günter, „Zum Problem der ästhetischen Versöhnung. Schiller und Hegel", in: *Schillers Briefe über die ästhetische Erziehung des Menschen*, ed. by Jürgen Bolten, Frankfurt a. M., 1984, pp. 314-333.

Sensen, Oliver (ed.), *Kant on Moral Autonomy*, Cambridge, 2009.

Tafani, Daniela, *Virtù e felicità in Kant*, Firenze, 2006.

Taminiaux, Jacques, *La nostalgie de la Grèce à l'aube de l'idéalisme allemand*, The Hague, 1967.

Ware, Owen, "Fichte's Normative Ethics: Deontological or Teleological?", in: *Mind* 127, 2018, pp. 565-584.

Herder
Perfectibility, Plasticity, and Pluralism

Stefanie Buchenau & Douglas Moggach

Introduction

The stated ambition of J.G. Herder (1744-1803) is to "reconcile philosophy with humanity and politics,"[1] making it genuinely fruitful for human activities and culture. A renewed interest in Herder's practical and political philosophy[2] attests to his ongoing relevance for contemporary efforts to combine ideas of human development and personal autonomy (or, better, spontaneity) in various kinds of perfectionist liberalism.[3] His thought confers central importance upon the principles of "perfection" or "perfectibility". In his view, perfectibility is the external and indirect expression of a spontaneous force which, from a metaphysical viewpoint, one may be able to stipulate but which lies forever hidden beyond the grasp of our faculties. It is a human property, which, together with "corruptibility", "distinguishes the character of the species"[4] and endows the individual with unique traits. Partly manifest to the eye, partly not, it serves as a necessary principle of heuristics and morals. It allows us to grasp the human creative capacity to develop and even transform oneself, and it directly confronts human beings with the practical challenges linked to their status as agents in the world and as citizens. As Herder is among the first to emphasize, one of the major challenges of such perfectibility is that it expresses itself in many possible life plans: paradoxically, human beings all share this *same* property that they can develop in *different* directions. They do not fit the same mold, nor do they obey a single standard of self-perfection, excellence or virtue – they are highly plastic and adaptable beings who creatively

---

1 See *HW* I, 108.
2 Herder's philosophy has been famously misused to promote certain political ideologies. In recent times, there have been several attempts to acknowledge its genuine political interest. See for example the recent work of Michael Forster (2018), who presents Herder's liberalism, republicanism and egalitarianism in "Political philosophy"; see also Forster (2017); Barnard (1965), (1969), (1988); Dreitzel (1987); Noyes (2015); Sikka (2011); Willoweit/Fehn (2007).
3 See, for example Raz (1986) and (2003); Hurka (1993); Sher (1997).
4 *HW* VI, 111.

relate to their particular situations, and embrace *consistent* and yet *diverse* and sometimes *conflicting* life plans. The spontaneous adaptability of human beings, their self-shaping in light of their relations to their material and social circumstances, is the key to Herder's perfectionist ethic.

Our aim here is to retrace Herder's original approach to this paradox of unity and multiplicity. We will examine several aspects of his multi-faceted philosophy of perfectibility, and several moments of an itinerary that leads from metaphysics to natural history, the history of humanity, ethics and politics,[5] in the hope that this inquiry may elucidate the historical origins of concepts of perfection in the Enlightenment, and better differentiate competing ethical positions.

1. Perfectibility, Spontaneity, Self-Perfection

Herder's perfectionism or doctrine of perfectibility strikingly contrasts with the Aristotelian teleological doctrine of human nature: it cannot be cast in the language of human nature precisely because it dispenses with the idea of a direction or an end posited prior to action. Humankind, decisively, makes itself. Charles Taylor has perhaps best captured the particularity and modernity of Herder's doctrine of power or "expressivism"[6]: "Where Aristotle speaks of the nature of a thing tending toward its complete form, Herder sees growth as the manifestation of an inner power (...) striving to realize itself externally."[7] Such inner potency is already a plurality of powers, variously (but never exhaustively) displaying themselves in concrete forms. The potentiality is always greater than any specific, given expression; the power remains distinct from the organ or the means through which it makes itself manifest.[8] It is open and indeterminate, in that its ends are not prescribed by any outside source. The final cause does not precede the action, as it does in Aristotle,[9] but reveals

---

5 Important material on "perfection" and "perfectibility" can be found in Herder's correspondence with Moses Mendelssohn in 1769, *Abhandlung über den Ursprung der Sprache* (Treatise on the Origin of Language), *Vom Erkennen und Empfinden* (On the Cognition and Sensation of the human Soul), *Ideen* and Letter 23-25 from the *Briefe zu Beförderung der Humanität* (*HW* VII) (Letters on the Promotion of Humanity).
6 "Fulfilling my nature means espousing the inner élan, the voice or impulse. And this makes what is hidden manifest for both myself and others. But this manifestation also helps to define what is to be realized. The direction of this élan wasn't and couldn't be clear prior to this manifestation". Taylor (1989), 374-75. See also Taylor (2017).
7 Ibid., 14.
8 *HW* VI, 171.
9 Aristotle, *Metaphysics*, 1013b.

itself, tentatively and provisionally, within the very action. The emphasis has shifted from the final to the efficient cause, which is, significantly, highly individual: each expression of powers is particular to a self, and represents an effort at the harmonious blending of the diverse into a (partial or provisional) unity. As the young Herder puts it: "every soul builds itself its own body" (*bildet sich einen Körper zu*).[10] Later, in the *Ideen*, Herder states that every individual ought to view herself as her own end; he affirms the existence of a dynamic natural order in which each person can secure well-being not through the arbitrary will of another, or even of the Creator, but through action in accord with the laws of reason that lie within the self.[11] Human perfectibility is what invites agents to live up to their own individuality, to find their own original path while recognizing their fellows' respective paths or individual measures, and treating them, in Kantian terms, as "ends in themselves." Actions are spontaneous in that they derive from one's inner powers, and are not prefigured according to external standards, nor completely necessitated by external causes (though these remain operative in establishing the natural and social context in which actions are undertaken, as well as the instrumental means at the disposal of the actors). One's deeds are formative of the self, and contribute to shaping its objective, social world as a manifestation of collective human capacities.

In its indeterminacy and openness that carves out a new space for human agency in history, Herder's perfectibility closely resembles that of Rousseau. In his *Discours sur l'origine et les fondements de l'inégalité parmi les hommes* (Discourse on the Origin and the Foundations of inequality between Men) of 1755, Rousseau famously introduces the word "perfectibility," as the most fundamental attribute of the human being which, contrary to metaphysical freedom, is accessible to experience. Rousseau writes:

> [L'homme] se reconnaît libre d'acquiescer, ou de résister ; et c'est surtout dans la conscience de cette liberté que se montre la spiritualité de son âme : car la physique explique en quelque manière le mécanisme des sens et la formation des idées ; mais dans la puissance de vouloir ou plutôt de choisir, et dans le sentiment de cette puissance on ne trouve que des actes purement spirituels, dont on n'explique rien par les lois de la mécanique.
>
> Mais, quand les difficultés qui environnent toutes ces questions, laisseraient quelque lieu de disputer sur cette différence de l'homme et de l'animal, il y a une autre qualité très spécifique qui les distingue, et sur laquelle il ne peut y avoir de contestation, c'est la faculté de se perfectionner ; faculté qui, à l'aide

---

10 See the letters to Mendelssohn from 1769 and the early draft: "Plato sagt: dass unser Lernen nur Erinnerung sei (1766-68) (Plato says: that our Learning is only Remembering)", reprinted in: Heinz (1994), 175-182.
11 *HW* VI, 15; *HW* V, 666.

des circonstances, développe successivement toutes les autres, et réside parmi nous tant dans l'espèce que dans l'individu, au lieu qu'un animal est, au bout de quelques mois, ce qu'il sera toute sa vie, et son espèce, au bout de mille ans, ce qu'elle était la première année de ces mille ans.[12]

For Rousseau, metaphysical freedom and perfectibility are closely linked concepts; but human freedom remains a "metaphysical" human attribute which escapes physical explanation if it is not expressed externally and empirically in perfectibility, or better, in either perfectibility or corruptibility. Human animals fundamentally differ from non-human animals insofar as they are capable of an "almost unlimited perfectibility". They can develop in two directions, either toward the good, or toward the bad. Herder, who, like many of his contemporaries, seems to be an attentive reader of Rousseau, adopts this general perspective on perfectibility early on in his thinking. But like his fellow German thinkers such as Moses Mendelssohn, Herder objects to Rousseau's visionary rhetoric, and is reluctant to endorse his philosophical terminology and genealogical method. Rather, Herder refines his own notion within the German debate, and with the help of its conceptual tools.[13]

For in the German territories, versions of ethical and political perfectionism and perfectibility are at the philosophical centre stage long before Rousseau introduces the term in his *Second Discourse*, and contrary to Isaiah Berlin's counter-Enlightenment reading, we contend that Herder is deeply influenced by this perfectionist tradition.[14] He connects, first, with a certain Protestant and Pietist[15] German tradition that revises Lutheran principles[16] by ascribing to the Christian believer the capacity and the duty to "ameliorate all faculties and aptitudes" as far as compatible with his or her own situation and place in society. According to the Pietist Siegmund Jacob Baumgarten, these may include both the natural and any supernatural faculties that God has chosen to bestow on

---

12   Rousseau (1964), 141-42. On Rousseau's perfectibility, see Binoche (2004). For a comparative approach to Rousseau and Herder, see Barnard (2011); and *La perfectibilité. Les Lumières allemandes contre Rousseau*, ed. Emmanuel Hourcade and Charlotte Morel, Paris, Garnier, in preparation.
13   See the illuminating analysis by Booher (2015). This paper adopts Booher's general outlook on Herder's perfectionism, in particular concerning Herder's reception of the German metaphysical tradition.
14   See Berlin (2000). For a recent discussion of Herder and the Enlightenment, see Zammito/Menges/Menze (2010).
15   See Baron/Soboth (2018).
16   See Schubert (2002).

the human being.¹⁷ This tradition restores the dignity and the salvific force of works within Lutheran thought, and assigns the task of perfection to each soul, not only as inner self-cultivation, but as a positive contribution to the order of creation. Herder also borrows elements from the rationalist Christian Wolff and his influential school, who introduce the duty of self-perfection as the first and most fundamental duty within their ethics, prior to the obligations toward God and toward one's fellow citizens.¹⁸ The Wolffian Georg Bernhard Bilfinger even describes a "perficibilitas facultatum,"¹⁹ as early as 1725. In this respect like the Pietists, from whom in other ways they markedly differ,²⁰ the Wolffians emphasize the human duty maximally to develop oneself and others, and, conversely, to omit anything that would cause the deterioration of one's state. Wolff himself derives the requirement to leave the putative state of nature and to enter into civil society from the impossibility, in pre-political relations, of securing one's own perfection or of contributing reliably to that of others, and he models the functions of the political state on their promotion of the general well-being of the population in its physical, intellectual, and spiritual aspects.²¹ While disagreeing strongly with Wolff's political conclusions, as we will see, Herder adopts some of his premises on the centrality and interrelationship of self- and social perfection.

The Wolffian programme undergoes a particular inflection and challenge in the debates on the destination of man that shake the German and *Berliner Aufklärung* in the 1760's. As Richard Booher²² has convincingly shown, it is from these debates that Herder derives his most crucial impetus. This controversy had been triggered in 1748 by Johann Joachim Spalding's treatise *Die Bestimmung des Menschen* (The Destination of Man), and had been revived in the circles of the Berlin *Aufklärung* by Thomas Abbt and Moses Mendelssohn in the 1760's. In response to Abbt's *Zweifel über die Bestimmung des Menschen* (Doubts about the Destination of Man),²³ Mendelssohn successively publishes a short treatise entitled *Orakel, die Bestimmung des Menschen betreffend* (Oracle

---

17 Baumgarten (1738), § 125: „Besserung aller Kräfte und Fertigkeiten (...) Christen (sind) verbunden, sich sowol überhaupt der möglichsten Besserung und Vermerung aller natürlichen und übernatürlichen Kräfte und Fertigkeiten zu befleißigen; als auch dabey insonderheit sich nach dem Beruf, darin sie Gott gesetzet, aufs sorgfältigste zu richten (...).''
18 Wolff (1976).
19 Bilfinger (1725), § 268.
20 On Wolff and the pietists, see Schneewind (1998), 442-44.
21 On perfection, Wolff (1969), § 43, §§ 106-108, §§ 186-189; Wolff (1988), 16, 41, 88-89; Moggach (2009).
22 See Booher (2015). For Herder's notes on Mendelssohn from 1766, *HSW* 32, 160.
23 Abbt, Thomas (1767).

concerning the Destination of Man, 1764)[24] and a more detailed version, *Phaedon, oder über die Unsterblichkeit der Seele* (Phaedo or the immortality of the soul), which is at the same time a rewriting of Plato's *Phaedo*. Mendelssohn here introduces a new Platonic perspective on human destiny or "calling" as perfection or progression. "What is the destination of man? Answer: To fulfil the intentions of God in a state of rational cognition, to persevere, to become more perfect, and to be happy in such perfection."[25] Mendelssohn conceives of perfecting, or progression (and the concurrent possibility of regression) in a dynamic pattern where human beings oscillate between the status of non-human animals and the divine. They strive toward and participate in the divine insofar as they have consciousness or, at least, "self-feeling" in exerting their own powers. No matter how far they reach, or what state of progression they may achieve, the basis for this striving lies in an initially inchoate feeling, a confused grasp and enjoyment of their own self or the exercise of their power; thus, the unborn and the "savage" are already human, because they possess a rudimentary awareness of their activity and capacity for perfectibility. It is perfectibility that at the same time accounts for human participation in a supernatural world. Mendelssohn abandons a certain Platonic two-world dualism, based on the idea of a progressive detachment from the material and an ascension toward the divine, and emphasizes instead the continuity between these two worlds. It is in establishing a contact with the divine, initially by means of their senses, and in applying their force within and for this world that human beings are conjointly members of two worlds, the natural and the supernatural.

Herder's direct comment on this debate and his interpretation of the concept of perfection can be found in two highly instructive letters to Mendelssohn from 1769.[26] In this correspondence, he seems to approve Mendelssohn's general setting of the problem, but notes certain necessary adjustments. In particular, he underlines the need to subject the notion of perfection itself to closer philosophical examination. In his view, "formation and development *in this life* is the end, is the vocation."[27] Here he stresses the immanent meaning of

---

24 Mendelssohn (1981), 19-27.
25 Ibid., 24.
26 See also DeSouza, (2014). Heinz (1992).
27 See Herder's letter to Mendelssohn, April 1769: „Diese Ausbildung u. Entwiklung *auf dieses Leben*, sie ist Zweck, sie ist Bestimmung; aber da ein unrechter Gesichtpunkt, zu leben, *damit man die Welt vollkomner verlaße*, als man sie betrat. Wir betraten sie, um hier vollkomner zu werden, zuzunehmen und abzunehmen, zu lernen u. anzuwenden, u. immer uns u. die Welt zu genießen: das war Absicht der Natur. Alles wird verrückt,

perfection, its concrete significance for betterment in real existence; he resists transcendent versions which seek perfection in religious reclusion or escape from the world. He considers that this point requires stronger emphasis in Mendelssohn's text. Herder also thinks that Mendelssohn has not drawn all the consequences of his own doctrine of the human being as a composite and sensuous being. In Herder's view, perfection needs to be reconceived as a *relational* and as a *contextual* notion, which receives its specific meaning in respect to a particular faculty and to the human being that it is supposed to qualify. Like "virtue", "perfection" belongs to those metaphysical concepts which, on account of their high level of abstraction and their speculative dimension, expose philosophers to the danger of reifying non-existent entities and of leading them astray:

> I believe that nothing in the world has engendered more opinions, and perhaps also more errors, than considering and treating abstract concepts as individual existences. So do we treat the words nature, virtue, reality, perfection. Originally these concepts were nothing but abstractions, relations between this and that, more or less shadows and colours of things. We make them into things, and think of them as things. And we likewise think of skills as realities, and attribute these perfections to the soul, which it collects like gold coins, although they were originally only relations which we have thought of as positions.[28]

This criticism reflects a more general philosophical programme of revising metaphysics and morals. Earlier on, Herder had expressed his dissatisfaction with the state of moral philosophy and its language. Moral philosophy remains empty and overly didactic – a "moral preaching," as he puts it,[29] as long it is not centered on individual human beings, and as long as it is not "popular," that is, as it does not speak to everyone, to philosophers and non-philosophers alike.[30] From his viewpoint, it is necessary to recur to alternative methods, and to preach a comprehensible kind of ethics by engraving a never-fading image of virtue into the human consciousness.[31]

---

        wenn ich mir eine einzige Vollkommenheit erwerbe, die bloß fürs *Verlaßen* der Welt Vollkommenheit sei."

28   Herder's letter to Mendelssohn, December 1769 [our translation; SB/DM].

29   See *HW* VI, 127-129.

30   Further on *Popularphilosophie*, see Maximiliano Hernández Marcos, "Rights-Perfectionism" in this volume.

31   *HW* VI, 127-129: („Wenn man ihm nicht die Tugend lehrt, sondern einprägt. (...) mache ich um diese Abstraktionen (der moralischen Begriffe) ein Gehege, so mache sich meine Philosophie am meisten nützlich (...) ich drücke ihm ein Bild ein, das nie verlöscht.") For the same programme, see also *HW* 9/2, 123.

2. Perfectibility as Flourishing? Change, Evolution, and Transformation in the Natural World

These thoughts will be further developed in Herder's later writings, such as *Abhandlung über den Ursprung der Sprache, Vom Erkennen und Empfinden, Ideen zur Philosophie der Geschichte der Menschheit, Briefe zu Beförderung der Humanität*. In order to describe the particular development, transformation, and tendency toward perfection characterizing human beings in general, Herder sets up an anthropological programme which approaches self-knowledge indirectly, via world-knowledge, and via the non-human as well as the human world, with the aim of exploring humanity in all times and places. In the 1770's and 1780's, Herder unfolds his highly innovative variant of perfectibility from the viewpoint of natural history. In order to reach self-knowledge, it is necessary to adopt a naturalistic approach and to posit continuity between matter and spirit, and between inorganic, organic, and human attributes.[32]

Such a natural history can dispense with "metaphysical speculation."[33] Like Buffon, Herder's ambition as a naturalist is to stick to observation and the description of external structure and outward experience; the naturalist eschews the reification of concepts in favour of close attention to concrete particulars. He must furthermore set all pride aside, humbly proceed bottom-up rather than top-down, and approach human differences and perfectibility by means of comparison with the animal.[34] What Herder calls a "philosophical and manly history of humanity" reaches even further than Buffon's *Natural history of man*. Instead of postulating an invisible difference, it includes the deduction of the "most divine" powers of man, such as a certain immateriality, reason, and infinite progression from the most primitive ones, such as irritability and sensibility, and from the analogy with animal 'perfectibility'.

The particular challenge of Herder's variant of natural history is to elucidate human development by means of its analogy with vegetal and, more particularly, animal development, through the resemblance or homology between animal and human organs and organisms. First of all, human perfectibility can be approached with regards to the deployment of certain faculties

---

[32] See Buchenau (2017; Zammito (2006), 209, 211. On the concept of *Kraft* as synthesis and a means of overcoming dualisms, see Nisbet (1970), 9-16, stressing its Leibnizian origins.

[33] See *HW* VI, Vorrede: „Wer bloß metaphysische Spekulationen will, hat sie auf kürzerem Wege; ich glaube aber, dass sie abgetrennt von Erfahrungen und Analogien der Natur, eine Luftfahrt sind, die selten zum Ziel führet [...]".

[34] Buffon (2007), 35: „Il doit se ranger lui-même dans la classe des animaux, auxquels il ressemble par tout ce qu'il a de matériel, et même leur instinct lui paraîtra peut-être plus sûr que sa raison, et leur industrie plus admirable que ses arts."

discovered in plants and animals. Like plants and animals, human beings experience "growth" – and Herder likes to compare human organic development to that of a tree. But humans share additional features and 'faculties' with the vegetal and animal kingdoms, such as reproduction and nutrition: animals, and in particular primitive organisms such as insects, can shed light on the human faculty of nutrition because nutrition seems to be their own unique or most central faculty: polyps, worms and shellfish are still "all mouth," as Herder puts it in the *Ideen*. Similarly, frogs and other cold-blooded animals exhibit an "excessive" form of irritability that warm-blooded animals lose. This seems to be a traditional idea of natural history, from Aristotle onwards, although thoroughly revised by Herder's doctrine of powers. We will shortly return to this point.

Human perfectibility can also be elucidated by particular animal modes of *evolution* and their finite form of adaptability to a given milieu or "sphere": as both Rousseau[35] and Samuel Hermann Reimarus appear to hold. The latter compares human and animal forms of evolution and perfectibility, and emphasizes the "drives, aptitudes and arts" of animals such as the web-building spider and the cocooning caterpillar. Such drives (or instincts) enable the animal to develop certain forms of life or 'arts', and they respect a certain 'economy' and 'order' that is favorable to the animal's self-preservation and seems to promote its ends, without the help of experience, exercise or reason. As Reimarus puts it, "nothing in the world, and in particular in the animal realm, lays before the eye with greater clarity the intentions of the creator, his wisdom and goodness, than the drives, the aptitudes or the arts of the non-rational animals."[36]

But Herder thinks that non-human animals can even elucidate human perfectibility in its "highest" sense of the term, where it denotes a faculty of change and transformation. He departs from the traditional Cartesian stance which was still defended, in some sense, by Reimarus and by Rousseau: the animal is not a machine, determined by its instincts, and opposable on this account to the human animal, who is endowed with free agency.[37] This distinction must be partly recast, because, interestingly, the non-human animal seems to be as capable of transforming and recreating itself as the human animal.

What seems particularly to retain Herder's interest here are the forms of animal change and metamorphosis that resemble human transformation. In the eighteenth century's lively debate on natural history and comparative

---

35 See, again, Rousseau (1964), 141-142.
36 Reimarus (1985), 311ff.
37 On challenges to Cartesianism and mechanism, see Gaukroger (2010), 58-64, 148-49; Beiser (1992), 152.

anatomy, these animal changes had attracted the attention of certain contemporaries and entomologists such as Swammerdam, Réaumur and Bonnet, whose results Herder enthusiastically praises in the *Ideen*.[38] This flourishing strand of Enlightenment entomology pays particular attention to those changing animals that undergo a programmed evolution, and to intermediate beings that traditionally fall outside the classificatory patterns, because they possess organs of two classes.[39] Animals such as caterpillars can change and adopt new shapes.[40] Polyps are so-called animal-plants, endowed with organs of both plants and animals, which can be apprehended as transitional beings, on a continuous scale: what we perceive as the function of a given organ may serve new ends in a future world.

Herder's originality is to apply the same naturalistic approach to human beings, by inquiring into their habits of nutrition and modes of life according to the standard catalogue of natural history, and by conceiving of the human organism as defined by a particular set of powers which are developed and blended in a well-proportioned whole. It is on these grounds that Herder, in the *Ideen*, characterizes humans as intermediate creatures (*Mittelgeschöpfe*). He thereby implies, first of all, that humans do not actually achieve *excellence* in any domain. In fact, human faculties are "average," and sometimes even below average, in comparison with certain animals: the elephant concerning the "delicacy of his nerves", the lion concerning "muscular strength", the sloth concerning the "elasticity of fibers". But it is precisely because they are so proportionate and attuned to each other, that humans have their own "measure" (*Maß*), that they are intermediate or transitional beings, according to a second meaning of the word "Mittelgeschöpf". Just like the amphibian, capable of living in a terrestrial and an aquatic ecosystem, they can inhabit two different "worlds". They are formed with organs allowing them to *develop* their own excellence for a future world. Like ostriches, they are flightless birds, endowed with wings but unable to fly. It is precisely the lack of rigid instinctual determination that allows human beings creatively to innovate in adapting to their environments, to follow diverse life-plans, to make their own history, never in

---

38 *HW* VI, 102.
39 See Aristotle, *De Partibus Animalium* IV 13 697a15-b26; *De Generatione animalium* I23 731b8-1; *De Incessu Animalium* 19 714B10-19.
40 Bonnet (1745), préface, IV: „Swammerdam nous a dévoilé le vrai sens des métamorphoses si chères à l'imagination & consacrés par les comparaisons les plus relevés. Il nous a appris que le Papillon existoit déjà sous la forme de Chenille, & que la Chrysalide dans laquelle celle-ci semble se transformer n'est que le papillon lui-même revetu de certaines enveloppes qui le tiennent comme emmaillotté."

abstraction from their surrounding natural world or the activities of their fellows, but in dynamic engagement with them.

This is some sort of principle of perfectibility that natural history has to offer to the human being. Animals mirror human beings and their perfection: not by telling humans who they are, but in displaying a harmonious balance or economy of forces and special organs or means to ends, thereby, on Herder's view, pointing to the human entitlement to citizenship in a supernatural and moral world. Such a second citizenship means, according to the *Abhandlung über den Ursprung der Sprache,* that humans have freedom of choice insofar as they can step back, reflect on the means at their disposal, and expand the boundaries of their actions.

The plasticity of human action and human nature exhibits common features with the other orders of nature in the non-mechanistic principle of adaptability to the environment, but also signals the presence of a distinctive human attribute, the power of reflection or *Besonnenheit*, rooted in our instinctual indetermination.[41] This power restricts the force of mere natural determination by making possible a reflective distancing, whereby humans are able to relate in diverse and unpatterned ways to their surroundings, displaying precisely that capacity for acquiescing or resisting, for exertion or self-restraint, that Rousseau had earlier invoked.[42] It is on this principle that the mutability of human nature, with its attendant perfectibility and corruptibility, rests.[43] Progress or progression in Herder is the sign of human freedom. The perfectibility of beings surrounding us, including animal beings, seems to mirror human perfectibility, or seems to offer humans contemplating and exploring such nature an empirical sign of their own possible direction, without any need for metaphysical statements about historical inevitability. Herder's redefined naturalism, biological, historical, and not mechanistic, conceives human plasticity as creative integration into the natural environment, in some ways analogous to animal adaptations and in some ways not; and it conceives further the cultural transformation of that environment, endowing both the world and the active self with new characteristics. Human agency is the deployment, differentiation, and realization of inner powers, achieving a fluid and dynamic accord between self and world, and eventuating in expressive harmony.

---

41   Barnard (1965), 131; Waldow (2017), 150, 152; Sikka (2011), 58.
42   Rousseau attaches a more negative meaning to reflection, however, linking it to amour-propre or egoistic self-love: (1964), 130. In Herder it acquires a broader signification.
43   Barnard (1965), 132, on the mutability of human nature.

3. Ethical Perfectionism

This principle of the life sciences and heuristics which allows us to explore the animal organism is more than just a theoretical and scientific exercise, insofar as it makes it possible to refine Herder's approach to self-formation and to understand why perfectibility is both a universal *and* an individual quality. Perfectibility is visible in nature, and its scientific exploration has a practical dimension insofar as it already lays some kind of universal human vocation or destination (*Bestimmung*) to self-perfection and *Humanität* before the eye. To follow a programme of self-perfection (or attain the highest good) means to develop such a "consistency", "health," "balance," or an equilibrated and harmonious usage of forces"[44], which Herder, from a particular eudaimonistic viewpoint, also designates as happiness (*Wohlsein, Glück*). This, however, does not yet provide a clear direction, an end or a human model that one could follow in ethics. As already mentioned above, in Herder's view, our equality as human beings reveals itself in our common perfectibility or adaptability, and, thus, in infinite difference. We all resemble each other insofar as we are capable of adapting to particular situations and projecting ourselves into individual life-plans which are suited to them. If individuals are supposed to find their own individual paths and to create their own particular life-plan, they cannot rely on any given model, and they do not seem to have any immediate sensual access or knowledge of such a standard of health and self-perfection either.

I of course can immediately feel an affinity, attraction and admiration toward certain figures, which produce in me a desire to imitate them, and it is ethically important for Herder to consider one's immediate moral feelings. But in order to acquire self-knowledge and truly understand what words such as "self-perfection", "excellence", "perfectibility" or "balance of forces" or "health" can possibly mean for myself, I will need to step back to reflect on these feelings and obtain self-knowledge via world-knowledge, the wandering around in the times and places of human geography and history. I will come to understand myself (my particular situation, means and powers which determine my self-perfection) better by understanding others, by some kind of *Einfühlung*, by putting myself at their place and understanding how they have developed their respective proportion and set of virtues. This comparative perspective is one of the ways in which reflection or *Besonnenheit* works.

From this vantage point, the study of human individuals and cultures *can* offer "models" for my own action and self-perfection. For example, Socrates and, more generally, ancient Greek culture, seem to fulfil an exemplary function for

---

44   On happiness as health, see *HW* VI, 327-330.

a modern European. In *Auch eine Geschichte* (This too a Philosophy of History for the Formation of Humanity) and in *Ideen*, Herder depicts Socrates as a model of virtue, humanity, sincerity, patriotism and humility.[45] "Only through his method and his art of living, through the moral education which he had given to himself and that he tried to give to others, and, first and foremost, through the manner of his death he was a model for the world."[46] However, even Socrates' exemplary function is restricted by his own sphere and his culture, and his virtue cannot be easily transposed to other situations. Each culture possesses virtues which describe its particular modes of adaptation to its surroundings, and its specific viewpoint on the world.

As a result, paradoxically, it is those cultures which do not endorse such an exemplary function because they are at a great cultural distance from my own that possess a more substantial interest for my own quest for happiness and self-perfection. They show that an excellence, a virtue that a particular age may produce, may turn out to be a vice in another age, and that the notion of "excellence" is always relative to a given situation. Any virtue or vice expresses a disproportion, occasioned by particular external circumstances. In Herder's account of the history of humanity, drawing on an eighteenth-century historiographical genre developed by Iselin, Lessing and Thomas Abbt[47], the religious devotion characterizing Middle Eastern cultures at the infancy of humanity changes into despotism in subsequent Oriental cultures.[48] But more importantly, cultural differences better lay before my eyes a plurality of particular excellences, which humans have developed and which, supposedly, still are available for my self-constitution. They better present my manifold virtual possibilities, "organs" or faculties.

And yet, such comparative reflection not only contributes to self-knowledge in that it offers possible goals for my own life, but it also makes me better understand my own social and historical nature. On Herder's account, one's ethical bearings are always provided by one's communal relations. These are infinitely varied, and are historical: there are no timeless absolutes, but always hypothetical imperatives governing the ways that human beings adjust to their social world, and express themselves in it. It is this normative relativism that

---

45   *HW* VI, 90f: „wenn du wie Sokrates handelst, demütig Vorurteilen entgegenstrebest, aufrichtig, menschenliebend, dich selbst aufopfernd Wahrheit und Tugend ausbreitest, wie du kannst (...)".
46   *HW* VI, 551.
47   Abbt (1978), 137-40. See also *Geschichte des menschlichen Geschlechts so weit selbige in Europa bekannt worden vom Anfang der Welt bis auf unsere Zeiten, aus dem großen Werke der allgemeinen Welthistorie ausgezogen und ausgearbeitet*, Bd. 1, Halle, Gebauer, 1766.
48   *HW* IV, 16 ff.

sharply distinguishes Herder from his teacher Kant, just as his historicized naturalism separates him from Kantian rationalism at the meta-ethical level. In a sense, Herder is both a universalist and a relativist in the manner that we have described: He thinks that all human beings are equal in that they are all adaptable, but each is adaptable in a distinctive way. It is not the case, however, that Herder is prepared to endorse any values without qualification as long as they (allegedly) express the will of a community.[49] Herder's position is thus markedly different from that of his contemporary August Wilhelm Rehberg, who wishes to defend persistent feudal inequalities on the basis of a putative original contract endowing landlords with irrevocable rights.[50] Instead, Herder repudiates irrational forms of domination and the willful destruction of human capacities: war, slavery, political tyranny, and colonialism.[51] His historical relativism is tempered by his democratic commitments.

4. Political Perfectionism

Herder's description of adaptation and perfecting is not a blithe account of continuities between self, nature, and the social world, but rather it evokes processes fraught with serious obstacles and challenges. In his expressivist view of freedom,[52] Herder postulates a metaphysical force which is expressive of an individual set of powers, but he also thinks that this kind of metaphysical supposition cannot claim any validity unless it is linked to experience, and to an empirical expression of such freedom in perfectibility. Such perfectibility is visible in nature, and its scientific exploration lays some kind of human vocation or destination (*Bestimmung*) before the eye: nature calls upon all individuals to deploy their specific powers to manifest their own particular content in the world. This in turn seems to presuppose the possibility that all agents can be confirmed in their deeds, and can recognise actions and their results *as their own work*. Thus, the totality of human powers is exerted, in historical time and through the active participation of many hands and minds. Herder follows Leibniz, and before him Stoic cosmopolitanism, in holding that all such individual and group perspectives, if properly understood, are ultimately compatible:[53] They are unique and irreplaceable facets of a single

---

49 Sikka (2011), 121.
50 On Rehberg, see Hernández Marcos, "Rights-Perfectionism" in this volume.
51 Sikka (2011), 93.
52 Taylor (1989), 368–90.
53 See, for example Sellars (2007).

composite human personality, a unity of unity and multiplicity. It follows that the suppression or assimilation of any part represents a diminution in overall systemic perfection. This position has been described as radical pluralism,[54] or co-operative pluralism.[55] The real political problem, from Herder's perfectionist vantage point, is that of unity and multiplicity; and especially the problem of maintaining diversity in the face of homogenizing and conformist pressures of different kinds. Herder's idea of politics or living together is not primarily focused on the setting up of political institutions allowing for individual recognition or the exercise of individual rights. His basic interest is not in political institutions (of which he is profoundly distrustful), but in fostering communal human bonds, and in aesthetic education as the cultivation of empathy and humanity, a concern that he shares with many of his contemporaries, such as Lessing, Mendelssohn and Schiller.[56] He admits no possibility of self-perfection outside society and human interaction: it is in society and through emulation and confrontation with human diversity (as attested by the growing encounter with non-European cultures in the eighteenth century) that human beings develop – because social interaction is what stirs their activity, because they measure themselves against others, reject them or identify themselves with them, and thereby, through knowledge of the surrounding natural and human world, expand their self-knowledge, which is also a knowledge of their own goals and values and of the "organs", means and faculties at their disposal. Hence historical perfection is not primarily a progress in the institutions and practices of rights, as it is among post-Kantians like Fichte, for example, but a free and full deployment of human cultural capacities, and creative engagement with the environment, whereby the implicit potential of each self or community comes to be realized. Progress in history does not proceed in a unilinear direction, and it is clearly not ineluctable, though its possibility seems to be underwritten (but not guaranteed) by the laws of nature.[57] From the empirical, practical and pragmatic viewpoint that he (Herder) favours (against dogmatic metaphysics), every generation projects its own history of human progress, and what appears to be a progress in its eyes can appear in a different light from the perspective of future generations. In some respects the modern European world has regressed behind the achievements of earlier eras. The critical task is to retrieve the prospects for free collective life that are currently in peril.

---

54   Forster (2019).
55   Barnard (1969), 54.
56   See, for example Nisbet (2008); Beiser (2005).
57   Beiser (2011), 164 f.

Herder is particularly attentive to three threats to pluralism that beset modern social relations: the division of labour, political authoritarianism, and the suppression of national identities in imperial regimes. It is most notably in the last respect that Herder will exert an important influence in subsequent political thought. Against the monotonous and constricting character of modern life, Herder celebrates the richness and diversity of mediaeval European civilization.[58] He stresses not its rigid and hierarchical nature, but its vivid and robust popular culture, the skilled labour and aesthetic achievements of its craftsmen, the intimacy and closeness to nature of the village community. In contrast, Herder detects a modern tendency toward the mechanistic reduction of social complexity: the division of labour, whose character can be discerned in incipient manufacturing centres,[59] represents not an increase in social differentiation, but an increase in uniformity, since labouring individuals become interchangeable and indistinguishable through their performance of standardised repetitive tasks. The modern division of labour reduces workers to identical, deskilled units, whose simple, repetitive movement is imparted from without, not self-directed through the experience and insight of the worker.[60] The mediaeval artisan is a master craftsman, deploying skills that demand lengthy and painstaking formation, and thus achieving self-expression; the modern worker is a thrall, reduced to fragmentary and soul-destroying motions. As Fichte will later do, Herder equates mechanism and heteronomy, understood not in a Kantian moral register, but as extraneous control and domination.[61] The culture of diremption,[62] of alienation and opposing economic interests, to be excoriated by Schiller and the Hegelian School, emerges here.

A second threat to the preservation of social diversity arises from a closely-related problem, that of authoritarian political rule, which succeeds by shattering the bonds of rich, sustaining communal life, and depriving the individual of the protection of intermediate bodies. The birth of early modern

---

58   Berlin (1976), p. 176.
59   Note that Herder's text, *Auch eine Philosophie der Geschichte zur Bildung der Menschheit* predates Adam Smith's *Wealth of Nations* by two years. Herder's critique is part of his general criticism of mechanism and its corresponding forms of domination. See esp. HW IV, 42-77. Manufacturing was far more advanced in Britain than elsewhere in Europe. See Kriedte/Medick/Schlumbohm (1981). On German receptions of Scottish political economy, see Waszek (2006). Nisbet (1970), 276-77, while offering an overall assessment of Herder's view of the role of trade in history, deems his contribution to economic science to be negligible.
60   *HW* IV, 42-77.
61   Cf. *SW* VII, 362 f.
62   See Moggach (2016), 71-98.

absolutism occurs through the destruction of the autonomy of local communities and their common subjugation under centralised power, a unity which effaces differences.[63] Without the safeguards afforded by dense and organic social relations, connections and solidarities among persons break. The result is twofold: the deformation of the individual, and political oppression. First, the individual who is released from social connectedness now appears as egoistic and competitive. Such egoism is not innate, but is a historically-conditioned perversion of individuality into possessive individualism, its ends shaped by the competitive struggle.[64] The model of historical deformation of the self as outlined by Rousseau in the *Discourse on Inequality*[65] has for Herder a certain applicability, though it here undergoes a reversal in its logic: the origin of the competitive individual does not lie in closer enforced connectedness to others and its related invidiousness, but precisely from the breakage of previous connections. Secondly, political oppression: such atomistic individuals are not freer than before, when they were members of a strong and articulated community. They are now especially susceptible to political control: each solitary self confronts the naked power of the state without buffering relations to shield it. Here the model defended in Hobbes' *Leviathan*, with its competing acquisitive individuals and its firm injunction against partial associations,[66] is decried as tyrannical. While later Romantics stress hierarchy and subordination in their idealisation of feudal Europe, Herder's organicism implies the diffusion of power and strong local communities. The late Romantics celebrate the mediaeval world for all the wrong reasons, Herder would doubtless say.[67]

The third kind of threat to diversity is posed if one nationality encroaches upon and absorbs another, to the detriment of human variety, and therefore to the detriment of collective perfection.[68] Herder's posing of the problem and its solution lies in his specific conception of society. Unlike the mechanical unity of the state, the nation is an organic entity, a shared popular life reflecting a dynamic inner principle.[69] Herder's expressivism takes freedom to be the translation into objectivity of a given, particular content, or the enactment of

---

63   *HW* IV, 42 ff. See Dallmayr (1997), 113.
64   *HW* IV, 77 ff; Macpherson (1962).
65   Rousseau (1964), 106, 140-146.
66   Hobbes (2012), esp. ch. 13, 14, and 29.
67   On differences with Burke and Romantic conservatives, see Barnard (1969), 51-52, 52-59. Contrastingly, in endorsing the aesthetics and skills of craft labour, Herder's thought displays affinities with that of William Morris in the late nineteenth century: see Weinroth/Browne (eds.) (2015).
68   *HW* IV, 42 ff; Dallmayr (1997), 115.
69   Helfer (1990).

a specific law of evolution proper to each actor or to each group.[70] His idea of the nation recasts Leibniz's monad in biological and organic language;[71] its contents evolve in an endogenously-propelled movement, an outpouring of its vital energies in the specific forms that give expression to its particular cultural perspective on the world. And yet he also adapts and modifies the Leibnizian model, making real interaction central to the formation of selfhood.[72] Action and expression presuppose reaction to external stimuli, though these are always undertaken in ways compatible with an underlying cultural identity. In following such an inner principle of change and progression, nations generate a spontaneous world order, of increasing complexity and differentiation of function. While responding to their inner drives and insights, all nations partake in a common task, making a unique contribution to the perfection of the world and of the species, which requires the widest possible range.[73] The suppression of any nation represents an undesirable reduction in complexity. Here, unlike later predatory nationalisms, the nation and the cosmopolis are complementary terms. Again, Herder does not succumb to blind optimism; he clearly recognises, and warns against, important disturbances in these processes of self-realisation, but he contends that such deviations are historically contingent and remediable.

It was particularly this latter aspect of Herder's thought that exerted enormous influence on national revolutionaries throughout Europe in the Revolutions of 1848, when the principle of nationality was mobilised against imperial powers.[74] Especially in the Habsburg territories and in the Baltic, nationalism of a Herderian stamp was affirmed as a means of democratic cultural renewal by suppressed or marginalised linguistic and ethnic groups. In striving for recognition and a measure of self-determination, this nationalism of the 'springtime of peoples' was frequently open and non-exclusive in orientation: cultures were taken not to be necessarily antagonistic among themselves, but to offer individualised and potentially harmonious expressions of human potentiality, as Herder too had believed. The voracious and militaristic

---

70 The question has been raised whether Herder's pluralism is sufficiently deep, or if he succumbs to an undifferentiated holism about groups, without attending to their inner multiplicity (Sikka (2011), 252; for a different perspective, cf. Barnard (1965), 134-37. The question of intersubjective relations, which becomes a central thematic in German Idealism with Fichte and Hegel, cannot be addressed here.

71 Nisbet (1970), 9.

72 DeSouza (2012).

73 On the critique of imperialist conquest and slavery, *HW* IV, *Auch eine Philosophie der Geschichte zur Bildung der Menschheit*. On nationalism in Herder, see Spencer (2012); Sauder (2003).

74 Manninen (1996); Barnard (1965), 153-77.

nationalism of later periods of European and world history, though not entirely absent in 1848, derives from other sources.[75]

It might be instructive to compare two central figures in the history of perfectionism for their contrasting views of nationhood. J.G. Fichte famously defended a version of German nationalism in his *Reden an die deutsche Nation*, whose political charge has been variously interpreted.[76] Herderian spontaneity, the more naturalistic unfolding of an innate principle, contrasts sharply with Fichtean rational autonomy, the conscious subordination of particularity under a universal. This is the fundamental difference, even if Fichte's conception of unity is itself subject to modifications.[77] Further, though one passage of the *Reden* strongly echoes Herder,[78] Fichte's conception of history, and the role played by nations within it, is of a chain of infinitely advancing moral perfection, rather than a spatially and temporally comprehensive depiction of the powers of the species; it is an eternal, sublime struggle, not a completed, beautiful whole.[79] The links in this chain, in Fichte's view, are not of equal worth, but are morally differentiated by their proximity to the Absolute. Their interrelationship is fundamental: they seek to emulate each other, reproducing in a new register the mutual elicitation of freedom which Fichte had earlier attributed to the interactions among juridical subjects in the sphere of right.[80] The aim is to advance along the chain, with the inspiration and help of the higher members. Herder's radical pluralism[81] would rather imply that the individual contributions of nations cannot be assigned differential weights; such a position at least accords with Herder's methodological principles, if not always with his practice.[82] Both authors emphasize the mutual education in freedom that occurs through creative engagement with other social formations, but Herder's naturalism lays greater stress on the fulfilment of inner possibility, in continuous interaction with its environment. The idea of humanity as an end to be approximated is also attested in Herder's thought, bringing him closer to Fichte in this respect; human beings need to represent themselves as members

---

75 Bohm (2009), 277-78, 291. See also Dreitzel (1987), 267-98.
76 *SW* VII, 263-499.
77 See Luca Fonnesu, "Teleology and Perfection. Law, Freedom and the Search for Unity, from Kant to the Post-Kantians," in this volume.
78 *SW* VII, 467-468.
79 *AA* V, 244-46.
80 *SW* III, §3-4.
81 Forster (2017), Section 8.
82 Sikka (2011), 5, 46, 86, 109.

of the human community as well as the local community, and as progressing within it.[83]

For Herder the idea of the nation offers a vantage point for the critique of modern atomistic individualism. His repudiation of ethical egoism has been taken as evidence of his distance from Enlightenment positions,[84] but is better seen as voicing an alternative within them. In his celebration of the achievements of Shakespeare, Herder stresses the latter's rootedness in the popular life of his period, and criticizes the effacement of present-day popular culture before sterile court and intellectual influences, manifest for example in the Germanic lands by the pre-eminence of French theatre, with its austere and derivative classicism.[85] The cultural hegemony of France threatens the extinction of Germanic originality, and the suppression of diversity that is necessary to the perfection of the species. Here too Herder expresses a judgment which appears similar in substance to Fichte's later position in the *Reden*. In Fichte's highly problematic rendering, German as a living language affords access to the supersensible domain, and thus to the realm of freedom; to this he contrasts dead languages, such as those derived from Latin, which remain mired in immediacy, and are thus devoid of resources to think the new, or to direct genuine change.[86] Herder's defence of German popular culture has distinct grounds from those adduced by Fichte, not admitting the sharp sensible/supersensible split, and looking to renewal primarily from below, from the welling-up of spontaneous popular energies and formative capacities. His nationalism is fundamentally democratic in spirit.

Further comparisons with other figures in the perfectionist tradition are instructive of Herder's specificity. He agrees with Christian Wolff that human beings unite in societies in the interests of perfection: "Why have men united, unless to become more perfect, better, happier men?"[87] Unlike Wolff, however, Herder rejects the view that the political state is the necessary and indispensable condition for such perfection. While he emphasizes in the *Briefe* the difficulties of conceiving of a unique model of state that could respond to his ethics of self-perfection,[88] some general considerations are possible. His characterization of the state of nature differs from Wolff's, in that Herder holds that principles of equity are not only present, but effective, outside the bounds

---

83   Forster (2017), Section 8.
84   Berlin (1976), 143-216; but see also Norton (2009).
85   *HW* II, 498-521.
86   *SW* VII, 318-326.
87   *HW* VII, 124: „Wozu hätten sich Menschen vereinigt, als dass sie dadurch vollkommenere, bessere, glücklichere Menschen würden?"
88   *HW* VII, 24 and 25.

of political obligation. Nor is the state of nature an artificial construct, as in Hobbes, introduced as a means of legitimating the transition to political authority. It describes, rather, the empirical condition of most of humanity, for most of its history; neither is there a Kantian imperative to leave the state of nature, on ethical grounds.[89] For Herder, the natural condition of humanity depends on kinship and ethno-cultural relations which do not require completion or transcendence in a legal or juridical framework. Instead, individuals, beginning from a position of self-regard, come to recognize the binding character of regard for others, even in the absence of the political realm and its authoritative or authoritarian impositions.

> From the first need man began to know and to test the powers of nature; his purpose was nothing more than his own wellbeing, that is, an even use of his own powers in rest and exertion. He came into relation with other beings, but his own existence was still the measure of this relation. The rule of equity (Billigkeit) imposed itself on him, for it is nothing else than the measure of the effect and countereffect of the social co-existence among beings of the same kind.[90]

Nor are we entitled to conclude with Wolff that without the state, no secure thriving is possible for individuals. The state is historically contingent, Herder affirms, and its existence far from universal in human experience. Moreover, political relations are often the source of oppression rather than of happiness:

> Even less comprehensible is the claim that man is made for the state, or that he necessarily owes his first real happiness to its foundation. (...) Millions on earth live without states, and even in artificial states, anyone wishing to be happy must begin where the savage begins, seeking to produce and sustain health and strength of soul, the happiness of his hearth and heart, not from the state, but from himself. Father and mother, husband and wife, child and brother, friend and man – these are natural relations, through which we become happy. What the state can give us are artificial tools, but it can unfortunately do something much more essential: it can rob us of our selves.[91]

Self-perfection is the task of individuals and social communities, more than of states.[92] It consists in deploying one's own nature-bestowed forces in ways that benefit the self and others, and in seeking to harmonise these forces, so that they present a dynamic unity, constructed and renewed. Progress consists

---

89   *AA* VI, 256, 267.
90   *HW* VI, 666.
91   *HW* VI, pp. 333 and 334 [our translation; SB/DM].
92   *HW* VII 25, 124.

in eliminating hindrances to life, health, and the common welfare.[93] What is paramount is not the interests of the rulers or *raison d'Etat*, but the common good of the people: "Nature does not count on rulers and states, but on the wellbeing of men in their state."[94]

Conclusion

Herder's legacy is a novel account of perfectibility as a universal human quality expressing itself in diversity and many possible life-plans. Human beings can be characterized by a particular indeterminacy, adaptability, and capacity to respond to different worlds. Perfectibility depends not only on human encounter and emulation, but also on the maximal preservation of diversity.

The dangers to the process of perfection lie in enforced uniformity and standardization, pressures arising from economic, political, and social sources. In his diagnoses of modernity and its possibilities for both emancipation and subjugation, Herder occupies an important position in the history of political thought. The naturalistic perspective that he adopts to account for these conflicting tendencies is not mechanistic, as in Hobbes, but biological and historical, linked in complex and perhaps fluctuating ways to Enlightenment humanism, but also anticipating later Romantic currents.[95] The pertinence of his approach for current conceptions of liberal naturalism,[96] non-reductive and non-mechanistic ideas of the self and its activities in relation to the natural world and the community, is a subject awaiting future examination.

The application of Herder's own theoretical approach suggests an alternative to the idea of a deep rupture between pre-Kantian and post-Kantian versions of perfectionism. He invites us to think instead of a continuum rather than an abrupt break in perfectionist traditions, with concepts and arguments combining, changing, and being reformulated in original and complex ways. And yet it is also possible to specify Herder's distinctive position along this continuum. Like the older perfectionisms of Aristotelian provenance, and unlike Kant, he takes the promotion of *eudaimonia* or happiness as the central *telos*. This theoretical stance would appear to align him with pre-Kantian positions; but he innovates here, endowing happiness with a new meaning, based

---

93 Ibid.
94 *HW* VI, 668 [our translation; SB/DM].
95 Beiser (2011), 142-43. His approach is also generative of later Romantic views of nature and society. Barnard (1965), 153-77; Forster (2019).
96 E.g. De Caro/Macarthur (eds.) (2008).

in a biological/adaptive model of human action and of thriving. The meta-ethical terrain is thus reconfigured through Herder's evolutionary naturalism; natural kinds and their ends are not given and permanent, but self-constituted and changing, in complex interrelations with their environments. Human nature is not fixed, but plastic: Herder's pluralism admits different standards of excellence and values in various societies and eras. He views these standards as distinctive modes of adjustment to empirical circumstances and to historical traditions, yet also expressive of a unique core insight into humanity and its potentialities that imparts unity and identity to a specific culture through its diachronic changes.

Nor, normatively, does Herder follow Christian Wolff and related pre-Kantian perfectionisms in politicizing happiness under the solicitous care of enlightened rulers. He shares Kant's repugnance toward these forms of paternalistic despotism,[97] and if he continues to base the legitimacy of forms of association on their contribution to welfare (in the broadest sense) and not to the practice of right, a profound commitment to individual and collective freedom is all-pervasive in his thought.

Herder bids us to reconsider the idealist criticisms of naturalism, and of the various senses of personal and collective autonomy.[98] The transition from Leibniz to Kant and German Idealism is not direct or unilinear, but follows multiple paths, all of which, in their own particularity, require open and attentive exploration.

Bibliography

Abbt, Thomas, *Zweifel über die Bestimmung des Menschen*, Amsterdam, 1767. Reprint in: Moses Mendelssohn, *Gesammelte Schriften*, vol. 6.1, 1981, pp. 7-27.
– *Vermischte Werke*, ed. by Friedrich Nicolai, 6 parts in 3 vol., Hildesheim: Olms, 1978.
Aristotle, *Select Works*, Cambridge (Mass.): Harvard University Press, 1926-60 ff.
Barnard, Frederick Mechner, *Herder's Social and Political Thought. From Enlightenment to Nationalism*, Oxford: Clarendon Press, 1965.
– *Herder on Social and Political Culture*, Cambridge: Cambridge University Press, 1969.
– *Self-direction and Political Legitimacy. Rousseau and Herder*, Oxford: Clarendon Press, 1988.
Baron, Konstanze/ Soboth, Christian, *Perfektionismus und Perfektibilität. Theorien und Praktiken der Vervollkommnung in Pietismus und Aufklärung*, Hamburg: Meiner, 2018.

---

97   AA VIII, 290. See also Herder's student Forster (1971).
98   AA VIII, 43-66.

Baumgarten, Siegmund Jakob, *Unterricht vom rechtmäßigen Verhalten eines Christen, oder Theologische Moral*, Halle: Bauer, 1738.
Beiser, Frederick C., *Enlightenment, Revolution, and Romanticism*, Cambridge (Mass.): Harvard University Press, 1992.
– *Schiller as Philosopher: A Re-Examination*, Oxford: Oxford University Press, 2005.
– *The German Historicist Tradition*, Oxford: Oxford University Press, 2011.
Berlin, Isaiah, *Vico and Herder. Two Studies in the History of Ideas*, London: Hogarth Press, 1976, pp. 143-216.
– *Three Critics of the Enlightenment: Vico, Hamann, Herder*, Princeton: Princeton University Press, 2000.
Bilfinger, Georg Bernhard, *Dilucidationes philosophicae de Deo, anima humana, mundo, et generalibus rerum affectionibus*, Tübingen: Cotta, 1725.
Binoche, Bertrand, *L'homme perfectible*, Ceyzerieu: Champ Vallon, 2004.
Bohm, Arnd, "Herder and Politics," in: *A Companion to the Works of Johann Gottfried Herder*, ed. by Wulf Köpke and Hans Adler, Rochester NY: Boydell and Brewer, 2009, pp. 277-304.
Bonnet, Charles, *Traité d'insectologie ou Observations sur les pucerons*, 1745.
Booher, C. Richard, *Perfection, Harmony and Harmonious Individuality. Herder's Ethical Thought, 1765-1791*, Dissertation, Syracuse University, 2015.
Buchenau, Stefanie, "Herder: Physiology and Philosophical Anthropology", in: *Herder. Philosophy and Anthropology*, ed. by Anik Waldow and Nigel DeSouza, Oxford: Oxford University Press, 2017, pp. 72-93.
Buffon, Georges-Louis Leclerc, *Œuvres*, Préface de Michel Delon, textes choisis, présentés et annotés par Stéphane Schmitt, Paris: Gallimard, 2007.
Dallmayr, Fred, "Truth and Diversity. Some Lessons from Herder", in: *Journal of Speculative Philosophy*, 11/2, 1997, pp. 101-124.
De Caro, Mario and Macarthur, David (eds.), *Naturalism in Question*, Cambridge (Mass.): Harvard University Press, 2008.
DeSouza, Nigel, "The Soul-Body Relationship and the Foundation of Morality: Herder contra Mendelssohn", in: *Herder Jahrbuch*, vol. 21, September 2014, pp. 145-161.
– "Leibniz in the Eighteenth Century: Herder's Critical Reflections on the Principles of Nature and Grace", in: *British Journal for the History of Philosophy*, vol. 20, no. 4, 2012, pp. 1-23.
Dreitzel, Horst, "Herders politische Konzepte", in: *Johann Gottfried Herder 1744-1803*, ed. by Gerhard Sauder, Hamburg: Meiner, 1987, pp. 267–98.
Fichte, J.G., *Sämtliche Werke*, ed. by Immanuel Hermann Fichte, Berlin: De Gruyter, 1971. (*SW*)
Forster, Georg, *Über die Beziehung der Staatskunst auf das Glück der Menschen*, Werke in vier Bänden, vol. 3, Leipzig, 1971, pp. 697-726.

Forster, Michael N., "Herder on human rights", in: *Herder: Philosophy and Anthropology*, ed. by Anik Waldow, Nigel de Souza, Oxford: Oxford University Press, 2017, pp. 224-229.
- *Herder's Philosophy*, Oxford: Oxford University Press, 2018.
- "Johann Gottfried von Herder", in: *Stanford Encyclopedia of Philosophy*, URL = https://plato.stanford.edu/archives/sum2019/entries/herder/, 25. 08. 2017.

Gaukroger, Stephen, *The Collapse of Mechanism and the Rise of Sensibility*, Oxford: Oxford University Press, 2010.

Herder, Johann Gottfried, *Sämmtliche Werke*. ed. by Bernhard Suphan, Berlin: Weidmann'sche Buchhandlung, 1877-1913. (*HSW*)
- *Werke. 10 in 11 Bänden*, ed. by Ulrich Gaier et all., Frankfurt: Deutscher Klassiker Verlag, 1985 ff. (*HW*)

Helfer, Martha, "Herder, Fichte, and Humboldt's 'Thinking and Speaking'" *Herder Today*, ed. by Kurt Mueller-Vollmer: Berlin: de Gruyter, 1990, pp. 367-381.

Heinz, Marion, "Die Bestimmung des Menschen. Herder contra Mendelssohn", in: *Philosophie der Endlichkeit. Festschrift für Erich Christian Schröder zum 65. Geburtstag*, ed. by Beate Niemeyer and Dirk Schütze: Würzburg, 1992, pp. 263-285.
- *Sensualistischer Idealismus. Untersuchungen zur Erkenntnistheorie des jungen Herder (1763-1778)*, Hamburg: Meiner, 1994.

Hobbes, Thomas, *Leviathan*, ed. by Noel Malcolm, vol. 2, Oxford: Oxford University Press, 2012.

Hurka, Thomas, *Perfectionism*, Oxford: Oxford University Press, 1993.

Jaumann, Herbert, *Rousseau in Deutschland. Neue Beiträge zur Erforschung seiner Rezeption*, Berlin: De Gruyter, 2011.

Kant, Immanuel, *Gesammelte Schriften*, ed. by Königlich Preussische Akademie der Wissenschaften (Akademie-Ausgabe), Berlin u.a., 1900 ff. (*AA*)

Kriedte, Peter/ Medick, Hans/ Schlumbohm, Jürgen, *Industrialization before Industrialization*, Cambridge: Cambridge University Press, 1981.

Macpherson, Crawford Brough, *The Political Theory of Possessive Individualism, Hobbes to Locke*, Oxford: Oxford University Press, 1962.

Manninen, Juha, *Feuer am Pol. Zum Aufbau der Vernunft im europäischen Norden*, Frankfurt/M.: Lang, 1996.

Mendelssohn, Moses, *Orakel, die Bestimmung des Menschen betreffend* (1764), in: *Gesammelte Schriften*, vol. 6.1 (1981), pp. 7-27. (*GS*)

Moggach, Douglas, "Freedom and Perfection: German Debates on the State in the Eighteenth Century", in: *Canadian Journal of Political Science*, Vol. 42, no. 4, 2009, pp. 1003-1023.
- „Die Kultur der Zerrissenheit und ihre Aufhebung", in: *Die Philosophie des Marktes, Deutsches Jahrbuch Philosophie*, ed. by Hans-Christoph Schmidt am Busch, vol. 7, 2016, pp. 71-98.

Nisbet, Hugh Barr, *Herder and the Philosophy and History of Science*, Cambridge: Modern Humanities Research Association, 1970, pp. 9-16.
– *Lessing. Eine Biographie*, München: C.H. Beck, 2008.
John K. Noyes, *Herder: Aesthetics against Imperialism*, Toronto: University of Toronto Press, 2015.
Norton, Robert, "Herder as Critical Contemporary", in: *A Companion to the Works of Johann Gottfried Herder*, ed. by Wulf Köpke and Hans Adler, Rochester/New York, 2009, pp. 351-372.
Raz, Joseph, *The Morality of Freedom*, Oxford: Oxford University Press, 1986.
– *The Practice of Value*, Oxford, Oxford University Press, 2003.
Reimarus, Hermann Samuel, *Die vornehmsten Wahrheiten der natürlichen Religion*, ed. by Günter Gawlick, Göttingen, 1985.
Rousseau, Jean-Jacques, Discours sur l'origine et les fondements de l'inégalité parmi les hommes, in: *Œuvres complètes*, vol. 3, Paris: Gallimard, 1964.
Sauder, Gerhard, „La conception herdérienne de peuple/langue, des peuples et de leurs langues", in: *Revue germanique internationale*, 2003, pp. 123-132.
Schubert, Anselm, *Das Ende der Sünde: Anthropologie und Erbsünde zwischen Reformation und Aufklärung*, Göttingen: Vandenhoeck und Ruprecht, 2002.
Sellars, John, "Stoic Cosmopolitanism and Zeno's 'Republic'", in: *History of Political Thought*, 28/1, 2007, pp. 1-29.
Sher, George, *Beyond Neutrality: Perfectionism and Politics*, Cambridge: Cambridge University Press, 1997.
Sikka, Sonia, *Herder on Humanity and Cultural Difference. Enlightened Relativism*, Cambridge: Cambridge University Press, 2011.
Spencer, Vicki, *Herder's Political Thought. A Study of Language, Culture, and Community*, Toronto: University of Toronto Press, 2012, pp. 129-57.
Taylor, Charles. *Sources of the Self. The Making of the Modern Identity*. Cambridge: Cambridge University Press, 1989.
– "Philosophy as Philosophical Anthropology", in: *Herder: Philosophy and Anthropology*, ed. by Anik Waldow and Nigel de Souza, Oxford: Oxford University Press, 2017, pp. 13-29.
Waldow, Anik/ DeSouza, Nigel, *Herder: Philosophy and Anthropology*, Oxford: Oxford University Press, 2017.
Willoweit, Dietmar/ Fehn, Janine, *Johann Gottfried Herder. Staat-Nation-Humanität. Ausgewählte Texte*. Würzburg: Königshausen & Neumann, 2007.
Waszek, Norbert, "The Scottish Enlightenment in Germany, and its translator, Christian Garve (1742-98)", in: *Scotland in Europe*, ed. by Tom Hubbard and R.D.S. Jack, Amsterdam: Rodopi, 2006, pp. 55-71.
Weinroth, Michelle/ Leduc Browne, Paul (eds.), *To Build a Shadowy Isle of Bliss*, McGill: Queen's University Press, 2015.

Wolff, Christian, „Vernünftige Gedanken von der Menschen Tun und Lassen zur Beförderung ihrer Glückseligkeit (Deutsche Ethik)", in: *Gesammelte Werke*, ed. by Hans Werner Arndt, Hildesheim: Olms, 1976.

– *Institutiones juris naturae et gentium* [1754]. *Gesammelte Werke*, Bd. 26, ed. by M. Thomann, Hildesheim: Olms, 1969.

– *Principes du droit de la nature et des gens, extrait du grand ouvrage latin*, par M. Formey, tome premier [1758] Caen, Centre de Philosophie politique et juridique, 1988.

Zammito, John, "(Re)discovering Johann Gottfried Herder", in: *Groniek Historisch Tijdschrift* 171, 2006, pp. 191-214.

– Zammito, John/ Menges, Karl/ Menze, Ernest. "Johann Gottfried Herder Revisited: The Revolution in Scholarship in the Last Quarter Century", in: *Journal of the History of Ideas* 71/4, 2010, pp. 661-684.

Schiller, das Gute am Schönen oder warum wir uns auf zweifache Weise verfehlen können

Eva Schürmann

Was hat Schönheit mit Selbstbestimmung zu tun? Mit dieser Frage sieht man sich konfrontiert, wenn man Schillers Autonomiebegriff klären möchte. In den frühen, nie von ihm selbst für den Druck überarbeiteten Kallias-Briefen schreibt Schiller an seinen Freund Körner:

> Es ist gewiß von keinem Sterblichen Menschen kein größeres Wort noch gesprochen worden, als dieses Kantische, was zugleich der Innhalt seiner ganzen Philosophie ist: Bestimme dich aus dir selbst: [...] Diese große Idee der Selbstbestimmung strahlt uns aus gewißen Erscheinungen der Natur zurük, und diese nennen wir Schönheit.[1]

Es ist eine merkwürdige Verbindung, die er da herstellt, und sie muss schrittweise entfaltet werden. Zuvor aber möchte ich einige systematische Vorbemerkungen machen, um zu erläutern, von wo aus ich eine Perspektive auf Schiller entwickeln werde. Peter Szondi zeigt verschiedentlich, dass es *dialektische* Lesarten von Schillers „Antinomien und Äquivokationen"[2] sind, die einen Schlüssel zu ihrer Deutung bereithalten. Denn auf den ersten Blick mögen seine antithetischen Leitunterscheidungen Sinnlichkeit und Sittlichkeit, Natur und Freiheit, Stoff und Form als zu schematische Gegensätze erscheinen und seine kühnen Volten von der Schönheit übers Spiel zum ästhetischen Zustand und der lebenden Gestalt können einen an Kants strenger begrifflicher Beweisführung orientierten Leser durchaus düpieren. Anders wird es, wenn man Schillers Grundbegriffe nicht als gegebene Dichotomien, sondern als *Vollzugsbestimmungen* und *Praxisbegriffe* liest. Ich werde dafür argumentieren, dass dadurch die Begriffe nicht allein dialektisch ineinander umschlagen, sondern chiastisch miteinander wechselwirken. Auf diese Weise kann in den Blick geraten, dass Schillers Denken nicht bloß in einer oszillierenden Bewegung zwischen einem binären Begriffsschema besteht,

---

* Für Diskussionen dieses Beitrags danke ich Levno von Plato, Antonio Roselli und den Teilnehmern meines Schiller-Seminars.
1 *NA* 26, 191. Die *Nationalausgabe* von Schillers Werken wird im Folgenden mit NA abgekürzt.
2 Szondi (1973), 97. Ferner: Szondi (1991), bes. 149ff.

sondern auf deren Komplementarität und wechselseitige Durchdringung zielt und darin zum Austragungsort eines wesentlichen Widerstreits wird. Die Entwicklung seiner Freiheitskonzeption realisiert sich in Prozessbegriffen, mittels derer die Theoriefiguren einer ästhetischen Anthropologie und einer existentiellen Ästhetik formulierbar werden und mit welchen Schiller die Oppositionen hinter sich lässt. Auf diese Weise wird es möglich, die doppelte Natur des Menschen weniger in eine harmonische Übereinstimmung als in einen Zustand des Aushaltens seiner inneren Zerrissenheit zu versetzen. Meine Lektüre soll erweisen, dass es letztlich ein Zustand der Enthobenheit über die Gegensätze und ihre schlechten Alternativen ist, den Schiller herauspräpariert. Ich beschränke mich dabei auf die Abhandlungen über Anmut und Würde (1793) bzw. über die ästhetische Erziehung des Menschen in einer Reihe von Briefen (1795).

Abschnitt I erörtert einige folgenreiche Unterschiede zwischen Kants und Schillers Willens- bzw. Freiheitsbegriffen. Abschnitt II erläutert, was die so verstandene Freiheit mit Schönheit und Spiel zu tun hat. Abschnitt III entfaltet Schillers Konzept des ästhetischen Zustands als einen Zustand unendlicher Bestimmbarkeit. Abschnitt IV diskutiert Schillers individualethisches Bildungsprojekt in seiner Bedeutung für ein politisches Gemeinwesen, mithin den Zusammenhang von Kunst und Politik. Abschnitt V verortet Schiller als Mittler im Verhältnis von Kant und dem Deutschen Idealismus.

1. Freiheit des Wollens

Beginnen wir mit Schillers Konzeption des Willens, die sich in wesentlichen Zügen von derjenigen Kants unterscheidet: Für Schiller steht der Wille „frey zwischen Pflicht und Neigung"[3], das heißt, er muss sich zwischen den Forderungen der Vernunftnatur des Menschen und denen seiner Gefühlsnatur entscheiden. Daraus folgt umgekehrt, dass er von zwei Seiten ‚Nöthigungen' erfährt, mithin fremdbestimmt ist, denn in beiden Fällen unterwirft er sich Ansprüchen, die ihn beherrschen. Wirkliche Freiheit besteht erst darin, sich beiden Forderungen gegenüber bestimmend zu verhalten.

„Die Gesetzgebung der Natur hat Bestand bis zum Willen, wo sie sich endigt, und die vernünftige anfängt. Der Wille steht hier zwischen beyden Gerichtsbarkeiten, und es kommt ganz auf ihn selbst an, von welcher er das Gesetz empfangen will"[4], heißt es in *Anmut und Würde*, wo der Wille als Vermögen der

---

3 *NA* 20, 316.
4 Ebd., 291.

Wahl bestimmt ist. „Aber er steht nicht in gleichem Verhältniß gegen beyde. Als Naturkraft ist er gegen die eine, wie gegen die andere, frey; das heißt, er muß sich weder zu dieser noch zu jener schlagen."[5]

Deswegen ist der Wille für Schiller anders als für Kant keineswegs sogleich ein guter Wille und Freiheit bedeutet durchaus auch, für das Böse frei zu sein, wie er es mit seinen Dramenfiguren durchspielt. Zwar gebraucht der Mensch seine Freiheit unwürdig, „wenn er [...] der Vernunft widersprechend handelt"[6]. Aber zugleich ist er darin erst wirklich frei; er ist an das Sittengesetz nicht unbedingt gebunden, sondern ihm lediglich ‚verbunden'.

Dies ist bereits eine bedeutende Abweichung von Kant. Für Kant ist das Bestimmtwerden durch die Natur die reine Heteronomie, während die freiwillige Unterwerfung unter die Vernunft höchste Selbstbestimmung bedeutet. Der Wille ist selbstgesetzgebend, insofern er Urheber des Gesetzes ist, dem er sich zugleich unterwirft.[7] Bei Schiller hingegen ist der Wille noch frei gegenüber den Nötigungen der Vernunft, denn es ist ja gerade eine einseitige Vernunftherrschaft, der er Zwanghaftigkeit und eine sträfliche Vernachlässigung der Neigung anlastet.

> So gewiß ich nehmlich überzeugt bin [...] daß der Antheil der Neigung an einer freyen Handlung für die reine Pflichtmäßigkeit dieser Handlung nichts beweist, so glaube ich eben daraus folgern zu können, daß die sittliche Vollkommenheit des Menschen gerade nur aus diesem Antheil seiner Neigung an seinem moralischen Handeln erhellen kann. Der Mensch nehmlich ist nicht dazu bestimmt, einzelne sittliche Handlungen zu verrichten, sondern ein sittliches Wesen zu seyn.[8]

Dieses Vollkommenheits- oder besser *Vollständigkeitsideal* ist der Grund dafür, dass Freiheit für Schiller im Unterschied zu Kant eine graduierbare Fähigkeit ist, so dass man mehr oder weniger Mensch sein kann. „In voller Bedeutung des Worts, Mensch"[9] ist man eben nur, wenn keine der beiden Seiten einseitige Schlagseiten hat. Warum das im Spiel der Fall ist, beschäftigt uns weiter unten.

Die ganze Argumentation gründet somit in den anthropologischen Grundspannungen der conditio humana. Weil der Mensch „weder ausschließend Materie, noch [...] ausschließend Geist"[10] ist, kann er vollständig nur sein,

---

5   Ebd.
6   Ebd.
7   *AA* IV, 431. Eine gute Darstellung jüngeren Datums zu Kant und den Folgen findet sich bei Noller (2016).
8   *NA* 20, 283.
9   So die berühmte Bestimmung des Spiels im 15. Brief (*NA* 20, 355-360).
10   Ebd., 356.

wenn und wo er seine sinnlich-sittliche Differenznatur aus jedem einseitigen Herrschaftsverhältnisse befreit hat.

> Das Begehrungsvermögen dringt also auf Befriedigung, und der Wille wird aufgefordert, ihm diese zu verschaffen. Aber der Wille soll seine Bestimmungsgründe von der Vernunft empfangen, und nur nach demjenigen, was diese erlaubt oder vorschreibt, seine Entschließung fassen. Wendet sich nun der Wille wirklich an die Vernunft, ehe er das Verlangen des Triebes genehmigt, so handelt er sittlich; entscheidet er aber unmittelbar, so handelt er sinnlich*.[11]

In dieser anthropologischen Doppelnatur, die zugleich seine Spaltung ist, gründet die Notwendigkeit dritter Vermittlungstätigkeiten. „Wäre der Mensch bloß ein Sinnenwesen, so würde die Natur zugleich die Gesetze geben und die Fälle der Anwendung bestimmen; jetzt theilt sie das Regiment mit der Freyheit"[12].

Schiller trennt terminologisch nicht strikt zwischen Autonomie, Selbstbestimmung und Freiheit. Von Autonomie ist ohnehin viel seltener die Rede als von Freiheit und diese besteht, wie wir noch sehen werden, in einem Zustand *aktiver Bestimmbarkeit*, mithin im Ausgleich von Bestimmend-Sein und Bestimmt-Werden. In den Kalliasbriefen hatte sich Schiller noch etwas von der terminologischen Unterscheidung zwischen Autonomie und Heautonomie[13] versprochen, aber er kommt darauf in den großen Abhandlungen nicht mehr zurück. Der Sache nach ist man ihm zufolge selbstbestimmt nicht vornehmlich dadurch, dass man sich selbst beherrscht oder sich Gesetzen unterwirft, sondern indem man zwischen zwei Extremen hindurch navigiert.

> Ueberall, wo der Trieb anfängt zu handeln, und sich herausnimmt, in das Amt des Willens zu greifen, da darf der Wille keine Indulgenz, sondern muß durch den nachdrücklichsten Widerstand seine Selbstständigkeit (Autonomie) beweisen.

---

11 *NA* 20, 292. Das * bezieht sich auf Schillers Anmerkung, die in unserem Zusammenhang ebenfalls interessiert: „Man darf aber diese Anfrage des Willens bey der Vernunft nicht mit derjenigen verwechseln, wo sie über die Mittel zu Befriedigung einer Begierde erkennen soll. Hier ist nicht davon die Rede, wie die Befriedigung zu erlangen, sondern ob sie zu gestatten ist. Nur das letzte gehört ins Gebiet der Moralität; das erste gehört zur Klugheit." Ebd.

12 Ebd., 262.

13 „Die Form muß im eigentlichsten Sinn zugleich selbstbestimmend und selbstbestimmt seyn, nicht bloße Autonomie sondern Heautonomie muß da seyn. Aber, wirst Du hier einwenden, wenn die Form mit der Existenz des Dinges zusammen eins ausmachen muß, um Schönheit hervorzubringen, wo bleiben die Schönheiten der Kunst, welche diese Heautonomie niemals haben können? Ich will Dir darauf antworten, wenn wir erst zu dem Schönen der Kunst gekommen sind, denn dieses erfordert ein ganz eignes Capitel." (*NA* 26, 207).

> Wo hingegen der Wille anfängt, und die Sinnlichkeit ihm folgt, da darf er keine Strenge, sondern muß Indulgenz beweisen.
> Dieß ist mit wenigen Worten das Gesetz für das Verhältniß beyder Naturen im Menschen, so wie es in der Erscheinung sich darstellet.[14]

Aus diesem Grund ist für Schiller die Achtung für das Sittengesetz weder das Höchste noch wirkliche Freiheit. „Von der Achtung, kann man sagen, sie beugt sich vor ihrem Gegenstände; von der Liebe, sie neigt sich zu dem ihrigen"[15]. Das heißt, auch die Achtung ist eine Form von Zwang oder jedenfalls ‚unschöne' Unfreiheit.

Schiller kommt auf diesen Gedanken in den *Briefen über die ästhetische Erziehung* zurück und erläutert ihn ausführlicher: „Wenn wir gegen einen andern feindlich gesinnt sind, der uns Achtung abnöthigt, so empfinden wir peinlich die Nöthigung der Vernunft. Sobald er aber zugleich unsre Neigung interessiert und unsre Achtung sich erworben, so verschwindet *sowohl der Zwang der Empfindung als der Zwang der Vernunft*, und wir fangen an, ihn zu lieben, d. h. zugleich mit unsrer Neigung und mit unsrer Achtung zu spielen."[16]

Aus Kantischer Sicht ist das Ansinnen, mit Achtung zu spielen, nachgerade ein Affront, und entsprechend hatte Kant bereits auf *Anmuth und Würde* ablehnend reagiert, indem er schreibt: „Ich gestehe gern, daß ich dem Pflichtbegriffe, gerade um seiner Würde willen, keine Anmut beigesellen kann. Denn er enthält unbedingte Nöthigung, womit Anmut in geradem Widerspruch steht"[17]. Das ist begrifflich richtig, verfehlt aber, wie wir in Abschnitt V sehen werden, auf symptomatische Weise Schillers systematische Pointe.

Vorläufig reicht es festzuhalten, dass die Freiheit sich in Schillers Konzeption gegenüber zwei schlechten Alternativen verwahren muss, und dass er damit gerade nicht die Subordinierung der Natur unter die Gesetzgebung der Vernunft betreibt. Vielmehr kritisiert er die einseitige Forderung nach Vernunftherrschaft als das, was in seiner Terminologie den Barbaren kennzeichnet, der ebenso wie sein Counterpart, der Wilde, das Ideal des ganzen Menschen verfehlt: „Der Mensch kann sich aber auf eine doppelte Weise entgegen gesetzt seyn: entweder als Wilder, wenn seine Gefühle über seine Grundsätze herrschen; oder als Barbar, wenn seine Grundsätze seine Gefühle zerstören."[18] Beide Typen von Verfehlungen macht Schiller verantwortlich für den Verlauf der französischen Revolution bzw. ihr Umschlagen in Terror. Der „gebildete

---

14   *NA* 20, 297.
15   Ebd., 302.
16   Ebd., 354 (Kursivierung von mir).
17   *AA* VI, 23.
18   *NA* 20, 318.

Mensch macht sich die Natur zum Freund"[19], und er vermeidet dergestalt das einseitige Regime der Pflicht ebenso wie die willenlosen Auslieferung an Gefühle.

Die Vernunft mag das Sittengesetz wohl aufstellen, heißt es im 8. Brief, aber erst „der muthige Wille, und das lebendige Gefühl"[20] realisieren seine praktische Geltung.

Kein Wunder, dass es für Schiller an diesem systematischen Punkt nötig wird, seine Leitdifferenzen im Rückgriff auf Reinholds und Fichtes Triebbegriffe zu reformulieren. Als Stoff- und Form*trieb* wird nun bezeichnet, was von vornherein prozessphilosophisch zu verstehen ist, „denn Triebe sind die einzigen bewegenden Kräfte in der empfindenden Welt"[21].

Es stützt meine These von den praktischen Vollzugsbegriffen als die die Oppositionen zu lesen sind, dass mit dem Triebbegriff Bewegungen und Strebungen aufgerufen werden, mit deren Hilfe die verdinglichenden Gegensätze dynamisiert werden. Man tut gut daran, den Willen ebenfalls als Prozessbegriff zu denken und nicht als ein Vermögen, das es substantiell oder ontisch immer schon gäbe. Wille entsteht vielmehr erst im Ergreifen einer partikularen Freiheit, und realisiert sich als Praxis selbstbestimmten Wollens, das sich sowohl zum Begehrten als auch zum Gesollten reflektiert verhält.[22]

Das Streben des sinnlichen Triebes zielt aufs Leben, das des Formtriebes auf Gestalt. Analog dazu wird das Gemüt bestimmt, wenn es empfindet, und bestimmt, wenn es denkt. Freiheit „muß [...] fehlen, so lang [...] [der Mensch] unvollständig und einer von beyden Trieben ausgeschlossen ist, und muß durch alles das, was ihm seine Vollständigkeit zurückgiebt, wieder hergestellt werden können."[23]

Es ist gerade das Ende der bloßen Herrschaft der Form über den Stoff, das den Spieltrieb qualifiziert und durch das die Freiheit wechselseitiger Anerkennung an die Stelle der hierarchischen Unterordnung gesetzt werden kann.

Der Spieltrieb vereint die Zielvorgaben von Stoff- und Formstreben in der lebenden Gestalt. Bloß weil man lebt, hat man noch keine selbstbestimmte Form, bloß weil der Künstler eine Form gestaltet, überzeugt sie noch nicht durch Lebendigkeit. Das Ganze kann nur in Übereinstimmung kommen, wenn weder die Materie über den Geist, noch die Vernunft über die Gefühle herrscht.

---

19   Ebd.
20   Ebd., 330.
21   Ebd., 330f.
22   Die systematische Nähe von Harry Frankfurts Konzeption von second order volitions bzw. seiner ganzen Theorie der Autonomie zu Schiller wird meinem Eindruck nach unterschätzt.
23   Ebd., 374.

Schillers zeitdiagnostisches Fazit lautet, „daß sich der Mensch auf zwey entgegen gesetzten Wegen von seiner Bestimmung entfernen könne, daß unser Zeitalter wirklich auf beyden Abwegen wandle, und hier der Rohigkeit, dort der Erschlaffung [...] zum Raub geworden sey. Von dieser doppelten Verirrung soll es durch die Schönheit zurückgeführt werden."[24]

2. Schönheit des Spielens

Es ist also eine zweifache Form der Selbstverfehlung, die durch freie Selbstbestimmung vermieden werden soll. Und hier erst taucht der Zusammenhang von Freiheit und Schönheit auf. Denn: In der Anschauung des Schönen befinden wir uns „in einer glücklichen Mitte zwischen dem Gesetz und Bedürfniß [...], dem Zwange sowohl des einen als des andern entzogen"[25].

Bereits in *Anmut und Würde* qualifiziert Schiller den Geschmack als Mitte zwischen Geist und Sinnlichkeit. Was den Geschmack anspricht, vermittelt solchermaßen zwischen Denken und Anschauung. „Durch die Schönheit wird der sinnliche Mensch zur Form und zum Denken geleitet; durch die Schönheit wird der geistige Mensch zur Materie zurückgeführt, und der Sinnenwelt wiedergegeben"[26]. Das Schöne ist der Name des anzustrebenden Ideals verwirklichter Freiheit. Die Kunst als systematisches Terrain des Schönen realisiert im ästhetischen Spiel eine sonst unmögliche Zwanglosigkeit.

Es geht um einen „Vernunftbegriff der Schönheit"[27], für den die Erfahrung ‚der Richterstuhl nicht ist'. Denn Schiller weiß um die Ambivalenzen des schönen Scheins, und kennt die guten Gründe für den Verdacht gegen das bloß Schöne. Und dass verfeinerte Sitten noch keine guten Menschen machen, kritisiert er ja gerade als ‚Erschlaffung des Zeitalters'. Er muss deswegen die Unterschiede zwischen seinem systematischen Programmbegriff des Schönen und empirischer Attraktivität herausarbeiten. Doch zugleich darf sich das Schöne in seiner Konzeption auch nicht gänzlich von der Empirie lossagen, da schließlich das Sinnliche mit dem Intelligiblen verschränkt werden soll. Dass das ein Spagat ist, versteht sich von selbst.

Diese paradoxale Gleichzeitigkeit des Ungleichen kann nicht mehr positiv ausgewiesen, sondern nur noch approximativ vorgestellt werden. Aber dieses Problem ist weder für Schiller noch für die Ästhetik spezifisch, sondern eines,

---

24 Ebd., 336.
25 Ebd., 357.
26 Ebd., 365.
27 Ebd., 340.

das auch Kant mit seiner Formel von der Kausalität aus Freiheit nicht löst.[28] Den dritten Trieb, der die entgegengesetzten Triebkräfte und die daraus resultierenden Konflikte zwischen Individuum und Gattung, Zeitlichem und Bleibendem vermitteln soll, bezeichnet er selbst als „schlechterdings [...] undenkbare[n] Begriff"[29] und affirmiert dessen paradoxale Verfassung mit der Formel von der ‚Aufhebung der Zeit in der Zeit'.

Die Frage, ob oder wie es einer Idee möglich werden soll, sinnlich sichtbar zu werden, hatte Schiller 1793 noch optimistisch beurteilt: „Die Freiheit in der Erscheinung ist also nichts anders, als die Selbstbestimmung an einem Dinge, insofern sie sich in der Anschauung offenbart."[30] Doch greift er diese frühe Formulierung der Kalliasbriefe nicht mehr bzw. nur noch in einer Anmerkung zum 23. Brief auf. Es ist Hegel, der affirmativ daran anknüpfen wird mit seinem Konzept der Kunst als dem sinnlichen Scheinen einer Idee.

Indessen heißt ‚Freiheit in der Erscheinung' meiner Lektüre zufolge nicht, ‚Freiheit, die erscheint', sondern so zu erscheinen, dass Freiheit darin *vollzogen* wird, das bedeutet, dass etwas aktualisiert wird und zum Ausdruck kommt, das dinglich ohne diese Vollzugsbewegung gar nicht vorhanden ist. Hier bewährt sich die prozessphilosophische Lesart der Begriffe, denn als performative Praxis des Hervorbringens von etwas, das es sonst nicht gäbe, ist das Schöne – das heißt sind Spiel und Kunst – *Maßnahmen der Verwirklichung*, nicht Abbildung eines Gegebenen. ‚Schönheit der Gestalt unter dem Einfluss der Freiheit' bedeutet deshalb nicht, dass etwas ohnehin Vorhandenes bloß noch illustriert würde. Lebende Gestalt heißt vielmehr, dass das Mögliche verwirklicht und eine Idee verkörpert wird. Wir werden noch sehen, warum hier das Allgemeine im Besonderen erscheint. Das heißt nicht, dass eine einzelne Idee im buchstäblichen Sinne anschaubar würde, aber es heißt sehr wohl, dass ein allgemeines Prinzip in einer besonderen Konstellation konkretisiert wird. Das eben ist es, wie ich zum Schluss erläutern werde, womit Schillers ästhetischer Standpunkt über Kants begrifflichen hinausweist, freilich als Geisteshaltung insgesamt, wie sie sich auch in seinem künstlerischen Œuvre ausdrückt.

Denn im Denken Schillers ist das Schöne keineswegs nur Symbol des sittlich Guten, sondern genau wie dieses im Moralischen ist jenes im Natürlichen die leitende Kategorie einer Sphäre, von der er erkennt, dass sie keine

---

28 Kontroverse Lesarten dazu versammelt der Band *Paradoxien der Autonomie*, aus der Reihe: *Freiheit und Gesetz* hg. von Thomas Khurana und Christoph Menke (2011), wo das freiheitslogische Paradox entfaltet wird, dass Autonomie selbst grundlos und willkürlich ist, oder aber durch Geltungsgründe bedingt, die dem Akt der Selbstgesetzgebung vorausgehen, und daher heteronom wären.
29 NA 20, 347.
30 NA 26, 192.

Nebensache ist. Vielmehr realisiert sie sich in der Ausbalancierung von Form und Stoff, Pflicht und Neigung, deren Übereinstimmung selbst schön *ist*, anstatt nur Schein eines anderen zu sein. Hierin liegt eine Abweichung von Kant, die zuletzt einen Unterschied ums Ganze macht, und an die sowohl Hegels Philosophie des Geistes als auch Schellings Identitätsphilosophie anknüpfen konnten.

Kommen wir nun zum Spielbegriff, indem wir uns vergegenwärtigen, – mit Schiller über Schiller hinaus – was der Sprachgebrauch damit im Allgemeinen bezeichnen kann. Zu denken ist hier ja nicht nur an selbstzweckhafte Tätigkeiten, die selbstgesetzten Regeln folgen, denen die Akteure sich freiwillig unterwerfen. Ebenso kann das selbstvergessene Spielen eines Musikinstruments gemeint sein, an dem jedes utilitaristische Kalkül scheitert, oder an den Realitätsüberstieg des Kinderspiels, das im So-tun-als-ob souverän über das Gegebene hinausgreift. Eine Art kosmogonische Kraft des Möglichkeitssinns über das bloß Reale hinaus ist jedenfalls eine wesentliche Bestimmung geistiger Freiheit, die sich im Spielen ausdrückt.

Auch Coleridges Formel „the willing suspension of disbelief"[31] im Umgang mit dem ästhetischen Schein ist, wie ich behaupte, ein bedeutsames Beispiel für die Freiheit des Spiels: Denn wir begeben uns freiwillig in einen Modus des Mitspielens noch des unwahrscheinlichsten Als-ob-Szenarios, wenn wir – bspw. bei fiktionaler Literatur oder als Zuschauer eines beliebigen Theaterabends oder Sciencefiction-Films – uns willentlich dazu entscheiden, uns allen künstlerischen Setzungen und unwahrscheinlichen Volten zu überlassen. Weder nehmen wir Anstoß daran, dass jemand, nachdem er erdolcht wurde, noch die geschliffensten Verse spricht, noch daran, dass jemand sich mit einer Tarnkappe unsichtbar macht – das heißt, sowohl auf der Ebene des Erzählens wie des Erzählten folgen wir den impliziten und expliziten Behauptungen eines Kunstwerks, weil eben darin der Witz ästhetischen Probehandelns und die Produktivität der Einbildungskraft liegen, welche letztere dem Möglichen genauso viel Bedeutung zubilligt wie dem Wirklichen. So würde man etwa die Pointe von Mozarts *Cosi fan tutte* schlechthin verfehlen, wenn man hier einwenden wollte, dass man es für unglaubwürdig hält, dass jemand seinen Liebhaber (bzw. den seiner Schwester) in einer Verkleidung nicht wiedererkennt. Man könnte vielmehr anbringen, dass die Figuren bereits auf Plotebene ein schönes Beispiel für das sind, was Coleridge gemeint haben könnte, weil die „freiwillige Aufhebung des Unglaubens" von den Figuren nicht weniger als von den Rezipienten praktiziert

---

31 Coleridge (1975), 169.

werden muss, wenn das Maskenspiel des Partnertausches durchgespielt wird, damit das Libretto vorangetrieben und die Musik ihre Kraft entfalten kann.

Gleichgültig ob Dostojewski eine Problemkonstellation aufstellt oder Beckett artifiziell verfremdet, stets handelt es sich um ein Durchspielen des Denkbaren jenseits des Wahrscheinlichen. Und jener Wirklichkeitsüberstieg durch Einbildungskraft im Spiel der Kunst ist eine qualitative Gestalt von Geistesfreiheit.

So versteht man vielleicht, warum Schiller meint, dass sich im Spielen freies Menschsein realisiere. Natürlich kann man mit Spiel auch Frivolität oder Unaufrichtigkeit assoziieren. Aber damit ginge man nicht mehr ‚mit Schiller über ihn hinaus', sondern ohne ihn in eine andere Richtung. Schiller versteht das Spiel als Konkretion der Freiheit.

Dem Theaterautor und -macher Schiller könnte beim Spiel auch die Verkörperungsleistung eines Schauspielers vorgeschwebt haben, die dem Anspruch der sinnlichen Darstellung von Ideenzusammenhängen vielleicht am nächsten kommen. Er schreibt indessen, den Namen Spiel „rechtfertigt der Sprachgebrauch vollkommen, der alles das, was weder subjektiv noch objektiv zufällig ist, und doch weder äußerlich noch innerlich nöthigt, mit dem Wort Spiel zu bezeichnen pflegt."[32]

Schönheit und Spiel sind also *Gestalten* der Freiheit im wörtlichen Sinne von Verkörperungsformen und im übertragenen von Aspektentfaltungen. Vergleichbar mit den unterschiedlichen Figuren, die in Vexierbilder hinein- bzw. herausgesehen werden können, realisiert sich die Freiheit in den Praxen und Formen des Spiels.[33]

Es gibt immer wieder Leute, die Anstoß daran nehmen, dass dies alles doch nicht wirklich funktioniere, weil das Schöne nun einmal mit dem Ernst des Lebens nichts zu tun habe, eine Idee im Übrigen ohnehin nicht erscheinen könne und was dergleichen Einwände mehr sind. Aber das verfehlt den Postulatcharakter, den Schiller von vornherein einräumt. Für ihn ist das Spiel gerade mehr als ‚nur ernst', wie es im 15. Brief heißt[34].

Natürlich gibt es die Schönheit nicht, wie es empirische Gegenstände gibt. Schönheit und Spiel sind regulative Ideen, die vorführen, was werden könnte,

---

32 *NA* 20, 357.
33 Sehr gute Kommentare zu den Möglichkeiten und Grenzen theatralen Spiels für das Verhältnis von Ethik und Ästhetik bzw. Kunst und Politik versammelt der Band von Ensslin (2006) *Spieltrieb. Was bringt die Klassik auf die Bühne? Schillers Ästhetik heute.*
34 „Ich würde also vielmehr gerade umgekehrt sagen: mit dem Angenehmen, mit dem Guten, mit dem Vollkommenen ist es dem Menschen nur ernst, aber mit der Schönheit spielt er." (*NA* 20, 358).

wenn man ihnen folgte. Das Ästhetische ist ein Versprechen[35], wie Jacques Rancière, der in unserer Zeit wie kaum ein anderer Schillers Aktualität betont, sehr zu Recht schreibt. Aber wir können an seiner Einlösung mitwirken und hierbei ist wichtig, daran zu erinnern, dass der Idealismus Schillers sich zur Unerreichbarkeit des Ideals bekennt.[36] Es ist allemal besser, ein unendliches Ideal zu verfehlen als ein endliches Ziel zu erreichen, schreibt Schiller in der Abhandlung *Über naive und sentimentalische Dichtung*.

Utopische Zielvorgaben stellen auch dann noch das Wünschenswerte vor Augen, wenn wir an ihnen scheitern, sie bleiben als Leitvorstellung dennoch orientierend. Deswegen kann Freiheit eine graduierbare Fähigkeit sein, und deshalb sind wir nur in Ausnahmefällen ganz vollständig. Im Normalzustand sind wir mehr oder weniger frei, verfehlen uns selbst und einander mehr oder weniger und sind mehr oder weniger weit vom Ideal entfernt.

3. Jenseits von Anmut und Würde: der ästhetische Zustand

Ein dialektisches Verständnis der Begriffe kann, wie ich meine, plausibilisieren, dass die Leitvorstellungen von Schönheit, Freiheit, Spiel und lebender Gestalt in Schillers Argumentationsgang *gleich Kippfiguren* ineinander umschlagen können, weil sie alle Aspekte desselben holistischen Ideals darstellen, dass die gedoppelte bzw. gespaltene Natur des Menschen vorübergehend ein Ganzes bilden könne. Im weiteren Verlauf der Briefe indessen geht Schiller noch einen Schritt weiter und reformuliert seine Überlegungen mit der Terminologie von aktiver Bestimmungsfähigkeit und passiver Bestimmbarkeit[37] und entwickelt mit dem Begriff des ‚ästhetischen Zustands' ein Konzept, das weniger auf Vollständigkeit abzielt als auf ein *Jenseits* der Gegensätze.

Gegenüber den doppelten Nötigungen des Willens durch Vernunft wie durch Sinnlichkeit geht es um einen Zustand der Neutralität oder Bestimmungslosigkeit, den Schiller ästhetisch nennt. Im 15. Brief bereitet er seine Argumentation mit dem monumentalen Frauenkopf der Juno Ludovisi vor, in der er diesen Zustand erblicken will: „Es ist weder Anmuth noch ist es Würde, was aus dem

---

35   Rancière (2004), 6-21.
36   „Aber diese Charakterschönheit, die reifste Frucht seiner Humanität, ist bloß eine Idee, welcher gemäß zu werden, er mit anhaltender Wachsamkeit streben, aber die er bey aller Anstrengung nie ganz erreichen kann" (*NA* 20, 289).
37   Wobei zu betonen ist, dass beide jeweils gedoppelt vorkommen: „Es lassen sich in dem Menschen überhaupt zwey verschiedene Zustände der passiven und aktiven Bestimmbarkeit, und eben so viele Zustände der passiven und aktiven Bestimmung unterscheiden." (Ebd., 368).

herrlichen Antlitz einer Juno Ludovisi zu uns spricht; es ist keines von beyden, weil es beydes zugleich ist."[38]

Jacques Rancière knüpft daran wiederholt an, um das Verhältnis von Kunst und Politik aus den falschen Disjunktionen von Autonomie versus gesellschaftlicher Bedeutung herauszuführen.[39] Doch bleiben wir zunächst noch bei Schillers weiterem Gedankengang:

> Es ist [...] nicht damit gethan, daß etwas anfange, was noch nicht war; es muß zuvor etwas aufhören, welches war. Der Mensch kann nicht *unmittelbar* vom Empfinden zum Denken übergehen; er muß einen Schritt zurückthun, weil nur, indem eine Determination wieder aufgehoben wird, die entgegengesetzte eintreten kann. Er muß also, um Leiden mit Selbstthätigkeit, um eine passive Bestimmung mit einer aktiven zu vertauschen, augenblicklich von aller Bestimmung frey seyn, und einen Zustand der bloßen *Bestimmbarkeit* durchlaufen. Mithin muß er, auf gewisse Weise zu jenem negativen Zustand der bloßen *Bestimmungslosigkeit* zurückkehren, in welchem er sich befand, ehe noch irgend etwas auf seinen Sinn einen Eindruck machte.[40]

Es handelt sich folglich nicht nur darum, bestimmend-sein und bestimmt-werden in ein harmonisches Verhältnis zu setzen, sondern auch darum, die negativen Modi von Bestimmungslosigkeit und Bestimmbarkeit miteinander zu verschränken.

> Das Gemüth geht also von der Empfindung zum Gedanken durch eine mittlere Stimmung über, in welcher Sinnlichkeit und Vernunft zugleich thätig sind, eben deswegen aber ihre bestimmende Gewalt gegenseitig aufheben, und durch eine Entgegensetzung eine Negation bewirken. Diese mittlere Stimmung, in welcher das Gemüth weder physisch noch moralisch genöthigt, und doch auf beyde Art thätig ist, verdient vorzugsweise eine freye Stimmung zu heißen, und wenn man den Zustand sinnlicher Bestimmung den physischen, den Zustand vernünftiger Bestimmung aber den logischen und moralischen nennt, so muß man diesen Zustand der realen und aktiven Bestimmbarkeit den ästhetischen heißen[41].

Der ästhetische Zustand ist vor allem eins: unendlich bestimmbar. Diese Form von Bestimmungslosigkeit ist positive Unendlichkeit.

---

38 Ebd., 359.
39 Die Griechenland zugeschriebene Geisteshaltung, in der die Gegensätze nicht aufgeteilt waren in gegeneinander abgegrenzte Sphären, verkörpere sich in der Juno Ludovisi, nämlich „ein Leben, in dem es keine Trennung in heterogene Erfahrungsbereiche gibt, in dem es deswegen keine ästhetische Erfahrung gibt, weil das Ästhetische zugleich ethisch, politisch oder religiös ist. Die Autonomie, die die Statue vor uns verkörpert, ist die Darstellung einer Autonomie, einer Ungetrenntheit." (Rancière (2006), 49).
40 NA 20, 374.
41 Ebd., 375.

„Was also das Denken in Rücksicht auf Bestimmung ist, das ist die ästhetische Verfassung in Rücksicht auf Bestimmbarkeit; jenes ist Beschränkung aus innrer unendlicher Kraft, diese ist eine Negation aus innrer unendlicher Fülle."[42]

Daher die merkwürdige Formulierung, der ästhetische Zustand sei ein ‚Nullzustand', die meist nur schlagwortartig zitiert wird, aber nicht im Kontext erläutert: „In dem ästhetischen Zustande ist der Mensch also Null, *insofern* man auf ein einzelnes Resultat, nicht auf das ganze Vermögen achtet, und den Mangel jeder besondern Determination in ihm in Betrachtung zieht."[43]

Die Beschreibung basiert erstens auf einer etwas sperrigen Analogie des Verhältnisses von Denken und Empfinden mit dem von Bestimmbarkeit und Bestimmungslosigkeit.[44] Und zweitens beruht sie auf der Unterscheidung von leerer und erfüllter Unendlichkeit: die „ästhetische Bestimmbarkeit" und „bloße Bestimmungslosigkeit" schlössen zwar „beyde jedes bestimmte Daseyn aus", seien aber im Übrigen „unendlich verschieden", denn Bestimmungslosigkeit sei „leere Unendlichkeit", während die „ästhetische Bestimmungsfreyheit [...] erfüllte Unendlichkeit"[45] ist. Die wesentliche Unbestimmtheit des ästhetischen Zustands besteht folglich in ‚erfüllter Unendlichkeit'. Diese kann jedoch nur noch negativ artikuliert werden als Weder-Noch von Leiden und Herrschen. Der ästhetische Zustand besteht in der Unterbrechung der Herrschaftslogik, der außerhalb der Kunst alles untersteht. Höchste Freiheit beherrscht weder die Vernunft noch die Gefühle, sondern sie spielt mit beiden.

4. Kunst und Politik

Kommen wir darauf zu sprechen, dass das ganze Schillersche Projekt zwei Großziele verfolgt: ein individualethisches, das Kunst und Lebenskunst verbindet, und ein politisches, das mit freien Individuen ein nicht nur vernünftiges, sondern auch gutes und gerechtes Gemeinwesen realisieren will. Hierfür muss der Einzelne allererst emanzipationsfähig werden, und zwar sowohl „durch Ausbildung des Gefühlvermögens" wie auch „des Vernunftvermögens"[46], das

---

42 Ebd., 377.
43 Ebd.
44 „So wie Empfinden und Denken einander in dem einzigen Punkt berühren, daß in beyden Zuständen das Gemüth determinirt, [...], sonst aber sich ins Unendliche von einander entfernen; gerade so" verhalte es sich auch mit dem Verhältnis von Bestimmbarkeit und Bestimmungslosigkeit, heißt es ebd.
45 Ebd.
46 Ebd., 348.

heißt nicht nur, indem er bestimmt *und* sich bestimmen lässt, sondern indem er sich unendlich *bestimmbar* macht.

Auf diese Weise konkretisiert Freiheit sich im Ästhetischen wie umgekehrt das Ästhetische die Möglichkeit der politischen Realisierung von Freiheit ist. Deswegen bezeichnet Schiller die Kunst als höchste Schenkung und qualifiziert sie als Instrument der Charakterbildung.[47] Dabei meint der spätere Schiller nicht mehr, das Theater sei eine moralpädagogische Veranstaltung. Denn er weiß, dass ein Stück über Karl Moor ‚die Landstraßen nicht sicherer' macht. Vielmehr ist es die Wiedergewinnung jenes bestimmungslosen Nullzustandes, von dem aus ein freier Aufbruch möglich wird:

> Durch die ästhetische Kultur bleibt also der persönliche Werth eines Menschen, [...] noch völlig unbestimmt, und es ist weiter nichts erreicht, als daß es ihm nunmehr, von Natur wegen möglich gemacht ist, aus sich selbst zu machen, was er will – daß ihm die Freyheit, zu seyn, was er seyn soll, vollkommen zurückgegeben ist. Eben dadurch aber ist etwas Unendliches erreicht. Denn sobald wir uns erinnern, daß ihm durch die einseitige Nöthigung der Natur beym Empfinden, und durch die ausschließende Gesetzgebung der Vernunft beym Denken gerade diese Freyheit entzogen wurde, so müssen wir das Vermögen, welches ihm in der ästhetischen Stimmung zurückgegeben wird, als die höchste aller Schenkungen, als die Schenkung der Menschheit betrachten. Freylich besitzt er diese Menschheit der Anlage nach schon vor jedem bestimmten Zustand, in den er kommen kann, aber der That nach verliert er sie mit jedem bestimmten Zustand, in den er kommt, und sie muß ihm [...] jedesmal aufs neue durch das ästhetische Leben zurückgegeben werden.[48]

Da kein direkter Übergang des Empfindens zum Denken möglich ist, bedarf es der Vermittlung des Ästhetischen. Schiller geht davon aus, dass ein Staatswesen nur so gut sein kann wie seine Bürger als Individuen, deswegen muss die Verbesserung der politischen Verhältnisse individualethisch anfangen. Die eminente Rolle, die der Kunst dabei zugewiesen wird, beklagen manche als Verlust ihrer Autonomie. Aber das ist nicht Schillers Standpunkt. Vielmehr beruht die analoge Verfassung von Individuum und Kollektiv darauf, dass beide derselben Herrschaftslogik unterliegen, die es zu unterwandern gilt:

„Erlaube mir", schreibt er an Körner,

> „dieß durch eine bildliche Vorstellung zu erläutern. Wenn ein monarchischer Staat auf eine solche Art verwaltet wird, daß, obgleich alles nach eines Einzigen Willen geht, der einzelne Bürger sich doch überreden kann, daß er nach seinem

---

47   Gute Kommentare dazu aus erziehungswissenschaftlicher Sicht bei Dörpinghaus (2006) und Meyer-Drawe (2006).
48   NA 20, 378.

eigenen Sinne lebe, und bloß seiner Neigung gehorche, so nennt man dieß eine liberale Regierung. Man würde aber großes Bedenken tragen, ihr diesen Nahmen zu geben, wenn entweder der Regent seinen Willen gegen die Neigung, des Bürgers, oder der Bürger seine Neigung gegen den Willen des Regenten behauptete; denn in dem ersten Fall wäre die Regierung nicht liberal, in dem zweyten wäre sie gar nicht Regierung. Es ist nicht schwer, die Anwendung davon auf die menschliche Bildung unter dem Regiment des Geistes zu machen. Wenn sich der Geist in der von ihm abhängenden sinnlichen Natur auf eine solche Art äußert, daß sie seinen Willen aufs treueste ausrichtet und seine Empfindungen auf das sprechendste ausdrückt, [...] so wird dasjenige entstehen, was man Anmuth nennt. Man würde aber gleich weit entfernt seyn, es Anmuth zu nennen, wenn entweder der Geist sich in der Sinnlichkeit durch Zwang offenbare, oder wenn dem freyen Effekt der Sinnlichkeit der Ausdruck des Geistes fehlte. Denn in dem ersten Fall wäre keine Schönheit vorhanden, in dem zweyten wäre es keine Schönheit des Spiels."[49]

Das Projekt ästhetischer Erziehung zielt auf die Bildung von sinnlich-sittlich bestimmbaren Bürgern, mit denen ein Staat zu machen ist, in dem Pflicht und Neigung keine unversöhnlichen Gegensätze mehr darstellen. Von allen zeitgenössischen Bemühungen um aktuelle Anschlüsse an Schillers Konzept ragt besonders diejenige Rancières[50] hervor, der Schillers Analogiebildung entschieden zustimmt: „Die Macht der Form über den Stoff, die der [...] Spieltrieb außer Kraft setzt, lässt sich in der Tat unmittelbar ins Politische übertragen. Sie ist die Macht des staatlichen Universellen über die [...] Individuen und Massen."[51] Innerhalb seiner eigenen Theorie des Ästhetischen knüpft Rancière an Schiller an, um das Verhältnis von Kunst und Politik einer grundsätzlichen Revision zu unterziehen.[52] „Kunst als solche identifizieren zu können, setzt eine bestimmte Aufteilung des Sinnlichen voraus, d.h. eine bestimmte Verteilung dessen, was machbar, spürbar und denkbar ist, die auch die Vorstellung von der Politik als Teilhabe an einem Gemeinsamen beinhaltet."[53]

Ich konzentriere mich hier auf seine autonomie-theoretische Lektüre: Während der Geist im Formtrieb allem seinen Stempel, nämlich „den Stempel seiner Autonomie"[54] aufdrücken wolle, und der Stofftrieb „die Anarchie seiner Begierden durchsetzen will"[55], erscheine im Spieltrieb „die ästhetische

---

49 NA 20, 278-279.
50 Rancière (2006) sowie Rancière (2010).
51 Rancière (2006), 43.
52 Ein sehr guter Kommentar zum Problem der Ästhetisierung von Politik in demokratie-theoretischer Absicht findet sich bei Rebentisch (2006), 71-81.
53 Rancière (2006), 41.
54 Ebd., 43.
55 Ebd.

Autonomie als rettende Antwort auf die Verstrickungen einer anderen Autonomie [...], nämlich derjenigen des Verstandes, der den Gegebenheiten seine Begriffe bzw. Formen aufzwingt"[56] und sei es auch im Namen eines noch so rationalen Willens. Was dabei jedoch nur fortgeschrieben werde, sei die Herrschaft des Universellen über das Partikulare bzw. die Opposition von Autonomie des Handelns und Heteronomie der Materialität. Diese Opposition will Rancière genauso verabschieden wie Schiller.

Anschlussfähig scheint mir darüber hinaus, wie stark auch Rancière den agonalen Charakter dieses Ringens um Schönheit und Freiheit betont: Dies habe „nichts mehr von einer gütlichen Einigung"[57], sondern sei höchst spannungsvoller Widerstreit. „Das Subjekt erfreut sich nicht heiteren Wohlgefallens an der Form. Es ist vielmehr einem Krieg ausgeliefert, der sich in seinem Inneren abspielt und in dem Autonomie auf Kosten einer anderen Autonomie erlangt wird."[58]

Schließlich halte ich seine Lesart für die maßgeblichste Argumentation gegen den Verdacht, die Kunst verlöre ihre Autonomie, wenn sie politisch etwas bewirken solle. „Es gibt keinen Gegensatz zwischen autonomer Kunst und einer Kunst, die der politischen Heteronomie unterworfen wäre. Es gibt eine spezifische Verknüpfung von Autonomie und Heteronomie"[59], bzw. zwei verschiedene Verknüpfungen, die nicht aufgehört haben, das Verhältnis von ästhetischer Erfahrung und politischer Gemeinschaft zu prägen.

5. Kunst und Philosophie

Aus Kantischer Sicht freilich stellt das ganze Problem sich anders dar. Autonomie als transzendentales Prinzip der Vernunft begründet ihm zufolge die Möglichkeit von Moral überhaupt, nicht nur dieser oder jener partikularen Freiheit. Schiller hingegen betrachtet Kants Formel vom unbedingten Sollen als *Zwangsherrschaft* der Vernunft. Und wenn er transzendentalphilosophisch argumentiert, dann nicht von der Möglichkeitsbedingung der Moralität her, sondern von der Freiheits*fähigkeit* des Menschen. Mehr noch aber geht es ihm um die *Konkretionen* der Freiheit, durch die ein gutes Leben des Einzelnen wie des Gemeinwesens befördert werden kann.

---

56 Ebd.
57 Ebd., 45.
58 Ebd., 46.
59 Ebd., 47.

So besteht die Vollkommenheitsvorstellung holistischen Menschseins weder im Abwechseln zwischen Sinnlichkeit und Sittlichkeit, noch in der Beherrschung der Natur durch Freiheit, sondern in jenen Figuren der chiastischen Komplementarität, die so oft in Schillers Formulierungen auffallen, etwa wenn es heißt, dass der Mensch empfindet, „weil er sich bewußt ist" und sich bewusst wird, „weil er empfindet"[60]. Erst in dieser Verschränkung entsteht das Ideal, dem wir uns, so Schiller, „im Laufe der Zeit immer mehr nähern [...] ohne es jemals zu erreichen."[61]

Auch die Frage nach dem Verhältnis von Begriff und Anschauung bzw. Idee und Erscheinung stellt sich vom Standpunkt des Kunstphilosophen aus anders dar als von dem begrifflichen Denken, nämlich nicht mehr als Problem der Urteilslogik, sondern als Tätigkeit des performativen Hervorbringens im Spiel und Schein der Kunst. Amphibolien und Paradoxien sind hier keine vermeidbaren begrifflichen Unklarheiten, sondern resultieren daraus, dass unterschiedliche Aspekte eines Entwicklungszusammenhangs prozessual entfaltet werden.

Wenn man den Standpunkt, von dem aus Schiller denkt, mitberücksichtigt, muss man den Spielbegriff vor dem Hintergrund seiner eigenen Theaterstücke lesen, in denen moralische Konfliktsituationen vors Auge gebracht werden. Hier wird nicht eine einzelne Idee mit Hilfe eines einzelnen Bildes irgendwie illustriert, sondern das Ganze einer philosophischen Problematik wird im Ganzen einer künstlerischen Anordnung anschaulicher Erfahrung zugänglich. Dadurch lassen wir die Disjunktion von Begriff und Anschauung insgesamt hinter uns, weil wir nicht mehr im Modus der Sprache begriffliche Probleme ventilieren, sondern im Modus der ästhetischen Erfahrung Probleme in Kontexten erschauen. Dabei kann und muss zwischen Intelligibilität und Sinnlichkeit nicht mehr strictu sensu unterschieden werden. An die Stelle von binären Ordnungsschemata, die das Denken blockieren, ist jene chiastische Durchdringung getreten, die Schiller als Wechselseitigkeit und Wechselwirkung bezeichnet: das Allgemeine und Gesetzmäßige am Besonderen und Freien aufzuzeigen. Das ist mehr als ein oszillierendes Spiel der Einbildungskraft und des Verstandes.

Schiller hat sich bekanntlich in der Frage nach der Rolle der Einbildungskraft mit Fichte überworfen.[62] Nachdem er als Herausgeber der Horen Fichtes Schrift *Über Geist und Buchstab*[63] als für die Veröffentlichung ungeeignet

---

60 NA 20, 353.
61 Ebd.
62 Ein Fichte-affiner Kommentar bei Franke (1987).
63 GA II 3.

befunden hat, was Fichte ihm sehr übel nahm, erläutert er sein eigenes Verständnis des Verhältnisses von Bild und Begriff in seiner Schrift *Über die nothwendigen Grenzen beim Gebrauch schöner Formen*.[64] Es geht darin um die prinzipielle Frage, was künstlerische Rede leisten kann, womit wir zurückkommen auf die Frage, ob Ideen erscheinen können. Ich kann das hier nicht mehr erörtern, möchte aber doch daran erinnern, dass Fichtes Vorwurf an Schiller gelautet hatte, er wolle ‚die Einbildungskraft zum Denken' zwingen.[65] Umgekehrt hat Schiller an Fichtes Schrift kritisiert, er wechsle Bild und Begriff nur miteinander ab, aber es komme zu keiner Wechselwirkung.[66]

Daran zeigt sich ein weiteres Mal die Erschließungskraft eines chiastischen Begriffsverständnisses, das ich mit meiner Lektüre plausibilisieren wollte. Denn ich hoffe gezeigt zu haben, dass Schiller nicht mit einer Entgegensetzung der Dualismen operiert, sondern so, dass die wechselseitigen Bedingungsverhältnisse darin zum Vorschein kommen und sie einander entweder aufheben oder sich miteinander verschränken.

Freilich kann diese oder jene partikulare Erscheinung eine allgemeine Idee nicht *unmittelbar* veranschaulichen. Sehr wohl aber kann im Gesamtsinn eines Kunstwerks ein allgemeines Prinzip individuiert werden. Und Schillers ästhetische Schriften handeln schließlich von der Kunst insgesamt bzw. von der ästhetischen Erfahrung als ihrem wesentlichen Realisationsmodus. Mit dem „Gebrauch schöner Formen" – mithin mit den Mitteln der Kunst – kann etwas gesagt und gezeigt werden, das nicht am Maßstab begrifflicher Widerspruchslosigkeit zu messen ist, sondern dessen Pointe darin besteht, Allgemeines und Besonderes zu verschränken.

Der Theatermacher Schiller denkt von der Performanz des Spieles her und in diesem ist das Schöne nicht nur stellvertretend symbolisiert, sondern es kommt praktisch zur Aufführung und wird ästhetisch erfahren, wenngleich nur in endlicher Weise. Im Kunstwerk mit seinem exemplarischem Modellcharakter[67] zeigt sich das Universelle am Partikularen und vice versa. Darin wird eine Wechselwirkung von Begriff und Anschauung praktisch vollzogen, die nicht in der Abwechslung von Bild und Begriff im Medium eines Textes besteht, sondern im Akt der Aufführung und seiner Rezeption aktualisiert wird. Es reicht, dass dadurch Anschauungen generalisiert und Grundsätze konkretisiert werden, um die Rede vom sinnlichen Erscheinen der Idee der Freiheit zu rechtfertigen.

---

64   *NA* 21, 3-27.
65   *GA* II 3, 339.
66   *NA* 27, 200 f.
67   Ausgeführt habe ich das in Schürmann (2017).

Vom Standpunkt gegen einander abgeschotteter Begriffssphären stellen sich die systematischen Probleme anders dar als vom Standpunkt ästhetischer Praxis. Deshalb lag mir daran, die performativen Prozessbegriffe herauszuarbeiten, mit denen Schiller die Disjunktionen unterwandert und die Übergänge beschreibt. In aestheticis ist die Freiheit des Geistes mehr als Gebrauch der Vernunft oder Subordination unter das Sittengesetz. Der Mensch ist freiheitsfähig der Anlage und Bestimmung nach, deswegen ist er bildbar und kann sich bilden. Nur „der physische Mensch [ist] wirklich, [...] der sittliche nur problematisch"[68], das heißt er ist bloß möglich. Freiheit ist nicht einfach gegeben, sondern möglicherweise zu erwirken. Das alles spricht für eine prozesstheoretische Lesart, für die ich argumentiert habe.

Zuletzt noch ein Wort zum Perfektionismus: Man mag Schillers Orientierung am Ideal perfektionistisch nennen. Mir indessen scheint es fruchtbarer, es perfektibilistisch zu nennen und zwar sowohl das Ideal ganzer Menschheit als auch das des Vernunftstaates. Es geht mehr um *Vervollkommnung* als um *Vollkommenheit*. Mit Herder[69] teilt Schiller die anthropologische Bestimmung einer grundlegenden Vervollkommnungsfähigkeit des Menschen, mit Fichte das Prinzip Bildsamkeit.[70] Begriffsgeschichtlich steht der Ausdruck Perfektibilität freilich im Kontext pietistischer und geschichtsphilosophischer Denktradition. Doch sahen wir wiederholt, dass Schiller davon ausgeht, Perfektion qua Idealität niemals erreichen zu können, immer aber anstreben zu sollen, also stets von Vervollkommnungsfähigkeit auszugehen. Freiheit, die Schiller meint, ist gleichermaßen individualethisch wie staatstheoretisch gedacht. Schillers Projekt einer ästhetischen Erziehung ist das politische Projekt einer perfektibilistischen Ethik und als Bildungsprojekt des Einzelnen ermöglicht es sogar Anschlüsse an tugendethische Modelle.[71]

Schiller ist in der Tat ein Mittler zwischen Kant und Hegel, ein Wegbereiter des Deutschen Idealismus und jemand, der zeigt, wie es aussehen könnte, wenn die Philosophie des Geistes wirklich ästhetisch[72] wird.

---

68 *NA* 20, 314.
69 *HW* I, 695 f.
70 Mit Bildsamkeit bezeichnet Fichte eine unendliche Entwicklungsfähigkeit und Veränderlichkeit, die den Menschen vom Tier unterscheidet. Er sei nichts Bestimmtes, „sondern lediglich eine Bestimmbarkeit ins unendliche; [...] nur Bildsamkeit. – Kurz, alle Tiere sind vollendet und fertig, der Mensch ist nur angedeutet und entworfen. [...] Jedes Tier ist, was es ist, der Mensch allein ist ursprünglich gar nichts. Was er seyn soll, muß er werden. [...] durch sich selbst werden. [...] Bildsamkeit als solche ist der Charakter der Menschheit" (*GA* I 3, 379).
71 Wie bspw. jenen von Iris Murdoch (1970).
72 „Die Philosophie des Geistes ist eine ästhetische Philosophie. Man kann in nichts geistreich sein [...] ohne ästhetischen Sinn." In Hegel, Georg Wilhelm Friedrich, „Das älteste Systemprogramm des Deutschen Idealismus" (Hegel (1986), S. 235).

Literatur

Coleridge, Samuel Taylor, *Biographia Literaria or Biographical Sketches of My Literary Life and Opinions*, London: J.M. Dent Orion Publishing Group, 1975.

Dörpinghaus, Andreas, „Die letzte Dankbarkeit gegen die Kunst: Friedrich Schillers Briefe „Über die ästhetische Erziehung des Menschen", in: *Schillers ästhetisch-politischer Humanismus*, hg. von Birgitta Fuchs und Lutz Koch, Würzburg 2006, S. 49-62.

Ensslin, Felix (Hrsg.), *Spieltrieb. Was bringt die Klassik auf die Bühne? Schillers Ästhetik heute*, Berlin: Theater der Zeit, 2006.

Fichte, Johann Gottlieb, „Grundlage des Naturrechts", in: *J.G. Fichte-Gesamtausgabe Reihe I: Werke 1794-1796*, Band I,3, hg. v. Hans Jacob u. Reinhard Lauth, Stuttgart-Bad Canstatt: Friedrich Frommann Verlag, 1966. (*GA* I 3)

– „292. Brief an Johann Christoph Friedrich Schiller, 27. Juni 1795", in: *J.G. Fichte-Gesamtausgabe Reihe II: Nachgelassene Schriften 1793-1795*, Band II,3, hg. v. Hans Jacob u. Reinhard Lauth, Stuttgart-Bad Canstatt: Friedrich Frommann Verlag, 1971. (*GA* II 3)

– „Ueber Geist, und Buchstab in der Philosophie", in: *J.G. Fichte-Gesamtausgabe Reihe II: Nachgelassene Schriften 1793-1795*, Band II,3, hg. v. Hans Jacob u. Reinhard Lauth, Stuttgart-Bad Canstatt: Friedrich Frommann Verlag, 1971. (*GA* II 3)

Franke, Ursula, „Poetische und Philosophische Rede. Die Kontroverse zwischen Schiller und Fichte zur Semiotik", in: *Modelle für eine semiotische Rekonstruktion der Geschichte der Ästhetik*, hg. v. Heinz Paetzold, Aachen: Rader, 1987, S. 149-169.

Hegel, Georg Wilhelm Friedrich, „Das älteste Systemprogramm des Deutschen Idealismus", in: *Georg Wilhelm Friedrich Hegel. Werke I. Frühe Schriften*, Frankfurt am Main: Suhrkamp, 1986.

Herder, Johann Gottfried, „Abhandlung über den Ursprung der Sprache, erster Teil", in: *Johann Gottfried Herder. Werke. Frühe Schriften*, Band 1, Frankfurt am Main: Klassiker Verlag, 1985. (HW)

Kant, Immanuel, *Gesammelte Schriften*, hg. v. Königlich Preussische Akademie der Wissenschaften (Akademie-Ausgabe), Berlin u.a., 1900 ff. (AA)

Khurana, Thomas u. Menke, Christoph (Hrsg.), *Paradoxien der Autonomie, Freiheit und Gesetz*, Band 1, Berlin: August Verlag, 2011.

Meyer-Drawe, Käte, Der „Weg zu dem Kopf durch das Herz'. Grundlinien von Schillers Bildungsbegriff", in: *Schillers ästhetisch-politischer Humanismus*, hg. von Birgitta Fuchs und Lutz Koch, Würzburg 2006, S. 33-48.

Murdoch, Iris, *The Sovereignty of Good*, London: Routledge, 1970.

Noller, Jörg, Die Bestimmung des Willens. Zum Problem individueller Freiheit im Ausgang von Kant, Freiburg/München: Karl Alber Verlag, 2016.

Rancière, Jacques, „Schiller et la promesse esthétique", in: *europe: revue littéraire mensuelle*, Nr. 900, 82. Jg., Paris: Europe, April 2004, S. 6-21.
- „Die ästhetische Revolution und ihre Folgen. Erzählungen von Autonomie und Heteronomie", in: *Ästhetisierung. Der Streit um das ästhetische in Politik, Religion und Erkenntnis*, hg. v. Ilka Brombach, Dirk Setton & Cornelia Temesvári, Zürich: Diaphanes, 2010, S. 23-40.
- „Schiller und das ästhetische Versprechen", in: *Spieltrieb. Was bringt die Klassik auf die Bühne? Schillers Ästhetik heute*, hg. v. Felix Ensslin, Berlin: Theater der Zeit, 2006, S. 39-55.

Rebentisch, Juliane, „Demokratie und Theater", in: *Spieltrieb. Was bringt die Klassik auf die Bühne? Schillers Ästhetik heute*, hg. v. Felix Ensslin, Berlin: Theater der Zeit, 2006, S. 71-81.

Schiller, Friedrich, „Über die ästhetische Erziehung des Menschen in einer Reihe von Briefen", 3./ 4./ 8./ 10./ 13./14./ 15./ 18./ 19./ 20. u. 21. Brief, in: *Schillers Werke. Nationalausgabe*, Band 20, Weimar: Hermann Böhlaus Nachfolger, 1992. (NA)
- „Über Anmuth und Würde", in: *Schillers Werke. Nationalausgabe*, Band 20, Weimar: Hermann Böhlaus Nachfolger, 1992.
- „Über die nothwendigen Grenzen beim Gebrauch schöner Formen", in: *Schillers Werke. Nationalausgabe*, Band 21, Weimar: Hermann Böhlaus Nachfolger, 1992.
- „154. Brief an Körner, 18. [und 19.] Februar 1793", in: *Schillers Werke. Nationalausgabe*, Band 26, Weimar: Hermann Böhlaus Nachfolger, 1992.
- „155. Brief an Körner, 23. Feb. 1793" in: *Schillers Werke. Nationalausgabe*, Band 26, Weimar: Hermann Böhlaus Nachfolger, 1992.
- „166. Brief an Fichte, 24. Juni 1795", in: *Schillers Werke. Nationalausgabe*, Band 27, Weimar: Hermann Böhlaus Nachfolger, 1992.

Schürmann, Eva, „Ästhetik als exemplarisches Philosophieren mit Kunst", in: *Ästhetik. Denken und Disziplin*, hg. v. Juliane Rebentisch, ‚Deutsche Gesellschaft für Ästhetik', http://www.dgae.de/wpcontent/uploads/2017/06/dgaeX_dud_schuermann.pdf?c=f9f15d&p0=5&p1=-3&p2=-7, 2017. Zuletzt aufgerufen: 04-10-2019.

Szondi, Peter, „Das Naive ist das Sentimentalische. Zur Begriffsdialektik in Schillers Abhandlung", in: *Lektüren und Lektionen*, hg. v. Peter Szondi, Frankfurt: Suhrkamp 1973, S. 59-105.
- *Poetik und Geschichtsphilosophie I*, Frankfurt: Suhrkamp, 1991.

The Reciprocal Cultivation of Self and State
Fichte's Civic Perfectionism

Dean Moyar

> The moral law, which extends to infinity, absolutely commands us to treat human beings *as if they* were forever capable of becoming perfected [*Vervollkommnung*] and remaining so, and this same law absolutely prohibits us from treating human beings in the opposite manner. One cannot obey such a command without believing in perfectibility [*Perfectibilität*].[1]

J.G. Fichte developed his Jena *Wissenschaftslehre* with the goal of overcoming the Kantian dualisms of theoretical and practical reason, of individual and community, of the finite conditions of human activity and the infinite goal of that activity. He embraced ethical perfectionism as the overall form of his ethical theory even as he sought to maintain Kant's insistence that autonomy, the formal freedom of the will, is an absolute requirement of moral action. Fichte saw in Kant's conception of the Highest Good (the unity of duty and happiness as the complete object of the will) a way to unite the claims of autonomy and perfection. But rather than think of postulates of practical reason that are indexed to a noumenal realm outside of time, Fichte thought of the perfection of reason and freedom as an ideal endpoint that orients moral action in the present. He did not want to theorize the merely possible, but rather to move from a formulaic philosophy to an applicable philosophy, and thus to derive from freedom the conditions of finite agency. Fichte does, however, retain a split between formal freedom as the inner condition of morality and material freedom as the outer achievement of morality. In his efforts to reconcile the two elements he demonstrates both the promise and the perils of basing a theory of perfection on an inherently indeterminate ideal of free activity.

Fichte's ethical goal of perfection makes reference to the ethical community, yet in his writings on politics Fichte argues against a connection of ethical perfection and political right. In his *Foundations of Natural Right*, with its famous arguments for a summons to freedom and mutual recognition, he argues

---

1 *SW* IV, 241; *SE*, 229.

for a conception of right that has nothing to do with the good, either with the good will or the final good of reason. At the same time, in *FNR* and *The Closed Commercial State*, he gives a theory of economic justice that rests on a substantive ethical ideal of equality. I argue in this paper that his political and economic theory can be considered a kind of civic perfectionism, directing the state not towards the goal of individual excellence but towards a proper distribution of well-being throughout the nation.

1. Perfection in "Some Lectures Concerning the Scholar's Vocation"

The theme of perfection is prominent in the first series of public lectures that Fichte delivered in 1794 in his new position as the successor to K.L. Reinhold in Jena. "Some Lectures Concerning the Scholar's Vocation" provide an accessible template for the intricate system of practical philosophy that Fichte works out during his Jena period. The lectures begin with a treatment of "the vocation of man as such"[2], which for Fichte is the development and realization of one's own freedom as a rational being. Central to Fichte's picture is a distinction between what he calls the pure I and the empirical I, between pure activity and the finite embodied subject.[3] He proposes that the vocation of man as a moral being is precisely to overcome the resistance to freedom within the finite self. He casts the point in Kantian terms:

> Man's ultimate and supreme goal is complete harmony with himself and – so that he can be in harmony with himself – the harmony of all external things with his own necessary, practical concepts of them (i.e., with those concepts which determine how things ought to be). Employing the terminology of the Critical Philosophy, this agreement is what Kant calls "the highest good".[4]

For Kant the Highest Good is the complete object of the will, the unity of duty and happiness as a world in which happiness would follow in proportion to dutifulness.[5] For reasons that go to the heart of his perfectionist turn, Fichte needs no such split between duty and happiness. He writes:

---

[2] *SW* VI, 294; *EPW*, 146.
[3] For good introductions to Fichte's *Wissenschaftslehre* or "Science of Knowledge," see Neuhouser (1990), Wood (1991), Martin (1997), and the essays collected in Breazeale (2013).
[4] *SW* VI, 299; *EPW*, 150.
[5] It is this idea with which Kant grounds the postulates of freedom, God and immortality. Fichte's transformation of the Highest Good thus both reflects his transformation of freedom and gives him an opening to reinterpret the concepts of God and immortality.

> this 'highest good' by no means consists of two parts, but is completely unitary: the highest good is the *complete harmony of a rational being with himself.* In the case of a rational being dependent upon things outside of himself, the highest good may be conceived as twofold: [firstly] as harmony between *the willing* [of such a being] and the idea of an eternally valid willing (i.e., as *ethical goodness*), and [secondly] as the harmony of our willing (...) with *external things* (i.e., as *happiness*).[6]

Fichte's twofold conception seems to reproduce Kant's divide between the pure willing of duty and the harmony of duty and happiness. But Fichte's point is that these two sides ought to be one and the same thing. He is in fact tempted by the Stoic idea of simply defining happiness in terms of morality. That would make the theoretical problem easier but it would lose the Kantian appeal to the ordinary (Epicurean) conception of happiness as connected with sensible drives.

Though many of Fichte's claims invoke the purity of the I and reason, he has a very important place in his theory for a conception of *culture* [*Kultur*] that involves both the sensuous and the rational. His philosophy is addressed to those who have become conscious of their freedom. He stresses the fact that one's inclinations will have already been developed in various ways at the time that one becomes aware of one's freedom. We cannot simply will away everything in ourselves that does not conform to reason. We need to acquire the skill [*Geschicklichkeit*] of self-transformation that he calls culture, "the skill to suppress and eradicate those erroneous inclinations which originate in us prior to the awakening of our reason and the sense of our own spontaneity, and ... to modify and alter external things in accordance with our concepts"[7]. Culture is both a means to perfection and a key indicator of the level of perfection that we have reached at any given time. Because it is an educative process, culture can cut across the divide between inner freedom and external circumstances, a divide that is both central to Fichte's theory and one of the greatest obstacles to understanding how that theory is to be put into practice.

The challenge of Fichte's ethics is to think of harmony as the purpose to be achieved in the infinite future, while also seeing each individual agent in the here and now as already capable of realizing that harmony in a determinate social world. In one of the clearest statements of his perfectionism Fichte stresses our capacity for self-improvement through ethical action:

---

6   *SW* VI, 299; *EPW*, 150-51; he adds: "And thus we may note in passing that it is not true that the desire for happiness destines man for ethical goodness. It is rather the case that the concept of happiness itself and the desire for happiness first arise from man's moral nature. Not *what makes us happy is good*, but rather, *only what is good makes us happy.*" (Ibid., 151)

7   *SW* VI, 298; *EPW*, 150.

> Man's final end is to subordinate to himself all that is irrational, to master it freely and according to his own laws. This is a final end which is completely inachievable and must always remain so – so long, that is, as man is to remain man and is not supposed to become God. It is part of the concept of man that his ultimate goal be unobtainable and that his path thereto be infinitely long. Thus it is not man's vocation to reach this goal. But he can and he should draw nearer to it, and his true vocation qua *man*, that is, insofar as he is a rational but finite, a sensuous but free being, lies in *endless approximation toward this goal*. Now if, as we surely can, we call this total harmony with oneself 'perfection,' in the highest sense of the word, then *perfection* is man's highest and unattainable goal. His vocation, however, is to *perfect himself without end*. He exists in order to become constantly better in an ethical sense, in order to make all that surrounds him better *sensuously* and – insofar as we consider him in relation to society – *ethically* as well, and thereby to make himself ever happier.[8]

A lot depends on whether or not we can give a determinate sense to this "*endless approximation.*" We can certainly make sense of the idea of an end that is in principle unobtainable because of our finitude. Another important question is whether the subject should be oriented more by her cultivation of herself or more by her cultivation of her environment. The Stoic dimension of Fichte's claim – that happiness is just being virtuous – might collide with the harmony-based element according to which it is only in actually achieving harmony with what is outside of myself that I can be both virtuous and happy.

The implication of Fichte's demand for external harmony is that freedom is essentially a social project. He is forthright that his conception of community is highly idealized, a community based on concepts, on rationality, rather than the type of social organization called the state. After acknowledging the differences among agents, he writes, "There is only one thing in which they are in complete agreement: their ultimate goal – perfection. Perfection is determined in only one respect: it is totally self-identical. If all men could be perfect, if they could all achieve their highest and final goal, then they would be totally equal to each other. They would constitute but one single subject."[9] We are to "approximate" this goal in society through a process that Fichte calls "unification" [*Vereinigung*]. We do this by constantly searching for perfection, by giving and asking for reasons, by holding up our ideals of what is best to others and receiving criticism and trying to raise others and ourselves to the highest standards. This too may seem rather empty as an end, but for resolving the main tension within Fichte's view it is crucial. The tension between formal inner freedom and material outer freedom can only be addressed through such

---

8   *SW* VI, 152; *EPW*, 299/300.
9   *SW* VI, 310; *EPW*, 159.

communicative action – action which is part of his overall theory of culture as the process of individual and social perfection.

When Fichte begins to give some definition to the social order appropriate to the human vocation, he quickly arrives at the idea of a *division of labor*. Fichte holds that the realization of the moral end requires the division of society into different *estates*. This theory of social differentiation is actually an integral part of his overall perfectionism, for the idea of perfection that Fichte adapts from Kant is that of a harmonious unity that preserves the differences among the elements of that unity.[10] Fichte argues that nature simply produces individuals with different talents, and this is a fact that philosophy cannot alter but must accommodate into the system of freedom. In principle, the moral law, as "the law of total self-harmony or absolute identity"[11] would dictate "that all of an individual's talents ought to be developed equally and that all of his abilities ought to be cultivated to the highest possible degree of perfection"[12]. This would in turn lead to "the demand *that all of the various rational beings ought to be cultivated or educated equally*"[13] and that "the final aim of all society is *the complete equality of all of its members*."[14] It would seem, then, that the ethical end is a manifestly social and political end directed at improving the educational and economic fortunes of all its members.

But Fichte does not imagine that there could ever be equality in the sense that there would be no division of labor. Rather, he argues for an element of "culture" that can serve as a metric of equality even though the actual circumstances of individuals are necessarily different. He writes,

> Everyone has the duty not only to want to be generally useful to society, but also the duty, according to the best of his knowledge, to bend all of his efforts toward society's final end: the constant improvement of the human species – liberating it more and more from natural compulsion, and making it ever more independent and autonomous. And thus, from this new inequality [of classes] there arises a new equality: the equitable advancement of culture in every individual.[15]

Fichte's idea here is that in entering a profession each person enters a program of education that equips him for the tasks within that part of the labor force. This education is a version of culture that is equitable in that each has a place she has chosen and develops her talents in the service of a part that

---

10   See Wood (2016), 220.
11   *SW* VI, 314; *EPW*, 162.
12   Ibid.
13   Ibid.
14   Ibid.
15   *SW* VI, 321; *EPW*, 167-68.

contributes to the whole. This theory of labor ties into Fichte's vision of the ultimate end as a social end: "an association in which one cannot work for others without working for himself; for the successful progress of any member is the successful progress of them all, and one person's misfortune is everyone's misfortune."[16] This is Fichte's vision of reciprocity, a simple vision underlying all the complexities of the practical philosophy he develops through 1800.

2. The Final End in the *System of Ethics*

The biggest interpretive difficulty with Fichte's 1798 *System of Ethics* as a whole is the split between a *formal* side, culminating in conscience, and a *material* side, culminating in Fichte's extensive account of the content of duties in light of the final purpose of reason. In trying to decipher Fichte's position on the relation of specific individuals' actions, on the one hand, and the final end of perfection, on the other, there are two closely intertwined issues that stand out. First, there is the issue of how the infinite end is related to the finite series of actions that are the duty of the specific individual. This issue is especially pressing for Fichte because he holds that there are *no indifferent actions*. One and only one action is demanded at every moment. Second, there is the issue of the focus of ethical activity: is my duty to cultivate my own moral feeling and disposition, to perfect my own capacities for doing what is right and good? Or should my focus be on producing good outcomes, creating a better overall condition of the world through my actions? On this second issue there is no strict either-or, for it makes sense for self-perfection to be a vehicle for the perfection of the world. Yet there are significantly different ways of thinking about the moral life depending on whether self-cultivation or the production of ethical outcomes is primary.

Fichte's bold proclamations on the final end of reason have the ring of ethical fanaticism, but this impression is misleading. He does sound extreme when he proposes that the ideal of perfection would be a world in which everything is determined by my rational will:

> self-sufficiency, which is our ultimate goal, consists in everything depending on me and my not depending on anything, in everything that I will to occur in my entire sensible world occurring purely and simply because I will for it to occur – just as happens in my body ... The world must become for me what my body is.

---

16   *SW* VI, 321; 168.

> This goal is of course unreachable ... This process of drawing ever nearer to my final end is my finite end.[17]

Yet Fichte qualifies this claim in many ways that make clear that it is not some kind of insane egoism.[18] In fact, the discussion that immediately follows is intended to make clear that what we think of as individuality is the contingent starting point for the pure I once the agent becomes conscious of her freedom. His emphasis is on "I-hood," the basic root of freedom and reason, the activity that determines our action in so far as we are moral. He writes,

> Since it is for I-hood as such a contingent fact that *I*, individual A, am precisely A, and since the drive for self-sufficiency is supposed to be a drive of I-hood, essentially as such, the aim of this drive is not the self-sufficiency of [the individual] A, but rather, the self-sufficiency of reason as such. Our ultimate goal is the self-sufficiency of all reason as such and thus not the self-sufficiency of one rational being, insofar as the latter is an individual rational being.[19]

Especially striking in this passage is the claim that our end does not single out reason in each of us as more important than reason in any other. The initial point is just that for all of his emphasis on the I, Fichte does not direct the ethical agent to self-perfection at the expense of the perfection of others.

But the fact remains that Fichte does think that each of us is in a privileged position to know the *morality* of our actions, for that is an inner quality of actions that is not open to the judgment of others.[20] This thesis is tied to Fichte's very strong thesis about the formal aspect of moral action, namely that the judgment of what action is right must come from the individual, be ratified in the individual's conscience. The heart of this doctrine is Fichte's transformation of Kant's idea that moral action is action done *from duty*, for the sake of duty, out of respect for the moral law, etc. Fichte's moral law is agreement with oneself, and conscience is a feeling of harmony, so one acts on duty when one acts from the feeling of conviction that is signaled in conscience's approval. Just how much work this feeling does in *determining* an individual's duty is a

---

17   *SW* IV, 229; *SE*, 217.
18   His analysis of the person who wills lawless dominion, and the contrast with the moral individual, is especially instructive. See *SW* IV, 184-191; *SE* 175-181.
19   *SW* IV, 231; *SE*, 220.
20   He writes, "Whether someone actually fulfills *his duty* within his estate is therefore something that he alone can calculate, before the witness of his own conscience" (*SW* IV, 326; *SE*, 309), and, "When it comes to morality, no human being can or ought to judge another." (*SW* III, 265; *GNR*, 230).

difficult question that is an ongoing subject of debate in the literature.[21] The important point for my account is that one cannot act morally unless one is motivated to act *from* one's sense of conviction, from one's conscience. This implies that there is simply no perspective from which one can aggregate the morality of the world at any given moment.[22] The morality of all may be our ultimate end, but that ultimate end includes a condition that rules out *ever* knowing that the end is realized.

The individual's inner life is an ineliminable element in the final end of perfection. This does not mean that each of us is shut up in the circle of our convictions. On the contrary, we need to communicate the content of our convictions to others in order to be secure in our subjective certainty. It is, indeed, this simultaneous emphasis on individual conviction and impersonal reason that makes Fichte the originator of discourse theory and communicative action.[23] He holds that "I am even obliged by my conscience to develop this same conviction just as self-sufficiently and as broadly as I can. // Such development, or at least the continuation of the same, is possible, however, only by means of reciprocal communication with others."[24] Only in conversation with others will I be able to get over the suspicion that "in the most secret depths of my own mind"[25] I am not certain of my conviction. Arguing against "blind enthusing" and "sterile brooding," he writes that "The mind as a whole must be trained completely and from all sides and by no means one-sidedly."[26] Part of our ethical end is the cultivation of the mental capacities of judgment.

Fichte is wary of thinking that there is a procedure that would allow us to generate judgments of duty in any situation. In the course of arguing that one must be prepared to die while doing one's duty, he writes, "Everyone ought to do and everyone simply must do whatever his situation, his heart, and his insight order him to do – this, and nothing else; and one simply must not do anything one is prohibited from doing by one's situation, heart, and insight."[27] These are not casual references to "heart" and "insight," for these subjective

---

21 Kosch has argued against the widely held view that conscience does have a first-order role that conscience is instead merely a second-order consciousness that one has reached conviction about one's duty. See Kosch (2014). Wood also now holds that conscience does not simply determine duty, but he does – in contrast to Kosch – still retain a first-order role for conscience. Wood (2016), Chapter 5.
22 See also the claim by Ware that *"There is only an inner condition of moral worth."* Ware (2017), 11.
23 See Wood (2016), 212.
24 *SW* IV, 245; *SE*, 233.
25 *SW* IV, 245; *SE*, 234.
26 *SW* IV, 262; *SE*, 251.
27 *SW* IV, 270; *SE*, 258.

elements of the individual are inescapable elements of morality. In an important passage he contrasts the world in which everyone acted "in accordance with reason," or legally, with the world in which the demand is met "that this should occur freely, in consequence of the moral law, and hence that genuine, true morality should rule."[28] His conclusion is that "every morally good human being's goal is the formal freedom of all rational beings"[29]. This seems sensible enough, but it does imply that our goal is a state of affairs to which we literally could not have access given the inner quality of formal freedom.

Each individual's formal freedom is the precondition of her moral worth, but the goal of moral action is impersonal, involves seeing through one's own freedom to the realization of reason in general. This comes out in Fichte's discussion of Kant's formula of humanity according to which each individual human being is an "end in itself." For this essay the important issue is the sense in which any individual takes her own perfection as an end.[30] Fichte elaborates his point with explicit reference to Kant's formula of humanity and clarifies that while others are ends in themselves for me, "no one is an end for himself" because "everyone is a *means* for realizing reason."[31] Turning to perfection and giving a non-egoistic interpretation of what moral perfection consists in, he writes,

> Those who think that perfection lies in pious meditations and devout brooding over oneself and who expect such exercises to produce the annihilation of their individuality and their merger with the godhead are very mistaken indeed. Their virtue is and remains egotism; they want only to perfect *themselves*. True virtue consists in acting, in acting for the community, by means of which one may forget oneself completely.[32]

The final end of morality is located in the community, in perfecting not oneself but reason in general as embodied in the community.

Yet a bit later in the text Fichte makes an argument that seems to undercut the above emphasis on the community. He argues against the temptation to forego marriage: "One is not permitted to sacrifice this end [marriage] to other

---

28   SW IV, 275; SE, 263.
29   SW IV, 276; SE, 263.
30   "Hence I am *for myself* – i.e., before my own consciousness – only an instrument, a mere tool of the moral law, and by no means the end of the same. – Driven by the moral law, I forget myself as I engage in action; I am but a tool in its hand. A person who is looking at the goal [of his action] does not see himself, for the goal in question lies outside that person." (SW IV, 256; SE, 244)
31   SW IV, 256; SE, 244.
32   SW IV, 256; SE, 245.

ends, such as service to the church, the aims of the state or the family, the calm of a life devoted to speculation, and the like; **for the end of being a complete human being is higher than any other end.**"[33] That is an emphatic statement of an individual-based end, *being a complete human being*, that would seem to take precedence over other ends that might lead one to avoid marriage. I do not think one can explain this away as an outgrowth of Fichte's strange and rather repugnant conception of marriage. He seems quite aware of the problems with any one-sided focus on the end of reason within an individual life. No amount of devotion to science can justify neglecting development of the whole range of one's capacities.

The picture that emerges from the *Sittenlehre* is that of a self-perfection that ought to take social perfection as its goal, and a social system that ought to take the perfection of individuals as its goal. But strictly speaking we are only talking about the ethics of the individual, not the policies of the rational state.[34] Fichte is quite well aware of the dangers of trying to impose a moral order on individuals. Morality must be freely chosen by individuals if it is to have the value of morality. This is nothing other than the central conundrum of a perfectionism of autonomy. A person can directly will only her own autonomy, and she can indirectly will the autonomy of others by willing the creation of a social world that provides options and avenues of autonomous action. Even so, we should be able to give some definition to the world that would realize freedom, and some real guidance to ethical judgment as to which action moves us further along the path to perfection.

3. Consequentialist and Deontological Perfectionism

In this section I review a current debate over Fichte's ethics with a view towards specifying the nature of his perfectionism. Michelle Kosch has recently defended a view of Fichte's ethics as a *consequentialist* theory anchored in the final end.[35] She contrasts Fichte's focus on the final end as the principle of morality with Kant's emphasis on universal legislation. She writes, "Kant emphasizes that this principle is 'formal'; a material principle, by contrast, would prescribe the production of an end and judge the goodness of acts, rules, or

---

33 *SW* IV, 333; SE, 315, my bold.
34 Though Fichte does include a provocative section near the very end on the duties of the state official.
35 Kosch (2014), (2015). The book (2018) appeared too late for me to incorporate into this article.

policies on the basis of their tendency to produce or further that end. Fichte's moral principle, by contrast, is material in just this sense."[36] According to Kosch's interpretation, Fichte's material principle determines an agent-neutral theory in which actions are determined by their "tendency to produce" the end of "broadening the scope of possible rational plans of action."[37] She gives further definition to her view of the final end (which she admits is too abstractly formulated in the *System of Ethics*) by emphasizing the role that greater control over nature plays in furthering this end. Specifically, she finds Fichte's consequentialism gives him a way to support "basic scientific research, education, and technological and social innovation."[38]

While not making perfectionism a central focus of her interpretation, Kosch does indicate that she wants to do justice to Fichte's references to perfection. This makes sense given her emphasis on the material end (that Fichte identifies with perfection) as the central and most distinctive aspect of his ethical theory. She writes at the outset of her account, "His moral principle requires, not that we act only on maxims suitable for universal legislation in a kingdom of ends, but instead that we pursue the substantive end of rational agency's perfection and material independence from external limitations of all kinds."[39] Note that there are two main components to the substantive end, one being the perfection of rational agency and the other being material independence from external limitations. She is surely right that Fichte requires both, but the question arises from her formulation of whether this is one end or two, for she seems to put perfection on the side of rational agency as distinct from material independence. This goes against the unity claim that we saw above with Fichte's reference to the Highest Good; perfection has to include the outer conditions of agency that Fichte aligns with happiness. At the conclusion of her paper she writes of Fichte's claim that self-sufficiency is our absolute final end, "It simply amounts to the claim that, beyond the perfection of the exercise of rational agency and the expansion of its scope, there is no further end that a rational agent must, *qua* rational agent, have."[40] The first component covers the internal activity and the second the external dimension contained in the demand that we bring the bring the external world under the dominion of reason. This makes the subject's capacities into the goal of perfection rather than

---

36   Kosch (2015), 349.
37   Ibid., 350.
38   Ibid., 350.
39   Ibid., 349-50.
40   Ibid., 371. In a footnote she suggests that Fichte's material principle might escape Kant's objections to all material principles because that Kantian argument did not really address all principles of perfection. Ibid., 373, n81.

taking the goal of perfection to include the realized material end in the social world.

In his critique of Kosch's interpretation, Allen Wood takes issue with both the characterization of the absolute end and with the way that Kosch proposes to use it to support her consequentialist reading. Wood denies that "the degree of *rational human control over nature*"[41] captures Fichte's conception of the final end of self-sufficiency. But he does not merely reject that specific formulation, for he argues that there is *no way of specifying the final end* that would allow us to think of specific actions as maximizing that end.

Wood argues that Fichte is a radical *deontologist* whose basic requirement of willing duty for its own sake cuts against the consequentialist reading. He writes that Kosch leaves out something crucial: "There is also clearly one crucial aspect of what Fichte means by 'independence and self-sufficiency' of which this interpretation takes no account at all: namely the human choice of dutiful actions for the sake of duty exhibiting the independence of our will from all natural drives and from every enjoyment of their satisfaction only for its own sake".[42] This choice is the side of formal freedom that appears ineluctably inner in Fichte's view and therefore cannot be assessed in any standard consequentialist manner. I think that Wood is somewhat uncharitable towards Kosch here, for, as we have seen, she does think that *part* of the final end is "the perfection of the exercise of rational agency," and she would surely admit that what Wood calls "exhibiting the independence of our will" is included in that perfection. The question is whether this willing can be included in the consequences in a way that would not cause trouble for other aspects of Kosch's view. Her split between a subject-oriented element ("the exercise of rational agency") and a world-oriented element ("the expansion of its scope") suggests that she does think there is such a way. But I take it that she does not think that Fichte gave us much guidance in how to unite the two elements into a single end.

Wood's alternative answer to how the final end informs ethical life is what he calls "a Recursive Projection of our Finite Ends".[43] He writes, "our choice of the next member of the series is not guided calculatively, by a conception of the final end and the action calculated as a means to it. It is guided instead by the actions we have already taken. The next action is chosen as the further extension or projection of these same actions, when they are considered as

---

41 Wood (2016), 176.
42 Ibid.
43 Ibid., 179.

a *series*."⁴⁴ The final end itself always remains indefinite, for it does not determine specific actions except insofar as there has to be a conception of the infinite end for the idea of the series to be coherent. But the specific actions tend towards the material end on their own terms, without adding to them the end of perfection: "Each recursion, moreover, involves setting *only* a new end within a determinate range, and not *also* setting the final end according to some determinate concept of it."⁴⁵ This formulation is true to Fichte's frequent emphasis on our determinate limitations, but it does render rather unclear what guidance the final end offers for our finite end-setting.

Wood's interpretation of the final end is reflected in his view of the moral life. Rather than taking practical reason to be a calculative operation on agent-neutral reasons, Wood's Fichte endorses a situation ethics oriented by the specificity of cases and the individual agent's commitments. He writes, "The facts that provide us with moral reasons always remain heterogenous and unsystematic – too varied in nature to admit of reduction to any deliberative procedure. There is no discursive criterion of right action."⁴⁶ He holds that this accords with the role that Fichte assigns individual conscience as the conclusion of deliberation.

The existentialist bent of Wood's interpretation comes out in his proposal that Fichte has a new way of answering philosophers who worry that the moral demand threatens to rob individuals of their integrity. Fichte's moral agent, on Wood's view, "reconceives morality in such a way that everything belonging to our ground project becomes our moral duty."⁴⁷ He holds that morality for Fichte "displaces any desire or project not integrated by moral reflection into my project of being the free self that I am. ... There is no conflict between the rational impartiality of the moral law and the concrete demands of my situation. For Fichte, they are the same. My care for other people, the projects and causes to which I devote myself, all belong to my moral vocation."⁴⁸ Wood thus argues that we should not divide agent-relative and agent-neutral reasons in Fichte, for care and integrity are the main hallmarks of agent-relativity. By integrating these in moral reflection, we do justice to the demands of impartiality that motivate the agent-neutral.

The Fichtean moral life looks so dramatically different on these two accounts, both of which can find support in Fichte's texts, that we may be led

---

44   Ibid., 180.
45   Ibid., 181.
46   Ibid., 151.
47   Ibid., 193.
48   Ibid., 194.

to suspect that the view is not in the end coherent. But it may be just that Fichte is pushing at the bounds of our categories. Owen Ware has argued for a middle position of sorts between Wood's radical deontological view and Kosch's calculative consequentialism, arriving at a view that he calls "social perfectionism."[49] Ware agrees with Kosch that Fichte's view is agent-neutral, but he argues against her consequentialism, citing many passages where Fichte denies that one should base ethical decisions on the expected consequences.[50] But he also argues that we should not read Fichte as deontological in Kant's sense because Fichte holds the formal moral law to be empty and that teleological arguments must be employed to generate the content of morality. Ware argues that Wood goes too far in claiming that the final end is indeterminate, for by Wood's own lights we can say that social harmony is the final end.[51]

For Ware, Fichte's teleology and his perfectionism come to the fore at the level of philosophical reflection while deontology predominates at the level of ordinary consciousness.[52] This theoretically specifiable end has to do with harmonization rather than maximization: "objects are measurable by their tendency to harmonize with a final end."[53] Ware holds that the end of social harmony is determinate enough to ground our duties, at least when that is understood as the grounding of ethical content from the philosophical point of view.[54] Ware's claim is that in the social end we have a determinate enough condition to provide an account of ethical duties, duties that are viewed as unconditionally binding for individuals not because of their consequences, but simply because they accord with the individual's moral feelings in free deliberation.

---

49   Ware (2017), 1.
50   Ibid., pp. 10-13.
51   "Human beings are different from one another by nature in their predispositions and talents. The perfection of society consists in combining their capacities and activities into a single harmonious whole." Wood (2016), 221.
52   See also Wood's suggestion ((2016), 175) that Kosch's consequentialism could be understood as part of a two level view in which the consequentialism defines the philosophical truth of how norms are justified in contrast to the agent's deontological viewpoint.
53   Ware (2017), p. 14.
54   Wood has replied that he is reluctant to use the perfectionist label because of its widespread use as a "pernicious stereotype. A perfectionist ethics is normally assumed to aim at the perfection of the individual agent. It is assumed that this agent has a 'nature' to be perfected, that we can have a determinate concept of this nature, and that everything the agent is or does can be determined by this nature and this concept". Wood (2017), cited by Ware (2017), p. 16, n16.

I agree with Ware's emphasis on the social character of Fichte's perfectionism, but we are left in an odd position if we accept a split-level view of justification. The idea is that an individual knows her duty and is in a position to act for the sake of duty simply in following the guidance of moral feeling in deliberation. This is not to say that feeling determines our duty but that it reliably identifies our duty in any given situation. The philosopher can give a general account of duties as those purposes that lead towards the final end of social harmony. The question this raises is why individuals should be barred from taking social harmony as guiding their own deliberation and, further, why they are not the ones actually setting the terms for that harmony. The latter would seem to be consonant with Fichte's Rousseauian understanding of the general will. It seems that what we need is not a two-level picture of ordinary and theoretical reasoning but rather a single view of reasoning internally differentiated by the different objects of deliberation: 1) actions that I believe it is right for me to perform here and now and 2) those norms and laws that constitute my social context. These two sets of objects could be united if we held that the moral life is the life devoted to social reform. Fichte's theory is among the first, if not *the* first, to make such a view of ethics seem attractive.[55] Fichte himself only partly drew this conclusion in his Jena period, for he thought we needed to separate morality and politics, and in fact took it as one of his main goals to establish grounds of (political) right independent of the moral law. It is to that split, and to the surprising ways in which Fichte also works to overcome it from the side of right, that I now turn.

4. Avoiding Political Perfectionism, Embracing Economic Justice

It is a social end that ultimately defines Fichte's ethical perfectionism, yet he denies that the political powers can be oriented towards this ethical purpose. From the side of ethics there are indeed duties of right, such as the duty to obey the laws of your state. But there do not seem to be grounds *within the relation of right* to make individual or communal perfection the goal of state action. Fichte makes claims that, taken literally, would give the domain of right and the domain of ethics *opposed purposes*. While ethics is oriented by a final end in which all individuality is to disappear, the whole theory of right consists of conditions to establish and secure individuality, and this can lead to a good

---

55 The clearest descendant of this program is that espoused by Bruno Bauer in his writings prior to 1848. See Chapter 9 of this volume.

deal of uncertainty about what the individual agent's aims should be.[56] Fichte is uncompromising in separating the validity of right from the well-being of ethical agents, insisting that justice must survive even if it means the world will perish.[57] But he does not support the kind of right libertarianism that often accompanies a focus on property and a non-moral state. Quite the contrary. And that brings us to the puzzle of his economic and political philosophy as a whole: how does a theory arguing for individual *independence* end up with one of the most robust theories of *interdependence* in modern political philosophy?

4.1 Consent, Reciprocity and Unification

Any direct move from *ethical* perfectionism to *political* perfectionism is blocked by Fichte's assertion of a very strong separation of morality and right.[58] In his *Foundations of Natural Right* he contrasts the moral law's unconditional commands of duty with the law of right's conditional permissions. Fichte situates himself within the social contract tradition and bases right on the voluntary consent of those who are subject to laws of right. He also thinks of right as strictly *external*, and thus as independent of anyone's good will. His theory is based largely on property right and coercion, and thus seems at first to belong more to the classical liberal tradition than to any potentially perfectionist doctrine. Yet Fichte's theory of sociality, mutual recognition, leads him into claims in the *Foundations* about the political that appear to go beyond his initial restrictions. These claims make the radical economic arguments of *The Closed Commercial State* rather less unexpected. The reciprocity at the heart of right is incompatible with an unjust social order, and to the extent that social reciprocity and ethical perfection are overlapping ideals, there is a way to understand the ethical and political theories as converging on a vision of social harmony.

There are in fact two distinct sociality arguments at the beginning of the *Foundations*, the "summons argument" and the "recognition argument." In order to become conscious of one's freedom one must be summoned to that freedom by the activity of another free individual. This summons argument concerns a necessary condition of freedom, and is, strictly speaking, about the

---

56 As Kosch writes, "He does not tell us, in any systematic way, how the imperatives of protecting individuality and expanding material self-sufficiency are to be balanced against one another, or against non-political associative duties, in practical deliberation." Kosch (2015), 374.

57 He writes, "it is an utterly false proposition that the government is instituted to serve the best interests of those who are governed. (*Salus populi suprema lex esto*) What is right is because it ought to be; it exists absolutely, and it ought to be enforced even if no one were to benefit from this (*Fiat justitia, et pereat mundus*)." (*SW* IV, 358; *SE*, 338)

58 On this point, see Neuhouser (2016) and Clark (2016).

development of the individual to the initial awareness of freedom.[59] The second argument does not establish the same kind of necessity, for it concerns a relation that individuals *voluntarily* enter into with each other and the consequences of that voluntary act.[60] It is this second argument that is decisive for the *Foundations*, for it turns on each individual recognizing the discrete sphere of activity of other persons, and all the subsequent requirements of right are just so many consequences of this original relation voluntarily entered into and maintained. This relation is a condition of one's individuality, for without this definition through secure contrast with another agent's sphere of freedom, one is not an individual. The groundbreaking claim is that I can only be an individual in community, and if I will the conditions of community I have to will all the conditions of right that follow from it. Yet – and here is the opening for a return to the more traditional contractualism – I cannot count on the good will of others or trust that they will continue to recognize me. By virtue of our mutual voluntary consent they are obligated to recognize me, but the *guarantee* of this recognition to which I am entitled comes only with the coercive laws of the state.

There is thus a strong strand of what I call *atomistic contractualism* running through the *Foundations*.[61] But beneath this superstructure of atomism there remains a stronger social element that irrupts in Fichte's presentation of the series of contracts with which he establishes the state's authority. His *holistic contractualism* comes out most strikingly in what he calls *the unification contract*.[62] This contract has the effect of nullifying contractualist logic in the sense that it takes individuals out of their bare individuality as atomistic property owners and unites them into an organic whole. He writes, "the individual becomes a part of an organized whole, and thus melts into one with the whole"[63]. We get an inkling of how such incorporation into a whole could lead to a perfectionist doctrine in Fichte's claim that "Apart from the state, human beings would experience only passing gratification, but never the least concern for the future"[64]. Entry into the organic whole is transformative, for it changes the way that we experience our desires, and, Fichte suggests, makes us into beings who can think ahead, delay gratification, etc.

---

59 *SW* III, 30-40; *FNR*, 29-39.
60 *SW* III, 41-53; *FNR*, 39-49.
61 For worries about how well this fits with Fichte's arguments for sociality, see Martin (2006) and Baur (2006).
62 For a longer discussion of this, see Moyar (2016).
63 *SW* III, 204; *FNR*, 177.
64 *SW* III, 208; *FNR*, 181.

The unification introduces elements into the *Foundations* that one might have thought were ruled out by his strict separation of morality and right. Though he does not go all the way towards making the political authorities responsible for cultivating the good will, there is a sense in which the state is the appropriate precursor to moral perfectionism. He writes, "Humanity was divided into several independent members; the natural institution of the state already cancels this independence provisionally and molds individual groups into a whole, until morality re-creates the entire species as one"[65]. Here again Fichte's ultimate goal, the ultimate perfection at which we aim, is universal agreement or oneness. This whole is not merely held together by the mechanical operation of coercive law, but also defines obligations. He writes of "an absolute civic duty"[66] to help those in need, and he argues that your property is not really yours when another citizen is suffering from lack of property. These terms of the unification contract do not present a clear argument for politics as the means to the perfection of individuals, but it does erect a political ideal of social harmony. We can call the view *civic perfectionism*, the point being that the state aims at the perfection of the whole, the *reciprocity* among members of the whole. The high standard set by these claims about property comes to the fore in the extreme measures Fichte entertains in the economic sphere to secure a system of labor that ensures the well-being of all.

4.2   Pleasure and Value in the Closed State

The radical economic proposals of Fichte's 1800 *The Closed Commercial State* certainly do not seem to lie in the ordinary classical liberal contractualist line of thought. The work does rely on some of the contractualist reasoning of the *Foundations*, but the thrust of the work is a strongly egalitarian centralized State that aims at complete control over economic forces. As Douglas Moggach has pointed out, Fichte frames his text as a middle path between the non-interventionist doctrines of Humboldt and the classical perfectionism of Christian Wolff.[67] Fichte takes it for granted that traditional perfectionism is no longer an option: "The opinion that the state is the absolute [*unumschränkt*] guardian of humanity in all its affairs, making it happy, rich, healthy, orthodox, virtuous, and, if God so wills, even eternally blessed, has been sufficiently refuted in our day."[68] Yet Fichte strongly resists the non-interventionist alternative. The state cannot just take existing property relations as given, or as irrelevant

---

65   *FNR*, 176; *SW* III, 203.
66   *FNR*, 220; *SW* III, 252.
67   Moggach (2011).
68   *SW* III, 399; *CCS*, 91.

to the basic justice of the laws, but rather must put itself in a position "to first *give* each what is his."[69] Fichte thus insists that the reciprocity at the heart of the state's authority depends quite fundamentally on economic justice. Unless each person is able to live from their labor, no one has a genuine claim to property in excess of what they require for mere life. Fichte puts a great deal of weight on our original equality and on the social institution of property. You only own something in so far as everyone else renounces their right to it. There is no reason for everyone to accept that some people are entitled to more property than others.

Because Fichte is committed to giving a social and political theory that stays away from appeals to the good will or other moral notions, he attempts to make his arguments in the basic and straightforward terms of life, pleasure and value. These are not terms external to subjectivity in general, for no mere quantities of stuff could serve as a measure for justice. The fundamental category for Fichte is *activity*, the purpose of which is first of all "to be able to live."[70] Life in turn can be translated into pleasure: "Everyone wishes to live as pleasantly as is possible. Since everyone demands this as a human being, and no one is more or less human than anyone else, everyone has an equal right in [making] this demand."[71] Fichte does not imagine that we could guarantee for each an equally pleasurable life. We need to make it *possible*, for each "must be able".[72] to live as pleasantly as others, but it is up to individuals to make this happen once they have been given the opportunity. Fichte's reference to pleasure and the teleological dimension of his thinking might give the impression that he is offering a utilitarian account here. But there is clearly no maximization *across* persons. Without equality *between* persons there is no right, so right is not there to maximize an overall amount of pleasure in the world.

The more pressing question is whether Fichte takes a position on which activities are more pleasant than others. Is it merely a question of subjective intensity? Or can we distinguish higher and lower pleasures in a way that would open the door to political perfectionism? If the state is in the business of distinguishing higher and lower, essential and inessential pleasures, this could lead to a perfectionist doctrine.

Fichte makes an important move towards an objective account of pleasure when he translates pleasantness into *value*. "Let one posit, as the first of two

---

69   Ibid.; In *Foundations* Fichte casts this point as an even more radical version of a similar point made by Rousseau. *SW* III, 204-05; *FNR*, 177.
70   *SW* III, 402; *CCS*, 93.
71   Ibid.
72   Ibid.

magnitudes, a determinate sum of potential activity within a certain sphere of efficacy. The value of this magnitude is the pleasantness of life resulting from this activity."[73] This does not at first seem to address the issue of the value of different pleasures, but rather seems to reduce value to pleasure, and thus simply to reformulate the question rather than to solve it. He admits that the "pleasantness of life" "is based on personal taste and inclination, and thus is not suitable, in and for itself, to serve as a universally valid standard measure."[74] He turns instead "to the possibility of living, the true intrinsic value of every free activity"[75], and on that basis argues for *bread* as having "value absolutely, and it is by this measure that we estimate the value of everything else."[76]

Things get trickier for Fichte's account when he returns to the issue of pleasure and formulates a way in which the value of diverse consumer goods can be measured in terms of bread. The greater pleasantness of items to be consumed (and I think this can be extended beyond food and drink to consumption in general) is to be determined by "a universally valid estimation" that amounts to the "greater expenditure" of "time, force, skill, and soil"[77] in producing those more pleasurable items. We can translate that expenditure back into an equivalent expenditure that would be required for producing bread.[78] What is important for Fichte at this point is that the luxury goods produced would represent an excess of effort beyond mere subsistence, and that this excess is also to be distributed by the state to prevent inequality.

Fichte's theory of equality is more complex than it might seem at first, for as we saw already in the *Vocation* lectures, he subscribes to a principle of the estates, or a division of labor that is also a division in manner of living. He thus glosses "relatively equal" with the claim that "each one will maintain the kind of force and well-being he needs for his specific occupation."[79] Comparing the scholar to the farmer, Fichte notes that someone engaged in thought requires different, and presumably more expensive nourishment, for it is "nourishment that satisfies in smaller quantities"[80]. It is also crucial for the scholar to have "an environment in which the cleanliness and nobility that should rule him within

---

73 Ibid.
74 *SW* III, 415; *CCS*, 104.
75 *SW* III, 415; *CCS*, 104.
76 Ibid.
77 *SW* III, 417; *CCS*, 105.
78 Adler criticizes Fichte on this point the it "sneaks in market forces through the back door" and he argues that "it is unlikely that this principle of substitution could provide a foundation for equating the value of heterogenous forms of activity." Adler (2012), 37.
79 *SW* III, 417-18; *CCS*, 106.
80 *SW* III, 418; *CCS*, 106.

is constantly placed before his eyes in the outside world."[81] Fichte does not shy away from distinguishing between lower and higher occupations, or from talking about what is truly human.[82] Thus, he writes, "Yet even the farmer, on his day of rest, when he enters into a thoroughly human existence, deserves to enjoy together with the others the better things that the soil of his land grants, and wear clothing worthy of a free man."[83] Fichte thereby balances a respect for the highest things that can be accomplished by individuals with a concern for the perfection of the whole. His *civic perfectionism* is on display when he writes that "the intrinsic essential state of prosperity consists in being able to procure for oneself the most truly human pleasures with the least difficult and time-consuming labor. This should be the state of prosperity of the *nation* as a whole and not only of a few individuals ..."[84] This passage does seem to set a scale of pleasures, with "the most truly human" at the top, and to set a goal for the nation of distributing this value in an optimal manner. Fichte is arguing, not unlike some contemporary consequentialists, that the final value is a certain distribution of value among individuals.[85]

In discussing the transition from an open to a closed state, Fichte raises the issue of existing needs and the right to continue to enjoy the pleasures that one has come to expect. "This habituation has turned these goods into needs that are indispensable to their well-being."[86] But what if these needs can only be sustained through trade with other countries? As much as possible the State must develop the production of these goods within its own borders. But there are limits here, limits with which Fichte distinguishes the element of perfection in his theory from an unlimited pursuit of luxury goods and refined needs. He writes, "a distinction must be made between those needs that can actually contribute something to well-being and those that only take opinion

---

81 Ibid.
82 Christopher Yeomans has put the worries with division of labor in these terms: "the very way that the individual's limited material independence is secured is precisely by removing from them the status of an end and making them into a means for the self-sufficiency of reason as such. The self-sufficiency of reason as such is not only consistent with paternalistic subordination of individuals, but in fact requires it." (2015), 67.
83 *SW* III, 418; *CCS*, 106.
84 *SW* III, 423; *CCS*, 110.
85 "Within the country agriculture and the factories have now been brought to the intended degree of perfection, and the ratio of each to the other, of trade to both of them, and of the public officials to all three, has been calculated, ordered, and fixed." (*SW* III, 504; *CCS*, 191)
86 *SW* III, 478; *CCS*, 165.

into account."[87] Is there a notion of well-being here that could be the basis of true needs, true pleasures, and the basis of the State's contribution to human perfection?

Fichte's position could simply be taken to rely on the common sense idea of necessity and luxury, but it is notoriously hard to distinguish what one really needs from what is superfluous. Fichte's gestures in this direction will no doubt seem self-serving, as when he writes about travel:

> Only the scholar and the higher artist will have to travel outside of a closed commercial state. Idle curiosity and the restless hunt for distraction should no longer be allowed to tote their boredom from land to land. The travels of the scholar and the higher artist happen for the benefit of humanity and the state, and the government, far from trying to prevent these trips, should even encourage them, sending scholars and artists on trips at public expense.[88]

Here is a selective allowance for scholars and artists, but one that is justified by a higher moral purpose of the perfection of humanity. The goods of mere tourism are not enough to justify the opening of the state, the anarchy of the market, and the proliferation of false needs. This case demonstrates better than any external criticism how the desire to reform the state for the good of all tends to favor certain elites of spirit over the elites of industry, and thus to put one class conflict in place of another.

Conclusion

As is often the case with Fichte, his boldest pronouncements lead us to expect more than he is able to deliver in the end. But this is by design, and it is a mark of his heroic honesty that he did not shy away from erecting roadblocks to the ends that he himself declares to be sovereign. Without the separation of morality and right, the moral end of perfection could be misunderstood as a doctrine that overrides the free choice of individuals to determine the right and good for themselves. But Fichte holds that obeying the existing laws, and thus respecting the expectations that they have brought into being, is itself

---

87   SW III, 479; CCS, 166; He notes, "it is hardly clear why the coat must be of sable or the dress of silk, when the country produces neither sable nor silk. And it is even less clear why it would be so terrible if one day our clothing suddenly lacked all that embroidery through which it is made neither warmer nor more durable." (SW III, 479; CCS, 166) See also Adler (2012), 38-39 on this passage.
88   SW III, 506-07; CCS, 193.

an ethical demand.[89] He is also willing to ascribe to heads of state the duty to bring about the ethical end, and he even invokes Plato's philosopher kings in support of the need for enlightened rule.[90] But Fichte stops short at calling for immediate change, or an immediate move to the equality that he clearly cherished. This comes at least in part from respecting those individuals who already exist and who cannot simply be reeducated to a new revolutionary condition. In the end Fichte's perfectionism finds its proper home in the progress of *culture*, which the State can encourage but not mandate. "As the level of culture rises and as culture spreads more widely such privileges will cease, and it is the end of both nature and of reason that they should cease and that there should arise a complete equality of all citizens according to *birth* ... The spread of culture is thus the end of both nature and of reason."[91] This faith is fully compatible with the imperative of reason that we each must act in order to bring about the transformation of culture, one step at a time, both in ourselves and in others. Perfectionism must be accompanied by realism about the limitations of human action and community.

Bibliography

Adler, Anthony Curtis, "Interpretive Essay: Fichte's Monetary History," in: J.G. Fichte, *The Closed Commercial State*, translated by Anthony Curtis Adler, Albany: SUNY Press, 2012.

Baur, Michael, "Fichte's Impossible Contract," in: *Rights, Bodies and Recognition: New Essays on Fichte's Foundations of Natural Right*, ed. by Daniel Breazeale and Tom Rockmore, Aldershot, Hampshire: Ashgate, 2006.

Breazeale, Daniel, *Thinking Through the Wissenschaftslehre: Themes from Fichte's Early Philosophy*, Oxford: Oxford University Press, 2013.

---

89 "It is a matter of conscience to submit unconditionally to the laws of one's state; for these laws contain the presumptive general will, against which no one may influence others. Everyone receives moral permission to have an effect on others only by virtue of the fact that the law declares their consent to be influenced in this way." (*SW* IV, 238; *SE*, 226-27)

90 "But reason still demands that the social bond should gradually approximate that bond that is the only rightful one, and this is also what is demanded by the arrangement of nature. Thus a governor [*Regent*] who has to govern the state with this end in mind must be acquainted with the latter. According to what was said above, a person who elevates himself above ordinary experience by means of concepts is called a scholar; hence the state official must be a scholar within his own field. Plato says that no prince could rule well who did not participate in the ideas, and this is exactly what we are saying here." (*SW* IV, 357; *SE* 337)

91 *SW* IV, 360; *SE*, 340.

Clark, James, "Fichte's Independence Thesis," in: *Fichte's Foundations of Natural Right: A Critical Guide*, ed. by Gabriel Gottlieb, Cambridge: Cambridge University Press, 2016, pp. 52-71.

Fichte, J.G., *Sämmtliche Werke*, ed. by Immanuel Hermann Fichte, Berlin: De Gruyter, 1971. (*SW*)

– *The Closed Commercial State*, translated by Anthony Curtis Adler, Albany: SUNY Press, 2012. (*CCS*)

– *Early Philosophical Writings*, translated and edited by Daniel Breazeale, Ithaca: Cornell University Press, 1993. (*EPW*)

– *Introductions to the Wissenschaftslehre and Other Writings (1797-1800)*, ed. and trans. by Daniel Breazeale. Indianapolis: Hackett, 1994. (*GNR*)

– *Foundations of Natural Right*, ed. by Frederick Neuhouser, trans. by Michael Baur, Cambridge: Cambridge University Press, 2000. (*FNR*)

– *The System of Ethics*, ed. and trans. by Daniel Breazeale and Günter Zöller, Cambridge: Cambridge University Press, 2005. (*SE*)

Kosch, Michelle, "Practical Deliberation and the Voice of Conscience in Fichte's 1798 *System of Ethics*", in: *Philosophers' Imprint* 14, 2014, pp. 1-16.

– "Agency and Self-sufficiency in Fichte's Ethics," in: *Philosophy and Phenomenological Research*, 91: 2, 2015, pp. 348-380.

– *Fichte's Ethics*. Oxford: Oxford University Press, 2018.

Wayne, Martin, *Idealism and Objectivity: Understanding Fichte's Jena Project*, Stanford, CA: Stanford University Press, 1997.

– "Is Fichte a Social Contract Theorist?", in: *Rights, Bodies and Recognition: New Essays on Fichte's Foundations of Natural Right*, ed. by Daniel Breazeale and Tom Rockmore, Aldershot Hampshire: Ashgate, 2006.

Moggach, Douglas, "Post-Kantian Perfectionism," in: *Politics, Religion, and Art: Hegelian Debates*, ed. by Douglas Moggach, Evanston: Northwestern University Press, 2011.

Moyar, Dean, "Fichte's Organic Unification: Recognition and the Self-Overcoming of Social Contract Theory," in: *Fichte's Foundations of Natural Right: A Critical Guide*, ed. by Gabriel Gottlieb, Cambridge: Cambridge University Press, 2016, pp. 218-238.

Neuhouser, Frederick, "Fichte Separation of Right from Morality," in: *Fichte's Foundations of Natural Right: A Critical Guide*, ed. by Gabriel Gottlieb, Cambridge: Cambridge University Press, 2016, pp. 32-51.

– *Fichte's Theory of Subjectivity*, Cambridge: Cambridge University Press, 1990.

Ware, Owen, "Fichte's Normative Ethics: Deontological or Teleological?", in: *Mind*, 2017.

Wood, Allen, *Fichte's Ethical Thought*, Oxford: Oxford University Press, 2016.

– "Fichte's Philosophical Revolution," in: *Philosophical Topics*, vol. 19, 1991, pp. 1-28.

Yeomans, Christopher, *The Expansion of Autonomy: Hegel's Pluralistic Philosophy of Action*, Oxford: Oxford University Press, 2015.

Hegelian Perfectionism and Freedom

Loughlin Gleeson & Heikki Ikäheimo

Introduction

In this chapter, we take up the connection between perfectionism and autonomy, or more generally freedom, from the Hegelian perspective. As one might expect of Hegel, his understanding of both concepts, as well as the nature of their interconnection, is highly original, at times difficult to discern and quite often misunderstood. On our interpretation, Hegel's perfectionism is a form of "evaluative essentialism", while his understanding of freedom turns around the concept of "concrete freedom" [*konkrete Freiheit*]. "Evaluative essentialism" refers to the view whereby an entity's essence, or in Hegel's terms "concept", is in effect its *immanent evaluative criterion*, the realization of which is a measure of the "goodness" specific to that entity.[1] "Concrete freedom", to give a preliminary characterization, is a relationship obtaining between self and other (whether other subjects, society, or internal or external nature) wherein the former is *genuinely reconciled* with the latter.[2] The connection between these two principles – perfectionism as evaluative essentialism and freedom as concrete freedom – is encapsulated in Hegel's claim that the "essence" [*Wesen*] of *Geist*, or as we interpret the latter, the "human life-form", is concrete freedom.[3] As we will show in more detail below, Hegel's conceptualization of the interconnection of the relevant concepts not only marks a continuation with the Kantian tradition, but also a partial break with it, to the extent that it embraces aspects of Aristotelianism. We will begin by introducing the main features of the unique brand of ethical perfectionism that Hegel espouses, evaluative essentialism that is (Section 1). Following this, we will adumbrate Hegel's concept of concrete freedom with specific reference to its various "dimensions" (Section 2). By way of conclusion (section 3), we will consider

---

1 A version of this position has already been set out in Ikäheimo, (2011), 155-159. We switch here from "normative" to "evaluative" as the latter term avoids the potentially misleading deontological connotations of the former.
2 Hegel, *Lectures on the Philosophy of Spirit* (1827-8) (2007), 67. Hereafter *LPS*.
3 Hegel, *Philosophy of Mind* (2007), §382. Hereafter *PM*. We are utilizing Inwood's excellent new edition of the Philosophy of Spirit, but we are replacing his use of "mind" as a translation for *Geist* with "spirit", as it covers more of the meanings Hegel gave to this central term.

the relationship of concrete freedom to autonomy, and discuss the various "opposites" of concrete freedom, in particular the alternative ideal of abstract freedom and its dialectical reversals into relations of domination. We will end by suggesting that the ideal of collective autonomy put in practice without the guidance of the meta-principle of concrete freedom amounts to a pathological development of the life-form.

1

Perfectionism is standardly interpreted within the context of moral philosophy as an ethical stance – different in kind both from deontological and consequentialist approaches – according to which human beings are to realize a certain conception of "the good." That "the good" has been differently conceived by various philosophers has given rise to competing perfectionist approaches. When the object whose realization is indicative of axiological desirability has not been designated by a putative "human nature", or the human *differentia specifica* as in Aristotle, it has usually been specified in terms of non-naturalistically derived "objective goods", perhaps most commonly happiness. Both approaches have been subject to rigorous criticism – for a-historicism and heteronomy, respectively – and in consequence perfectionism generally has for some time now found itself somewhat out of favor within ethical theory. The general theme of this volume is a specific version of perfectionism that combines the basic idea with a broadly Kantian notion of autonomy: post-Kantian or autonomy-perfectionism. As our reconstruction of Hegel's position should reveal not only is it meaningfully different from the naturalist and non-naturalist variants of perfectionism referred to above, it is also largely immune to the standard charges brought against perfectionist ethics. As to post-Kantian perfectionism in the sense specified by Douglas Moggach in this volume and elsewhere,[4] Hegelian perfectionism remains post-Kantian in so far as "the good" around which it turns is freedom. In many other respects however, Hegel's version of perfectionism is unique to him, and distinct from both pre-Kantian perfectionisms and from autonomy-perfectionism.

Nowhere is the fact that Hegel espouses a unique kind of post-Kantian perfectionism more evident than in the "Introduction" to the Philosophy of Spirit of his 1830 Berlin *Encyclopaedia* and in the corresponding passages of his 1827/8 *Lectures on the Philosophy of Spirit*. It is here, in introducing his readers and students to the theme and basic principle of the Philosophy of

---

4 Moggach (2011), 179-200.

Spirit, that Hegel declares freedom to be the "essence" of *Geist* or spirit. In §382 of the *Encyclopaedia* we read: "For this reason formally the *essence* of spirit is *freedom*, the concept's absolute negativity as identity with itself."[5] In the lectures Hegel reaffirms this claim, albeit with reference to the synonymous terminology of "essential determination" and "concept": "Freedom constitutes the essential determination of spirit, and we can say that freedom is the concept of spirit."[6] Whether freedom is referred to as the "essence", "concept" or "essential determination", such a claim requires delicate handling. Before explaining the concept of freedom – concrete freedom that is – in the next section, let us thus characterize his evaluative essentialism by means of four general characteristics:

(i) Hegel's essentialism is of an *immanent*, and in this sense broadly Aristotelian kind;
(ii) it is normative or *evaluative*, as opposed to purely descriptive;
(iii) *contra* Aristotle, or at least simple versions of Aristotelianism, Hegel's essentialism on *Geist* has a decidedly *anti-naturalistic* twist;
(iv) marking a further point of differentiation from Aristotelianism, Hegel's essentialism also encompasses, to an extent, *historicism*.

(i) In our view, both *Geist* and its essence are to be interpreted in a fundamentally *immanentist* vein. Many good reasons, both exegetical and philosophical, have been presented for resisting the equivalence established by Charles Taylor between *Geist* and "cosmic spirit."[7] Taylor's reading, which is selectively grounded on the *Phenomenology of Spirit*, ultimately exports to the discussion of *Geist* a transcendent plane which is detached from the down to earth descriptions and conceptualizations of the various elements of the human life-form which Hegel's Philosophy of Spirit actually consists of. The rival, "post-Kantian" conception of *Geist* developed more recently by Robert Pippin, Terry Pinkard, Robert Brandom and others, by contrast, rejects the cosmic spirit-reading, and turns around the general idea of self-generating, self-legitimating shared norms as set within a *sui generis* "space of reasons."[8] Though the self-generation and self-legitimation of norms is actually something done collectively by humans, this reading largely omits the "thicker" (psychological, affective, "ethical") aspects of human life that Hegel spends so much time and effort in conceptualizing in the Philosophy

---
5 *PM*, §382.
6 *LPS*, 67.
7 Taylor (1988).
8 See, for instance, Pippin (2008), 17.

of Spirit. Our approach seeks to do justice to the completely human content of Hegel's conception of *Geist*, as well as those moments which cannot be reduced to "thin" deontological-normative concepts. As we understand it, *Geist* encompasses the totality of all distinctly *human* activities, structures, capacities and achievements – from the most "immediate" naturally-founded, anthropological determinacies discussed at the beginning of the Philosophy of Spirit to the most elaborate ones of philosophical reflection discussed at the end. Otherwise expressed, *Geist* is a *title-word* for the "human life-form"[9] and it embraces all the partially given, partially self-produced and self-reflective moments – in Hegel's terminology the "subjective", the "objective" and the "absolute" – constitutive of our life-form. These – and nothing else – are the explicit topic of Hegel's Philosophy of Spirit.

What Hegel means by "essence" is equally immanent, in contrast to a Platonic "form" on the traditional interpretation. In the *Science of Logic* Hegel says that by the "essence" of a thing he means its "concept" or "universal":

> [...] the *nature*, the specific *essence*, that which is truly *permanent* and *substantial* in the manifold and accidentiality of appearance and fleeting externalization, is the *concept* of the thing, *the universal which is present in it* just as there is present in each human being, although universally unique, a specific principle that makes him human (or in each individual animal a specific principle that makes it animal).[10]

Essence, in this broadly Aristotelian sense, is hence the immanent principle that makes a given entity what it is[11]; or as James Kreines puts it, its "immanent concept."[12] An important feature of essences so conceived is also their "objectivity." Such entity-defining concepts are mostly not products of human construction or legislation *a la* Pippin and other post-Kantians,[13] but have a relative mind-independence, the more precise determinations of which depend on the general kind of thing in question.[14] For Hegel concrete freedom

---

9   See Stekeler-Weithofer (2013), 701-735.
10 Hegel, *Science of Logic* (2010), 16. Hereafter *SL*.
11 *LPS*, 67.
12 Kreines (2015), 22.
13 As we will show, nor is self-legislation all that the human essence amounts to. Compare Pippin (2008), 40.
14 Artifacts are of course human made and their human purpose defines their essence. This is not so with natural entities. Here we are focused only on the human essence, which for Hegel is what it is independently of what humans think it is, even though its actualization is not.

is *the* human essence, and he clearly does not think this is up to negotiation or re-legislation.

(ii) That Hegel's brand of essentialism is Aristotelian means that it is not simply descriptive. It is not focused on demarcating entities in terms of necessary properties or necessary and sufficient conditions on which something counts as a particular kind of entity. Rather, it is of a normative or *evaluative* type, whereby the "essence" or "concept" of a given entity is its *immanent ideal* and thus *evaluative principle*. From this perspective, evaluative judgements pertain to the correspondence of an entity to its essence, and the degree to which an entity instantiates or realizes its essence is the degree of its "goodness" or "badness" on criteria specific to it.[15] As to the human life-form and concrete freedom as its essence, the more instantiations of the life-form instantiate concrete freedom, or the "freer" they are in this sense, the better (and "truer"[16]) they are. Conversely, any non-insignificant failures to realize concrete freedom count as defects or imperfections, forms of "badness" that is, of human life. As should become clear in the next section, the goodness and badness at stake here are of a broadly *ethical* kind.

(iii) Associating Hegel with Aristotelian essentialism will no doubt be cause for concern both within and outside of Hegel-scholarship, as it may seem to imply some sort of reductive *naturalism* on *Geist*, or humanity. The worry is that this involves positing a fixed or invariant conception of "human nature" and negating the self-constituting character of the human life-form – a position categorically rejected by the post-Kantian Hegelians such as Pippin and others.[17] At least part of this worry can be allayed by a consideration of what the realization of the essence in question actually involves. It is significant, in this respect, that Hegel himself disavows the thought that concrete freedom is something to which we as humans tend *naturally*, as flowers turn to light or bees to honey. Instead, he characterises our essence as a "vocation" [*Bestimmung*], the achievement of which necessarily involves human activity and thus at least potentially explicit thought. Hegel says:

> If it is asked, what is spirit? The proper sense of this question is what is essential in spirit, and this is equivalent to the question, what is the vocation [*Bestimmung*]

---

15   *SL*, 712: "In the concrete things, together with the diversity of the properties among themselves, there also enters the difference between the *concept* and its *realization*. [...] Therefore, although an actual thing will indeed manifest in itself what it *ought* to be, yet, in accordance with the negative judgment of the concept, it may equally also show that its actuality only imperfectly corresponds with this concept, that it is *bad*."
16   This involves an ontological concept of truth. See Halbig (2006), 234-35.
17   Pippin (2008), 17.

of the human as such? Vocation expresses on the one hand a difference [between what is, and what is supposed to be], an end, a purpose that is supposed to be achieved. [...] On the other hand, vocation means the origin, what the human being is in himself [*an sich*]. The human being is supposed to bring himself about, but he cannot make himself to be anything other, and can have no other end, except what he originally is in himself. [..] The nature of spirit is to bring forth what it is, to bring it to manifestation, to discourse, to consciousness. The vocation of spirit is to make itself be what it is in itself.[18]

Though Hegel's substantializing turns of phrases on *Geist* at the end of the quotation may initially suggest a naturalistic determinism with respect to the realization of the essence, what he is actually talking about is the determination and vocation of human being or beings which can only be "brought about" through individual and collective human action. It is only through an activity of *self-realisation* that, invoking Hegelian terminology, our essence becomes "for itself" [*für sich*], actual and determinate, as opposed to merely "in-itself" [*an sich*], an implicit potentiality.[19] This connects with the next point and we will also return to it in the third section.

(iv) Whereas the above may allay some of the post-Kantian worries about naturalism, it does not address the related worry of an uncritical *a-historicism*. Here it is important to understand that Hegel conceives of the relevant essence at a high degree of abstraction, or, if you like, *formally*. For concrete freedom to be realized in human affairs, it necessarily requires specification and thus "fitting into" the specific historical and cultural conditions pertaining to the social reality in question. Whereas Hegel himself construed a particular institutional complex as the ideal system of concrete freedom overall that he could think of for the conditions of his time and place, the details and attendant evaluative judgments pertaining to the realization of concrete freedom in, for instance, continental Europe today would be rather different, despite the "context-transcending" general form of concrete freedom. Hegel's *formal* evaluative essentialism does not as such determine the details of any particular specification thereof. Rather, it is here that the real-philosophical labor actually begins, and that is what Hegel undertook in his *Philosophy of Right*. Even if not operating with exactly the same concept of freedom, a close enough analogue tuned to the social, economic and cultural conditions of contemporary Germany (or perhaps Western Europe) can be found in Axel Honneth's *Freedom's Right*.[20] It too operates on a fairly formal concept of

---

18   *LPS*, 67.
19   *PM*, §382z.
20   Honneth (2014).

("social") freedom, and applies it to social reality by specifying what it means in the different contemporary social and institutional spheres. To return to the previous point, however exactly one thinks of the connections between philosophical theory, practice, and historical development, it is clear that the realization of concrete freedom in institutions and in social structures and practices does not happen naturally, but requires human activity, philosophical work as activity of "absolute Spirit" included.

Bringing together the various threads set out above, concrete freedom hence figures in Hegel's thought as *the* immanent evaluative criterion of the various instantiations of the human life-form. The relevant essence is such that its realization requires human activity and this necessarily involves its specification under determinate contexts. The more or the better concrete freedom is realised by instantiations of human life – and more exactly, as we will see next, relations to necessarily determining others – the better or more perfect those instantiations are on a criterion immanent to them, hence exemplifying the "goodness" proper to our kind.

2

Having briefly reconstructed the main features of Hegel's evaluative essentialism, it is time now to explicate what exactly the essence in question – *concrete* freedom – is on his account. In the "Introduction" to the Philosophy of Spirit and in the accompanying lectures, Hegel emphasizes that by freedom as the essence of *Geist* he does not mean merely "abstract freedom", or *freedom from* something.[21] His critique of and polemic against abstract freedom spread across his writings is that it cannot apply to what we are necessarily determined by (e.g., other subjects, society, internal and external nature).[22] The concept of abstract freedom is logically incoherent with regard to such necessarily determining "others,"[23] and practical attempts to apply it relation to them are doomed to fail, the more catastrophically so the harder the attempt (as evidenced for example by the infamous "reign of terror" during the French revolution[24]). Hegel's point of departure with respect to his *concrete*

---

21 PM, 65-67.
22 Hegel, *Elements of the Philosophy of Right* (2011), §5. Hereafter PR. Also see Hegel, *The Phenomenology of Spirit* (1977), §549.
23 As Hegel puts it, "the one who flees, however, is not yet free, for in fleeing he is still dependent on what he flees." In Hegel, *Encyclopedia of the Philosophical Sciences in Basic Outline: Part I: Science of Logic*, (2010), 94 A. Hereafter EL.
24 PR, §5 Z.

conception of freedom is marked by the idea that the necessary determinants or necessarily determining others referred to above should not be conceived of as restrictions to the subject, but as *constitutive* of it, and that freedom in relation to them cannot be freedom from them, but, if you like, freedom *with them* or *with regard to them*. Concrete freedom is thus a certain kind of relation in which the subject is *reconciled* with constitutive otherness, whether epistemically or practically, whether affectively or in reflective thought. Importantly, concrete freedom as reconciliation with necessarily determining others, or, as Hegel puts it, "being with oneself in the other" [*bei sich selbst sein in anderem*], does not amount to the complete overcoming of the other in question.[25] Nor does it mean the subject merging with or being engulfed by the other. Rather, freedom *in concreto* amounts to the "sublation" [*Aufhebung*] of the other's alienness or inimicality.

Another way in which Hegel attempts to capture just this is by the formal expression "unity of unity and difference." Simply put, all finite things are constituted not only by an immediate (abstract) relation-to-self, but also by what they are *not*, an "other."[26] Being maximally constituted and thereby free in the relevant concrete sense is not a matter of abstractly negating such "difference"; on the contrary, it implies incorporating it within a mediated (concrete) self-relation.[27] "What exists concretely," Hegel writes, "is [...] not abstractly for itself but only in an other, but in this other it is the relation to itself and the relationship is the unity of the relation to itself and the relation to an other."[28] Here, of course, we are only interested in human beings and in the ways in which they, or we, realize our essence with regard to constitutive others, as expressed by the formulas of "unity of unity and difference' or "being with oneself in otherness." As to the "objectivity" or relative mind-independence of concrete freedom's status as *the* essence of the human life-form, for Hegel this clearly at least partly stems from his ontology of finite being and thus from something not up to human legislation. Whatever human *autonomy* in the sense of self-legislation encompasses, it does not have the power to change or legislate over these fundamental ontological facts about finite being, including human existence.

---

25   To claim as much, as figures as otherwise diverse as Adorno, Habermas or Deleuze have, is to effectively conflate the overcoming of the other's otherness with the overcoming of the other *tout court*. Only the former can be said to accurately characterise Hegel's position.

26   *SL*, 46: "[...] *there* is nothing, nothing in heaven, or in nature or in mind or anywhere else which does not equally contain both immediacy and mediation [...]".

27   Ibid., 89.

28   *EL*, §135 A.

The practical relevance of the concept of concrete freedom that is beginning to come into view now will undoubtedly hinge on spelling out in more detail what it means to be concretely free with regard to necessarily determining others, and this requires a general conception of what those others are. To speak at the level of the human individual we can discern four kinds: (i) her "internal" physiological and psychological processes, features and capacities; (ii) external nature; (iii) other humans; and (iv) social institutions and social reality broadly speaking. As different as these "others" and the relations with them constitutive of the human individual are, they all represent essential determinants of human life in whose absence it is not conceivable. We are *physiologically and psychologically determinate beings constitutively connected to other similarly constituted subjects and our natural and social environments*. No account of human freedom that tries to abstract from what we are, that is, our constitutive determinatedness, can be adequate to its subject matter. Further, whatever the historical and local specifications of concrete freedom, they clearly need to be attentive to all four above mentioned dimensions. To grasp the fundamental difference of this framework of thinking of freedom to the Kantian moral philosophical framework, consider the fact that the latter starts from a wholesale abstraction from what we are as empirical beings. Whatever the Kantian elements present in Hegel's thought, this difference is crucial for understanding Hegel's particular combination of perfectionism and freedom.

Let us now try to spell out in brief what concrete freedom might mean in its different dimensions – the "'subjective'', "natural", "intersubjective", and "social" – which can be rationally reconstructed from Hegel's Philosophy of Spirit. In the first place (i), the "subjective" dimension concerns the relationship to our "psycho-physiology" (body, first-order motivations, psychological capacities). Beginning in his "Anthropology" (*PM*, §§391-412), Hegel accounts for the emergence and gradual cultivation of an initially inchoate, pre-intentional "self", or "soul" [*Seele*],[29] which is endowed with a variety of internal-natural determinacies (sensations, feelings, and potentials of the human body). The course of its cultivation portends its liberation in the concrete sense of freedom whereby it gains an organized "self-feeling" [*Selbstgefühl*], which is present in and gives structure to all of its various determinations. The "cultivated" [*gebildete*] human subject is constituted through an organization of the sentient unity of the body, and at the same time gradually gains reflective distance to it. To put this in other words, the cultivated subject, or the "I" as Hegel calls

---

29   The "soul" is Hegel's Anthropology is to be understood in broadly Aristotelian, "hylomorphic" sense as the organizing principle of the body. See *PM*, §389: "The soul is not only immaterial for itself. It is the universal immateriality of nature, its simple ideal life."

it, is more or less at home in and thus reconciled with its psycho-physiology; it is necessarily determined by it, and yet not as if by something alien or unruly, but rather as by something that is its own.[30] With his usual acuteness, however, Hegel notes that the body is never *completely* shed of its "difference": part of our bodiliness is inescapably natural, beyond our powers to change or legislate over.[31]

Hegel's account of the internal constitution of the human subject continues in the "Psychology" section of the Philosophy of Spirit (*PM*, §§440-82), where he discusses the *intentional* processes and activities of the "I" and their organization into a rational whole or "system."[32] Again, what is at stake is a development through which the subject comes into its own *qua* a subject of knowledge and action, at once identical with its various cognitive and volitive capacities (i.e., memory and drives) and capable of reflecting and further developing those aspects. Though we cannot go into details here,[33] to avoid a false impression of dualism, it is important to see that for Hegel the "psychological" and the "anthropological" determinations are not abstractly separate but internally connected. To pick just one example, even abstract philosophical thought requires bodily habituation, and as Hegel somewhat humorously puts it, it can cause headache for those not accustomed to it.[34]

Secondly (ii), to grasp what concrete freedom in relation to external nature means, it is useful to distinguish between the *pre-intentional* and *intentional* relations of human beings to this particular dimension of their constitutive determinatedness or "otherness". Though these form a concrete whole, we can roughly locate Hegel's discussion of the *pre-intentional* side in the "Anthropology" section (*PM*, §§388-98). To underline the thoroughly empirical

---

30 Ibid., §412 Z.: "the self has [...] actualised itself in the soul's reality, in its bodiliness, and conversely, has posited being within itself; so that now that self or the I intuits its own self in its other and is this self-intuiting." The familiar formulation of 20th century phenomenology comes close to this: I both am and have my body.

31 Ibid., §412 Z.: "The soul's pervasion of its bodiliness [...] is not *absolute*, does not completely sublate the difference of soul and body. On the contrary, the nature of the logical Idea, developing everything from itself, requires that this difference still be given its due. Something of bodiliness remains, therefore, purely organic and consequently withdrawn from the power of the soul, so that the soul's pervasion of its body is only one side of the body."

32 Ibid., §408 Z.: "The sober and healthy subject has an alert consciousness of the ordered totality of its individual world, into the system of which it subsumes each particular content of sensation, idea, desires, inclination etc., as it arises, and inserts in its intelligible place in the system."

33 Ikäheimo (2016), 424-449.

34 *PM*, §410 Z.

nature of human subjectivity, Hegel discusses the various *affects* of external nature on it. External natural determinacies such as our distance from the sun, or the cyclical changes of seasons are inescapable determinations without which human life as we know it would not be possible.[35] Though *Geist* liberates itself from nature, both at the collective and individual level, this should not be read as meaning liberation according to the abstract concept of freedom. Thought in terms of the concrete concept of freedom, as Hegel prompts us to do in his "Introduction" to the Philosophy of Spirit, we should neither be completely immersed in natural determinacies, as this would simply amount to animal unfreedom,[36] nor try to deny them or try to abstract ourselves from them – a project doomed to failure or catastrophe, as we know all too painfully today.

Hegel discusses the reconciliation with external nature at the *intentional* level in the "Phenomenology" section of the Philosophy of Spirit (§§413-439).[37] His discussion of the *theoretical* aspect of that relation (§§418-423) tracks an ideal development from an immediate "sensuous" relation to nature to a refined, philosophical form of intellectual comprehension that grasps nature *both* as intelligently organised and thus not alien to the subject *and* yet fully independent from it.[38] His discussion of the *practical* aspect (§§424-437) begins with animal "desire" [*Begierde*], which refers to a purely destructive way of relating to nature by devouring it.[39] It proceeds to "labour", a form-giving relation or activity, which finds nature amenable to thoughtful utilization, while at the same time acknowledging its genuine separateness from the subject and its resistance to attempts of simply reducing it to subjective ends.[40] A concretely free relation with nature at an intentional level is therefore one in which it is both *epistemically familiar* and *practically habitable* to us, while retaining its "difference" from us. Though environmentalist concerns were not thematic to Hegel as they are for us today, it is not difficult to discern the outlines of an environmental ethics here, one which emphasizes our constitutive dependence on nature: concrete freedom with regard to natural

---

35   Ibid., §§392-94.
36   Ibid., §392: "In the case of man, the more cultivated he is and the more his whole condition rests on a free, spiritual foundation, the less the significance that such connections have."
37   The "Phenomenology" section deals with intentionality in general, but here we narrow our focus to this aspect of it.
38   See ibid., §§422-3, and the related discussion in "Psychology" in §§465-8.
39   Ibid., §427.
40   Ibid., §428: "In so far as self-consciousness relates as fashioning activity to the object, the object get only the form of the subjective, a form acquiring a *subsistence* in it, while in its matter the object is preserved."

determinacies is a matter of critically appropriating and cultivating them, to the point where we are individually and collectively more or less reconciled with external nature as something inescapable and separate from us, yet as not frighteningly hostile – a place in which we can build a home. As that home consists to a large extent of social institutions, it is potentially dangerous to conceptualize them and the norms they consist of as a *sui generis* reality constituted by collective self-legislation "spinning frictionlessly in [a] void", to invoke the allegory made famous by John McDowell.[41]

Thirdly (iii), the *intersubjective* dimension of concrete freedom, the idealized development and basic structure of which Hegel discusses in the "Self-consciousness" section of Philosophy of Spirit (*PM*, §§427-37), is a matter of *horizontal* relations of recognition between two or more human subjects.[42] The progressive movement considered therein begins with an encounter between two irreconcilable "desiring" intentionalities,[43] it transitions to the famous lord-bondsman-relation (also thematizing the theme of work just discussed) with an imperfect reconciliation by means of one yielding to the other,[44] and it ends in a relationship of subjects who mutually recognize each other as free and are thereby concretely free with regard to each other ("universal self-consciousness" in Hegel's shorthand).[45] Concrete freedom consists here, on the one hand, of the *independence* of the subjects with regard to each other, and, on the other hand, of the *unity* of their intentionalities in that they affirm each other by means of attitudes of recognition and find themselves thereby affirmed by each other. As Hegel puts it, subjects have "affirmative awareness" of themselves in and through one another, or they have "absolute independence" from one another, and yet they do not "distinguish [themselves] from the other."[46] Whereas post-Kantian readers of Hegel tend to spell this out in *deontological* terms of mutual attribution of authority on shared norms or of normative statuses[47], Hegel's own paradigmatic example of

---

41   McDowell (1994).
42   For details on the different senses of 'recognition' involved here, see Ikäheimo (2013), 11-38.
43   *PM*, §430.
44   Ibid., §433-45.
45   Ibid., §436-37.
46   Ibid., § 436: "*Universal self-consciousness* is the affirmative awareness of oneself in the other self. Each self as free individuality has *absolute independence*, but in virtue of the negation of its immediacy or desire does not distinguish itself from the other; it is universal and objective; and it has real universality in the form of reciprocity, in that it is aware of its recognition in the free other, and is aware of this in so far as it recognises the other and is aware that it is free."
47   Pippin (2008), 25.

recognition – "love" – is in the *axiological* register.⁴⁸ Abstracting from details, both mutual respect and mutual love are concretizations of unity of unity and difference in intersubjective relations, or of mutual consciousness of oneself in an independent other.

Finally (iv), concrete freedom also encompasses the "vertical" relation of subjects to the social institutions and the social whole, which Hegel treats under the banner of *objective spirit* both in the Philosophy of Spirit (*PM*, §§488-502; 513-52), and in greater detail in his *Philosophy of Right*. This dimension can be analysed either *objectively*, in terms of "ethical" [*Sittliche*] norms and institutions (family, civil society, modern nation-state),⁴⁹ or *subjectively*, from the perspective of individual subjects and their roles with regard to such norms and institutions.⁵⁰ In Hegel's view, subjects are first *integrated* into a "rational" social whole via the formative process of *Bildung*,⁵¹ a whole which they then in turn help to *reproduce* through various modes of recognitive identification and practical participation.⁵² In the ideal social-institutional setting, properly socialized individuals "find themselves" in established norms and institutions (that possess relative ontological independence from any particular individual's will),⁵³ in these reflect their personal-identity-defining attachments,⁵⁴ are amenable to their ends, and generally such that individuals can acknowledge them as just and good.⁵⁵ Both Kantian, explicitly reflexive endorsement,⁵⁶ and Aristotelian, habitual or "second natural" acceptance of the norms and institutions and the roles that they prescribe,⁵⁷ are modifications of these. Either sense would require further treatment beyond what it is possible here, but together they make up a complete picture of what it is to be both *reflectively* and *affectively* "at home" in a human world structured by social institutions.⁵⁸

---

48   *PM*, §436 and 436 Z.; *PR*, §7 Z.
49   *PR*, §142.
50   *PM*, §484.
51   *PR*, §151 Z.
52   *PM*, §514 Z.
53   *PR*, §146.
54   Ibid., §147.
55   Ibid., §260.
56   Pippin (2008), 261.
57   See, for example Lumsden (2013), 220-243.
58   A worrying detail for egalitarians is that in Hegel's ideal society different estates embody the different modes of being at home in the institutional whole of the society or state: the "substantial estate" the unreflective or affective mode, and the "universal estate" the educated and reflective mode. But this is a detail in Hegel's application and specification of the principle of concrete freedom for his time and place open to challenge, not something determined by that principle.

A further way in which one can be said to be concretely free with regard to social norms and institutions, and thus roles they prescribe, is that one has some "legislative" authority over them. The general ontological fact that human societies are the sole authorities of their norms is clearly not enough for genuine collective autonomy. In addition, there has to be awareness of this fact in the society, and at the individual level actual opportunities to exercise legislative authority over the norms and institutions. This aspect of concrete freedom is one that Hegel did not show much interest in in the *Philosophy of Right*, but clearly it is much too important to ignore. And yet is it equally important to acknowledge that it – autonomy that is – is far from all there is to concrete freedom.

Interpreted holistically, then, Hegelian concrete freedom encompasses all of the constitutive and thus necessarily determining dimensions of otherness in individual and collective human existence. Above we have merely sketched some of the general features of what this means on each dimension, and treated them by and large in abstraction from each other. It is clear that they are in many ways interconnected: think of especially the ways in which the cultivated habits and inner dispositions of feeling, as well as the perceptions and thoughts of a person, the quality of her inter-human attitudes and relations, and the social and institutional roles prescribed by and available in her society must form a harmonious enough whole. Lack of concrete freedom in one of these dimensions is likely to reverberate as trouble in the others as well. And ultimately, the life-form as a whole will fail if its relation to the external nature of which it lives does not sufficiently exhibit concrete freedom, or unity of unity and difference in Hegel's sense. What all of this means more concretely is a matter for thoughtful application in the given natural, cultural and historical circumstances, and thus a task for social and political philosophy with an emancipatory interest.

3

Towards the end of the last section we suggested that autonomy – the core normative principle in autonomy-perfectionism as understood in this volume – is one aspect of what it means to be concretely free with regard to norms and institutions governing social life. And since social norms and institutions and the roles they prescribe are internalized and structure also our embodied psychological lives – our "subjectivities" – as well as our relations to others and the world in general, it is clearly a very important aspect of concrete freedom more generally. But there is also another, equally valid way to look at the relation of concrete freedom and autonomy: this is to say that concrete freedom is a meta-principle, or principle of a higher order to which autonomy as self-legislation can and on the Hegelian view should be subjected. Unlike more historicist interpretations of Hegel would have it, for him it is not merely a subjective principle or ideal adopted in particular historical and cultural conditions (roughly, those of the "Germanic world"), but an objective principle grounded on facts about the ontological structure of finite beings in general, and of conscious living beings in particular. Finite beings are by definition determined, not only logically, but in many "real" ways discussed in Hegel's *Realphilosophie*, by things other than themselves. For animal life the relations to determining otherness are partly relayed through the medium of sensations; and for conscious beings in Hegel's sense, humans that is, they are in addition mediated by theoretical and practical intentionality. These general ontological facts form the inescapable setting within which human autonomy in the sense of legislation of norms or principles inevitably operates.

It is worth invoking here the double meaning of "autonomy" according to the Greek etymology, referring on the one hand to "one's own laws" in general, and "one's own laws" in the specific sense of self-legislated laws. On Hegel's account, concrete freedom is not a law or principle in the *subjective*, self-legislated, or in general legislated sense, but rather the *objective*, in important senses mind-independent evaluative principle of *Geist* or the human life-form.[59] And yet, its realization in human affairs, and thus Geist's realizing of its essence, depends on humans appropriating it as their evaluative essence or ideal subjectively. In the subjective sense of autonomy, humans are free to legislate the laws they live by, and it is also up to them whether or not they appropriate the higher order *nomos* of concrete freedom as the meta-principle guiding their legislation. However, if they do not, Hegel's message is that they are violating inescapable ontological strictures and thus doomed to fail, one way or another.

To illustrate the applicability and potential usefulness of the meta-principle of concrete freedom in critical social philosophy, let us finish by a brief sketch of a catalogue of such failures, or of the "opposites" of concrete freedom on the four dimensions we discussed in the previous section: inner and outer nature, other humans, and social institutions. Of particular interest here is abstract freedom as an alternative ideal, one which Hegel never tires of criticizing, and its tendency to morph in practice into relations of domination. Hegel's characterization of the structure of concrete freedom – unity of unity and

---

59   For elaboration of the "passive" sense of autonomy in relation to Kant's and Hegel's thoughts on living beings see Khurana (2013).

difference – is of heuristic use in this regard. Thought in terms of it, concrete freedom contrasts with two general kinds of "opposites":

(1) difference without the right kind of unity, which is therefore also a wrong kind of difference, and
(2) unity without the right kind of difference, which is therefore also a wrong kind of unity.

Formulated somewhat more concretely, the first opposite represents the structure of abstract freedom, whereas the second represents attempts to deny the independence or difference of the other – or in other words *domination*. Expressed in terms of the subject-other-relation, the latter can mean either (2a) domination of the other by the subject, and (2b) domination of the subject by the other.

Relation to Internal Nature

As to the relation with internal nature, Hegel's critique of ascetism or "monkishness" is here a case in point.[60] The attempt to abstract oneself from one's bodily needs, or to be (1) abstractly free from them – perhaps, as they are deemed sinful – is bound to fail one way or another, since, contrary to "Cartesian" theoretical abstractions of an ego abstractly distinct from the body, human existence is necessarily bodily existence. That abstract freedom in relation to one's body is a failed ideal shows also in its practical instability: if it does not take the form of suicide,[61] in practice it turns into one or the other form of domination. The attempt to be free from bodily urges demands (2a) a repression of them, a harsh regime that does not effect a positive cultivation of them; hence they remain "irrational" in content, pestering us with their unruliness. In the extreme, this can turn to the opposite of (2b) a pathological overtaking of the subject by its inner nature in which the subject ends up stripped of its capacity for rational self-determination.[62] In short: try to be (1) abstractly free from your bodiliness, and you will either eventually die, or end up in a vicious struggle in which you are trying to dominate your body (2a) while it is at the same time 'trying' to take over or dominate you (2b).

---

60 *PM*, §410 and 410 Z.
61 Ibid., §4.
62 See Hegel's discussion of the various forms of "derangement" in Hegel *PM*, 408 Z. 20th century and contemporary psychoanalysis has of course much to add on the importance of appropriating and being reconciled with one's mental and emotional life – not all of which can be perfectly mastered and thus part of which always retains some degree of otherness. Try to simply repress it, and it will return with a revenge.

Relation to External Nature

What holds true of the nature *within us* also partly holds true of the nature *around us*. The folly of (1) abstract freedom, difference without unity with regard to external nature, or the image of human beings as wholly free from external nature – frictionlessly hovering above it, if you like – can similarly only take one of two forms in practice: either death (the collective species-sense of death included), or a struggle in which both sides try to dominate the other (2). There is no overcoming of humanity's dependence on the natural conditions of our planet, and thus no use in trying to conceive of freedom with regard to them in terms of abstract freedom. We can try to force our will (2a) upon the planet and its biological, chemical and other elements and processes without a serious acknowledgement of their "otherness" or irreducibility to human ends or legislation. Yet, invariably, this results in consequences that are difficult or impossible to control, and in the worst case in nature metaphorically turning against us with a vengeance (2b).[63]

Relation to Others

Hegel's famous lord-bondsman scenario is, from one perspective, a reflection on how an attempt to be (1) abstractly free from other subjects effectively institutes (2) domination within horizontal relations.[64] Not exercising the Hegelian details here, it is enough to point out the obvious: humans cannot live without other humans, and thus fantasies of omnipotent abstract freedom from determination by others are unstable, involving a tendency of turning in practice into either domination *over them* (2a), or *by them* (2b), due to lack of genuine reconciliation in the relationship. Structurally, domination implies an asymmetrical and thereby a wrong kind of "unity" whereby the dominating party rules over and exploits the dominated party denying, the latter's independence and difference.[65] The history of liberal political philosophy from Hobbes to Fichte and beyond contains many variations of

---

63 What about a "return to nature" in the sense of an undifferentiated unity with it? Just as abstract difference, abstract unity is a folly with regard to external nature: it actually means nature at large taking over humans, just as it takes or rules over other animal species. Alternatively, "return to nature" can be a somewhat misleading expression for another and perhaps better kind of unity of unity and difference with nature – say, small farming instead of industrial farming. (Whether or not this is an example of an actually workable application of the principle is an empirical question, not something that can simply be deduced from the principle.)

64 PM, §§433-35.

65 Again, psychoanalysis has much to say about the importance of a balance between unity and difference with others for a non-pathological development of human subjectivity, and of the various failures or opposites of this. See Benjamin (1988).

the interplay of abstract freedom and domination. Fichte provides one of the most illustrative examples for our purposes: he thinks of freedom according to the abstract concept, in terms of individuals inhabiting "spheres of freedom" that are mutually exclusive and thus separate from one another, and ends up with a conception of the state that is largely coercive – the kind of state required to ensure that individuals abstractly free within their respective spheres (although in many other ways interdependent) do not encroach upon each other's spheres and thus try to dominate each other.[66] Fichte's solution to lack of adequate harmonizing factors on the horizontal dimension, and thus to the danger of intersubjective domination, is establishing vertical domination by a higher power, that of the state.

Relation to Society

The coercive or dominating images of the state, or of the social whole, the kinds of which one finds in Fichte and even certain (mis-)readings of Hegel, are bound to create fantasies of escaping from or denying it. The underlying theoretical mistake here is the idea that norms, laws or social institutions are abstractly separate from us, and hence we from them, and the consequent lack of understanding of genuine freedom with regard to them – not abstract (1), but concrete. A core idea in Hegel's thinking of *Sittlichkeit*, to speak in the deontological register of Hegel's post-Kantian interpreters, is that human life is necessarily governed by shared norms, and the system of institutionalized norms, or the various spheres of the state broadly conceived, should be largely in harmony with norms (habits and customs) *de facto* governing the life of the collective or nation. This image is of course still compatible with a simple immersion in established habits and customs and thus with an unreflective, uncritical relation to the institutional whole from which individual autonomy or in Hegel's terms "subjective freedom"[67] is absent (2b). A picture of *Sittlichkeit* that realizes concrete freedom must indeed include autonomy or self-legislation: social norms and their institutionalizations, and thus the interlocking and identity-defining social and institutional roles that they imply, being authorized by those whose life they govern. There is of course always a possibility that particular groups within society may aspire to dominate the social whole (2a) by taking over the authority on the shared norms, and the more so the less horizontal relations are imbued with a culture of mutual recognition and thus realize concrete freedom in that dimension. Here, as elsewhere, the various dimensions of Hegelian concrete freedom and

---

66 Fichte (2000).
67 *PR*, §§124, 185, 260, 262.

attendant defects are deeply interconnected. However, and to conclude, even collective autonomy with a fair and equal distribution of normative authority will fail to live up to the evaluative essence or immanent ideal of the human life-form according to Hegel if it is, implicitly or explicitly, guided by images of abstract freedom from, or domination over, all of the constitutive aspects of our being, or the dimensions of otherness, that we cannot be free from, nor legislate over. If anything deserves the name of "social pathology",[68] or more broadly a pathological development of the human life-form, then it is the ideal of collective autonomy put in practice without proper guidance by the meta-principle of concrete freedom.

Bibliography

Benjamin, Jessica, *The Bonds of Love*, New York: Pantheon Books, 1988.

Fichte, J.G., *Foundations of Natural Right: According to the Principles Wissenschaftslehre*, transl. by Michael Baur. Cambridge and New York: Cambridge University Press, 2000.

Halbig, Christoph, "Varieties of Nature in Hegel and McDowell", in: *European Journal of Philosophy* 14 (2), 2006, pp. 234-35.

Hardimon, Michael O., *Hegel's Social Philosophy: The Project of Reconciliation*, Cambridge: Cambridge University Press, 1994.

Hegel, G.W.F., *Philosophy of Mind*, transl. by W.W. Wallace and A.V. Miller, Oxford: Clarendon Press, 2007. (*PM*)

– *Science of Logic*, ed. and transl. by George di Giovanni, Cambridge: Cambridge University Press, 2010. (*SL*)

– *Lectures on the Philosophy of Spirit* (1827-8), transl. by Robert R. Williams, Oxford: Oxford University Press, 2007. (*LPS*)

– *Elements of the Philosophy of Right*, ed. by Allen Wood, Cambridge: Cambridge University Press, 2011. (*PR*)

– *The Phenomenology of Spirit*, transl. by A.V. Miller, Oxford: Oxford University Press, 1977.

– *Encyclopedia of the Philosophical Sciences in Basic Outline: Part I: Science of Logic*, transl. by Klaus Brinkman and Daniel O. Dahlstrom, Cambridge, 2010. (*EL*)

Honneth, Axel, *Freedom's Right: The Social Foundations of Democratic Ethical Life*, transl. by Joseph Ganahl, Cambridge: Polity Press, 2014.

– "Pathologies of the Social: The Past and Present of Social Philosophy", in: *Disrespect: The Normative Foundations of Critical Theory*, Cambridge, Polity, 2007, pp. 3-48.

---

68 See Honneth (2007).

Ikäheimo, Heikki, "Holism and Normative Essentialism in Hegel's Social Ontology", in: *Recognition and Social Ontology*, ed. by Heikki Ikäheimo and Arto Laitinen, Leiden: Brill, 2011, pp. 155-159.

– "Hegel's Psychology", in: *The Oxford Handbook of Hegel*, ed. by Dean Moyar, Oxford: Oxford University Press, 2017, pp. 424-449.

– "Hegel's Concept of Recognition – What is it?", in: *Recognition – German Idealism as an Ongoing Challenge*, ed. Christian Krijnen, Leiden: Brill, 2013, pp. 11-38.

Khurana, Thomas, "Life and Autonomy: Forms of Self-Determination in Kant and Hegel", in: *The Freedom of Life: Hegelian Perspectives*, ed. by Thomas Khurana, Berlin, August Verlag Verlag, 2013, pp. 155-193.

Kreines, James, *Reason in the World: Hegel's Metaphysics and Its Philosophical Appeal*, Oxford: Oxford University Press, 2015.

Lumsden, Simon, 'Habit, *Sittlichkeit* and Second Nature', in: *Critical Horizons*, 13 (2), 2013, pp. 220-243.

McDowell, John, *Mind and World*, Cambridge, Massachusetts: Harvard University Press, 1994.

Moggach, Douglas. "Post-Kantian Perfectionism", in: *Politics, Religion, and Art: Hegelian Debates*, ed. by Douglas Moggach, Evanston: Northwestern University Press, 2011, pp. 179-200.

Pippin, Robert, *Hegel's Practical Philosophy: Rational Agency as Ethical Life*, New York: Cambridge University Press, 2008.

Stekeler-Weithofer, Pirmin, "Intuition, Understanding, and the Human form of Life", in: *Recognition and Social Ontology*, ed. by Heikki Ikaheimo and Arto Laitinen, 11, Leiden: Brill, 2011, pp. 85-113.

Taylor, Charles, *Hegel and Modern Society*, Cambridge: Cambridge University Press, 1988.

Thompson, Michael, "Forms of Nature: 'first', 'second' and 'living', 'rational' and 'phronetic", in: *Freiheit: Stuttgarter Hegel-Kongress 2011* (Veröffentlichungen der Internationalen Hegel-Vereinigung), ed. by Gunnar Hindrichs and Axel Honneth, Frankfurt am Main, 2013, pp. 701-735.

Ergänzung und Überschreiten von Hegels politischer Philosophie durch Eduard Gans

Norbert Waszek

Im Zentrum von Hegels politischer Philosophie steht die Freiheit und die ganze Weltgeschichte ist für ihn bekanntlich „der Fortschritt im Bewusstsein der Freiheit".[1] Den verschiedenen Ebenen der Hegelschen Rechtsphilosophie entsprechen allerdings sich wandelnde und sich bereichernde Konzeptionen der Freiheit. Die elementare Wahlfreiheit des „abstrakten Rechts"[2] muss sich im Rahmen der „Sittlichkeit" weiter entfalten durch die *bewusste* Teilnahme der Subjekte an den sittlichen Einrichtungen, den Institutionen der Familie, der bürgerlichen Gesellschaft und des Staates. Der Fortschritt artikuliert sich eben nicht nur in verbesserten Bedingungen, sondern auch „im *Bewusstsein* der Freiheit" und so muss die „Sittlichkeit" eben auch *bewusstere* Formen der Freiheit zeitigen. Dazu gehört auch die Autonomie oder Selbstbestimmung[3] der Subjekte, wie es Douglas Moggach in der Einleitung zu seiner grundlegenden Studie über Bruno Bauer treffend dargestellt hat.[4] Obwohl Hegel in seinem berühmten Bild der Eule der Minerva, am Ende der Vorrede seiner Rechtsphilosophie, die Rolle der Philosophie auf die zurückblickende Aufgabe beschränkt, die Vernunft in den vergangenen historischen Entwicklungen zu erkennen, eben wenn „eine Gestalt des Lebens alt geworden" war, darf diese Perspektive keinesfalls auf eine Rechtfertigung des *status quo* reduziert werden, wie es in den überholten Legenden von Hegel als Staatsphilosophen Preußens geschah.[5] Seine Position der Vorrede überschreitend hat sich Hegel nicht nur gelegentlich ungedeckt vorgewagt und sich, wenn auch nur kurz, geradezu prophetisch über die zukünftige, weltgeschichtliche Rolle von Amerika und

---

1 Hegels Schriften werden, wenn keine andere Quelle genannt wird, zitiert nach der weitverbreiteten *TWA*-Edition: hier *TWA* 12, 32.
2 Vgl. hierzu die drei einschlägigen Beiträge von Pippin (1997), Ritter (1997) und Quante (1997) in Siep (Hrsg.) (1997).
3 In der weitgehenden Identifikation der Begriffe ‚Autonomie', ‚Selbstbestimmung' und ‚Selbstständigkeit' lehne ich mich an Gans selbst an, der sie nahezu synonym verwendet; vgl. zum Beispiel Gans (2005), 133 und Gans (1825), 357.
4 Moggach (2003), 7-12.
5 Wie sie Rudolf Haym vielleicht am wirkungsmächtigsten verbreitet hat: Haym (1857).

Russland geäußert⁶, sondern auch für Preußen selbst ist Hegel eindeutig über den *status quo* hinausgegangen, wie es schon Karl Rosenkranz überzeugend gegen Haym betont hat:

> Preußen war damals kein konstitutioneller Staat; er besaß keine Öffentlichkeit und Mündlichkeit der Rechtspflege, keine Pressfreiheit, keine Gleichheit der Bürger vor dem Gesetz, keinen Antheil des Volkes an der Gesetzgebung und Steuerbewilligung – und alles das lehrte Hegel als philosophische Notwendigkeit.⁷

Der Auffassung, dass Hegel in der Ausführung, sozusagen im Eifer des Gefechts, über das in der Vorrede formulierte Programm hinausgeht, kann auch eine andere Lesart an die Seite gestellt werden. Da Vorworte oder Vorreden in der Regel als chronologisch letzter Textabschnitt eines Buches geschrieben werden, im Falle der Hegelschen Grundlinien ist die Vorrede auf den 25. Juni 1820 datiert, könnte die rückblickende Perspektive am Ende der Vorrede auch einer gewissen Resignation darüber Ausdruck geben, dass die Verwirklichung der im Buch selbst artikulierten Ziele doch noch länger auf sich warten ließe.⁸

Wie dem auch sein mag, lässt sich schon für Hegel selbst eine Spannung zwischen dem bereits Erreichten und der noch ausstehenden Verwirklichung seiner politischen Ziele konstatieren, eine Spannung, die den Ambivalenzen zwischen Reform und Restauration der preußischen Realität entsprach, blieb seine eigene Haltung durch Erwartung und verhaltenen Optimismus⁹ charakterisiert – eine Haltung, die sich wie folgt zusammenfassen lässt: ‚was an der Zeit war, würde sich mittelfristig auch durchsetzen'. Diese Haltung beizubehalten wurde für seine Schüler indessen immer schwieriger. Durch die andauernde, ja, sich mitunter verschärfende Restauration – zwischen dem Bewusstsein und der Verwirklichung der Freiheit schien sich eine Kluft geöffnet zu haben – gerieten diese *nolens volens* in die Lage, sich stärker als oppositionelle Gruppe positionieren zu müssen, die in ihren Forderungen ‚lauter' wird, politische und soziale Fortschritte präziser als Ziele artikuliert und auch zu verwirklichen sucht. Am Beispiel von Eduard Gans können solche Entwicklungen nicht nur aufgezeigt werden, sondern sein Beispiel drängt sich geradezu auf, wenn einerseits an die Führungsrolle gedacht wird, die er in den wenigen, aber bedeutsamen Jahren, um welche er Hegel überlebte (Hegel

---

6 Schon Shlomo Avineri hat die wichtigsten Stellen – darunter das oft zitierte Wort über Amerika, „das Land der Zukunft" (*TWA* 12, 114) – zusammengetragen und kommentiert; Avineri (1972), 234-238.
7 Rosenkranz (1870), 152.
8 Vgl. Lucas (1986), 218.
9 Hermann Lübbe findet einen treffenden Ausdruck für Hegels Haltung, wenn er von „relativer politischer Versöhnung" spricht: Lübbe (1974), 93.

starb 1831, Gans schon 1839), zweifellos spielte[10], andererseits wegen des Lehrer-Schüler Verhältnisses, in welchem Gans zu so bedeutenden Vertretern der nächsten Generation wie David Friedrich Strauß, August von Cieszkowski und Karl Marx stand.

Wie bei anderen Hegelschülern und Hegelianern im weiteren Sinne[11] stehen auch bei Gans unter den Themenbereichen, in denen er Hegel zu vervollkommnen sucht, zwei besonders markant hervor: a) die Verfassungsfrage und die inhaltliche Ausgestaltung des Verfassungsstaates; b) eine innovative Antwort auf die „soziale Frage". Als Textkorpus der folgenden Analyse dieser Themen dienen einerseits die von Gans selbst veröffentlichten Schriften[12], inklusive der bekanntlich von ihm auf der Grundlage von studentischen Nachschriften redigierten „Zusätze" zu den mitunter spröden Paragraphen von Hegels Rechtsphilosophie[13], andererseits die posthumen Editionen (H. Schröder, M. Riedel, J. Braun) von Gans' eigenen Vorlesungen.[14]

Verfassungsfrage und Verfassungsstaat
Nicht nur für Preußen, sondern auch für die anderen deutschsprachigen Länder erwuchs die Forderung nach einer Verfassung auch aus der damaligen Rechtslage, denn der Artikel XIII der Bundesakte vom Juni 1815 (zeitlich nicht allzu weit vom Entstehen von Hegels *Grundlinien der Philosophie des Rechts* entfernt) versprach: „In allen Bundesstaaten wird eine landständische Verfassung stattfinden." Diese Ankündigung, „wird" (Zukunft), schien einerseits bereits auf frühkonstitutionelle Aspirationen zu antworten, andererseits ermutigte sie solche Bestrebungen weiter. Als Schwäche dieser Regelung muss allerdings erscheinen, dass weder ein zeitlicher Rahmen (bis wann?) für die Verwirklichung fixiert wird, noch eine inhaltliche Präzisierung (welche Inhalte sollten solche Verfassungen mindestens enthalten?) erfolgte. Dieser vage Charakter war dem Artikel XIII wohl absichtlich gegeben worden, um es den einzelnen Ländern zu erlauben, die Verfassungsgebung beliebig aufzuschieben, oder Richtlinien zu erlassen, die den Titel „Verfassung" kaum verdienen. Tatsächlich wurden bald nach der Bundesakte erste Landständische Verfassungen gewährt (z.B. Sachsen-Weimar-Eisenach 1816, Baden und Bayern

---

10   Vgl. die diversen Belege in Waszek (2015), besonders 29-33.
11   Vgl. Moggach (2003), 10.
12   Vgl. die Bibliographien in Gans (1836/1995), 435-437 und in Braun (1997), 225-231.
13   Erstmals wurden die „Zusätze" veröffentlicht in der als Band 8 von Hegels frühester Werkausgabe (‚Freundesvereinsausgabe') von Gans bearbeiteten Edition: Hegel, *Grundlinien der Philosophie des Rechts*. Berlin, Duncker & Humblot, 1833; wiederabgedruckt in vielen späteren Ausgaben (z.B. *TWA* 7).
14   Gans (1971); Gans (2005).

1818, Württemberg 1819) und bis 1848 folgten fast alle Länder des Bundes, mit Ausnahme von Preußen (!) und Österreich, den beiden größten Mächten.

Da sich Hegel in Preußen niederließ, nachdem er den Ruf der Universität Berlin 1818 angenommen hatte – doch wohl in Anerkennung der dort kurz vorher durchgeführten Reformen und der Hoffnung auf deren Fortsetzung, aber auch überzeugt von der kulturellen Rolle, die für ihn zu Preußens Bestimmung gehörte[15] – und Berlin auch der Wirkungskreis von Gans blieb (sowie ohnehin im Zentrum der Hegelschen Schule stand), müssen den Bedingungen in Preußen besondere Aufmerksamkeit entgegengebracht werden. Gerade durch das von König Friedrich Wilhelm III. mehrfach wiederholte Verfassungsversprechen[16], welches er aber in seiner über vierzigjährigen Regierungszeit nie einlöste, erwuchs aus der Verfassungsfrage eine der zentralen politischen Debatten der Periode des Vormärz.

Die Grundüberzeugung, dass die Verfassung der Vernunft und dem Zeitbedürfnis entspricht, wie sie Hegel ab den §§ 271-273 seiner *Grundlinien*[17] deutlich zum Ausdruck bringt, scheint der Philosoph bereits aus Heidelberg nach Berlin mitgebracht zu haben, denn in der Nachschrift des Jurastudenten Peter Wannenmann seiner Vorlesung des Wintersemesters 1817/18[18] ist sie ebenso nachweisbar. Beide Texte enthalten diverse Aussagen, die zumindest als implizite Kritik am preußischen *status quo* zu verstehen sind.

> Ein Monarch an der Spitze eines Staates ohne vernünftige Verfassung fasst das Ganze in seine Willkür und kann alles verderben. Das, was durch den Begriff notwendig ist – dass dieses ist, muss Zutrauen einflössen. In den großen

---

15   Wie es Hegel in seiner Berliner Antrittsvorlesung (vom 22. Oktober 1822) deutlich zum Ausdruck bringt: „Und es ist insbesondere dieser Staat [i.e. Preußen], der mich nun in sich aufgenommen hat, welcher durch das geistige Übergewicht sich zu seinem Gewicht in der Wirklichkeit und im Politischen emporgehoben, sich an Macht und Selbständigkeit solchen Staaten gleichgestellt hat, welche ihm an äußeren Mitteln überlegen gewesen wären. Hier ist die Bildung und die Blüte der Wissenschaften eines der wesentlichsten Momente selbst im Staatsleben; auf hiesiger Universität, der Universität des Mittelpunktes, muß auch der Mittelpunkt aller Geistesbildung und aller Wissenschaft und Wahrheit, die Philosophie ihre Stelle und vorzügliche Pflege finden." (*TWA* 10, 400)

16   Er stellte eine Verfassung für Preußen mehrfach in Aussicht, z.B. im Finanzedikt von 1810, besonders in der „Verordnung über die zu bildende Repräsentation des Volkes" vom 22. Mai 1815, auch noch im Staatsschuldengesetz von 1820. Weitere Einzelheiten in der umfangreichen Biographie von Stamm-Kuhlmann (1992).

17   *TWA* 7, 431-440.

18   Von dieser Nachschrift liegen gleich zwei Ausgaben vor, diejenige von Ilting (1983) und diejenige des Hegel-Archivs Hegel-Wannenmann (1983), aus der im Folgenden mit der Sigle *„Hegel-Wannenmann"* zitiert wird.

Forderungen an den Fürsten liegt überhaupt die Vorstellung eines despotischen Staates, wo die vernünftige Verfassung fehlt.[19]

Nur durch die Einbindung der Monarchie in eine Verfassung, durch die Umwandlung einer absoluten zu einer konstitutionellen Monarchie, kann sie zu einem „notwendigen Moment des Ganzen"[20] werden. Im obigen Zitat, ist Hegels Satzbau auch ein wenig kompliziert, stecken letztlich Aussagen, die unter den damaligen Gegebenheiten als radikal erscheinen müssen. Kann aus dem ersten Satz nicht herausgelesen werden, dass eine absolute Monarchie, eine Monarchie „ohne vernünftige Verfassung", eine Willkürherrschaft ist und aus dem letzten Satz, dass die Machtausübung des Herrschers, außerhalb eines konstitutionellen Rahmens ein Despotismus ist?[21] Schon die zwei Seiten vorher auftretende Äußerung: „das Vernünftiggöttliche ist die Verfassung, der Monarch ist [nur ?!] das Natürlichgöttliche"[22] hätte der König von Preußen, ob der derzeitige Friedrich Wilhelm III. oder der 1840 folgende Friedrich Wilhelm IV., wohl kaum als Kompliment aufgefasst.

Klingen die Formulierungen der *Grundlinien* nicht ganz so scharf, hält Hegel auch in seiner publizierten Rechtsphilosophie nicht nur an seiner Option für die konstitutionelle Monarchie fest, sondern auch dort lassen sich viele Stellen als Kritik an den damaligen Bedingungen Preußens verstehen. Wenn es im § 273 heißt, dass „die Ausbildung des Staates zur konstitutionellen Monarchie [...] das Werk der neueren Welt" ist, und diese Ausbildung im nächsten Satz auch als „Vertiefung des Geistes der Welt in sich"[23] bezeichnet wird, kann an Hegels positiver Würdigung dieses historischen Prozesses nicht gezweifelt werden, auch wenn er die systematische Zuordnung der konstitutionellen Monarchie zum Prozess der Weltgeschichte, wie er sie in der Anmerkung zum § 273 andeutet[24], eigentlich erst in seinen Vorlesungen über die Philosophie der Geschichte (ab 1822/23) ausarbeitet. Werden damit aber die Monarchien, denen, wie Preußen, eine Verfassung noch fehlt, nicht zu überkommenen Resten der alten Welt herabgesetzt? In der von Dieter Henrich edierten Nachschrift der Vorlesung von 1819/20 (schon in Berlin) heißt es jedenfalls eindeutig:

---

19 *Hegel-Wannenmann*, 206.
20 Ibid.
21 Vgl. Lucas (1986), 211.
22 *Hegel-Wannenmann*, 204.
23 *TWA* 7, 435.
24 Ibid., 436: „die Geschichte dieser wahrhaften Gestaltung des sittlichen Lebens ist die Sache der allgemeinen Weltgeschichte."

„In allen anderen Verfassungen [als der konstitutionellen Monarchie] ist die wahrhafte Freiheit noch nicht zu ihrer Wirklichkeit gekommen."[25]

Auch in der inhaltlichen Ausgestaltung des Verfassungsstaats gibt es schon bei Hegel zahlreiche Elemente, die über die Verhältnisse im Preußen seiner Zeit hinausgehen. Insofern hat Rosenkranz mit seinem bereits zitierten Katalog von fortschrittlichen Bestimmungen, die bei Hegel als philosophisch notwendig, weil der Vernunft entsprechend, ausgewiesen werden, ganz recht. Mag sich der Philosoph dabei in seinen Vorlesungen einer deutlicheren Sprache als in den *Grundlinien* bedient haben, werden doch auch dort entscheidende Desiderate der preußischen Verhältnisse sichtbar gemacht. Hatte Friedrich Wilhelm III. jedenfalls keine gesamtstaatliche Repräsentation mit Gesetzgebungs- und Steuerbewilligungskompetenz zugelassen (1823 hatte er lediglich Provinziallandtage mit sehr beschränkten Funktionen einrichten lassen), wird diese in Hegels Grundlinien ausdrücklich begründet:

> Das *ständische* Element hat die Bestimmung, dass die allgemeine Angelegenheit nicht nur *an sich*, sondern auch *für sich*, d.i. dass das Moment der subjektiven *formellen Freiheit* [...] darin zur Existenz komme.[26]

Wird die Aufteilung der „Ständeversammlung in zwei Kammern" in Hegels Vorlesungen vielleicht deutlicher angesprochen[27], findet sie sich der Sache nach (§§ 302 ff) und mindestens einmal auch ausdrücklich[28] in den *Grundlinien* wieder. Ebenso werden die „Öffentlichkeit der Ständeversammlungen" (§ 314) als „Bildungsmittel" (§ 315), als „die Bürger vorzüglich bildendes Schauspiel"[29] gefordert, die „öffentliche Meinung [...] geachtet"[30], und die Freiheit der Presse als mit der „konsequenten Verfassung" zusammenhängend zugelassen.[31] Zumindest die Vorlesung des Wintersemesters 1817/18 enthält zudem eine Begründung der Notwendigkeit einer Opposition innerhalb der Ständeversammlung:

> Eine Ständeversammlung kann erst insofern als in wirkliche Tätigkeit getreten angesehen werden, insofern sie eine Opposition in sich hat [...]

---

25 *Hegel-Henrich*, 238.
26 *TWA* 7, § 301, 468f.
27 Zum Beispiel: *Hegel-Wannenmann*, 230-232.
28 *TWA* 7, § 312, 481: „die ständische Versammlung wird sich somit in *zwei Kammern* teilen."
29 Ibid. § 315 Zusatz, 482.
30 Allerdings auch „verachtet": „Die öffentliche Meinung verdient daher ebenso *geachtet* als *verachtet* zu werden." (*TWA* 7, § 318, 485)
31 Vgl. *TWA* 7, § 319, 486-489 und Hegel-Wannenmann, 238-240.

Es muss daher notwendig eine Opposition innerhalb der Ständeversammlung selbst sein [...].³²

Mit allen diesen, gemessen an den zeitgenössischen preußischen Verhältnissen, fortschrittlichen Bestimmungen geht Hegel sicher bewusst in Richtung auf die Selbstbestimmung der Bürger, wie es im § 147 der Wannenmann Nachschrift besonders deutlich zum Ausdruck kommt:

> Das Hauptmoment in ihr [d.i. die gesetzgebende Gewalt; N.W.] ist das *Ständische*, damit das, was als allgemeiner Wille und als das Vernünftige festgesetzt wird, es nicht nur *zufällig* und *an sich*, sondern auch *für sich*, <u>mit tätigem Anteil und mit selbstbewusstem Zutrauen der allgemeinen Bürgerschaft</u> und mit Notwendigkeit sei.³³

Am Anfang seiner Lehre an der Universität Berlin, z.B. in der Naturrechts-Vorlesung des Wintersemesters 1828/29³⁴, als Hegel noch lebte, blieb auch Gans noch bei der Strategie seines Meisters, die preußischen Zustände nur implizit zu kritisieren, durch die Darstellung von verfassungsstaatlichen Institutionen, die der Vernunft entsprächen und an der Zeit wären, aber in Preußen noch nicht erreicht waren. Doch schon damals setzte er einen deutlichen Akzent, fast eine Provokation, indem er aus den wenigen Sätzen über die Opposition, die sich bei Hegel nur in der Wannenmann Nachschrift finden³⁵, einen eigenen Abschnitt macht „Die Lehre von der Opposition"³⁶, welcher nicht nur grundsätzlich die Notwendigkeit der Opposition betont, sondern recht drastische Formulierungen enthält wie „Hat der Staat es nicht mit der Opposition zu tun, so verfällt er in Faulheit."³⁷ Schon bald wurde Gans noch deutlicher: so benutzte er eine Rezension³⁸, dadurch ein wenig versteckt, dazu, das „Eigentümliche des preußischen Staates" seiner Zeit schonungslos offenzulegen: „Ist er ein absoluter, ein väterlicher, ein konstitutioneller Staat?"³⁹, fragt Gans und weist in der Folge⁴⁰ eine um die andere Bezeichnungen zurück. Dass Preußen

---

32 *Hegel-Wannenmann*, § 156, 240f.
33 *Hegel-Wannenmann*, § 147, 221 (meine Unterstreichung; N.W.).
34 Nach einer Nachschrift unbekannter Hand teilweise von Horst Schröder ediert; Gans (1971), 37-154.
35 *Hegel-Wannenmann*, § 156, 240f.; vgl. § 149, 226.
36 Gans (1971), 135-137.
37 Ibid., 136. Bei der „Faulheit" denkt Gans sicher nicht nur an ‚Trägheit', sondern eben auch an ‚Verrottung'.
38 Gans (1832), 450-479. Es handelte sich scheinbar um die Rezension des folgenden Werkes, wenn es in Wirklichkeit dabei um viel mehr ging: Gaertner (1832).
39 Gans (1832), 468.
40 Ibid., 468-471.

noch kein konstitutioneller Staat sei, begründet Gans damit, dass die Regierten dort weder „die Steuern bewilligen" noch „die Gesetze mit errichten". Im Hinblick auf die gesetzgebende Gewalt sei Preußen „wesentlich absolut". Es könne noch nicht einmal gesagt werden, dass schon „ein Grundstein zu der künftigen Verfassung gelegt worden wäre."[41] Für Gans offenbart sich Preußen (um 1830) letztlich als ein „vormundschaftlicher Staat", der seine Bürger als unreife Mündel behandelt, und den Gans mit einer Ironie geißelt, die an seine Jugendfreundschaft mit Heinrich Heine erinnert:

> Man muss sagen, der Bevormundete ist an sich frei – er ist es nur nicht in der Wirklichkeit; was er tun könnte und sollte, vollführt ein anderer, weil eben angenommen wird, er würde es nicht recht tun.[42]

Bei Gans geht es also nicht einfach um die Erörterung der Kategorie der konstitutionellen Monarchie als solche, sondern eher darum, konkret die damalige preußische Situation anzuprangern. Dass diese Kritik am Ort der Macht sehr wohl verstanden wurde, dürfte dazu geführt haben, dass Gans daraufhin die Publikation seiner *Beiträge* nicht fortsetzen konnte, wie er selbst vorsichtig aber für den zeitgenössischen Leser nachvollziehbar ausführt.[43] Für unser vorliegendes Thema ist indessen entscheidend, dass Gans als Ziel und Zukunftserwartung des Ausgangs aus der Unmündigkeit die „Emanzipation zu einer höheren und freieren Stellung" formuliert und damit junghegelianische Positionen der frühen 1840er Jahre ankündigt:

> Ein vormundschaftlicher Staat kann wie die Vormundschaft selbst nur immer eine Zeitlang dauern. Die Emanzipation zu einer höheren und freieren Stellung liegt in seiner Natur; er kann sie eine Zeitlang verleugnen und aufschieben, er kann sich aber nicht von ihrem endlichen Resultate befreien.[44]

Ein weiterer Text, „Ueber Opposition", der, wohl gegen Ende 1837 geschrieben, erstmalig 1838 publiziert wurde[45], scheint diese Kontinuitätslinie, etwa zu Arnold Ruge, deutlicher hervortreten zu lassen. In seiner Rechtfertigung der

---

41   Ibid., 470.
42   Ibid., 471f.
43   Ibid., Vorwort, III f. So kann es auch nicht überraschen, dass der mit Gans befreundete Karl August Varnhagen von Ense am 16. Mai 1839, also kurz nach Gans' Tod, in sein Tagebuch schrieb „Am Hofe sind sie recht froh, dass Gans tot ist, nun sind sie ihn los." Varnhagen von Ense (1861), 129.
44   Gans (1832), 476f.
45   Eduard Gans „Ueber Opposition", zuerst in Dorow (1838), 9f.; wenig später auch in Dorow (1841), 90-93; jetzt leichter zugänglich in Gans (1991), 155f.

Opposition im Staate rückt Gans sie nämlich, was nicht unbedingt selbstverständlich ist, nahe an Widerspruch und Negation heran:

> Wie kann dieser [der Staat] vermeinen, dass Widerstand gegen seine Fort- oder Rückschritte etwas anderes bedeute, als die Seite des Negativen, die im Handeln wie im Denken immer auftritt, und nach deren Besiegung oder Beseitigung erst die Wahrheit besteht.[46]

Für die eingeweihten Leser lag darin eine Anspielung auf Hegels *Wissenschaft der Logik*, genauer auf die Anmerkung 3 „Satz des Widerspruchs"[47], worin die produktive Rolle des Widerspruchs „gegen eines der Grundvorurteile der bisherigen Logik" mehrfach hervorgehoben wird: er ist z.B. „die Wurzel aller Bewegung und Lebendigkeit; nur insofern etwas in sich selber einen Widerspruch hat, bewegt es sich, hat Trieb und Tätigkeit."[48] Wenn Gans' Argumentationsweise tatsächlich eine Anspielung auf Hegels *Logik* enthält, könnte darin der Versuch liegen, diese Logik gegen die resignativen Züge der Hegelschen Rechtsphilosophie auszuspielen.

Diese Strategie scheinen Arnold Ruge und die Brüder Bruno und Edgar Bauer aufzugreifen. In seinem Aufsatz „Kritik und Partei" (1842)[49] bemüht sich jedenfalls auch Ruge darum, die produktive Kraft von Negation, Widerspruch und Gegensatz aus der „Wissenschaft" – wo die „Negation" bereits „als Moment anerkannt" sei und sich die Erkenntnis durchgesetzt habe, dass „nur dort überhaupt Entwicklung und Leben existiert, wo noch Gegensätze auszugleichen sind, wo es Kampf kostet und Überwindung"[50] – auf die Politik zu übertragen, woraus sich für ihn die Konsequenz ergäbe, gegensätzliche politische Parteien zuzulassen:

> Jedenfalls ist das Freigeben und Konstituieren der Parteibewegung in der Politik ganz das, was das Freigeben der geistigen Gegensätze in der Wissenschaft, die Freiheit der Forschung und der Geltendmachung des Gedankens in der Theorie ist.[51]

Im IV. Abschnitt der anonymen Broschüre des Jahres 1843, *Staat Religion und Parthei*[52], welche gelegentlich Bruno Bauer zugeschrieben wird, aber eher

---

46 Gans (1991), 156.
47 *TWA* 6, 74-80.
48 Ibid., 75.
49 Ruge (1842), 1175-1182.
50 Ibid., 1179.
51 Ibid., 1182.
52 Anon. (1843).

von seinem Bruder Edgar stammt, wird, ohne Gans zu nennen, wiederum der Gedanke einer legitimen Opposition aufgegriffen, welche, wie bei Ruge, als „Partei" bezeichnet wird:

> Parteien wird es geben, so lange es Staaten gibt, aber es ist ein großer Unterschied, ob die Parteien anerkannt werden, indem man sie alle zur Sprache kommen lässt, oder ob nur Eine als die einzig berechtigte angesehen und sie daher ganz mit dem Staate identifiziert wird. [... Das wahre Leben des Staates] besteht in nichts Anderem, als in dem gegenseitigen Wetteifer der Parteien, welcher, da jede Partei sich aussprechen und alle ihre Kräfte entwickeln darf, auch stets den wahren Gehalt, den echten Geist des Staates offenbaren wird.[53]

Gerade der Gegensatz, die erlaubte Auseinandersetzung der Parteien würde die Zukunftsperspektive einer Selbstbestimmung der Bürger näherbringen und diese Perspektive wird, wenn nicht explizit mit den Namen von Hegel oder Gans verbunden, so doch mit der Position des „Philosophen" identifiziert:

> Wie der Philosoph das ganze Gebiet des Wissens nach jenem obersten Satze von der selbstständigen Hoheit des menschlichen Geistes regelt, so begnügt sich auch das philosophisch-politische Bewusstsein nicht mehr mit der gläubigen Unterwürfigkeit, sondern es will in seiner Regierung den Ausdruck seiner selbst sehen; es verlangt eine Selbstregierung.[54]

Armut, soziale Frage und die Erhebung des Pöbels zur Sittlichkeit

Über Hegels Analysen der Armut und seine Diskussion von Lösungsansätzen ist schon oft geschrieben und gestritten worden und es würde zu weit führen, diese ganze Debatte hier wieder aufzurollen.[55] Nur an zwei Punkte, über die in der Forschung ein weitgehender Konsens herrscht, sei hier erinnert:

(1) Für Hegel ist die Armut nicht mehr, wie deren ‚klassische' Form (Armut, die es immer gab), nur Resultat kontingenter Ereignisse[56], wie Missernten, Zerstörungen durch Kriege, krankheits- oder unfallbedingte Arbeitsunfähigkeit, sondern eine Konsequenz der „bürgerlichen Gesellschaft" selbst, gerade wenn diese „sich in ungehinderter Wirksamkeit befindet"[57]. Da die „bürgerliche

---

53 Ibid., 19f.
54 Ibid., 18.
55 Aus der jüngsten Literatur seien hervorgehoben: Ruda (2011); Schildbach (2018).
56 TWA 7, § 241, 387: „zufällige, physische und in den äußeren Verhältnissen liegende Umstände".
57 TWA 7, § 243, 389.

Gesellschaft" selbst eine „Schöpfung [...] der modernen Welt"[58] ist, denkt Hegel offenbar quantitativ an ein neues Ausmaß und qualitativ an neue Formen der Verarmung und materiellen Bedrohung, wie sie mit der Industrialisierung assoziiert werden. Benutzt er selbst den Begriff „soziale Frage" noch nicht – dieser scheint sich im Deutschen erst in den späten 1830er und frühen 1840er Jahren, mit Autoren wie Heinrich Heine und Lorenz von Stein, also nach Hegels Tod, eingebürgert zu haben[59] –, hat er die Sachverhalte, für die knapp zwanzig Jahre später der Begriff „soziale Frage" geläufig wurde, schon in seiner Rechtsphilosophie „gründlich erfasst", wie z.B. S. Avineri ausführt.[60] Dass die Armut (bei Hegel wörtlich „Abhängigkeit und Not") wie „die Anhäufung der Reichtümer"[61] konsequent und mit Notwendigkeit durch die „bürgerliche Gesellschaft" erzeugt wird, darf sicher als eine Innovation bezeichnet werden.

(2) Für Hegel ist wichtig, dass Armut nicht nur ein objektiver Sachverhalt (wie immer er genau definiert wird), sondern auch ein subjektives Befinden ist[62], welches er unter der Bezeichnung „Gesinnung"[63] behandelt, also ein unmittelbares Betroffensein beinhaltet. Seine Sensibilität gegenüber den psycho-sozialen Konsequenzen[64], den Demütigungen, die mit der Armut einhergehen, stammt aus dieser Einsicht. Dass Hegel die öffentliche Fürsorge für die Bedürftigen stärken und die private Mildtätigkeit „entbehrlicher [...] machen" will[65], dürfte nicht nur mit der größeren Effizienz der staatlich organisierten Armenpflege zusammenhängen[66], sondern auch seiner Intention entsprechen, den Bettlern, die z.B. vor der Kirchentür stehen, die Erniedrigung zu ersparen. Denn auch für ihn geht es nicht nur um Subsistenz und Lebensstandard, sondern, um Dostojewskis Titel aufzugreifen, um die

---

58 Ibid., § 182 Zusatz, 339; vgl. auch den Zusatz – ein Satz, der später noch in einem anderen Kontext behandelt wird – zum § 244: „Die wichtige Frage, wie der Armut abzuhelfen sei, ist eine *vorzüglich die modernen Gesellschaften* bewegende und quälende." (TWA 7, 390 (meine Hervorhebung; N.W.))
59 Vgl. Waszek (2018), besonders 246-250.
60 Avineri (1976), 185: „Nur wenige Personen haben um 1820 die Situation der modernen Industriegesellschaft [...] so gründlich erfasst wie Hegel."
61 TWA 7, § 243, 389.
62 Am Anfang des § 242 spricht Hegel ausdrücklich „das Subjektive der Armut" an: TWA 7, 388.
63 Zum Beispiel: TWA 7, § 241, 388 und § 244 Zusatz, 389.
64 TWA 7, § 241, 388: „sie aller Vorteile der Gesellschaft, Erwerbsfähigkeit von Geschicklichkeit und Bildung überhaupt, auch der Rechtspflege, Gesundheitssorge, selbst des Trostes der Religion usf. mehr oder weniger verlustig macht."
65 Ibid. § 242, 388: „in der Notdurft und ihrer Abhilfe das Allgemeine herauszufinden und zu veranstalten und jene Hilfe [private Mildtätigkeit; NW.] entbehrlicher zu machen."
66 Weil die private Mildtätigkeit „für sich und in ihren Wirkungen von der Zufälligkeit abhängt" (ibid.).

‚Erniedrigten und Beleidigten'. Damit nimmt Hegel viele Aspekte vorweg, die in der aktuellen Armutsforschung wieder zum Tragen kommen.[67]

Zudem ergeben sich (oder können sich zumindest ergeben, wenn dieser Tendenz nicht entgegengesteuert wird) politische Konsequenzen aus der Armut.[68] Wie bereits ausgeführt, steht die „Freiheit" im Mittelpunkt von Hegels Denken. Ihm war aber schmerzhaft bewusst, dass für die Armen Gefahr besteht, dass sie ihren Zugang zur politischen Partizipation und zur „Freiheit" verlieren. Mit der „Not", führt Hegel aus, hängt „die Unfähigkeit der Empfindung und des Genusses der weiteren Freiheiten und besonders der geistigen Vorteile der bürgerlichen Gesellschaft" zusammen.[69] Sozialstaatliche Maßnahmen, wie sie Hegel anregt, sind zentral auf diese Bedrohung ausgerichtet, keineswegs auf die Herstellung materieller Gleichheit. In der zeitgenössischen politischen Philosophie und Verfassungstheorie begegnet uns diese Problematik unter der Bezeichnung „freiheitsfunktionaler Sozialstaat"[70]. Vereinfacht gesagt, geht es bei diesem Ausdruck um einen Sozialstaat im Dienste der Freiheit, wie es auch Hans Michael Heinig im Titel seines lehrreichen Buches ausspricht.[71] Wenn es einem ausufernden, paternalistischen Wohlfahrtsstaat zwar (aber eben auch nur) um die Versorgung der Bedürftigen geht, muss der „freiheitsfunktionale Sozialstaat" der gesellschaftlich ständig entstehenden Ungleichheit entgegentreten, damit Freiheit und Chancengleichheit der Bürger bewahrt bleiben bzw. wiederhergestellt werden. Wenngleich der große philosophiegeschichtliche Bezugspunkt der Debatte um den „freiheitsfunktionalen Sozialstaat" Kant blieb[72], passt auch Hegel nicht nur ausgezeichnet in diesen Kontext, man könnte mit Heinig sogar sagen, dass Hegels „sittliche[r] Staat gleichsam *per se* ein freiheitsfunktionaler Sozialstaat"[73] ist.

Trotz dieser wichtigen Entwicklungen, denen hier nicht weiter nachgegangen werden kann, glaubte Gans, über seinen Meister hinausgehen zu müssen. Seine diesbezügliche Haltung lässt sich mit Hilfe schon älterer und neuerer Hegel-Forschungen verständlicher machen. Dürfte es auch gerade Hegel selbst gewesen sein, der seine Schüler durch seine subtile Analyse der

---

67 Vgl. hierzu Schildbach (2018), 9-15, 331ff.
68 In ihrer neuen Studie thematisiert Schildbach (2018, 12-15 u.ö.) diese Konsequenzen unter dem Stichwort „Selbstverwirklichung" und deren notwendiger Bedingungen.
69 *TWA* 7, § 243, 389.
70 Meines Wissens hat Ottfried Höffe den Begriff in den späten 1970er und frühen 1980er Jahren geprägt und verbreitet; z.B. Höffe (1981), hier 241, 255; ehe er dann von anderen Philosophen (Wolfgang Kersting) und Juristen aufgegriffen und weiterentwickelt wurde.
71 Heinig (2008).
72 Waszek (2011).
73 Heinig (2008), 234.

„bürgerlichen Gesellschaft", mit ihren Möglichkeiten, aber auch ihren Grenzen, auf deren Aporien aufmerksam machte[74], erschienen ihnen, und Gans vermutlich an erster Stelle, Hegels Lösungen unbefriedigend. Die Hegel-Forschung hat diese Skepsis oft geteilt. Vor fast 50 Jahren (1972, dt. 1976) hatte schon S. Avineri ausgeführt, dass Hegel

> offen zugegeben [habe], dass er für die Probleme der modernen bürgerlichen Gesellschaft keine Lösung sieht. Das ist der einzige Punkt in seinem System, an dem Hegel ein Problem sieht – und es offen lässt. Obgleich seine Theorie des Staates darauf abzielt, die widerstreitenden Interessen der bürgerlichen Gesellschaft unter einem gemeinsamen Band zu integrieren, weiß er zu dem Problem der Armut letztlich nicht mehr zu sagen als dass es ‚eine vorzüglich die modernen Gesellschaften bewegende und quälende'[75] Frage ist. An keiner Stelle sonst lässt Hegel ein Problem in dieser Weise ungelöst.[76]

In jüngster Zeit hat Frank Ruda in seinem glänzenden Debüt[77] Hegels Überlegungen zur Linderung der Armut rekonstruiert und daraus sieben Arten von Maßnahmen analytisch unterschieden.[78] Auch in der Art, wie Ruda unter Heranziehung aller Quellen (auch der diversen Vorlesungsnachschriften) Hegels Differenzierung zwischen der ‚bloßen' Armut als materielle Not, in Hegels Sprache „Armut an sich"[79], und einer besonderen Schicht der Armen, die Hegel „Pöbel" nennt, nachzeichnet, liegt eine Stärke seines Buches.[80] Schafft die „Not", die eine größere Gruppe betrifft, die Bedingungen für die Entstehung einer kleineren Anzahl von Armen, die Hegel „Pöbel" nennt, muss dabei doch zu den objektiven Voraussetzungen noch eine „Gesinnung" treten, die dann den „Pöbel" konstituiert. Diese „Gesinnung" des „Pöbels" wird durch die „Abwerfung" von „Ehre und Scham", „innere Empörung"[81] und „eine Skepsis bis Ablehnung gegenüber den gesellschaftlichen und politischen Institutionen"[82] charakterisiert. Wenngleich Hegel alle Lösungsansätze des Problems, die er

---

74 Vgl. Waszek (2007), 21-24.
75 Das Zitat entstammt dem Zusatz zum § 244 (*TWA* 7, 390).
76 Avineri (1976), 185f.; in der englischen Originalausgabe (1972), 154.
77 Ruda (2011); die Studie geht auf seine Dissertation des Jahres 2009 an der Universität Potsdam zurück.
78 Vgl. ibid., 37-59.
79 *TWA* 7, Zusatz zum § 244, 389.
80 Ruda (2011), 65-81; aus diesem Kapitel ist die Erinnerung daran, dass es für Hegel auch „reichen Pöbel" gibt, besonders hervorzuheben, weil die einschlägigen Ausführungen – besonders deutlich in *Hegel-Hoppe Die Philosophie des Rechts: Vorlesung von 1821/22*, § 244, 222 – sonst oft vernachlässigt werden. Diesen Ausführungen über den „reichen Pöbel" nachzugehen, muss ich mir für eine andere Gelegenheit vorbehalten.
81 *TWA* 7, § 245, 390 und Zusatz zum § 244, 389.
82 Wie Schildbach (2018), 74 formuliert.

anführt, gleich selbst auch kritisch diskutiert (ist dies nicht gerade Teil seiner argumentativen Stärke?), scheint es überzogen zu behaupten, dass sie alle scheitern, worauf Rudas Untersuchung hinausläuft. Gegen Ruda könnte Hegel mit Hinweisen auf seine „Redlichkeit" (Avineri) oder auf seinen Pragmatismus (Waszek) verteidigt werden.[83] Zudem hat Hegel jenseits des „objektiven" im Systemteil des „absoluten Geistes" noch weitere Lösungsansätze bereitgestellt. Wenn der „Pöbel" u.a. durch eine entsittlichte Gesinnung charakterisiert wird, dann muss auch die Aufhebung der sittlichen Entzweiung, die im Abschluss des Systems, dem „absoluten Geist" (Kunst, Religion, Philosophie) intendiert ist, für die Untersuchung von Armut und Pöbel relevant werden.[84]

Ziel der letzten Ausführungen war nicht so sehr die Auseinandersetzung mit Rudas Studie, auch wenn diese es verdienen würde, als vielmehr der Nachweis, wie aktuell Eduard Gans mit seiner Haltung geblieben ist.[85] Hielt Hegel die Erzeugung des „Pöbels" für perennierend, will Gans diese „Kruste der bürgerlichen Gesellschaft dünner"[86] machen, ja, sie sogar „aufheben":

> Muss der Pöbel bleiben? Ist er eine notwendige Existenz? [...] Die Polizei muss daher wirken können, dass kein Pöbel mehr existiert. Er ist ein Faktum, aber kein Recht. Man muss zu den Gründen des Faktums kommen können und sie aufheben.[87]

Dass bei dieser optimistischen Einschätzung von Gans seine Rezeption der saint-simonistischen Schule, wie sich diese besonders in dem Sammelwerk *Doctrine de Saint-Simon*[88] ausgedrückt hat, eine wichtige Rolle gespielt hat, ist schon öfter untersucht worden[89] und soll hier nicht erneut aufgerollt werden. Betont sei indessen, dass die von Gans intendierte „Aufhebung" der Ursachen der Entstehung des „Pöbels" eine Innovation darstellt und ein zukunftsträchtiges Bewusstsein der ‚sozialen Frage' innerhalb der Hegelschen Schule markiert. Gans verortet seine Überlegungen, insofern lehnt er sich noch an Hegel an, am Ende seiner Ausführungen zur bürgerlichen Gesellschaft, also bei „Polizei" und Korporation. Als Teil der öffentlichen Gewalt

---

83 Vgl. Avineri (1976), 185; in der englischen Originalausgabe (1972), 154. Waszek (2007), 22 f.
84 Auch daran erinnert die Studie von Schildbach (2018), 281-330.
85 Tatsächlich zitiert Ruda ((2011), 187) indirekt aus Riedel und ohne dessen Namen zu nennen!) ein gewichtiges Wort von Gans als Motto seines 11. Kapitels, ohne dessen Ausführungen näher darzustellen.
86 Gans (1836/1995), 100.
87 Gans (1981), 92; vgl. Gans (2005), 388 (Anm. 252).
88 Vgl. [Saint-Simon, aus der Schule von](1830) – dt. Ausgabe: Salomon (1962).
89 Zum Beispiel von Bienenstock (2002), 153-175 – englische Fassung in Moggach (2011), 164-178.

hat die „Armenpolizei" die besondere Pflicht, „für die Armen zu sorgen"[90]. Sie organisiert also die öffentliche Fürsorge für die Armen. Die dazu durchgeführten „Veranstaltungen sind vielfältig" und Gans behandelt nur Beispiele, betont aber, dass „Armut durch Arbeit zu heben" gegenüber einer bloßen Unterstützung („Armentaxe") vorzuziehen und dass dafür zu sorgen sei, dass „wer Arbeit haben will, Arbeit finden kann".[91]

Trotz ihres großen Wirkungskreises sei die „Polizei" aber bloß eine „äußerliche Vorsorge" und „nicht versittlichend"[92]. Die Versittlichung bleibt der „freien Korporation" vorbehalten, eine Institution, die Gans zwar wiederum von Hegel übernimmt, doch deren fortschrittlichen Sinn (im Unterschied zu den geschlossenen Zünften des Mittelalters) er deutlicher hervortreten lässt und mit Anregungen aus dem schillernden Assoziationsbegriff der Saint-Simonisten verbindet. Gans' „freie Korporationen" führen zur „Vergesellschaftlichung der zerrissenen Teile der bürgerlichen Gesellschaft". Sie verleihen einem atomisierten Haufen eine Standesehre, „das Bewusstsein, einem Allgemeinen anzugehören, und dadurch etwas zu erlangen, was sonst nicht in ihm ist"[93], sie erfüllen eine wichtige (auch politische) Bildungsfunktion und schaffen somit die subjektiven und objektiven Bedingungen zu einer weitergehenden Partizipation in Richtung auf Selbstbestimmung.

An einer Stelle scheint mir Gans dieses Überschreiten von Hegels Lehre durch seine Textauswahl und redaktionellen Eingriffe sogar in einem der „Zusätze", die er seiner Ausgabe (1833) von Hegels Rechtsphilosophie beigab, zu artikulieren.

> Man hat seit einiger Zeit immer von oben her organisiert [...] aber das Untere, das Massenhafte des Ganzen ist leicht mehr oder weniger unorganisch gelassen; und doch ist es höchst wichtig, dass es organisch werde, denn nur so ist es Macht, ist es Gewalt, sonst ist es nur ein Haufen, eine Menge von zersplitterten Atomen. Die berechtigte Gewalt ist nur im organischen Zustande der besonderen Sphären vorhanden.[94]

Wenn er ziemlich unverblümt eine Organisation ‚von unten' fordert, welche einem zersplitterten Haufen zu einem größeren Maß an Selbstbestimmung verhelfen soll, dann scheint Gans mit seinen Termini „freie Korporation" und „Assoziation" Organisationsformen zu antizipieren[95], die sich in Deutschland

---

90   Gans (2005), 195.
91   Ibid.
92   Gans (1981), 93.
93   Ibid.
94   TWA 7, Zusatz zum § 290, 460.
95   Eine These, die ich erstmal 1988 publizieren konnte: Waszek (1988), 355-363.

erst viel später als ‚Gewerkschaften' konstituieren und artikulieren durften.[96] Zentrale Aufgabenbestimmungen einer Gewerkschaft wie kollektive Tarifverhandlungen, Vertretung der sozialen und kulturellen Interessen der Arbeitnehmer sind bei Gans jedenfalls bereits vorweggenommen. Ohne behaupten zu wollen, dass sich die Berliner Zigarrendreher Texte von Gans vorlesen ließen,[97] ist es zumindest eine bemerkenswerte Koinzidenz, dass der Erste Zigarrenarbeiter-Kongress (Berlin, 25.-29. September 1848), oft als eine der ersten frühgewerkschaftlichen Verbindungen in Deutschland gewürdigt, sich nicht nur unter dem Namen „*Assoziation* der Zigarren-Arbeiter Deutschlands" konstituiert, sondern in seinen Statuten des folgenden Jahres (1849) neben dem „materiellen Wohl" der Arbeiter auch weitergehende Ziele wie deren Bildung und „moralisches" Wohl befördern will[98] – lauter Ziele und Forderungen, die Gans schon zehn Jahre vorher artikuliert hatte.

Literatur

A) *Quellen und zeitgenössische Texte*

Anon. [manchmal Bruno Bauer zugeschrieben, aber eher von Edgar Bauer], *Staat Religion und Parthei*. Leipzig: O. Wigand, 1843.

Gaertner, Gustav Friedrich, *Kritik des Untersuchungs-Principes des Preußischen Civil-Processes*. Berlin: Duncker & Humblot, 1832.

Gans, Eduard, *Das Erbrecht in weltgeschichtlicher Entwickelung. Eine Abhandlung der Universalrechtsgeschichte*. 4 Bände. Berlin: Maurer, 1824-1825, Stuttgart & Tübingen: Cotta, 1829-1835.

– „Ueber die Untersuchungsmaxime des Preußischen Civilprocesses (Eine Rezension), in: *Beiträge zur Revision der preußischen Gesetzgebung*, hrsg. von Eduard Gans, Berlin: Duncker & Humblot, 1832, 450-479.

– *Rückblicke auf Personen und Zustände*, Berlin: Veit, 1836; Nachdruck mit Einleitung, Anmerkungen und Bibliographie von Norbert Waszek, Stuttgart-Bad Cannstatt: Frommann-Holzboog, 1995.

– *Philosophische Schriften*, hrsg. und eingeleitet von Horst Schröder, Glashütten im Taunus: Auvermann, 1971.

---

96 Erst nach Gewährung der ‚Koalitionsfreiheit' in der „Gewerbeordnung" des Norddeutschen Bundes (1869) und „Reichsgewerbeordnung" von 1872; vgl. Wehler (1995), 160.

97 Belegt, ja geradezu legendär, ist nicht nur die Gestalt des „Vorlesers" in der Zigarrenherstellung, sondern auch, dass gern aus den Texten von oppositionellen und radikalen Autoren vorgelesen wurde; vgl. Schröder (2011), besonders 208 f.; Dahms (1965), 72 u.ö.

98 „Statut der Assoziation der Zigarren Arbeiter Deutschlands" (vom 13. September 1849), zitiert nach Schröder (2011), 232f.; vgl. Dahms (1965), 21-30.

- *Naturrecht und Universalrechtsgeschichte*, hrsg. von Manfred Riedel, Stuttgart: Klett-Cotta, 1981.
- *Eduard Gans (1797-1839): Hegelianer – Jude – Europäer. Texte und Dokumente*, hrsg. von Norbert Waszek, Frankfurt/Main: Peter Lang, 1991.
- *Naturrecht und Universalrechtsgeschichte: Vorlesungen nach G. W. F. Hegel*, hrsg. von Johann Braun, Tübingen: Mohr Siebeck, 2005.

Hegel, Georg Wilhelm Friedrich, *Theorie Werkausgabe*. 20 Bände, Frankfurt/Main: Suhrkamp, 1969-71. (*TWA*)
- *Die Philosophie des Rechts: Die Mitschriften Wannenmann Heidelberg 1817/18 und Homeyer Berlin 1818/19*, hrsg. von Karl-Heinz Ilting, Stuttgart: Klett-Cotta, 1983.
- *Philosophie des Rechts: die Vorlesung von 1819/20 in einer Nachschrift*, hrsg. von Dieter Henrich, Frankfurt/Main.: Suhrkamp, 1983. (*Hegel-Henrich*)
- *Vorlesungen über Naturrecht und Staatswissenschaft, Heidelberg 1817/18, mit Nachträgen aus der Vorlesung 1818/19, nachgeschrieben von P. Wannenmann*, hrsg. von [den Mitarbeitern des Hegel-Archivs], Hamburg: Meiner, 1983. (*Hegel-Wannenmann*)
- *Die Philosophie des Rechts: Vorlesung von 1821/22*, hrsg. von Hansgeorg Hoppe. Frankfurt/Main: Suhrkamp, 2005. (*Hegel-Hoppe*)

Rosenkranz, Karl, *Hegel als deutscher Nationalphilosoph*, Leipzig: Duncker & Humblot, 1870.

Ruge, Arnold, „Kritik und Partei. Der Vorwurf gegen die neueste Geistesentwicklung", in: *Deutsche Jahrbücher für Wissenschaft und Kunst*. 5, 1842, S. 1175-1182.

[Saint-Simon, aus der Schule von], *Doctrine de Saint-Simon: exposition*. Paris: Au bureau de l'Organisateur et du Globe, 1830 – dt. Ausgabe: *Die Lehre Saint-Simons*, übersetzt von Susanne Stöber, hrsg. von Gottfried Salomon, Neuwied: Luchterhand, 1962.

Varnhagen von Ense, Karl August, *Tagebücher*, Bd. 1, Leipzig: Brockhaus, 1861.

B) *Sekundärliteratur*

Avineri, Shlomo, *Hegel's Theory of the Modern State*, Cambridge: Cambridge University Press, 1972 – dt. Übersetzung von Rolf und Renate Wiggershaus, *Hegels Theorie des modernen Staates*, Frankfurt/Main: Suhrkamp, 1976.

Bienenstock, Myriam, „Die ‚soziale Frage' im französisch-deutschen Kulturaustausch: Gans, Marx und die deutsche Saint-Simon Rezeption", in: *Eduard Gans (1797-1839). Politischer Professor zwischen Restauration und Vormärz*, hrsg. von Reinhard Blänkner et alii. Leipzig: Universitätsverlag, 2002, 153-175 – englische Fassung: "Between Hegel and Marx: Eduard Gans on the 'Social Question'", in: *Politics, Religion, and Art: Hegelian Debates*, hrsg. von Douglas Moggach, Evanston/IL: Northwestern University Press, 2011, S. 164-178.

Braun, Johann, *Judentum, Jurisprudenz und Philosophie: Bilder aus dem Leben des Juristen Eduard Gans (1797-1839)*, Baden-Baden: Nomos, 1997.

Dahms, Ferdinand, *Geschichte der Tabakarbeiterbewegung*, Hamburg: Weinacht, 1965.

Dorow, Wilhelm (Hrsg.), *Facsimile von Handschriften berühmter Männer und Frauen aus der Sammlung des Herausgebers*, bekannt gemacht und mit historischen Erläuterungen begleitet von Wilhelm Dorow, Teil 4, Berlin: Sachse, 1838.

– *Denkschriften und Briefe zur Charakteristik der Welt und Litteratur*, N.F. Bd. 5, Berlin: Duncker, 1841.

Haym, Rudolf, *Hegel und seine Zeit. Vorlesungen über Entstehung und Entwickelung, Wesen und Werth der Hegel'schen Philosophie*, Berlin: Gaertner, 1857.

Heinig, Hans Michael, *Der Sozialstaat im Dienst der Freiheit: zur Formel vom „sozialen" Staat in Art. 20 Abs. 1 GG*, Tübingen: Mohr Siebeck, 2008.

Höffe, Otfried, „Die Menschenrechte als Legitimation und kritischer Maßstab der Demokratie", in: *Menschenrechte und Demokratie*, hrsg. von Johannes Schwartländer. Kehl am Rhein: Engel, 1981, S. 241-274.

Lübbe, Hermann, *Politische Philosophie in Deutschland: Studien zu ihrer Geschichte* [1963], 2. Auflage, München: DTV, 1974.

Lucas, Hans-Christian, „Wer hat die Verfassung zu machen, das Volk oder wer anders?: zu Hegels Verständnis der konstitutionellen Monarchie zwischen Heidelberg und Berlin", in: *Hegels Rechtsphilosophie im Zusammenhang der europäischen Verfassungsgeschichte*, hrsg. von Hans-Christian Lucas und Otto Pöggeler, Stuttgart-Bad Cannstatt: Frommann-Holzboog, 1986, S. 175-220.

Moggach, Douglas: *The philosophy and politics of Bruno Bauer*, Cambridge: Cambridge University Press, 2003.

Pippin, Robert, „Hegel, Freedom, The Will. *The Philosophy of Right*: §§ 1-33 – 23", in: *G.W.F. Hegel, Grundlinien der Philosophie des Rechts* [Klassiker auslegen, Bd. 9], hrsg. von Ludwig Siep, Berlin: Akademie Verlag, 1997, S. 31-53.

Quante, Michael, „„Die Persönlichkeit des Willens' als Prinzip des abstrakten Rechts. Eine Analyse der begriffslogischen Struktur der §§ 34-40 von Hegels *Grundlinien der Philosophie des Rechts*", in: *G. W. F. Hegel, Grundlinien der Philosophie des Rechts* [Klassiker auslegen, Bd. 9], hrsg. von Ludwig Siep. Berlin: Akademie Verlag, 1997, S. 55-72.

Ritter, Joachim, „Person und Eigentum. Zu Hegels *Grundlinien der Philosophie des Rechts* (§§ 34-81)", in: *G. W. F. Hegel, Grundlinien der Philosophie des Rechts* [Klassiker auslegen, Bd. 9], hrsg. von Ludwig Siep, Berlin: Akademie Verlag, 1997, S. 73-94.

Ruda, Frank, *Hegels Pöbel: eine Untersuchung der "Grundlinien der Philosophie des Rechts*, Konstanz: Konstanz University Press, 2011.

Schildbach, Ina, *Armut als Unrecht: Zur Aktualität von Hegels Perspektive auf Selbstverwirklichung, Armut und Sozialstaat*, Bielefeld: transcript, 2018.

Schröder, Wilhelm Heinz, „Arbeit und Organisationsverhalten der Zigarrenarbeiter in Deutschland im 19. und frühen 20. Jahrhundert: ein Beitrag zur Erklärung der Führungsrolle der Zigarrenarbeiter in der frühen politischen Arbeiterbewegung", in: *Historical Social Research*, Supplement 23, 2011, S. 195-251.

Siep, Ludwig (Hrsg.), *G. W. F. Hegel, Grundlinien der Philosophie des Rechts* [Klassiker auslegen, Bd. 9], Berlin: Akademie Verlag, 1997.

Stamm-Kuhlmann, Thomas, *König in Preußens großer Zeit. Friedrich Wilhelm III., der Melancholiker auf dem Thron*, Berlin: Siedler, 1992.

Waszek, Norbert, „Eduard Gans und die Armut: Von Hegel und Saint-Simon zu frühgewerkschaftlichen Forderungen", in: *Hegel-Jahrbuch 1988*, Bochum, 1988, S. 355-363.

– „Saint-Simonismus und Hegelianismus – Einführung in das Forschungsfeld", in: *Hegelianismus und Saint-Simonismus*, hrsg. von Hans-Christoph Schmidt am Busch, Ludwig Siep, Hans-Ulrich Thamer & Norbert Waszek, Paderborn: Mentis, 2007, S. 13-35.

– „Peut-on, avec Kant, passer de l'État de droit (*Rechtsstaat*) à un État de droit social (*sozialer Rechtsstaat*)?", in: *Kant: Anthropologie et l'Histoire*, hrsg. von Olivier Agard und Françoise Lartillot, Paris: L'Harmattan, 2011, S. 185-200.

„War Eduard Gans (1797-1839) der erste Links- oder Junghegelianer?", in: *Die linken Hegelianer. Studien zum Verhältnis von Religion und Politik im Vormärz*, hrsg. von Michael Quante und Amir Mohseni, Paderborn: Fink, 2015, S. 29-51.

– „Die soziale Frage bei Lorenz von Stein", in: *La Question sociale à l'ordre du jour. Sociétés et économie entre représentations et conceptualisation: France/Allemagne 1830-1848*, hrsg. von Wolfgang Fink et al. Reims: EPURE, 2018, S. 245-279.

Wehler, Hans-Ulrich: *Deutsche Gesellschaftsgeschichte, Band 3: Von der „Deutschen Doppelrevolution" bis zum Beginn des Ersten Weltkrieges 1845/49-1914*, München: C.H. Beck, 1995.

'The Republic of Self-Consciousness'
Bruno Bauer's Post-Kantian Perfectionism

Michael Kuur Sørensen & Douglas Moggach

In the decade preceding the Revolutions of 1848, the Left-Hegelian Bruno Bauer developed a paradigmatic post-Kantian perfectionist ethical programme, and applied it in his relentless critique of religion and politics, in pursuit of a new republicanism, the impending 'Republic of Self-Consciousness' [‚Republik des Selbstbewußtseins'].[1] While he took his concrete engagements and polemics to be exemplifications of his perfectionist ethics, the critical potential of the theory exceeds the particular applications that Bauer himself made of it in the heated polemics of the *Vormärz*.

Post-Kantian Perfectionist Ethics

Bauer's post-Kantian perfectionism is an ethical theory whose supervening end is the promotion of freedom and the conditions for its exercise. It differs from earlier perfectionisms in that it accepts the Kantian critique of *eudaimonia* or happiness as the appropriate goal of ethical action,[2] but does not take this critique as precluding all forms of teleological ethics. Freedom or autonomy, as self-determining action in the objective world, and as realising itself in political and social relations and institutions, becomes the directive ethical value, and the criterion for critical assessment of claims to legitimacy. The aim is to expand the capacity for rational agency and autonomous thinking, and not primarily to further any substantive idea of happiness or thriving.[3] In the Kantian triplicity of practical reason, encompassing happiness, right, and morality,[4] the domain of post-Kantian perfectionism is in the operation of right and rightful interaction. The question of right is the use of freedom in its external aspect, and the appropriate institutional forms through which this freedom can be exercised, singly and collectively.

---

1 *Anekdota* II, 111. *Anekdota* II, 150: „es werden Staaten kommen, die sich zuversichtlich auf der Freiheit des Selbstbewußtseins gründen werden." Further on Bauer's republicanism, see Barbour (2016), 77-92.
2 *AA* III, 441-43.
3 Moggach (2018).
4 *AA* VI, 203-243.

In Bauer's elaboration, the theory functions in two dimensions. At the meta-ethical level, it offers an account of historical development as the unfolding of human self-consciousness to higher levels of reason and autonomy, achieved through struggle and opposition. For Bauer this position was supported by an interpretation of Hegel that emphasised the concept of self-consciousness as the propulsive force of history: "Self-consciousness, reason means everything to him [Hegel]; it is the aim of all history as well as the medium and material through which it unfolds." ["Das Selbstbewußtsein, die Vernuft ist ihm Alles, Zweck, Mittel und Material der Geschichte"][5] The higher levels of reason are achieved by actors self-consciously confronting the existing order, theoretically and practically: holding to account its claims to validity, and acting to change it. The struggle reveals the potential for establishing a new, but always provisional, political and social system, where freedom and autonomous action can be expanded. But Bauer's stringent ethical programme placed still further demands on the historical subject. Not only the institutional network, but the self, is to refashion its aims and values in the light of emancipatory reason. Universal self-consciousness, a term that Bauer distilled from Hegel, becomes the critical examination of particular interests, one's own and those of others, in order to assess their compatibility with the demands of historical progress, and thus to test their admissibility and legitimacy. In this version of post-Kantian perfectionism, acts are validated by their contribution to the expanding space of freedom;[6] all discourses and institutions are open to rational assessment and challenge. Nothing is valid simply in virtue of its positive existence, or because some group or individual happens to will it, but only if it stands the test of critical interrogation, as contributing to the space of free activity for all. Following Kant's famous dictum in the *Critique of Pure Reason*, the defining characteristic of the modern world is that all existing institutions and principles are required to justify themselves in the light of critical rationality,[7] through rational discourse. In Bauer's usage, the Kantian moral "ought" is historicised and politicised through its application to social and juridical categories and forms. "Only the 'ought' is true," ["Das Sollen aber ist allein das Wahre."],[8] Bauer asserted, but this ought now refers to the historical process of bringing the objective order under the command of reason, which itself evolves in contestation. Ethics is no longer a question of a timeless duty, but is bound up with the critique of existing institutions

---

5 Bauer (1842), 162.
6 Moggach (2011).
7 *AA* IV, 9 n.
8 Bauer (1841), 82.

as hindrances or as facilitators of freedom. Although his underlying theory of history is not deterministic, in that it admits no metaphysical guarantees of progress, Bauer held that history tends in general to uncover new domains of autonomous action, whose attainment depends on free, unconstrained human effort and choice.[9]

Secondly, at the normative level, the theory focuses on the realisation of freedom and the concrete obstacles to its exercise. Bauer's perfectionism directs critical attention to the institutions that are impeding freedom and political autonomy, and it unveils their unsustainable claims to legitimacy. Yet in accord with the meta-ethics of historical perfection, Bauer's own normative applications have a merely provisional status. His particular political views in the *Vormärz* are only a momentary and problematic version of neo-Kantian perfectionism, whose conclusions would be transcended in time, as the theory prescribes. Bauer's judgements make no claim to permanent validity, but demand revision and reformulation as the consciousness of freedom grows. The theory invites actors to enter the public sphere, to contest all validity claims, and continuously to subject existing institutions, and their own actions and beliefs, to rational critique. For Bauer, the course of human history is not predetermined, but is (potentially) shaped by such critical reason and interventions: only insofar as rational actors drive universal self-consciousness beyond the limits of the present will historical progress ensue. To promote these processes is the vocation of the critic. Bauer's specific applications of post-Kantian perfectionism to contemporary events and ideologies in the 1840s serve merely to adumbrate the general theory, which claims for itself a broader scope, to accompany and guide future developments of practical reason and its specific forms in ethics, politics, and science.

Philosophical Criticism as the Vehicle for Perfection

The vehicle for perfection is the philosophical endeavour designated as 'criticism'. Beyond his derivation of central categories from Kant, Fichte, and Hegel,[10] Bauer's philosophical criticism drew on the critical thinking of the Enlightenment, which he further refined into a general theory of historical progress. Criticism is the tool of progress, in that it seeks to reveal the inconsistencies and contradictions in the conceptions of freedom and other categories that guide human thought and action. The goal is to enhance

---

9   On the historicising of the Kantian "ought", see Moggach (2001-02).
10 Moggach (2015), 177-198.

freedom and autonomy through the critique of existing obstacles to freedom. That philosophical criticism can play a vital role in the transformation of consciousness is central for Bauer's neo-Kantian position. It is only by being active, by constantly subjecting the existing to rational interrogation, that new avenues of freedom and human autonomy can be opened:

> No intellectual being can be elevated to a higher level if it is not changed, and no such being will be changed without putting up the strongest possible resistance against such efforts. One must combat what one wants to elevate. [Ein geistiges Wesen kann aber nicht gehoben werden, wenn es nicht verändert wird, und verändern läßt es sich nicht, ehe es nicht den äußersten Widerstand geleistet hat. Was man heben will, muß man bekämpfen.][11]

Yet one can never genuinely elevate another, but only labour to remove general obstacles to freedom: one can facilitate the task of individual emancipation, but one can never enact it on behalf of another. Freedom cannot be bequeathed, but only won, singly, in struggle. The act of emancipation is always a self-determined act.

Yet if freedom must be self-positing, this does not imply for Bauer, at least in the *Vormärz*, that it can be achieved in abstraction from existing political relations. It is not merely an internal orientation, but an active engagement with objectivity, in order to bring the latter into closer accord with reason. It implies participation in the struggle against the historically given institutions of church and state, and not indifference to them. This attitude of principled and open critical opposition is one of the distinguishing marks in Bauer's polemics with Max Stirner. Stirner has been described in recent work as promoting a weak version of anarchism:[12] weak in the sense that active resistance to the state is not theoretically mandated; it suffices merely to escape its clutches. If we apply a similar category to Bauer, we could describe him as a strong republican: the struggle for republican institutions is implicit in the current meaning of freedom itself. One frees oneself by committing to the combat, theoretically and practically.[13]

---

11   Bauer (1968a), 212.
12   Leopold (2006).
13   Bauer (1841), 82: „Die Opposition muß ernstlich seyn, scharf, durchdringend, rücksichtslos und der Sturz des Bestehenden die Hauptabsicht." Cf. *Anekdota* II, 163, 185.
    „Die Krisis is nicht mehr die theoretische der Prinzipien, sondern die praktische, ob ein geschlagenes Prinzip, welches durch seine Sprache und durch sein ganzes Auftreten seine Niederlage beweist, in der wirklischen Welt herrschen, ob es in einer Welt herrschen soll, die es nicht mehr geistig leben sieht, nicht mehr lebensehen kann, oder ob das

Bauer's philosophical criticism is a method for 'unmasking', 'unveiling' and 'revealing' irrational ideas and institutions that stand in the way of human progress. His philosophical criticism is the vehicle for human emancipation, and its application to social problems is intended to contribute to the expansion of human autonomy and freedom. The exact targets for philosophical criticism are not given in advance, but emerge in the course of social struggles, as the various parties define their own roles and objectives, and expose themselves to critique. Nor is this criticism a precise blueprint for the future; it is intended to expose the limitations of existing views, and to elicit their reformulation. The task is rather, as in Hegel, to identify specific contradictions which hamper historical progress, and not to prescribe a singular solution. History offers no metaphysical guarantees that reason will always prevail in opposition to the irrational principles that it encounters. The theory is normative in the sense that the faculty of reason ought to determine the course of history, and it functions hypothetically: only *if* subjects posit the need for rational justification as the deciding principle, and *if* they act practically to remove such obstacles, once unveiled.

This idea is spelled out in Bauer's *Die Gute Sache der Freiheit*, after his politically-motivated dismissal from the University of Bonn in 1842.[14] Here the transformative function of philosophical criticism is explained in terms of the battle between the old and the new principles which underlie and justify competing forms of consciousness and social life. The new principles that Bauer adhered to in his polemical defence of his procedure were human rights and the expansion of human domains of freedom: he proclaimed the intrinsic instability and performative contradiction at the heart of conservatism. In the clash with a more progressive adversary, the old order that conservatives defend ceases to be what it had been, as something merely given or taken for granted, and becomes itself a new configuration of consciousness and values.

> The old that stands against the new ceases in reality to be actually the old. Through the opposition, it has become rather a new shape of Spirit: its rights lie not in the past, but must first be proven. [Das Alte, welches dem Neuen sich widersetzt, ist nicht mehr wirklich das Alte, durch den Gegensaß ist es vielmehr selber zu einer neuen Gestalt des Geistes geworden: seine Rechte liegen nicht in der Vergangenheit, sondern sind erst zu beweisen].[15]

---

neue siegreiche Prinzip praktische Anerkennung erhalten soll ... Dem Volke gehört die Zukunft."
14   Bauer (1842b).
15   Bauer (1842b), 2.

Philosophical criticism is a method for the promotion of freedom and human autonomy in two ways; first as a universal tendency of man's application of reason to the contemporary world and the problems identified in it, and second as a particular engagement between two or more principles. When confronted with philosophical criticism, the old principles must justify their existence against the new and more comprehensive principles. In so doing, they acquire a degree of reflexivity that they previously lacked, and this shift from mere givenness to conscious articulation changes their character fundamentally. They can no longer rely on tradition or customary acceptance to justify them, because their engagement with their critical adversaries forces them to try to formulate a rational justification for what, in light of the new principle, is merely contingent and arbitrary, or 'positive' in Hegel's terms.[16] In the 1840's, Bauer was confident that if the newly-emergent concepts were of higher ethical worth, they would tend to prevail in combat: eventually, and always with the possibility of regression. He viewed the development of human freedom as the movement from particular statuses, privileges, and exemptions, towards the universal recognition of human rights. This progress was announced in the French Revolution, and was now extending its sway across Europe; yet even the new principle is never definitive. Bauer would not consider human rights, as formulated at the time, to be the ultimate expression of the human consciousness, but to represent the provisionally most advanced and comprehensive principles available to contemporary society. These principles ought to be defended as such, but never fetishised or deemed immutable. When the spirit of the old order, still predominant though decisively challenged by new insights into freedom, comes into conflict with these new ideas, the forces that reject these human rights are, in their particularistic notions of freedom, revealed as 'inhuman,' as rationally indefensible. In his contemporary setting, Bauer argued that the opponents of philosophical criticism, in their rejection of its principles of universal freedom and human rights, put out into the open *"the true meaning of the old, its proper execution, and its unveiled secret"* [„der richtige Sinn, die richtige Durchführung desselben, das aufgedeckte Geheimniß des Alten"][17]; in light of the new principle, the intrinsic oppressiveness and inhumanity of the old order is laid bare. In order to better illustrate the position, we can apply Bauer's general indictment of conservatism to a specific example from his time, consistent with Bauer's own logic and political stance, even if not expressly addressed by him. The institution of serfdom in Prussia had only recently come to a difficult and hesitant end under the efforts of the reform

---

16 See, for example, *TWA* 1, 104-229.
17 Bauer (1842b), 2-3.

movement, prompted initially by the Napoleonic conquests. Serfdom had been defended, however, by proponents of the Historical School of Law: the long existence of the institution of serfdom pointed to its accord with human nature, or to the implicit consent of those affected by it.[18] The latter claim, however, that institutions are only valid as long as those subject to them give consent, is an admission of the new revolutionary principle of popular sovereignty, which undermines the traditionalist case. From the moment when the old principle is challenged by a new, superior principle, it must seek its justification in terms that validate the new principle itself. The old thereby concedes its defeat and impotence. In another example of this transformation of consciousness, this time explicit in Bauer's works, he showed how the *Vormärz* Prussian state was revealed as the enemy of freedom of expression, in its efforts to quell all dissenting voices in the universities:

> In claiming and exercising authority over the evaluation of university faculties, the government admits that its existence is incompatible with the freedom of thought [...].The rupture is the real liberation of [academic] freedom and the transformation of [the principle of] restrictiveness into the essence of the enemies of freedom. [[...] die Regierung, die sich zum Urtheil der Facultäten bestimmen läßt, spricht damit aus, daß ihre Existenz mit der Freiheit des Gedankens unverträglich ist [...]. Der Bruch ist die wirkliche Befreiung der Freiheit und die Umwandlung der Beschränktheit zum Wesen der Gegner der Freiheit].[19]

Post-Kantian Perfectionism and Religious Critique

Bauer offered two major fields of application of his post-Kantian perfectionism, religion and politics. Since Christianity and the alliance of throne and altar constituted a major bulwark of the existing order, Bauer's religious critique was a daring attempt to undermine the regime. It was fundamentally political in its inspiration and execution. The criticism of religion was an avenue for the criticism of broader social institutions. For Bauer, religion stands in opposition to mankind's capacity to shape the world in light of reason. In religion, the self has alienated itself, by making the universal which originates within the self become its own negation as God, a subject distinct from the self, and a master over it.[20] Religion falsely imbues the world with a magical existence, a sacrosanct order in which human beings are fundamentally passive and dependent. It thus negates human spontaneity and formativity, the

---

18   Bauer (1841b), 465-479. See also *MEW* 1, 78-85.
19   Bauer (1842b), 3.
20   Bauer (1841), 77.

potential to remould the world and the self through the agency of reason. For Bauer, the Enlightenment and the French Revolution have demonstrated that human beings are able to become the masters of their own destiny, and thereby carve out an area of freedom, of free thought as the basis for creating greater realms of concrete freedom and autonomy:

> Religion is the fixation of human passivity, intuited, made, willed, and elevated to the essence of man. It is the worst kind of suffering that man could possibly inflict upon himself. [die Religion ist die fixierte, angeschaute, gemachte, gewollte und zu seinem Wesen erhobene Passivität des Menschen, das höchste Leiden, das er sich selbst zufügen konnte ...].[21]

Bauer viewed religion in general as a hindrance for rational thought and for the capacity of human beings to deal creatively and freely with objective reality. In all religions the self is alienated, by making human creations, the institutions in society, and the development of philosophy, which all originate within self-consciousness, appear as divine gifts from a God: "For philosophy, God is dead, and only the I as self-consciousness [...] only the I lives, creates, has effect, and is everything." ["Gott ist todt für die Philosophie und nur das Ich als Selbstbewußtsein [...] nur das Ich lebt, schafft, wirkt und ist Alles"].[22] Bauer argued that it is a paradox that a free being seals itself off from its own essence, and in its place creates an alien subject, God, who becomes the master of humanity. The elimination of religion would be conducive to higher degrees of human autonomy and freedom: autonomy because man's self-consciousness is set free to unfold the works of reason as its own creation; and freedom because the oppressive institutions in society can no longer be disguised behind the veil of religion. The Enlightenment and its aftermath have driven the contradiction between the church, a static and conservative force, and the emancipatory claims of science, to an extreme pitch, where it demands resolution. The religious consciousness imputes to man a sense of fear and preaches man's abject submission to authority, and therefore hinders the development of autonomous reason. In Christianity, the self is alienated because the historical movement of reason appears as the work of a divine being, when it in reality is the product of man's own thought, separated from its origin in human self-consciousness.[23] By projecting the invention of religious dogmas onto divine revelation, religion becomes inhuman because it attributes mankind's central property of reason to a divine being. The essence of religion is heteronomy, in

---

21   Bauer (1843), 201.
22   Bauer (1841), 77.
23   *Anekdota* II, 105.

that mankind substitutes for its essential characteristic, namely reason, a set of unalterable holy scriptures and divine revelations, prescribed by an alien source: "Whoever wants to be human, whoever wants to think and wants to be free, cannot but commit high treason against the sect." ["Wer Mensch sein, denken, frei sein will, begeht den höchsten Verrat an der Sekte"][24] Because of the innate danger of free thinking, the sect must always appear as an internal tyrant confronting its members, ready to punish the slightest deviations from orthodoxy and to preserve dogma. The sect thus requires that reason and free thinking be suppressed: "The sect is suspicious of everything that is human and therefore has to punish it." ["Alles Menschliche ist ihr verdächtig und muß bestraft werden"].[25] When some of his fellow Left Hegelians applauded the form of religion (if not its historical substance) and sought to retrieve it for the progressive cause, Bauer opposed this tendency, on the grounds that it was colluding in the enslavement of reason to dogma. For him, faith and reason are antinomies.

The prevailing Christian religion in particular was a principal target for Bauer. He claimed that Christianity presents itself as a religion of love and freedom, but is in reality the negation of both. The freedom offered by Christianity is a supernatural freedom, because real human freedom, the advance of the human self-consciousness, is trapped within a religious doctrine that is unable to change, since it is an eternal mandate of God: "This freedom is therefore the unconditional slavery under an authority from which there are no possible appeals." ["Diese Freiheit ist daher die unbedingte Knechtschaft unter einer Autorität, gegen die es keine Möglichkeit der Appellation gibt."][26] Christian freedom therefore turns out to be its opposite, the slavery of human beings. Since the Prussian state of the Restoration period was formally based on Protestant Christianity, such accusations marshaled here by Bauer constituted a direct challenge to the established order. The heteronomy at the heart of Christian theology is replicated in the Christian state, from whose grip the decisive task of the present is to liberate oneself.

If Christianity is not a religion of freedom but of tutelage and domination, neither is it a religion of love. Having demolished the idea of Christian freedom, Bauer also shows that Christianity with its numerous competing sects cannot but spur conflicts that are irresolvable, because they are based on dogmas asserted as unconditionally true and valid, and immune to rational thought. Unlike human rights which are available for all mankind,

---

24 Bauer (1843), 199.
25 Ibid., 200; see also 201.
26 Ibid., 215.

Christian freedom and charity are exclusively reserved for practitioners of this creed, and are further restricted to the adherents of particular sectarian congregations.[27] Christianity has therefore no love for humanity as such, despite what its believers profess, but only for the members of limited circles of faith, the particular Christian sects. All others, including rival sects, become the enemy, to be damned, combated, and destroyed. "The mystery of religious love is thereby resolved, when it is recognized as hate." [„Das Rätsel der religiösen Liebe ist damit gelöst, daß sie als der Haß anerkannt wird."][28] Bauer argues that the particularistic and sectarian form intrinsic to the Christian religion, based on adherence to irrational and arbitrary doctrines, leads to a condition of permanent war. The differences between religions and sects are viewed as eternal and impossible to overcome: "Each party believes it possesses the only true expression of human nature. It follows from this that each of them has to repudiate all the others and declare them inhuman." [„Jede Partei glaubt der wahre Ausdruck des menschlichen Wesens zu sein, jede muß daher die andere verleugnen, für unmenschlich erklären ..."][29] The doctrinal differences in various religious texts are forever beyond the scope of rational discourse, are a permanent source of hatred and conflict, and cannot accompany the further development of man's rational faculties. While philosophical criticism allows reason to resolve conflicts between opposing principles, religion, as an uncritical faith in divine dogmas, precludes such a resolution.[30]

Bauer was also resistant to his fellow Left Hegelians' flirtation with the form of secularised religion. He rejected the idea temporarily entertained by some Left Hegelians like Arnold Ruge, to create a religion of humanism.[31] "Even Ruge concluded the edition of the Deutsche Jahrbücher by propagating a new religion." [„Auch Ruge beschloss die Redaktion der Deutschen Jahrbücher mit der Verkündigung einer neuen Religion"].[32] Ruge believed that the masses could become mobilised in the cause of reason and progress if they believed in the progressive political views of the time – not as something that they fully understood, but as an article of faith, a form of secular religion. As a vehement critic of religion, Bauer opposed this idea strenuously. His critical stance followed from his conception of self-consciousness, as autonomy and freedom.

---

27 On Bauer's critique of exclusivity, see Tomba (2006).
28 Bruno (1843), 216.
29 Ibid., 195.
30 Ibid., 198.
31 On Ruge's complex engagements with the relations between social emancipation and religious beliefs, see Calvié (2011).
32 Bauer (1847), 151.

If reason regresses into the form of religion, then man betrays his own essence, the essential human capacity of reflection and critique.

> You think that whoever eliminates one barrier [to human self-consciousness] has to replace it with another one? [...] If I unmask the hypocrisy of the theologians, must I invent a new mask [to replace it]?
> [Sie meinen, wer eine Schranke auflöst, muß wieder eine Schranke seßen? [...] Wenn ich die Heuchelei der Theologen entlarve, muß ich eine neue Larve erfinden?][33]

For Bauer, the historically-given religions should not be replaced by a new religion, but by the open affirmation of autonomous reason capable of setting its own ethical standards. Bauer advocated the transcendence of religion and religious dependency, and resisted efforts to render philosophy as the new religion. To do so would be to enact the dialectic of the old and the new in reverse, to regress to the indefensible standpoint of the outmoded principle.

> Criticism will destroy religion – do you hear me? –, it will demolish all religion. But what will we put in its place? Mr. Gruppe thinks that we do not yet know this, or that whatever comes in its place is only a matter for the future. Just one page before he writes that we will replace religion with some sort of philosophy. No, Mr. Gruppe! Not some sort of philosophy, nor, for that matter, philosophy as such. [Die Religion – hören Sie? – die Religion schlechthin wird von der Kritik gestürzt. Und an ihre Stelle: was seßen wir? Herr Gruppe meint, wir wüßten es nicht, oder es sey etwas nur Zukünftiges – eine Seite vorher sagte er, wir wollten eine Philosophie an die Stelle der Religion seßen – Nein, Herr Gruppe! weder eine Philosophie, noch die Philosophie][34]

The subjugation of religion to criticism carves out a whole new area of human freedom. No compromise with the old principles ought to be entertained. If the creations of reason are propagated as a matter of faith, they cease to be reasonable. The dilution of philosophy into a secular faith would only destroy the very essence of philosophy. Ruthless criticism was the path to liberation.

Despite his virulent critique of the religious consciousness, Bauer was careful to distinguish his own position from that of Enlightenment materialism, which he nonetheless acknowledged as a precursor. Bauer contended that the Enlightenment could only grasp religion as error and manipulative deception, but not in its inner essence as a form of self-estranged consciousness.[35] Because of its limited philosophical base in a crude materialism, Enlightenment

---

33 Bauer (1842b), 201.
34 Ibid., 201-202.
35 Bauer (1838), 160-161; here applied to Judaism and pagan deities.

criticism could not conceive the history of the loss and redemption of spirit as an immanent and necessary process, or view religion as an alienated but essential stage in the dawning of human self-awareness.[36] On Bauer's Hegelian account, the externalisation of the human essence in the form of the divine, and the immersion of the self in a community of shared values, is a transitional passage toward the recognition of the genuine universality and freedom of human consciousness.[37] The next historical step is for subjects to assume the burden of universality themselves, to express and defend the common interests of historical progress, and to create new institutions adapted to the current critical standpoint. Religion is not merely an external imposition by power-hungry clerics, as the materialists had held, but a (temporarily) necessary dialectical illusion, whose time has however passed. Bauer saw his own thought as completing and transcending the Enlightenment standpoint. Unlike the perspective attained by infinite self-consciousness, which recognises only rational freedom as its essence, the Enlightenment clung to the sensuous self, and mistook the quest for material satisfaction or happiness to be the defining characteristic of modern subjects. As Hegel had said, the supreme principle of the Enlightenment is that everything exists for the subject,[38] but it did not yet possess an adequate understanding of that subject, continuing to represent it as the repository of particular, immediate interests. Contrasting his own standpoint with that of the French Enlightenment, Bauer asserted:

> [The French] have generally conceived the movement of self-consciousness at the same time as the movement of a common essence, of matter, but could not yet see that the movement of the universe first becomes genuinely for-itself, and is brought together into unity with itself, only as the movement of self-consciousness. [[Die Franzosen] haben die Bewegungen des Selbstbewußtseins allerdings zugleich als die Bewegungen des allgemeinen Wesens, der Materie gefaßt, aber noch nicht sehen können, daß die Bewegung des Universums erst als die Bewegung des Selbstbewußtseins wirklich für sich geworden und zur Einheit mit ihr selbst zusammengegangen ist.][39]

This limitation had important political consequences. By asserting the primacy of matter over spirit, eighteenth-century criticism was unable to detect the exercise of spontaneous, creative activity. For Bauer, self-consciousness had advanced since its Enlightenment manifestations: enriched by these earlier

---

36 On the historical role of religion as a necessary transitional stage in the history of self-consciousness, see Bauer (1841), 42-57.
37 Ibid., 45.
38 *TWA* 20, 332-333.
39 Bauer (1843), 161.

struggles, the forces of progress were now able to build on previous revolutions, and to propel the political and social movement forward. The criterion was no longer immediate subjectivity and utility, but rational subjects who understand and transform themselves in the course of historical becoming.

> This transition consists in nothing other than the freeing of the atoms which up till now have been fixed in their own right, but which from now on can only win their equal justification by giving up the immediate rigidity with which they had held fast to their presupposed rights, and by setting themselves in unity with each other through the conquest of themselves. Self-denial is the first law, and freedom the necessary consequence. [Dieser Umschwung besteht in nichts anderem als in der Befreiung der bisher durch ihr eigenes Recht fixierten Atome die von jetzt an ihre gleiche Berechtigung haben und dadurch gewinnen können, daß sie zunächst ihre unmittelbare Sprödigkeit, mit der sie an ihrem vorausgesetzten Recht festhielten, aufgeben und jenes durch die Überwindung seiner selbst mit dem andern sich in Einheit setzt. Die Selbstverleugnung ist das erste Gesetz und die Freiheit die notwendige Folge.][40]

The Hegelian dialectic, dissolving the givenness and rigidity of the human subject and its values, allows self-consciousness to reclaim the idea of universality in the activities of the subjects themselves, and in their concrete political and social relations. Religious alienation is overcome when both the political community, and its individual citizens, exhibit self-directed rationality in their ethical decisions, and no longer rely on transcendent powers, earthly or divine, to provide authoritative direction; nor are they confined by their own particular interests, but can evaluate, discard, or reconfigure these in emancipatory struggle. The principle of freedom, enunciated in the Enlightenment and the French Revolution, now needed to be further developed, and practically elaborated, in order to sweep away the vestiges of alienated spirit, and all irrational forms of ethical life. The progress in the comprehension and practice of freedom, the essential aim of post-Kantian perfectionism, is thus doubly marked in the critique of religion: in the revelation of religion as the alienated work of self-consciousness, and in the advance effected by the critical principle itself, from external, contingent critique, to an inner engagement with the history of human spirit.

---

40   Bauer (1968), 26.

Bauer's Post-Kantian Perfectionist Politics

Extending his criticism of religion, Bauer sought to identify central social and political contradictions in order to advance rational autonomy and freedom:

> Philosophy must also affect the political, and it has the duty to attack and to stir up all those existing social and political conditions that are not in accordance with self-consciousness. [Auch im Politischen mus daher die Philosophie wirken und die bestehende Verhältnisse, wenn sie ihrem Selbstbewusstsein widersprechen, unumwunden angreifen erschüttern][41]

Bauer maintained that it was the existing state, and not religion, which was the principal adversary of freedom.[42] He insisted that the decisive political question in the revolutionary struggles of 1848 was the source of the state's authority, whether in tradition and religious sanction, or in the popular will. Thus he attacked the absolutist state and its conservative proponents in the prelude to 1848, criticising the defects and incoherences of the old order, in its reactionary efforts to reassert itself after the decisive shocks of the French Revolution. He also engaged polemically with other partisans of the opposition movement, notably liberals and socialists, who in his view distorted the emancipatory tendencies of modern society. In each case, his perfectionist ethics invokes the criterion of historical progress against irrational and outmoded ideas, values, and institutions. The ends of political action require rational justification, based on enhancing the conditions for free activity in general, rather than advancing particularistic notions of personal privilege or traditional status. Perfection in the political sphere is for Bauer closely linked to his meta-ethical theory of the historical development of self-conscious freedom. Bauer attributed epochal significance to the *Vormärz* revolutionary moment, as a fundamental political, social, and cultural transformation. The task was to complete the unfinished work of the French Revolution, but also to address the unprecedented challenges posed by modern civil society. A republican league of equal right, eliminating irrational privileges, refashioning social relations, and eradicating religious and political alienation, was the properly-conceived goal of the movement. The new revolution would be a decisive step in forwarding the emancipatory strivings of modernity, fulfilling the promise of the transcendental project initiated by Kant, and elaborated by Hegel. It is

---

41   Bauer (1841), 83.
42   Bauer (1842b), 218-19: „Nicht die Kirche wird uns lästig – auch wir fallen ihr nicht zur Last – sondern der Staat ist es, der uns durch seine christlichen Aufforderungen zur Läst fällt."

this post-Kantian philosophical context which shapes Bauer's understanding of the current political struggle.

The major adversary in Bauer's critical campaign in the *Vormärz* was the *ancien régime*, and its Restoration supporters. He denounced feudalism as a system of tutelage and irrational privilege, monopoly, and exemptions.[43] In the feudal world, from which the current regime had newly emerged and to which it nostalgically clung, the political community is dispersed into multiple local, competing points, at which predatory private interests, both individual and corporate, cluster and oppose each other, seeking to consolidate and extend their particular advantages. The authoritarian state which gradually arises over these rigidly exclusive particulars, and which assumes the mantle of a sham universality, represses the self-activity of its people, turning them into passive, administered subjects.[44] The state invokes religious sanctification to bolster its authority, and, struggling against the emergent new principles of freedom, seeks to halt historical development in retrograde political forms.[45] The analogy with Bauer's criticism of religion is striking, in the irreconcilable rivalries among sectarian and local/status interests, and in the arrogation of universality by a seemingly transcendent force. This was the oppressive order to which the French Revolution had delivered a decisive, but not fatal, blow. The powers of the ancient regime were now reconstituting themselves in the post-1815 Restoration, and continued to resist the demands of emancipation. The correct ethical stance in response was implacable opposition.[46]

Yet these demands of freedom too could be misconstrued. From his republican vantage point, Bauer contested the emancipatory potential of emergent liberalism. Drawing on the example of the *Girondins* in the French Revolution, and on contemporary German events, Bauer argued that because it equates freedom with property, liberalism has been demonstrated to be historically

---

43 Bauer (1842a), 98-99: „So lange das Christentum herrschte, galt allein der Feudalismus; als sich zuerst Völker sittlich auszubilden anfingen – gegen das Ende des Mittelalters – erhielt das Christentum den ersten gefährlichen Stoß, und ein freies Volk, wirkliche Freiheit und Gleichheit und der Sturz der feudalistischen Privilegien wurde erst eine Möglichkeit, als in der französischen Revolution das religiöse Prinzip richtig gewürdigt wurde."

44 Bauer (1841a), 310: „wenn die Eine Alles ist und die reine Allgemeinheit des Selbstbewußtseins allein repräsentiert, so blieb den Anderen die Dummheit und höchstens die Bosheit." Cf. ibid., 46, 108-109.

45 Bauer (1844a), 36-37, Brief 8 an Edgar Bauer (Feb. 4, 1840): „Der Staat muß an sich selber ein religiöses Interesse nehmen und die Fortentwicklung der Philosophie beschränken. Sie war bisher durch ihre Verbindung mit dem Staate konsolidarisch verpflichtet, also auch eingeengt; sie hatte sich, da sie scheinbar freigelassen und ohnehin begünstigt war, d.h. an der Vorteilen der Regierung teilnahm, selbst ihre Grenze gesetzt."

46 Bauer (1841), 82.

incapable of sustained combat against the old order. It will seek compromise with the forces of order whenever property is threatened, or it will misdirect emancipatory efforts toward accumulation and egoistic privilege.[47] Moreover, the dominance of private economic interest, and the hegemony of civil society over the state, against which Hegel had warned in the *Philosophy of Right*, imply the evacuation of citizenship in favour of a particularised mass society: inert, apolitical, and incapable of determined, principled exertion.[48] Liberal constitutionalism is the political translation of private interest. It is riven with internal contradictions between two diametrically opposed principles of sovereignty, popular and princely, and represses the essential contention between them, thus impeding their historical resolution. It is "a system in which the government acts purely from 'raison d'etat', and confronts a mass of individuals possessing rights equally, i.e. equally little, and determines the worth of the individual according to the monetary contribution which his taxes make to the maintenance of the state machine."[49] Here is no solid basis for genuine progress in rational freedom: liberalism is repudiated on historically perfectionist grounds.

Bauer waged his *Vormärz* critical campaign on a third front, against incipient schools of socialism. The centrality of the social question, the emergence of new forms of urban poverty and exclusion linked to the depopulation of the countryside and the onset of industrialisation, meant that the new revolution could not be a mere reprise of older struggles. Hegel had already identified the crisis-laden and polarised character of civil society as a deep, unresolved problem for the modern rational state, and his successor Eduard Gans had made this issue thematic in his own lectures on history and politics, at the genesis of the Left-Hegelian school.[50] Bauer pursued this line in his *Vormärz* polemics. He described the proletariat as the determinate negation of the existing order, the central unresolved issue that impeded the progress of the state in

---

47   Bauer (1843a), 101: „Der constitutionale Liberalismus ist das System der Bervorrechteten, der beschränkten und interessierten Freiheit. Seine Basis ist noch das Vorurteil, sein Wesen noch religiös."

48   Bauer (1843-1844), 6: „Die Bourgeoisie hat der Zeit angehört, welche nach dem Sturze des alten Königthums in Frankreich folgte; die Bourgeoisie hat selbst die Schreckens-Herrschaft gestürzt und die goldenen Früchte geerntet, die aus dem mit Blut gedüngten Saat des 18. Jahrhunderts hervorgingen; sie hat die revolutionären Ideen, für die nicht sie sondern uneigennützige oder leidenschaftliche Männer sich aufopferten, sich allein zu gute kommen lassen, den Geist in Geld verwandelt – freilich nachdem sie jene Ideen die Spitze, die Konsequenz, den zerstörenden und gegen allen Egoismus fanatischen Ernst genommen hatte."

49   Bauer (1846), 230.

50   Waszek (2006) and Bienenstock (2011).

its mission of representing rational freedom. Yet he disagreed fundamentally with contemporary socialist prescriptions. For him, the social question could be resolved, and the proletariat liberated, not by direct appeals to the particular interests of any one class, but only by a common struggle against unjustified advantages and violations of rights in all their forms, a struggle animated by republican convictions of the general good. Otherwise freedom is distorted into sectarian privilege. The result of this combat, waged unremittingly, would be progress in justice and its generalisation throughout the spheres of social life. Bauer asserted that the objective of his new republicanism was not merely political, but social emancipation: a society in which the possibility of free self-definition was not structurally precluded for anyone. Consistent with the post-Kantian ethical basis of this position, it implies, beyond equality of opportunity in the quest for happiness or material satisfaction, an enhanced capacity for rational agency or freedom, that is, a heightened ability to adjudicate the proper ends of action, in pursuit of general interests.

In his defence of the republican constitution in the prelude to 1848 and during the uprisings themselves, Bauer stressed two features, prescribed by his ethical theory, that the revolutionary regime ought to exhibit. First, it must firmly maintain the principle of popular sovereignty, without dilution or compromise. The constitution must be self-determined and self-given by the people's Assembly, and not humbly received as a privilege accorded from on high. King Friedrich Wilhelm IV's offer to grant a constitution from the fullness of his own powers must be rebuffed, because such a grant would always be revocable at the royal whim, and would amount to a concession by the Assembly that sovereignty remains vested in the crown. It would treat freedom as a gift, and not as a hard-won victory.[51] For Bauer, emancipation is always self-emancipation.

Secondly, the post-Revolutionary regime must be a dynamic agent of historical change. Bauer envisioned a constitution in constant mutation, not permanently fixed by its founders' reputed intentions, but consistent with the advancement of reason and universal values among its members:

> Every people, with the progression of time, must make changes to its existing constitution so that it comes ever closer to the true one. [Jedes Volk muß mit dem

---

51   Bauer (1972). Cf. Bauer (1842b), 221-22: „Wir sind schlechthin unmündig: die Macht, die unseres Wesen zu ihrem Privilegium gemacht hat, denkt, spricht, handelt für uns oder vielmehr für sich und uns kommt ihr Tun und Denken nur deshalb zu Gute, weil wir ihm als Privateigentum angehören. Wir sind nur Privateigentum und die Leibeigenen eines Andern, dem wir unseres Wesen als sein ausschließliches Privilegium zuerteilt haben."

Fortgange der Zeit solche Veränderungen mit seiner vorhandenen Constitution machen, welche sie der wahren immer näher bringen]⁵²

A republican regime would be flexible in its ability to respond to changes in its citizens' understandings of freedom, and to incorporate these changes into its own practices and institutions. This dynamism of the concept of freedom is the hallmark of republican constitutionalism for Bauer in the 1840's. The rational state is

> the result of the struggle through which the purpose of morality, and its reality, are raised to a higher content, and the initially empty infinity has made itself into moral purpose and has attained legal recognition. The State is then again the reaction against the result, since after the resolution of the struggle it lets its pure infinitude appear again against the particular form of the result. It is immortal, eternal. [Er ist das Resultat des Kampfes, durch den der Zweck der Sittlichkeit und dessen Realität zu einer höhern Stufe erhoben ist, und die im Anfang leere Unendlichkeit sich zum sittlichen Zweck gemacht und rechtliche Anerkennung errungen hat. Der Staat ist dann wieder selbst die Reaktion gegen das Resultat, indem er nach der Auflösung des Kampfes die reine Unendlichkeit seiner selbst gegen die bestimmte Form des Resultats wieder hervortreten läßt. Er ist unvergänglich, ewig.]⁵³

Such a state is now within the grasp of the revolutionary forces, if they act with decisiveness, courage, and insight. So Bauer admonished them in his electoral addresses of 1848-49, the synopsis of his critical campaigns throughout the *Vormärz*.⁵⁴

As Fichte in his *Vocation of the Scholar*⁵⁵, Bauer attributed a special place to philosophy in the oversight of future development of society toward higher standpoints of freedom and human rights, more universal in scope, instead of privileges imbued with religious or particularistic connotations:

> The philosophers are the rulers of the world, and with their deeds, that are deeds of destiny, they determine the fate of humankind. They formulate the decisions of the cabinet that makes world history and all peoples must therefore obey them. The worldly kings that rule over their peoples are nothing but the scribes who copy in their decrees what the philosophers have put down in their writings – at least if they follow reason, and if there is any reason in their decisions. [Die Philosophen sind die Herren der Welt, sie machen das Schicksal der Menschheit, ihre Thaten sind Thaten des ‚Schicksals'. Sie ‚schreiben die cabinetsordres der

---

52 Bauer (1841), 83.
53 Bauer (1840), 107-08.
54 Bauer (1972); Bauer (1972a).
55 *GA* I 3, 27-68.

Weltgeschichte gleich im Original', Völker müssen ihnen also gehorchen und die Könige, wenn in ihren Cabinetsordres und so weit in diesen Vernunft enthalten ist, sind nur Copisten der Actenstücke, welche die Philosophen schreiben.]⁵⁶

Yet all citizens of the future rational republic share a common mission, to assume the burden of universality themselves, to devote themselves to the common cause of freedom, and to criticise and renounce private interests when they impede the general interest. Despite his severe critique of the masses as the adversaries of freedom and progress,⁵⁷ Bauer's political position is not attached to the idea of a static intellectual elite but of a self-defining citizenry, practicing public virtues and repudiating particular interests.⁵⁸ It sets a stringent ideal of self-transcendence, consistent with its meta-ethical basis.⁵⁹ This status of citizen is potentially open to all, though Bauer anticipated that many would fail to seize the new opportunities for rational political agency, but would remain sunken in torpor and imbecility.⁶⁰ Still, the French Revolution had demonstrated that the mass, too, did not constitute a fixed historical category, but was capable of elevating itself into a self-determining people through decisive political action.⁶¹ Whether such heroic exertion was again forthcoming would decide the fate of the modern revolutions.

Bauer's own political prescriptions were clear on principles but not closely detailed. This was a deliberate choice. They followed the logic of the Hegelian determinate negation, where the decisive historic task is set with necessity, but the manner of its resolution remains open.⁶² The precise shape of future institutions cannot be anticipated, but critical theory can identify what the major obstacles to progress are, and can clarify the central issues in need of redress. This approach Bauer shared with Karl Marx, who likewise always repudiated the efforts of 'utopian socialists' to provide exhaustive accounts of emancipated future life.⁶³ Bauer's own assessments also invited constant revision and critique, as his theory requires. There are also contingent historical grounds for rethinking his polemical positions. In the intense confrontations

---

56 Bauer (1841), 80.
57 Rosen (1971), 399.
58 *Anekdota* II, 111: „die Entwicklung fortschreitet, und eben deshalb, weil sie dem allgemeinen Interesse dient."
59 Cf. Bauer (1968), 26, on self-denial [Selbstverleugnung] and freedom.
60 *Anekdota* II, 89.
61 Bauer (1847), vii: „[the mass] [...] verwandelte sich mit einem Schlage in ein Volk, das durch seine heroische Anstrengung Kraft, Mut und Fähigkeit erhielt, alle Vorrechte auch draußen überhaupt die Privilegien der Nationalitäten zu stürzen."
62 For an analysis of this procedure in Hegel, see Bourgeois (1992), ch. 1.
63 *MEW* 4, 459-493.

of the *Vormärz*, with its numerous competing voices and its emergent ideological schools, political orientations were often confused or ambiguous, and the possibility of dubious judgements was especially marked. Such was the case, for example, with Bauer's own stance on Jewish emancipation in Prussia. Because he considered the political emancipation of the Jews to be a particularistic claim to freedom in view of a private religious affiliation, he deemed it inadmissible as a progressive demand.[64] Jewish emancipation had to be resolved into the struggle for general liberation from religion and the absolutist state, and not construed as the grant of a privilege or status to a specific group. It would appear, however, that Bauer's meta-ethical theory does not uniquely prescribe this conclusion.[65] We can reconstruct this question from a Bauerian perspective in the following way, while deviating from Bauer's own application. A group has been disadvantaged and disempowered by the existing regime because of its particular beliefs and practices. To eliminate those political disadvantages is to make the universal interest formally accessible to the previously excluded group, rather than to endow the group with a new special status. Nor is the demand for emancipation equivalent to seeking a favour from the existing state; rather, it is to offer principled resistance to the state and to its traditional hierarchies, in the name of political equality. Whether the formal possibility of emancipation is acted upon or not by the members of the group remains a question of self-definition and individual choice; yet the opening of this formal possibility for all, and the removal of irrational restraints, appear to be mandated by the perfectionist ethical theory. If the republican struggle cannot directly emancipate individuals, it can, and must, eliminate obstacles, wherever possible, to their achieving their own liberation. The critical potential of the theory is not exhausted in Bauer's *Vormärz* debates.

After the defeats of 1848, Bauer abandoned his historical perfectionism, and the sublime and arduous struggle for freedom that it entailed. He redefined the correct practical stance as the disinterested withdrawal from active ethical engagement, awaiting new social agencies, produced under disciplinary duress if not by reflective personal exertion.[66] Bauer now anticipated the emergence of transnational blocs locked in deadly rivalry, with the prospect of permanent global war. Strongly authoritarian states would rise above depoliticised mass society, homogenised and conformist; but under this crushing pressure, new forces of freedom and individuality might possibly be able to extrude

---

64 See also Leopold (1999) for a contrasting assessment.
65 A related criticism is offered in Moggach (2006), 114-135.
66 Bauer's late idea of the disciplinary levelling of particularity is foreshadowed in some of his *Vormärz* texts. See, for example, Bauer (1840), 19-33.

themselves. A new dialectic of the will, structurally similar to that enacted by the religious consciousness in its emergence from particularity to genuine selfhood,[67] cannot be precluded, though it cannot be guaranteed.

Bauer's later thought, after 1848, falls outside the scope of perfectionist ethical and political projects. His *Vormärz* republicanism interpreted freedom as the power of reason to reshape objective social relations, and to refashion the self and its interests as an agent of historical advance. His critical theory assessed the claims to emancipation and legitimacy raised by the diverse political actors in the German Restoration states, and reclaimed the heritage of Hegel, the Enlightenment, and the French Revolution for the new problems of the age. In a spirited defence of his work against the censors in 1844, he described himself as 'the friend of freedom' ["der Freund der Freiheit"].[68] The dynamic freedom at the heart of his theory can best be understood as a specific variant of post-Kantian perfectionism.

Bibliography

Barbour, Charles, "Acts of Emancipation. Bauer, Marx, and the 'Jewish Question', in: *The Aporia of Rights*, ed. by Peg Birmingham and Anna Yeatman, New York: Bloomsbury, 2016, pp. 77-92.

Bauer, Bruno, *Kritik der Geschichte der Offenbarung. Die Religion des alten Testaments in der geschichtlichen Entwicklung ihrer Prinzipien dargestellt*, vol. 1, Berlin: Ferdinand Dümmler, 1838. (Bauer 1838)

– (anon.), *Die evangelische Landeskirche Preußens und die Wissenschaft*, Leipzig: Otto Wigand, 1840. (Bauer 1840)

– (anon.), *Die Posaune des jüngsten Gerichts über Hegel den Atheisten und Antichristen. Ein Ultimatum*, Leipzig: Otto Wigand, 1841. (Bauer 1841)

– *Kritik der evangelischen Geschichte der Synoptiker*, vol. 2, Leipzig: Otto Wigand, 1841. (Bauer 1841a)

– „Theologische Schamlosigkeiten," in: *Deutsche Jahrbücher für Wissenschaft und Kunst*, 15-18. November 1841, no. 117-120, pp. 465-479. (Bauer 1841b)

– (anon.), *Hegels Lehre von der Religion und Kunst von dem Standpuncte des Glaubens aus beurtheilt*, Leipzig: Otto Wigand, 1842. (Bauer 1842)

– *Kritik der evangelischen Geschichte der Synoptiker und des Johannes*, vol. 3, Braunschweig: Fr. Otto, 1842. (Bauer 1842a)

---

67   See above, note 35.
68   Bauer (1844), 53.

- *Die Gute Sache der Freiheit und Meine eigene Angelegenheit*, Zürich/Winterthur: Verlag des literarischen Comptoirs, 1842. (Bauer 1842b)
- „Rezension: "Die Geschichte des Lebens Jesu mit steter Rücksicht auf die vorhandenen Quellen dargestellt von Dr. von Ammon. Leipzig, 1842." In: *Anekdota zur neuesten deutschen Philosophie und Publizistik*, vol. 2, ed. by Arnold Ruge, Zürich/Winterthur, 1843, pp. 160-185. (*Anekdota* II)
- „Rezension: ‚Einleitung in die Dogmengeschichte' von Theodor Kliefoth." in: *Anekdota zur neuesten deutschen Philosophie und Publizistik*, vol. 2, ed. by Arnold Ruge, Zürich/Winterthur, 1843, pp. 135-159. (*Anekdota* II)
- „Leiden und Freuden des theologischen Bewußtseins", in: *Anekdota zur neuesten deutschen Philosophie und Publizistik*, vol. 2, ed. by Arnold Ruge, Zürich/Winterthur, 1843, pp. 89-112. (*Anekdota* II)
- *Das entdeckte Christenthum. Eine Erinnerung an das 18. Jahrhundert und ein Beitrag zur Krisis des 19.*, Zürich and Winterthur: Verlag des literarischen Comptoirs, 1843. (Bauer 1843)
- *Die Judenfrage*, Braunschweig: Fr. Otto, 1843. (Bauer 1843a)
- „Die Septembertage 1792 und die ersten Kämpfe der Parteien der Republik in Frankreich," in: *Denkwürdigkeiten zur Geschichte der neueren Zeit seit der Französischen Revolution*, nach den Quellen und Original Memoiren bearbeitet und herausgegeben von Bruno Bauer und Edgar Bauer, Charlottenburg: Egbert Bauer, 1843-1844, Part 1. (Bauer 1843-44)
- (ed.), *Acktenstücke zu den Verhandlungen über die Beschlagnahme der ‚Geschichte der Politik, Kultur und Aufklärung des achtzehnten Jahrhunderts' von Bruno Bauer*, Part I, Christiania: C.C. Werner, 1844. (Bauer 1844)
- (ed.), *Briefwechsel zwischen Bruno Bauer und Edgar Bauer während der Jahre 1839-1842 aus Bonn und Berlin*, Charlottenburg: Egbert Bauer, 1844. (Bauer 1844a)
- *Geschichte Deutschlands und der französischen Revolution unter der Herrschaft Napoleons. Zweiter Band. Drei Jahre Kontrerevolution*, Charlottenburg: Egbert Bauer, 1846. (Bauer 1846)
- *Vollständige Geschichte der Parteikämpfe, Vollständige Geschichte der Parteikämpfe in Deutschland während der Jahre 1842-1846*, vol. I, Charlottenburg: Egbert Bauer, 1847. (Bauer 1847)
- „Der christliche Staat und unsere Zeit," in: *Bruno Bauer, Feldzüge der reinen Kritik*, ed. by H.-M. Sass, Frankfurt am Main: Suhrkamp, 1968, pp. 7-43. (Bauer 1968)
- „Was ist jetzt der Gegenstand der Kritik", in: *Bruno Bauer, Feldzüge der reinen Kritik*, ed. by H.-M. Sass, Frankfurt am Main: Suhrkamp, 1968, pp. 200-212. (Bauer 1968a)
- „Erste Wahlrede von 1848," in: *Bruno Bauer, Studien und Materialien*, ed. by Ernst Barnikol, aus dem Nachlass ausgewählt und zusammengestellt von P. Riemer und H.-M. Sass, Assen: van Gorcum, 1972, pp. 525-531. (Bauer 1972)

- „Verteidigungsrede Bruno Bauers vor den Wahlmännern des Vierten Wahlbezirkes am 22.2. 1849," in: *Bruno Bauer: Studien und Materialien*, ed. by Ernst Barnikol, aus dem Nachlass ausgewählt und zusammengestellt von P. Riemer und H.-M. Sass, Assen: van Gorcum, 1972, pp. 518-525. (Bauer 1972a)
Bienenstock, Myriam, "Between Hegel and Marx: Eduard Gans on the 'Social Question', in: *Politics, Religion, and Art*, ed. by Douglas Moggach, Evanston, Ill.: Northwestern Univ. Press, 2011, pp. 164-178.
Bourgeois, Bernard, *Etudes hégéliennes. Raison et décision*, Paris: Presses universitaires de France, 1992.
Calvié, Lucien, "Ruge and Marx: Democracy, Nationalism, and Revolution in Left Hegelian Debates," in: *Politics, Religion, and Art*, ed. by Douglas Moggach, Evanston, Ill.: Northwestern Univ. Press, 2011, pp. 301-320.
Fichte, J.G., „Einige Vorlesungen über die Bestimmung des Gelehrten," in: *Gesamtausgabe der bayerischen Akademie*, vol. I/3, Stuttgart: Frommann Holzboog, 1966, pp. 27-68. (*GA*)
Hegel, Georg Wilhelm Friedrich, *Theorie Werkausgabe*. 20 volumes, Frankfurt/Main: Suhrkamp, 1969-71. (*TWA*)
- „Die Positivität der christlichen Religion", in: *Theorie Werkausgabe*, vol. I, Frankfurt am Main, 1986, pp. 104-229.
- „Vorlesungen über die Geschichte der Philosophie" III, in: *Theorie Werkausgabe*, vol. 20, Frankfurt am Main, 1971.
Kant, Immanuel, *Gesammelte Schriften*, ed. by Königlich Preussische Akademie der Wissenschaften (Akademie-Ausgabe), Berlin u.a., 1900 ff. (*AA*)
- „Grundlegung zur Metaphysik der Sitten", in: *Akademie-Ausgabe*, vol. 3, Berlin, 1903.
- „Kritik der reinen Vernunft", in: *Akademie-Ausgabe*, vol. IV, Berlin, 1978.
- „Metaphysik der Sitten", in: *Akademie-Ausgabe*, vol. VI, Berlin, 1968.
Leopold, David, "The Hegelian Antisemitism of Bruno Bauer", in: *History of European Ideas* 25/4, 1999, pp. 179-206.
- "The State and I: Max Stirner's Anarchism," in: *The New Hegelians*, ed. by Douglas Moggach, Cambridge: Cambridge University Press, 2006, pp. 176-199.
Marx, Karl: „Das philosophische Manifest der historischen Rechtschule", in: *Karl Marx, Friedrich Engels, Werke*, vol. 1, Berlin, 1964, pp. 78-85. (*MEW*)
- „Manifest der kommunistischen Partei," in: *Karl Marx, Friedrich Engels, Werke*, vol. 4, Berlin, 1972, pp. 459-493.
Moggach, Douglas, "'Free Means Ethical': Bruno Bauer's Critical Idealism," in: *Owl of Minerva*, 33/1, Fall/Winter 2001-02, pp. 1-24.
- "Republican Rigorism and Emancipation in Bruno Bauer", in: *The New Hegelians*, ed. by Douglas Moggach, Cambridge: Cambridge University Press, 2006, pp. 114-135.

- "Post-Kantian Perfectionism", in: *Politics, Religion, and Art*, ed. by Douglas Moggach, Evanston, Ill.: Northwestern Univ. Press, 2011, pp. 179-200.
- "Subject or Substance: The Meta-Ethics of the Hegelian School", in: *Die linken Hegelianer. Studien zum Verhältnis von Religion und Politik im Vormärz*, ed. by Michael Quante and Amir Mohseni, Paderborn: Fink, 2015, pp. 177-198.
- "German Republicans and Socialists in the Prelude to 1848," in: *The 1848 Revolutions and European Political Thought*, ed. by Douglas Moggach and Gareth Stedman Jones, Cambridge: Cambridge University Press, 2018, pp. 216-235.

Rosen, Zvi, "The Radicalisation of a Young Hegelian: Bruno Bauer" in: *The Review of Politics*, 33/3, 1971, pp. 377-405.

Tomba, Massimiliano, "Exclusiveness and Political Universalism in Bruno Bauer," in: *The New Hegelians*, ed. by Douglas Moggach, Cambridge: Cambridge University Press, 2006, pp. 91-113.

Waszek Norbert, "Eduard Gans on Poverty and on the Constitutional Debate", in: *The New Hegelians*, ed. by Douglas Moggach, Cambridge: Cambridge University Press, 2006, pp. 24-49.

Perfektionistische Gehalte der Rugeschen Geschichtsphilosophie?
Historische Zuordnungsfrage und systematische Herausforderung

Tim Rojek

> Der Mensch muß theoretisch und ethisch autonom sein.[1]
> (Arnold Ruge)

1. Einleitung

Der vorliegende Beitrag verfolgt zwei Ziele: *Erstens* soll es darum gehen, mögliche perfektionistische Gehalte der Rugeschen Philosophie offenzulegen. Hierzu soll im zweiten Teil (2) eine Klärung der Rede von ‚Perfektionismus' für die Zwecke dieses Beitrags vorgenommen werden. Im dritten Teil (3) soll dann geprüft werden, ob sich entsprechende Merkmale bei Ruge wiederfinden lassen. Damit ist die erste Frage, ob Arnold Ruges (1802-1880) Geschichtsphilosophie in einem bestimmten Sinne als perfektionistisch aufgefasst werden sollte, beantwortet. Im vierten und letzten Teil des Beitrags soll das *zweite* Ziel verfolgt werden. Es gilt mögliche Einwände und systematische Schwierigkeiten zu diskutieren, die mit den perfektionistischen Elementen bei Ruge einhergehen. Mithin lautet die Frage, was sich für die systematische Ausarbeitung einer perfektionistischen Position aus den Schwierigkeiten der Rugeschen Position lernen lässt.

Dabei wird sich zeigen, dass perfektionistische Gehalte sich insbesondere in der Geschichtsphilosophie Arnold Ruges tatsächlich nachweisen lassen. Bei dieser handelt es sich um denjenigen theoretisch-philosophischen Teil seines Denkens, den Ruge im Rahmen seiner allgemeinen Zielsetzung einer publizistischen Intervention zur Demokratisierung der Verhältnisse in Preußen ausgearbeitet hat. Diese Gehalte der Rugeschen Philosophie sind – so meine These – perfektionistisch, womit die erste, diesen Beitrag leitende Frage positiv beantwortet wäre. Ruge ist – in noch näher zu bestimmendem Sinne – ein Perfektionist.

---

[1] Ruge (1841a), 31.

In der abschließenden Diskussion wird die Frage behandelt, inwiefern eine perfektionistische Konzeption von Autonomie attraktiv sein kann, selbst wenn die Rugesche Konzeption, aufgrund der gegen sie vorgebrachten Einwände als (guter) Kandidat einer perfektionistischen Autonomietheorie nicht in Frage kommt. Eine gelingende Konzeption perfektionistischer Autonomie kann dann *ex negativo* durch das Vermeiden der identifizierten Komplikationen entwickelt werden. Aus der Kritik an Ruges Konzeption folgt also nicht ohne weiteres, dass eine perfektionistische Konzeption von Autonomie obsolet würde. Auch wird es kaum genügen, bei der Ausarbeitung einer solchen lediglich diejenigen Komplikationen zu vermeiden, die Ruges Position mit sich führt. Wohl aber sollte eine bessere Konzeption diese Schwierigkeiten vermeiden, worin dann der systematische Teilbeitrag einer Auseinandersetzung mit Ruge liegt.

2. Perfektionismus der Autonomie nach Kant?

In seinem konzeptionellen Beitrag „Post-Kantian Perfectionism" von 2011, als Fortsetzung philosophiehistorischer Thesen von 2009,[2] hat Douglas Moggach den Vorschlag gemacht, dass sich ein entsprechend benannter systematischer Theorietyp im Rahmen der linkshegelianischen Unternehmungen identifizieren lasse (zur Weiterentwicklung seiner Thesen vgl. auch seinen Beitrag in diesem Band).

Auf den ersten Blick scheint eine solche theoretische Zuordnung der Linkshegelianer durchaus ungewöhnlich. Dies deshalb, weil der prä-kantische Perfektionismus, wie er paradigmatisch in der Rechts-, Staats- und Moralphilosophie von Christian Wolff (1679-1754) verkörpert wurde, seit der fundamentalen Kritik, die Kant in seinen Schriften zur praktischen Philosophie daran übte, indem er diesen Theorietyp unter grundsätzlichen Heteronomieverdacht stellte, scheinbar ausgedient.[3]

Die spezifische Pointe des post-kantischen Perfektionismus (= PkP) soll nun gerade darin bestehen, dass in ihm der ethisch und politisch zu befördernde und zu realisierende Wert die Freiheit, Autonomie bzw. rationale Selbstbestimmung darstellt. Mithin kam hierin das Ziel zum Ausdruck, die fundamentale Rolle, die Kant der Autonomie zugewiesen hatte mit der prä-kantischen perfektionistischen Vorstellung von zu realisierenden

---

[2] Vgl. Moggach (2011) sowie Moggach (2009).
[3] Vgl. die Abschnitte 2 „Pre-Kantian Perfectionism" und 3 „Kantian Criticisms" aus Moggachs Beitrag von 2011.

Bedingungen des guten und gelingenden Lebens zu versöhnen. Attraktiv kann ein solcher systematischer Theorietyp *prima facie* etwa dadurch erscheinen, dass er hinsichtlich der Realisierungsbedingungen eines guten menschlichen Lebens in einer politischen Gemeinschaft nicht bei der bloßen (normativen) Forderung stehen bleibt, sondern der spezifischen, historischen Dynamik und den sozialen Rahmenbedingungen, die es in einer Gesellschaft bedarf, um Autonomie für alle zu ermöglichen, Rechnung trägt und an konkrete, bereits vorliegende Praxen anknüpfen kann, um von dort aus eine weitere Realisierung von autonomen und autonomiebewahrenden sozialen Verhältnissen anzumahnen.

Gesteht man eine erste Attraktivität dieses Theorietyps zu und damit, dass sich eine weitere Diskussion von PkP lohnt, dann sind im Folgenden zwei Fragen auseinanderzuhalten:

Q1: Wie lässt sich PkP systematisch so ausgestalten, dass eine auf dem ‚Markt' ethischer und politischer Theoriebildung konkurrenzfähige und vertretbare Theorie entsteht, die man bereit wäre gegenüber perfektionistischen (und nicht-perfektionistischen) Alternativen zu verteidigen?

Q2: Lassen sich historische Positionen identifizieren, die sich unter PkP subsumieren lassen und damit ggf. als Inspirationsquelle für eine systematische Ausarbeitung im Sinne von Q1 dienen können?

Der Beitrag von Moggach ist vorrangig mit der zweiten Frage befasst. Auch in diesem Beitrag soll es primär um Q2 gehen. Zwar ist es nicht im methodischen Sinne zwingend, eine Antwort auf Q2 zu geben, um sich Q1 zu widmen, gesteht man aber zu, dass philosophiehistorische Auseinandersetzungen ein – wenn auch nicht notwendiges – doch aber hilfreiches Mittel zur Konstruktion eines verteidigungs- und vertretungswürdigen Theorietyps darstellen, dann gilt es zuerst einmal die philosophiehistorische Angebotslage daraufhin kursorisch zu prüfen, wie bisherige Ausgestaltungen von PkP aussehen, um diese hinsichtlich ihrer systematischen Stärken und Schwächen beurteilen zu können.[4]

---

4 Die Unabhängigkeit von Q1 und Q2 zeigt sich auch daran, dass man einen Streit darüber, ob eine bestimmte historisch vorliegende Theorie (und historisch umfasst hier auch zeitgenössische Theoriebildung) unter PkP fällt, führen kann, ohne deren systematische Plausibilität diskutieren zu müssen. Sofern man aber keine rein philosophiegeschichtlichen Interessen verfolgt, sollte jedoch klar sein, dass der Streit darum, welche historischen Theorien unter PkP fallen, gerade deshalb von Interesse ist, weil entsprechende Theorien herangezogen werden können, um die systematischen Stärken und Schwächen von PkP einschätzen zu können, mithin deren Geltung letztlich Zweck auch der philosophiehistorischen Bemühungen ist.

Dass die nähere Bestimmung der Merkmale von PkP immer noch eine ziemlich heterogene Sammlung spezifischer Theorievorschläge zu subsumieren erlauben, machen die beiden historischen Theorien deutlich, die Moggach als Fälle von PkP identifiziert. Es handelt sich einmal um Fichtes politisch-ökonomische Theorie im *Geschlossenen Handelsstaat* von 1800, zum anderen um die politischen Schriften Bruno Bauers (1809-1882) bis zu dessen konservativer Wende nach der gescheiterten Revolution von 1848 mit der die revolutionäre Epoche des Vormärz und auch der linkshegelianische Diskurs zu ihrem Ende kamen. Gerade Fichtes Vorschlag im *Handelsstaat* sollte einen skeptisch stimmen, ob tatsächlich jede Ausgestaltung eines PkP schon als systematisch attraktiv gelten kann. Denn Fichte (1762-1814) realisiert in seiner Schrift das geradezu paradoxe Ziel, Freiheit durch soviel Sicherheit zu ‚schützen', dass zu guter Letzt von konkreten Freiheitsrechten (Sicherheit der Wohnung, freie Berufswahl, Reisefreiheit, um nur einige eingängige Beispiele zu nennen) nahezu nichts mehr übrig bleibt und diese in einer Art Polizei-, Überwachungs- und Planungsstaat verloren gehen.[5]

Demgegenüber weisen die Überlegungen Bruno Bauers eher in Richtung eines demokratischen Staatsgefüges, dass die Autonomie der einzelnen – z.B. durch das Wahlrecht und Pressefreiheit – sichern soll. Sicherlich hängt die nähere Einschätzung der Attraktivität und Plausibilität der genannten Ausgestaltungen von PkP in der von Moggach skizzierten Gestalt, von weiteren Annahmen darüber ab, was eine ethische und politische Theorie leisten können soll. Hier ging es mir vorerst nur darum, klar zu machen, dass mit der Zuordnung zu PkP erst einmal nur wenige spezifische Rechte und Ansprüche verteidigt oder eingeführt sind. Vielmehr handelt es sich bei dieser Zuordnung um eine allgemeine Strategie, einen evaluativen und normativen Rahmen für ethische, rechtliche und politische Ansprüche bereitzustellen, die sich auf signifikante Weise sowohl von der kantischen als auch von der wolffianisch-perfektionistischen Variante unterscheiden soll. Möchte man konkrete Ausgestaltungen von PkP näher bestimmen, wäre zudem entweder der Theorietyp mit weiteren Merkmalen auszustatten oder aber die jeweiligen Theorievorschläge an der modernen und zeitgenössischen Debatte, die den Perfektionismus primär vom Liberalismus abgrenzt, zu bemessen. Denn auch in dieser gegenwärtigen Debatte wird das Schlagwort ‚Perfektionismus' für zahlreiche Projekte in Anspruch genommen.[6] Als Haupteinwand gegen perfektionistische Ansätze hat sich in der modernen Diskussion der Einwand des Paternalismus

---

5 Vgl. *SW* III zur stark beschränkten Reisefreiheit etwa 419 zu den planwirtschaftlichen Konsequenzen der fichteschen Wirtschaftslehre etwa 421-424.
6 Zu den modernen Vorschlägen instruktiv Düber (2016), 71-126, vor allem 71-95. Zu modernen Perfektionismen vgl. auch Wall (2019).

herauskristallisiert. Ob dieser jedoch – in der einen oder anderen Gestalt – tatsächlich alle Perfektionismen zu diskreditieren vermag, ist allerdings nach wie vor fraglich.[7] Jedenfalls erscheint es aussichtsreich, auch den vorliegenden Theorietyp PkP auf etwaige paternalistische Gehalte hin abzuklopfen. Zuvor gilt es allerdings zu klären, inwiefern man Arnold Ruges Philosophie unter den PkP subsumieren kann. Doch bevor ich mich dieser Aufgabe im dritten Kapitel stellen werde, gilt es zuvor noch den Theorietyp PkP hinsichtlich seiner metaethischen und normativen Merkmale näher zu charakterisieren, um so Prüfmittel in die Hand zu bekommen, an denen sich dann bewähren muss, ob Arnold Ruge als Verfechter eines solchen ethisch-politischen zählen kann.

‚Perfektionismus' lässt sich grob als eine Theorie charakterisieren, die der Förderung und Entwicklung bestimmter Fähigkeiten oder Talente einen intrinsischen, nicht rein-instrumentellen Wert beimisst. Die Realisierung dieses Wertes (oder einer Menge an als ethisch-politisch intrinsisch gewerteten Fähigkeiten) liefert das vorherrschende Ziel ethischer Orientierung. Einzurichtende oder zu kritisierende Normen sollten mithin so gestaltet sein, dass sie die Realisierung der Werte oder des Wertes befördern, die als intrinsisch förderungswürdige Fähigkeiten anerkannt oder behauptet worden sind. Wie weiter oben bereits angemerkt, stellt der förderungswürdige Wert des PkP die menschliche Freiheit, d.h. Autonomie, in der Gestalt rationaler Selbstbestimmung dar. Der prä-kantische Perfektionismus eines Christian Wolff dagegen sei auf das Ziel der Glückseligkeit resp. Vollkommenheit ausgerichtet gewesen, dies eröffnet Kant die Möglichkeit seiner fundamentalen Kritik aus dem Prinzip der Autonomie heraus.[8]

Man hat es bei PkP also mit einer monistischen, auf den Wert der Freiheit gerichteten, perfektionistischen Theorie zu tun. Der unterstellte Autonomiebegriff ist zudem relational und historisch, die Autonomie der Individuen realisiert sich (resp. soll historisch realisiert werden) dadurch, dass spezifische freiheitsherstellende und verbürgende Institutionen geschaffen werden, die es erlauben, Autonomie wirklich werden zu lassen.[9] Ein Individuum ist mithin autonom nur relativ zum Hintergrund spezifischer Institutionen und Praxen.

---

7 Vgl. hierzu ebenfalls die moderne und zeitgenössische Varianten des Perfektionismus auf diesen Einwand hin prüfende Studie von Düber (2016).
8 Zur Bestimmung der „Glückseligkeit" bei Wolff vgl. Wolff (1980), § 118; zu den Hintergründen in der Vollkommenheitslehre und Anthropologie vgl. § 11 und § 36. Einen historisch-entwicklungsgeschichtlichen Überblick über Wolffs Vollkommenheitsethik bietet Schwaiger (2018).
9 Für eine moderne Fassung einer relationalen Autonomietheorie, die politische Realisierung und historischen Wandel zu integrieren versucht vgl. Christman (2009). Eine solche relationale Autonomietheorie, die Autonomie auch und gerade in Institutionen verortet und nicht nur in den Fähigkeiten und Eigenschaften einzelner Handlungssubjekte, lässt sich bereits bei Hegel (1770-1831) finden. Vgl. hierzu etwa Yeomans (2015).

Die Entwicklung dieser Institutionen und Praxen wiederum ist – etwa im Falle Bruno Bauers – eingebettet in eine normative Geschichtsphilosophie, die – auch im Blick auf die Zukunft – die Geschichte als Realisierung und Durchsetzung des Wertes der Freiheit versteht. Als Vorbild dient hier offensichtlich die – allerdings auf die Dimension der Zukunft verzichtende – Geschichtsphilosophie Hegels, die sich als eine Begriffsgeschichte der Freiheit verstehen lässt.[10] Da das Verständnis von Freiheit und Autonomie selbst historisch-relativ bestimmt ist, stellt eine (normative) Geschichtsphilosophie ein notwendiges Ingredienz des PkP dar, jedenfalls sofern man Moggachs Lektüre von Bruno Bauer nicht einfach nur als Illustration, sondern als Festsetzung eines paradigmatischen Falles von PkP auffasst.

Metaethisch stellt PkP einen nicht-naturalistischen Kognitivismus bereit, in dem sich wahrheitswertfähige bzw. begründbare Behauptungen darüber, was zu tun sei, aus einer theoretisch (d.h. hier genauer: geschichtsphilosophisch) angeleiteten Reflexion auf den historischen Prozess ergeben sollen. Nicht-naturalistisch ist PkP, da die Annahmen über den Menschen sich nicht auf historisch-empirische Bedingungen oder eine als fix angenommene menschliche Natur beschränken lassen, sondern transzendentale Fähigkeiten miteinbeziehen. Autonomie wird dabei als monistischer Wert gesetzt, der nicht lediglich der Instanz des ‚freien Willens' – wie bei Kant – zukommt, sondern relational konzipiert wird und sich daher in der sozialen Wirklichkeit selbst in angemessenen Institutionen und Praxen Ausdruck verschaffen muss und soll. Damit wird der Grundgedanke Hegels aufgegriffen, dass die Philosophie nicht nur Normen zu rechtfertigen habe, sondern diese zugleich an bereits historisch vorliegende ‚Gestaltungen' anbinden müsse, in denen sich diese Normen und damit Freiheit Ausdruck zu verleihen vermögen.[11]

---

10 Vgl. zu diesem Verständnis der hegelschen Geschichtsphilosophie Rojek (2017), 221-246. In den linkshegelianischen Debatten war es insbesondere der Beitrag von August von Cieszkowski (1804-1894), der die hegelsche Geschichtsphilosophie um die Dimension der Zukunft ergänzte. Vgl. hierzu Cieszkowski (1981), insbesondere 8-9, 20; und Schweikard (2015). Dass eine Geschichtsphilosophie im hegelianischen Geist nicht zwingend auf PkP festlegt, zeigt das Beispiel Cieszkowskis aber auch. Dieser ist jedenfalls kein Vertreter des PkP, da er als perfektionistischen Wert, der in der Geschichte zu realisieren sei, nicht ‚Freiheit', sondern ‚Glückseligkeit' angibt und damit eher in die wolffische Tradition fiele. Vgl. Cieszkowski (1981), 70, wo von der „Endbestimmung der Glückseligkeit" die Rede ist.

11 Man denke etwa an Hegels Bestimmungen von ‚Idee', ‚Begriff' und ‚Verwirklichung' des Rechts in seinen Grundlinien der Philosophie des Rechts. „Die philosophische Rechtswissenschaft hat die Idee des Rechts, den Begriff des Rechts und dessen Verwirklichung zum Gegenstande.

Die Philosophie hat es mit Ideen, und darum nicht mit dem, was man bloße Begriffe zu heißen pflegt, zu thun, sie zeigt vielmehr deren Einseitigkeit und Unwahrheit auf, so wie

PkP lässt sich somit als die Verknüpfung des kantischen Wertes der individuellen Autonomie mit dem hegelschen Gedanken der Realisierung oder Verwirklichung dieser Autonomie in Institutionen und Praxen begreifen. Als Hintergrund zur Generierung spezifischer Normen zur Durchsetzung dieser Autonomie in adäquaten Praxen im Rahmen einer spezifischen historischen Realität bedarf es dann der informierenden normativen Geschichtsphilosophie, der also für die Attraktivität dieses Theorietyps ein nicht unwesentliches Gewicht zukommt.

Während August von Ciezkowski (wegen des Wertes der Glückseligkeit) und Max Stirner (1806-1856)[12] (wegen seines Nonkognitivismus) zu den linkshegelianischen Denkern gehören, die klarerweise nicht unter den PkP fallen, denen gegenüber Bruno Bauer paradigmatischerweise darunter fällt, so gilt es im dritten Kapitel zu prüfen, ob sich auch Arnold Ruge diesem Theorietyp zuordnen lässt.

3. Perfektionismus der Autonomie bei Arnold Ruge?

Vergleicht man Arnold Ruge mit Ludwig Feuerbach (1804-1872), Bruno Bauer oder selbst August von Cieszkowski, so wird man feststellen müssen, dass er – philosophiehistorisch gesehen – nicht zu den führenden Theoretikern der linkshegelianischen Diskurse gehört. Während sich die übrigen Denker, insbesondere durch theoretische Grundlegungsarbeiten um die Weiterentwicklung des Linkshegelianismus bemüht haben, lässt sich dies für Arnold Ruge nur in eingeschränkterem Maße geltend machen. Er hat weder zur Debatte um die Religionskritik, die für die Genese der Differenzierung in Links-, Rechts- und Zentrumshegelianer wesentlich war,[13] noch zum Streit um die Rolle der Philosophie als kritische Instanz gegenüber der eigenen

---

  daß der Begriff, [...] allein es ist, was Wirklichkeit hat und zwar so, daß er sich diese selbst giebt. Alles, was nicht diese durch den Begriff selbst gesetzte Wirklichkeit ist, ist vorübergehendes Daseyn, äußerliche Zufälligkeit, Meynung, wesenlose Erscheinung, Unwahrheit, Täuschung u.s.f. Die Gestaltung, welche sich der Begriff in seiner Verwirklichung giebt, ist zur Erkenntnis des Begriffes selbst, das andere von der Form, nur als Begriff zu seyn, unterschiedene wesentliche Moment der Idee." (*GW* 14, §1 & §1 A, 23)

12 Zu Johann Kaspar Schmidt alias Max Stirner vgl. Rojek (2019), 77f.
13 Diese Ausdrücke sind hier zur groben Andeutung dienende historische Zuordnungstermini. Sie sollen den evaluativen Gehalt, der ihnen als Selbst- und Fremdzuschreibungen in der damaligen Debatte zukam, nicht mittransportieren.

politisch-sozialen Gegenwart, d.h. des Streits um das Verhältnis von Theorie und Praxis, grundlegende Beiträge monographischen Umfangs geliefert.[14]

Nichtsdestotrotz handelt es sich bei Arnold Ruge um eine „organisatorische Zentralfigur des Junghegelianismus"[15]. Seine Stärke lag in seiner Tätigkeit als Herausgeber und leitende Figur der *Hallischen Jahrbücher* und nach deren Verbot durch die preußische Zensur der, dann in Sachsen publizierten *Deutschen Jahrbücher für Wissenschaft und Kunst*. Hierbei handelt es sich um die zentralen Diskursorgane der Linkshegelianer, die Ruge mit Geschick leitete, das Auftreten von Konkurrenzorganen zu unterbinden wusste und so einen wesentlichen Beitrag zur politischen Publizistik des Vormärz leistete. Erst durch den Streit mit Marx in Paris während der kurzfristigen Zusammenarbeit an den Deutsch-Französischen Jahrbüchern, den Zerfall der linkshegelianischen Diskursgemeinschaft ab 1845 und das Exil im englischen Brighton, verlor sich die zentrale organisatorische Rolle, die Ruge zwischen 1838 und 1843 für sich beanspruchen konnte.[16] Ruges philosophische Beiträge, sofern sie für den linkshegelianischen Kontext relevant sind, beschränken sich auf ‚tagespolitische' Interventionen im Rahmen der von ihm herausgegebenen Zeitschriften.[17]

Ruge setzt sich in diesen publizistisch-politischen Interventionen insbesondere für eine Demokratisierung des preußischen Staates sowie die Pressefreiheit ein. Die argumentative Hintergrundfolie seiner Beiträge bildete die hegelsche Philosophie, die er jedoch – typisch für die Linkshegelianer – zum einen um die Dimension des absoluten Geistes depotenziert, indem er diesen in den Bereich des objektiven Geistes und dort letztlich in die Geschichtsphilosophie integriert, und zum anderen Hegels Philosophie selbst in Teilen historisch relativiert, indem er diese als bloß theoretischen Ausdruck ihrer Zeit deutet. Inzwischen habe sich die Zeit geändert und die Forderung nach Verwirklichung von Freiheit müsse über die in Hegels *Grundlinien der Philosophie*

---

14 Nichtsdestotrotz lassen sich auch Ruges Geschichtsphilosophie und seinem Plädoyer für Reform statt Revolution durchaus eigenständige Überlegungen abringen. Vgl. hierzu Rojek (2015). Zum Streit um Theorie und Praxis, d.h. die Rolle und Funktion der Philosophie oder eines ihr nachfolgenden Wissenschaftstyps, die neben dem Streit um das Verhältnis von Religion und Philosophie einen der beiden Hauptdiskussionsstränge der linkshegelianischen Debatten ausmacht (vgl. Quante (2010), 198-210), siehe Rojek (2019), zu Arnold Ruge ebd., 76f.

15 Bunzel/Hundt/Lambrecht (2006), 50.

16 Zu Ruges Biographie vgl. knapp Rojek (2015), 143-144, sowie die ausführliche Zeittafel über Ruges Leben in Meyer (2010), 22-47.

17 Seine Schriften und Übersetzungen nach 1845 sowie die teils altphilologischen Arbeiten zur Antike sowie seine Arbeiten zur hegelschen Ästhetik bleiben hier also außer Betracht.

des Rechts geforderten und rekonstruierten Institutionen und Praxen hinausgehen und diese wirklich werden lassen:

> [E]r [Hegel; T.R.] war wirklich der *philosophische* Abschluß seiner Zeit, und nun ignorierte er auch die Schranke oder die Negation der Zukunft, weil diese dem absoluten Wissen widerspricht; diese Schranke offenbart sich nun unmittelbar an ihm selber, und diese Negation ist bereits eingetreten: wir können weder seine Zurechtmacherei des Christentums, noch die Konstruktion der bereits historisch überwundenen Zustände, wie z.B. der englischen Verfassung, weder die ‚absolute Religion', noch die ‚absolute Kunst', und noch weniger ‚das absolute Wissen' anerkennen, und werden ihm überall beweisen, daß solche Unfreiheit seinem eigenen, dem ewigen Prinzip der Freiheit und der Geschichte, d.h. der Entwicklung, zuwider ist. Die entwickelte Freiheit und der weltbewegende Anstoß zu ihrer Verwirklichung und Ausbreitung ihres Begriffs hat Hegel uns übrig gelassen.[18]

In diesem Zitat aus einer Kritik des Staats- und Völkerrechts, die Ruge 1840 für seine *Hallischen Jahrbücher* verfasst hat, bündeln sich die einzelnen Motive und philosophischen Vorstellungen Ruges, in ihrer Aktivierung für eine Kritik der politisch-sozialen Verhältnisse seiner Zeit, wie in einem Brennglas.

Das Zitat macht deutlich, dass Ruge Hegel für den *philosophischen* Abschluss seiner Zeit, d.h. Hegels Zeit hält. Doch anders als Hegel glaubte, ist damit keineswegs auch ein politisch-institutioneller Abschluss erreicht. Diese praktische Realisierung politisch einzufordern, wie dies Ruge mit seinen Beiträgen beansprucht, sei nun die Aufgabe der Gegenwart, wie insbesondere der letzte Satz der zitierten Passage deutlich macht. Dass Hegel als philosophischer Abschluss seiner Zeit gelten könne, ist allerdings mehrdeutig. Auf der einen Seite bedarf es eben nicht nur der schlichten Realisierung der bei Hegel zu entdeckenden Gehalte in der preußischen Realität, sondern auch einer neuen Philosophie, die allerdings bei den Linkshegelianern in weiten Teilen von den hegelschen Begründungsfiguren und Ansprüchen zehrt. Wie der mittlere Teil des Zitats zeigt, entfällt der absolute Geist und damit die gesamte ‚Abgeschlossenheitsrhetorik' des hegelschen Systems und die Zukunft wird nun in Hegels Geschichtsphilosophie integriert. Dass damit erhebliche neue Ansprüche auf die Schultern einer hegelsch inspirierten systematischen Geschichtsphilosophie geladen werden, stellt ein Problem dar, dem sich Ruge an keiner Stelle explizit gewidmet hat. Mutmaßlich hatte der politische Forderungs- und Realisierungscharakter in seinen Texten und seinen Interessen das Primat vor einer systematisch ausgearbeiteten Absicherung der Geltung seiner Forderungen. Zudem versteht Ruge Hegels Philosophie, ebenso

---

18 Ruge (1840), 403-404.

wie diejenige etwa Kants in Teilen als Akkomodationen an ihre repressiven Zeitverhältnisse, diese ‚uneigentlichen' Gehalte müssten also aufgedeckt, beseitigt und strikt von den Gehalten unterschieden werden, die auch für die jeweilige Gegenwart noch Geltung beanspruchen.[19] Dazu, wie eine solche Trennung möglich sein soll, hat Ruge allerdings kein klares Kriterium etabliert. Die Ziele Pressefreiheit und Wahlrecht resp. ein demokratisches Staatsgebilde werden einfach als Forderungen der Zeit gesetzt, ohne das klar wird, wieso diese aus Hegels Philosophie konsequent gelesen ebenso folgten wie deren Realisierung in der Zukunft (also in Ruges Gegenwart) zwingend sei.[20]

Während Hegels Geschichtsphilosophie *rekonstruktiv* verfährt und daher die Philosophie nicht beanspruchen kann, über die Zukunft irgendetwas Sicheres zu sagen oder aber für diese zu fordern, beansprucht Ruge – ebenso wie Cieszkowski oder Bauer – dass Hegel gezeigt habe, dass sich die Freiheit notwendig, auf die eine oder andere Weise in der Geschichte realisiere, so schreibt Ruge:

> Ans Ende jeder Geschichtsentwicklung tritt die Forderung ihrer Zukunft, welche als religiösen und gewissenhaften Trieb die Verwirklichung des Gewußten zum praktischen Pathos des Subjekts macht, aus der faulen Beschaulichkeit des Hegelianismus die Fichtische Thatkraft wieder auferweckt, und die Polemik gegen das Sollen, gegen den praktischen Liberalismus, gegen den wahren Rationalismus, gegen die durchgeführte Aufklärung verwirft; denn das inhaltsvolle Sollen der sich selbst erkennenden geschichtlichen Gegenwart ist die Dialektik der Geschichte selbst.[21]

Zu den Problemen, denen sich Ruges Uminterpretation des hegelschen Systems sowie dessen Umbau ausgesetzt sieht, zählen unter anderem, das er keinen klaren Abschlusspunkt mehr für die geschichtliche Durchsetzung des Freiheitsprinzips anzugeben in der Lage ist und damit letztlich unklar bleibt, welches Maß an Freiheit eigentlich als das für die gesellschaftlich-politische Wirklichkeit angemessene gelten kann.[22] Weiterhin bleibt problematisch,

---

19　Das Ziel, die bloß zeitabhängigen Gehalte der Philosophien Kants und Hegels zu identifizieren, setzt sich Ruge in Ruge (1841b).

20　Zur Forderung der Demokratie etwa: „Die deutsche Welt, um ihre Gegenwart dem Tode zu entreißen und ihre Zukunft zu sichern, braucht nichts als das neue Bewußtsein, welches in allen Sphären den freien Menschen zum Princip und das Volk zum Zweck erhebt, mit Einem Wort *die Auflösung des Liberalismus in Demokratismus*." (Ruge (1843), 116) Zur Forderung nach Pressefreiheit, Ruge (1841), 25.

21　Ruge (1840), 404.

22　Dass man sich, sofern man Interesse an einem gelingenden Staatsaufbau hat, der mit der Freiheit aller verträglich ist, mit der Maßstabsfrage befassen sollte, zeigt die Wehrlosigkeit mit der Ruge und andere Linkshegelianer der radikalen Freiheitsemphase Max Stirners

dass seine Version einer hegelschen Geschichtsphilosophie sich zu einer Art Historismus wandelt, der selbst die Geltungsdimension der hegelschen Logik nicht unaffiziert lässt, von der doch Ruge selbst in seinen Beiträgen permanent zehrt. Damit negiert er gewissermaßen die Geltungsmittel, die er doch benötigt, um seine Forderungen aufstellen zu können.[23]

Doch unabhängig von diesen Problemen und Beweislasten mit denen sich Ruges Vorschläge konfrontiert sehen, lässt sich vor dem Hintergrund der bisher dargestellten Gehalte der Rugeschen Geschichtsphilosophie noch nicht klar erkennen, ob wir es hier mit einer Ausgestaltung des Theorietyps PkP zu tun haben.

Zwar hat sich bisher gezeigt, dass Ruge sowohl die Freiheit resp. Autonomie für den zentralen Wert hält, als auch dass es diesen Wert zu realisieren gelte, mithin Autonomie perfektionistisch aufgefasst wird. Auch verortet Ruge das Ziel der Philosophie nicht im theoretischen, d.h. im bloßen Erkennen des Wahren, sondern in der Praxis, d.h. der Realisierung von Freiheit in konkreten Institutionen und Praxen. So schreibt Ruge:

> Die Philosophie, die ihren radikalen Zweck aus dem Sinne verliert, läuft eben so wie die allgemeine Weltbildung der reinen Privatmenschen, immer Gefahr, an Selbstbespiegelung und eitler Bewegung in ihrer eignen Subjektivität sich zu Grunde zu richten.[24]

Dass die Praxis, mithin realisierende und realisierte Autonomie von Ruge demgegenüber als Selbstzweck gesetzt wird, belegt die folgende Passage aus dem gleichen Beitrag:

---

gegenüberstanden, die deren Theorien allesamt auf die Seite paternalistischer und damit gerade nicht freiheitsförderlicher Theorien fallen ließ. Vgl. hierzu Quante (2015).

23 Deutlich macht dies etwa die folgende Passage: „Die Wissenschaft geht nicht in die Logik zurück, sondern in die Geschichte, und die Logik selbst wird in die Geschichte hineingezogen, sie muß es sich gefallen lassen, als Existenz [Dies ist z.B. selbst eine hegelsche Kategorie! |T.R.] begriffen zu werden, weil sie dem Bildungsstande *dieser* Philosophie angehört, d.h. die Wissenschaft, die selbst eine historische Form des Geistes ist, fasst die Wahrheit nicht in der absoluten Form, sie wirft *den ganzen Inhalt der Idee* (oder der Wahrheit) in ihre Form, so wie sie aber als Existenz begriffen, also der *Kritik* unterworfen ist, geht die Geschichte über sie hinaus. Die Kritik ist die Bewegung, der Sekretionsprozeß, der zugleich Zeugungsprozeß ist." (Ruge (1841b), 285-286.) Zur Kritik an Ruges ‚Historismus' vgl. Rojek (2015), 156-158.

24 Ruge (1843), 106.

> Die Wahrheit ist sich selbst Zweck heißt: ihr Zweck ist im Bewußtsein der Welt und als lebendiges, bewegendes Princip, zu sein, d.h. der Zweck der Theorie ist die Praxis der Theorie.[25]

Da Ruge seine Forderungen zudem nicht als Ausdruck eines ‚blinden Triebs' ausgibt oder aber anthropologisch in der Menschennatur verankert, sondern vielmehr dem Leben des Geistes, d.h. spezifischen kulturellen Gegebenheiten zuweist, wird man ihm kaum einen Nonkognitivismus unterlegen können, der auch mit seinen hegelschen Hintergründen schwerlich verträglich wäre. Für einen Kognitivismus und zugleich für den zentralen Eigenwert der ‚Autonomie' lässt sich zudem der folgende Passus anführen:

> Das Princip, um das sich jetzt Alles dreht, ist die *Autonomie des Geistes*, und zwar im Wissenschaftlichen die Fortbildung des *Rationalismus* und im Staatlichen des *Liberalismus*. Alle Wahrheit in der Wissenschaft hat gegenwärtig die allgemeine Form des Selbstbewußtseins, ist der Prozeß des denkenden Menschen. Die Einheit des geschichtlichen und reingeistigen Processes, weil sie als dieselbe Bewegung der Vernunft erkannt worden, läßt nichts übrig, als die Welt der Vernunft selbst.[26]

Wenn diese Beobachtungen zutreffen, dann stellt ‚Freiheit' in der Tat für Ruge einen in einer monistischen und kognitivistischen Konzeption verankerten intrinsischen Wert dar, dessen jeweilige Realisation zudem über seinen geschichtsphilosophischen Hintergrund, von dem Ruge zehrt ohne ihn zu explizieren, an historisch spezifische Umstände gebunden wird. Da Ruge zudem als Realisationsinstanzen nicht allein individuelle Autonomie und deren Wahrung einfordert, sondern zudem die Verwirklichung derselben in demokratischen Strukturen, treffen die Kernmerkmale, die Moggach für PkP ausgegeben hat, auch auf die praktisch-philosophischen Überlegungen Arnold Ruges zu. Man hat es bei Ruge also mit einer Instanz des PkP zu tun.

Damit ist die eingangs gestellte Frage Q2 einer Antwort zugeführt. Ruges Geschichtsphilosophie stellt eine Ausgestaltung des PkP dar und weist die wesentlichen Merkmale auf, die es erlauben, eine historische Position unter diesen systematischen Theorietyp zu subsumieren.

---

25   Ruge (1843), 108.
26   Ruge (1841a), 30. Die zeitindikatorischen Ausdrücke ‚jetzt' und ‚gegenwärtig' belegen zudem den Rugeschen Historismus mit den oben genannten Problemen.

4. Herausforderungen für den Post-kantischen Perfektionismus am Beispiel Arnold Ruges

Abschließend soll nun auf einige der Herausforderungen eingegangen werden, denen man sich gegenübersieht, sofern man Ruge auch für die Frage Q1 heranziehen möchte, d.h. seine konkreten Vorschläge und theoretischen Angebote als ‚Inspirationsquelle' für eine systematisch gehaltvolle Ausarbeitung eines PkP für die systematischen Teildisziplinen Ethik und Politische Philosophie bereitzustellen.

Hier muss die Antwort freilich weitaus skeptischer ausfallen, als bei der Frage der berechtigten Subsumtion Ruges unter den Theorietyp des PkP. Nicht nur stellt Ruge selbst kaum gehaltvolle Argumentationen für seine Position vor, so findet sich erstens keine Argumentation dafür, dass ‚Freiheit' einen (oder *den*) intrinsischen Wert darstellt, den es historisch zu realisieren und zu vervollkommnen gilt. Doch selbst dann, wenn man diesen Wert bloß über ‚Intuitionen' absichern mag oder lediglich negativ darüber absichert, dass wir in unserer gelebten moralischen und politischen Praxis Verstöße gegen Freiheitsrechte oder aber deren Instrumentalisierung als bloße Mittel ablehnen,[27] so gibt uns Ruge doch kaum Hinweise an die Hand, welche Institutionen und Praxen wir auf welche Weise weiterzuentwickeln oder zu reformieren hätten, um den Ansprüchen des Wertes der Freiheit gerecht zu werden.

Auch über die geschichtsphilosophischen Details, die es erlauben, nicht nur rekonstruktiv die Geschichte als Realisierung des Begriffs der Freiheit (und dessen partieller Verwirklichung in Institutionen und Praxen) zu verstehen, sondern auch für die Zukunft *berechtigte* Ansprüche auf deren weitere Realisierung zu stellen, hat Ruge nichts verlauten lassen. Dies kann entweder als Ausdruck politischer Kampfrhetorik oder aber eines bemerkenswerten Vertrauens auf bloß implizit bleibende theoretische Hintergründe interpretiert werden. Während eine geschichtsphilosophische Rekonstruktion der Weltgeschichte als zunehmende Realisierung und begriffliche Entfaltung von ‚Freiheit' noch einen gewissen Anhalt an den methodischen Normen und Vorschlägen nehmen kann, die Hegel selbst in seiner Geschichtsphilosophie vorgelegt hat, jedenfalls soweit dies aus seinen hinterlassenen Manuskripten und spärlichen Textpassagen in den *Grundlinien der Philosophie des Rechts* und den

---

27 Wie ein Blick in die Tagespresse zeigt, steht aber auch diese Intuition auf eher schwachen Füßen und über den Umstand hinaus, dass ‚Freiheit' ein Ausdruck ist, dem man semantisch gern Tribut zollt, gehen hier die politischen und kulturellen Kämpfe früh los, so dass es schwer sein dürfte, hier einen gemeinsamen Hintergrundkonsens zu finden, der nicht bereits durch wechselseitige petitio-principii Vorwürfe attackiert wird.

drei Fassungen der *Enzyklopädie der philosophischen Wissenschaften im Grundrisse* ersehen werden kann, ist Ruge für die Dimension der Zukunft völlig auf sich selbst und die methodisch fragwürdigen Ausführungen bei August von Cieszkowski angewiesen.[28]

Da Ruge mithin zu diesen drei zentralen Aufgabenbereichen einer begründeten und argumentativ gehaltvollen Ausgestaltung des PkP wenig mitzuteilen weiß, fällt er als Inspirator für eigene systematische Arbeit weitestgehend aus, so sehr uns sein Einsatz für Demokratie und Pressefreiheit trotz einer mehrjährigen Gefängnisstrafe in den 1820er Jahren auch imponieren mag. Dass auch die Rede von ‚Freiheit' selbst semantisch und damit institutionell unterbestimmt bleibt, obgleich Ruge einige Positionen als nicht mit ihr verträglich angesehen hat, stellt ein weiteres Monitum dar.[29]

Dennoch lässt sich, wenngleich nur negativ, aus Ruges Texten einiges für eine potentielle eigenständige Vertretung eines PkP lernen. Seine Beiträge machen deutlich, welchen Beweislasten man sich zu stellen hat, möchte man einen PkP als konkurrenzfähige Position etablieren. Die größte Herausforderung liegt m.E. darin, eine systematische Geschichtsphilosophie bereitzustellen, durch die sich ein Perfektionismus der Autonomie sowohl erklären als auch rechtfertigen oder aber stützen lässt, je nachdem, wie man diese genau ausarbeitet. Eine solche Geschichtsphilosophie müsste zweierlei leisten: Im Rahmen der theoretischen Philosophie muss sie erklären, wie sich die Vergangenheit, deren Institutionen, Diskurse und Praxen als Ausdruck des Wertes der Freiheit rekonstruieren und verstehen lässt. Eine nicht geringe Teilaufgabe bestünde dann darin, diese philosophische Zielbestimmung mit den Kompetenzen und Mitteln der Geschichtswissenschaften disziplinär adäquat abzugleichen oder an diese anzupassen. Zum anderen aber muss die Geschichtsphilosophie normativ zeigen, welche Realisationen der Freiheit für die jeweilige Zukunft als sinnvoll und vertretbar gefordert werden sollten,

---

28 Zu den methodischen Eigenheiten der hegelschen Philosophie der Weltgeschichte, insbesondere zum komplexen Verhältnis von Geschichts*philosophie* und nicht-philosophischer Geschichtswissenschaft vgl. Rojek (2017), Kap. 2 und Kap. 3.

29 So stand Ruge dem Sozialismus, den er für tendenziell freiheitsgefährdend hielt, äußerst skeptisch gegenüber. Er hielt ihn für utopisch und damit nicht an die geschichtlichen Realisationstendenzen von Freiheit in seiner Zeit anschlussfähig. Vgl. seine beißende Kritik an Moses Heß, die er im Rückblick auf seine erfolglose Zeit in Paris formulierte. Vgl. Ruge (1846), 29-45. Zudem spricht er sich in Ruge (1841a), 31 gegen den „Polizeistaat" als Realisation von Freiheit aus. Leider hat Ruge die semantischen Konturen einer adäquaten Realisation von ‚Freiheit' relativ zu den Herausforderungen und Spannungen seiner Zeit nicht näher konturiert. Warum etwa ist Demokratie eine adäquate Realisation, nicht aber der Sozialismus? Eine systematische Ausarbeitung des PkP hätte hier zumindest gute Gründe zu offerieren.

dafür wird es – zumindest in Maßen – auch der Erkennbarkeit der Zukunft, mithin theoretisch-geschichtsphilosophischer Aussagen bedürfen. Lässt man einen naiven Geschichtsdeterminismus außer acht, so kommt hier heute wohl nur noch der Rückgriff auf mehr oder weniger plausible Prognosen in Frage, was ebenfalls eine inter- oder transdisziplinäre Aufgabenstellung verlangt, die neben der Philosophie sicher auch die Rechtswissenschaften, die Ökonomie, Soziologie und Psychologie umfassen müsste, sofern man nicht so optimistisch ist, alle diese Aufgaben mit rein philosophischen Mitteln leisten zu wollen.

Macht man sich klar, welche gewaltigen systematischen Aufgaben hier für die Ausarbeitung eines PkP liegen, so wird man sich wohl nicht ohne Weiteres auf die Sicherheit stützen wollen, mit der Ruge schrieb:

> Der Geist unserer gegenwärtigen Geschichte ist *der bewußte*; von jetzt an täuscht er sich über sein Ziel nicht mehr; wir wissen Alle, daß uns die Freiheit der literarischen Oeffentlichkeit und die Oeffentlichkeit des freien Staates gewiß ist (...).[30]

Eine realistische Geschichtsphilosophie als Stützung von oder Teil eines PkP wird hier zum einen die Option der Täuschung zulassen müssen und damit eine gewisse Offenheit gegenüber der Paternalismusgefahr zugestehen müssen,[31] zum anderen ist die Rede von Gewissheit auch insofern doppeldeutig, als sich die normative Dimension der Geschichtsphilosophie und die Dimension desjenigen, was sich deskriptiv über die Zukunft sagen lässt, hier in einem unklaren Verhältnis zueinander befinden. Ähnlich doppeldeutig, zwischen normativer und deskriptiver Aussage schwankend, formuliert Ruge etwa auch: „Der Mensch muß theoretisch und ethisch autonom sein."[32] Hier drohen Ruges Geschichtsphilosophie Paradoxien, wie sie im Marxismus etwa aus den Debatten des sogenannten Austromarxismus bekannt sind. Wenn die Ankunft der Freiheit sicher ist, wieso muss man sich dann noch um sie bemühen – was ist der normative Geltungsgrund der eigenen politischen Motivation?[33] Eine modernisierte Geschichtsphilosophie als trans- oder interdisziplinäres Projekt hätte hier klar(er) zu unterscheiden.

Was sich an Ruge exemplifizieren lässt, ist dass mit der Zuordnung zum Typ des PkP systematisch nur ein erster Schritt getan ist, der deutlich macht, wo

---

30 Ruge (1841a), 25.
31 Damit ist freilich nicht gesagt, dass es nicht Formen von Paternalismus geben mag, die sich rechtfertigen lassen, man denke etwa an die Anschnallpflicht im Auto oder Warnhinweise auf Zigarettenpackungen.
32 Ruge (1841a), 31.
33 Klar ins Auge gefasst wird das Problem etwa von Otto Bauer (1881-1938). Vgl. Bauer (1970).

die eigentliche systematische Arbeit zu beginnen hätte und das weitere ‚Inspirationsquellen' herangezogen werden müssten, um die Ansprüche eines PkP auf eine nicht nur historisch diskutable, sondern systematisch plausible Weise einlösen zu können.

Literatur

Bauer, Otto, „Marxismus und Ethik", in: *Austromarxismus*, hg. v. Raffael De La Vega/ Hans-Jörg Sandkühler, Frankfurt am Main, 1970, S. 485-499.

Bunzel, Wolfgang/Hundt, Martin/Lambrecht, Lars (Hrsg.), „Einführung", in: *Zentrum und Peripherie. Arnold Ruges Korrespondenz mit Junghegelianern in Berlin*, Frankfurt am Main, 2006, S. 7-64.

Christman, John, *The Politics of Persons. Individual Autonomy and socio-historical Selves*, Cambridge, 2009.

Cieszkowski, August von: *Prolegomena zur Historiosophie*. Mit einer Einleitung von Rüdiger Bubner und einem Anhang von Jan Garewicz, Hamburg, 1981 [1838].

Düber, Dominik, *Selbstbestimmung und das gute Leben im demokratischen Staat. Der Paternalismus-Einwand gegen den Perfektionismus*, Münster, 2016.

Fichte, Johann Gottlieb, „Der geschlossene Handelsstaat" (1800), in: *Fichtes Werke herausgegeben von Immanuel Hermann Fichte*, Bd. III, Berlin, 1971, S. 387-513. (*SW*)

Hegel, Georg Wilhelm Friedrich, „Grundlinien der Philosophie des Rechts", in: *Gesammelte Werke*, hg. v. Klaus Grotsch und Elisabeth Weisser-Lohmann, Band 14.1, Hamburg, 2009. (*GW*)

Meyer, Regina (Hrsg.), „Zeittafel", in: *Ästhetische Lehre und Lehren in Halle. Arnold Ruge. Rudolf Haym. Johannes Schmidt. Heinrich von Stein*, Halle (Saale), 2010, S. 22-47.

Moggach, Douglas, „Freedom and Perfection: German Debates on the State in the Eighteenth Century", in: *Canadian Journal of Political Science*, 42/4, 2009, S. 1003-1023.

– „Post-Kantian Perfectionism", https://carleton.ca/bhum/wp-content/uploads/ Moggach-9-Moggach-edited.pdf (Januar 2011; letzter Aufruf 16.06.2019).

Quante, Michael, „After Hegel: The Actualization of Philosophy in Practice", in: *Routledge Companion to Nineteenth Century Philosophy*, hg. v. Dean Moyar, London, 2010, S. 197-237.

– „Max Stirners Kreuzzug gegen die Heiligen, oder: Die Selbstaufhebung des Antiperfektionismus", in: *Die Linken Hegelianer. Studien zum Verhältnis von Religion und Politik im Vormärz*, hg. v. Michael Quante u. Amir Mohseni, Paderborn, 2015, S. 245-263.

Rojek, Tim, *Hegels Begriff der Weltgeschichte. Eine wissenschaftstheoretische Studie*. Berlin/Boston, 2017.

- „Zwischen Reform und Revolution. Arnold Ruges Geschichtsphilosophie", in: *Die Linken Hegelianer. Studien zum Verhältnis von Religion und Politik im Vormärz*, hg. v. Michael Quante u. Amir Mohseni, Paderborn, 2015, S. 141-159.
- „Die Einheit von Theorie und Praxis – Praxiskonzepte vom Linkshegelianismus bis zum historischen und dialektischen Materialismus", in: *Philosophien der Praxis: Ein Handbuch*, hg. v. Thomas Bedorf u. Selin Gerlek, Tübingen, 2019, S. 73-104.

Ruge, Arnold, „Zur Kritik des gegenwärtigen Staats- und Völkerrechts [1840]" in: ders. *Werke und Briefe Band 2, Philosophische Kritiken 1838-1846*, hg. v. Hans-Martin Sass in 12 Bänden, Aalen, 1988, S. 397-433. (Ruge 1840)

- „Das Verhältnis von Theorie und Praxis. Vorwort zu dem Jahrgange der Hallischen Jahrbücher 1841", in: ders. *Werke und Briefe Band 2. Philosophische Kritiken 1838-1846*, hg. v. Hans-Martin Sass, Aalen, 1988, S. 24-41. (Ruge 1841a)
- Ruge, Arnold, „Über das Verhältnis von Philosophie, Politik und Religion. (Kants und Hegels Akkomodation)", in: ders. *Werke und Briefe Band 2. Philosophische Kritiken 1838-1846*, hg. v. Hans-Martin Sass, Aalen, 1988, S. 254-297. (Ruge 1841b)
- „Selbstkritik des Liberalismus", in: ders. *Werke und Briefe Band 2. Philosophische Kritiken 1838-1846*, hg. v. Hans-Martin Sass, Aalen, 1988, S. 76-116. (Ruge 1843)
- Ruge, Arnold, *Werke und Briefe Band 5, Zwei Jahre in Paris 1843-1845*, hg. v. Hans-Martin Sass, Aalen 2007. (Ruge 1846)

Schwaiger, Clemens, „Ethik", in: *Handbuch Christian Wolff*, hg. v. Robert Theis u. Alexander Aichele, Wiesbaden, 2018, S. 253-268.

Schweikard, David P., „Die Erkennbarkeit der Zukunft. Zu einem grundlegenden Postulat der Geschichtsphilosophie August von Ciezkowskis", in: *Die Linken Hegelianer. Studien zum Verhältnis von Religion und Politik im Vormärz*, hg. v. Michael Quante u. Amir Mohseni, Paderborn 2015, S. 199-215.

Wall, Steven, "Perfectionism in Moral and Political Philosophy", in: *The Stanford Encyclopedia of Philosophy* (Summer 2019 edition), hrsg. von Edward N. Zalta, forthcoming URL=https://plato.stanford.edu/archives/sum2019/entries/perfectionism-moral/ (letzter Aufruf: 10.06.2019).

Wolff, Christian, *Grundsätze des Natur- und Völkerrechts*. Mit einem Vorwort von Marcel Thomann 1754, ND: Hildesheim/New York, 1980.

Yeomans, Christopher, *The Expansion of Autonomy. Hegel's Pluralistic Philosophy of Action*, Oxford, 2015.

Karl Marx – ein postkantischer Perfektionist?

Michael Quante

> Die Frage, ob dem menschlichen Denken gegenständliche Wahrheit zukomme – ist keine Frage der Theorie, sondern eine *praktische* Frage.
>
> (Karl Marx)

Einleitung

Unstrittige Voraussetzungen sind im Kontext der Interpretation des Werkes von Karl Marx nur wenige zu finden.[1] Eine davon ist die Annahme, er sei in seinem Denken wesentlich von der Philosophie Hegels beeinflusst worden (strittig ist dabei aber sowohl, was dieser Einfluss systematisch für die Marxsche Theoriebildung austrägt, als auch, wie lange dieser Einfluss Hegels für das Marxsche Denken formierend gewesen ist). Eine andere ist die Annahme, Marx habe sein philosophisches Denken im Kontext der linkshegelianischen Debatte und auf der Grundlage linkshegelianischer Konzeptionen begonnen (strittig ist dabei aber sowohl, was genau unter linkshegelianischen Konzeptionen verstanden werden sollte, als auch, wie lange dieser Einfluss systematisch für die Marxsche Theoriebildung bedeutsam gewesen ist).

Strittig sind dagegen, wenn es um die grundlegendsten Voraussetzungen bzw. Interpretationshypothesen geht, zum einen die Frage, welcher wissenschaftstheoretische Status dem *Kapital* bzw. dem Marxschen Forschungsprogramm einer Kritik der politischen Ökonomie zugeschrieben werden müsse. Eng damit verbunden ist zum anderen die Frage, ob sich im Denken von Karl Marx irgendwo ein Theoriebruch diagnostizieren lässt: Vertreter der *Diskontinuitätsthese* gehen davon aus, dass sich irgendwann ab 1847 (das genaue Datum und die einen solchen Bruch belegenden Textzeugen sind innerhalb dieses Lagers strittig) ein solcher Bruch vollzogen habe. Marx breche mit seiner philosophischen Anthropologie und seinen linkshegelianischen Prämissen;

---

[1] In diesem Beitrag beziehe ich mich ausschließlich auf Karl Marx und lasse die Position von Friedrich Engels (sowie seine unterschiedlichen Rollen bei der Ausarbeitung der Marxschen Texte und Konzeptionen) gänzlich unerörtert.

er verfolge, so die starke Lesart, ab dann ein Theorieprogramm, welches von seinen methodologischen, epistemologischen und geltungstheoretischen Ansprüchen her nicht mehr als Philosophie gewertet werden könne. Einer schwächeren Lesart der Diskontinuitätsthese zufolge vollziehe sich dieser Bruch innerhalb der Philosophie: Marx verwerfe den anthropologischen Essentialismus der *Ökonomisch-philosophischen Manuskripte* zugunsten einer strukturalistischen, nicht mehr dem anthropologischen Humanismus verpflichteten Theorie sozialer Institutionen. Vertreter der *Kontinuitätsthese* gehen stattdessen von der Annahme aus, dass zentrale philosophische Konzeptionen, die Marx im Kontext seiner philosophischen Anthropologie entwickelt hat, auch in seinen zum Forschungsprogramm einer Kritik der politischen Ökonomie gehörenden Texte weiterhin gültig sind. Innerhalb dieses Lagers finden sich unterschiedliche Auffassungen darüber, in welchem Ausmaß und auf welcher Ebene der Theoriebildung diese Kontinuität bestehe. Ein weiterer Aspekt, der für die Fragestellung des vorliegenden Beitrags zentral ist, zugleich allerdings quer zur Opposition von Kontinuitäts- und Diskontinuitätsthese steht, kommt in der Frage zum Ausdruck, ob der Marxschen Theorie, insbesondere seiner Kritik der politischen Ökonomie, überhaupt eine ethische Dimension eingeschrieben sei?[2]

Die Titelfrage meines Beitrags zielt mitten in dieses Wespennest widerstreitender Interpretationen und exegetischer Schulstreitigkeiten hinein. Ihre Beantwortung setzt daher Prämissen voraus, die an dieser Stelle nicht zu begründen sind. Sie ruft zugleich Folgefragen und systematische Probleme auf, die im Folgenden nicht behandelt werden können. Die soeben genannten Streitfragen betreffen keine interpretatorischen Feinheiten einzelner Marxscher Konzeptionen, Theoreme oder Argumentationen (auch von diesen gibt es sehr viele nebst nahezu unüberschaubar vieler, miteinander nicht kompatibler Antworten). Die von mir aufgerufenen Streitfragen betreffen die grundlegendsten Aspekte des Marxschen Denkens; die Uneinigkeit über sie ist bis heute ein prägender Zug der Debatte um Marx und der vielen

---

2 Die Frage nach der ethischen Dimension des Marxschen Denkens liegt quer zur Opposition von Kontinuitäts- und Diskontinuitätsthese. Zum einen kann man (die Kontinuitätsannahme vorausgesetzt) die Position vertreten, dass Marx eine essentialistische Anthropologie und Geschichtsphilosophie entwickelt habe, die zwar Philosophie, aber frei von einer ethischen Dimension sei. Zum anderen kann man (die Diskontinuitätsthese in ihrer schwächeren Form vorausgesetzt) zwischen der frühen und der späteren Philosophiekonzeption einen Bruch verorten und zugleich behaupten, es handele sich um zwei unterschiedliche ethische Konzeptionen. Für viele Anhänger der Diskontinuitätsthese (in starker wie schwacher Lesart) ist aber gerade der Wegfall der ethischen Dimension der zentrale Gesichtspunkt dieses Theoriewechsels.

Auseinandersetzungen innerhalb (bzw. zwischen den unterschiedlichen Arten) des Marxismus. Meine Antwort auf die Titelfrage des Beitrags liegt einerseits quer zu diesen großen Wasserscheiden der Marx- und Marxismusforschung, ist andererseits aber mit vielen darin zu finden Positionen nicht vereinbar. Deshalb werde ich mich hier, gleichsam zur Eröffnung einer komplexen Debatte, ausschließlich auf Marx und meine Leitfrage fokussieren.[3]

Aus diesem Grund lege ich im ersten Teil meine Vorannahmen, meine Ziele und das Vorgehen, mittels dessen ich sie erreichen möchte, offen (1.). Anschließend stelle ich die philosophische Anthropologie, die Marx in der Mitte der 1840er Jahre entfaltet hat, als eine spezifische Version des postkantischen Perfektionismus dar (2.). Im dritten Schritt wende ich mich dem *Kapital*, und damit dem Marxschen Forschungsprogramm einer Kritik der politischen Ökonomie, zu. Auch diese Konzeption, die Marx ab den 1850er Jahren in seinen theoretischen Schriften entwickelt hat, werde ich als einen Baustein seines postkantischen Perfektionismus explizieren (3.). Im abschließenden Fazit weise ich dann auf interpretatorische und systematische Fragen bzw. Probleme hin, die durch meinen hier vorgelegten Versuch, Karl Marx als Vertreter eines postkantischen Perfektionismus zu deuten, aufgeworfen werden.

1.   Voraussetzungen, Vorgehen und Ziele

Erstens ist die *Kernfrage* dieses Beitrags explizit zu formulieren: Stellt die philosophische Anthropologie von Marx, eventuell inklusive seiner Kritik der politischen Ökonomie, eine Version des postkantischen Perfektionismus dar? Angesichts der vielen Forschungsbeiträge, die eine Analyse der Marxschen Ethik vorgelegt haben, ist es wichtig, meine Kernfrage zu präzisieren. Dies kann durch die Angabe dreier Fragen bzw. Interpretationsstrategien geleistet werden. In diesem Beitrag geht es *erstens* ausschließlich um das Denken von Karl Marx; die Frage nach einer möglichen Ethik des Marxismus wird nicht gestellt. *Zweitens* verfolge ich bei meinen Überlegungen ausdrücklich nicht das Ziel, die Marxsche Ethik als Version einer von mir selbst aus systematischen Gründen favorisierten Metaethik auszuweisen. Anders gesagt: Ich möchte klären, ob wir Marx als postkantischen Perfektionisten verstehen können,

---

3   Auch den Bezug zu der selbst schon sehr umfangreichen Literatur, in der nach (dem Typ) der Marxschen Ethik gefragt wird, werde ich nur ganz kursorisch herstellen; ein Grund dafür ist die in ihr häufig stattfindende Vermengung exegetischer Interpretationsziele mit je eigenen systematischen Erkenntnisinteressen; vgl. zu dieser Debatte insgesamt stellvertretend die Beiträge in Angehrn/Lohmann (1986), Cohen et al. (1980) oder Nielsen/Patten (1981).

unabhängig davon, ob es sich dabei um eine plausible oder gar systematisch attraktive Theorieoption handelt. Darüber hinaus zielt dieser Beitrag *drittens* explizit nicht auf die systematische Frage ab, was man im Rahmen der Marxschen Kritik der politischen Ökonomie (heute oder prinzipiell) sinnvoller Weise vertreten kann oder soll. Selbstverständlich kann und muss man die Texte von Marx interpretieren und dabei eigenständige systematische Interessen verfolgen dürfen. Dieser Beitrag beschränkt sich jedoch ausdrücklich auf eine immanente Explikation (das hermeneutische Wohlwollen, das an jeden Autor heranzutragen ist, erstreckt sich also nicht darauf, Marx Ziele oder Positionen zuzuordnen, die der Interpret relativ zu den eigenen Prämissen und Erkenntnisinteressen für plausibel hält).

Zweitens ist die *Textgrundlage*, auf die sich mein Interpretationsvorschlag stützt, festzulegen; damit sind zugleich auch die Texte von Marx benannt, an denen sich mein Vorschlag messen lassen muss. Meine Deutung soll alle seine philosophischen Texte von 1843 an, d.h. sowohl die zur philosophischen Anthropologie und zum linkshegelianischen Diskussionskontext gehörigen Texte, als auch die Texte, in denen Marx die konzeptionellen Grundlagen seines Forschungsprogramms einer Kritik der politischen Ökonomie entfaltet, einschließen. Der Einfachheit halber beziehe ich mich in diesem Beitrag auf die *Ökonomisch-philosophischen Manuskripte* des Jahres 1844 (inklusive der sogenannten Mill-Exzerpte) für ersteres und auf den ersten Band des *Kapital* in den Marx selbst besorgten ersten beiden Auflagen der deutschsprachigen Ausgabe für letzteres.[4] Maßgeblich für meine interpretatorischen Ansprüche ist dabei der Textbestand in der kritischen Ausgabe, also der sogenannten MEGA²; angesichts der überaus komplexen, teilweise verworrenen und zumeist von eigenen Interessen der Editoren und Herausgeber gelenkten Editionen, in denen zentrale Schriften von Karl Marx nach seinem Tod und im gesamten 20. Jahrhundert veröffentlicht worden sind, ist dies als Grundlage einer soliden Marxforschung, d.h. einer an der Interpretation der Texte von Marx interessierten Forschung, unerlässlich. Auch wenn das damit beschriebene Vorgehen keinesfalls den Ist-Zustand der gegenwärtigen Marxforschung beschreibt, ist es doch als Grundlage einer wissenschaftlich soliden Erforschung des Werkes von Karl Marx unverzichtbar.

Zwei weitere Aspekte sind in Bezug auf die Textgrundlage noch anzusprechen: Marx hat *zum einen* Texte ganz unterschiedlicher Textgattungen verfasst. Diese sind nur zum geringen Teil von ihm selbst veröffentlicht worden; vieles (z.B. die Briefe oder auch die Exzerpte) waren niemals zur

---

4 Zur weiteren Erläuterung siehe die jeweils erste Anmerkung zum zweiten und zum dritten Teil dieses Beitrags.

Veröffentlichung gedacht. Die Texte, die von Marx zur Veröffentlichung vorgesehen waren, liegen zumeist als unveröffentlichte Manuskripte mit teilweise sehr divergierendem Ausarbeitungsgrad vor. Die zeitliche Abfolge ihrer posthumen Publikation deckt sich in vielen Fällen, dies ist insbesondere für die zur Kritik der politischen Ökonomie gehörenden Texte systematisch relevant, nicht mit der zeitlichen Abfolge ihrer Entstehung (oder teils mehrfachen Überarbeitung). Beides, sowohl die Textgattung als auch der Grad der Ausarbeitung durch Marx selbst, ist bei der Verwendung als Begründung für eine systematisch orientierte Interpretation zu beachten. Nicht selten werden in der Forschungsliteratur Konzeptionen oder Theoreme, an denen Marx auch bei Überarbeitungen (oder, im Falle des *Kapital*, auch bei der zweiten Auflage) festgehalten hat, mit Bezug auf Äußerungen in Briefen, in programmatischen Vorworten oder als argumentative Skizzen in Manuskripten außer Kraft gesetzt. Oder sie werden zu zentralen Belegen aufgewertet, Marx eine bestimmte systematische Position zuschreiben zu können. Eine solide Marxforschung wird hier wesentlich behutsamer vorgehen müssen. *Zum anderen* sind die verschiedenen Projekte zu unterscheiden, die Marx als Journalist, als Politiker und als Theoretiker verfasst hat. Das holzschnittartig skizzierte Theoriegerüst im *Kommunistischen Manifest* kann selbstverständlich die im *Kapital* entfaltete Analyse weder präzisieren, geschweige denn ersetzen. Auch seine als politische Analysen mit dem Ziel direkter Intervention verfassten Texte lassen sich mit dem Geltungsanspruch einer systematischen Theoriebildung nicht sinnvoll belasten. Angesichts der Leerstellen im Bereich der politischen Philosophie, die sich bei Marx finden, mag die Versuchung, sie zu diesem Zweck heranzuziehen, zwar nachvollziehbar und groß sein. Die Unterscheidung der verschiedenen Publikationsarten erlaubt ein solches Vorgehen jedoch letztlich nicht. Selbstverständlich ist in Bezug auf einzelne Texte unklar, ob und in welchem Maße sie zum Theorieprogramm von Marx gehören. Wenn ein solcher Text mit nachvollziehbaren Gründen hinzugezählt werden kann, muss er in die Deutung mit einbezogen werden. So gesehen hat bereits die Festlegung des für die Interpretation relevanten Textkorpus mit Gründen zu erfolgen und kann strittig sein; in einzelnen Fällen wird diese Festlegung sogar nicht unabhängig von den eigenen Prämissen oder Erkenntnisinteressen der Interpreten erfolgen können. Die bei den folgenden Überlegungen vorgenommene Einschränkung des Fokus vermeidet diese Probleme weitestgehend, erkauft dies jedoch mit der entsprechenden Einschränkung ihrer Geltungsansprüche.

Drittens sind vier *Prämissen meiner Argumentation* offenzulegen: Ich gehe (i) von der Kontinuitätsthese aus und fasse (ii) sowohl die philosophische Anthropologie als auch das Forschungsprogramm einer Kritik der politischen Ökonomie als philosophische Projekte auf. Außerdem (iii) unterstelle ich, dass die mit letzterem von Marx entfaltete kritische Sozialphilosophie erstere konzeptuell voraussetzt (und in diesem Sinne kein unabhängiges philosophisches Projekt von ihm) ist. Schließlich (iv) verstehe ich die philosophische Anthropologie als eine Konzeption, die durchgängig und in nicht eliminierbarer Weise evaluativ ausgerichtet ist; daraus folgt (in Verbindung mit meiner dritten Prämisse), dass auch seine Kritik der politischen Ökonomie eine nicht eliminierbare evaluative Geltungsdimension aufweist.

Viertens ist vorab eine, wenn auch grobe *Arbeitsdefinition des postkantischen Perfektionismus* zu geben, um die Kernfrage dieses Beitrags beantworten zu können. Ich lege hier die von Douglas Moggach in der Einleitung zu diesem Band vorgeschlagene Definition zugrunde, der zufolge es um eine neue Konzeption geht,

> which focuses not on the substantive goods toward which human nature putatively tends, but rather on the perfection of autonomy itself. Its starting point is the new concept of rational self-legislation which the Kantian account of practical reason had revealed, and new interrogations of its possible field of application: it is the enhancement of the capacity for free, rational self-determination, and not any given substantial end, that defines the objective of this perfectionism after Kant. Accompanying this change are close explorations of the objective, institutional, and intersubjective conditions for the practice of freedom, and demands for the reform, extension, and consolidation of these conditions. It is in this broad sense that we employ the concept of autonomy-perfectionism here.[5]

Der Hinweis von Douglas Moggach, er schlage damit eine Konzeption des postkantischen Perfektionismus im weiten Sinne vor, hat eine doppelte Stoßrichtung. Zum einen ist sie gegenüber der Kantischen Konzeption weiter, weil es allgemein um Autonomie und nicht um die spezifische Fähigkeit zur moralischen Selbstgesetzgebung geht. Zum anderen ist die unserem Band zugrunde gelegte Definition auch weiter als Definitionsvorschläge, die Douglas Moggach an anderer Stelle gemacht hat. In einem Beitrag, der schwerpunktmäßig auf Fichte ausgerichtet ist, wird als zusätzliches Element das Ziel

> to consolidate the sphere of right, to expand the scope of rightful interactions in the sense-world, and to secure the objective conditions for effective action in pursuit of our self-given ends[6]

---

5 Vgl. Moggach in diesem Band S. 1f.
6 So Moggach (2018), 135; vgl. auch die ähnliche Explikation des postkantischen Perfektionismus in Moggach (2020).

als weiteres Definitionsmerkmal des postkantischen Perfektionismus mit aufgenommen. In einem früheren Beitrag zum postkantischen Perfektionismus schlägt Douglas Moggach, insbesondere mit Blick auf die Philosophie Bruno Bauers, zwei weitere Charakteristika vor. Die Entwicklung dieser "historiced doctrine of freedom" sei "linked to ideas of republican virtue and citizenship" und vom "impact of the social question on republicanism" geprägt.[7] Diese anderen Definitionsvorschläge legen den postkantischen Perfektionismus auf eine deontologische Version fest und nehmen überdies die Institutionen des Rechts und des Staates als konstitutive Elemente mit auf. Die in diesem Band zugrunde gelegte Definition verzichtet dagegen auf diese Einengung; lediglich das Merkmal, es müsse um Autonomie als das zu perfektionierende Ziel gehen, bleibt erhalten.[8]

Angesichts der allseits bekannten und markanten Kritik von Karl Marx an deontologischen Moralkonzeptionen einerseits sowie den sozialen Institutionen des Rechts und des Staates andererseits ist die neue und weitere Definition des postkantischen Perfektionismus, die Douglas Moggach hier vorschlägt, unerlässlich; zumindest ist sie argumentationsstrategisch überaus hilfreich.[9] Denn nun sind im Prinzip auch rechts- und staatskritische Konzeptionen als Spielarten mit ihr kompatibel; es ist nicht mehr definitorisch gefordert, jede Variante eines postkantischen Perfektionismus müsse deontologisch verfasst sein. Vor diesem Hintergrund können wir unsere zentrale Frage auch so formulieren: Stellt die Marxsche Konzeption einer Selbstverwirklichung der Gattung eine Variante des so definierten postkantischen Perfektionismus dar?

Fünftens sind schließlich noch die *Ziele* meines Beitrags zu nennen. Primär geht es mir um die Beantwortung der Titelfrage im Rahmen der hier einlösbaren Geltungsansprüche. Darüber hinaus verfolge ich mit meinen Überlegungen zwei weitere Zwecke: Zum einen, dies ist ein weitergehendes Interpretationsziel, möchte ich den hier gewählten Fokus nutzen, um Unterbestimmtheiten und Probleme sichtbar zu machen, mit welchen die Konzeption von Karl Marx behaftet ist. Zum anderen, dies stellt ein eigenständiges systematisches Erkenntnisinteresse dar, möchte ich anhand der Marxschen Konzeption auf ethische und metaethische Erfordernisse hinweisen, denen sich eine Konzeption des postkantischen Perfektionismus zu stellen hat.

---

7 Vgl. Moggach (2011), 181.
8 Somit ist in diesem Beitrag jede Variante des postkantischen Perfektionismus per definitionem ein Autonomieperfektionismus. Aus Gründen der stilistischen Vereinfachung verwende ich daher im Folgenden stets „postkantischer Perfektionismus" anstelle von postkantischer Autonomieperfektionismus.
9 Zu meiner Deutung dieser Marxschen Kritik vgl. Quante (2013a).

2. Das gegenständliche Gattungswesen ein postkantischer Perfektionismus?

In seinen 1844 verfassten Schriften, auf die ich mich an dieser Stelle als Textgrundlage stütze, entwickelt Karl Marx eine philosophische Anthropologie, deren Zentrum seine Konzeption des gegenständlichen Gattungswesens bildet.[10] Ich werde der Frage, ob sich diese Konzeption als eine Version des postkantischen Perfektionismus verstehen lässt, in zwei Schritten beantworten: Zuerst stelle ich die zentralen Elemente dieser Konzeption kurz vor (2.1); dann diskutiere ich drei Interpretationsalternativen sowie drei systematische Probleme, die die von Marx entwickelte Version des postkantischen Perfektionismus aufwirft (2.2).

2.1 *Die Konzeption des gegenständlichen Gattungswesens*

Nur wenige Begriffe haben in der Marxforschung so viel Aufmerksamkeit auf sich gezogen, wie sie dem Begriff der Entfremdung zuteilgeworden ist. Die ca. zehn Seiten, die Marx dazu überhaupt nur in systematisch zusammenhängender Form verfasst hat, erschienen 1932 erstmals in den posthum veröffentlichten *Ökonomisch-philosophischen Schriften*. Analysiert man diesen Entfremdungsbegriff, dann stellt man zum einen fest, dass er sich nur explizieren lässt, wenn man zwei weitere Marxsche Konzeptionen hinzunimmt: seine Vergegenständlichungstheorie des Handelns[11] und seine philosophische Anthropologie, für die bei ihm der Terminus „gegenständliches Gattungswesen" steht. Eine tiefergehende Analyse der Marxschen Gesamtkonzeption zeigt dann, dass „Entfremdung" bei ihm zwei Kontrastbegriffe hat: den der Aneignung und den der Anerkennung.[12] Aus diesem Grund muss man zu der in den *Ökonomisch-philosophischen Manuskripten* zu findenden

---

10   Für eine umfassende Interpretation vgl. meine Darstellung in Quante (2009) und (2018).

11   Auf die Handlungstheorie von Karl Marx kann ich in diesem Beitrag nur soweit eingehen, wie es für die Explikation seiner philosophischen Anthropologie als Version eines postkantischen Perfektionismus notwendig ist; für eine ausführliche Darstellung vgl. Quante (2009) und (2016).

12   Diese Dopplung entsteht systematisch dadurch, dass Marx zum einen „Entäußerung" und „Entfremdung" gelegentlich gleichsetzt, gelegentlich aber auch unterscheidet (letzteres ist bei Hegel terminologisch klar vorgebildet). Zum anderen können sich beide sowohl auf Objekte als auch auf andere Subjekte beziehen. Die Aufhebung der Entäußerung oder Entfremdung von einem Objekt ist dann die Aneignung desselben, während die Aufhebung der Entfremdung von einem Subjekt eine Form der Anerkennung dieses Subjekts darstellt.

Entfremdungskonzeption auch die von Marx in seinen Mill-Exzerpten skizzierte Konzeption der Anerkennung hinzunehmen.[13]

Die Konzeption des gegenständlichen Gattungswesens geht davon aus, dass Menschen leiblich bedürftige und handelnde Wesen sind, die philosophisch in einem dreifachen Sinne als „gegenständlich" charakterisiert werden können: Sie lassen sich als Bewusstsein und Selbstbewusstsein nach dem Subjekt-Objekt-Modell explizieren (i); sie sind selbst als Organismen gegenständlich im Sinne raumzeitlich existierender Einzeldinge (ii); und sie realisieren ihre Absichten und zugleich ihr Wesen durch Vergegenständlichung (iii). Zugleich sind Menschen „Gattungswesen", was sich philosophisch ebenfalls in einem dreifachen Sinne explizieren lässt: Sie sind Individuen einer Spezies (i); als selbstbewusst denkende Wesen machen sie sich das Wesen (die Gattung) der Dinge (darunter auch ihr eigenes) im Denken begrifflich zum Gegenstand (ii); und als genuin soziale Wesen können sie ihr individuelles Wesen und ihr Gattungswesen nur durch die Interaktion mit anderen menschlichen Individuen realisieren (iii).

Das menschliche Gattungswesen ist darauf ausgerichtet, seine Wesenskräfte handelnd durch Vergegenständlichung zu realisieren, was – hier übernimmt Marx geschichtsphilosophische und bildungstheoretische Modelle des Deutschen Idealismus – nur über einen geschichtlichen Selbstrealisierungs- und Selbstbildungsprozess möglich ist. Das Ziel dieser Entwicklung ist die sich perfektionierende Realisierung des Gattungswesens (in Form individuell gelingenden Lebens und vernünftiger sozialer (inklusive ökonomischer) Institutionen). Dieser historische Prozess verläuft jedoch nicht gradlinig, sondern durch sich immer weiter verschärfende Gegensätze und Entfremdungsstadien hindurch. Erst am Ende dieser Entwicklung, die nach Marx die Vorgeschichte des Gattungswesens Mensch darstellt, wird die Aufhebung der Entfremdung und damit die adäquate Realisierung des Gattungswesens erreicht.

Um zu verstehen, weshalb Marx aus seinen Prämissen die Notwendigkeit dieser entfremdeten Zwischenschritte ableiten kann, muss man noch eine aus dem Vergegenständlichungsmodell und dem Subjekt-Objekt-Modell des Selbstbewusstseins sich ergebende epistemologische Prämisse hinzunehmen: Selbsterkenntnis ist nur möglich, indem der Mensch seine Wesenskräfte im

---

13 Vgl. MEGA², IV. Abteilung, Band 2, 447-459 und 462-466; diese in dem Exzerpt zusammenhängende Skizze ist eine der ganz wenigen Stellen, an denen Marx einen Grundriss der zwischenmenschlichen Beziehungen entwirft, in denen die durch Privateigentum und Lohnarbeit konstituierte Entfremdung der Menschen voneinander und jedes Menschen zu sich selbst aufgehoben ist.

Handeln (absichtlich, aber auch in nicht intendierter Form) vergegenständlicht. Der produzierte Gegenstand (dies kann ein materielles Objekt oder auch eine Tatsache sein) weist dann Eigenschaften und Fähigkeiten auf, die eigentlich solche des Gattungswesens selbst sind. Sie sind entäußert und, soweit dieser Vergegenständlichungszusammenhang nicht durchschaut ist, auch entfremdet. Selbsterkenntnis ist erst möglich, wenn ein Subjekt die an ein solchermaßen vergegenständlichtes Objekt verlorenen Eigenschaften und Fähigkeiten als seine eigenen erkennt und sie sich praktisch wie theoretisch selbst aneignet.[14] Als denkendes Gattungswesen kann der Mensch sich sein Gattungswesen erst aneignen, wenn er alle Formen des sozialen Zusammenlebens, einschließlich seiner Interaktion mit der Natur, als Realisierungen seiner Gattungskräfte theoretisch erkennt und ihm die Aneignung durch soziale Veränderungen auch praktisch gelingt. Da Selbsterkenntnis aber zum Gattungswesen gehört, muss sie realisiert werden, was nur über die Entäußerung geschehen kann. Im Gegensatz zu einem nicht raumzeitlich existierenden, unendlichen Selbstbewusstsein kann der Mensch als raumzeitlich gebundenes und endliches Wesen diese Entäußerung nur schrittweise durchschauen und beherrschen lernen. Daraus ergibt sich die Notwendigkeit der Entfremdung als nicht zu überspringender Schritt im Selbstverwirklichungsprozess der menschlichen Gattung.

Je mehr die Menschen in ihrer sozialen Interaktion ihre individuellen und Gattungseigenschaften auf entfremdete Weise vergegenständlichen, desto mehr realisiert sich ihr Gattungswesen als verdinglichte und sie beherrschende Welt von Sachzwängen. Im Kapitalismus, so die geschichtsphilosophische Prämisse von Karl Marx, ist diese Entfremdung bis zum äußersten fortgeschritten. Die Wesenskräfte der Gattung sind in entfremdeter Form freigesetzt und müssen nun, als letzter Schritt der Selbstverwirklichung, bewusst angeeignet werden. Daraus entsteht dann die neue Gesellschaftsformation als gewusste und gelebte Realisierung des Gattungswesens, die den Abschluss der Perfektionierung der Gattung bildet. In ihr, so Marx, können sich alle menschlichen Individuen frei entfalten und in den richtigen sozialen Formen gemeinsam ihr Gattungswesen realisieren. Zu diesem Endzustand gehört die historische Erfahrung und das Wissen um die Möglichkeit der Entfremdung hinzu; aus diesem Grund ist der vorentfremdete Zustand, hier folgt Marx wiederum Hegels Dialektik der Negation der Negation, nicht mit dem der

---

14   Die Übernahme der Grundfigur von Feuerbachs Religionskritik ist an dieser Stelle unverkennbar; die Grundstruktur entspricht dabei weitestgehend der bewusstseinstheoretischen Gesamtkonzeption von Hegels *Phänomenologie des Geistes*; vgl. dazu Quante (2018).

aufgehobenen Entfremdung gleichzusetzen. Der Endzustand selbst bleibt bei Marx störanfällig und bedarf auch aus diesem Grund der Erinnerung an die Vorgeschichte, um Rückfälle bewusst verhindern zu können. Zugleich stellt er sich Marx zufolge nicht mit einer geschichtsphilosophisch verbürgten Gewissheit ein: Diese Realisierung kann, so ist Marx zu verstehen, auch scheitern und die Perfektionierung des Gattungswesens kann misslingen. In dem Fall ginge die historische Entwicklung hin zu dem zu erreichenden Endzustand wieder von vorne los.[15]

Die damit skizzierte geschichtsphilosophisch dynamisierte Konzeption des gegenständlichen Gattungswesens qualifiziert sich als eine Version des postkantischen Perfektionismus. Ihr ist eine perfektionistische Ethik im Sinne der angemessenen Ausbildung sozialer (inklusive ökonomischer) Institutionen sowie der angemessenen ethischen Haltungen (Anerkennung) der Individuen untereinander eingeschrieben. Das Ziel der Entwicklung ist die vollständige (perfekte) Entfaltung aller Wesenskräfte der Gattung, welche die Freiheit von Hemmnissen einschließt. Diese Perfektionierung wird als Selbstverwirklichung und Realisierung der eigenen Fähigkeiten konzipiert, nicht als Umsetzung eines externen Maßstabs oder Plans. Der zu erreichende Endzustand garantiert überdies, so die Marxsche Überzeugung, nicht nur die freie Entfaltung aller Gattungskräfte, sondern zugleich auch die freie Entfaltung aller Individuen. Das Ziel dieser Entwicklung ist die perfekte Ausübung und Verwirklichung theoretischer und praktischer Selbstbestimmung innerhalb der dazu erforderlichen sozialen Institutionen und evaluativen Umgangsformen der Menschen miteinander.

2.2 Drei Interpretationsalternativen und drei systematische Probleme

Es ist nicht mein Ziel, die Plausibilität oder systematische Attraktivität dieser Konzeption von Karl Marx zu erörtern. Stattdessen werde ich im ersten Schritt kurz auf drei mögliche Interpretationsalternativen und im zweiten Schritt auf drei systematische Probleme hinweisen.

Die evaluative Dimension, die im Rahmen eines postkantischen Perfektionismus ethisch – sei es in axiologischer, sei es in deontologischer Version – entfaltet wird, lässt sich im Prinzip im Rahmen essentialistischer Prämissen, dies ist die *erste* Interpretationsalternative, auch auf eine andere Weise explizieren: Die spezifische modallogische Normativität ergibt sich aus der Differenz eines Ist-Zustands zum essentialistisch definierten Soll- oder Ziel-Zustand. Ohne

---

15 Die Möglichkeit, dass die menschliche Spezies sich bei diesem Scheitern komplett selbst auslöscht, hat Marx, soweit ich sehe, noch nicht als theorierelevante Option in seine Version des postkantischen Perfektionismus eingebaut.

weitere Annahmen (wie beispielsweise diejenige, dass Wesensverwirklichung ethisch geboten oder ethisch gut ist), kann man aus dem Essentialismus allein keine Ethikkonzeption ableiten. Dies gilt selbst dann, wenn es beim Zielzustand um die perfekte Realisierung von Autonomie geht. Solange dieses Ziel nicht selbst als ein ethisches Gut oder dessen (maximale) Realisierung als ethisches Gebot formuliert wird, kann man im Rahmen eines ethikfreien Essentialismus verbleiben.[16]

Eine *zweite* Interpretationsalternative besteht darin, die evaluative Dimension durch eine rein metaphysisch ausgelegte Geschichtsphilosophie zu explizieren, die nötige Soll-Ist-Differenz also durch eine historisch angelegte Teleologie zu erzeugen. Diese Strategie kann allerdings nur dann erfolgreich sein, wenn evaluative Begriffe wie z.B. der des Fortschritts eliminiert werden können. Ob dies überhaupt geht, ist schon fraglich. Dass es bei Marx eine plausible Interpretationshypothese abwirft, ist jedenfalls mehr als unwahrscheinlich.[17]

Als *dritte* Alternative ist dann noch die Strategie zu erwähnen, die essentialistischen Prämissen von Marx durch eine empirische (zumeist szientistische) Reduktion zu ersetzen. Die von Friedrich Engels und Karl Marx als Reaktion auf Max Stirners Fundamentalkritik vorgenommene Umorientierung kann diesem Interpretationsprojekt einige Nahrung liefern.[18] Allerdings wird es dabei nicht nur schwierig, die von Marx getätigten starken modalen Aussagen reduktionistisch zu übersetzen; auch die geschichtsphilosophischen Grundlagen müssen in einem solchen Projekt als kaum zu überwindende Hürden angesehen werden.

Damit gehe ich zu drei systematischen Problemen über. Eine Schwierigkeit, die man mit dem postkantischen Perfektionismus haben kann, besteht in der

---

16 Meine hier vorgelegte Interpretation der Marxschen Konzeption des gegenständlichen Gattungswesens muss deshalb im Detail gegen eine solche Alternative entwickelt werden. Anders herum müsste aber auch ein solcher Essentialismus durch eine detaillierte Interpretation der Marxschen Konzeption etabliert werden; vgl. zu diesem Themenkomplex auch Archibald (1989) und Meikle (1985).

17 Diese geschichtsphilosophische Alternative ist nicht mit folgendem Einwand zu verwechseln: Marx könne keine ethische Konzeption entwickelt haben, weil er von einem geschichtsphilosophischen Determinismus ausgehe. Selbst wenn man Marx, wofür einiges spricht, eine Version eines solchen Determinismus unterstellen kann, folgt die Konsequenz nicht, setzt sie doch die Unvereinbarkeit von Ethik und Determinismus voraus. Dies ist aber eine jedenfalls keineswegs unumstrittene Position; zu den geschichtsphilosophischen Aspekten des Marxschen Denkens vgl. Quante (2019a).

18 Die mittlerweile in der MEGA² vorliegende kritische Ausgabe dieser Manuskripte spricht auch vom Textbefund her gegen eine solche Lesart; vgl. insgesamt zur Rolle Stirners in der linkshegelianischen Debatte auch Quante (2015).

Gefahr paternalistischer Bevormundung auf der Basis essentialistischer Vorgaben. Diese der individuellen Selbstbestimmung externen Maßstäbe werden dann als ethisch unzulässig zugunsten der Autonomie zurückgewiesen. Indem der postkantische Perfektionismus diese Autonomie selbst als zu perfektionierendes Gut ansetzt (und dabei nicht auf eine Maximierungsstrategie utilitaristischer Prägung festgelegt ist), wird diese Gefahr (zumindest auf der prinzipiellen oder kategorischen Ebene) vermieden. Doch selbst unter dieser Voraussetzung bleibt eine *erste* systematische Schwierigkeit bestehen: Soll man diese essentialistische Voraussetzung, wie sie auch der Marxschen Konzeption des gegenständlichen Gattungswesens eingeschrieben ist, als einen unseren sozialen Praxen externen, oder aber als einen wenn auch impliziten internen Standard der Evaluation und Kritik begreifen?

Ein *zweites* systematisches Problem zeigt sich in der Konzeption von Marx als nicht nur metaethisch, sondern als ganz praktisch überaus dringlich: Um wessen Autonomie geht es bei der Perfektionierung? Die der Gattung oder die eines jeden einzelnen Individuums? Ohne hier in die Detailerörterung eintreten zu können, muss mit Blick auf die von Marx entwickelte Variante festgestellt werden, dass er den sich aus dieser Frage ergebenden Problemen wenig Beachtung geschenkt hat. Seine Vorstellung von Perfektion scheint auf eine nach der Vorgeschichte des Menschen sich einstellende Harmonie der Individuen ausgerichtet zu sein, in der es keiner sozialen Institutionen des Schutzes individueller Ansprüche oder der normativ angemessenen Regelung von konfligierenden Interessen bedarf. Ob Marx tatsächlich einer solchen Vorstellung angehangen hat, kann hier offenbleiben. Festzuhalten ist aber eine empfindliche Lücke in seiner Konzeption, da er sich über die zur Lösung dieser Fragen benötigten sozialen Institutionen nicht geäußert hat.[19]

Ein *drittes* systematisches Problem, welches der postkantische Perfektionismus (zumindest) in der Marxschen Version aufwirft, lässt sich mit dem Stichwort der Überforderung benennen. Wenn man die Perfektionierung nicht als unendlichen, niemals abschließbaren Prozess zu einem ontologischen Sollen oder in Form moralischer Forderungen, die für endliche Wesen niemals erfüllbar sind, zu einem moralischen Sollen umgestaltet: Wird mit dieser Perfektion nicht ein Maßstab an reale soziale Institutionen und menschliche Handlungen angelegt, denen sie niemals genügen können? Anders gefragt: Ist das Ideal der universellen und konfliktfreien Anerkennung zwischen Individuen und das Ziel einer vollständigen Aufhebung von Entfremdung ein Maßstab, dem

---

19 Die radikale Kritik von Marx an Recht und Staat verschärft die damit aufgerufene Problematik zusätzlich, da sie den Gestaltungsspielraum zur Füllung dieser Theorielücke empfindlich einschränkt.

menschliche Gesellschaften prinzipiell nicht genügen können? Noch anders gefragt: Wie sähe ein postkantischer Perfektionismus aus, der diese Überforderungsgefahr ernst nähme und in seiner Theoriebildung berücksichtigte? Wie wir im dritten Teil sehen werden, hat Karl Marx in seinen späteren Schriften zumindest geahnt, dass er in seiner Kritik der politischen Ökonomie diese Schwierigkeit berücksichtigen muss.

3. Die Kritik der politischen Ökonomie: Teil des postkantischen Perfektionismus?

Einer der zentralen Streitpunkte in der Marx- und der Marxismusforschung gleichermaßen dreht sich um die Frage, ob die Kritik der politischen Ökonomie von ihrem Theorietyp her als ein philosophisches Projekt zu verstehen ist.[20] Alternativ dazu kann sie entweder einer einzelwissenschaftlichen Disziplin (beispielsweise der Ökonomie, den Politikwissenschaften oder der Soziologie) zugeschlagen werden, oder man stellt sich auf den Standpunkt, Karl Marx habe mit seinem *Kapital* einen vollkommen neuartigen Theorietyp entwickeln (der dann beispielsweise als „historischer" oder „dialektischer" Materialismus, gelegentlich auch als „wissenschaftliche Weltanschauung" charakterisiert wird). Es ist sicher nicht unangemessen zu behaupten, dass außer proklamatorischen Bekundungen oder programmatischen Ankündigungen bisher keine wissenschaftstheoretisch belastbaren Forschungsergebnisse vorliegen, die dafürsprächen, es sei Karl Marx gelungen, einen vollkommen neuen Typ von Wissenschaft zu entwickeln, geschweige denn zu etablieren. Genauso wenig ist zu bestreiten, dass sich in den zum Forschungsprogramm einer Kritik der politischen Ökonomie sowohl extensive Quellenstudien und Einbeziehungen

---

20 Der Einfachheit halber beschränke ich meine Aussagen zum Marxschen Forschungsprogramm einer Kritik der politischen Ökonomie hier, wie im ersten Teil bereits gesagt, auf die von ihm selbst besorgten deutschsprachigen Ausgaben des *Kapital*; vgl. für eine ausführlichere Interpretation meine Darstellung in Quante (2018) und (2019b). In einem umfassenderen Sinne gehören zu diesem Forschungsprogramm selbstverständlich alle in der zweiten Abteilung der MEGA² edierten Bände sowie die für diese Texte von Marx angefertigten Exzerpte, die bisher nur teilweise in der vierten Abteilung der MEGA² erschienen sind. Zur Ermittlung des Kontextes, in dem Marx seine Überlegungen entfaltet, wird eine umfassende Rekonstruktion dieses Forschungsprogramms auch den Briefwechsel sowie die journalistischen und politischen Arbeiten von Marx einzubeziehen haben. Es liegt auf der Hand, dass diese Texte sich aufgrund ihrer Textgattungen per se und aufgrund ihres aus editionsphilologischer Sicht sehr unterschiedlichen Status nur sehr begrenzt für die Bestimmung des Theorietyps der Kritik der politischen Ökonomie heranziehen lassen.

von Forschungsresultaten diverser einzelwissenschaftlicher Disziplinen finden als auch Argumente und Theoreme, die sich als Züge in diesen diversen Einzeldisziplinen verstehen lassen. Anders gesagt: Im *Kapital* finden sich sowohl Behauptungen von Marx, die sich durch einzelwissenschaftliche Befunde falsifizieren (oder stützen) lassen, als auch Thesen und Begründungen, die problemlos als Argumente innerhalb dieser Einzelwissenschaften zu interpretieren sind. Daraus lässt sich jedoch nicht die stärkere Schlussfolgerung ziehen, es handele sich bei diesem Werk von seiner Gesamtanlage her um einen Beitrag zu einer dieser Einzelwissenschaften.

Wie eingangs bereits offengelegt, gehe ich hier von der Prämisse aus, dass sich das theoretische Werk von Karl Marx, dies schließt sowohl seine Frühschriften der 1840er Jahre als auch die zum Forschungsprogramm einer Kritik der politischen Ökonomie gehörenden Texte ein, als Beitrag zur Philosophie interpretieren lässt.[21] Karl Marx zielte mit seiner kritischen Abkehr stets auf die Hegelsche Philosophie und die diversen linkshegelianischen Versionen derselben ab. Aus seiner Philosophiekritik folgt daher nicht zwingend, dass es sich bei der Kritik der politischen Ökonomie nicht um ein philosophisches Projekt handeln kann.

Sachlich mit diesem zentralen Zankapfel der Marx- und Marxismusforschung eng verbunden ist der Dissens bezüglich einer zweiten Fragestellung: Liegt zwischen den (mehr oder weniger) unbestritten als Philosophie eingeschätzten theoretischen Arbeiten der 1840er Jahre und den Schriften von Karl Marx, die ab den 1850er Jahren als Beiträge zu seiner Kritik der politischen Ökonomie anzusehen sind, ein – epistemologischer oder methodologischer – Bruch? Es handelt sich hierbei jedoch um zwei zu unterscheidende Fragestellungen. Denn zum einen könnte Marx auch nach diesem ‚Bruch' ein philosophisches Projekt verfolgt haben (indem er beispielsweise mit der linkshegelianischen Philosophie ‚bricht', nicht aber mit der Philosophie im Allgemeinen). Zum anderen ließe sich die Hinwendung zu einem nicht mehr als Philosophie zu verstehenden Forschungsprojekt auch als Umorientierung konzipieren, die keinen ‚Bruch' einschließt (dies wäre z.B. dann der Fall, wenn Marx seine philosophischen Prämissen und Theoreme aus den 1840er Jahren als Grundlage verwendet, um dann mit ihnen andere Zwecke zu verfolgen).

---

21 Mit dieser Prämisse ist die Annahme vereinbar, dass sich sein Werk auch fruchtbar oder sinnvoll als Beitrag zu einer anderen wissenschaftlichen Disziplin deuten lässt (dies hängt letztendlich von den Erkenntnisinteressen und Prämissen der jeweiligen Interpretationen ab).

Wie oben bereits offengelegt, gehe ich in diesem Beitrag sowohl davon aus, dass es sich beim *Kapital* um einen Beitrag zur Philosophie, genauer zur kritischen Sozialphilosophie, handelt, als auch davon, dass sich auf der grundlegenden Ebene der Theoriebildung zwischen den Schriften der 1840er Jahre und den ab 1850 im Rahmen der Kritik der politischen Ökonomie verfassten Schriften kein Bruch im Denken von Karl Marx feststellen lässt.[22] Damit ist der Weg frei für die Frage, ob sich auch das *Kapital* in das Projekt des postkantischen Perfektionismus einfügen lässt. Denkbar wäre ja auch, dass sich zwar die philosophische Anthropologie der 1840er Jahre, nicht aber die kritische Sozialphilosophie, die Marx im *Kapital* entfaltet hat, als postkantischer Perfektionismus verstehen lässt.

Für eine solche skeptische Vermutung lassen sich einige gute Gründe anführen: So führt Marx erstens seine Analyse nicht auf der Ebene der individuellen Akteure durch, sondern bezieht sich explizit auf funktionale Strukturen, die sich hinter (und auf) den Rücken der Akteure realisieren. Diese lassen sich, so Marx, philosophisch als Zweckverwirklichungen nichtintendierter Folgen kollektiver Interaktionen explizieren. Zweitens orientiert Marx sich dabei an Hegels *Wissenschaft der Logik*; damit ist eine Theorie im Spiel, die sich ebenfalls nicht auf der Ebene der Explikation konkreter Redehandlungsakteure, sondern der Explikation funktionaler Strukturen von Kategorien bewegt. Hinzu kommt dann noch, dass mit der Hegelschen Logik ein Anspruch auf Abgeschlossenheit und Totalität in die Marxsche Theoriebildung aufgenommen wird, der zumindest prima facie mit der Vorstellung eines postkantischen Perfektionismus der Autonomie nicht gut vereinbar zu sein scheint. Schließlich ist mit Blick auf einen dritten Grund noch zu

---

22 Zu einem großen Teil speist sich der Dissens hinsichtlich dieser zweiten Streitfrage aus zwei Quellen: Zum einen werden die von den jeweiligen Diskutanten vorausgesetzten Prämissen und Ziele nicht expliziert, sodass die Argumente sehr leicht aneinander vorbeigehen. Zum anderen ist auch die Rede vom ‚Bruch' mit diversen Unklarheiten verbunden. Niemand kann ernsthaft bestreiten, dass es zu jedem Zeitpunkt des Marxschen Denkens ‚Brüche' (im Sinne von Inkonsistenzen, Unschärfen oder nicht abgetragenen Beweislasten) gibt. Genauso wenig ist zu bestreiten, dass in jedem zeitlichen Intervall in der sich darin vollziehenden Theoriearbeit zahlreiche ‚Brüche' (im Sinne des Verwerfens oder auch Weiterentwickelns von Thesen oder Konzeptionen) zu identifizieren sind. Was es aber, so meine Prämisse, bei Marx nicht gibt, ist ein konversionsähnlicher „vollständiger Bruch" mit den philosophischen Grundlagen und Erkenntnisinteressen, die er in den 1840er Jahren herausgearbeitet hat. Nur diese Vorstellung eines Bruchs, die sowohl in der von Friedrich Engels nach dem Tode von Karl Marx begonnenen Selbsthistorisierung als auch in der im Marxismus-Leninismus weitergeschriebenen Narration eines ‚Durchbruchs zur wissenschaftlichen Weltanschauung' kanonisch geworden ist, wird durch meine Prämisse einer Kontinuität des philosophischen Charakters der Theorie zurückgewiesen.

erwähnen, dass Marx eine Deutung seiner Kapitalismuskritik als moralische explizit zurückweist. Auch dies passt nur schlecht zum Theorietyp eines postkantischen Perfektionismus, der ausdrücklich als Praktische Philosophie konzipiert ist.

Trotz dieser relevanten Einwände kann auch das *Kapital* (und das Forschungsprogramm einer Kritik der politischen Ökonomie insgesamt) als Bestandteil der für Marx spezifischen Version eines postkantischen Perfektionismus aufgefasst werden. Eine solche Interpretation setzt, wofür in diesem Beitrag im zweiten Teil die Argumente vorgestellt worden sind, voraus, dass sich die philosophische Anthropologie von Marx als postkantischer Perfektionismus verstehen lässt. Denn nur dann lässt es sich plausibel machen, dass sich auch seine Kritik der politischen Ökonomie (trotz der drei soeben formulierten Bedenken) darin einfügt, weil sie diesen Charakterzug von der Konzeption des Gattungswesens erbt.

Damit die hier vorgeschlagene Deutung gelingen kann, muss also *erstens* vorausgesetzt werden, dass die konzeptionellen Grundlagen, die Marx in seiner philosophischen Anthropologie entwickelt hat, auch (zumindest ein Teil der) Grundlage seiner Kritik der politischen Ökonomie sind. Für diese Annahme spricht eine Vielzahl von Belegen: So ist das Vergegenständlichungsmodell im *Kapital* das handlungstheoretische Grundmodell. Es unterliegt nicht nur seinem Begriff der Arbeit, sondern ist zudem ein notwendiger Bestandteil der Wertanalyse und damit der konzeptionellen Grundlage der gesamten Theorie. Auch die These, der Mensch müsse sich seine Gattungseigenschaften über den Weg der vergegenständlichenden Entäußerung aneignen, liegt dieser Analyse zugrunde. Dass Marx die Waren selbst als Akteure auftreten lässt, ergibt systematisch Sinn, wenn sich auf dieser funktionalen Ebene die entfremdet entäußerten Absichten der interagierenden Subjekte philosophisch explizieren lassen.[23] Schließlich ist die Rede vom Kapital als einem automatischen Subjekt und das gesamte von Marx aufgerufene Metaphernfeld von Zombies, Vampiren, lebendiger vs. toter Arbeit oder dem Bild des Aussaugens der lebendigen Arbeitskraft durch das Kapital ebenfalls nahtlos in dieses Grundmodell der Vergegenständlichung einzufügen. Dass sich diese Entäußerung qua Gattungswesen durch den Antagonismus von Kapitalist und Arbeiter realisiert sowie

---

23 Auch die für die adäquate Realisierung des Gattungswesens notwendigen Anerkennungsverhältnisse kommen hier in ihrer entfremdeten Gestalt vor: Marx organisiert seine Wertformanalyse als anerkennungstheoretisch rekonstruierbare Geltungsverhältnisse zwischen Waren (inklusive sozialer Rollen von Charaktermasken). Die damit aufgespannten sozialen Strukturen sind damit als eine Verdinglichung der dem Gattungswesen inhärenten evaluativen Anerkennungsstrukturen philosophisch explizierbar, vgl. dazu Quante (2013b).

zugleich durch den Antagonismus von Natur und Kapital bestimmt ist, passt ebenfalls zur Grundkonzeption des gegenständlichen Gattungswesens: Weil es sich um eine entfremdete Entäußerung handelt, befindet sich das Gattungswesen (auf individueller und kollektiver Ebene) in einem Widerspruch zwischen seiner leiblich-naturalen und seiner intentional-sozialen Dimension. Dieser Grundwiderspruch manifestiert sich, dies ist ein zentrales Theorem der Marxschen Entfremdungskonzeption, auch in den sozialen Relationen zwischen den Menschen (auf individueller und kollektiver Ebene). Dass Marx die kapitalistische Produktionsform als doppelten Antagonismus (zwischen Kapital und Arbeit sowie zwischen Kapital und Natur) konzipiert hat, ist nicht bestreitbar. Dieser Befund fügt sich bruchlos in seine Konzeption des gegenständlichen Gattungswesens ein. Gleiches gilt für die positive Dimension der bewussten Aneignung dieser in entfremdeter Form entäußerten Gattungseigenschaften. An den wenigen Stellen im *Kapital*, an denen Marx überhaupt auf die Überwindung der kapitalistischen Produktionsform eingeht, verwendet er nicht nur Hegels Konzeption einer ‚Negation der Negation', sondern stellt diesen Prozess zudem als Versöhnung mit der Natur und als Aneignung durch die Arbeiter dar. Letztere ist, worauf Marx in seiner Darstellung Wert legt, zugleich die Enteignung der Kapitalisten; erstere wird, anders als noch in den *Ökonomisch-philosophischen Manuskripten*, nicht mehr als vollendet durchgeführte Naturalisierung des Menschen und Humanisierung der Natur konzipiert. Die Versöhnungsemphase der Frühschriften weicht im *Kapital* einer realistischeren Darstellung, die implizit die Standards korrigiert (oder präzisiert), die in der philosophischen Anthropologie aufgerufen worden sind. Durch die Aufhebung der Entfremdung wird die Arbeit nicht zum Spiel und die Sphäre der materiellen Produktion bleibt konstitutiv von Notwendigkeiten bestimmt, welche rational gestaltbar, aber niemals eine widerstandslose Verwirklichung unbegrenzter menschlicher Freiheit sein können.

Eine weitere Gelingensbedingung für meinen Interpretationsvorschlag besteht *zweitens* darin, eine evaluative Dimension zu identifizieren (ohne diesen Schritt würde die Kritik der politischen Ökonomie zwar möglicherweise eine mit dem postkantischen Perfektionismus von Marx kompatible kritische Sozialphilosophie sein, aber eben selbst kein Bestandteil seines postkantischen Perfektionismus). Zuerst einmal ist zuzugestehen, dass sich die mit dem Begriff der Kritik analytisch verbundene Normativität eines Kritikstandards auch ohne Bezug auf evaluative (sei es axiologische, sei es deontologische) Standards ausweisen lässt. Würde man die Geschichtsphilosophie von Marx als einen metaphysischen Essentialismus ohne interne evaluative Dimension rekonstruieren, dann wäre im Prinzip eine rein modallogische Normativität (im Sinne einer Soll-Ist-Differenz der Wesensverwirklichung) denkbar. Doch wie im zweiten Teil angedeutet, ist dies weder eine systematisch attraktive noch eine interpretatorisch plausible Option. Fügt man die Marxsche Analyse der kapitalistischen Gesellschaftsformation in seine philosophische Anthropologie ein, ergibt sich ein stimmiges Gesamtbild: Der Kapitalismus ist dasjenige Stadium im historischen Gang der Selbstverwirklichung des Gattungswesens, der durch die vollständige und radikalste Form der Entfremdung charakterisiert ist. Damit sind erstmals alle Gattungskräfte entäußert und somit der Aneignung zugänglich; zugleich liegen sie unter der Herrschaft des Kapitals als automatischem Subjekt in entfremdeter Form, d.h. in für die realen Akteure nicht durchschaubaren sozialen Strukturen vor. Die Aneignung dieser Gattungskräfte soll, so Marx, dann durch rationale Kontrolle (Planung) und die Schaffung transparenter sozialer Institutionen (Durchsichtigkeit) sowie die Aufhebung der entfremdenden Effekte vereinseitigender Arbeitsteilung und die Kürzung der für die Reproduktion einzusetzenden Arbeitszeit auf Dauer gestellt werden. Die damit verbundenen sozialen Veränderungen umschreibt Marx, ohne auf die politische Gestaltung dieser Prozesse näher einzugehen, als Enteignung der Kapitalisten, welche zugleich als Aneignung der Gattungskräfte durch die Arbeiter zu verstehen ist. Unauflöslich verbunden mit dieser Aneignung ist die Aufhebung der ideologischen Verzerrungen, durch welche sich die Menschen über ihre Rollen täuschen und in entfremdeten sozialen Beziehungen miteinander leben. Weil, so unser Befund im zweiten Teil dieses Beitrags, auch die richtige evaluative Haltung zueinander ein wesentlicher Bestandteil der Realisierung des Gattungswesens ist, gehört zu dem Marxschen Gesamtkonzept damit eine evaluative Dimension irreduzibel dazu.

Insgesamt stellt Marx im *Kapital* den Kapitalismus als eine scheiternde Gestalt der menschlichen Lebensform dar. Seine Kritik durch Darstellung ist dabei methodologisch Hegels *Phänomenologie des Geistes* und *Wissenschaft der Logik* gleichermaßen verpflichtet: Unter der Voraussetzung der philosophischen Anthropologie (inklusive der ihr eingeschriebenen Geschichtsphilosophie und ihrer evaluativen Dimension) kann Marx den Kapitalismus an einem Maßstab messen, der den Menschen inhärent ist, auch wenn die mit ihm einhergehenden Standards den Akteuren nur in verzerrter Form bekannt oder sogar ihrem Handeln nur implizit eingeschrieben sind. Die Marxsche Auskunft, er kritisiere den Kapitalismus genauso wenig wie einzelne Kapitalisten (oder deren Handlungen) moralisch, ist hiermit vereinbar: Zum einen setzt Marx Moral mit einer apriorisch-deontologischen Konzeption Kantischen oder Fichteschen Typs gleich, die an ihren Gegenstand einen ahistorischen, abstrakten und damit externen Maßstab anlegt. Zum anderen organisiert Marx die evaluative Dimension seiner Kritik durch die Darstellung der sich vollziehenden Entfremdung, ohne diese Phänomene selbst mittels einer solchen ethischen Kategorie als unangemessen zu klassifizieren. Marx möchte, dass sich seine evaluative Kritik zeigt, ohne dass er sie explizit aussprechen muss. Der Maßstab dieser Kritik, den Marx seiner philosophischen Konzeption insgesamt zugrunde legt, lässt sich, so der hier unterbreitete Vorschlag, als eine spezifische Form des postkantischen Perfektionismus entfalten: Durch die Geschichte und die mit diesem Prozess verbundenen Entfremdungsstufen hindurch realisiert der Mensch seine Wesenskräfte. Dies ist eine philosophisch explizierbare historische Entwicklung, die auf die maximale Entfaltung aller seiner Gattungseigenschaften angelegt ist. Diese vollständige Verwirklichung ist, so Marx, die Entwicklung der Freiheit von Naturgewalt und sozialer Fremdbestimmung. Sie schafft zugleich den Rahmen, innerhalb dessen jeder Mensch auch seine individuellen Eigenschaften und Fähigkeiten entfalten kann. Die vollständige nicht mehr entfremdete Entfaltung des Gattungswesens ist dann zugleich die vollständige Realisierung seiner Autonomie.

Fazit

Es ist nicht überraschend, wenn das Werk eines historischen Autors nicht nahtlos in eine 150 Jahre später an es angelegte metaethische Systematik passt. Wie die Argumentation in diesem Beitrag gezeigt hat, wirft die hier verfolgte Fragestellung dennoch einen doppelten philosophischen Ertrag ab: Zum einen legt unsere Perspektive systematische Unschärfen oder Probleme der Philosophie von Karl Marx offen. Zum anderen ergeben sich aus unseren Befunden auch für die systematische Weiterentwicklung des postkantischen Perfektionismus Anschlussfragen und Entwicklungsaufgaben, um die Unschärfen, welche dieser metaethischen Option eingeschrieben sind, zu beheben.

1.   *Erste Unschärfe: Individuum oder Gattung?*
Auf die erste Unschärfe, die sich explizit bei Marx, implizit aber auch bei anderen Vertretern des postkantischen Perfektionismus ausmachen lässt, stößt man, wenn man fragt, um wessen Autonomie es in diesem Perfektionismus geht. Die philosophische Anthropologie von Marx ist geprägt durch die Rede von der Gattung und dem Gattungswesen. Nach der Reaktion auf die Intervention von Max Stirner, der die Rede von *dem* Menschen oder *der* Gattung als eine spezifische Form des „Heiligen" kritisiert hat, beginnt Marx zwar damit, seiner Konzeption ein empirisches Fundament zu geben, doch die Unschärfe in seiner Rede von den Menschen bleibt unaufgeklärt: Geht es um das einzelne Individuum und dessen Autonomie? Oder zielt die Perfektionierung der Autonomie auf die Realisierung und Entfaltung der Gattungspotentiale? Selbst in

den Arbeiten, die zu seinem Projekt einer „Kritik der politischen Ökonomie" gehören, bleibt die Vorstellung, die Produktivkräfte der Gattung zu entwickeln und zu entfalten, zentral.

Im ersten Band des *Kapital* analysiert Marx die sozialen Strukturen des Kapitalismus auf der Ebene der verdinglichten Relationen zwischen Waren. Die einzelnen Akteure werden dabei lediglich als Träger von Handlungsabsichten („Charaktermasken") berücksichtigt, soweit ihnen durch das kapitalistische Produktionssystem zuschreibbare funktionale Absichten zukommen. Diese Absichten müssen vom einzelnen Akteur nicht als die eigenen Absichten seiner Handlungen gewusst werden. Außerdem ist die kritische Sozialphilosophie von Marx darauf ausgerichtet, die als Verwirklichung nicht intendierter Folgen kollektiver Kooperationen explizierbaren Systemeffekte des Kapitalismus zu analysieren. Beides führt dazu, dass in seinem Theorieprogramm einer Kritik der politischen Ökonomie der Zusammenhang zwischen Systemebene und individueller Handlung einerseits sowie von nicht intendierten Folgen kollektiver Kooperationen und individuellen Handlungen andererseits nicht expliziert wird.[24] Ein solcher Theoriebaustein ist jedoch unverzichtbar, um das Verhältnis der Realisierung der Produktivkräfte der Gattung und die Realisierung der individuellen Potentiale der einzelnen Gattungsmitglieder zu bestimmen.

Die handlungstheoretischen und methodologischen Fragen, die mit dem Fehlen dieses Theoriebausteins verbunden sind, haben in der Marxforschung keine sonderliche Beachtung gefunden.[25] Etwas besser steht es dagegen um die normative Dimension dieses Problemkomplexes. In der Debatte um den metaethischen Status der Marxschen Theorie im Allgemeinen und seines Programms einer Kritik der politischen Ökonomie im Besonderen ist die Frage nach dem Verhältnis von individueller Freiheit, Selbstverwirklichung von Individuum und Selbstrealisierung der Gattung erörtert worden.[26] Da diese Debatte jedoch die handlungstheoretischen Grundlagen ausgeblendet hat, wurde die Frage zumeist darauf reduziert, ob die Marxsche Theorie überhaupt als eine evaluative Konzeption verstanden werden dürfe. Diejenigen, die hierauf eine bejahende Antwort geben, erörtern dann, ob es sich hierbei um eine deontologische, eine konsequentialistische oder eine perfektionistische Konzeption handelt.

Wie eingangs (vgl. 1.) gesagt, soll hier kein Beitrag zu dieser Debatte geleistet werden. Zu beachten ist jedenfalls, dass die berühmte Rede vom „Reich der

---

24   Vgl. hierzu exemplarisch Coleman (1990) sowie Hoffmann-Rehnitz et al. (2019).
25   Vgl. dazu aber Lange (1980) und Quante (2009).
26   Vgl. dazu exemplarisch Brenkert (1983) und Peffer (1990).

Freiheit" als Opposition zu fourierschen (und anderen frühsozialistischen) Vorstellungen, nicht aber als deontologisches Bekenntnis von Marx zu werten ist. Mit dieser Opposition korrigiert Marx unbestreitbar emphatische Obertöne seiner Entfremdungskonzeption. Daraus aber lassen sich keinerlei Schlüsse mit Blick auf die Beantwortung der Frage ziehen, wie Marx sich das Verhältnis von individueller Selbstverwirklichung und Realisierung der Gattungskräfte vorgestellt hat. Um diese Frage überhaupt sinnvoll stellen zu können, benötigt man im Marxschen Theorieprogramm zum einen den hier als Desiderat identifizierten Theoriebaustein, in dem individuelles Handeln und systemische Funktionen aufeinander bezogen werden. Zum anderen muss man, um diese Frage normativ adäquat stellen zu können, in Rechnung stellen, dass Marx in seiner Entfremdungskonzeption der 1840er Jahre sämtliche institutionellen Vermittlungen des Konflikts individueller und allgemeiner Ansprüche als inadäquat zurückweist und dem Ideal einer unmittelbaren Auflösung von Gegensätzen und Konflikten verpflichtet ist. Die Frage, welche Auswirkungen die im *Kapital* zu beobachtende Deflationierung der Entfremdungskonzeption für das systematische Fundament des Theorieprogramms einer Kritik der politischen Ökonomie nach sich ziehen muss, ist komplex; und Marx selbst hat zu ihrer Beantwortung wenig beigetragen. Aber systematische Antworten auf diese Frage sind keine Antwort auf die andere Frage, wie Marx sich das Verhältnis von Individuum und Gattung in Konfliktfällen normativ vorgestellt hat. Antworten auf diese beiden Fragen werden voraussichtlich nicht vollkommen unabhängig voneinander zu entwickeln sein. Aber es bleiben dennoch zwei verschiedene Fragen. Gemeinsam ist ihnen allerdings, dass die Texte, die Karl Marx im Rahmen seines Theorieprogramms einer Kritik der politischen Ökonomie verfasst hat, keine expliziten und nur sehr wenige indirekte Antworten auf sie enthalten.

2. *Zweite Unschärfe: Postkantischer Perfektionismus und die Ambivalenz der Autonomie*

Akzeptiert man den in diesem Beitrag entfalteten Befund, dass die Philosophie von Karl Marx sich als eine Variante des postkantischen Perfektionismus verstehen lässt, dann werden durch die kritische Erörterung der Marxschen Konzeption Fragen und Probleme sichtbar, denen sich eine systematische Weiterentwicklung dieses metaethischen Theorietyps stellen muss. Nicht nur die Frage, um wessen Autonomie es eigentlich geht (Individuum oder Gattung), ist zu klären. Auch die Frage, was genau unter Autonomie zu verstehen ist, muss beantwortet werden. Handelt es sich um ein deontologisch zu explizierendes Grundprinzip, welches formal als Fähigkeit zur und normativ als Recht auf Selbstbestimmung zu verstehen ist? Wenn dem so wäre, was bedeutet dann die Rede davon, Autonomie zu perfektionieren? Handelte es sich dagegen um einen im Rahmen einer Axiologie auszubuchstabierenden Wert, dann wäre zu klären, ob es sich hierbei um die einzige Währung einer solchen Ethik handelt, ob dieser Wert quantifiziert und die Perfektionierung damit als Maximierung verstanden werden kann (dies wäre eine utilitaristische Konzeption). Oder handelt es sich um eine Fähigkeit des Menschen, die analog zu tugendethischen Konzeptionen zu explizieren wäre?

Die Darstellung der Konzeption von Karl Marx hat verschiedene Aspekte der freien Selbstverwirklichung des Gattungswesens identifiziert, die für unterschiedliche metaethische Ausdeutungen und Präzisierungen sprechen.[27] Deshalb belegt auch sein Werk die Notwendigkeit, die Konzeption des postkantischen Perfektionismus systematisch weiter auszudifferenzieren.[28]

Literatur

Angehrn, Emil/Lohmann, Georg (Hrsg.), *Ethik und Marx*, Königstein / Ts.: Athenäum Verlag, 1986.

Archibald, W. Peter, *Marx and the Missing Link: Human Nature*, Atlantic Highlands, NJ: Humanities Press, 1989.

Brenkert, George G., *Marx's ethics of freedom*, London: Routledge & Kegan Paul, 1983.

Cohen, Marshall et al. (Hrsg.), *Marx, Justice, and History* (a Philosophy & Public Affairs Reader), Princeton: Princeton University Press, 1980.

Coleman, James S., *Foundations of social theory*, Cambridge: Harvard University Press, 1990.

Hoffmann-Rehnitz, Philip et al., „Diesseits von methodologischem Individualismus und Mentalismus", in: *Angewandte Philosophie / Applied Philosophy*, 2019, S. 133-152.

Lange, Ernst Michael, *Das Prinzip Arbeit*, Frankfurt am Main: Ullstein Verlag, 1980.

Meikle, Scott, *Essentialism in the Thought of Karl Marx*, La Salle, Illinois: Open Court Publishing Company, 1985.

Moggach, Douglas, "Post-Kantian Perfectionism", in: ders. (Hg.), *Politics, Religion, and Art*, Northwestern University Press: Evanstone, Illinois, 2011, S. 179-200.

– "Contextualising Fichte: Leibniz, Kant, and Perfectionist Ethics", in: *Fichte-Studien* 45, 2018, S. 133-153.

– "The Limits of State Action: Humboldt, Dalberg, and Perfectionism after Kant", in: James Clarke and Gabriel Gottlieb (Hg.), *Practical Philosophy between Kant and Hegel: Freedom, Right and Revolution*, Cambridge: Cambridge University Press, 2020 (im Erscheinen).

---

27 Vgl. zu den unterschiedlichen metaethischen Optionen in der Debatte zur Ethik von Marx, die ein Spiegelbild dieses Befundes bildet, die Darstellung von Sweet (2002).

28 Siehe hierzu auch den systematischen Ausblick von Mooren und Quante in diesem Band.

Nielsen, Kai/Patten, Steven C. (Hrsg.), *Marx and Morality* (Canadian Journal of Philosophy, Supplementary Volume VII), Ontario: Canadian Association for Publishing in Philosophy, 1981.

Peffer, Rodney G., *Marxism, Morality, and Social Justice*, Princeton: Princeton University Press, 1990.

Quante, Michael, „Kommentar", in: *Karl Marx: Ökonomisch-Philosophische Manuskripte. Studienausgabe mit Kommentar*, Frankfurt am Main: Suhrkamp Verlag, 2009 (dritte Auflage 2018), S. 209-410.

– „Bruno Bauer, Karl Grün und Karl Marx zur Emanzipation der Juden", in: A. P. Olivier/E. Weisser-Lohmann (Hrsg.), *Kunst – Religion – Politik*, München: Fink, 2013, S. 321-336. (2013a)

– "Recognition in *Capital*", in: *Ethical Theory & Moral Practice* 16, 2013, S. 713-727. (2013b)

– „Max Stirners Kreuzzug gegen die Heiligen, oder: Die Selbstaufhebung des Antiperfektionismus", in: M. Quante/A. Mohseni (Hrsg.), *Die linken Hegelianer*, Fink: München, 2015, S. 245-263.

– „Handlung, System der Bedürfnisse und Marktkritik bei Hegel und Marx", in: H.-C. Schmidt am Busch (Hrsg.), *Die Philosophie des Marktes / The Philosophy of the Market*, Hamburg: Meiner, 2016, S. 153-175.

– *Der unversöhnte Marx. Die Welt in Aufruhr*, Münster: Mentis, 2018.

– „Auf dem Weg zur materialistischen Geschichtsauffassung?", in: K. Bayertz/ M. Hoesch (Hrsg.), *Die Gestaltbarkeit der Geschichte*, Hamburg: Meiner, 2019, S. 117-136. (2019a)

– „Einleitung", in: *Karl Marx: Das Kapital. Kritik der politischen Ökonomie. Erster Band*, Hamburg: Meiner, 2019, S. IX-XLVII. (2019b)

Sweet, Robert T., *Marx, Morality and the Virtue of Beneficence*, Lanham: University Press of America, 2002.

The Non-Essentialist Perfectionism of Max Stirner

David Leopold

§1

Max Stirner is a fine advertisement for what is sometimes called the history of philosophy 'without the gaps'.[1] That slogan refers to a narrative which proceeds not from 'peak' to 'peak', but with due attention to all the foothills, false summits, dead ends, and plains, that surround and extend beyond them. The hope is that paying attention to the wider landscape might not only alter our identification, understanding, and evaluation of the peaks, but also lead us to discover and reappraise previously neglected topographical features which are interesting and important in their own right.

'Stirner' was the student nickname – reflecting a high forehead (*'Stirn'*) and the way he parted his hair – of Johann Casper Schmidt (1806-1856). 'Max Stirner' became both a pseudonym – some cannot resist saying *nom de guerre* – and his preferred identity. The basic circumstances of Stirner's adult life are easily listed: an extensive exposure to Hegelian philosophy at university and beyond; a short period of regular employment as a teacher at a respectable private girls' school; two short and unhappy marriages; a brief burst of minor literary notoriety; followed by a longer period of social isolation, poverty, and financial precariousness (including two spells in a debtors' prison); before an unexpected and early death. However, information about his interior life and personality remains sparse, largely frustrating attempts to identify meaningful affinities between his life and work.

What survives, above all, is a single book; for one critic, 'the most revolutionary ever written'.[2] The first edition of *Der Enzige und sein Eigentum* is dated 1845, although copies circulated from the end of October the previous year.[3] The book is known in English as *The Ego and Its Own* – after the title chosen

---

[1] As propounded, not least, by Adamson (2014), and elsewhere.
[2] Huneker (1909), 350.
[3] References to Stirner's text are to two editions, divided by a forward slash: Stirner (1972); and Stirner (1995).

(when Steven Tracy Byington,[4] George Schumm,[5] and others, were unable to agree) by Benjamin R. Tucker[6] – but a more literal translation would be *The Unique Individual and their Property*. In comparison, Stirner's other writings are slight in both extent and content, and remain of interest primarily because, and to the extent that, they illuminate the genesis and character of *Der Einzige*.

The historical impact of Stirner's work should not be underestimated. Most immediately, it was not only an impulse to, and reflection of, the fracturing of 'left' Hegelianism as a coherent intellectual movement, but also played a crucial, and related, role in the intellectual formation of the young Karl Marx, accelerating and shaping the latter's emergence from a period of ardent Feuerbachian enthusiasm. Over a longer period, Stirner was a progenitor of individualist anarchism (in America and elsewhere), and has been seen as prefiguring the intellectual avant-garde of a variety of subsequent generations, including those with existentialist, neo-Nietzschean, and post-structuralist, sensibilities.

Claims for the intrinsic philosophical interest of Stirner's work are wide-ranging. In part this reflects the scope of *Der Einzige*, with Stirner variously providing: a developmental account of an individual life; an outline philosophy of history; a genealogical portrait of modernity (as an asylum); a distinctive critique of morality; an attack on the state; and a positive portrayal of egoism and the kind of social relations that it requires and promotes. The critical threads of the book are perhaps the most resonant today; not least, Stirner's systematic attempt to portray a variety of ostensibly emancipatory projects as tightening, rather than loosening, tyranny over the individual. Complete converts to his constructive vision might remain few, but Stirner plays the role of provocateur with verve and conviction. In challenging progressive beliefs, he pressures even those who disagree with him to think hard about what precisely it is that they want to resist and how they might best do so.

That said, some of Stirner's views on these, and other topics remain elusive. In part, this is due to the form of his prose, and his refusal to restrict his own modes of expression and reasoning to those licensed by conventional views

---

4   Steven T. Byington (1868-1957) was the translator of *Der Einzige*. (His other translations include *The Bible in Living English* published posthumously by the Watchtower Bible and Tract Society.) He was a teacher, linguist, and contributor to Tucker's anarchist journal *Liberty*.

5   George Schumm (1856-1941) was a compositor, printer, and assistant to Tucker. In addition to helping copy edit and proofread the Byington translation, Schumm translated John Henry Mackay's *Die Anarchisten*.

6   Benjamin R. Tucker (1854-1939) was a publisher and writer; editor of the individualist anarchist periodical *Liberty* between 1881 and 1908, and author of the wonderfully titled *Instead of a Book, By a Man Too Busy to Write One* (1893).

of truth and language (which he sees as oppressive). In part, there remains uncertainty about the sincerity of some of his argumentation, about how literally he should be read. For instance, whether – in his 'dialectical' treatment of individual and historical development (as progressing through stages of 'realism', 'idealism', and 'egoism') – Stirner is best understood as parodying rather than endorsing certain Hegelian forms of argumentation.[7]

Given that range and uncertainty, I should perhaps stress the modesty of my own ambitions in the present chapter. I examine only a single thread in *Der Einzige*; offering an outline characterisation of, and some initial reflection on, Stirner's relation to perfectionism.

§2

'Perfectionism' is a term of art which can mean very different things in different contexts. Accordingly, I begin with some remarks about how it will be understood here. This understanding is not idiosyncratic, but I do not wish to deny the legitimacy and utility of alternative usages. In particular, my comments in the present section are intended to clarify what follows in this chapter, and not to police the use of the term 'perfectionism' elsewhere, including elsewhere in the present volume.

I understand perfectionism as an ethical standpoint which values the development and deployment of certain human capacities apart from any happiness or pleasure that they might bring.[8] It is perhaps most familiar in the form of an ethical theory that characterises the good life in terms of the development and deployment of our essential human nature. The name of this broad standpoint is said to derive from the somewhat antiquated characterisation of such capacities, whose promotion constitutes the good, as 'perfections' of human character. The relevant human capacities here are much contested, but the capacity for intellectual reflection and the capacity for productive labour, can stand as examples of the kind of capacities whose development and deployment might be said to constitute the good life. Because the development and deployment of those capacities is valued apart from any pleasure or happiness that they might bring, perfectionism is usually said to constitute an 'objective' account of the good. Of course, perfectionists can allow that the development and deployment of the relevant capacities

---

7 See, for example De Ridder (2007).
8 The account here draws on Hurka (1993).

brings us pleasure – and indeed welcome that fact – but they do not (qua perfectionists) hold that goodness consists in the pleasure that it brings.

Perfectionism can take a wide variety of forms, as suggested by the diversity of authors – from Aristotle to Nietzsche – who have been characterised as holding such a view. Disagreements amongst perfectionists often concern the precise constitution of human nature, and consequently the various ingredients of a perfected human life, but other intra-perfectionist disputes are available. They might disagree about whether perfectionism is one element, or the entirety, of a satisfactory moral theory. They might also take different views about the relation between perfection and moral pluralism. They might share an account of human nature but disagree about the social and political conclusions that supports. They might take different, more or less 'egoistic', approaches to the relation between one's own perfection and the perfection of others. And so on.

§3

Stirner's relation to perfectionism, so understood, might appear obvious enough. In particular, the author of *Der Einzige* is fiercely critical of characterisations of the good life in terms of the development and deployment of our essential human nature. Consequently, whatever we make of his substantive views, it seems clear that Stirner, as one recent commentator has it, 'is not at all a perfectionist'.[9] I intend – in the next section – to put this view under pressure, but, for the moment, acknowledge that it has much to recommend it.

One of Stirner's main critical ambitions is to demonstrate that modernity fails to escape from the very thing that it claims to have outgrown, namely religious modes of thought. His ostensible target is 'liberalism', which he sees as having played a significant role in world history, and in the emergence of modernity in particular. That looks sweeping enough, but Stirner's subsequent characterisation of its character appears a little more parochial. The various forms of 'liberalism' are said to share a perfectionist problematic, whereby individuals are separated from their human essence, and then that essence is set above them as something to be striven for. This problematic is exemplified by the philosopher Ludwig Feuerbach, whilst its various modern forms seemingly owe much to 'the free', the eponymous group of Berlin Hegelians which whom Stirner had associated. The latter are sub-divided into 'political', 'social', and 'humane', liberalisms, which share the perfectionist problematic, but disagree

---

9 Moggach (2011), 187.

about the exact nature of our humanity, identifying the species with citizenship, labour, and critical activity, respectively.

(In this context, a passing reference may be of interest to modern readers. Marx was not a well-known, or well-published, figure in 1844, but Stirner had noticed his recent essay *'Zur Judenfrage* [On the Jewish Question]' and sought to locate it within this contemporary intellectual landscape.[10] Stirner's remarks are interesting partly because Marx is not identified with those socialists and communists who associate the human essence with productive activity, insisting that 'labour is man's "destiny [*Bestimmung*] and calling"'.[11] Instead, Marx appears later, as something closer to a radical Feuerbachian, confirming the religious character of liberalism by advancing the demand that we should strive to become a *'wirkliches Gattungswesen'*, a true species being.[12] It is a historical reminder: that his contemporaries often knew less about Marx than we now do; that the evolution of his communist commitments is complicated; and that the writings in which he most clearly identified humankind with a certain kind of productive activity were mainly unpublished at this time.)

The centrality of the critique of Feuerbach to Stirner's project is clear from this account of the former's emblematic status, exemplifying the perfectionist problematic of 'liberalism'. It is also apparent from the form of the book, which constitutes a structural parody of Feuerbach's best-known work. Where the two halves of Feuerbach's *Das Wesen des Christentums* had been entitled *God* and *Man* – with the first attacked, and the second celebrated – the two corresponding parts of Stirner's opus are named *Man* and *I*.

Stirner seeks to challenge the progressive verdict on Feuerbach's achievement. He suggests that the celebration of Feuerbach for having completed the critique of religion, is not merely mistaken but nearer the opposite of the truth. Far from undermining religion, the Feuerbachian problematic is said to reproduce its central features. To anticipate Stirner's punchline, we might say that the experience of alienation – a dysfunctional relationship between self and other – remains the same, whether we strive to be more like God or more like the 'true man'.[13]

---

10 Marx's essay appeared in the one and only edition of the *Deutsch-französische Jahrbücher* in February 1844.
11 Stirner (1972), 134/110. Proudhon is the only author mentioned by name in this section on 'social liberals', but Hess and Weitling are mentioned serially elsewhere.
12 Ibid., 192/158.
13 Ibid., 359/283.

In *Das Wesen des Christentums*, Feuerbach undertakes a philosophical analysis of Christian religious experience.[14] He maintains that the proper meaning of religious experience is obscured to those who undergo it; indeed, ignorance of its real object is portrayed as a defining feature of religion. (Feuerbach often, and unhelpfully, conflates Christianity and religion, perhaps in part because he viewed the former – in its Protestant variants, of course – as the culmination of the latter.) Feuerbach seeks to excavate the hidden meaning of Christianity, although his conclusion can look disarmingly simple. In Christianity individuals worship the predicates of human nature projected onto an ideal and imaginary entity; that is, the Christian God is revealed as a collection of essential human predicates, 'purified from the limits of the individual man', and viewed as if they belonged to an objective being existing apart from humankind.[15] Such a stark summary is not inaccurate, but it misses out much that is interesting and important. Those omissions include: the extensive and detailed supporting evidence that Feuerbach provides; his account of theological reflection on religious experience so understood; and the educative and emancipatory ambitions of the project as a whole. The last of these is especially pertinent here.

Feuerbach's emancipatory ambitions become clearer once we recognise that he saw religious belief as a necessary step in the progress of humankind to self-understanding. It is through transformative criticism – recovering the correct relation of subject and predicate from its inversion in Christianity – that we first come to understand what human nature is. Moreover, confirming his perfectionist commitments, Feuerbach maintains that, once liberated from their otherworldly form, these essential human characteristics – and especially perhaps our love for others – would come to form the basis of the unalienated social and political life of the future. This emancipatory ambition also helps to clarify Feuerbach's insistence that he should be seen as a friend, and not an enemy, of religion; in particular, he sought not to destroy Christianity, but to liberate its content from otherworldly forms. This claim is also at the heart of his distinctive – and perhaps idiosyncratic – denial that he was an atheist. Feuerbach maintains that 'true atheism' requires the rejection not only of God as subject, but also of those predicates – love, wisdom, justice, and so on – traditionally associated with divinity.[16]

Where Feuerbach declines to take this second step, Stirner might be said to pick up this (idiosyncratic) characterisation of 'true atheism' and run with it.

---

14 References to Feuerbach's text are to two editions, divided by a forward slash: Feuerbach (2006); and Feuerbach (1957).
15 Feuerbach (2006), 48/14.
16 Ibid., 58/21.

Stirner maintains that religion, properly understood, is characterised by the subordination of the individual to 'spirit' in any of its guises. The rejection of God as transcendental subject consequently leaves the essential failing of religion intact. Feuerbach's perfectionist problematic, Stirner remarks, might have altered 'the tinsel' (the divine subject) but it leaves 'the main thing' (the divine predicates) unchanged.[17] The sacred is allowed to remain, if not as God, then as 'Man with a capital M' in Byington's inspired English rendering of Stirner's '*Der* Mensch'.[18]

Stirner portrays religion as some monstrous protean adversary, a 'gigantic opponent', which humankind has sought to conquer for over two thousand years, but which 'is constantly rising anew under a changed form and name'.[19] The perfectionist deification of the human essence, he insists, is simply the most recent incarnation, 'nothing more or less than a new – religion'.[20] Stirner rejects Feuerbach's self-description – as having revealed human nature as it is – and portrays him instead as having deified a prescriptive account of what being human required. In this way, the 'real kernel' of religion – the positing of an 'essence over me' – is left intact.[21]

Indeed, Stirner maintains that matters are worse than that description might suggest. The perfectionist problematic has actually increased, and not merely reproduced, religious tyranny over the individual. Feuerbach's 'Man', Stirner predicts, will prove 'capable of pinching us still more torturingly' that 'God' ever did.[22] Stirner sees the 'change of masters' here – deifying human nature in place of God – as extending and intensifying religious domination.[23] It extends domination because this new deity is no longer the preserve of the faithful, but can possess everyone, believers and unbelievers alike.[24] And it intensifies domination because divinity is now attached to us 'with indelible *immanence*'.[25] The scrutiny of my own conscience is harder to evade than that of a transcendent subject that flutters 'over our heads as a dove'.[26]

---

17   Stirner (1972), 63/56.
18   Ibid., 62/55.
19   Ibid., 103/86.
20   Ibid., 62/55.
21   Ibid., 50/46.
22   Ibid., 191/156.
23   Ibid., 62/55.
24   See Ibid., 103/86.
25   Ibid., 52/47.
26   Ibid., 103/86.

It is worth trying to identify the locus of Stirner's disapproval of the perfectionist problematic, as paradigmatically found in Feuerbach's writings, with a little more precision. There look to be four main threads here.

First, Stirner worries about the account of selfhood that perfectionism seems to assume, and its enthusiasm for *division*, and 'dualistic essences', in particular.[27] He warns the reader that Feuerbach, and his ilk, would 'cut your identity in two'.[28] I take it that the fact of plurality is less the issue here – despite a joke about the dangers of overcrowding once the divine predicates have been moved out of their 'heavenly dwelling' and taken up residence in us – than the specific character of, and relationship between, these two subjects.[29]

Second, Stirner characterises the perfectionist division here as involving a *contradiction* – in some suitably expansive sense – between a fictitious generic human essence, on the one hand, and a real particular individual, on the other. Feuerbach's love for humankind, for instance, is described as 'the love of *man*, the unreal concept, the spook', and emphatically not the love of any real individual.[30] The human nature of the perfectionists is essentially a fictitious entity, 'only an ideal', or 'only something thought of'.[31] And Stirner consequently insists that it will always remain something 'alien' and 'otherworldly' to the flesh and blood individual.[32]

Third, Stirner portrays the perfectionist problematic as *subordinating* the individual to the species. This is one source of its religious character; it is religious 'because it separates my essence from me and sets it above me, because it exalts "man" to the same extent as any other religion does its God or idol'.[33] We are told that 'we are worth nothing' when 'we are not "human"', but Stirner insists that embracing this goal makes little sense.[34] Human nature properly understood is neither universal, nor does it have any prescriptive content. As a result, it cannot ground any claim about how we *ought* to live. Indeed, Stirner concludes that: 'I am a man just as the earth is a star. As ridiculous as it would be to set the earth the task of being a "thorough star", so ridiculous it is to burden me with the call to be a "thorough" man'.[35]

---

27   Ibid., 87/74.
28   Ibid., 32/32.
29   Ibid., 35/35.
30   Ibid., 84/72.
31   Ibid., 200/163.
32   Ibid., 192/158.
33   Ibid., 192/158.
34   Ibid., 203/166.
35   Ibid., 199/163.

Fourth, Stirner understands the perfectionist relation between human nature and individual as involving *subjection* and *frustration* for the latter. The so-called '"proper self"' – the scare quotes are in the original – is set 'to be the ruler of the paltrier remainder'.[36] And, insofar as I strive to be more human, 'I yield myself a prisoner' to that spook.[37] Moreover, when it 'sets me beneath man' the perfectionist problematic 'creates for me a "vocation"' which I can never fulfil.[38] The human essence, Stirner insists, always 'remains otherworldly to you', and the striving 'to become wholly man' will prove 'just as fruitless as the Christian's to become wholly a blessed spirit!'[39] Simply put, we cannot become what is alien to us.

In short, Stirner's hostility to the perfectionist problematic looks emphatic enough. He insists that perfectionism divides the person into two contradictory parts, a fictitious true self and the prosaic remainder, it then sets the latter the ambition of becoming more like the former, establishing a relationship which involves subjection and frustration for the individual.

§4

The Stirnerian critique of perfectionism, sketched in the previous section, appears clear and forceful. It might easily seem that there is little to be said against it, at least as confirming Stirner's own hostility towards perfectionism, and correctly identifying his views as resolutely anti-perfectionist. However, as previously trailed, I think that matters are more complicated. Indeed, perhaps surprisingly, I want to suggest that Stirner's own standpoint is actually a perfectionist one.

In order to introduce this potentially surprising suggestion, consider a distinction that can be drawn between perfectionist approaches. In earlier remarks, I neglected to draw attention to the difference between perfectionism in the expansive sense, and one of its narrower varieties.[40] Perfectionism in the expansive sense is an ethical standpoint which values the development and deployment of certain human characteristics apart from any happiness or pleasure that they might bring. However, we can think of that broad picture as being elaborated in two different ways. In the first, perfectionism is an ethical

---

36 Ibid., 32/32.
37 Ibid., 183/150.
38 Ibid., 193/158.
39 Ibid., 192/157.
40 The distinction between broad and narrow perfectionism is also used by Hurka, but in a slightly different way. See Hurka (1993), 4.

theory that characterises the good life, so understood, in terms of the development and deployment of our essential human nature. On this account, which might be called 'essentialist perfectionism', certain characteristics of the individual are valued *because* they realise some aspect of human nature. In the second, this element – the relating of the relevant characteristics to our essential human nature – is missing. This variant is still perfectionist in that it identifies perfections of character whose promotion constitutes ethical goodness, but neither the relevant perfections, nor their goodness, are related to any account of our essential human nature. Let us call this latter variety 'non-essentialist perfectionism'.

(I can imagine readers worrying about these labels and their use of the slippery term 'essentialism' in particular. Non-imaginary readers in the same position should note that I am not especially attached to these particular terms, and am happy for them to be replaced with something else. What I am attached to is the idea of a conceptual space for a variety of perfectionism which values certain 'excellences' of character, but does not understand those excellences as forming part of an ideal of realising our essential human nature. That conceptual space, and not any particular label for it, is what matters here. And it matters, not least, because I will maintain that Stirner can plausibly be understood as occupying it.)

In short, in the remainder of this chapter I seek to demonstrate that Stirner is plausibly understood as what is here called a 'non-essentialist perfectionist'. That is, notwithstanding his fierce attack on 'essentialist perfectionism' and its associated idea of human nature, Stirner endorses an ethical standpoint which values certain excellences of character apart from any happiness or pleasure that they might bring.

§5

The presence of a character ideal is already trailed in Stirner's critique of 'liberalism'. If alienation is to be overcome, he maintains that the human essence of the 'liberals' has to be recognised and rejected as the enemy of selfhood rather than its true content and aspiration. However, that is already to accept that there is a kind of selfhood which not only survives, but whose existence and expression necessitates, the death of 'Man' as well as 'God'.

The name that Stirner gives to his character ideal is intended to indicate its distance from accounts of our essential human nature. It is the 'un-man [*Unmensch*]' whose existence and expression Stirner values.[41] And he is

---

41 Stirner (1972), 194/159.

sanguine that what 'an un-man is is not particularly hard' to describe 'in blunt words'.[42] Progress can be made by distinguishing two threads in the characterisation that follows: a negative account of what the 'un-man' is not; and a positive account of what the 'un-man is'.

Stirner's (negative) account of what the 'un-man' is not, rests on the critique of 'essentialist perfectionism'. The 'un-man' is simply 'a man who does not correspond to the *concept* man'.[43] So understood, we might say that the 'un-man' is *not*, for instance: divided into two parts; which are, in some sense, contradictory; with the prosaic remainder set to strive after a fictitious true self; in a way that involves subjection and frustration for the individual. For example, in the first person that he sometimes uses to characterise the 'un-man', Stirner notes that in order to reach that point 'I cease ... to measure myself and let myself be measured by man, cease to recognise anything above me'.[44] However, we would still seem to need more in the way of positive content if the character ideal here is not to remain somewhat under-described.

Stirner's (positive) account of what the 'un-man' is, identifies this character type with the 'egoist'.[45] In this context, we might recall Stirner's injunction to give up the 'foolish mania to be something else' and become 'what you really are', 'become egoists'.[46] This identification of the 'un-man' and the 'egoist' is important, but requires some interpretative care. In particular, Stirnerian egoism is not synonymous with egoism as conventionally understood. As Stirner recognises, 'egoists in the usual sense' are 'selfish people, looking out for their advantage'.[47] However, so understood, egoism includes 'one-sided, unopened, narrow' forms that Stirner himself denounces.[48] The egoism that Stirner admires and endorses is not simply self-seeking, but is associated with the idea of individual autonomy, the elusive idea of an agent who governs herself.

On the account offered here, the 'perfection' at the heart of Stirner's character ideal is the radical notion of autonomy, or self-rule, that he calls 'ownness'. 'I am my own', Stirner writes, 'only when I am master of myself, instead of being mastered ... by anything else.'[49] This association of egoism and autonomy appears throughout *Der Einzige*. Considering the antonym of 'egoism', for instance, Stirner reaches not for altruism, but rather identifies

---

42   Ibid., 194/159.
43   Ibid., 194/159.
44   Ibid., 162/131.
45   Ibid., 136/112.
46   Ibid., 181/149.
47   Ibid., 81/70.
48   Ibid., 82/70.
49   Ibid., 187/153.

'thraldom, service, self-renunciation' as paradigmatically '*not egoism*'.[50] Similarly, elucidating his provocative claim that 'God' is best understood as an egoist, Stirner explains that this is because 'He serves no higher person'.[51]

The appeal of individual autonomy is often taken for granted in modern intellectual culture, with self-rule treated as obviously desirable and unproblematic. However, it is an idea which can be developed in a variety of ways, not all of which are attractive and uncontroversial. Stirner's account of 'ownness' is a case in point. He not only ranks 'ownness' above any other consideration, but also makes it incompatible with any moral requirement to act in a particular way. As will become apparent, the impact of these moves is stark and unsettling.

In order to elucidate these concerns, the idea of 'ownness' needs a little more unpacking. We might think of Stirnerian self-rule as having both external and internal dimensions. I fail to be autonomous if I submit to an external power, whether that be an institution or another individual.[52] And my autonomy is also undermined if I allow myself to be 'mastered' by one of my own appetites or desires.[53] I will discuss both of these dimensions, but begin with the latter.

§6

Stirner's character ideal has an important 'internal' dimension. The egoist will, of course, have ideas and emotions, but they must not come to dominate or rule the individual. Stirner is concerned that 'if anything plants itself firmly in me, and becomes indissoluble, I become its prisoner and servant' and the 'anything' here would appear to include the individual's own thoughts and feelings.[54]

The Stirnerian egoist can consequently be understood as having to cultivate a kind of emotional detachment towards their own thoughts and feelings.[55] Stirner often presents the egoist as located in a conflict with various 'others', a fight for submission that they cannot afford to lose. On this account, the various 'others' include her own thoughts and feelings, in that the egoist must

---

50 Ibid., 182/149.
51 Ibid., 4/6.
52 Ibid., 187/153.
53 Ibid., 187/153.
54 Ibid., 157/127.
55 Stirner's biographer, John Henry Mackay, uses a related idea in a different context; presenting Stirner's own social isolation as the authentic expression of the 'ataraxic' dimension of egoism. See Mackay (1914), 212.

never allow either to 'subjugate' her, or make her 'a tool of its realisation'.[56] The appropriate strategic response involves emotional detachment, the flexibility and willingness to abandon particular ideas and emotions if the egoist finds herself getting too attached to them, if they threaten her sovereignty.

Recognising this internal dimension of egoistic self-rule can help elucidate the distance between Stirnerian and other more conventional kinds of egoism. There are forms of self-seeking which Stirner rejects precisely because they neglect or frustrate this internal condition for 'ownness' or autonomy. Consider the character and behaviour of what we can call 'the avaricious man'.[57] Since 'the avaricious man' will go to any length 'to gather treasures' he is conventionally, and not implausibly, portrayed as an egoist.[58] However, for Stirner, this is a 'one-sided, unopened, narrow' form of egoism that we should reject.[59]

For Stirner, 'the avaricious man' is an unsatisfactory character type because he is not self-governing, but rather 'wholly absorbed' by one of his own desires.[60] The conventionally egoistic desire for riches has broken loose, and come to subjugate and enslave its creator. Consequently, 'the avaricious man' exemplifies, not 'ownness' (or autonomy), but rather 'possessedness' (or heteronomy).[61] Greed 'becomes our – master' when it starts to 'inspire, enthuse, fanaticize' the individual.[62] We might say that the avaricious man, rather than being self-determining, is 'dragged along' by one of his own appetites.[63]

The case of 'the avaricious man' might also help to clarify the place of pleasure or desire satisfaction here. Stirner assumes that the egoist will typically do what she desires, or what pleases her. However, it is autonomy rather than pleasure or desire-satisfaction that gives egoistic character and behaviour its value. It might be that 'the avaricious man' gains huge pleasure from his pursuit of riches, but that clearly counts for nothing here. For Stirner, the crucial feature of his situation is the lack of autonomy; the avaricious man 'is a slave of lucre', he 'belongs to lucre, the moneybag, not to himself; he is not his own'.[64] In short, egoism and happiness might typically go together, but the former is not defined by the latter. No matter how pleased he might be with

---

56 Stirner (1972), 385/302.
57 Ibid., 81/70.
58 Ibid., 82/70.
59 Ibid., 82/70.
60 Ibid., 81/70.
61 Ibid., 82/70.
62 Ibid., 66/58.
63 Ibid., 64/56.
64 Ibid., 335/266.

himself and his life, 'an avaricious man is not a self-owned man, but a servant' of his own appetites.[65]

§7

Stirner's character ideal also has an important 'external' dimension. The egoist, of course, will stand in some relation to social institutions and other individuals, but these latter must never be allowed to dominate or rule. Not least, the attitude and behaviour of the egoist towards these external others must take a certain form, if her autonomy is to be preserved.

The egoist's relations with social institutions and other individuals are driven, as ever, by Stirner ranking of 'ownness' above any other consideration, and his conceptualising it as incompatible with the constraints of duty and obligation. The institutional casualties of these moves are many. However, to keep the discussion manageable, I focus on the case of the state, and the attitude that the egoist should adopt towards it.[66] Egoism emerges here as the opponent, not the ally, of statehood; as Stirner insists 'we two, the state and I, are enemies'.[67]

Stirner portrays the state as a repressive and illegitimate institution, whose 'sole purpose' is 'to limit, tame, subordinate the individual'.[68] The antipathy between the individual and the state is, on this account, a necessary one, based on the conflict between individual autonomy and the subject's obligation to obey the law. 'No one', Stirner maintains, 'has any business to command *my* actions, to say what course I shall pursue and set up a code to govern it', and yet the state is unable to forego 'the claim to determine the individual's will'.[69] The form of the state has no impact on this basic conflict. 'Every state is a despotism', he insists, 'be the despot one or many'.[70]

Note that Stirnerian egoism rules out the most familiar way of reconciling autonomy with a moral requirement to obey the law, through appeals to contract and consent. When Stirner maintains that 'no one has any business to command *my* actions, to say what course I shall pursue and set up a code to govern it', he explicitly identifies the 'no-one' here as including myself.[71]

---

65   Ibid., 335/266.
66   The discussion of the state that follows draws on Leopold (2006), 176-199.
67   Stirner (1972), 196/161.
68   Ibid., 249/201.
69   Ibid., 214/174.
70   Ibid., 215/175.
71   Ibid., 213-4/174.

Simply put, self-binding conflicts with 'ownness'. A self-assumed obligation still involves a moral or other requirement to act, and Stirner, of course, insists that 'ownness' can be realised 'only by recognising no *duty*, not *binding* myself nor letting myself be bound'.[72] Moreover, to require obedience to a law that I 'gave myself' would be to allow my will of yesterday to restrict my will of today, as if because 'I was a fool yesterday I must remain such my life long'.[73]

However, Stirner does not suggest that the individual has a positive duty to oppose, or seek to eliminate, the state. Such a suggestion would conflict with Stirner's considered account of autonomy and his scepticism towards political movements. To endorse a positive duty of this kind would be to seek to command and limit the individual's behaviour in a way that 'ownness', of course, proscribes. And to call for the overthrow of the state would seem liable to attract the scorn that Stirner directs at 'plans for the redemption or improvement of the world'.[74] Egoism, he maintains, rejects any sense of idealistic devotion to 'a great idea, a good cause, a doctrine, a system, a lofty calling'.[75]

Instead of a frontal assault on state power, Stirner recommends a strategy combining a general withdrawing of attitudinal support, with a case-by-case evasion of constraints. He offers historical role models for both strands. First, we should adopt an 'insurrectionary', rather than 'revolutionary', posture towards the state, declining to seek its approval or be judged by it. This attitude is said to have been exemplified by Jesus. Stirner denies that Jesus had been engaged in a political fight with the temporal power, and portrays him instead as having 'wanted to walk his own way, untroubled about, and untroubled by, these authorities'.[76] Second, in those 'cases where his advantage runs against the state's' the egoist should evade the demands of the political authorities, insofar as that is possible.[77] Here we should take our lead, not from the 'fool' Socrates, who conceded to the Athenians the right to condemn him, but rather the 'intriguer of genius' Alcibiades, who fled Athens rather than face trial.[78] To join Jesus and Alcibiades together as role models is a typically provocative Stirnerian conceit.

Stirner maintains that the institutional impact of these attitudinal and behavioural changes spreading should not be underestimated. Indeed, he suggests that they might even undermine the existence of the state. The

---

72 Ibid., 215/175.
73 Ibid., 215/175.
74 Ibid., 28/29.
75 Ibid., 82/70.
76 Ibid., 355-356/281.
77 Ibid., 263/212.
78 Ibid., 235-236/190-191.

argument here appeals to what might be called an idealist sociology, according to which the state is based on the idea of sovereignty, and held together by the deference of its citizens. Now if you hold that the state exists only because of 'the disrespect that I have for myself', then it might indeed follow that 'with the vanishing of this undervaluation' the state itself would be 'extinguished'.[79] Alluding to Hegel's discussion of '*Herrschaft*' and '*Knechtschaft*' in the *Phänomenologie des Geistes* – and seemingly promoting the moment of 'recognition' into a complete account of state power – Stirner suggests that if 'submissiveness' ceased 'it would be all over with lordship'.[80] The cumulative effect of a growing disrespect for law would be to 'scuttle [*anbohren*]' – literally, to drill holes into – 'the ship of state [*Staatsschiff*]'.[81]

I now turn to Stirner's understanding of egoistic social relations, and to the attitude and behaviour that the egoist should adopt towards other individuals. One complication here is that there exists something of a tension between what might be called – *mis*appropriating the language of Ernst Bloch – the 'warm stream' and 'cold stream' account of these matters in *Der Einzige*.

In 'warmer' mode, Stirner strives to present the egoistic future in a rosy manner, and downplay its distance from the present. In particular, he suggests that many familiar and worthwhile relationships, including 'love', might survive being reconstructed on egoistic lines, and he promotes 'the union of egoists' as an attractive, fluid, and spontaneous set of alliances, enabling individuals to unite without loss of sovereignty, without swearing allegiance to anyone else's 'flag'.[82] In his reply to critics – to Moses Hess, Ludwig Feuerbach, and 'Szeliga'[83] – Stirner imagines two heart-warming street scenes to illustrate egoistic union: in the first, children happen upon each other and spontaneously engage in the 'comradeship of play [*Spielkameradschaft*]'; and in the second, Hess himself bumps into friends before adjourning for a drink, not out of loyalty, but in the expectation of pleasure.[84]

I will be comparatively brief with this 'warmer' thread. It is a little submerged in the book, and Stirner subsequently regretted that readers had not always noticed the 'union of egoists', and rushed instead to associate the exclusivity of the egoist with 'isolation, separation, loneliness [*Isolirtheit, Vereinzelung,*

---

79 Ibid., 316/252.
80 Ibid., 214/175.
81 Ibid., 61/54.
82 Ibid., 261/210.
83 'Szeliga' was the pseudonym of Franz Zychlin von Zychlinsky (1816-1900), a Prussian officer, and sometime contributor to periodicals published by Bruno Bauer in the early 1840s.
84 Stirner (1914), 395-396.

Vereinsamung]'.⁸⁵ There are also many questions about its coherence and plausibility which are not easily and briefly dealt with. In this mode, Stirner sometimes recognises the benefits of cooperation – the union can strengthen and secure – in a way that he is reluctant to do elsewhere, and without seriously asking whether that concession creates difficulties for other parts of his argument.⁸⁶ He also seems to exaggerate the likely continuity between non-egoistic and egoistic variants of worthwhile relationships; for instance, failing to appreciate the involuntary and 'disinterested' character of love, and mistakenly thinking that it might easily be transplanted into egoistic social relations. And he helps himself to assumptions that might not be readily available on the egoistic account; perhaps underestimating the complexity and fragility of cooperation, and erroneously thinking that meaningful social cooperation could survive the erosion of trust that egoism would seem likely to engender.

In 'colder' mode, Stirner seems rather to revel in the iconoclastic standing of the egoist, and even celebrate the gulf between conventional attitudes and the arguments of *Der Einzige*. The language that he uses to describe egoistic social relations varies, but typically appeals to the idea of instrumental treatment. We are to think of other persons as, for instance, property and food. Both images might mislead a modern reader. In the first case, the reader needs to forget conventional juridical, or moral, notions of property, which, after all, rest on ideas of right, and involve constraints on use and control, that Stirner rejects. In contrast, egoistic property involves 'unlimited dominion' over the world, and is a way of insisting that there are no moral constraints on how an individual might chose to relate to things and other persons.⁸⁷ In the second, the reader has to forget the possibility of animal rights, or duties to the environment. The egoist, Stirner explains, has no obligations to others, but rather treats them as 'food' to be 'fed upon and turned to use' just as she is minded.⁸⁸ These images are intended to suggest that we can treat other person as we wish, that there are no moral constraints on what we can do to them. 'We have only one relation to each other, that is usableness, of utility, of use. We owe each other nothing.'⁸⁹

This lack of moral constraint impacts predictably on the permissible behaviour of the egoist. At various points, Stirner condones a variety of activities which are conventionally judged morally troublesome. The list includes: incest

---

85   Ibid., 375.
86   See Stirner (1972), 287/229.
87   Ibid., 279/223.
88   Ibid., 331/263.
89   Ibid., 331/263.

(the man who touches 'his sister as wife also');[90] infidelity;[91] filial impiety;[92] infanticide (the dying widow who strangles her child);[93] political and religious disloyalty ('ownness permits everything, even apostasy, defection');[94] breaking one's word ('yes, even his oath');[95] and murder (the egoist does not renounce 'even the power over life and death').[96] Indeed, the egoist does not fear, nor forbid, murder as a 'wrong', and views it as permissible provided only that 'it is right for me [*ist es Mir recht*]', or – in a more colloquial translation – provided only that 'it suits me'.[97] The egoist is justified in acting in all of these ways, and more, 'in order to determine himself instead of being determined by moral considerations'.[98] And the status of other persons, on this account, seems clear. 'For me', Stirner explains, 'no one is a person to be respected', but only 'an *object* in which I take an interest or not'.[99]

Many will find this vision of a social world – in which the egoist may 'think and act' as she will, utilizing others as she chooses – a repugnant one.[100] I sympathise with that response, but will not belabour it here. Instead, I note both that Stirner anticipates it, and remains unmoved. He acknowledges that 'very few' of his readers will 'draw joy' from this vision of a world without duties or obligations towards others, and expresses indifference at this predictable response, which reflects the emotional pull of conventional ideas that should be abandoned.[101] Insofar as his book promotes the spread of egoism, Stirner allows that 'trouble, combat, and death' might well result from its publication, and adds that these consequences are of no concern to him.[102] Indeed, if he had cared about the welfare of others, he would have kept *Der Einzige* from entering general circulation.

---

90   Ibid., 48/45.
91   Ibid., 48/45.
92   Ibid., 48/45.
93   Ibid., 356/281.
94   Ibid., 261/210.
95   Ibid., 261/210.
96   Ibid., 357/282.
97   Ibid., 208/170.
98   Ibid., 261/210.
99   Ibid., 312/276.
100 Ibid., 233/189.
101 Ibid., 331/263.
102 Ibid., 331/263.

§8

Stirner is widely thought of as a staunch opponent of perfectionism. He mounts a fierce attack on 'essentialist perfectionism', and its associated idea of human nature. This perfectionist problematic, exemplified by Feuerbach, stands accused of dividing the person into two parts, a fictitious true self which 'contradicts' the prosaic remainder, before setting the latter the task of striving to become more like the former, thereby establishing a relationship which involves subjection and frustration for the individual.

However, Stirner goes on to endorse an ethical standpoint which values certain excellences of character apart from any happiness or pleasure that they might bring. The character ideal that he promotes – the 'un-man' or 'egoist' – centres on the autonomous individual, whose capacity for self-determination, once developed and deployed, is objectively valuable. As a result, I have suggested that Stirner is better understood as a 'non-essentialist perfectionist'.

Stirner's evaluation and understanding of egoistic self-rule is a distinctive and surprising one. 'Internally', the egoist must cultivate an attitude of emotional detachment, and avoid becoming too attached to her own ideas and emotions. (Unlike 'the avaricious man' who, rather than being self-determining, is dragged along by one of his own appetites.) 'Externally', the egoist must recognise no constraints of duty or obligations; even self-assumed restrictions are deemed illegitimate. As a result, the state emerges as one of egoism's main institutional enemies. However, Stirner recommends that the egoist pursue, not a frontal assault on state power, but a strategy of (generally) withdrawing attitudinal support and (on a case by case basis) evading legal and political constraints. As for other individuals, Stirner recommends that they be treated as objects in which we might have an interest or not, rather than as persons who have any moral claims on us. He allows that such a view might licence a variety of activities – up to, and including, the taking of another's life – conventionally judged unacceptable. And he concedes – indeed, can seem to revel in this – that few readers will draw comfort from this result.

There is much that might be said about Stirner's discussion of these issues. However, in the remaining space I want to respond to a possible doubt about this proposed interpretation of Stirner as a ('non-essentialist') perfectionist. A reader might accept much of the account here – allowing, for example, that Stirner proffers the egoist as an ideal of character, with autonomy rather than some subjective good at its heart – but still be concerned about the status of Stirner's views. In particular, given that Stirner criticises and rejects morality, they might question whether he is rightly portrayed as occupying an ethical standpoint (as perfectionism, on the account adopted here, requires). These are difficult issues, and my defence of this interpretation of Stirner as a ('non-essentialist') perfectionist will utilise a controversial distinction between 'ethics' and 'morality'. I should acknowledge both that Stirner does not explicitly adopt this distinction, and that there is little wider scholarly consensus about its boundaries or coherence. Nonetheless, I think that it can help make sense of, and has some broad conceptual fit with, Stirner's own position.

When Stirner rejects morality, it seems certain that he is operating with a narrow notion of its boundaries. Morality is seen as preoccupied with the idea of duties and obligations towards others, and Stirner consequently rejects it because – on his distinctive account – these demand the sacrifice of autonomy. The moral individual is required to give up her own will 'for an alien one which is set up as rule and law'.[103] Yet, despite this rejection of morality, Stirner remains preoccupied with wider ethical questions about how we should live and how we should act. In this context, he does not hesitate to celebrate and champion the attitude and behaviour of the egoist; for instance, ranking the egoist's *'enjoyment of life'* above the mere *'longing for life'* exhibited by the pious.[104]

A distinction of this kind – between broader and narrower evaluative perspectives – allows us to understand how Stirner can consistently reject morality, and yet evaluate egoism as ethically superior to other modes of existence, or types of character. Consider, for instance, his discussion of Nero. The egoist and 'the moral man' are interestingly united in their condemnation of the Roman emperor, but the grounds of their disapproval are very different. Nero is 'a "bad" man' in the eyes of morality, because he failed to respect the rights of others.[105] Whereas, for Stirner, Nero is 'a *possessed* man', to be criticised because his obsessive predilections violated his self-mastery.[106]

Stirner portrays the 'the moral man' as having an unhelpfully impoverished understanding of the conceptual landscape in this area. In particular, Stirner appears to regret that 'the moral man' allows no space for ethical behaviour outside of the moral sphere. 'The moral man' imagines that whoever is not moral must consequently be immoral, as if those two categories exhausted all the options here. This 'narrow' perspective is said to generate a mistaken verdict regarding the egoist; namely that 'the moral man [...] throws the egoist into the only class of men that he knows besides moral men, into that of the – immoral'.[107] Stirner not only rejects this classification, but also suggestively

---

103   Ibid., 88/75.
104   Ibid., 322/284.
105   Ibid., 57/51.
106   Ibid., 57/51.
107   Ibid., 59/53.

observes that, lacking a more sophisticated account of the normative terrain, 'the moral man can never comprehend the egoist'.[108]

Bibliography

Adamson, Peter, *Classical Philosophy*, Oxford: Oxford University Press, 2014.

De Ridder, Widukind, "Max Stirner, Hegel and the Young Hegelians: A Reassessment", in: *History of European Ideas*, 34/3, 2007, pp. 285-297.

Feuerbach, Ludwig, *The Essence of Christianity*, trans. by George Eliot, New York: Harper & Row, 1957.

– *Das Wesen des Christentums*, in: *Gesammelte Werke*, Band 5, hg. v. Werner Schuffenhauer, Berlin: Akademie Verlag, 2006. (Feuerbach 2006)

Huneker, James, *Egoists. A Book of Supermen*, New York: Scribner, 1909.

Hurka, Thomas, *Perfectionism*, Oxford: Oxford University Press, 1993.

Leopold, David, "The State and I: Max Stirner's Anarchism", in: *The New Hegelians*, ed. by Douglas Moggach, Cambridge: Cambridge University Press, 2006, pp. 176-199.

Mackay, John Henry, *Max Stirner. Sein Leben und sein Werk*, Berlin: John Henry Mackay, 1914.

Marx, Karl: „Zur Judenfrage", in: *Deutsch-französische Jahrbücher*, hg. v. Arnold Ruge u. Karl Marx, Paris, 1844.

Moggach, Douglas, "Post-Kantian Perfectionism", in: *Politics, Religions, and Art. Hegelian Debates*, ed. by Douglas Moggach, Evanston/Illinois: Northwestern University Press, 2011.

Stirner, Max, *Der Einzige und sein Eigentum*, hg. v. Ahlrich Meyer, Stuttgart: Reclam, 1972. (Stirner 1972)

– *The Ego and Its Own*, ed. and introduced by David Leopold, Cambridge: Cambridge University Press, 1995. (Stirner 1995)

– *Max Stirner's Kleinere Schriften und seine Entgegnungen auf die Kritik seines Werkes „Der Einzige und sein Eigentum". Aus den Jahren 1842–1848*, hg. v. J.H. Mackay, Berlin²: Zack, 1914. (Stirner 1914)

Tucker, Benjamin R., *Instead of a Book, By a Man Too Busy to Write One: A Fragmentary Exposition of Philosophical Anarchism*, New York: Benjamin R. Tucker, 1893.

---

108 Ibid., 59/53.

Søren Kierkegaard's Critique of Eudaimonism and Autonomy

Roe Fremstedal

1. Introduction: Eudaimonism and Autonomy

This article focuses on how Kierkegaard criticizes both eudaimonism and Kantian autonomy for failing to account for unconditional obligations and genuine other-regard. Like Kant, Kierkegaard argues that eudaimonism makes moral virtue contingent on prudence. Kierkegaard views eudaimonism as an anthropocentric and self-regarding doctrine, which he contrasts not with Kantian autonomy but with theocentrism and proper other-regard. Kierkegaard then criticizes Kantian autonomy in much the same way as he criticizes eudaimonism. Whereas eudaimonism makes morality contingent on prudence, autonomy makes morality contingent on revocable decisions, he argues. As a result, human autonomy can account for hypothetical imperatives but not for categorical imperatives. This line of reasoning seems problematic, however, since Kierkegaard takes Kantian autonomy to not only represent a form of moral constructivism, but also a form of moral relativism and decisionism. Still, Kierkegaard's critique of autonomy indicates that morality and practical rationality need unconditional commitment towards what is objectively good.

2. Kierkegaard on Eudaimonism – The Kantian Heritage

We begin by exploring Kierkegaard's explicit criticism of ethical eudaimonism in *Concluding Unscientific Postscript* (1846) and his *Journals and Papers* from the 1839-54 period.[1] In these texts, Kierkegaard offers a Kantian critique of ethical eudaimonism (while seemingly accepting psychological eudaimonism,

---

1 Other writings, notably *Upbuilding Discourses in Various Spirits* (1847), also deal with eudaimonism, although less explicitly. Since the criticism of eudaimonism is essentially the same in the signed writings and in *Concluding Unscientific Postscript*, Kierkegaard appears to share Climacus' views on eudaimonism in the *Postscript*. See also Matthew Mendham (2007); Carson Webb (2017).

the view that we generally act with happiness in mind). Kierkegaard can be seen as radicalizing Kant's critique of eudaimonism, so that it amounts not just to a critique of egoism (and instrumentalism about moral virtue) but also to a critique of autonomy. This radicalization of Kant's critique of eudaimonism has not attracted much research attention, although it provides an informative example of Kierkegaard's ambivalent and eclectic attitude towards Kantian philosophy.[2]

Kierkegaard was familiar with Kant's critique of eudaimonism from his studies at the University of Copenhagen.[3] In *Anthropology from a Pragmatic Point of View*, Kant describes eudaimonism as a form of moral egoism that is motivated by personal happiness and utility instead of moral duty.[4] Kant thinks that ethical eudaimonism involves *instrumentalism* about moral virtue, since virtue is conditioned on pre-moral notions of self-interest and personal happiness (in a wide sense that includes sensuousness). Eudaimonists therefore view moral obligations as hypothetical imperatives based on personal happiness. Additionally, normative moral reasons are seen as being subjective and partial rather than objective and impartial.[5] This is something to which both Kant and Kierkegaard object because they think that it undermines the proper role and authority of morality. Like Kant, Kierkegaard takes morality and prudence to represent *categorical* and *hypothetical* imperatives, respectively.[6]

In the marginal notes of his personal copy of *Either/Or*, Kierkegaard writes that "'To choose oneself' is no eudaimonism".[7] Kierkegaard thus contrasts eudaimonism with the famous existential choice of oneself, a choice that is identified with the choice of the ethical by Judge William in the second part of *Either/Or*. Clearly, Kierkegaard denies that the position of William – the ethical stage – involves eudaimonistic ethics.

---

2 Like some of his German predecessors, Kierkegaard uses some Kantian ideas to break with the historical Kant, following the spirit instead of the letter of the critical philosophy. Unlike some of the German Idealists, however, Kierkegaard never claimed to be a consistent Kantian. Rather, he viewed Kant as an exemplary philosopher who provided a prolegomena for Christian faith. See Roe Fremstedal (2015a) and (2014), ch. 11. To some extent, the discussion of eudaimonism and autonomy in this article draws on my earlier work, including Roe Fremstedal and T.P. Jackson (2015); Roe Fremstedal (2015b).
3 *B&A* 1, 10 / LD, doc 12, 10; Green (1992), pp. 7f. I use the standard abbreviations for Kierkegaard's works.
4 Irwin (1996) (referencing Kant: *AA* VII, 130; cf. *AA* 6, 377f.).
5 For this distinction, see Parfit (2012), chs. 2-6.
6 Cf. *SKS* 9, 123, 133f., 194f. / *WL*, 119f., 130f., 195f.; *SKS* 22, 78, *NB* 11, 131 / *JP* 1, 975; Knappe (2004), chs. 3-5.
7 *Pap.* IV A246 / *JP* 5, 5636.

Like Kant, Kierkegaard (and William) does not appeal to prudence in order to justify morality. Nevertheless, this leads to a *dilemma* about how morality can be justified. The first horn of the dilemma understands being moral as requiring that we act for moral reasons, something that is circular and unconvincing to an amoralist or a practical moral skeptic (aesthete in Kierkegaard's terminology).[8] The second horn, takes the form of being moral for non-moral (notably prudential) reasons, something that appears self-defeating, because it implies instrumentalism about virtue (or *self*-regard instead of *other*-regard) and legality instead of morality. Indeed, Kantians and eudaimonists tend to agree that morality requires not just the right actions but also proper motivation.

Neither Kant nor Kierkegaard consider it problematic to ascribe a secondary role to prudence, in which prudence provides normative reasons for actions that are constrained and limited by morality. Both Kant and Kierkegaard are *non*-eudaimonists rather than *anti*-eudaimonists. Non-eudaimonists hold that "we have sufficient reason to pursue virtue above all other goods or advantages even if it conflicts with happiness or it does not affect it either way".[9] Still, happiness is important for morality in other respects, because it can provide reasons for action and a second defense of morality. Anti-eudaimonists, by contrast, hold that "any thought of the benefits one gains from" virtue to be "entirely out of place, and incompatible with" virtue.[10] Virtue should therefore not be seen as a means to, or part of, personal happiness or self-interest.

In Kierkegaard's early work (1843-46), he views the relation between virtue and happiness as contingent in this life (as opposed to the afterlife),[11] whereas the late Kierkegaard (1847-55) suggests that there is an inverse relation between virtue and happiness in history. More specifically, in his later works, Kierkegaard claims that Christian virtue, which is ethical and religious, requires following Christ, something that involves suffering, martyrdom, humiliation, and crucifixion in this life.[12] Despite this, both the early and late Kierkegaard

---

8   Reflected aesthetes only seem to allow moral considerations insofar as morality is secondary to non-moral, aesthetic concerns. Kierkegaard takes the aesthetic in the original sense of *aesthesis*, as perception from the senses, but associates it with sensation, sensibility, and sensuousness more generally. The aesthetes then prioritize sensuousness above morality, even if they act morally on occasion.
9   Irwin (2011), 289.
10 Irwin (2011), 549. Irwin views Kant as a non-eudaimonist and Kierkegaard as an anti-eudaimonist.
11 *SKS* 4, 123, 156 / *FT*, 27, 63; *SKS* 7, 126 / *CUP1*, 134.
12 *SKS* 20, 249, *NB* 3, 11 / *JP* 1, 954; *SKS* 20, 293, *NB* 4, 13 / *JP* 1, 956; *SKS* 27, 486, *Papir* 407 / *JP* 1, 958; *SKS* 21, 152, *NB* 8, 17 / *JP* 1, 964; *SKS* 8, 220, 319-431 / *UD*, 119, 217-341; *SKS* 12, 170 / *PC*, 167; *SKS* 25, 370, *NB* 29, 107 / *JP* 3, 2908; *SKS* 13, 307 / *M*, 251.

think that the theological virtues and the second use of the law prepare, or contribute to, personal salvation and eternal happiness (the highest good). Instead of ruling out the idea that God may save unbelievers, Kierkegaard presents Christianity as demanding faith, hope, and charity. Indeed, these theological virtues seem to partially anticipate the happiness or bliss that we may later enjoy eternally.[13] Hope, for instance, expects the good for oneself and for one's neighbor alike. And neighbor-love, which appears to anticipate the kingdom of God, involves loving both yourself and your neighbor (in the right way). Instead of viewing eternal happiness as incompatible with virtue (or denying that virtue contributes to eternal happiness), Kierkegaard is a non-eudaimonist.

Kierkegaard's general approach to eudaimonism seems broadly Kantian. Consider this passage from 1843-44:

> The transition from eudæmonism to the concept of duty is a leap, or, assisted by a more and more developed understanding of what is most prudent, is one finally supposed to go directly over to virtue? No, there is a pain of decision which the sensuous (the eudæmonistic), the finite (the eudæmonistic) cannot endure. Man is not led to do his duty by merely reflecting that it is the most prudent thing to do; in the moment of decision reason lets go, and he either turns back to eudæmonism or he chooses the good by a leap.[14]

First, this quote aligns eudaimonism with the sensuous, the finite, and with prudence. On this account, prudence is not only something that serves personal happiness and self-interest, but ultimately something that serves sensuousness and inclination. This involves a very broad understanding of prudence (and happiness) that seems Kantian.[15] For instance, a radically evil fanatic may not be prudent in the sense of rationally pursuing personal happiness and self-interest. Still, he could be prudent in the broader sense that he follows sensuousness and his inclinations rather than moral duty.

Second, Kierkegaard describes the transition from eudaimonism to virtue, duty, and the good as a leap. This is significant as it clearly shows that, for Kierkegaard, there is no gradual transition from eudaimonism to morality, because they represent different normative domains. Kierkegaard here points to a much-discussed problem, namely how to get from self-concern to genuine (non-instrumental) other-concern. The eudaimonist is initially concerned with personal happiness and only later develops other-regarding virtues such

---

13 Cf. Fremstedal and Jackson (2015); Fremstedal (2014), chs. 4-6.
14 *SKS* 27, 277, *Papir* 283, 1 / *JP* 3, 2349.
15 Cf. Irwin (1996); Fremstedal (2014), chs. 2-4.

as justice. Nevertheless, on this account virtue seems to require *self-effacement* which undermines the very self-concern that eudaimonists view as initially motivating the development of virtues.[16]

Kierkegaard expands upon this idea in his *Concluding Unscientific Postscript*, where he describes the relation between morality and prudence as follows:

> [T]here actually are not two [different] paths, or there are two [similar] paths of pleasure [*Lystens Veie*], one of which is a little more sagacious [*klogere* – prudent] than the other, just as when climbing a mountain to enjoy [*nyde*] the view it is more sagacious not to turn around too soon – in order to enjoy it all the more. Then what? Then the sensualist [*Vellystningen* – the libertine] (the eudaemonist) is not only lunatic because he chooses the path of pleasure [*Lystens Vei*] instead of the path of virtue, but he is a lunatic sensualist [*gal Vellystning*] for not choosing the pleasurable [*lystige*] path of virtue.[17]

This passage associates eudaimonism with hedonism, libertinism, and sensualism.[18] Like Kant, Kierkegaard understands eudaimonists as relying on pre-moral notions of happiness that are in principle accessible to amoralists and instrumentalists about virtue. Of course, this is something most virtue ethicists – or self-described eudaimonists – would deny, since they take virtue to be constitutive of happiness.[19]

The passage above suggests that prudence supports libertinism and vice. This clearly indicates *conflict* between prudence and morality.[20] Nevertheless, in *Concluding Unscientific Postscript*, Kierkegaard denies that this conflict is total:

> All worldly wisdom is indeed abstraction, and only the most mediocre eudaemonism has no abstraction whatever but is the enjoyment of the moment. To the same degree that eudaemonism is sagacious [*klog*], it has abstraction; the more sagacity, the more abstraction. Eudaemonism thereby acquires a fleeting resemblance to the ethical and the ethical-religious, and momentarily it can seem as if they could walk together. And yet this is not so, because the first step of the ethical is infinite abstraction, and what happens? The step becomes too great for eudaemonism, and although some abstraction is sagacity, infinite abstraction, understood eudaemonistically, is lunacy.[21]

---

16 Cf. Justin Clark (2016), ch. 7.
17 *SKS* 7, 367 / *CUP1*, 403. Pleasure and enjoyment seem identical in the original, although the Danish uses both *"Lyst"* and *"at nyde"*.
18 Elsewhere Kierkegaard also interprets eudaimonism in hedonistic terms. Cf. *SKS* 20, 223, *NB* 2, 211 / *JP* 2, 1510. See also Mendham (2007).
19 Cf. Irwin (1996); Annas (1993).
20 Cf. *SKS* 7, 313 / *CUP1*, 342f.
21 *SKS* 7, 387 / *CUP1*, 426.

Kierkegaard (Climacus) here distinguishes between mediocre and abstract eudaimonism. The former is concerned with "the enjoyment of the moment," with short-term egoistic pleasure, whereas the latter has a broader focus, referring to enlightened self-interest or an enlarged or idealized form of prudence. Although he does not spell it out in detail, the abstract eudaimonism seems to be concerned with long-term interests instead of those relating to the present moment, or with other prudential values (or goods) than mere pleasure. Perhaps it even includes the interests of some other human beings. Kierkegaard (Climacus) therefore concedes that this abstract eudaimonism resembles morality to some extent. Conflict between morality and prudence (or eudaimonism) is not total, and idealized forms of prudence may partially resemble morality.

In the 1847-54 period, Kierkegaard repeatedly criticizes Christian eudaimonism for being egoistic.[22] In 1848, for instance, he attacks the Danish congregation and cultural movement established by N.F.S. Grundtvig:

> [T]he Grundtvigians imagine they are the only true Christians [...] They must be reproached for [...] that they do not do anything to communicate Christianity to other men. It is a kind of eudaimonism [...] to live on enjoying Christianity, to keep it for themselves [...].[23]

The Grundtvigians focus on their own salvation, instead of the salvation of others. Kierkegaard suggests that this 'kind of eudaimonism' involves sectarianism, parochialism and group egoism that is incompatible with the universalistic and egalitarian character of Christianity. He objects to the self-regarding nature of sectarianism, which lacks proper regard for humanity as a whole.[24]

3. Anthropocentrism and Kierkegaard's Radicalization of Kantianism

Kierkegaard goes a step further than Kant by viewing eudaimonism as an anthropocentric and self-regarding doctrine, which he contrasts with theocentrism and proper other-regard. He contends that the starting point of eudaimonism is irreducibly anthropocentric and self-referential, because

---

22   SKS 20, 223, NB 2, 211 / JP 2, 1510; SKS 26, 248f., NB 33, 5 / JP 6, 6927; SKS 25, 376, NB 29, 114 / JP 4, 3878; SKS 25, 390, NB 30,12 / JP 4, 3881-3882.

23   SKS 20, 336, NB 4, 106 / JP 5, 6122. The translation leaves out Kierkegaard's description of this position as *"en Art Utroskab mod det Christelige,"* as "a type of betrayal of what is Christian" (my translation).

24   Kierkegaard also accuses the Grundtvigians of confusing Christianity with Danish national identity. See Backhouse (2015).

it concerns individual-striving for personal happiness or flourishing. Even if eudaimonia involves moral excellence or virtue, eudaimonism still starts from the individual desire of permanent possession of eudaimonia or the highest good.[25]

By contrast, Kierkegaard's Christian ethics in *Works of Love*, starts from God's descent to us, not from our ascent to God. More specifically, the second ethics is based on the acceptance of divine grace (after the collapse of pre-Christian ethics). Its starting point is not personal interests (or interest in personal salvation) but rather the theological virtue of agape, in the dual sense of loving both one's neighbor and God. Kierkegaard denies conflict between loving neighbor and loving God, since we can only love God by loving our neighbor. For this reason, in *Works of Love*, he develops a Christian ethics that is simultaneously theocentric and other-regarding. This ethics is based on the imitation of Christ's selfless concern for all human beings. Kierkegaard emphasizes that Christian charity requires willingness to sacrifice personal interests (including happiness) for the sake of other humans who are in need. This is what Kierkegaard means by following Christ, something which he associates with the experience of suffering in this life.[26]

4. Evaluation of Kierkegaard's View of Eudaimonism

Recently, eudaimonists have developed responses to Kant's critique of eudaimonism, which argue that this criticism has limited validity, because it mainly holds for hedonistic and instrumentalist forms of eudaimonism.[27] Much the same may apply to Kierkegaard's (related) critique of eudaimonism, even if the latter goes beyond Kant's own.

First, even if Kierkegaard were right about philosophical ethics, he may not be right about theological forms of eudaimonism. Thinkers such as Augustine and Thomas Aquinas combine the eudaimonistic framework of classical ethics with Christian revelation (by viewing the highest good as the key to both ethics and soteriology). It is not clear that these types of theological eudaimonism need to be anthropocentric or subjective in any problematic sense. Within the perspective of theological eudaimonism, the human starting point (which Kierkegaard criticizes) is not invalid or mistaken as such, because this (albeit limited) starting point partially leads to the kingdom of God and salvation.

---

25 Fremstedal and Jackson (2015), 3.
26 See note 12.
27 See Annas (1993); Irwin (1996).

Virtue and happiness are not only good from our (limited) perspective, but also good for God. In other words, virtue and happiness are objectively good and there need not be a fundamental conflict between anthropocentrism and theocentrism (or a conflict between mere reason and faith), at least not if we understand both correctly.

Second, it is not completely clear that Kierkegaard's point holds for philosophical forms of eudaimonism which do not rely on divine revelation. Like Kant, Kierkegaard suggests that eudaimonism wrongly understands morality as relying on hypothetical imperatives instead of on categorical ones. Because virtue is contingent on the agent's desire (or even his strongest desire or inclination), the contention is that eudaimonism involves a problematic form of subjectivism about morality. Nevertheless, as Terrence Irwin argues, this is problematic as an interpretation of eudaimonism. Irwin quotes Bishop Butler who writes "'my reason for pursuing my happiness justifies my inclination to do it, not the other way around'".[28] It is not the case that I only have reason to pursue my happiness, or to look after my interests, if I happen to care about happiness or self-interest in the first place. For it does make sense to criticize someone who ignores their interests or their happiness. Our lives would be better than they otherwise would be if we are happy or achieve human excellence and virtue. A happy life is better than an unhappy life, and human excellence and virtue is preferable to vice, even if the agent involved fails to realize it. Whether we recognize it or not, personal happiness and self-interest can therefore represent objective goods that benefit us.[29] Eudaimonistic reasons for action can therefore hold independently of an agent's given desires. As a result, these reasons can be objective rather than subjective and categorical rather than hypothetical (although they need not always be overriding).

Third, we can debate whether eudaimonism needs to involve substantial egoism or instrumentalism about virtue. Virtue can be constitutive of happiness, so that no happiness is to be had unless one is virtuous. The Stoics see virtue as necessary and sufficient for happiness, whereas Aristotelians see it as necessary but not sufficient (since external goods are also needed). Nevertheless, there are forms of eudaimonism that are more vulnerable to the criticism of Kierkegaard and Kant. This is especially salient in the case of hedonistic eudaimonism (although any type of eudaimonism that does not see virtue as constitutive of eudaimonia is vulnerable). Hedonists (Epicureans) may insist that virtue leads to happiness, but is not clear why that must be the case, since the connection between virtue and happiness seems contingent

---

28   Joseph Butler quoted from Irwin (1996), 76.
29   Haybron (2010), 187. Cf. Parfit (2012), chs. 2-6.

and empirical. As long as happiness is not at least partially defined in terms of virtue, but in terms of pleasure (or anything non-moral), the charge of instrumentalism and substantial egoism seems valid. More specifically, if personal happiness by definition, or necessity, requires other-regarding virtues such as justice, there need not be anything problematic about pursing this happiness (even if it involves formal egoism that is concerned with personal happiness).[30]

Nevertheless, the broadly Kantian critique of eudaimonism found in Kierkegaard is reconstructed and defended by J.J. Davenport. He discusses various cases that clearly indicates that if I were to lose self-interested motives for action, I could still have an other-regarding motive left. But this implies that an other-regarding motive is operative alongside self-concerned motives. Other-regard and self-regard, then, represent two independent motives that may conflict. The intrinsic role of virtue, its role as a final end, cannot serve as a mere means to happiness because happiness is at best an unintended by-product of genuine virtue.[31] Acting for the good of a friend, for instance, may involve personal benefit as a side-effect, but it may also require personal sacrifice. Nevertheless, eudaimonism rules out self-forgetfulness or moral purity that does good *only* because it is good. Unless it contributes to personal happiness, therefore, eudaimonists cannot rationally sacrifice anything significant for the sake of others. Non-instrumental other-regard then seems incompatible with the eudaimonistic focus on the agent's happiness as the highest good.[32]

In cases of conflict, we must prioritize either morality or prudence. For instance, someone may sacrifice his career in order to adopt a child, or he may lose his job and social standing by refusing to side with a culture of racism, sexism, or corruption. Moral sacrifices like these are difficult to reconcile with eudaimonism because eudaimonists ultimately deny conflicts between morality and prudence.[33] One exception to this, however, would be a eudaimonism which requires that morality be prioritized *above* prudence at the level of particular actions, local deliberations and motives, while still maintaining that prudential considerations justify morality (primarily) at the global level of life as a whole.[34]

---

30 See Annas (1993); Irwin (1996).
31 See Davenport (2007), chs. 5-7. This argument is developed independently of Kierkegaard, although Davenport is a MacIntyrian Kierkegaardian. Davenport does not discuss Kierkegaard's "highest good," a concept that makes happiness (a) second to virtue and (b) something that only results from divine grace. Cf. Fremstedal (2014), chs. 4-6.
32 Still, eudaimonism can overcome this problem by denying individuality. See Davenport (2007), chs. 6-8.
33 See Fremstedal (2018).
34 See Clark (2016).

5. Kierkegaard's Critique of Autonomy

Although it has not attracted much scholarly attention, Kierkegaard criticizes autonomy in much the same way as he criticizes eudaimonism. Both here and elsewhere, Kierkegaard radicalizes Kantian ideas to the point that they almost become unrecognizable.[35] In 1850, he writes:

> Kant was of the opinion that man is his own law (autonomy) – that is, he binds himself under the law which he himself gives himself. Actually, in a profounder sense, this is how lawlessness or experimentation are established [...] If I am bound by nothing higher than myself and I am to bind myself, where would I get the rigorousness as A, the binder, which I do not have as B, who is supposed to be bound, when A and B are the same self.[36]

If I can bind myself, I can also unbind myself at will. In 1847, Kierkegaard writes:

> [T]he adult is simultaneously master and servant; the one who is to command and the one who is to obey are one and the same. [...] It can so easily happen that the servant meddles in the deliberation about the task, and conversely, that the master pays too much attention to the servant's complaints about the difficulties in carrying out the tasks. Then, alas, confusion develops; instead of becoming his own master a person becomes unstable, irresolute, vacillating [...] Finally [...] all his energy is expended in thinking up ever new changes in the task [...].[37]

Like the German Romantics and Idealists, Kierkegaard points to a *dilemma* inherent to autonomy.[38] The first horn of the dilemma takes the form of self-determination based on reasons that are *antecedently* valid and therefore have authority prior to self-legislation. In this case, autonomy is constrained by standards that are not self-imposed, something that appears to involve *heteronomy*.

By contrast, the second horn only recognizes the authority of self-determination. It insists on setting all the rules of conduct itself. Indeed, it also sets the rules for setting the rules (and the rules for setting these rules again) and so on. Nevertheless, any given rule would *contingently depend* on a decision that creates normative content. Because there are no external constraints or antecedent reasons that limit it, any self-imposed decision would be valid.[39] Norms or rules are only authoritative if self-imposed by contingent *fiat*. This

---

35 See note 2.
36 SKS 23, 45, NB 15, 66 / JP 1, 188.
37 SKS 8, 389f. / UD, 294f. See also SKS 11, 182f. / SUD, 68f.
38 The Kantian paradox of autonomy is one of the key topics of Pinkard (2010). See also Stern (2012).
39 Kierkegaard refers to a "constraining [...] factor," see SKS 23, 45, NB 15, 66 / JP 1, 188.

amounts to a *decisionism* that accepts any self-imposed decision, irrespective of normative content.[40] Any normative content is valid, contingent on a relevant decision (or perhaps contingent on a dominating decision). Since there is nothing that prevents a change of will, the normative content could *change anytime*, and is therefore only *provisionally* valid. Arbitrary change of normative content cannot be ruled out, except by a contingent principle that is itself only provisionally valid.

On this picture, autonomy collapses into a *motiveless and arbitrary* choice that is fundamentally *groundless*. It is possible to justify derived content in terms of more fundamental content, however, just as a theorem is derived from an axiom. But there can be no justification for the fundamental normative content – or axiom, in the analogy – itself; for there is no higher authority or principle that could ground or support it. The autonomous normative source must then constitute itself through a bootstrapping operation that is groundless, motiveless, and arbitrary.

The lawgiver is *identical* to a subject that is finite, fallible, and imperfect. Moreover, this lawgiver and subject is prone to whims and moods, on the one hand, as well as laxness, procrastination, and corruption on the other. For this reason, Kierkegaard suggests that the motiveless choice of the lawgiver can be affected by whims and moods. Worse still, the choice of the lawgiver can be unduly influenced by the special interests of the subject. The subject can influence the lawgiver to change or lessen his obligations instead of fulfilling them (something that can be quite demanding). Indeed, one can constantly change one's mind about what to do, by lazily concocting new tasks instead of realizing given tasks.[41] Instead of acting morally, one deliberates about what one's obligations are or what they could and should be. Autonomy, then, facilitates an unrestrained reflection that is self-consuming, something Kierkegaard associates with late modern European society.

Kierkegaard is criticizing a subjectivist form of autonomy that is anti-realistic and relativistic. In this way, his notion of autonomy is closer to Jena Romanticism and Sartre's notion of radical choice than anything that could be found in Kant (or Hegel).[42] Although Kierkegaard seems to focus on individual

---

40 For a contemporary defense of a similar meta-ethical position, which claims that it is possible to reject rational agency and by doing this to become insane or to die, see Cohen (2008).
41 SKS 8, 389f. / UD, 294f.
42 See Pinkard (2010); Stern (2012); Fremstedal (2014). We may ask why Kierkegaard associates this form of autonomy with Kant. Although Kant specialists discuss whether Kant is a meta-ethical realist or constructivist, many have taken autonomy to involve constructivism that creates valid norms by following valid procedure. Not just Rawls and

autonomy, the points I have made above would also largely apply to collective autonomy. Indeed, Kierkegaard makes similar points about moral autonomy and political democracy, suggesting that they overlap insofar as both represent modern subjectivism in which normatively speaking everything is up for grabs. Unless restricted by antecedent moral or legal constraints, both favor a never-ending, self-consuming reflection instead of moral action or political action. Kierkegaard's diagnosis of late modern European society in *A Literary Review* indicates that democratization and autonomy, together with the public sphere and mass media, contribute to unconstrained reflection, levelling, nihilism, and secularization. Still, he views these modern phenomena not just as problems, but also as benefitting us insofar as they indirectly contribute to religious faith at the individual level.[43]

Despite his critique of Kantian autonomy, Kierkegaard is concerned with a form of personal autonomy that allows us to take responsibility for ourselves as agents who shape our ends and priorities. John Davenport comments:

> Formal autonomy involves volitional identification with some first-order motives and alienation of others [...] Caring about first-order ends rationally commits us to caring^2 [second-order caring] that the putative values to which we respond in our central commitments, relationships, and life goals are objectively or intersubjectively sound [...] [and] mutually consistent [...].[44]

Moral agency requires a capacity for strong evaluation of first-order motives that presuppose evaluative judgments that must be capable of being (more or less) objectively correct. We can only shape our identity in a substantially rational manner if we can make ourselves better or worse by standards *external* to our wills. In order to examine our higher-order cares and commitments in a rational manner, therefore, we need the idea of the good, in an objective or realist sense, at least as a regulative ideal.[45]

Habermas, but also Kierkegaard and some German Romantics and Idealists associated Kantian autonomy with constructivism. See Fremstedal (2014), ch. 10; Pinkard (2010), 59f., 115, 162f., 187-89, 207, 277.

43   Conway (2015).
44   Davenport (2012), 117.
45   Rudd (2012), 91-95, 112-116. In meta-ethics, Kierkegaard is a non-naturalist cognitivist who is interpreted either as a moral realist or as a divine command ethicist. Even the latter interpretation, however, tends to view Kierkegaard as a moral realist, one who typically denies that the whole content of morality is contingent on God's will. On this interpretation, God's commands explain not so much the content of morality as its strictly obligatory form, which goes beyond what is merely good for us. For divine command ethics, see Evans (2014); Evans (2006); cf. Stern (2012), chs. 6-7. For realism, see Rudd (2012); Davenport (2012).

Kierkegaard insists that wholeheartedness, or consistency, requires unconditional moral commitment, since immorality is parasitic on morality and therefore involves double-mindedness or despair.[46] Nevertheless, this does not prevent autonomy from playing some kind of role beyond the formal autonomy analyzed by Davenport. Kierkegaard writes: "[I]n the world of spirit, precisely this, to become one's own master, is the highest – and in love to help someone toward that, to become himself, free, independent, his own master, to help him stand alone – that is the greatest beneficence."[47] Kierkegaard maintains, however, that we only become free and independent by loving our neighbor. By relying on commanded love that loves all humans without exception, we avoid being dependent on specific human beings. Charity makes us free, for "without law, freedom does not exist at all, and it is law that gives freedom."[48] This suggests that autonomy is a moral virtue of independent-mindedness rather than a source that creates moral obligations.[49]

6. Conclusion

For Kierkegaard, there is a deep similarity between eudaimonism and autonomy. Eudaimonism views moral obligations as hypothetical imperatives based on personal happiness, whereas autonomy views obligations as hypothetical imperatives based on contingent decisions (that may or may not relate to our pursuit of personal happiness). Eudaimonism allegedly views normative reasons as given by sensuousness or even the strongest inclination or desire. Autonomy, by contrast, views these reasons as given by human freedom (in the form of the strongest decision). The type of freedom involved here, however, is not Kant's notion of the will (*Wille*) as practical rationality. Instead, Kierkegaard takes autonomy to rely on *Willkür*, the power of choice. As such, autonomy involves arbitrariness rather than pure practical reason. It may be instrumentally rational but not substantially rational. Moreover, both eudaimonism and autonomy are susceptible to change. Eudaimonism puts virtue second-place to desires, which may change; whereas autonomy puts

---

46 *SKS* 8, 138ff. / *UD*, 24ff. This assumes that it is impossible to be morally indifferent in general.
47 *SKS* 9, 272 / *WL*, 274.
48 *SKS* 9, 46 / *WL*, 38f. The reference to the law here probably includes the two great commandments of Christian ethics.
49 See the distinction between independent-mindedness in the theory of virtue and meta-ethical constructivism in Adams (2016).

laws second-place to arbitrary decisions, which may also change (particularly if influenced by the all-too-human subject).

Kierkegaard argues that neither eudaimonism nor autonomy account for categorical reasons or unconditional imperatives. Neither can they account for normative reasons that are objective and impartial. Instead, eudaimonism and autonomy are special cases of subjectivism and special interests. This argument seems to hold for extreme forms of autonomy based on *Willkür*, but not moderate forms of autonomy based on *Wille*. In the case of eudaimonism, a Kierkegaardian critique of egoism and instrumentalism about virtue seems defensible, even if it is rather contentious.[50] Kierkegaard may be right to suggest that eudaimonism *can* involve subjectivism, anthropocentrism and hypothetical imperatives. But it is not clear that eudaimonism *must* be based on any of these, since it can be combined with objectivism, theocentrism, and categorical imperatives instead.

The argument sketched above can *either* be taken to count in favor of eudaimonism and (extreme) autonomy *or* against them. Although some readers have associated Kierkegaard with the former view,[51] we have seen that he clearly opts for the latter view. More specifically, he consistently interprets moral obligations as being categorical or unconditional.[52] Additionally, he identifies the good with the divine,[53] describing the moral demand as the "infinite ethical requirement"[54]. Finally, he also seems to view moral (ethico-religious) reasons as being categorically overriding, although this is controversial (due to what he calls the "teleological suspension of the ethical" in *Fear and Trembling*). In any case, he distinguishes between the first and second ethics, between philosophical ethics and Christian ethics, respectively. The former is seen as the default position that collapses internally and by doing so necessitates Christian ethics. On my view, this means that the first ethics is replaced (at least partially) not by an amoralism or immoralism but by Christian ethics.

Kierkegaard's relation to the post-Kantian debates on perfectionism and autonomy is generally ambiguous. Kierkegaard could be considered a perfectionist, concerned with the development of capacities of intrinsic and supervening value that are neither eudaimonist nor Kantian. Rather than being concerned with (mere) human self-perfection, he is concerned with how morality leads to guilt-consciousness and thereby prepares divine assistance. For Kierkegaard,

---

50 Cf. Davenport (2007), chs. 5-12.
51 E.g. Cohen (2008).
52 Cf. Knappe (2004), chs. 3-5. Kierkegaard appears to view moral obligations as objective, overriding, and partially universal. See Evans (2006), 15.
53 Rudd (2012), 45f.; Evans (2006), 88, 105, 183.
54 *SKS* 7, 455ff. / *CUP1*, 502ff.

our highest perfection lies in the acceptance of divine grace. In particular, he is concerned with the theological virtues (faith, hope and charity), and the reinterpretation of Christianity after eudaimonism, Kantianism, Idealism, and Liberal theology.

For Kierkegaard, the final end is not eudaimonia, but he thinks of the highest good in broadly Kantian terms, comprising virtue, happiness, and the kingdom of God.[55] Obstacles to perfection are mainly original sin and the corruption of the Christian church (although liberal theology, secularization, democracy, and the modern press are also viewed as hindrances). Kierkegaard believes that the church should teach, preach, and minister in this world, even though the realization of the kingdom of God belongs to the afterlife, when humanity will broadly be redeemed. He is wary of all historical collectives and emphasizes the inner transformation of the person, not the outer reformation of society: "Christianity does not want to make changes in externals; neither does it want to abolish drives or inclination – it wants only to make infinity's change in the inner being."[56]

Kierkegaard warns against the "disastrous confusion of politics and Christianity," but he is still concerned with what he regards as the rightful place of politics and Christianity, understood as external reforms and religious inwardness, respectively.[57] He strongly denies that the divine and transcendent can be identified with a worldly order without being corrupted.[58] For this reason, Kierkegaard is opposed to privileging religious citizens, and against the very idea of Christian states and state churches. He also repeatedly criticized contemporaries – Hegelians and Grundtvigians – for confusing Christianity with politics, culture, civilization, patriotism, nationalism, and national identity.[59]

---

55 Fremstedal and Jackson (2015); Fremstedal (2014), ch. 4-6.
56 *SKS* 9, 141 / *WL*, 139. Still, Kierkegaard's attack on the Danish state church (1854-55) arguably involves an increasing dissatisfaction with this strict inner versus outer divide. The kingdom of God has not yet come, and no temporal institution is redemptive as such, but the visible church, like the singular individual, must be responsible to and for the salvific truth of the Gospel here and now (Fremstedal and Jackson (2015)).
57 *SKS* 14, 112 / *COR*, 53. Kierkegaard is concerned with politics in a wide sense that includes formation of identity, common life, social morality, establishment, political communication, populism, patriotism, nationalism and national destiny. He is concerned with ideology, assumptions and actions that affect public welfare and the understanding of social life. See Backhouse (2015).
58 Evans (2006), 7, 329.
59 See Backhouse (2015). Kierkegaard supports Danish absolutism, while criticizing the 1848 revolution, communism, populism, and the Danish state church. Kirmmse argues that Kierkegaard went from being a conservative aristocrat to an egalitarian liberal, whereas

Nevertheless, Kierkegaard's contribution to political theory seems negative rather than positive. Indeed, it is not even clear if he rules out a normative political theory or not, although he has a basic social ontology that emphasizes the social formation of individuality and how the self takes responsibility for a traditional (conventional) identity that it transcends.[60] Even though his social ontology is conceived of in normative, ethico-religious terms, politics still has a somewhat unclear normative role in his theory. Partly as a result of this, and partly as a result of his support of absolutism, Kierkegaard seems more relevant as an existential, ethical, and religious thinker than as a political thinker.[61]

Bibliography

Adams, R.M., "Human Autonomy and Theological Ethics", in: *European Journal for Philosophy of Religion*, 8 (3), 2016, pp. 3-20.

Annas, Julia, *The Morality of Happiness*, Oxford: Oxford University Press, 1993.

Backhouse, Stephen, "Politics, Society, and Theology in Golden Age Denmark: Key Themes and Figures", in: *A Companion to Kierkegaard*, ed. by Jon Stewart, Oxford: Wiley-Blackwell, 2015, pp. 385-412.

Clark, Justin, "Eudaimonistic Virtue Ethics and Self-Effacement", in: *The Journal of Value Inquiry*, 50, 2016, pp. 507-524.

Cohen, A.J., "Existentialist Voluntarism as a Source of Normativity", in: *Philosophical Papers*, 37, 2008, pp. 89-129.

Conway, Daniel, "Reflections on Late Modernity: Kierkegaard in the 'Present Age'", in: *A Companion to Kierkegaard*, ed. by Jon Stewart, Oxford: Wiley-Blackwell, 2015, pp. 399-412.

Davenport, J.J., *Narrative Identity, Autonomy, and Mortality: From Frankfurt and MacIntyre to Kierkegaard*, London: Routledge, 2012.

– *Will as Commitment and Resolve: An Existential Account of Creativity, Love, Virtue, and Happiness*, New York: Fordham University Press, 2007.

Evans, C.S., *Kierkegaard's Ethics of Love: Divine Commands and Moral Obligations*, Oxford: Oxford University Press, 2006.

– *God and Moral Obligation*, Oxford: Oxford University Press, 2014.

Hannay thinks that Kierkegaard should side with the social democrats against the conservatives. See Hannay (1991), 297; Kirmmse (1990), 4, 264.

60 See Tilley (2015). Tilley emphasizes Kierkegaard's claim that social unity lies behind us, not ahead of us. Nevertheless, Kierkegaard still seems to believe in the communion of the saints in the afterlife and the invisible church in this life (Fremstedal (2014), ch. 5).

61 Thanks to Attila Tanyi and the Ethics Research Group, at University of Tromsø – The Arctic University of Norway, for comments on earlier versions of this article.

Fremstedal, Roe, *Kierkegaard and Kant on Radical Evil and the Highest Good: Virtue, Happiness, and the Kingdom of God*, Basingstoke: Palgrave Macmillan, 2014.

– "Kierkegaard's Use of German Philosophy: Leibniz to Fichte", in: *A Companion to Kierkegaard*, ed. by Jon Stewart, Oxford: Wiley-Blackwell, 2015a, pp. 36-49.

– "Kierkegaard's Views on Normative Ethics, Moral Agency, and Metaethics", in: *A Companion to Kierkegaard*, ed. by Jon Stewart, Oxford: Wiley-Blackwell, 2015b, pp. 113-125.

– "Morality and Prudence: A Case for Substantial Overlap and Limited Conflict", in: *The Journal of Value Inquiry*, 52, 2018, pp. 1-16.

Fremstedal, Roe and T.P. Jackson, "Salvation/Eternal Happiness", in: *Kierkegaard's Concepts: Salvation to Writing*, ed. by Steven Emmanuel, William McDonald and Jon Stewart, Farnham: Ashgate, 2015, pp. 1-8.

Green, R.M., *Kierkegaard and Kant: The Hidden Debt*, Albany: State University of New York Press, 1992.

Hannay, Alastair, *Kierkegaard*, London: Routledge, 1991.

Haybron, Daniel, *The Pursuit of Unhappiness: The Elusive Psychology of Well-Being*, Oxford: Oxford University Press, 2010.

Irwin, Terence, "Kant's Criticism of Eudaemonism", in: *Aristotle, Kant, and the Stoics: Rethinking Happiness and Duty*, ed. by Stephen Engstrom and Jennifer Whiting, Cambridge: Cambridge University Press, 1996, pp. 63-101.

– *The Development of Ethics: A Historical and Critical Study*, 3 vols., Oxford: Oxford University Press, 2011.

Kierkegaard, Søren, *Breve og Aktstykker vedrørende Søren Kierkegaard*, 2 vols., edited by Niels Thulstrup, Copenhagen: Munksgaard, 1953-54. (*B&A*)

– *The Corsair Affair and Articles Related to the Writings*, Princeton: Princeton University Press, 1982. (*COR*)

– *Concluding Unscientific Postscript to Philosophical Fragments*, Princeton: Princeton University Press, 1992, vol. 1. (*CUP1*)

– *Fear and Trembling*, Princeton: Princeton University Press, 1983. (*FT*)

– *Søren Kierkegaard's Journals and Papers*, 7 vols. Bloomington: Indiana University Press, 1967-78. (*JP*)

– *Letters and Documents*, trans. by Henrik Rosenmeier, Princeton: Princeton University Press, 1978. (*LD*)

– *Søren Kierkegaards Papirer*, 2nd. Edition, 16 vols., Copenhagen: Gyldendal, 1968-78. (*Pap.*)

– *Practice in Christianity*, Princeton: Princeton University Press, 1991. (*PC*)

– *Søren Kierkegaards Skrifter*, 55 vols., Copenhagen: Gad, 1997-2013. (*SKS*)

– *Sickness unto Death*, Princeton: Princeton University Press, 1983. (*SUD*)

– *Upbuilding Discourses in Various Spirits*, Princeton: Princeton University Press, 2009. (*UD*)

– *Works of Love*, Princeton: Princeton University Press, 1998. (*WL*)
Kirmmse, Bruce, *Kierkegaard in Golden Age Denmark*, Indianapolis: Indiana University Press, 1990.
Knappe, Ulrich, *Theory and Practice in Kant and Kierkegaard*, Berlin: de Gruyter, 2004.
Mendham, Matthew, "Eudaimonia and Agape in MacIntyre and Kierkegaard's *Works of Love*", in: *Journal of Religious Ethics*, 35, 2007, pp. 591-625.
Parfit, Derek, *On What Matters*, Oxford: Oxford University Press, vol. 1, 2012.
Pinkard, Terry, *German Philosophy 1760-1860: The Legacy of Idealism*, Cambridge: Cambridge University Press, 2010.
Rudd, Anthony, *Self, Value, and Narrative: A Kierkegaardian Approach*, Oxford: Oxford University Press, 2012.
Stern, Robert, *Understanding Moral Obligation: Kant, Hegel, Kierkegaard*, Cambridge: Cambridge University Press, 2012.
Tilley, J.M., "Prolegomena for Thinking of Kierkegaard as a Social and Political Philosopher", in: *A Companion to Kierkegaard*, ed. by Jon Stewart, Oxford: Wiley-Blackwell, 2015, pp. 480-488.
Webb, Carson, "Kierkegaard's Critique of Eudaimonism: A Reassessment", *Journal of Religious Ethics*, 45, 2017, pp. 437-462.

Antipaternalismus und Perfektionismus in Mills Axiologie der Selbstentwicklung

Simon Derpmann

1. Zwang zur Freiheit?

Zu den an den liberalen Rechtsstaat gerichteten Rechtfertigungsanforderungen gehört die Bestimmung der Freiheitssphäre seiner Bürgerinnen und der damit korrespondierenden Pflichten, diese Sphäre zu respektieren und zu schützen. Darüber hinaus schuldet er Rechenschaft über die zulässigen Mittel der Beförderung derjenigen Bedingungen, Kompetenzen, Einstellungen und Unabhängigkeiten, ohne die Freiheit nicht zu realisieren ist. Denn die Abwesenheit physischen oder legalen Zwangs ist keine hinreichende Bedingung für das Vorliegen individueller Freiheit. Während die neuzeitliche politische Theoriebildung sich zunächst primär mit den Grenzen staatlicher Gewalt im Sinne der Abwehr von Eingriffen in die individuelle Selbstbestimmung befasst, zeigt sich in modernen grundsätzlich freiheitlich verfassten Gesellschaften eine Spannung zwischen der Unverhandelbarkeit basaler Abwehrrechte gegen Eingriffe in die Freiheit einerseits und einem auf die Freiheit ausgerichteten Paternalismus andererseits.[1] Theorien der relationalen Autonomie berücksichtigen die besondere Bedeutung von Formen internalisierter Unterdrückung, die keinen unmittelbaren Zwang darstellen, aber das Ausüben von Autonomie verunmöglichen und damit womöglich Eingriffe in die Freiheit der Einzelnen unter Rekurs auf ebenjene Freiheit zulässig oder gar erforderlich machen. Ein solcher Paternalismus der Autonomie, der zunächst nur für solche Eingriffe in den Freiheitsraum des oder der Einzelnen eine Rechtfertigung anbietet, die seine oder ihre Freiheitsausübung sichern,

---

1 Als ‚paternalistisch' sollen im Weiteren diejenigen Versuche der Einflussnahme auf den Einzelnen gelten, die allein um seines eigenen Wohls willen – aber gegen seinen oder gleichgültig gegenüber seinem Willen – durch Machtausübung in Form von Zwang, Drohung oder Gewalt auf seine Entscheidungen einwirken. Siehe hierzu die debattenprägende Diskussion in Dworkin (1972). Mir geht es dabei nicht um jede Form des Paternalismus, sondern besonders um Versuche der paternalistischen Sicherstellung von Selbstbestimmung.

ist mit der paradoxen Konstellation der Unmöglichkeit der wirksamen freiwilligen Aufgabe der eigenen Freiheitsausübung konfrontiert.²

Ich möchte im folgenden Beitrag darlegen, inwiefern John Stuart Mills Freiheitskonzeption, die auf den ersten Blick als strikt antipaternalistisch einzustufen ist, gleichzeitig eindeutig perfektionistische, und womöglich paternalistische, Züge trägt. Als *Handlungsnorm* formuliert Mills Freiheitsprinzip einen – wenngleich begrenzten – deontologischen Vorrang eines absoluten Freiheitsrechts vor der Förderung material bestimmter Zwecke wie Glück, Wohlergehen oder Kultiviertheit. Die *Begründung* dieser Norm erfolgt jedoch nicht innerhalb eines deontologischen moralphilosophischen Rahmens. Der Vorrang der Freiheit ist in Mills Konzeption nur indirekt, und damit womöglich auch nur instabil, über den Wert der Selbstentwicklung begründet.³ Mills Freiheitstheorie ist daher nur zu erschließen, wenn die *Beschaffenheit der indirekten Rechtfertigung* absoluter Freiheitsrechte zum Gegenstand gemacht wird. Nach einigen Vorbemerkungen zum Skopus der Millschen Freiheitstheorie hinsichtlich der untersuchten *Quellen* und *Formen* äußeren Zwangs (2) stelle ich kurz Mills Freiheitsprinzip und dessen moralphilosophische Fundierung (3) dar. Die Vermittlung der Begründung des deontischen Schadensprinzips über die axiologische Bedeutung der Selbstentwicklung erzeugt dort Konflikte, wo das Eingreifen in den Freiheitsraum der Einzelnen erforderlich ist, um das Fundament ihrer Selbstentwicklung herzustellen (4). Ein Anwendungsfall, der die Tragweite der Wahl der Begründungsstrategie des Schadensprinzips verdeutlicht, zeigt sich in Mills und Harriet Taylors gemeinsamer Positionierung zu den gebotenen Antworten auf die gesellschaftliche Unterdrückung der Frau im Viktorianischen England, insofern hier neben anderen gesellschaftlichen Missständen eine persönliche Unfreiheit manifest wird, in die sich zumindest manche Frauen – wenn auch mit unterschiedlichen vorstellbaren Gründen oder Ursachen – selbst fügen (5). Mill muss womöglich aufgrund der spezifischen Begründung des Freiheitsprinzips in diesem Fall paternalistische Eingriffe zur Sicherstellung der Bedingungen

---

2 Siehe etwa die Debatte um das paternalistisch motivierte Verbot der Vollverschleierung unter Rekurs auf den Schutz der Freiheit der sich verschleiernden Person, beispielsweise in Fateh-Moghadam (2014).

3 Sandel (1982), 179 etwa markiert diesen Unterschied anhand voneinander unabhängiger Begriffe von *Deontologie*, die sich einerseits auf der Ebene des Gehalts moralischer Normen und andererseits auf der Ebene der Begründungsmuster zeigen kann. Zur umstrittenen Frage, ob konsequentialistische Moralkonzeptionen in der Lage sind, absolute Rechte zu begründen, siehe beispielsweise Pettit (1997); oder mit Blick auf Mills konsequentialistische Rekonstruktion von moralischen Rechten Lyons (1994) oder Brink (2007). Zur Kritik der konsequentialistischen Fundierung des Freiheitsprinzips siehe Gutmann (2014).

der Selbstentwicklung erlauben, insofern nicht das Recht der Freiheit, sondern der Wert der Selbstentwicklung die entscheidende moralische Begründungsressource des Freiheitsprinzips ist.

2. Vorbemerkungen zu Mills Freiheitsbegriff

Mills *On Liberty* formuliert eine wirkmächtige Bestimmung der Natur und der Grenzen der Gewalt, die Staat und Gesellschaft rechtmäßig über die Einzelne ausüben dürfen.[4] Sein Freiheitsprinzip, das die Abwendung des Schadens von Dritten als unerlässliche Bedingung rechtmäßiger Eingriffe in die individuelle Freiheit ausweist, hat als Essenz der Millschen Freiheitstheorie eine breite Rezeption erfahren, die zunächst seinen strikten Antipaternalismus aufgreift und in dessen Bestimmung vordringlich den Begriff des Schadens thematisiert, anhand dessen sich erst der Umfang der Unterlassungspflichten von Staat und Gesellschaft bestimmen lassen.

Der persönliche Freiheitsraum, der dem äußeren Einwirken auf das Individuum eine strikte Grenze setzt, wird oftmals über die Grenzen *staatlicher Gewalt* bestimmt. Freiheit, so die verkürzte Auffassung, die Mill ergänzen will, beschränkt sich auf die wirksame Abwehr staatlicher Eingriffe in die individuelle Lebensgestaltung. Mill entscheidet sich in seiner Untersuchung explizit für einen von diesem Zugriff verschiedenen Ansatzpunkt, mit dem er insgesamt eine andere Perspektive auf den Gegenstand der politischen Philosophie einnimmt. Sein Perspektivwechsel zeigt sich darin, dass Mill sowohl andere *Quellen* als auch andere *Formen* der Beschränkung der Freiheit der Einzelnen behandelt als etwa durch die Machtausübung tyrannischer Herrschaft.

Erstens macht Mill in der Bestimmung bürgerlicher und sozialer Freiheit nicht nur die Grenzen *despotischer* Gewalt über den Einzelnen, sondern die Grenzen *politischer* Macht insgesamt zum Gegenstand. Zur Veranschaulichung dieses Unterschieds legt er zu Beginn der Abhandlung verschiedene Stadien der Absicherung individueller Freiheit dar, die zunächst in der Zurückdrängung despotischer Herrschaft – etwa durch die Grundlegung bürgerlicher Rechte oder durch die Kontrolle politischer Herrschaft durch Verfassungen

---

[4] Siehe *CW* 18, 217. Verweise auf Mills Werke beziehen sich auf die kritische Gesamtausgabe, hg. von John Robson. Verwendet werden: *De Tocqueville on Democracy in America [I]* (1835): *CW* 18, 47-90; *De Tocqueville on Democracy in America [II]* (1840): *CW* 18, 153-204; *On Liberty* (1859): *CW* 18, 213-310; *Utilitarianism* (1861/1863): *CW* 10, 203-259; *Considerations on Representative Government* (1861): *CW* 19, 371-577; *The Subjection of Women* (1869): *CW* 18, 259-340; *Autobiography* (1873): *CW* 1, 1-290.

oder demokratische Entscheidungsprozesse – Niederschlag finden. Mill betont, dass zur Abwendung der Beschränkung individueller Freiheit diese rechtsstaatlichen und demokratischen Fortschritte allerdings nicht hinreichend sind. Die von Alexis de Tocqueville beschriebene *Tyrannei der Mehrheit* begreift auch Mill als eine von demokratischer Herrschaft ausgehende Gefahr.[5] Denn Demokratie im Sinne der Selbstbestimmung eines Staatsvolkes und der Kontrolle seiner Regierung schließt die unrechtmäßige Herrschaft über eine Minderheit durch eine Mehrheit nicht aus. In seinen Überlegungen zu repräsentativen Regierungsformen ergründet Mill daher, welches institutionelle Rahmengefüge sich eignet, um eine solche Tyrannei – also nicht nur die Tyrannei von Despoten, sondern auch von demokratischen Mehrheiten – zu verhindern.[6] An diesem ersten Aspekt von Mills Perspektivwechsel ist entscheidend, dass die Opponenten in dem beschriebenen Gegensatz nicht mehr Staat oder Regierung auf der einen Seite und Bevölkerung oder Bürger auf der anderen sind, sondern dass mit ihm auch *innergesellschaftliche* Unterdrückung im Rahmen demokratischer Selbstbestimmung behandelt wird.

Zweitens gehen Mills Überlegungen der Freiheitsschrift über die klassische Staatsphilosophie hinaus, insofern sie nicht nur die Herrschaft von – despotischen oder gewählten – *politischen Regierungen* betreffen, sondern von *Gesellschaft insgesamt*, die ebenfalls als Tyrann in Erscheinung treten kann. Dieser Unterschied hinsichtlich der Urheber gesellschaftlichen Zwangs überträgt sich auch auf die Mittel seiner Ausübung. So behandelt Mill nicht allein den unmittelbaren äußeren Zwang, den Gerichte, Bürokratie oder Polizei ausüben oder durchsetzen, sondern ebenso den geistigen Zwang öffentlicher Meinung, informeller Sitten und Anstandsnormen, die in die persönliche Lebensführung eingreifen. Damit geraten neben der Einschränkung der Freiheit durch Gesetzgebung, Rechtsprechung und Normdurchsetzung, auch die freiheitsgefährdenden Einflüsse von Abhängigkeit und Konformitätsdruck ins Blickfeld der politischen Philosophie. Mill betont, dass exekutive oder staatliche Gewalt, unabhängig von ihrer jeweiligen politischen Legitimation, nicht die einzige und auch nicht die gravierendste Form der Einschränkung individueller Freiheit ist, die es zu verurteilen und zu bekämpfen gilt:

> Society [...] practises a social tyranny more formidable than many kinds of political oppression, since, though not usually upheld by such extreme penalties, it leaves fewer means of escape, penetrating much more deeply into the details of life.[7]

---

5 Siehe *CW* 18, 49-90; 153-204. Hierzu auch Rosen (2013), 152.
6 Siehe hierzu beispielsweise *CW* 19, 435-466.
7 *CW* 18, 220.

Denn während die meisten Formen öffentlicher Regeln und Normen zwar individuelle Entscheidungen bestimmen und begrenzen, nicht aber zwingend in persönliche Überzeugungen und Wertvorstellungen eingreifen, werden Gewohnheit und öffentliche Meinung von Handlungssubjekten verinnerlicht. Sie setzen nicht nur Rahmenbedingungen für individuelles Handeln in Form von Verboten und Sanktionen, sondern formen die Entscheidungsfindung selbst, indem sie Wertvorstellungen, Ängste, Vorurteile und Tabus einprägen. Daher warnt Mill auch in seinen demokratiekritischen Abhandlungen nicht nur vor politischer Unterdrückung, sondern vor der Tyrannei über den Geist.[8] Diese Form der Einflussnahme auf das Individuum ist in Mills Beschreibung mitunter weit ausgereifter als der Zwang, den öffentliche Autoritäten auszuüben vermögen. Die politische Tyrannei von Despoten oder demokratischen Mehrheiten ist demnach von der sozialen Tyrannei vorherrschender Meinungen und Gewohnheiten zu unterscheiden, und beide Formen der Einflussnahme sind für Mill in einer politischen Theorie der Freiheit zu berücksichtigen. Der von Mill verfolgte Freiheitsbegriff umfasst in diesem Sinne sowohl politische als auch soziale Freiheit und die Grenzen, die sie der Gesellschaft setzt. Diese Grenzen der gesellschaftlichen Gewalt zu bestimmen und wirksam zu ziehen, ist in seiner Einschätzung ebenso unverzichtbar wie die Grenzen staatlicher Gewalt zu formulieren, die meist zuerst die Aufmerksamkeit der politischen Philosophie einnehmen. Mills Einschätzung der Durchschlagskraft gesellschaftlicher Zwänge erzeugt eine aufschlussreiche Spannung für diejenigen Eingriffe in die Freiheit des Einzelnen, die der Vorbeugung seiner Selbstunterwerfung angesichts sozialer Zwänge dienen.

3. Das Freiheitsprinzip

Vor dem Hintergrund dieses ausgedehnten Begriffs politischer und gesellschaftlicher Einflussnahme legt Mill (CW 18, 223) eine basale Norm zum Schutz persönlicher Freiheiten vor:

> [...] the sole end for which mankind are warranted, individually or collectively, in interfering with the liberty of action of any of their number, is self-protection [...] the only purpose for which power can be rightfully exercised over any

---

[8] „The despotism, therefore, of the majority within the limits of civil life, though a real evil, does not appear to us to be a formidable one. The tyranny which we fear, and which M. de Tocqueville principally dreads, is of another kind – a tyranny not over the body, but over the mind." (CW 18, 178).

> member of a civilized community, against his will, is to prevent harm to others. His own good, either physical or moral, is not a sufficient warrant.

Mills Freiheitsnorm formuliert ein Prinzip der uneingeschränkten Ablehnung bestimmter Formen von Zwang und Kontrolle. In einem ersten Zugriff besagt diese Norm, dass Handlungen, aus denen kein Schaden für Dritte entsteht, in eine für Staat und Gesellschaft unverfügbare persönliche Freiheitssphäre fallen. Das Freiheitsprinzip formuliert eine strikte Zurückweisung bestimmter Formen der Machtausübung, sowohl durch die Gewalt staatlicher Institutionen als auch durch den Zwang der öffentlichen Meinung. Es bestimmt eine notwendige Bedingung für die Zulässigkeit jedes staatlichen oder gesellschaftlichen Eingreifens in die persönliche Freiheit und damit im Umkehrschluss eine hinreichende Bedingung seiner Unzulässigkeit. Zulässig ist ein solches Eingreifen *nur dann*, wenn es den Zweck verfolgt, Schaden von Anderen abzuwenden, und somit dem Selbstschutz der Gesellschaft – bzw. einzelner Mitglieder – dient, weshalb das Freiheitsprinzip mitunter auch als Schadensprinzip bezeichnet wird. Umgekehrt ist das Eingreifen in die individuelle Freiheit *immer dann* unzulässig, wenn diese Bedingung der Schadensabwendung nicht erfüllt ist.

Dieses Verbot der Ausübung von Zwang greift dann, wenn das zur Disposition stehende Handeln einer Person – oder ihre Geisteshaltung oder ihre Lebensführung – nur die Handelnde selbst betrifft. Allein zur Schadensabwehr ist ein Eingriff in ihre individuelle Freiheit legitim; und er ist auch dann nur unter zusätzlichen Bedingungen legitim, weil die Schadensbedingung zwar notwendig, aber nicht hinreichend für die Zulässigkeit eines Freiheitseingriffes ist.[9] Mill formuliert dementsprechend vorsichtig, dass unter diesen Umständen lediglich etwas für einen solchen Eingriff spricht, denn es sind weitere Erwägungen erforderlich – etwa der Verhältnismäßigkeit, der Wirksamkeit des Eingriffs oder der Beurteilung der Relevanz damit einhergehender Formen des Schadens. Diese Unterscheidung des verbotenen und gebotenen Eingreifens in die individuelle Freiheit zeigt sich darin, dass Mill (CW 18, 292) an einer anderen Stelle nicht von einem Prinzip spricht, sondern von zwei Maximen, die bestimmte Eingriffe als unzulässig und andere als gerechtfertigt begreifen:

> The maxims are, first, that the individual is not accountable to society for his actions, in so far as these concern the interests of no person but himself. [...] Secondly, that for such actions as are prejudicial to the interests of others, the individual is accountable, and may be subjected either to social or to legal

---

[9] Siehe hierzu beispielsweise Brink (2013), 177-187.

punishment, if society is of opinion that the one or the other is requisite for its protection.

Da nahezu alle Handlungen Dritte in irgendeiner Art betreffen, lässt sich kaum eine Klasse von Handlungen als bloß selbstbezüglich und deshalb uneingeschränkt zu schützen bestimmen. Allerdings sind umgekehrt bestimmte Arten von Ansprüchen der Nichtschädigung als unzulässig auszuweisen. Mill unterscheidet daher zwischen Handlungen, die Andere *nicht betreffen*, und solchen, die *ihre Interessen nicht berühren*.[10] Nicht jede Form von Beeinträchtigung kann als Schaden im Sinne der rechtfertigenden Grundlage eines Freiheitseingriffs gelten, da für die Legitimation von Zwang ein besonderer Schaden – etwa in Form der Verletzung eines *begründeten* Anspruchs – vorliegen muss.[11] In diesem Zusammenhang legt Mill dar, dass jeder die Existenz abweichender Lebensstile, sexueller Orientierungen oder religiöser Einstellungen aushalten muss, selbst wenn er sie als übergriffig begreift, weil er sie abstoßend oder empörend findet. Nicht jede *Leid*erfahrung ist also prinzipiell geeignet, um einen Freiheitseingriff zu rechtfertigen. Diejenigen Formen von *Schaden*, die zur Begründung der Einschränkung von Freiheit vorgebracht werden können, umfassen zwar nicht nur körperliche, sondern auch geistige oder seelische Verletzungen, etwa in Form von Demütigung oder Kränkung, aber nicht jede Form der Empörung, des Ekels, oder der Aversion. In diesen Fällen muss Mill nicht bestreiten, dass der Verstoß gegen religiöse Vorschriften, ein gleichgeschlechtlicher Kuss oder das Aufbrechen traditioneller Rollenmuster für manche Personen empörend, verstörend oder verletzend sein kann, insofern sie dadurch ihre Moralvorstellungen oder ihren Lebensentwurf in Frage gestellt sehen. Dennoch sind diese Formen der Beeinträchtigung nicht geeignet um Freiheitseingriffe unter Rekurs auf die Abwehr solchen Schadens zu begründen, weil sie nicht mit dem gleichen Recht wie der Freiheitsanspruch auftreten können.[12] Die Verantwortung für diese Formen der Empörung ist demnach nicht der beurteilten Person, sondern vor allem der urteilenden Person zuzuschreiben.

Mill will demnach vor allem zwei Begründungen für den Eingriff in die Angelegenheiten einer Person als unzureichend zurückweisen. Die Berufung auf einen Paternalismus, mit dem ein Eingriff allein unter Verweis auf das Wohl der Bevormundeten gerechtfertigt wird, und die Berufung auf Moralismus, mit

---

10 Siehe hierzu insbesondere Rees (1960).
11 Siehe hierzu beispielsweise Riley (1998), 91 ff. oder Brink (2013), 135-141.
12 Siehe hierzu etwa Skorupski (1989), 367-368 oder Riley (1998), 98.

dem ein Eingriff unter Verweis auf Anstandsnormen und die bloße Empörung über eine bestimmte Lebensweise gerechtfertigt wird.[13]

Neben diesen Auslegungsfragen muss Mills Freiheitsprinzip im Kontext seiner moralphilosophischen Fundierung geprüft werden. Denn angesichts der Begründung, die Mill für das Freiheitsprinzip vorbringt, ist sein vermeintlich strikter Antipaternalismus in Zweifel zu ziehen, oder zumindest unzureichend begründet. Wie sich zeigt, bietet die Formulierung des Freiheitsprinzips Anlass zu einer Reihe von Rückfragen, die weitere Bestimmungen erforderlich machen. So ist zu klären, wie Mill den Schutz persönlicher Freiheit in Form einer *kategorischen* Zurückweisung bestimmter Formen staatlicher oder gesellschaftlicher Eingriffe begründen kann. Das Schadensprinzip formuliert zwar hinsichtlich des Gehalts der Verpflichtung deontische Verbote im Sinne Nozickscher *side constraints*[14], dies aber nicht auf der Grundlage eines deontologischen Verständnisses moralischer Freiheitsrechte, sondern auf der Grundlage einer axiologischen These zu Bedeutung persönlicher Selbstentfaltung, für die ein negativer Freiheitsraum faktisch zuträglich ist. Es ist somit nicht die Freiheit, sondern die Selbstentfaltung, die für Mill die normative Arbeit leistet.

4. Die axiologische Fundierung des Freiheitsprinzips

Eine zum Verständnis der Millschen Freiheitskonzeption unbedingt notwendige Klärung bezieht sich auf die Quelle der *Rechtfertigung* des Millschen Freiheitsprinzips. Denn hier zeigt sich der perfektionistische Zug der Millschen Freiheitskonzeption. Mill muss erläutern, wie die im Freiheitsprinzip formulierte Norm als kategorisches Verbot zu begründen ist. Er bringt hier eine Reihe von Argumenten vor. Erstens ist jede Person qua Subjekt ihres Wohlergehens die alleinige und angemessene Hüterin ihres jeweils eigenen Wohls. Dieses Argument verweist auf einen epistemischen Mangel seitens der in die persönliche Freiheit eingreifenden Gesellschaft, die sich mit nicht geringer Wahrscheinlichkeit über die Bedingungen des gelingenden Lebens

---

13 Die beiden Motive der Freiheitsbeschränkung, Paternalismus und Moralismus, unterscheidet etwa Gray (1996), 90-102. Zu einer alternativen Unterscheidung der ausgeschlossenen Freiheitseingriffe siehe Brink (2013), 137-139.

14 Siehe etwa Nozick (1974), 33, in dessen Terminologie *side constraints* sich durch die Absolutheit des Geltungsanspruchs, bzw. ihre Unabwägbarkeit gegen andere Güter auszeichnen. Mill (*CW* 18, 224) bringt dies über das Postulat einer absoluten rechtsförmigen Souveränität der Person über die allein sie betreffenden Angelegenheiten: „In the part which merely concerns himself, his independence is, of right, absolute. Over himself, over his own body and mind, the individual is sovereign."

des Einzelnen irrt, wenn sie versucht diese gegen seinen Willen hervorzubringen. Demnach ist es bereits aufgrund der Urteilsposition des Einzelnen wahrscheinlich, dass er die für ihn besseren Entscheidungen hinsichtlich seines eigenen Wohls – beispielsweise der für ihn geeigneten Glaubensvorstellungen oder Sexualmoral – trifft als wenn die Gesellschaft dies für ihn tut, denn er kennt seine Bedürfnisse und Wünsche besser als die Gesellschaft. Wohlgemerkt bezieht sich dieses Argument auf eine Wahrscheinlichkeit. Der individuelle Irrtum über die eigenen Wünsche und Lebensvorstellungen ist nicht *begrifflich* ausgeschlossen. Daher ist es zumindest denkbar, dass Außenstehende ein zutreffendes Urteil darüber treffen, was für eine Person das Beste ist, mit dem sie dem Urteil der betroffenen Person berechtigterweise widersprechen. Mills Argument kann auf dieser Grundlage daher zunächst kein kategorisches Verbot, sondern nur einen Vorbehalt begründen.

Gemäß dem zweiten Argument profitiert die Gesellschaft insgesamt von der Sicherung der Freiheit des Einzelnen, denn sie zieht mehr Vorteile aus der Gewährung individueller Selbstbestimmung als sie durch Fehlentscheidungen oder die Empörung Dritter verliert. Selbstbestimmung kommt dieser Argumentation zufolge ein instrumenteller Wert zu, insofern von der Vielfalt der auf diese Weise möglichen oder wahrscheinlichen Lebensweisen ein für den gesellschaftlichen Fortschritt förderlicher Erkenntnisgewinn zu erwarten ist.

Das für Mills Gesamtposition zentrale Argument rekurriert auf den besonderen Wert der individuellen Selbstentwicklung, d.h. die individuelle Freiheitssphäre wird *indirekt* als moralisch bedeutsam ausgewiesen. Die *Souveränität* innerhalb der persönlichen Handlungssphäre, die durch das Freiheitsprinzip geschützt wird, ist in dieser Grundlegung deshalb so wertvoll, weil sie Bedingung der *Individualität* ist. Mill verteidigt also das Prinzip der negativen Freiheit von äußerem Zwang über den Verweis auf den positiven Wert von Selbstentwicklung und Individualität.[15]

Mill selbst scheint in der hier vorgenommenen Bestimmung von Individualität als Element menschlichen Wohls daher das *eigentliche Thema* der gesamten Abhandlung zu sehen.[16] Im Eingangszitat der Untersuchung verweist Mill auf

---

15 Die Unterscheidung von positiver und negativer Freiheit findet sich programmatisch bei Berlin (1969), 121-122. Zur Unterscheidung des negativen Begriffs der Freiheit von Eingriffen und dem positiven Begriff der Freiheit der Selbstentwicklung siehe Skorupski (1989), 342-343.

16 In seiner Autobiographie nennt Mill (*CW* 1, 259) *On Liberty* ein philosophisches Lehrbuch „of a single truth [...]: the importance, to man and society, of a large variety in types of character, and of giving full freedom to human nature to expand itself in innumerable and conflicting directions."

Wilhelm von Humboldt, dass „[t]he grand, leading principle, towards which every argument unfolded in these pages directly converges, is the absolute and essential importance of human development in its richest diversity."[17] Auch an anderer Stelle seiner Abhandlung zu den *Grenzen der Wirksamkeit des Staats* wird genau diese zentrale Bedeutung der Selbstentwicklung unterstrichen:

> Der wahre Zweck des Menschen [...] ist die höchste und proportionierlichste Bildung seiner Kräfte zu einem Ganzen. Zu dieser Bildung ist Freiheit die erste und unerläßliche Bedingung. [...] Gerade die aus der Vereinigung Mehrerer entstehende Mannigfaltigkeit ist das höchste Gut, welches die Gesellschaft gibt, und diese Mannigfaltigkeit geht gewiß immer in dem Grade der Einmischung des Staates verloren.[18]

Entscheidend an diesen Passagen ist die instrumentelle Bedeutung der individuellen Freiheitssphäre für einen von ihr unterschiedenen moralischen Wert, sei es Individualität, Selbstentwicklung, oder die Ausbildung der menschlichen Kräfte. Genau wie v. Humboldt begreift Mill gesellschaftliche Freiheit als Bedingung von menschlicher Entwicklung und persönlicher Individualität. Im Anschluss an diese Bestimmung stellt sich die Frage, worin der Wert der Selbstentwicklung besteht, über deren Bedeutung der abgeleitete moralische Status der individuellen Freiheitssphäre begründet ist.

So, wie eine Gesellschaft das Äußern verschiedener Meinungen zulassen – wenn nicht gar fördern – sollte, sollte sie auch offen gegenüber verschiedenen Experimenten der Lebensführung sein. Die Vielfalt dieser Experimente, die durch die Freiheitssphäre geschützt wird, ist jedoch nicht nur aufgrund ihrer gesamtgesellschaftlichen Bedeutung erstrebenswert. Selbstentwicklung und Individualität werden von Mill nicht bloß als *Mittel* zur Beförderung des menschlichen Wohls angesehen, sondern als seine *Bestandteile*.[19] In seiner Darstellung der Fehleinschätzung von Freiheit durch die Gesellschaft, die sie teils indifferent und teils nicht als eigenständig wertvoll begreift, legt Mill offen, welche Bedeutung er selbst der Freiheit, – nun nicht im Sinne der rechtlichen

---

17   *CW* 18, 215. Im Gegensatz zur englischen Übersetzung von Joseph Coulthard ist bei v. Humboldt allerdings nicht von einem zentralen Grundsatz die Rede. Dort schreibt v. Humboldt weniger eindringlich: „Nach dem ganzen vorigen Räsonnement kommt schlechterdings alles auf die Ausbildung des Menschen in der höchsten Mannigfaltigkeit an." Siehe v. Humboldt (1851), Kap 10.

18   v. Humboldt (1851), Kap. 3.

19   So bedauert Mill etwa, dass auch wenn weitestgehend der instrumentelle Wert von Individualität anerkannt ist, dennoch nicht berücksichtigt wird, dass „the free development of individuality is one of the leading essentials of well-being." (*CW* 18, 261).

Freiheitssphäre, sondern verstanden als freie Entwicklung der Individualität und individuelle Spontaneität – in seiner eigenen Konzeption zuschreibt.

Freiheit geht für Mill nicht nur mit gesellschaftlicher Entwicklung einher, sondern ist gleichzeitig Bedingung und Bestandteil von Zivilisation, Bildung, Erziehung und Kultur. Der entscheidende Zug ist, dass Individualität nicht nur instrumenteller Wert zukommt, sondern ein eigenständiger, oder intrinsischer Wert. Mill formuliert dies vermittelt über die Beobachtung des misslichen Umstandes, dass Freiheit für gewöhnlich nicht in dieser Weise begriffen wird: „the evil is, that individual spontaneity is hardly recognised by the common modes of thinking, as having any intrinsic worth, or deserving any regard on its own account."[20] Mill bezieht sich in der Erläuterung des Werts der Individualität abermals auf v. Humboldt, der die Bedeutung von Freiheit über den Zweck des Menschen zur Entwicklung zu einem vollständigen und stimmigen Ganzen begründet. Der Zusammenhang der hierfür relevanten Prinzipien Freiheit, Mannigfaltigkeit, Eigentümlichkeit oder Individualität und Originalität ist bei von Humboldt nicht systematisch dargestellt. Entscheidend ist, dass es Mill in seiner Bezugnahme auf Humboldt auf eine besondere Bedeutung der freien Entwicklung von Individualität ankommt, die es genauer zu verstehen gilt. In Mills Beschreibung besteht die freie Entwicklung der Individualität darin, dass Personen ihre Charakterzüge, Vorlieben oder Lebensweisen nicht unter dem Zwang gesellschaftlicher Einflüsse ausbilden, sondern in einer jeweils für sie selbst kennzeichnenden Weise. Die Merkmale, die sie ausbilden, sollten zum einen *ihrer persönlichen Natur* und nicht allein den sie umgebenden sozialen Erwartungen oder Gewohnheiten entsprechen. Spontaneität betont darüber hinaus zum anderen einen reflexiven Aspekt, der mit einer Entwicklung in dieser Weise einhergeht. Sie besteht darin, dass Personen *eigene Entscheidungen* über die von ihnen zu verfolgenden Lebenspläne treffen. Dementsprechend spricht Mill auch von der Selbstentfaltung, in der es nicht nur um eine angemessene Entwicklung einer Person, sondern um das Vorantreiben ihrer Entwicklung *durch* diese Person selbst geht.[21]

Diese beiden Bestimmungen sollten nicht so verstanden werden, dass die Einzelne ihre Entwicklung allein aus sich selbst erzeugen sollte und damit jeder gesellschaftliche Einfluss als problematische Fremdbestimmung zu verstehen ist. Dass Entscheidungen der eigenen Lebensgestaltung und Selbstentwicklung von Individuen selbst getroffen werden sollten, erfordert – entgegen

---

20 *CW* 18, 261.
21 Siehe *CW* 18, 265-266 und Skorupski (1989), 348-349. Obwohl es sinnvoll ist, diese beiden Begriffe zu unterscheiden, stellt Mill an späterer Stelle wieder ihren Zusammenhang her („Individuality is the same thing with development').

einem nahe liegenden Einwand – nicht das Ausblenden bereits vorliegender Erfahrungen. In allen Gesellschaften liegen Erfahrungen über die Attraktivität verschiedener Konzeptionen des gelingenden Lebens in Form von Sitten und Gebräuchen vor, an denen sich Personen orientieren können, wenn sie gemeinhin bekannte Sackgassen und Irrtümer vermeiden wollen. Gewohnheit und Sitte dürfen ihnen demnach als Anhaltspunkt ihrer eigenen Entscheidungen dienen. Um ihre Individualität zu wahren, müssen Personen in der Verfolgung des für sie Guten auf soziale oder historische Erfahrung demnach nicht verzichten. Sie sollten Mill zufolge aus drei Gründen gleichwohl eine eigene kritische Perspektive auf diese Erfahrungsbestände einnehmen.

Erstens ist kein Verlass darauf, dass eine vorherrschende Deutung der menschlichen Erfahrung nicht irrt, etwa weil sie von bestimmten Vorurteilen belastet ist. Womöglich hängen Vorstellungen darüber, welche Lebenspläne eine Person eines bestimmten Geschlechts oder aus einer bestimmten gesellschaftlichen Schicht zu ihrem eigenen Wohl sinnvollerweise verfolgen sollte, von gesellschaftlichen Konstellationen ab, die nichts mit der Attraktivität dieser Vorstellungen, sondern mit partikularen Machtkonstellationen zu tun haben. Wenn Frauen etwa suggeriert wird, dass sie sich nicht für öffentliche Ämter oder Führungspositionen eignen, muss sich dies nicht einer verlässlichen gesellschaftlichen Erfahrung verdanken, sondern ist schlicht durch eine von partikularen Interessen geleitete historisch etablierte Unterdrückung zu erklären.[22]

Zweitens mag eine gesellschaftliche Erfahrung mit einer bestimmten Vorstellung des gelingenden Lebens tatsächlich valide sein, aber nur für bestimmte Charaktere mit bestimmten Merkmalen. Womöglich ergibt die unvoreingenommene Beobachtung individueller Lebensverhältnisse, dass Menschen dazu neigen, ohne soziale Nahbeziehungen zu verkümmern, dass sie Familien gründen oder stabile Partnerschaften eingehen sollten. Diese tendenzielle Aussage beschreibt aber nicht jeden besonderen Einzelfall. Selbst wenn soziale Einbindung in Nahbeziehungen den Bedürfnissen der meisten Menschen entspricht, besagt sie nichts über diejenige, der das Dasein als Einsiedlerin liegt. In diesem Fall ist die gesellschaftliche Erfahrung zwar zutreffend, aber nicht zutreffend *für sie*.

Drittens sollten auch funktionierende gesellschaftliche Lebenspraxen und Gewohnheiten beständig der Prüfung unterzogen werden, um das menschliche Urteilsvermögen zu erhalten. Selbst, wenn eine Gewohnheit durch ihre Angemessenheit in der Verfolgung eines bestimmten Ziels begründet ist, sollte sie nicht *als* Gewohnheit befolgt werden, weil wichtige Vermögen des

---

22   Siehe hierzu *CW* 18, 263ff.

Wahrnehmens, Empfindens und Überlegens wie ein Muskel betätigt werden müssen, um nicht zu verkümmern.[23] Jede Person bedarf dieser Vermögen zur Ausgestaltung und Verfolgung der eigenen Lebenspläne, entwickelt sie aber nur in dem Maße, in dem sie selbst über ihr eigenes Handeln entscheidet. Wer über längere Zeit keine eigenen Entscheidungen treffen kann oder will, verliert allmählich die Fähigkeit, dies selbst zu tun, d.h. sie büßt womöglich mit gravierenden Folgen ihre Urteilskraft ein. Selbst wenn der Charakter einer Person so beschaffen sein sollte, dass die gesellschaftliche Erfahrung und die dadurch vorgegebenen Entscheidungen ihr vollends entsprechen, sollte sie dieser Erfahrung nur nach eigenem Urteil folgen, damit sie in der Situation, in der dies nicht der Fall ist, noch eine davon abweichende Entscheidung zu treffen vermag und nicht auf die Beständigkeit ihrer Umgebung angewiesen ist.

Diese drei von Mill angeführten Begründungen – möglicher Irrtum, Unangemessenheit des nur der Tendenz nach berechtigten gesellschaftlichen Urteils sowie der Erhalt des eigenen Urteilsvermögens – führen keinen Eigenwert der Individualität oder Originalität der Person im Sinne ihrer eigenständigen Entwicklung an, sondern argumentieren über die Bedeutung, die ihr in der Verfolgung eines gelingenden Lebens zukommt. Demnach gibt es eine oder mehrere Vorstellungen des gelingenden Lebens, die zu einer Person passen. Mills Behauptung, dass, „[if] a person possesses any tolerable amount of common sense and experience, his own mode of laying out his existence is the best, not because it is the best in itself, but because it is his own mode"[24] verdeutlicht zunächst, dass die Verschiedenheit persönlicher Anlagen eine Verschiedenheit persönlicher Lebensstile erfordert, oder in v. Humboldts Terminologie eine *Mannigfaltigkeit*, die jedoch kein Merkmal der Entwicklung einer einzelnen Person, sondern einer plural verfassten Gesellschaft ist. Die Selbstbestimmung in der Verfolgung des je eigenen Lebensstils ermöglicht es, aus den vorgelebten Experimenten eine passende Wahl zu treffen. Der Wert der Individualität ergibt sich in dieser Bestimmung allerdings aus dem Beitrag von Freiheit und Mannigfaltigkeit zur Möglichkeit der Findung der besten

---

23 Mill schreibt: „He who lets the world, or his own portion of it, choose his plan of life for him, has no need of any other faculty than the ape-like one of imitation." (*CW* 18, 263) Es ist nicht nur das Resultat der verfolgten Lebenspläne, das Mill als problematisch empfindet, sondern auch der Prozess der Wahl der zu verfolgenden Lebenspläne und die menschlichen Vermögen, die in diesen Prozess eingebracht werden.

24 *CW* 18, 278.

Gestaltung des eigenen Lebens, nicht aber aus einem *eigenständigen Wert* der Individualität selbst.[25]

Wie kommt Mill nun zu einer moralphilosophischen Einordnung von Selbstentwicklung, die zur Grundlegung des Freiheitsprinzips angeführt werden kann? Mill glaubt, die im Freiheitsprinzip formulierten, absolut geltenden gesellschaftlichen Grenzen gesellschaftlicher Einwirkung ohne Rückgriff auf einen Rechtsbegriff begründen zu können, der basaler ist als der Wert von Individualität und Selbstentwicklung. Die umfassende Beschreibung der menschlichen Natur als fortschreitend oder sich entwickelnd ist der erste Schritt in der axiologischen Untermauerung der Bedeutung persönlicher Freiheit.[26]

> Among the works of man, which human life is rightly employed in perfecting and beautifying, the first in importance surely is man himself. [...] Human nature is not a machine to be built after a model, and set to do exactly the work prescribed for it, but a tree, which requires to grow and develope [sic!] itself on all sides, according to the tendency of the inward forces which make it a living thing.[27]

In dieser Passage will Mill nicht die Beschreibung der Bedeutung des menschlichen Urteilsvermögens fortführen, sondern er trifft ein von den vorausgehenden Argumenten fundamental verschiedenes Werturteil. Er beschreibt nun nicht mehr den instrumentellen Wert dieses Vermögens in der Verfolgung eines gelingenden Lebens, sondern schreibt der Individualität *eigenen* Wert zu. Es geht in der Verfolgung des gelingenden Lebens demnach nicht allein darum, welche Handlungs- und Lebensoption eine Person verwirklicht, sondern *dass* und *in welcher Weise* sie ihre eigenen Entscheidungen trifft. Der Einzelnen mag kein Schaden aus ihrem Unvermögen, eigene Entscheidungen zu treffen, entstehen, so dass die zuvor genannten Nachteile aus kontingenten Umständen

---

25   Die Freiheitsschrift wird oftmals zum Nachweis der Inkonsistenz des Millschen Werks angeführt, weil seine Darlegung der Bedeutung persönlicher Freiheit und Individualität unvereinbar mit dem utilitaristischen Wertsystem begriffen zu sein scheint. Eine umfassende Kritik mit dieser Stoßrichtung findet sich etwa bei Stephen (1967). Zur Darstellung dieser klassischen Kritik siehe Gray (1996) 1-8; und insbes. 160-161. Mill behauptet unmissverständlich, dass „[it] is proper to state that I forego any advantage which could be derived to my argument from the idea of abstract right, as a thing independent of utility. I regard utility as the ultimate appeal on all ethical questions; but it must be utility in the largest sense, grounded on the permanent interests of man as a progressive being." (*CW* 18, 224).

26   Skorupski (1989) nimmt dies als Ausgangspunkt der Verteidigung der Millschen Position: „There is no inconsistency in Mill's position; there is simply a large, substantive claim about human nature and society [...]." (345).

27   *CW* 18, 263.

nicht zum Tragen kommen. Dennoch diagnostiziert Mill in diesem Fall einen Mangel. Eine solche Person verfehlt ihr Potential als menschliches Wesen. An dieser Stelle wird deutlich, was für Mill Selbstentwicklung und Individualität bedeutet. Mills Individualitätskonzeption hat einerseits eine *anthropologische* Dimension, insofern Selbstentwicklung als Wesensmerkmal des Menschen begriffen wird. Diese Bestimmung des Menschen als sich selbst entwickelndes Wesen individuiert ein moralisch bedeutsames Gattungsmerkmal. Es liegt demnach in der Natur des Menschen, seine Potenziale selbst und bewusst zu entwickeln. Darüber hinaus hat Mills Konzeption der Individualität eine *persönliche* Dimension, insofern die konkrete Ausprägung dieser Entwicklung der spezifischen Veranlagung und Entscheidung des Einzelnen entsprechen muss. Individualität betont die Bedeutung der Eigenheit im Sinne der Passung der Entwicklung zum sich entwickelnden Subjekt, Selbstentwicklung die Bedeutung der Eigenregie in diesem Prozess. In dieser Konzeption hat jede Person ein ihr eigentümliches Entwicklungsprinzip, das sie nur dann adäquat verfolgen kann, wenn sie sich selbst gemäß ihrer eigenen – persönlichen, nicht menschlichen – Natur entwickelt. Dies ist – neben der zugestandenen Bezugnahme auf soziale Erfahrung – die zweite Weise, in der Selbst*entwicklung* nicht als bloße Selbst*erzeugung* zu begreifen ist. Selbstbestimmung ist zwar an die Möglichkeit, eigene Entscheidungen zu treffen, gebunden. Diese Entscheidungen können aber Ausdruck einer persönlichen Veranlagung sein, für die sich Personen nicht lediglich entscheiden, sondern die sie zum Teil entdecken und entwickeln müssen.[28]

Mit der Einordnung von Selbstentwicklung als menschlichem Wesenszug ist also ein Pluralismus der Formen der Selbstentwicklung vereinbar, das heißt, welche Tätigkeiten angemessener Ausdruck der eigenen Individualität sind, mag sich von Person zu Person unterscheiden. Mill geht gleichzeitig davon aus, dass Menschen höhere Freuden in Tätigkeiten finden, in denen sich ihre eigenen Entscheidungen und ihre Individualität manifestieren. Er beschreibt ein Ideal von Autarkie, in dem Individualität nicht nur als Abwesenheit von äußeren Einflüssen, sondern als Bestimmung des eigenen Handelns nach einem selbst gewählten Muster ist. Einerseits, weil Mill annimmt, dass der Gebrauch höherer Vermögen selbst wertvoll und anzustreben ist, andererseits, weil die Selbstentwicklung gemäß der eigenen Natur wertvoll ist. In jemandes Individualität zeigt sich ihre persönliche Natur. Der Wert der Betätigung des Vermögens zur Selbstentwicklung ist in ihrer menschlichen Natur begründet.

---

28   Zur Unterscheidung und dem Zusammenhang von Entdeckung und Wahl siehe Gray (1996), 72ff.

Mills Freiheitskonzeption ist also nicht nur mit dem perfektionistischen Ideal menschlicher und persönlicher Entwicklung *vereinbar*, sondern sie *setzt* es in der Begründung der Freiheitsnorm *voraus*. Mill ist Perfektionist, insofern er dafür argumentiert, dass gesellschaftliche Institutionen eine bestimmte Lebensweise befördern sollten, er bleibt aber in zweifacher Hinsicht Liberaler, insofern die zu befördernde Lebensweise nicht material bestimmt ist, sondern sich auf die individuelle Selbstentwicklung beschränkt, der wiederum nur durch die Einziehung persönlicher Freiheitsräume gedient ist.[29] Individuen *sollten* ihr Leben in einer bestimmten Weise gestalten, und zwar so, dass sie es *selbst* formen. Hier findet sich also kein Perfektionismus, der eine evaluative Position hinsichtlich material konkretisierter Güter vertritt, und auf dieser Grundlage durch Zwang oder Anreize in die individuelle Lebensgestaltung eingreifen würde. Es bleibt der Einzelnen überlassen, ob sie ein Leben in Einsamkeit, Naivität, Verwahrlosung oder Selbstzerstörung führt, weil a priori nicht – schon gar nicht mit universaler Geltung – festzustellen ist, ob diese oder jene Lebensführung mit mehr oder weniger Wohl einhergeht. Unabhängig von der konkreten Ausgestaltung individueller Lebensentwürfe ist jedoch auf einer übergeordneten Ebene für Mill zentral, dass das jeweilige Subjekt der Entwicklung selbst bewusst mit diesem Prozess befasst ist.

Im Lichte dieser moralphilosophischen Begründung stellen diejenigen Fälle eine Herausforderung für Mills Freiheitsprinzip dar, in denen sich Individuen in die Beschneidung der Vermögen ihrer eigenen Selbstentwicklung fügen. Die Beschäftigung mit der gesellschaftlichen Stellung der Frau in Mills England etwa legt in diesem Zusammenhang eine Spannung offen, da in dieser patriarchalen oder androzentrischen Gesellschaftsformation sowohl externe Eingriffe in Form von legalem Zwang oder gesellschaftlichem Druck als auch internalisierte soziale Rollenmuster der freien Selbstentfaltung von Frauen in besonderer Weise entgegenstehen.

---

29 Zu den Problemen einer antipaternalistischen Variante eines solchen Autonomieperfektionismus siehe Gutmann (2014), der zwar zugesteht, dass sich über das axiologische Gewicht der Selbstentwicklung ein Argument gegen paternalistische Eingriffe entwickeln lässt, aber keine abwägungsresistente Zurückweisung. Gutmann argumentiert darüber hinaus, dass der durch den Rekurs auf Autonomie vermeintlich eingeschränkte Paternalismus nicht zu begrenzen ist, insofern es aus dieser Perspektive nur folgerichtig scheint, nicht nur gegen ideologische Verblendung vorzugehen, sondern die körperlichen und geistigen Grundlagen der Autonomieausübung insgesamt in den Blick zu nehmen und zu regulieren.

5. Das Problem der (Selbst-) Unterwerfung der Frau

Gemeinsam mit Harriet Taylor formuliert Mill in *The Subjection of Women* eine für ihre Zeit radikale Kritik der ungleichen sozialen Stellung der Frau. Die Zurückweisung der Unterdrückung der Frau könnte zunächst als klarer Anwendungsfall der Überlegungen aus Mills Freiheitsschrift begriffen werden, insofern sich die geschlechtliche Ungleichbehandlung vor allem in einer ungerechtfertigten Beschränkung persönlicher Entfaltungsmöglichkeiten manifestiert: im Ausschluss von politischer Partizipation und Ämtern, in der Verweigerung von Bildung, in Berufsverboten, in eingeschränkten Eigentumsrechten, in der absoluten Ausgeliefertheit in der Ehe und der gleichzeitigen ökonomischen Notwendigkeit der Bindung an einen nahezu zwangsläufig männlichen Versorger. Allerdings ergibt sich eine Besonderheit daraus, dass die vorliegende Form der Beschränkung der Freiheit sich auf einen spezifischen Teil der Gesellschaft beschränkt. Gesellschaftliche Anstandsnormen, Sexualmoral, religiöse Vorschriften oder staatliche Zensur bedeuten meist einen allgemeinen Eingriff in die Freiheit, der – zumindest der Möglichkeit nach – jedes Mitglied einer Gesellschaft betrifft. Die geschlechtsspezifische Einschränkung der Freiheit hingegen ist selektiv. Mills und Taylors Widerstand richtet sich aus diesem Grund nicht allein gegen die gesellschaftliche *Bevormundung* der Frau, sondern darüber hinaus gegen die moralisch bedenkliche *Ungleichbehandlung*, auf der sie fußt. In dieser Zurückweisung der Ungleichheit ist noch kein spezifisch moralphilosophisches Argument vorzubringen, sondern allein eine Rationalitätsanforderung, mit der Gleichheit selbst noch nicht als normatives Ideal ausgewiesen werden muss.[30] Sachverhalte sind aus Vernunftgründen moralisch gleich zu beurteilen, sofern kein moralischer Unterschied zwischen ihnen angeführt werden kann. Die Begründung der Unterdrückung der Frau scheitert daher – insofern sie bloß auf den Geschlechtsunterschied verweisen kann – bereits auf derselben Ebene wie die Begründung von Aristokratie oder Rassismus.

Die geschlechtliche Ungleichbehandlung stellt eine Verletzung eines derart fundamentalen Anspruchs dar, dass es offenbar keiner weiteren Argumente bedarf, um sie zurückzuweisen. So kann Mill über utilitaristische Erwägungen ein sekundäres moralisches Prinzip der Gleichbehandlung begründen. Er legt in *Utilitarianism* dar, dass „All persons are deemed to

---

30   Gleichwohl ist es nicht unplausibel, auch den Utilitarismus als moralische Theorie zu begreifen, die auf der moralischen Bedeutung der Gleichberücksichtigung aufbaut. Siehe hierzu beispielsweise Kymlicka (2002), 32ff.

have a *right* to equality of treatment, except when some recognized social expediency requires the reverse."[31] Die Gleichbehandlung lässt sich wie auch andere moralische Rechtsnormen als grundlegender persönlicher Anspruch utilitaristisch fundieren. Mill und Taylor widersprechen der naheliegenden Antwort, dass es einen mit der Ungleichheit verbundenen sozialen Vorteil gibt. Daher verweisen sie auch auf die Auswirkungen der Ungleichstellung auf sozialen Fortschritt und menschliche Entwicklung. Gemäß diesem Argument beraubt sich die Gesellschaft selbst einer Unmenge von Talenten, Ideen und Tugenden, indem sie es einem Teil der Menschheit verunmöglicht, diese in vollem Umfang zu entwickeln und in die Gesellschaft einzubringen. Nicht allein die von Frauen erlittene Benachteiligung und Bevormundung sprechen demnach gegen die geschlechtliche Ungleichbehandlung, sondern auch die nachteiligen Folgen für die gesamte Gesellschaft. Wer die Zurückweisung der Ungleichbehandlung auf ihre nachteiligen Folgen reduzieren will, mag daher den Vorwurf gegen diese Argumentation erheben, das eigentliche Problem der Ungleichheit zu verfehlen, das sich nicht erst im geringeren Wirtschaftswachstum oder dem verlangsamten wissenschaftlichen oder sozialen Fortschritt zeigt. Dieser zweite von Mill und Taylor genannte Punkt zu den Folgen der Ungleichheit macht jedoch weder den einzigen, noch den primären Einwand gegen die Unterdrückung der Frau aus. Ungleichbehandlung wird als eigenständiges Übel für die von ihr Betroffenen ausgewiesen.

Mill und Taylor setzen sich im Verlauf der Schrift mit einer Reihe von zurückzuweisenden Argumenten und Fehlauffassungen der Befürworter der Ungleichheit auseinander. Neben der Zurückweisung jeglicher Möglichkeit Unterschiede in den Naturen der Geschlechter auszumachen, die nicht gleichermaßen oder besser durch unterschiedliche Sozialisationen erklärt werden könnten, und die darüber hinaus gleichzeitig hinreichen würden, um eine gesellschaftliche Ungleichbehandlung zu rechtfertigen, antworten sie auf die von Gegnern vorgebrachte Unterstellung der freiwilligen Selbstunterwerfung der Frau. Neben den Verteidigern des Unterschiedes zwischen Mann und Frau argumentieren einige Verteidiger der Ungleichbehandlung, dass die gesellschaftliche Position der Frauen von ihnen selbst angenommen und befürwortet wird. Ein vermutetes Übel der Ungleichbehandlung müsste sich aber in einer Opposition von Frauen gegen die Ungleichheit zeigen, die – so der Einwand – sich bei vielen Frauen nicht finden lässt. Anhand dieses Einwands lässt sich eine Doppeldeutigkeit hinsichtlich des philosophischen Gegenstands, den Mill und Taylor vor Augen haben, ausmachen. Denn der

---

31 *CW* 10, 258.

Begriff ‚subjection' im Titel der Abhandlung lässt zwei Deutungen zu, insofern ‚subjection of women' sowohl im *genitivus objectivus* – in dem ‚women' das grammatikalische direkte Objekt sind – als auch im *genitivus subjectivus* – in dem ‚women' das grammatikalische Subjekt sind – zu lesen ist. Es macht offensichtlich einen gewaltigen Unterschied, ob die Frauen als Objekt oder Subjekt der Unterwerfung in dieser Formulierung auftreten, insofern sie im ersten Fall unterworfen werden und sie sich im zweiten Fall selbst unterwerfen. Diese Doppeldeutigkeit sollte nicht aufgelöst werden, denn sie entspricht dem Untersuchungsgegenstand der Abhandlung. Die Untersuchung befasst sich einerseits mit den Formen, in denen gesellschaftliche Strukturen Frauen unterwerfen. Andererseits versteht sich die Untersuchung in dieser Formulierung aber auch als Erklärung, warum Frauen *sich* diesen gesellschaftlichen Strukturen unterwerfen, und natürlich der Frage des gebotenen Umgangs mit dieser Form der Unterwerfung. In der deutschen Übersetzung des Titels ist oftmals von der ‚Hörigkeit der Frau' die Rede, was die Schrift allein im Sinne der zweiten Bedeutung versteht. Mills und Taylors Ausführungen, die gleich zu Beginn auf die rechtliche Ungleichheit als Grundlage gesellschaftlicher Ungleichheit hinweisen, deuten zumindest darauf hin, dass ‚subjection' primär im ersten Sinn zu begreifen ist, obwohl gleichzeitig auch die gesellschaftlich mehr oder minder breite Einwilligung in die männliche Herrschaft im zweiten Sinn von passiver Unterwerfung zum Gegenstand gemacht wird.

Mills und Taylors Antwort in diesem Punkt der vermeintlichen Fügung von Frauen in ihre gesellschaftliche Rolle fällt ähnlich aus wie die Zurückweisung der Annahme natürlicher Unterschiede zwischen den Geschlechtern. Zunächst weisen sie die empirische Behauptung innerhalb des Einwands als faktisch nicht zutreffend zurück. Sie verweisen auf eine Reihe von gesellschaftlichen Bewegungen, in denen zutage tritt, dass eine Vielzahl Frauen keineswegs in die männliche Herrschaft einwilligen, sondern unter dieser Unterdrückung leiden und sich gegen sie wehren. Aber auch für den Teil der Frauen, die sich in die ihnen zugeschriebene Position einfügen, stehen zwei Antworten offen. Erstens kann die Befürwortung der Unterwerfung der Frau in Einzelfällen allenfalls dafür sprechen, es *zuzulassen*, dass Frauen – oder natürlich Männer – sich selbst in eine bestimmte gesellschaftliche untergeordnete Position fügen. Wieder aber spricht nichts dafür, diese Position durch die Gewalt der Durchsetzung eines diskriminierenden Arbeits-, Mitbestimmungs-, Eigentums-, oder Eherechts zu *erzwingen*. Wenn Frauen tatsächlich mit ihrer untergeordneten und freiheitlich eingeschränkten gesellschaftlichen Rolle einverstanden sind, oder diese befürworten, bedarf es auch des Zwangs faktisch nicht.

Dennoch stellt sich die Frage, wie aus freiheitstheoretischer Perspektive mit diesen paradoxen Formen der in einem gewissen Sinne gewählten Unfreiheit umzugehen ist, und ob hier gegebenenfalls ein Zwang zur Selbstbestimmung zulässig wäre. *The Subjection of Women* bietet keine explizite Positionierung zu diesem Problem. Welche Antwort aber ergibt sich aus der bisherigen Einordnung der systematischen Freiheitskonzeption aus *On Liberty*? So verwirft doch diejenige Frau, die sich – nicht nur im Viktorianischen England – in eine mit der freien Selbstentwicklung unvereinbare Position begibt, etwa durch die Annahme einer untergeordneten Rolle in einer Partnerschaft, oder durch die Eingliederung in eine patriarchalische Religionsgemeinschaft, die Möglichkeit der Realisierung eines der für Mill zentralsten moralischen Werte, der gleichzeitig erst die Grundlage ihres Freiheitsschutzes – inklusive der Wahl der Unterordnung – bereitstellt. Mill müsste demnach auf der Grundlage seines philosophischen Urteils über den Wert von Selbstbestimmung und Individualität argumentieren, dass die Befürwortung der eigenen Ungleichbehandlung aus einer für die Selbstentwicklung unzureichenden Position getroffen wird. Demnach begründet der Freiheitsanspruch vermeintlich unterwerfungswilliger Frauen nicht den Respekt vor ihrer Entscheidung zur Unmündigkeit, sondern er spricht im Gegenteil gegen die gesellschaftliche Vorprägung von Lebenswegen. Hier zeigt sich der perfektionistische Zug der liberalen Grundhaltung, mit der Mill eine materiale Position zum gelingenden Leben vertritt, insofern er Selbstentwicklung als im Wesen der menschlichen Natur angelegt sieht, bzw. diese mit einem normativen Begriff des gelingenden Lebens verknüpft. Er positioniert sich zwar gegen das Eingreifen in die persönliche Entscheidungssphäre von Individuen, betont aber gleichzeitig die moralische Bedeutung der für Selbstentwicklung essentiellen gesellschaftlichen Rahmenbedingungen und persönlichen Vermögen.[32]

Die vorausgehende Erörterung der Millschen Begründung des Freiheitsprinzips verdeutlicht, dass Mill keinen strikten Antipaternalismus fundieren kann, weil Eingriffe zur Sicherstellung der Bedingungen der Selbstentwicklung nicht auszuschließen sind. Insofern nicht das Recht der Freiheit, sondern der Wert der Selbstentwicklung die entscheidende moralische Begründungsressource des Freiheitsprinzips ist, muss die Selbstentwicklung in Konfliktfällen trumpfen. Der perfektionistische Zug der Begründung des Freiheitsprinzips hat somit Konsequenzen für die Millsche politische Moral,

---

32 Zur Beschreibung dieser Position als ‚Perfektionismus' siehe beispielsweise Brink (2013), 60-63.

die weitgehend als antipaternalistisch bestimmt werden kann, aber nicht mit Blick auf die Bedingungen der Selbstentwicklung. Dies betrifft allerdings nur derart gelagerte Fälle, in denen gesellschaftliche Unterordnung und damit einhergehende Beschneidung von Freiheiten vermeintlich selbst gewählt sind, aber die Position, aus der heraus dies geschieht, nicht als eine der freien Selbstentwicklung beschrieben werden kann.

Zunächst muss diese Konzeption der Freiheit für gesellschaftliche Rahmenbedingungen plädieren, auf deren Grundlage die Einzelne in die Lage versetzt wird, sich der unterjochenden Wirkung sozialen Drucks oder ökonomischer Abhängigkeit zu entziehen. Dies gelingt nicht primär durch Eingriffe in die Freiheit, sondern durch die Bereitstellung von Alternativen zur Selbstunterwerfung. Die selbstgewählte freiheitsgefährdende Unterordnung erfordert in dieser Abwägung daher womöglich keinen Eingriff in die Freiheitssphäre des Einzelnen, sondern zuerst die Herstellung gesellschaftlicher Rahmenbedingungen, unter denen diese Wahl nicht bereits vorgegeben ist, und die Gewährleistung der Möglichkeit, eine solche Entscheidung zu widerrufen.

Weiterhin müssen diejenigen Formen der selbstgewählten Freiheitseinschränkung, die *Ausdruck* der Selbstentwicklung sind, von denjenigen unterschieden werden, die mit einem basalen Verständnis von Selbstentwicklung unvereinbar sind. Die praktischen Folgen dieses mit Blick auf die Selbstentwicklung durchlässigen Antipaternalismus beschränken sich daher auf spezifische Konstellationen und erlauben keine weitreichenden Eingriffe in die Freiheit der Einzelnen. Denn die einschneidenden Beschränkungen der individuellen Verfolgung der Selbstentwicklung, auch in Fällen der Selbstunterwerfung, gehen von meist äußeren Einflüssen aus. Selbst wenn der Wert der Selbstentwicklung paternalistische Eingriffe rechtfertigt, ist ein Zwang zur Autonomie nur zulässig, nachdem alle Formen äußeren Zwangs durch Recht, Erziehung, Sitte, Familie und öffentliches Ansehen in die Schranken gewiesen sind. Bevor eine Gesellschaft der Einzelnen den Verzicht auf Selbstentwicklung versagt, muss sie diejenigen selbstentwicklungsfeindlichen Einflüsse unterbinden, die aus Erziehung, Bildung und sozialer Abhängigkeit resultieren. Diese Eingriffe sind aber nicht paternalistisch, sondern richten sich auf diejenigen Einwirkungen Dritter, die Selbstentwicklung unterminieren. Wie gegenwärtige Debatten zum Autonomiepaternalismus zeigen, ist in vielen Konstellationen des Mangels an Optionen zur Selbstentwicklung unklar, ob dies der Fremd- oder Selbstunterwerfung zuzuschreiben ist. Dass in Fällen der Unsicherheit ein Primat der Nichteinmischung begründet ist, bedeutet jedoch nicht, dass ein striktes Prinzip des Antipaternalismus der Komplexität von Freiheit und Selbstentwicklung angemessener ist als der durchlässige Antipaternalismus des Millschen Selbstentwicklungsperfektionismus.

Literatur

Anderson, Elizabeth, "John Stuart Mill and Experiments in Living", in: *Ethics*, 102; 1991, S. 4-26.

Berlin, Isaiah, *Four Essays on Liberty*, Oxford: Oxford University Press, 1969.

Brink, David, "Mill's Ambivalence about Rights", in: *Boston University Law Review*, 90, 2007, S. 1669-1704.

Brink, David, *Mills Progressive Principles*, Oxford: Clarendon Press, 2013.

Brudney, Daniel, "Grand Ideals: Mill's Two Perfectionisms", in: *History of Political Thought*, 29, 2008, S. 485-515.

Dworkin, Gerald, "Paternalism", in: *The Monist*, 56, 1972, S. 64-84.

Fateh-Moghadam, Bijan, „Religiöse Neutralität und Geschlechterordnung – Europäische Burka-Verbote zwischen Gender Mainstreaming und Rechtspaternalismus", in: *Als Mann und Frau schuf er sie. Religion und Geschlecht.* hg. v. Barbara Stollberg-Rilinger, Würzburg: Ergon, 2014, S. 181-213.

Gray, John, *Mill on Liberty: A Defence*, London: Routledge, 1996.

Gutmann, Thomas, „Paternalismus und Konsequentialismus", in: *Paternalismus und Konsequentialismus*, hg. v. Michael Kühler und Alexa Nossek, Paderborn: mentis, 2014.

Kymlicka, Will, *Contemporary Political Philosophy: An Introduction*, Oxford: Oxford University Press, 2002.

Lyons, David, "Utility and Rights", *Nomos*, 24, (1982), S. 107-138.

Mill, John Stuart, *Collected Works of John Stuart Mill*, hg. v. John Robson, London/Toronto: Routledge and Kegan Paul/ University of Toronto Press, 1963-1991. (*CW*)

Pettit, Philip, "The Consequentialist Perspective", in: *Three Methods of Ethics*, hg. v. Marcia W. Baron, Philip Pettit, Michael A. Slote, Malden: Blackwell, 1997, 92-174.

Rees, J.C., "A Re-reading of Mill on Liberty", in: *Political Studies*, 8, 1960, S. 113-129.

Riley, Jonathan, *Mill on Liberty*, London: Routledge, 1998.

Rosen, Frederick, *Mill – Founders of Modern Political and Social Thought*, Oxford: Oxford University Press, 2013.

Skorupski, John, *John Stuart Mill*, London: Routledge, 1989.

Stephen, James Fitzjames, *Liberty, Equality, Fraternity*. Cambridge: Cambridge University Press, 1967 [1874].

v. Humboldt, Wilhelm, *Ideen zu einem Versuch, die Grenzen der Wirksamkeit des Staats zu bestimmen*, Breslau: Eduard Trewendt, 1851 [1792].

Becoming Artists of One's Own Life
Perfectionist Thinking in Friedrich Nietzsche

Maria Cristina Fornari

1

That Nietzsche is an excellent historian of morality is beyond question, but can Nietzsche be considered as a *moral* thinker, that is, as a philosopher whose thought can find application in life: can it be lived and practised? Certainly, Nietzsche does not possess a complete moral theory and, coherently with his whole philosophy, he refuses to assign a positive value to any normative ethic; nonetheless, he does not fail to propose lines of conduct that can help individuals to modify their own status, with a view to improving their existence.[1] Let us assume provisionally that Nietzsche not only suggests to us an ethic, but a performative ethic, aiming in some sense at the acquisition of consciousness about one's own form of life and its requisites. In this sense, can we consider him a perfectionist? And in cases where this has been done (as with Cavell or Hurka), on what theoretical and textual elements is this designation based? Are such positions still defensible, or, as Brian Leiter thinks, are they now obsolete, even if they continually re-emerge?

Even though it is he who contributed to giving the term 'perfectionism' a pre-eminent place in political debate, John Rawls' definition of the concept in the 1970's can now be considered reductive. As has been noted, Rawls, in seeking a definition of the good in relation to justice, characterised perfectionism as a moral theory related to utilitarianism, which instead of maximising the useful, or pleasure – as in classical utilitarianism – specifies the good as the "achievement of human excellence in art, science, and culture"[2], and prescribes its maximisation. Rawls has little difficulty in seeing Nietzsche as a representative of this kind of theory, maintaining, however, a major reservation: the Nietzschean prescription to maximise human excellences not only denies the primacy of the principle of justice, but it especially provides

---

1 The term 'improvement' must already be taken with caution, as it might induce one to think of change in a progressive sense. But from a Nietzschean point of view this would be a very problematic assumption. In the 'improvement' process, there inhere a condition of belonging and a system of evaluation, and thus a moral order to which the system of evaluation refers, and in which it is inscribed.
2 Rawls (1971), 325.

that it is permissible to produce some "great human beings" to the detriment of others.

> "Mankind must work continually to produce individual great human beings – this and nothing else is the task [...] For the question is this: how can your life, the individual life, retain the highest value, the deepest significance?"

This is, according to Rawls, the key idea of *Schopenhauer als Erzieher*: "Only by your living for the good of the rarest and most valuable specimens".[3] The idea that the intrinsic value of some human beings is inferior to that of others, and that the many can be sacrificed for the greatness of the few (as Rawls reads the Nietzschean exhortation to work for the production of the great man) lays the basis for social inequality and is naturally unacceptable to any liberal.[4] Nietzsche thus becomes, in Rawls' reading, the principal representative of an extreme form ("a strong version") of elitist perfectionism, and simultaneously the mirror of its distortions.[5]

It scarcely need be noted that the passage used by Rawls as evidence for his interpretation, taken from *Schopenhauer als Erzieher* (1874), is deprived of any contextualisation: he offers a reading which is no longer possible after the historical-philological references by the editors of the international critical edition of Nietzsche's works, Giorgio Colli and Mazzino Montinari.[6]

---

3 "[...], die Menschheit soll fortwährend daran arbeiten, einzelne grosse Menschen zu erzeugen – und dies und nichts Anderes sonst ist ihre Aufgabe' [...] Denn die Frage lautet doch so: wie erhält dein, des Einzelnen Leben den höchsten Werth, die tiefste Bedeutung? Wie ist es am wenigsten verschwendet? Gewiss nur dadurch, dass du zum Vortheile der seltensten und werthvollsten Exemplare lebst, nicht aber zum Vortheile der Meisten, das heisst, der, einzeln genommen, werthlosesten Exemplare." (Nietzsche, *Schopenhauer als Erzieher*, § 6, KSA 1, 383).

4 "A political theory might be non-elitist in its view of the nature of human good and the proper principle for regulating its distribution, but illiberal in its conception of how politics should be arranged so that human good is achieved. A perfectionist doctrine could follow Plato but not Nietzsche. But it is immediately obvious that perfectionism can be yoked to many different moral, metaphysical, and empirical claims, only some combinations of which support illiberal governance. John Stuart Mill, along with Thomas Hill Green and other nineteenth-century British writers, sees a liberal political order as the best vehicle for delivering perfectionist values." (Arneson (2000), 42).

5 An attempt to go beyond the debate between 'aristocratic' and 'democratic' readings of Nietzsche's perfectionism is made by Jeffrey Church (2015).

6 Just as recourse to the compilation *Will to Power* is no longer possible. As is well known, this is not an authentic work by Nietzsche but a more-or-less arbitrary assemblage of posthumous writings, put together, in its first edition of 1901, by Elisabeth Förster-Nietzsche and her collaborators at the Nietzsche-Archiv in Weimar. The position held by some, that a legitimate

The solicitation for the maximisation of excellences in the scope of the *Unzeitgemässe Betrachtungen* (1874-1876) emerges from the political and cultural preoccupations that Nietzsche shared at that time with Richard Wagner: the cult of genius, of clear Kantian-Schopenhauerian hue, is linked to a metaphysical vision of the world that the late Nietzsche will resolutely refute. In the initial phase of Nietzsche's philosophy, the romantic genius, like the saint and the artist, is invested with a cosmic function, fully explicated in *Die Geburt der Tragödie* and implied and referenced often in the writing dedicated to Schopenhauer. The genius and the artist occasion the encounter of truth with itself: such figures, endowed with superhuman sensitivity, are the privileged sites where the ontological principle that Nietzsche places at the basis of his youthful philosophy manifests itself.[7]

If, therefore, Rawls' judgement of an elitist and antiliberal Nietzschean perfectionism is based on an unwarranted extension and overestimation of the German philosopher's early positions, the Rawlsian vision of perfectionism itself came to lose its pre-eminence in the 1990's, opening to other, more conciliatory definitions, in which Nietzsche still finds a place. Under the name of perfectionism today, a wide variety of theoretical aspects is assembled, sharing the same *ratio*: the necessity of presenting a moral theory based on the ideal of human improvement, with critical application to teleological conceptions of subjective good such as happiness or wellbeing.[8]

---

use of the text is warranted because it consists of authentically Nietzschean elements, is not sustainable. Amalgamation, dismemberment, and the arrangement of posthumous writings in thematic rather than chronological order – in addition to errors of decipherment and transcription – lead to distorted interpretations.

7 Besides Schopenhauer, the influence of Friedrich Schlegel is strong here, as shown particularly by Conant (2001), 191-196. On the influence of Romantic genius on Nietzsche's early thought, see also Araldi (2009). Nietzsche's reflections on 'genius', especially 'the great man', change their significance but do not cease, implying readings like *Inquiry into Human Faculty* by Francis Galton, *Psychologie des grands hommes* by Henri Joly, and perhaps *Great Men and Their Environment* by William James: on this topic, see Fornari (2004).

8 If, historically, perfectionism is associated with ethical theories characterising an objective good in terms of a development of human nature (authors like Aquinas, Spinoza, Kant, Marx are perfectionists in this sense), Aristotle is generally considered to be the founder of all the Western perfectionist theories, with his conception of virtue as the ideal of human perfection, pertaining to the person who knows how to do the right thing at the right moment (*phronimos*); who knows how to articulate action in space and time (an 'exemplar', in Stanley Cavell's sense, as we will see): "Excellence [*aretè*] then, is a disposition issuing in decisions, depending on intermediacy of the kind relative to us, this being determined by rational prescription and in the way in which the wise person would determine it [*kai o an o phronimos oriseien*]." (Aristotle (2002), 1106b 36-1107a 2).

2

We owe it to Stanley Cavell, himself profoundly indebted to Nietzsche, Heidegger and Wittgenstein, and engaged in the philosophical re-reading of thinkers like Emerson and Thoreau, that perfectionism abandons the strict hierarchy of ends proposed by Rawls. He proposes instead the individual ethical injunction to be 'the best that one can be', exploring the many alternatives of conduct that are presented to each person. The problem at the heart of Cavell's perfectionism is not that of morally right action, but of the *comprehension* or *clarification* of the self.[9]

For Cavell, perfectionism is a 'register' or a 'dimension of the moral life' defined by a type of difficulty different from that which characterises normative moral theories: if the latter concentrate on the problem of an action to be performed, perfectionism in the sense of Cavell (close to Emerson's) examines a series of difficulties relative to self-consciousness, or 'becoming intelligible to oneself', 'being true to oneself', etc.[10] In this perspective we can turn again to Nietzsche and ask if in *this* sense he ought to be included among perfectionist philosophers, with the reservation, however, that he will never enjoin an Apollonian self-consciousness (given the impossibility of introspection into a self already exploded), but rather the Pindaric 'becoming what one is', in no way immediately accessible to knowledge.[11]

---

9   "What is essential to Cavell's thought, as I read it, is that this further self is not given to us from the outside, as it were, but constitutes the development of our present self to its state of fullness and clarity with itself." (Donatelli (2006), 39).

10 Cf. Falomi (2014), 16. The idea that the sphere of ethics should also include the comprehension and transformation of the self is shared by other contemporary authors, like Iris Murdoch and Cora Diamond; but we can also place in this constellation the spiritual exercises of Pierre Hadot and the late Foucault's reflections on 'care of the self'.

11 Cf. Nehamas (1983), 385-417. Nehamas maintains, however, that to stress the moment of self-creation (as for example in Harold Aldermann (1977)) involves a kind of paradox: "This interpretation would hold that to become what one is would be to actualize all the capacities for which one is inherently suited; it might be inaccurate but not positively misleading to call such an interpretation 'Aristotelian'. Appealing to actuality and potentiality may account for some of the logical peculiarities of Nietzsche's phrase, since one (actually) is not what one (potentially) is. But this view faces two difficulties. The first is that if one actualizes one's capacities, one has become what one is; becoming has now ceased, it has 'flowed into being' just in the sense that we have seen Nietzsche deny that this is possible. The second is that construing becoming as realizing inherent capacities makes the creation of the self be more like the uncovering of what is already there. Yet Nietzsche seems to be trying to undermine precisely the idea that there are antecedently existing possibilities grounded in the nature of things, even though (as on the view we are considering) we may not know in advance what they are." ((1983), 393).

Precisely in response to Rawls, Cavell turns to *Schopenhauer als Erzieher* to show how it has been misunderstood, including at the lexical level. In what Cavell defines as the focal passage, on which Rawls' interpretation had been based, the German term *Exemplar* was translated by R.J. Hollingdale (1965) as specimen, in a biological perspective (specimen as the sample used to study the properties and distinctive traits of a species), which tends to favour an elitist reading ("This sounds bad," is Cavell's *caveat*).[12] As James Conant later explains, "Specimens are characterized by their *traits*; exemplars (in Nietzsche's sense) by their *excellence*"[13].

When, in this text, Nietzsche exhorts us, among other things, to 'live for the good of the rarest and most precious individuals', he is not offering us an objective conception of the good that we have the duty to maximise, but is exhorting us, according to Cavell, to confront ourselves with an 'exemplary type', or with a figure onto which to project our own still-unexpressed potentialities, so as to be able to become conscious of them.[14]

Living for genius thus does not mean: "there is genius, such that every self is to live for it," but rather: "for each self, there is a genius," understanding by 'genius' – still following Emerson – "the capacity for self-criticism, the capacity to consecrate the attained to the unattained self, on the basis of the axiom that each is a moral person."[15] The sacrifice that Nietzsche recommends is not therefore the sacrifice of a majority of ordinary people in favour of a super-endowed few, but the effort, possible for all, to become original individuals, emancipated from prejudice and faithful to themselves. Living for the good of

---

12   The revised Cambridge University Press edition now translates *Exemplar* as *instance* and *Vortheil* as *advantage*.
13   Cavell (1991), 146 ff.; Conant (2001), 194.
14   As Conant confirms, 'exemplar' is a term referring to the debate on the Kantian concept of genius within German nineteenth-century Romantic philosophy: "In this context, exemplars are those individuals who have attained excellence in respect to the qualities that are common to all human beings. The genius does not possess particular talents or natural gifts that render him constitutively different from the rest of us; between him and us is no difference of kind, but only of degree, a difference measured by the perseverance with which the exemplar has cultivated the sum of his qualities. In the Romantic frame, it is exactly the similarity between us and those we admire that is at the base of their educative power. Precisely because their exemplary character does not depend on the exercise of an innate talent, the admiration that they elicit is not what separates the work of genius from its public, but the mark of its capacity to awaken in its admirers a desire to emulate, without merely imitating, its exemplarity." (Vaccari (2011), 133; [translation by D. Moggach).
15   Cavell (1991), 146.

the exemplars, in Cavell's perfectionist perspective, is devoting one's own life to the ideal of a more genuine self-consciousness.[16]

As in the case of Rawls, Cavell also overlooks the periodization of the third *Betrachtung* and its metaphysical context. Let us repeat how the term *Exemplar* refers to the debate on the concept of genius that animated the German Romantic scene. Here Nietzsche stakes the claim of the philosophical genius to indicate a different direction for *Bildung* and to underline its privileged role, in which the true essence of the real is manifest.[17] Situated in its context, the third *Betrachtung* is far from the simplifications and the intentions that its first perfectionist readers attributed to it;[18] yet it is still interesting to take up their suggestion, especially Cavell's and subsequently Conant's, to consider *Schopenhauer als Erzieher* as an invitation to promote one's own individual expression and to embrace an ideal of self-perfection:[19] a personal vision of

---

16 According to Vaccari, "The relationship with the exemplar provokes two deeply-connected effects: self-consciousness and disquiet. The confrontation with what we admire reveals the existence of a higher self. A self in whose light what we are seems false, deceptive, empty. A self with whom we can no longer fully identify. Still, our higher self presents itself as something that we are not yet, and as distant from us. This relation is the source of a particular disquiet, caused by the discrepancy between what we are now and what we perceive as our true self, still remote from us. Such a feeling of dissatisfaction is the source of the desire to look beyond the present, and to seek to realise our higher self. According to Nietzsche, this constitutes the nucleus of the transformative power of every educational experience, emulative and not imitative, with our teachers." (Vaccari (2011), 135; translation by D. Moggach). If this reading were plausible for the Nietzsche of the period of the *Betrachtung* on Schopenhauer, it is again not extensible to Nietzschean though in its entirety, as it denotes a dualism to which the later Nietzsche would not subscribe in the least: namely, a reversion to a doubling between an 'empirical I' and an 'ideal I' which, as Isaiah Berlin explains, transforms the relation to ourselves into a kind of metaphysical struggle between butcher and victim, see Berlin (1969).

17 "Nietzsche expresses an attitude of marked activism and agonism, crystallised around the early metaphysic of the artist, and he attempts to use the 'untimely' elements of Schopenhauer while repudiating the security of metaphysical guarantees. The 'superstition of the genius' that in the shadow of Wagner seems to him in his first period to be the necessary foundation for a new civilisation will come to be criticised as a privileged and immediate, but illusory, exit from bad modernity." (Barbera-Campioni (2010), 37; translation by D. Moggach).

18 Conversely, but just as ineffectively, the position of Lemm (2007), who presents subsequent passages from *Schopenhauer as Educator* to conclude from them that Nietzsche is *not* a perfectionist in the sense of Cavell.

19 Even if Cavell detaches himself from Emerson on some essential points, the role that the American philosopher played in the elaboration of his theories is well-known. The same can be said of Nietzsche, who from his early period reads and appreciates many Emersonian essays, takes up their metaphors, and mediates on their suggestions, right up to the final period of his philosophical life. His personal library contained the German

individual care that is not necessarily in opposition or contrast to the socially defined ideals cherished by liberalism,[20] and one that opens as well to a perfectionist conception involving the style of philosophical communication.[21]

3

Having dismissed more or less definitively Nietzsche's brutal and naïve elitism (cf. Conant 2001: 183 ff.), and having admitted "as uncontroversial that Nietzsche's positive moral views fall under the general heading of what today is called perfectionism," a debate has arisen on the recent proposal of Thomas Hurka, for whom the moral ideas of the German philosopher "are centred on a conception [objective] of the good, which they commend actions for instantiating or promoting. But this conception does not equate the good with anything like pleasure or the satisfaction of desires; instead, it locates the good in objective human excellences that for Nietzsche centre on the concepts of power and strength."[22] According to Hurka, in fact, if Nietzsche identifies the good with the perfection of human nature, and human nature with those properties essential to a human being, then he must identify the good with the maximization of *will to power*, the fundamental property essential to all things:

---

translation of three essays by Emerson (*Versuche, Die Führung des Lebens, Neue Essays*), besides a notebook of extracts from the *Essays* compiled at the beginning of 1882. On the Nietzsche-Emerson relation, see Stack (1992); Zavatta (2019).

20 For Cavell, democracy and self-realisation ought to be deeply integrated: individual perfection is not only "tolerable for a life of justice in a constitutional democracy but [...] it is essential for that life." (Cavell (1990), 56) "What is the pertinence, for example, of perfectionism's emphasis, common from Plato and Aristotle to Emerson and Thoreau and Nietzsche, on education and character and friendship for a democratic existence? That emphasis on perfectionism, as I have said, may be taken to serve an effort to escape the mediocrity of leveling, say vulgarity, of equal existence, for oneself and perhaps for a select circle of like-minded others. There are undeniably aristocratic or aesthetic perfectionisms. But in Emerson it should, I would like to say, be taken as a part of the training for democracy." (Cavell (1991), 152-153)

21 "It will emerge that Nietzsche's perfectionism does not (as is often assumed) take the form of a teleological (moral or political) theory that seeks to maximize certain social or cultural goods. It will emerge further that one cannot grasp the sense in which his philosophy *is* perfectionist apart from an understanding of why he thinks there is a problem about how philosophy, as he seeks to practice it, should be written and read. For the perfectionist moment in his work is tied to his conception of the manner in which that work seeks to engage its reader." (Conant (2000), 182). See also Vaccari (2011).

22 Hurka (2007), 9.

hence, "the best individuals are therefore those who are most powerful"[23], and not those who excel in terms of rational capacity or characteristics.

According to Donald Rutherford, who resolutely opposes this reading, the pervasive "antirealism" of Nietzsche and his perspectivism suffice to contrast the position more genuinely held by the German philosopher, with one that, he suspects, derives more from the hermeneutic desire of the interpreter:

> Nietzsche's pervasive antirealism about the ground of value is in tension with the main lines of Hurka's perfectionist interpretation, which assumes an objective human good. If anything like Hurka's account can be recovered from Nietzsche's writings, it will have to be reconciled with the thesis that value judgments are expressions of kinds of life and that they are not answerable to external standards in terms of which life itself can be valued.[24]

---

23   Hurka (2007), 10.
24   Rutherford (2017), 5. Added to this is the intensive, substantial critique that Nietzsche makes of utilitarianism and eudaemonism. If every individual, as Nietzsche maintains, possesses his or her own individual measure of value, the good and the happiness of each will be absolutely personal: "Dem Individuum, *sofern* es sein Glück will, soll man keine Vorschriften über den Weg zum Glück geben: denn das individuelle Glück quillt aus eigenen, Jedermann unbekannten Gesetzen, es kann mit Vorschriften von Aussen her nur verhindert, gehemmt werden. – Die Vorschriften, welche man 'moralisch' nennt, sind in Wahrheit gegen die Individuen gerichtet und wollen durchaus nicht deren Glück. Ebenso wenig beziehen sich diese Vorschriften auf das 'Glück und die Wohlfahrt der Menschheit,' – mit welchen Worten strenge Begriffe zu verbinden überhaupt nicht möglich ist, geschweige dass man sie als Leitsterne auf dem dunklen Ozean moralischer Bestrebungen gebrauchen könnte." (*Morgenröthe*, aphorism 108; KSA 3, 95). Here is the core of the Nietzschean critique of the social moralities of evolutionism and positivism, which misconceive the value of the individual by grasping it as a species-homogeneity. But the criticism also touches classical perfectionism and Kantian deontological morality: "[...] Insofern haben Plato und Aristoteles Recht, in den Freuden der Erkenntniß das Erstrebenswertheste zu sehen – vorausgesetzt daß sie damit eine persönliche Erfahrung und nicht eine allgemeine aussprechen wollen: denn für die meisten Menschen gehören die Freuden der Erkenntniß zu den schwächsten und stehen tief unter den Freuden der Mahlzeit". (*Nachgelassene Fragmente*, KSA 9, 49). Or again, in the well-known aphorism 43 of *Jenseits von Gut und Böse* (KSA 5, 60): "Man muss den schlechten Geschmack von sich abthun, mit Vielen übereinstimmen zu wollen. 'Gut' ist nicht mehr gut, wenn der Nachbar es in den Mund nimmt. Und wie könnte es gar ein 'Gemeingut' geben! Das Wort widerspricht sich selbst: was gemein sein kann, hat immer nur wenig Werth. Zuletzt muss es so stehn, wie es steht und immer stand: die grossen Dinge bleiben für die Grossen übrig, die Abgründe für die Tiefen, die Zartheiten und Schauder für die Feinen, und, im Ganzen und Kurzen, alles Seltene für die Seltenen. –". On Nietzsche's critique of utilitarism and eudaemonism, see Fornari (2006/2009).

Situating *Schopenhauer als Erzieher* chronologically,[25] Rutherford wants to show that Hurka's interpretation, besides not taking account of the prospective character to the tables of values and their inscription in history,[26] also fails at the textual level, and if one may speak of perfectionism in Nietzsche, this concerns the recuperation of the values specific to a 'noble', affirmative individual, who can emerge in the wake of the transvaluation of Christian values – in opposition to an objective and commonly-shared ideal of human perfection.[27]

It is in these terms that we can begin to delineate the form of Nietzsche's perfectionism. There are a variety of ways in which the noble mode of valuation can be

---

[25] "*Schopenhauer as Educator* is an early work in which Nietzsche has not yet found his feet as a philosopher. The argument is premised on a teleological conception of nature that is foreign to his later thought. Nature as a whole is understood to have 'a metaphysical goal [*einem metaphyischen Zwecke*], that of its own self-enlightenment' or 'self-knowledge' (KSA 1, 383). This goal is realized in the appearance of 'great redemptive men', whom each of us should seek to produce. All of this belongs to a stage of his thought that Nietzsche leaves behind. Moreover, it does not entail that a person should act without regard to her own good. The 'task', he says, is 'to promote the production of the philosopher, the artist and the saint within us and without us and thereby to work at the perfecting of nature' (ibid., emphasis in original). The life of each person receives its 'highest value' and 'deepest significance' to the extent that it is dedicated to promoting the 'metaphysical goal' of nature wherever it can be realized, in oneself or in others. This is not Hurka's 'maximax' principle." (Rutherford (2017), 6).

[26] "All values are 'created', in the sense that they come to exist as a result of human beings' affective responses to the world and have no reality independently of those responses. What distinguishes the values of the noble type is that they are a spontaneous expression of its life and reflect its affirmation of its life, whereas the values of the common type are essentially reactive and reflect an underlying dissatisfaction with life [...]. If this is correct, then the significance of Nietzsche's revaluation of values lies less in the support it offers for a return to master morality, which involves the dominance of the noble type over a class of inferior people, than in its claim for a space in which the noble mode of valuation can be exercised by those who seek to do so. This conclusion is supported by the models Nietzsche offers of new manifestations of the noble mode of valuation. Artists, free spirits, and philosophers of the future exemplify in different ways the characteristic mode of valuing of the noble type: they feel themselves to stand above the common run of life and they insist on the right of independence – to judge value for themselves." (Rutherford (2017), 10 and 12).

[27] Similarly Vaccari (2011), 141: "The positive ethic that Nietzsche opposes to Christian culture in the *Genealogy of Morals* implies that primacy of self-respect that in *Schopenhauer as Educator* was the mark of characters who live their uniqueness with rigorous coherence. These are exactly the themes that explain the refusal of a morality based on resentment, which derives its values from a reaction to factors external to the self. The positive ethic develops within an educative relation that each of us has to our own higher self, that is, along that creative path that allows us to become what we really are." [Translation by D. Moggach].

manifested: an aristocratic political order, Dionysian art, new philosophers who are 'commanders and legislators' of values. Along with these we may include a value perspective that incorporates features of perfectionism: an individual identifies her good with the realization of an ideal version of her life, conceived in terms of the elevation or perfection of her powers. This value perspective preserves the characteristics of the noble mode of valuation – spontaneity, the pathos of distance, normative independence – but modulates their expression in ways that distinguish the resulting perspective from the original form of master morality. [...] In these ways, Nietzsche lays the ground for a new noble type that adopts the ethical perspective of perfectionism. While preserving the affirmative stance of the noble mode of valuation, the perfectionist perspective is premised on an individual's heightened awareness of the distance between what is common in her and the individual she might become; and she conceives of the realization of the latter in terms of her meeting the demands of specific virtues, including intellectual conscience, honesty, courage, and a capacity for solitude.[28]

The noble type identifies perfection with the spontaneous development of one's own qualities, and is capable of standing forth as an example of a superior form of life. This constitutes an ideal, even if not of universal extension ("there is no single ideal for human life. There are only *ideals* projected by individuals as higher versions of their lives"[29], if not a solipsistically subjective ideal[30], which keeps Nietzsche anchored in perfectionism:

---

28 Rutherford (2017), 12-13. So Giorgio Colli, in his *Nota introduttiva* to the Italian edition of *Beyond Good and Evil* (1986), XII-XIII: "Here, in *Beyond Good and Evil*, the designation of the aristocratic classes and aristocratic virtues is not the principal aim, even if Nietzsche highlights it. Being explained is what in the historical world manifests the aristocratic instinct, and what the vulgar, to allude to the nature of the instincts themselves. The primitive interiority with which an individual feels the surrounding world, and reacts in consequence, is what interests Nietzsche. The coarse, macroscopic documentation of these instincts is the story of men. But the aristocratic and the vulgar taste are then traced back to their origin, before the intervention of mediation by the collective [...] It is the instinct of separation that is, perhaps, the root of the aristocratic. The dividing, the setting oneself against everything around one, the holding oneself apart, distant, separate, in thought and in action. This appears to be the subterranean 'pathos' at the basis of all the configurations of aristocratic taste." [Translation by D. Moggach].

29 Rutherford (2017), 18.

30 It seems to us rather that this ideal shifts with the 'political' projects of Nietzsche: the noble individual to whom the fates not only of Europe, but of future humanity, are entrusted, must present himself as a renewed subjectivity: no longer as the rigid and exclusionary configuration born of constrictive power (be it the power of nature, the state, morals, or religion), but as a man who is 'concentrated', spiritually rich, endowed with a new awareness of his own value, his own freedom, and his own destiny (see the definition of the 'sovereign individual', *Zur Genealogie der Moral*, Zweite Abhandl., 2.; KSA 5, 293-294). Note, in relation to his liberty, that "The agent's self-ascription of absolute freedom belongs essentially to Kant's concept of moral agency, and the self-ascription

The desire to live above and apart from a common humanity is one that Nietzsche shares and that he invests with the highest value. The explanation of how it is possible to do this – what it means to perfect oneself, the source of the ideals in terms of which one represents one's perfection, and the sense in which one is accountable to those ideals – are innovations of his philosophy; but for all that, in his ethical outlook, Nietzsche remains deeply indebted to perfectionism.[31]

4

Remaining in the optic of self-perfecting, it seems interesting at this point to return to Cavell's suggestions, or better still, to his practice of utilising performative texts. The perfectionist position is that the textual dimension is not purely instrumental, but that it participates actively, we might say, in the *autopoiesis* of the reader. Certain texts, certain authors, induce a transformation: this is the idea of a consciousness that produces or constitutes a change or a turn, an immediate practical awareness that alters the way that the person experiencing it thinks of him- or herself (or, the text functions as an *Exemplar*, in the sense we saw above).

One of the basic presuppositions of Cavell's perfectionism is that an understanding of the specific modalities through which a text enters into relationship with its own reader is crucial for the type of philosophical thought that the reader practices. The text not only provides us with theses and arguments, but places us before a series of resistances, something that the reader rejects, only eventually to become conscious of it. In this sense the text makes accessible to

---

of 'freedom' to Nietzsche's sovereign individuality. But the 'freedom' the sovereign individual ascribes to itself and to its peers is not absolute spontaneity, which for Nietzsche is a self-contradictory concept; and this self-ascription of a rare freedom does not have the same function as the postulate of absolute freedom in Kant's practical philosophy. It is, rather, the main way in which the sovereign individual's 'pathos of distance' is expressed, and hence a form of self- affirmation" (Brusotti (2017), 220).

31 Rutherford (2017), 19. According to Conway's thesis, on the other hand, 'ethical perfectionism' conveys, in Nietzsche, a "political perfectionism". Conway speaks of a "micro-politics" of resistance, as against a "macro-politics" of transformation. Macropolitics concerns the „production of great individuals through the organisation of institutional resources", whereas micropolitics operates outside institutional frameworks, within the "network of ethical life" that is their source: „[a]utochthonous folkways, tribal rituals, ethnic customs, and memory traces, familial habits and mores, hieratic regimens of diet and hygiene" (Conway (1997), 48). Conway also underlines the performative dimension of Nietzsche's writings and reads in the political means no more than a semiotics of self-creation.

us a part of ourselves, making us conscious of something to which we offered resistance, but which, precisely for that reason, belongs to us.³²

> In other words, there are communicative intentions, and corresponding methodologies, which do not concentrate on the pure transmission of the message as an item of knowledge, but which grasp this transmission as a transformation of the recipient to whom the message is directed. Neither the communication, nor the importance of the message, nor the quality of the method utilised, are measured self-referentially according to the *quid* of the message, but according to the effect it has upon the recipient. The philosophical text is constructed in these cases as the site of an activity in which the reader is involved, at the term of which there can and should be observed a change in the reader, [a process] which has nothing to do with the intellectual acquisition of new notions and new concepts.³³

Secondly, Cavell offers a series of indications describing the characteristics of a perfectionist text: for example, a text which reports a form of conversation among persons, of whom one is more authoritative than the others, so as to elicit their emulation; a text in which the interlocutors undergo a process of education, of ascent toward a higher state of consciousness and self-cultivation. The main example of this literature is Plato's *Republic*, but it is inevitable to think of *Also sprach Zarathustra*, where the text seeks to establish a performative relation first among its characters, then with the reader.³⁴

---

32 Donatelli considers this "the paradox of perfectionism": "If the thoughts of a text such as Emerson's (say the brief text on rejected thoughts) are yours, then you do not need them. If its thoughts are not yours, they will not do you good. The problem is that the text's thoughts are neither exactly mine nor not mine. In their sublimity as my rejected – say repressed – thoughts, they represent my further, next, unattained but attainable, self. To think otherwise, to attribute the origin of my thoughts simply to the other, thoughts which are then, as it were, implanted in me – some would say caused – by let us say some Emerson, is idolatry" (2006), 40). "If truth is not yours already it will not do you good; but if it is yours already you will not need it. The paradox signals the special problem that perfectionism has in establishing the relation between my present point of view and that of truth." (*ibid.*).

33 Piazzesi (2009), 16 [translation by D. Moggach]. Piazzesi's book is dedicated to Pascal, Kierkegaard, and Wittgenstein, who himself becomes the object of a new reading in a perfectionist key, giving rise to the so-called *New Wittgenstein*: cf. Crary/Read (2000).

34 As James Conant has observed, "It is a characteristic trait of the [perfectionist] writing that a relation obtaining between voices *in* the text mirrors a relation into which the reader is invited to enter *with* the text." (Conant (2001), 208). For Piazzesi, Nietzsche's Zarathustra offers us a notion of truth dependent upon the contingency of its reception and transmission: "To ask oneself questions not *about*, but *to* one's own path, Zarathustra continues, means learning too to answer these questions. The answer is not already available to whoever asks the right question, independently of who asks it and how it is asked. [The answer] results instead from a learning process, that defines what qualifies as a

In general, Nietzsche's entire philosophical communication can perhaps be reread in this light. The reading modality that Cavell defines as 'therapeutic' requires a particular form of sagacity, of attention to the text, to its undertones and allusions, its instructions, to enable us to free ourselves from our ordinary representations. And Nietzsche, as we know, asks us to read him well,[35] often defining himself, a *nuance* to be taken up with particular knowledge and caution. He asks us to put ourselves in relation to his own experiences, to that *Erlebnis* from which he says his writings are uniquely composed, and of which the sharing remains the sole adequate presupposition for their comprehension.[36] The *Erlebnis*, the lived life, represents not only a hermeneutic disposition, not only an accessory circumstance, but more essentially the content and the object of the text.[37]

Such recommendations are comprehensible in light of the therapeutic or educative role that Nietzsche assigns to his own texts. In 1886, pleading with his editor the cause of a new edition of his previous works supplied with prefaces, Nietzsche does not conceal that, if properly understood, these could activate a real process of self-education:

> You will have noticed that *Human, All Too Human, Daybreak* and the *Gay Science do not have* a preface. I had good reasons for taking a vow of silence after

---

response to the questions posed and what would be the correct response to the singular, specific question. Learning to answer means that the criterion to locate the answer (and the truth) is not already available; nor is the answer itself universally available, but depends on the criterion adopted to associate it with the question. There is no previous or a priori competence that makes this acquisition possible according to universal rules; it is a transformation of the subject, through a new learning process, that enables this." (Piazzesi (2009), 13).

35 Cf. *Morgenröthe*, "Vorrede", 5.; KSA 3, 17. "Nietzsche's work is unquestionably esoteric; but the esotericism of his writings is not a function of the way in which it seeks to delimit the class of its readers in advance. It is rather a function of its criterion for what counts as its having been seriously read. It demands the *transformation* of its reader as the mark of its reception" (Conant (2001), 198).

36 "Daß man sich versteht, dazu gehört noch nicht, daß man dieselben Worte gebraucht: man muß dieselben Worte auch für dieselbe Gattung innerer Erlebnisse brauchen – und man muß *diese* GEMEINSAM HABEN. [...] Dies ist gesagt, um zu erklären, warum es schwer ist, solche Schriften wie die meinigen zu verstehen: die inneren Erlebnisse, Werthschätzungen und Bedürfnisse sind bei mir anders." (*Nachgelassene Fragmente* 34[86], KSA 11, 448).

37 Let us also recall the importance for Nietzsche of the question of style, which must correspond to the theoretical horizon it intends to communicate: "Hat nicht die Absicht einer Schrift nicht immer erst das Gesetz ihres Stils zu schaffen? Ich verlange, daß, wenn diese Absicht sich ändert, man auch unerbittlich das ganze Prozedurensystem des Stils ändert." (Letter to J.V. Widmann, 4 Feb. 1888, KSB 8, 244).

composing these works, I was still too close, too 'inside' and I practically did not realize what had happened to me. Now that I am able to explain fully and more clearly the characteristics of these works and what makes them unique and to what point they inaugurate a new literary genre for Germany (the prelude to a self-education and a moral culture that so far has been missing for the Germans). I would willingly decide to compose these *retrospective* prefaces with hindsight. My writings represent a *constant development*, and I shall not be alone in living this experience and destiny – I am only the first, a generation that is forming will understand for itself what I have lived through and will have the refinement of taste necessary to savour my books.[38]

An additional trait of a perfectionist text is to invite the reader to retrace the path of formation that the text itself represents: here it is interesting that Nietzsche recognises having himself effected this trajectory, which has enabled him to clarify to himself 'who he is'.[39]

Retrospectively retracing the experience of all his past writings, with the aim of making himself understandable for action in the present through the projected *transvaluation of all values*[40], Nietzsche sketches a personal evolution of which he himself can only become conscious *a posteriori*, and in which he discovers a destinal coherence. Nietzsche's own path is that of a *Selbstbildung*, effected through his works. It is therefore no accident that the autobiography that he leaves us at the end of his conscious life restores a kind of identity throughout his writings, and that it should bear the subtitle "Wie man wird, was man ist"[41].

---

38 "Sie werden bemerken, daß Menschl<iches> Allzum<enschliches> die Morgenröthe, die fröhliche Wissenschaft einer Vorrede *ermangeln*: es hatte gute Gründe, daß ich damals als diese Werke entstanden, mir ein Stillschweigen auferlegte – ich stand noch zu nahe, noch zu sehr „drin" und wußte kaum, was mit mir geschehn war. Jetzt, wo ich selber am besten und genauesten sagen kann, was das Eigene und Unvergleichliche an diesen Werken ist und inwiefern sie eine für Deutschland neue Litteratur inauguriren (das Vorspiel einer moralistischen Selbst-Erziehung und Cultur, die bisher den Deutschen gefehlt hat) würde ich mich zu solchen *zurückblickenden* und nachträglichen Vorreden gerne entschließen. Meine Schriften stellen eine *fortlaufende Entwicklung* dar, welche nicht nur mein persönliches Erlebniß und Schicksal sein wird: – ich bin nur der Erste, eine heraufkommende Generation wird das, was ich erlebt habe, von sich aus verstehn und eine feine Zunge für meine Bücher haben." (Letter to E.W. Fritzsch, 7 August 1886, KSB 7, 224).

39 Cf. *Ecce homo*, "Vorwort", 1.; KSA 6, 257.

40 In this respect, see particularly the letters from 1885 onward; and see Fornari (2012).

41 "Nietzsche recognises that it is not at the epistemological level but in lived experience that subjectivity constitutes itself, and to express this decisive shift Nietzsche considers as more appropriate than the Delphic imperative, 'Know thyself', the other imperative, inspired by Pindar, 'Become what you are.' [...] A paradoxical injunction that refers to an inner dynamism, to a form of self-construction characterised by movement, thus takes the place of a finalistic imperative. Not knowing where one is going, or the absence

Sharing Dewey's idea that the aesthetic object is not the intellectual fruition of the work of art but its entire life, Richard Schusterman defines this ethical path as "the stylisation of the self"[42]: he finds it in Emerson, Nietzsche, and Wittgenstein, once again the key authors of perfectionism, capable of exercising (as Nietzsche exhorts in *Gay Science*, 290) that "great and rare art" which is "to give a style to one's own character," in the name of the originality of one's own most personal views. It is not merely a question of the idea that:

> l'originalité est synonyme d'expression honnête de soi, ou consiste simplement à être ce que l'on est. L'idée d'un moi supérieur, stylisé, semble au contraire exiger que nous déguisions et transformions ce que nous sommes afin de devenir meilleurs. Comment devrons-nous résoudre la contradiction apparente entre ces exhortations à être ce que nous sommes et à être ce que nous ne sommes pas, mais espérons devenir ? Comment réconcilier la notion de style original en tant qu'expression honnête de soi avec celle d'une transformation artificielle de soi? [...] La solution la plus plausible, me semble-t-il, est d'avancer que les tentatives d'autotransformation artistique ont pour préalable la reconnaissance et l'expression de ce que l'on est déjà. Comme le suggère Wittgenstein lui-même, "une confession doit faire partie de votre vie nouvelle"; car "un homme ne sera jamais grand s'il se méprend sur lui-même".[43]

Moreover, the dissolution of the categories of traditional psychology and morality (subject, consciousness, will) entails a revision of one's own experience of the self. As Piazzesi pertinently recalls: "Personality is not only a fact, it is a *destination* that could easily remain unexplored, ignored, misunderstood, without the ethical work of genuinely taking responsibility for what this means."[44]

And such an exploration, it seems to me, is exactly the theme of *Ecce homo*: right from the second chapter, Nietzsche imputes his double nature ("Abgerechnet nämlich, dass ich ein décadent bin, bin ich auch dessen Gegensatz"[45]) to the fatality of his own existence, but also to a conscious

---

of a predetermined goal of movement, and 'deviation', are indicated by Nietzsche as preconditions for 'becoming what one is.' (Lupo (2012), 22-23n; translation by D. Moggach).

42   Schusterman (1997), 103.
43   Schusterman (1997), 107-108.
44   Cf. Piazzesi (2007), 258-295. Again, citing Nehamas: "the unity we are looking for is not a final stage which follows upon others, but the total organization of everything that one thinks, wants and does". "It begins to seem, then, that Nietzsche has in mind not a final state of being which follows upon and replaces an earlier process of becoming. Rather, he is thinking of a continual process of greater integration of one's character-traits, habits and patterns of interaction with the world." (1983), 403 and 404). For Foucault, too, Nietzsche substitutes, for the project of an authentic self, that of the creative construction of the self. (cf. Schrift (2001), 50).
45   *Ecce homo*, "Warum ich so weise bin", 2.; KSA 6, 266.

construction, which displays itself as symptom and as consequence alike of his physico-psychic state. What one is, as long as one knows how to listen, guides and settles our vital choices – Nietzsche is proud of having theorised 'cornarism'[46] –, elaborates strategies for mobilising our resources, but at the same time demands active abilities to choose and direct, in view of what our instincts have in store for us.[47]

This mixing of fate and the conscious construction of one's own form of life may appear contradictory, since the first would render the second superfluous[48]. In reality, recognising own's own, fated configuration is what will effectively guide our destiny ("Fatum ist ein erhebender Gedanke für den, welcher begreift, daß er *dazu* gehört"[49]): not to lose one's way in the face of such knowledge, but instead to work to favour its becoming concretely real, is the sign of a superior culture. The marvelous harmony born from the sounds of our instrument, "eine Harmonie, welche zu gut klingt, als dass wir es wagten, sie uns selber zuzurechnen"[50], is the encounter of chance with the capacity to extend fully the uniqueness of our own condition, in a happy coincidence of will and fate.[51]

If we want to continue to consider Nietzsche as a 'perfectionist', we must look, beyond the labels, to that will to educate oneself that permeates his writings and that takes shape through and by means of them: an education that Nietzsche effects in the first place at the personal level and then, he

---

46 Cf. *Götzen-Dämmerung*, "Die vier grossen Irrthümer", 1.; KSA 6, 88.
47 "Inzwischen wächst und wächst die organisirende, die zur Herrschaft berufne 'Idee' in der Tiefe, – sie beginnt zu befehlen, sie leitet langsam aus Nebenwegen und Abwegen *zurück*, sie bereitet *einzelne* Qualitäten und Tüchtigkeiten vor, die einmal als Mittel zum Ganzen sich unentbehrlich erweisen werden, – sie bildet der Reihe nach alle *dienenden* Vermögen aus, bevor sie irgend Etwas von der dominirenden Aufgabe, von 'Ziel', 'Zweck', 'Sinn' verlauten lässt. –Nach dieser Seite hin betrachtet ist mein Leben einfach wundervoll." (*Ecce homo*, "Warum ich so klug bin", 9.; KSA 6, 293).
48 Cf., for example, KSA 2, 580.
49 *Nachgelassene Fragmente* 26[442]; KSA 11, 268.
50 *Die fröhliche Wissenschaft*, 277.; KSA 3, 522.
51 In this sense, what Nietzsche writes to Paul Deussen, on the occasion of his birthday, is illuminating: "Ich habe einen so hohen Begriff von Deiner thätigen und tapfren Existenz, daß es wenig Sinn hat, besondre Wünsche auszudrücken. Wer einen eigenen Willen in die Dinge zu legen hat, über den werden die Dinge nicht Herr; zuletzt arrangieren sich die *Zufälle* noch nach unsern eigentlichsten Bedürfnissen. Ich erstaune oft, wie wenig die äußerste Ungunst des Schicksals über einen Willen vermag. Oder vielmehr: ich sage mir, wie sehr der Wille selbst Schicksal sein muß, daß er immer wieder auch *gegen* das Schicksal Recht bekommt, ὑπὲρ μόρον –, ὑπὲρ μόρον" (3 January 1888, KSB, 8, 220).

contends, in view of our emancipation.[52] Despite the possible accusation that this 'moralising' reading misconstrues Nietzschean naturalism, we believe that Nietzsche offers us the instruments to perfect ourselves on the path of coherence, intellectual honesty, and fidelity to ourselves, looking ahead to a new human 'type' that he so often invoked.

> – Sollte mein Erlebniss – die Geschichte einer Krankheit und Genesung, denn es lief auf eine Genesung hinaus – nur mein persönliches Erlebniss gewesen sein? Und gerade nur *mein* ‚Menschlich-Allzumenschliches'? Ich möchte heute das Umgekehrte glauben; das Zutrauen kommt mir wieder und wieder dafür, dass meine Wanderbücher doch nicht nur für mich aufgezeichnet waren, wie es bisweilen den Anschein hatte –. Darf ich nunmehr, nach sechs Jahren wachsender Zuversicht, sie von Neuem zu einem Versuche auf die Reise schicken? Darf ich sie Denen sonderlich an's Herz und Ohr legen, welche mit irgend einer ‚Vergangenheit' behaftet sind und *Geist* genug übrig haben, um auch noch am Geiste ihrer Vergangenheit zu leiden? Vor allem aber Euch, die ihr es am schwersten habt, ihr Seltenen, Gefährdetsten, Geistigsten, Muthigsten, die ihr das *Gewissen* der modernen Seele sein müsst und als solche ihr *Wissen* haben müsst, in denen was es nur heute von Krankheit, Gift und Gefahr geben kann zusammen kommt, – deren Loos es will, dass ihr kränker sein müsst als irgend ein Einzelner, weil ihr nicht ‚nur Einzelne' seid ..., deren Trost es ist, den Weg zu einer *neuen* Gesundheit zu wissen, ach! und zu gehen, einer Gesundheit von Morgen und Uebermorgen, ihr Vorherbestimmten, ihr Siegreichen, ihr Zeit-Ueberwinder, ihr Gesündesten, ihr Stärksten, ihr *guten Europäer*! – –.[53]

Translated from Italian by Douglas Moggach

---

52 According to Piazzesi "*The* route [...] does not exist: there is not *the* way, disconnected from trials and errors, from points of reference and wanderings of those who seek their *own* way, and most of all, who go. This series of instructions cannot be communicated as knowledge, as a series of instructions, because, it is legitimate to affirm, it does not exist independently of the person who, in traversing it, defines it, because, in traversing it, he traces it out. This 'truth', whatever it might be, is not transmissible as such: if its status is tied singularly to certain conditions of the person who appropriates it and how he appropriates it, it cannot be learned or passed along *ex cathedra* to others." (Piazzesi (2009), 13; translation by D. Moggach). If this cannot be doubted, still education in such a prospective view has the appearance of a 'truth', undoubtedly connected to the objective virtues of honesty: „Redlichkeit, gesetzt, dass dies unsre Tugend ist, von der wir nicht loskönnen, wir freien Geister – nun, wir wollen mit aller Bosheit und Liebe an ihr arbeiten und nicht müde werden, uns in *unsrer* Tugend, die allein uns übrig blieb, zu „vervollkommnen": mag ihr Glanz einmal wie ein vergoldetes blaues spöttisches Abendlicht über dieser alternden Cultur und ihrem dumpfen düsteren Ernste liegen bleiben!" (*Jenseits von Gut und Böse*, 227; KSA 5, 162). On *Redlichkeit* as an explicit Nietzschean virtue, much has been written: see, for example, White 2001.

53 *Menschliches, Allzumenschliches II*, "Vorrede", 6.; KSA 2, 376.

Bibliography

Araldi, Clademir Luis, "O gênio romântico no pensamento de Nietzsche", in: *Artefilosofia, O uro Preto*, n. 6, 2009, pp. 183-193.

Aristotle, *Nicomachean Ethics*, trans. Christopher Rowe, Oxford: Oxford University Press, 2002.

Arneson, Richard J., "Perfectionism and Politics", in: *Ethics*, vol. 111, No. 1 (2000), pp. 37-63.

Barbera, Sandro/Campioni, Giuliano, *Il Genio Tiranno. Ragione e dominio nell'ideologia dell'Ottocento. Wagner, Nietzsche, Renan*, ETS: Pisa, 2010².

Berlin, Isaiah, *Two Concepts of Liberty*, London: Oxford University Press, 1969 (1958).

Brusotti, Marco, "Spontaneity and Sovereignty Nietzsche's Concepts and Kant's Philosophy", in: Tom Bailey, João Constancio (eds.), *Nietzsche and Kantian Ethics*, London/New York: Bloomsbury, 2017, pp. 219-256.

Cavell, Stanley, "Aversive Thinking: Emersonian Representations in Heidegger and Nietzsche", in: *New Literary History*, vol. 22 (1991), pp. 129-160.

– *Conditions Handsome and Unhandsome: The Constitution of Emersonian Perfectionism*, University of Chicago Press, 1990.

Church, Jeffrey, "Nietzsche's Early Perfectionism: A Cultural Reading of 'The Greek State'", in: *Journal of Nietzsche Studies*, vol. 46, No. 2 (Summer 2015), pp. 248-260.

Colli, Giorgio, *Nota introduttiva* a Friedrich Nietzsche, *Al di là del bene e del male*, Milano: Piccola Biblioteca Adelphi, 1986.

Conant, James, "Nietzsche's Perfectionism: A Reading of Schopenhauer as Educator", in: Schacht (ed.), *Nietzsche's Postmoralism. Essays on Nietzsche's Prelude to Philosophy's Future*, Cambridge: Cambridge University Press, 2001, pp. 181-257.

Conway, Daniel W., *Nietzsche and the Political*, Routledge, London, 1997.

Crary, Alice/Read, Rupert (eds.), *The New Wittgenstein*, London/New York: Routledge, 2000.

Donatelli, Piergiorgio, "Bringing Truth Home: Mill, Wittgenstein, Cavell, and moral Perfectionism", in: John Andrew Norris (ed.), *The Claim to Community: Essays on Stanley Cavell and Political Philosophy*, Stanford University Press, 2006.

Falomi, Matteo, "Il perfezionismo di Cavell". Introduzione all'edizione italiana di: Stanley Cavell, *Condizioni ammirevoli e avvilenti. La costituzione del Perfezionismo Emersoniano. Carus Lectures*, 1988, Armando, Roma, 2014.

Fornari, Maria Cristina, "And so I will tell myself the Story of my Life". Nietzsche in his last Letters (1885-1889), in: João Constancio (ed.), *As the Spider Spins: Essays on Nietzsche's Critique and Use of Language*, Berlin/New York: de Gruyter, 2012, pp. 281-296.

- *La morale evolutiva del gregge. Nietzsche legge Spencer e Mill*, ETS, Pisa 2006; German translation: *Die Entwicklung der Herdenmoral. Nietzsche liest Spencer und Mill*, Wiesbaden: Harrassowitz Verlag, 2009.
- "Superuomo ed evoluzione", in: *Nietzsche e la provocazione del superuomo*, ed. by Francesco Totaro, Carocci, Roma, 2004.

Hurka, Thomas, "Nietzsche: Perfectionist", in: Leiter Brian & Sinhababu Neil (eds.): *Nietzsche and Morality*, Oxford: Oxford University Press, 2007, pp. 9-31.

Lorenzini, Daniele, *Éthique et politique de soi. Foucault, Hadot, Cavell et les techniques de l'ordinaire*, Vrin, Paris, 2017^2.

Lupo, Luca, *Filosofia della Serendipity*, Napoli: Guida, 2012.

Nehamas, Alexander, "How One Becomes What One Is", in: *Philosophical Review*, 92 (1983), pp. 385-417.

Nietzsche, Friedrich, *Sämtliche Briefe, Kritische Studienausgabe in 8 Bänden*, hrsg. von G. Colli und M. Montinari, Berlin: de Gruyter, 1975-1984. (KSB)
- *Sämtliche Werke, Kritische Studienausgabe in 15 Bänden*, hrsg. v. G. Colli und M. Montinari, Berlin/New York: de Gruyter, 1988^2. (KSA)

Piazzesi, Chiara, *La verità come trasformazione di sé, Terapie filosofiche in Pascal, Kierkegaard e Wittgenstein*, ETS, Pisa, 2009.

Piazzesi, Chiara, "Pathos der Distanz et transformation de l'expériénce de soi chez le dernier Nietzsche", in: *Nietzsche Studien*, 36 (2007), pp. 258-295.

Rutherford, Donald, "Nietzsche as Perfectionist", in: *Inquiry: An Interdisciplinary Journal of Philosophy*, 2017, pp. 42-61.

Schacht, Richard (ed.), *Nietzsche's Postmoralism. Essays on Nietzsche's Prelude to Philosophy's Future*, Cambridge: Cambridge University Press, 2001.

Schrift, Alan D., "Rethinking the Subject: Or, How One Becomes-Other Than What One Is", in: Schacht (ed.), *Nietzsche's Postmoralism. Essays on Nietzsche's Prelude to Philosophy's Future*, Cambridge: Cambridge University Press, 2001, pp. 47-62.

Shusterman, Richard, "Style et styles de vie: originalité, authenticité et dédoublement du moi", in: *Littérature*, 105 (1997), pp. 102-109.

Stack, George J., *Nietzsche and Emerson: An Elective Affinity*, Ohio University Press, 1992.

Vaccari, Alessio, "Perfezionismo e critica della morale in Friedrich Nietzsche", in: *Iride*, 62 (2011), pp. 129-144.

White, A., "The Youngest Virtue", in: Schacht (ed.), *Nietzsche's Postmoralism. Essays on Nietzsche's Prelude to Philosophy's Future*, Cambridge: Cambridge University Press, 2001, pp. 63-78.

Zavatta, Benedetta, *Individuality and Beyond: Nietzsche Reads Emerson*, Oxford, 2019.

Neukantianische Autonomie
Hermann Cohens Beitrag

Myriam Bienenstock

Bei all seiner Bewunderung für Kant hat Hermann Cohen (1842-1918), das berühmte Schulhaupt des Marburger Neukantianismus, doch immer eine gewisse Distanz gegenüber dem Königsberger Philosophen beibehalten. Er glaubte, sogar in Kants Begriff der Autonomie gewisse Schwierigkeiten und Zweideutigkeiten entdecken zu können und unternahm es, den Begriff weiterzuentwickeln, teils im Rahmen des Kantischen Denkens, teils über Kant hinausgehend. Seine Weiterentwicklung des Autonomiebegriffs darf zu den stärksten Elementen seiner Lehre gerechnet werden: einer Lehre, die origineller und in historischer Hinsicht von größerer Wahrnehmungskraft ist, als viele andere Thesen, die seitdem zur Frage der Autonomie entwickelt worden sind. Die folgenden Ausführungen streben das Ziel an, die ursprüngliche Kraft der Autonomielehre Hermann Cohens nachvollziehbar zu machen und von ihr zu zeigen, dass sie keineswegs so ungenau war, wie unter begriffsgeschichtlichem Blickwinkel hätte angenommen werden können, auch wenn sie sich tatsächlich von der Lehre Kants entfernte bzw. über diese hinausgehen wollte.

Für viele Leser von Hermann Cohen sind es folgende, von Cohens Schüler Ernst Cassirer am 7. April 1918 am Grabe seines Lehrers geäußerten Sätze, welche die Autonomielehre des Marburger Philosophen, sowie dessen Bild insgesamt, bleibend geprägt haben:

> Das Wort ‚Bestimme dich aus dir selbst', das Schiller als größtes und tiefstes bezeichnet, das vielleicht jemals von einem Menschen gesprochen worden sei, wurde auch ihm zum Schlüssel der Kantischen Philosophie. Er begriff sie als die große Lehre von der Selbsttätigkeit des Geistes: von der logischen, der ethischen, der künstlerischen Spontaneität des Bewußtseins. Und damit war ihm nun zugleich der Weg vorgezeichnet, auf dem er in seinen eigenen systematischen Schriften, in der Logik der reinen Erkenntnis, in der Ethik des reinen Willens und in der Ästhetik des reinen Gefühls über Kant hinauszugehen versuchte. Der Vorrang der Aktivität vor der Passivität, des Selbständig-Geistigen vor dem Sinnlich-Dinglichen sollte rein und vollständig durchgeführt werden. Jede Berufung auf ein bloß ‚Gegebenes' sollte wegfallen …[1]

---

1 Cassirer (1994), 70f.

Bringt diese Würdigung den Leitfaden von Cassirers eigener Konzeption ausgezeichnet zum Ausdruck, wird sie den Kerngedanken des Werkes Cohens, insbesondere im Hinblick auf seine Konzeption der Ethik, dennoch weniger gerecht. Denn es war nicht die Idee der Selbstbestimmung, sondern eher diejenige der Autonomie, oder – um einen Terminus griechischen Ursprungs auf Deutsch auszudrücken – der ‚Selbstgesetzgebung', die Cohen als grundlegend für seine Ethik betrachtete, und beide Termini besitzen weder denselben Ursprung noch denselben Sinn. Cohen selber setzte die beiden Begriffe nicht gleich. Eher glaubte er, in Kants Begriff der Autonomie und insbesondere in seiner Bezeichnung der Freiheit als „Wechselbegriff der Autonomie"[2] gewisse Schwierigkeiten und Zweideutigkeiten entdecken zu können. So nahm er sich vor, diesen Begriff weiterzuentwickeln.

In diesem Beitrag wird zuerst gezeigt (I), dass ‚Selbstbestimmung' und ‚Autonomie' nicht einfach austauschbar sind bzw. als Synonyme behandelt werden dürfen, wie dies öfters geschieht. Danach wird (II) Cohens Auslegung und Weiterführung des kantischen Begriffs der Autonomie als ‚Autotelie'[3], und (III) seine eigene Auffassung des Verhältnisses der Ethik zur Politik und zum Recht erörtert: Meistens wird seine Position im Zusammenhang der damaligen Debatten um einen ‚ethischen Sozialismus' erörtert[4], doch soll in diesem Aufsatz gezeigt werden, dass diese Position auch problemlos in die heutigen Diskussionen um einen ‚postkantianischen Perfektionismus' passt und diese bereichern kann.

1. Autonomie vs. Selbstbestimmung

In der Kant-Forschung wird bis heute nicht ausreichend betont, dass Kant selber die beiden Begriffe ‚Autonomie' und ‚Selbstbestimmung' keineswegs gleichsetzte. Wenn er hin und wieder ein deutsches Äquivalent für das Fremdwort *Autonomie* benutzte, dann war das der Terminus *Selbstgesetzgebung*[5] und nicht etwa der der *Selbstbestimmung*, der in seinem Werk nur selten auftritt.

Dass Kant den Begriff ‚Selbstbestimmung' nur selten benutzt, ist leicht nachvollziehbar. Im Gegensatz zu dem alten Begriff der Autonomie, der griechischen Ursprungs ist, ist der Terminus der Selbstbestimmung, so wie er

---

2 Vgl. *AA* IV, 450.
3 Vgl. z.B. die *Ethik des reinen Willens* in Werke 7, hier: 322.
4 Vgl. hier insbesondere die Aufsatzsammlung von Holzhey (1994).
5 Zum Beispiel in der *Grundlegung zur Metaphysik der Sitten* und in Kants Vorlesungen von 1784-1785. Vgl. *AA* IV, 450; *AA* XXIX, 628 f.

heute benutzt wird, relativ neuen Datums: Vor Beginn des 19. Jahrhunderts ist er kaum aufgetreten.[6] Es sind Autoren wie Schiller und Fichte, die dem Begriff zu philosophischen Ehren verhalfen. Wenn man den Sinn verstehen will, den der Begriff ‚Selbstbestimmung' vor Kant hatte, also etwa bei Leibniz oder bei Wolff, so muss er auf die Logik und Ontologie bezogen werden, nicht jedoch auf die praktische Philosophie. Wichtig ist hierbei, dass zwar der griechische Terminus der ‚Autonomie' zunächst ein Begriff war, der vorzugsweise auf den Gebieten des Rechts und der Politik Verwendung fand – auch Kant benutzt ihn noch so – der Begriff der ‚Selbstbestimmung' aber in einen ganz anderen Zusammenhang gehört. Ausdrücke wie ‚sich bestimmen' oder auch bestimmt werden ‚durch sich', durch sich selbst, finden sich in Kontexten, in denen es sich darum handelt, die ‚Bestimmung' eines Gegenstandes oder eines Begriffes zu erklären. Einen Begriff oder einen Gegenstand bestimmen, hieß ihn begrenzen oder ihn auf gewisse Weise definieren. Es handelte sich darum, ihn durch Adjektive oder Prädikate zu beschreiben und dabei diejenigen auszuschließen, die unangemessen sind, aber alle diejenigen beizubehalten, die passen und die eine hinreichende oder vollständige Charakterisierung geben. In einem solchen Falle liegt eine Bestimmung durch sich oder durch sich selbst vor. So ging auch Kant vor, zum Beispiel wenn er in seiner *Kritik der reinen Vernunft* von den Kategorien der Modalität (möglich, wirklich, notwendig) sagt, „daß sie den Begriff, dem sie als Prädikate beigefüget werden, als Bestimmung des Objekts nicht im mindesten vermehren"[7]; oder etwa auch, wenn er in der „transzendentalen Dialektik" der *Kritik der reinen Vernunft* bekräftigt, dass die „durchgängige Bestimmung" eines Dings sich auf eine Idee oder besser gesagt auf ein Ideal der reinen Vernunft gründe, „das einzige eigentliche Ideal, dessen die menschliche Vernunft fähig ist; weil nur in diesem einzigen Falle ein an sich allgemeiner Begriff von einem Dinge durch sich selbst durchgängig bestimmt und als die Vorstellung von einem Individuum erkannt wird"[8].

So benutzt auch Fichte den Begriff, wenn er zum Beispiel in seiner *Zweiten Einleitung in die Wissenschaftslehre* aus dem Jahre 1797 daran erinnert, dass „Denken und Objecte bestimmen [...] ganz dasselbe ist; beide Begriffe identisch

---

[6] Wie Volker Gerhardt in seinem Artikel im *Historischen Wörterbuch der Philosophie* richtig feststellt, findet der deutsche Terminus der Selbstbestimmung in den philosophischen Wörterbüchern des 18. Jahrhunderts nicht einmal eine Erwähnung: Vgl. Gerhardt (1995).

[7] *KrV*, A 219; weiterhin *AA* III, 186: „Die Kategorien der Modalität haben das Besondere an sich: dass sie den Begriff, dem sie als Prädikate beigefüget werden, als Bestimmung des Objekts nicht im mindesten vermehren, sondern nur das Verhältnis zum Erkenntnisvermögen ausdrücken ..."

[8] *KrV*, A 576/B 604; *AA* III, 388.

sind" und dass „die Logik die Regeln dieser Bestimmung angibt"[9]. Er erläutert auch, diesmal in der *Ersten Einleitung* (ebenfalls aus dem Jahre 1797), dass „der Idealismus [...] die Bestimmungen des Bewusstseins aus dem Handeln der Intelligenz" erkläre; dass jedoch, um ein Bestimmtes ableiten zu können, die Intelligenz aufgefasst werden muss, wie „ein *durch sie selbst* [...] bestimmtes Handeln"[10]. Festzuhalten ist, dass auch hier die Bezeichnungen ‚Bestimmung' und ‚Bestimmung durch sich selbst' verwendet werden, um eine Erkenntnistätigkeit, also eine theoretische Tätigkeit zu erklären, nicht jedoch in einem politischen oder ethischen Kontext. Ein solcher Sachverhalt trifft selbst auf Hegel noch zu, denn wenn er sich zum Beispiel im Vorwort der *Phänomenologie des Geistes* auf den „sich bewegenden und seine Bestimmungen in sich zurücknehmenden Begriff"[11] beruft, wenn er von der „Selbstbewegung", oder wie in den *Grundlinien der Philosophie des Rechts* sogar von der „Selbstbestimmung des Begriffs"[12] spricht, dann handelt es sich dabei zunächst auch für ihn um einen Erkenntnisvorgang der Wirklichkeit: also um Logik und Ontologie und nicht um Moral und Politik. Wie Cassirer in seiner oben zitierten Rede andeutet, waren es Schiller[13], aber auch Fichte und ihr Zeitgeist, in dem sich das Wort ‚Selbstbestimmung' in eine Art Kampfbegriff verwandelte, der in allen Bereichen Verwendung finden konnte: in der Moral, aber auch in der Ästhetik und sowohl auf theoretischem, als auch auf praktischem Gebiet. Hatte Cassirer aber Recht, wenn er Cohen in dieser Hinsicht in der Nachfolge Schillers interpretierte?

Wird diese Frage nur auf der Grundlage dessen betrachtet, was Cohen ausdrücklich über Schiller sagte, wird sie wohl mit nein beantwortet werden müssen. Es ist bekannt, dass Cohen Schiller vorgeworfen hat, die Bedeutung der ästhetischen Erziehung und der Ästhetik überhaupt ‚überspannt' zu haben, indem er glaubte, der ästhetische Sinn könne zur Moral und zur Religion führen[14]. Aber es geht hier nicht nur um die Weise, wie Cohen Schiller beurteilt, sondern vielmehr um seine Bewertung des Deutschen Idealismus insgesamt. Denn Cohen war sich durchaus der zentralen Rolle bewusst, welche die Ästhetik in der Herausbildung des Deutschen Idealismus – bei Schiller aber auch über ihn hinaus – gespielt hat. „Das ist ja eben die tiefe Kraft des Idealismus", so Cohen,

---

9 *SW* I, 498.
10 *SW* I, 440f.
11 *TWA* 3, 57.
12 *TWA* 7, 33.
13 Vgl. Schillers Brief an Körner vom 18. Februar 1793: „Es ist gewiß von keinem sterblichen Menschen kein größeres Wort gesprochen worden als dieses Kantische, was zugleich der Inhalt seiner ganzen Philosophie ist: Bestimme Dich aus Dir selbst ..." (*NA* 26, 190-197).
14 Vgl. die *Ethik des reinen Willens* in *Werke* 7, 336.

„dass er auch die ästhetische Vernunft zur ästhetischen Selbstgesetzgebung zu erwecken vermag."[15] Doch gerade diese Stärke des Idealismus – von Cassirer, daran sei erinnert, hochgeschätzt – versucht Cohen in Frage zu stellen. Gegen Goethe und Schiller hebt Cohen hervor: „[...] aber ein Fehler ist es und bleibt es, die Ethik auf Ästhetik zu gründen. Das ist nichts als Heteronomie."[16] Und er geht sogar so weit zu behaupten, dass „die wahre Kunst [...] die Ethik immerdar zur Voraussetzung"[17] habe. Viele werden die Gültigkeit dieser These sicher bestreiten wollen. Welche Position im Hinblick auf diese These aber auch eingenommen wird, sie zeigt auf jeden Fall, wie weit sich die Auffassungen Cohens von denen Schillers (und auch Cassirers) unterscheiden.

Cohens Spezifizität offenbart sich noch deutlicher, wenn die Haltung untersucht wird, die er gegenüber Fichte einnahm, also gerade gegenüber demjenigen Philosophen, der sich als größter Verteidiger der Selbstbestimmung erwiesen hat. Hier geht es nicht um Fichtes politische Philosophie, also auch nicht um die Anerkennung von Fichtes „patriotischen Verdiensten", die Cohen ihm bekanntlich in seinem Aufsatz „Deutschtum und Judentum" dafür ausspricht, dass er „in der nationalen Konkretheit", „im nationalen Ich seiner Deutschheit [...] die wahrhaftige ethisch-soziale Realisierung des Idealismus der Menschheit" erkannt habe. Cohen geht sogar so weit, in Fichte „einen Höhepunkt der deutschen Philosophie"[18] zu sehen. Aber neben diesen lobenden oder zumindest apologetischen Einschätzungen Fichtes erinnert er auch daran – und dieser Teil seiner Bewertung verdient besondere Aufmerksamkeit – dass „die Ich-Philosophie Fichtes [...] ein theoretischer Rückschritt hinter Kant"[19] sei. Fichtes Philosophie des Ichs und damit die Grundlegung seiner Wissenschaftslehre sind hier von besonderem Interesse. Der Zusammenhang zwischen dieser Philosophie und der Art und Weise, wie sich Fichte darin auf die Idee der Selbstbestimmung bezieht, und seiner politischen Philosophie selbst ist weniger direkt als auf den ersten Blick angenommen werden könnte.[20] Fichtes

---

15 Ebd., 329.
16 Ebd., 330.
17 Ebd., 343.
18 *JS* II, 283.
19 Ebd., 282.
20 So ist es auffällig, dass Fichte in seinen *Reden an die deutsche Nation* von 1807/8 die ‚Selbstbestimmung' nicht ausdrücklich behandelt, obwohl dies häufig erwartet wurde. Aber wie zum Beispiel Peter L. Oesterreich (1992) in seinem Aufsatz „Aufforderung zur nationalen Selbstbestimmung" schreibt, verwirklicht er sie auf gewisse Weise schon – oder er fordert mit einer „Rhetorik der Aufforderung" zu dieser Verwirklichung auf, eine Rhetorik, die sich nicht an individuelle Subjekte, sondern an ein kollektives Subjekt richtet, an ein „Wir", das sich als solches selbst noch konstituieren muss – auch wenn Fichte sie nicht behandelt.

Philosophie des Ichs konstituiert vermutlich die bestmögliche Illustration der Konzeption, die Cassirer auf Cohen bezog: die Konzeption „von der Selbsttätigkeit des Geistes: von der logischen, der ethischen, der künstlerischen Spontaneität des Bewußtseins". Es ist Fichte (und nicht Cohen, wie es noch näher gezeigt werden wird), der als Prinzip der Philosophie – der praktischen Philosophie, die als Grundlage des ganzen Wissens konzipiert ist – das Ich setzt, welches seinem innersten Wesen nach als „Selbsttätigkeit"[21] oder auch als „Selbstbestimmen seiner selbst durch sich selbst" gedacht wird.[22] Es ist Fichte, der die Schulphilosophie und den logischen und ontologischen Sinn, den die Tradition der Schulphilosophie von Leibniz und Wolff dem Begriff der Selbstbestimmung gegeben hatte, wiederaufnimmt. Und es ist Fichte, der diesen Begriff als Grundlage seiner Philosophie setzt, die er als praktische Philosophie versteht – um ihn mit dem Begriff der ‚Selbstgesetzgebung' zu identifizieren. Denn er bezeichnet als *„Autonomie, Selbstgesetzgebung"* nicht nur die Voraussetzung eines Gesetzes, dem sich das Ich frei unterwirft, und woraus es eine Maxime seines Willens macht, nicht nur die Verwirklichung dessen, was dieses Gesetz in jedem besonderen Falle fordert, sondern vor allem auch – was den Inhalt des Gesetzes anbelangt – nichts gefordert wird, als absolute Selbständigkeit und absolute Unbestimmbarkeit. Um zu erklären, was der Begriff der *„Autonomie"* oder *„Selbstgesetzgebung"* ist, beruft er sich auf die „Selbständigkeit", das „wahre Wesen" des Ichs. Im Zentrum seiner Konzeption der Autonomie steht also das *„Selbst"* und nicht das Gesetz.[23]

---

21   Zum Beispiel, Fichte (1982), 18, § 5.
22   Vgl. zum Beispiel *SW* IV, 22.
23   Vgl. z.B. den folgenden Passus: „Man hat [...] diese Gesetzgebung *Autonomie*, Selbstgesetzgebung genannt. Sie kann in dreifacher Rücksicht so heißen. Zuvörderst, den Gedanken des Gesetzes überhaupt schon vorausgesetzt, und das Ich lediglich als freie Intelligenz betrachtet, wird das Gesetz *überhaupt* ihr nur dadurch zum Gesetze, dass sie darauf reflectirt, und mit Freiheit sich ihm unterwirft, d.i. selbstthätig es zur unverbrüchlichen Maxime alles ihres Wollens macht; und hinwiederum, was in jedem *besonderen* Falle dieses Gesetz erfordere, muss sie erst [...] durch die Urtheilskraft finden, und abermals frei sich die Aufgabe geben, den gefundenen Begriff zu realisiren. Sonach ist die ganze moralische Existenz nichts anderes, als eine ununterbrochene Gesetzgebung des vernünftigen Wesens an sich selbst [...] – Dann, was den Inhalt des Gesetzes anbelangt, wird nichts gefordert, als absolute Selbstständigkeit, absolute Unbestimmbarkeit durch irgend etwas außer dem Ich. Die materielle Bestimmung des Willens nach dem Gesetze wird sonach lediglich aus uns selbst hergenommen; und alle *Heteronomie*, Entlehnung der Bestimmungsgründe von irgend etwas außer uns, ist geradezu gegen das Gesetz. – Endlich, der ganze Begriff unserer nothwendigen Unterwerfung unter ein Gesetz entsteht lediglich durch absolut freie Reflexion des Ich auf sich selbst in seinem wahren Wesen, d.h. in seiner Selbständigkeit." (*SW* IV, 56 f.).

Gerade dieser Aspekt ist hier entscheidend: es wird nämlich deutlich, dass Fichtes Konzeption derjenigen Cohens ausgesprochen antithetisch gegenübersteht. Cohen verwischt niemals die Grenzen zwischen Autonomie und Selbstbestimmung; und es ist nicht die Idee der Selbstbestimmung, sondern eher diejenige der Autonomie oder Selbstgesetzgebung, die für ihn die Grundlage seiner praktischen Philosophie bildet. Zwar bekräftigt auch er, in seiner *Ethik des reinen Willens*, dass dem Begriff der Selbstbestimmung ein „umfassender Sinn"[24] gegeben werden solle. Wenn aber näher untersucht wird, was er unter Selbstbestimmung versteht, dann wird deutlich, dass er damit meint, es sei unzulässig, die Selbstbestimmung auf die Handlung eines isolierten Individuums einzuschränken, welches für sich selbst entscheiden müsste. Das ‚Selbst' von dem gesagt wird, dass es sich selbst ‚bestimmt', ist immer dasjenige eines Individuums, das eine bestimmte, einzelne Handlung auszuführen hat: es ist gerade die Einzelheit der Handlung, welche die Selbstbestimmung im Unterschied zur Autonomie ausmacht. Aber niemand kann ohne Selbstbewusstsein handeln, und das Selbstbewusstsein eines jeden kann nur im Verhältnis zu anderen erweckt werden: zu denjenigen, die ihn erziehen und zu denjenigen, mit denen er in einer Gesellschaft und in einem Staat zu einer historisch bestimmten Periode zusammenlebt. Die bestimmte, auszuführende Handlung darf also nicht wie eine vereinzelte, isolierte Handlung betrachtet werden, sondern muss vielmehr wie eine historisch verortete, politische und soziale Tat und darüber hinaus vor allem wie eine rechtlich begründete, eine ethische Tat verstanden werden.

Was die Selbstbestimmung begründet, ist die Autonomie. Und was nach Cohen für die Idee der Autonomie von Bedeutung ist, ist der *nomos*, das Gesetz, auf dessen Basis allein das ‚Selbst' verstanden werden muss. Im Hinblick auf diese Frage ist Cohens These radikal: Autonomie einklagen, besteht nicht etwa darin zu verkünden, dass das Gesetz vom Selbst, vom Subjekt oder vom als Subjekt verstandenen Individuum, *ausgeht*. Eher handelt es sich darum, zu bekräftigen, dass das Selbst, das Subjekt, durch das Gesetz gebildet ist, oder besser, durch das Gesetz gebildet werden soll: durch das moralische Gesetz, das Gebot. Der Hauptirrtum, den die meisten derjenigen begehen, welche die Autonomie fordern – Kant inbegriffen – sei es tatsächlich gewesen, das Subjekt, das Selbst, auf welches die Vorsilbe ‚auto' im Begriff der ‚Autonomie' verweist, als ein schon vorhandenes zu betrachten, als eines, das da und vorausgesetzt sei. Das heißt als ein Subjekt, welches sich nur noch in seinem ethischen Handeln auszudrücken und zu entfalten bräuchte, in Handlungen, die seine Manifestationen wären. Aber das Selbst ist keineswegs im

---

24 Werke 7, 359.

Voraus gegeben: es muss sich zunächst erst herstellen und dies kann es nur *in der Gesetzgebung*, in der Legislation im aktiven Sinne des Wortes oder sogar im wörtlichen Sinne als ‚Gebung des Gesetzes':

> Die Handlung ist nicht mehr lediglich die Entfaltung des Selbsts; sondern sie ist bedingt durch die Gesetzgebung, welche die Gesetzgebung des Selbst ist, so dass auch das Selbst bedingt ist durch die Gesetzgebung. Also *die Selbstgesetzgebung ist nicht etwa die Gesetzgebung aus dem Selbst, sondern zum Selbst.* Auf die Gesetzgebung kommt es an; in ihr erst bezeugt sich das Selbst; in ihr erzeugt es sich. Der Gedanke der Autonomie geht also nicht dahin, dass das Gesetz vom Selbst ausgehen müsse.[25]

Zweifellos sind diejenigen zahlreich, die Cohen nicht so weit folgen wollen, dass alle wirkliche Autonomie letztlich auf dem moralischen Gesetz, dem Sittengebot basiert, das heißt auf einem *Gebot*, einem Imperativ; dass man also umso autonomer, der Autonomie umso näher sei, wenn man die Gebote befolgte, anstatt sich lediglich an dasjenige zu halten, was man für aus dem ‚Selbst', aus seiner eigenen Person oder Subjektivität, sich begründend annimmt. Cohen weiß übrigens ganz genau, dass er in diesem Punkte weiter geht als Kant. Aber er erinnert schon am Anfang seiner Analyse[26] daran, dass das 'Selbst', auf welches Kant das Gesetz bezieht, nicht mit dem ‚Subjekt' im psychologischen Sinne des Begriffs vermischt werden sollte: wenn Kant in diesem Zusammenhang vom ‚Selbst' oder vom ‚Selbstbewusstsein' spricht, dann benutzt er diese Begriffe nicht in dem psychologischen oder anthropologischen Sinne, in welchem sie in der neueren Zeit gewöhnlich gebraucht werden. Er denkt eher an die Idee, auf welche schon Platon das ‚Selbst' bezog: an die Vernunft, das heißt an ein *a priori*. Die Vorgehensweise ist hier eher metaphysisch als psychologisch. Aber selbst der Terminus ‚metaphysisch' ist als Beschreibung nicht angemessen: die Metaphysik, die dem *a priori* der Erkenntnis nachspürt, läuft nach Cohen Gefahr, in die Psychologie zurückzufallen, wenn sie sich nicht als transzendentale Vorgehensweise begreift, deren ganzes Ziel oder deren Zweck es sei, die Erkenntnis und die Moral zu begründen. Dies ist genau der Vorwurf, den Cohen gegen Fichte erheben sollte, als er ihm vorwarf, das Transzendentale dem Metaphysischen anzugleichen. Diese Assimilation führt für ihn zum Psychologismus und würde Fichtes „Rückfall in die Scholastik und den Cartesianismus" erklären, so wie „jenen abenteuerlichen Subjectivismus, mit seinem scholastischen Gebaren".[27]

---

25 Ebd., 339 (Cohens Hervorhebung; M.B.).
26 Vgl. ebd., 327f.
27 *Werke* 2, 289.

Diesen Vorwurf hatte schon Kant formuliert.[28] In seinem *Opus postumum* – den Notizen, die Kant genau in den Jahren niederschrieb, in welchen Fichte an seiner *Wissenschaftslehre* arbeitete[29], hatte er auch eine ausführliche Überlegung über das Wesen der Transzendentalphilosophie in ihren Bezügen zur Metaphysik entfaltet.[30] Hier kann die schwierige Frage nicht ausführlich beantwortet werden, wie Kant – der alte Kant seiner letzten Schaffensperiode – diese dunkle Idee eines „Überschritts" versteht, die er in seinem *Opus postumum* so oft wiederholt, womit der Überschritt von der Metaphysik zur Transzendentalphilosophie gemeint ist. Angemerkt sei lediglich, dass sich die Terminologie, die er in diesen späten Aufzeichnungen benutzt, wandelt. Häufig benutzt er nun nicht nur den Begriff der Autonomie, sondern auch denjenigen der

---

28 Bereits im Jahre 1799, in einer Erklärung, die er in der *Allgemeinen Literaturzeitung* veröffentlichen ließ und mit welcher er Fichte sehr verletzte, hatte Kant die *Wissenschaftslehre* Fichtes als „gänzlich unhaltbar" beurteilt und hervorgehoben, dass „reine Wissenschaftslehre nichts mehr oder weniger ist als bloße *Logik*, welche mit ihren Prinzipien sich nicht zum Materialen des Erkenntnisses versteigt, sondern vom Inhalte derselben als *reine Logik* abstrahirt, zu welcher ein reales Object herauszuklauben vergebliche und daher auch nie versuchte Arbeit ist, sondern wo, wenn es die Transcendental-Philosophie gilt, allererst zur Metaphysik übergeschritten werden muss." (*AA* XII/3, 396 f.) Fichte war über diese Kritik völlig empört: er sollte Kant daraufhin der Senilität beschuldigen und er hatte sogar hinzugefügt, dass der Alte in der Tat unfähig geworden sei, seine eigene Philosophie [die Kantische] noch zu verstehen. Wie Fichte Schelling schrieb, der ihm darin ganz zustimmte, „bezeichnet *meinem Sprachgebrauch nach*, das Wort Wissenschaftslehre gar nicht die Logik, sondern die Transzendental-Philosophie oder Metaphysik selbst" (*GA* III/4, 76). Und es ist Fichte zuzustimmen, dass Kant zweifellos zu weit geht, wenn er ihn beschuldigt, die Transzendentalphilosophie auf die reine Logik zu reduzieren und aus dieser Logik einen wirklichen Gegenstand abzuleiten.

29 Bei dem *Opus postumum* handelt es sich um eine Zusammenstellung von sehr späten Notizen, die aus der Zeit nach 1796 stammen, also nach der ersten *Wissenschaftslehre* Fichtes (1794-1795), und teilweise auch nach der praktischen Philosophie dieses Autors, d.h. nach der *Grundlage des Naturrechts* (1796-1797), und nach dem *System der Sittenlehre* (1798). Kant spielt sogar zweimal auf Schelling an und auf dessen *System des transzendentalen Idealismus* (1800): Vgl. *AA* XXI, 87, 97.

30 Wenn die Metaphysik, so schreibt er dort, gegebene „Begriffe" befragt oder analysiert, wie denjenigen von Gott – dabei nachforscht, welche Inhalte in diesen Begriffen stecken, und wie sie sich bestimmen – so beschäftige sich die Transzendentalphilosophie vielmehr mit der Untersuchung, was synthetische Urteile a priori ermöglicht, und auf welche Prinzipien sie sich gründen. „In der moralisch//practischen Vernunft ist das Princip der Erkenntnis meiner Pflichten als Gebote (*praecepta*) d.i. nicht nach der Regel die dem Subject zum G. macht sondern die aus der Freyheit hervorgeht sich selbst vorschreibt und doch gleich als ob es ihm ein Anderer und Höherer als Person dem Subject zur Regel machte (*dictamen rationis practicae*) enthalten und denen es zu gehorchen durch seine eigene Vernunft sich genötigt fühlt (nicht analytisch nach dem Princip der Identität sondern synthetisch als einem Überschritt von Metaphysik zur Transc: Philos.)." (*AA* 22, 129).

Selbstbestimmung, den er in seinen früheren Schriften nur selten gebrauchte[31] und bekräftigt so, dass die ganze Transzendentalphilosophie „Autonomie" sei[32]; oder genauer, dass sie geregelt werde durch das „Princip der Autonomie", „das Gesetzgebende Princip für alle Philosophie". Es gibt, so schreibt er, eine „Autonomie der theoretisch//speculativen in Verbindung mit der moralisch// practischen Vernunft zum Behuf möglicher Erfahrung welche (als Princip) das Ganze der Transc.Ph. ausmacht."[33] Er erweitert also den Sinn des Terminus, indem er ihn nicht nur zur Charakterisierung der Tätigkeit des Subjekts in der praktischen Philosophie, also in einem moralischen Sinne verwendet, sondern auch um die Tätigkeit des Subjekts in der theoretischen Philosophie, der Erkenntnistheorie zu charakterisieren.

Bemerkenswert ist auch, dass er die Autonomie auf die Vernunft bezieht: auf die Vernunft als Kraft der Ideen im Kantischen Sinne, das heißt der „Formen"; oder auch auf das denkende Subjekt als „Vernunft". Dieser Aspekt ist ganz besonders wichtig, wenn man verstehen will, wie er den Gedanken der ‚Selbstbestimmung' benutzt; denn er benutzt ihn als von der Vernunft ausgehend, also von dem Vermögen der Ideen – und damit nicht vom Verstand oder vom Selbstbewusstsein. Wenn er die Transzendentalphilosophie zum „System des reinen Idealismus der Selbstbestimmung des denkenden Subjekts" macht, dann hebt er auch stark hervor, dass es sich dabei um einen *Idealismus* handelt und dass sich das Subjekt nicht durch „bloße Begriffe" selbst bestimme, sondern durch *Ideen* – die Ideen der Vernunft, das heißt die „Gesetze des Denkens", die es sich selbst vorschreibt. Wenn Kant von der Transzendentalphilosophie schrieb, dass sie die „Selbstbestimmung des denkenden Subjekts" sei, so wollte er damit zum Ausdruck bringen, sie sei

> das Bewusstseyn des Vermögens vom System seiner Ideen in theoretischer so wohl als practischer Hinsicht Urheber zu seyn. Ideen sind nicht bloße Begriffe sondern Gesetze des Denkens die das Subjekt ihm selbst vorschreibt

und in diesem Sinne ist die Selbstbestimmung „Autonomie".[34] – „Urheber vom System seiner Ideen", „Urheber seiner selbst" zu sein, „sich gleichsam selbst

---

31 Vergleiche aber die These, die er in seiner *Anthropologie* aufstellt, die These nach welcher die *„Begierde (appetitio) Selbstbestimmung"* sei, die „Selbstbestimmung der Kraft eines Subjekts durch die Vorstellung von etwas Künftigen, als einer Wirkung derselben" (*AA* VII, 251): es ist nicht der *Willen*, auf den er die Autonomie bezieht, sondern die *Macht* oder die *Kraft*, die sich irgendwie *selbst bestimmt*.
32 Vgl. z.B. *AA* XXI, 106f.
33 *Opus postumum*, in *AA* XXI, 106-110, hier: 109.
34 *AA* XXI, 93.

machen"³⁵: so enthalten diese Seiten des *Opus postumum* eine vollständige Reflexion – und gerade darin dürfte seine Innovation liegen – über die Frage, in welchem Sinne das Subjekt „sich selbst macht"; wie es sich – weit davon entfernt, einen gegebenen Gegenstand bloß mit Hilfe der Wahrnehmung zu empfangen – ihn vielmehr als „Gegenstand" erst konstituiert, und sich dadurch selbst schafft, sich durch seine Ideen als Gegenstand konstituiert – und dadurch ebenfalls als denkendes Wesen.³⁶

Mit diesem Sprachgebrauch setzt Kant sicher die Diskussion mit Fichte fort, der erklärt hatte, es sei zum Aufweis der Wirklichkeit der Freiheit keineswegs nötig einen Umweg über den kategorischen Imperativ und über das Moralgesetz zu machen. Sich als denkendes oder verstehendes Wesen zu denken oder auch als sich selbst bestimmend, als Selbstbestimmung, das wäre tatsächlich das gleiche wie sich als frei zu fassen: die Intelligenz, schreibt Fichte, würde „bloß dadurch, dass sie sich als Intelligenz fasst, frei"³⁷. Von der Idee der Selbstbestimmung glaubte Fichte den Begriff des *Sollens* ableiten zu können,

---

35 „Transc.[endental] Phil.[osophie] ist nicht ein Aggregat sondern ein System nicht von objectiven Begriffen sondern von subjectiven Ideen welche die Vernunft sich selbst schafft, und zwar nicht hypothetisch (problematisch oder assertorisch) sondern apodictisch indem sie sich selbst schafft. Transc.[endental] Phil.[osophie] ist das Vermögen des sich Selbstbestimmenden Subjects durch den systematischen Inbegriff der Ideen welche a priori die durchgängige Bestimmung desselben als Objects (die Existenz desselben) zum Problem machen sich selbst als in der Anschauung gegeben zu constituiren" (*AA* XXI, 93).

36 Denn es handelt sich hier durchaus darum, sich als denkendes Wesen zu schaffen, und nicht nur als bewusstes oder gar selbstbewusstes Wesen. Die Transzendentalphilosophie, welche die „Selbstbestimmung des denkenden Subjekts" behandelt, setzt das Bewusstsein oder das Selbstbewusstsein – das „Subjekt" als Bewusstsein von sich in gewisser Weise voraus. Dies ist aber nicht ihr Gegenstand. Im *Opus postumum* widmet Kant zwar auch den Fragen des Bewusstseins, des Selbstbewusstseins – oder um dies noch anders auszudrücken, der Frage des cogito, der Frage nach der Bedeutung des Satzes 'Ich denke darum bin ich' zahlreiche und umfangreiche Ausführungen. Aber was er dort schreibt, ist, dass der „Akt der Apperception", durch den ich mich selbst vorstelle, dieser Akt, durch den sich das Subjekt selbst zum Gegenstand macht, „blos logisch" und „ohne Bestimmung des Gegenstandes" ist; dass es ein Akt ist, der „allem Urtheil" und damit in gewissem Sinne jeder Erkenntnistätigkeit voraus geht (z.B. *AA* XXII, 89f.) Für ihn geht das Selbstbewusstsein der Erkenntnis oder dem Denken voraus: es ist eine Bedingung des Denkens. Um eine Formulierung Bernard Bourgeois' aufzugreifen, so ist das ‚ich denke' für Kant dasjenige, was alles Denken ‚bedingt' (*conditionne*) und nicht, wie es bei Fichte der Fall sein wird, dasjenige was dieses Denken ‚bestimmt' (*détermine*): die Transzendentalphilosophie Kants ist eine Philosophie des ‚Bedingens' (*du conditionner*), nicht eine des ‚Bestimmens' (*de la détermination*) (vgl. Bourgeois (2000)). Diese These bleibt gültig, selbst wenn Kant in seiner letzten Schaffensperiode – derjenigen des *Opus postumum* – die Terminologie der Bestimmung und der Selbstbestimmung benutzt.

37 *SW* IV, 36.

als „absolutes kategorisches Sollen"; also den Begriff einer Regel: „es soll seyn, schlechthin, weil es seyn soll". Die Reflexion über die Selbstbestimmung des Selbst durch sich selbst, das heißt über das Wollen führte für Fichte von selbst zum Bewusstsein des Moralgesetzes, das heißt zum kategorischen Imperativ. Kant hatte etwas ganz anderes sagen wollen – und wenn er in seinem *Opus postumum* so sehr auf dem indirekten Charakter des Beweises der Freiheit, auf dem Vorrang des kategorischen Imperativs vor der Freiheit beharrte, so könnte darin sehr wohl eine Antwort auf Fichte gesehen werden:

> Nicht der Begriff der Freiheit begründet den categorischen Imperativ sondern dieser begründet zuerst den Begriff der Freyheit. – Der Pflicht//Begriff geht noch vor der Freyheit vorher u. beweiset die Realität der Freyheit – Die Möglichkeit der Freyheit kann direct nicht bewiesen [werden], sondern nur indirect durch die Möglichkeit des categorischen Pflichtimperativ der gar keiner Triebfedern der Natur bedarf ...[38]

Die Autonomie wird auf der Grundlage des kategorischen Imperativs, der Idee der ‚Pflicht', des Moralgesetzes als ‚Pflicht' verstanden; und es verhält sich ebenso mit dem Begriff Gottes: die Idee Gottes als ein moralisches Wesen entsteht in uns nur auf der Grundlage des kategorischen Imperativs, wie es Kant zum Beispiel in folgender Textstelle hervorhebt:

> Es giebt zweyerley Arten wie die Menschen das Daseyn Gottes postuliren; Sie sagen bisweilen: Es ist ein Göttlicher *Richter* und *Rächer* denn die Bosheit und *Verbrechen* erfordern Vertilgung dieser Abscheulichen Race. – Andererseits denkt sich die Vernunft ein *Verdienst* dessen der Mensch fähig ist sich selbst in eine höhere *Classe* nämlich sich selbst gesetzgebender Wesen (durch moralisch//practische Vernunft) setzen zu können und sich über alle blos sinnenfähige Wesen setzen zu können und einen *Beruf* es zu thun und ist als ein solcher nicht ein blos *hypothetisches* Ding sondern eine Bestimmung darin zu treten: von seinem Range selbst Urheber zu seyn d.i. verpflichtet und dabey sich selbst verpflichtend zu seyn.[39]

Hier wird ganz deutlich, was Autonomie für Kant bedeutet: eine „*Zwangspflicht*"; „verpflichtet [zu sein] und doch dabey sich selbst verpflichtend". Kant hatte dies schon seit seiner *Grundlegung zur Metaphysik der Sitten* bekräftigt, wenn er erklärte, dass sich der moralische Imperativ an seinem imperativen Charakter erkennen lässt, am *Sollen* – das die Form eines ‚du sollst' annimmt, also einen Zwang darstellt; und dass gerade an seiner Legalität seine Universalität erkennbar wird. Die Fassung des kategorischen Imperativs als Autonomie,

---

38 AA XXII, 60, 52, 53.
39 Ebd., 117f.

und die Grundlegung in der Freiheit kommen hier bekanntlich erst ganz am Ende zum Tragen.

2. Autonomie als Autotelie: ein Reich der Zwecke

Hermann Cohen hat also nicht ganz Unrecht, wenn er in seiner Studie *Kants Begründung der Ethik* bedauert, dass Kant in seiner *Grundlegung zur Metaphysik der Sitten* von der Freiheit und der „eigenen Gesetzgebung des Willens" gesagt habe, „beides seien Autonomie, mithin Wechselbegriffe". Kant hatte sofort hinzugefügt, dass „eben um deswillen einer nicht dazu gebraucht werden kann, um den anderen zu erklären."[40] Aber die Gefahr blieb bestehen, dass gerade dieser Fehler begangen, dass die Freiheit also zur Erklärung und Verdeutlichung der Autonomie benutzt werde. Gegen diesen Irrtum, der also von Fichte begangen wurde, betont Cohen, so zum Beispiel in seinem Artikel über „Autonomie und Freiheit" (1900), wie falsch es sei, die Freiheit bei Kant als einen Grundsatz der Ethik zu betrachten, der seinem Status nach dem Prinzip der Kausalität in den Naturwissenschaften entspräche; und er erinnert daran, dass diese Idee der Freiheit erst in der mittelalterlichen Ethik, und in der christlichen Welt, ihre Bedeutung erlangte, wenn sie nämlich gewissermaßen „der Ausdruck und der Wertmesser für den Anteil [wird], den die Religion an der Philosophie erobern und behaupten möchte. Mehr aber soll die Freiheit nicht besagen und nicht bedeuten dürfen".[41] Für ihn ist der Begriff der Freiheit lediglich „der historische Ursprungsbegriff der Autonomie".[42]

Die Freiheit kann nicht als Prinzip der Ethik dienen und es wäre falsch, sie gewissermaßen als ›Ursache‹ einer Handlung zu betrachten – oder auch, um einen Ausdruck aufzugreifen, der von Kant stammt – als „das Vermögen, die Handlung ‚von selbst anzufangen'."[43]

„*Wo aber ist dieses Selbst?*", fragt Cohen in seinem langen Aufsatz über „Religion und Sittlichkeit" aus dem Jahre 1907:

> Ist es etwa schon da? Dann wäre es ja die absolute Substanz, die von der dogmatischen Seite behauptet, hier aber kritisch bestritten wird. Und wenn es schon da wäre, dann wäre auch die Freiheit schon da, die in ihm besteht, wie es in ihr. Dann wäre die Freiheit nicht, was sie doch allein sein soll, eine Aufgabe. Wenn aber die Freiheit nur die Idee einer Aufgabe sein kann, und nicht

---

40   *AA* IV, 450.
41   *JS* III, 37.
42   Ebd.
43   *KrV*, A534/B562.

die Kausalität eines Naturvermögens, so kann auch das Selbst nur als Aufgabe zu denken sein, wenn es doch nur in dieser Aufgabe der Freiheit sein Sein hat.[44]

Die Freiheit als „eine Aufgabe" zu denken, würde bedeuten, sie als „Zweck" zu denken. Und es ist gerade der Idee des „Zweckes", der Cohen die Aufgabe zuweisen möchte, die Ethik zu begründen: „Diese regulative Bedeutung der Zweckidee bildet die Hauptaufgabe einer Begründung der Ethik", sagte er schon im Jahre 1877, in *Kants Begründung der Ethik* (1877).[45] Diese Aufgabe versteht er ganz anders als Fichte, denn es handelt sich für ihn darum, den Imperativ der Autonomie nicht auf die Selbstbestimmung eines „Selbst" zu beziehen, das wesentlich frei konzipiert sei, sondern vielmehr um die Konstituierung eines „Reichs der Zwecke", oder anders ausgedrückt einer „Gemeinschaft autonomer Zwecke", einer „Gemeinschaft von Gesetzen"[46]. Die Autonomie ist „Autotelie":

> Das Sittengesetz hat sich als identisch herausgestellt mit der Idee, der Maxime, dem Gesichtspunkt der Freiheit. Denn diese, als Verfassungsgesetz gedacht, ergibt jene Gemeinschaft autonomer Wesen, deren regulative Realität wir als den Inhalt des Sittengesetzes erkannt haben. Damit aber war die Identität der Freiheit und des Endzwecks gegeben. Denn nur absolute Zwecke können jene eine autonome Gemeinde bilden. Damit ist hinwiederum unzweifelhaft gegeben der Begriff des Endzweckes als einer Art von Endgesetz; der Gedanke von einer Erfüllung alles Denkens durch die Erkenntnis dieser Autotelie; der Gedanke von dem Primat der praktischen Vernunft[47].

Die Freiheit „unter dem Grundgesetz der Autonomie" zu denken, heißt, die Freiheit als eine Idee zu denken, im platonischen Sinne des Begriffs. In seinem Artikel über „Autonomie und Freiheit" rückt Cohen diese Idee sehr nahe an Platons Idee des Guten heran und betont, dass die Idee der Autonomie an der Platonischen Idee des Guten vorgebildet sei, die bereits für Platon die Grundlage der Ethik bildete: „... eine Idee, keine sinnliche Realität. [...] Eine Idee, das heißt aber nicht: ein Hirngespinst, ein frommer Gedanke; sondern das will sagen, eine Aufgabe, und *immerdar Aufgabe*."[48]

Diese Aufgabe bezieht er auf die Sittlichkeit und hebt „die überall durchwirkende ethische Tendenz und Kraft der christlichen Gottesidee"[49] stark hervor. Der Grund, weshalb er die Idee der Autonomie dem Christentum

---

44 *JS* III, 149f.
45 *Werke* 2, 110.
46 Ebd., 227.
47 Ebd., 288.
48 *JS* III, 40f.
49 Ebd., 134f.

annäherte, ist aber wesentlich kulturgeschichtlicher Art: Ohne die Idee der Menschwerdung Gottes fehle uns nämlich die Möglichkeit, die Autonomie des Sittengesetzes geschichtlich zu verstehen. Diese Lehre hat eine „kulturgeschichtliche Mission"[50] erfüllt, in dem Maße, wie sie es erlaubt hat zu verstehen, „daß die Sittlichkeit das Werk des Menschen sein müsse."[51] Auch betont Cohen, dass es keinen Widerspruch zwischen dieser Idee und dem jüdischen Gottesbegriff gibt, denn dieser ist wesentlich ein ethischer Begriff: für den jüdischen Monotheismus ist und bleibt

> das Wesen Gottes [...] das Wesen der menschlichen Sittlichkeit. Und dieses Wesen der menschlichen Sittlichkeit hat die strenge Bedeutung: daß der Mensch seine Sittlichkeit selbst sich zu erschaffen, zu erbauen, zu erhalten, und daher auch zu verantworten habe.[52]

Es gäbe keinen Widerspruch zwischen dieser jüdischen Konzeption der Sittlichkeit und der christlichen Konzeption, und Cohen hebt „die überall durchwirkende ethische Tendenz und Kraft der christlichen Gottesidee" stark hervor.[53] Was den jüdischen Gottesbegriff im Gegensatz zur christlichen Konzeption charakterisiert, ist für ihn vielmehr, dass er sich in jener ethischen Konzeption „erschöpfe".[54] Die Frage nach dem Wesen Gottes sei für das Judentum nicht zentral, wie sie es aber im Christentum ist.

Diese ethische Konzeption des Judentums lässt sich überall in Cohens Werk wiederfinden, bis hin zu seinen allerletzten Schriften. Und es ist von daher wohl nicht überflüssig an dieser Stelle erneut hervorzuheben, dass der Begriff der Autonomie für ihn nicht nur kein Problem, sondern vielmehr den Grundinhalt seiner Konzeption bildet. Für die Ethik des Judentums, wie für Kant, soll

> [d]ie Sittlichkeit [...] als ein Gesetz zu denken sein, welches ohne Ausnahme für jeden Menschen und von jedem Menschen gültig ist. Dieses Gesetz soll zwar auf der Selbstgesetzgebung (Autonomie) der Vernunft beruhen; aber die Vernunft darf keine andere Beziehung zum Willen einnehmen, als dass sie ihm ein allgemeines Gesetz auferlegt. Wir dürfen nicht ‚Voluntäre der Sittlichkeit' sein. Es ist, als ob Kant diesen Ausdruck von einem jüdischen Philosophen und im Talmud selbst vernommen hätte. ‚Grösser der unter dem Gebot handelt als der ohne Gebot'.

---

50   JS II, 76.
51   JS III, 136.
52   Ebd., 134f.
53   Ebd.
54   Ebd., 135: „so erschöpft sich der jüdische Gottesbegriff in der ethischen Bedeutung der Gottesidee."

Denjenigen, die ihm doch einen grundlegenden Unterschied zwischen dem Gesetzesbegriff des Judentums und dem kantischen Begriff entgegenhalten möchten, antwortet Cohen, dass der Unterschied zwar wesentlich sei – bei Kant gründet sich die Autonomie auf der menschlichen Vernunft – dass aber auch für Kant „Gott der Urheber und der Bürge des Sittengesetzes" sei[55].

3. Autonomie und ethischer Sozialismus

Zur Erhellung der Bedeutung und Tragweite dieser Erklärung ist Cohens allererstes Gespräch mit Friedrich Albert Lange (1828-1875) zweifellos am besten geeignet: Auf den Einwand Langes – seit jeher Sozialist, Autor eines viel beachteten Pamphlets *Zur Arbeiterfrage*[56] und einer noch viel berühmteren *Geschichte des Materialismus*[57], dank dessen Unterstützung Cohen seine erste Stelle als ‚außerordentlicher Professor' erhielt –, dass beide jedenfalls vom Christentum wohl sehr verschiedene Vorstellungen hatten, hatte Cohen geantwortet:

> Nein, sagte ich: Denn was Sie Christentum nennen, nenne ich prophetisches Judentum. Und sogleich war innige Übereinstimmung unter uns hergestellt. [...] So hat der ethische Sozialismus uns mit einem Schlage über die Schranken unserer Religionen hinweg geeinigt.[58]

Der „Gott", auf welchen sich Kant Hermann Cohen zufolge berufen würde, ist also der ‚Gott' des Christentums genauso wie der des ‚prophetischen Judentums' – und es ist zum allerersten als „Urheber" und „Bürge des Sittengesetzes", dass dieser Gott nötig wäre. Der Einigungspunkt beider Religionen sei aber nicht nur allgemein die Ethik, sondern genauer der „ethische Sozialismus".

Cohens Ausarbeitung der Kantischen Autonomieauffassung steht tatsächlich im Zeichen eines dezidiert politischen, ethischen Sozialismus. Besonders deutlich ist in dieser Hinsicht seine „Einleitung mit kritischem Nachtrag" (erste Auflage, 1896) zur neunten Auflage der *Geschichte des Materialismus* von Friedrich Albert Lange, in welcher Cohen so weit geht zu schreiben, dass Kant „der wahre und wirkliche Urheber des deutschen Sozialismus" gewesen

---

55   Die genannten Ausführungen stammen aus einem Vortrag, den Cohen im Jahre 1910 über die „Inneren Beziehungen der Kantischen Philosophie zum Judentum" gehalten hat: vgl. *Werke* 15, 311-345, hier: 324ff.
56   Vgl. Lange (1865/1910).
57   Vgl. Lange (1866).
58   *Werke* 5, 104.

sei – und dies dank derjenigen Formulierung des kategorischen Imperativs, welche „*die Idee der Menschheit* als seinen Inhalt erklärt", und „den Menschen als *Selbstzweck* von allem unterscheidet, was ‚bloß Mittel' sei".[59] Auch in seiner *Ethik des reinen Willens* (erste Fassung, 1904) hat Cohen behauptet, dass die zweite und insbesondere die dritte Fassung des kategorischen Imperativs in Kants *Grundlegung zur Metaphysik der Sitten* „in herrlicher Klarheit [...] die Idee der Menschheit und die politische Idee des Sozialismus" deklarieren:

> *Die Idee der Menschheit bedeutet den Zweckvorzug der Menschheit.* Der Zweckbegriff, den jede Idee für ein bestimmtes Problem zu vertreten hat, kommt hier zu inhaltlicher Anwendung. Die Menschheit wird durch den Zweck bestimmt. [...] *Das ist der neue Sinn der Freiheit.* [...] Kein Zweck darf als sittlich gelten, für den der Mensch, der eine wie jeder andere, nur als Werkzeug zu arbeiten hätte; in dem er nicht vielmehr den Zweck seines eigenen Daseins, seines eigenen Begriffs vollzöge; in dem er nicht als Endzweck fungierte. *Die Idee des Zweckvorzugs der Menschheit wird dadurch zur Idee des Sozialismus, dass jeder Mensch als Endzweck, als Selbstzweck definiert wird.*[60]

Über einen langen Zeitraum wurde Cohens „Einleitung mit kritischem Nachtrag" (1896) zur neunten Neuausgabe von Langes *Geschichte des Materialismus* so gelesen, wie Eduard Bernstein (1850-1932) es tat – und dann als ‚revisionistisch' verurteilt wurde. Dies wegen ihrer grundsätzlichen, radikalen Opposition zum ‚Materialismus', welcher den politischen Sozialismus jener Epoche kennzeichnete[61], und dessen Neigung, „auf die schiefe Ebene der Revolution hinüberzugleiten"[62]. Cohen selber hat die revolutionäre Option aber keineswegs durchgängig verneint und es ist kein Zufall, dass einige seiner treuesten Anhänger ‚rote Kantianer' genannt wurden[63]; doch jenseits dieser Debatte[64] lohnt es sich, seinen neukantianischen Begriff des Sozialismus wieder in Betracht zu ziehen, zumal er nicht nur eine eigenständige Konzeption des Sozialismus darstellt, sondern auch bis zum Begriff der ‚Gesellschaft' zurückgreift, in welchem Cohen die Ankündigung des Sozialismus erblickt:

> Schon die *societas*, die in der römischen Rechtssprache des Kompagniegeschäft bedeutet, ist in der Stoa die *Societas generis humani*, aus welcher in dem späteren

---

59 Ebd., 111-113.
60 *Werke* 7, 319-323. Vgl. dazu van der Linden (1994).
61 Vgl. *Werke* 5, 115f.
62 Ebd., 117.
63 Insbesondere Karl Vorländer (1860-1928) und Franz Staudinger (1849-1921), vgl. Holzhey (2004), 81.
64 Vgl. über diese Debatte Holzhey (1994), S. 8-15 und Sieg (1994), 225-234.

Gelehrtenlatein die *socialitas* sich abzweigte. Während die Verbindung von Menschen zu einer Korporation als *universitas* sich bestimmte und gliederte, fließt in der *societas* der moralische, der revolutionäre Blutstropfen, auch wo sie nur ein Rechtsverhältnis bedeutet: *societas jus quodammodo fraternitatis in se habet*. Und die Assoziation bildet auch rein juristisch ein Moment des Fortschritts im Recht (...).[65]

Wenn Cohen den Begriff der Gesellschaft auf denjenigen der Brüderlichkeit (*fraternitas*) bezieht, dann deshalb, weil er die Verbindung mit rechtlichen Assoziationen verdeutlichen will, wie es auch Ferdinand Lassalle (1825-1864) getan hatte, an diesem Punkt von Fichte und sogar von Hegel inspiriert, den Cohen in diesem Kontext zitiert[66], was er sonst doch selten tat. Geht es darum, den Sozialismus zu rechtfertigen, ist Hegel also kein ‚toter Hund' gewesen, nicht einmal für Hermann Cohen.[67]

Literatur

Bourgeois, Bernard, „Cogito kantien et cogito fichtéen", in: *L'idéalisme allemand. Alternatives et progrès*, hg. v. Bernard Bourgeois, Paris: Vrin, 2000, S. 13-25.

Cassirer, Ernst, „Hermann Cohen. Worte gesprochen an seinem Grabe am 7. April 1918", in: *Hermann Cohen*, hrsg. von Helmut Holzhey, Frankfurt: Peter Lang, 1994, S. 67-74.

Cohen, Hermann, *Werke*, hg. v. Hermann-Cohen-Archiv am Philosophischen Seminar der Universität Zürich unter Leitung von Helmut Holzhey, Hildesheim: Olms, 1977-. (*Werke*)

– *Jüdische Schriften*, 3 Bände, hg. v. Bruno Strauß mit einer Einleitung von Franz Rosenzweig, Berlin: Schwetschke, 1924. (*JS*)

Fichte, Johann Gottlieb, *Sämtliche Werke*, hg. v. Immanuel Hermann Fichte, Berlin: De Gruyter, 1971. (*SW*)

– *Gesamtausgabe der Bayerischen Akademie der Wissenschaften*, hg. von Reinhard Lauth und Hans Gliwitzky, Stuttgart-Bad Cannstatt: Frommann-Holzboog, 1973. (*GA*)

– *Wissenschaftslehre nova methodo. Kollegnachschrift K. Chr. Fr. Krause 1798/99*, Hamburg, 1982. (Fichte 1982)

Friedrich Albert Lange, *Die Arbeiterfrage in ihrer Bedeutung für Gegenwart und Zukunft*, Duisburg: W. Falk & Volmer, Erstausgabe 1865, zweite stark veränderte Ausgabe

---

65 *Werke*, 5, 113f.
66 Vgl. *Werke*, 7, 254f.
67 Vgl. *G. W. F. Hegel und Hermann Cohen. Wege zur Versöhnung. Festschrift Myriam Bienenstock*, hg. v. N. Waszek, Freiburg & München, Alber, 2018.

1870, dritte Ausgabe 1875. Die Erstausgabe wurde im Jahre 1910 mit einer Einleitung von Franz Mehring wieder abgedruckt, Berlin: Buchhandlung Vorwärts.
– *Geschichte des Materialismus*, Iserlohn: Baedeker, 1866.
Gerhardt, Volker, „Selbstbestimmung", in: *Historisches Wörterbuch der Philosophie*, 12 Bde., hg. v. Joachim Ritter und Karlfried Gründer, Basel: Schwabe, 1971-2005, Band 9, 1995.
Hegel, Georg Wilhelm Friedrich, *Hegel: Theorie-Werkausgabe*, 20 Bände, hg v. Eva Moldenhauer und Karl Markus Michel, Frankfurt am Main: Suhrkamp, 1969-1972. (*TWA*)
Holzhey, Helmut (Hrsg.), *Ethischer Sozialismus. Zur politischen Philosophie des Neukantianismus*, Frankfurt am Main: Suhrkamp, 1994.
– „Der Neukantianismus", in: *Die Philosophie des ausgehenden 19. und des 20. Jahrhunderts 2*, hg. v. Helmut Holzhey u. Wolfgang Röd, Geschichte der Philosophie Bd. 12, München: Beck, 2004.
Kant, Immanuel, *Gesammelte Schriften*, hg. v. Königlich Preussische Akademie der Wissenschaften (Akademie-Ausgabe), Berlin u.a., 1900 ff. (*AA*)
Oesterreich, Peter L., „Aufforderung zur nationalen Selbstbestimmung", in: *Zeitschrift für philosophische Forschung*, 46, 1992, S. 44-55.
Schiller, Friedrich, *Werke. Nationalausgabe*, Historisch-kritische Ausgabe, begründet von Julius Petersen, fortgeführt von Lieselotte Blumenthal, Benno von Wiese, Siegfried Seidel, jetzt hg. v. Norbert Oellers, Weimar: Böhlau, 1943 ff.
Sieg, Ulrich, *Aufstieg und Niedergang des Marburger Neukantianismus. Die Geschichte einer philosophischen Schulgemeinschaft*. Würzburg: Königshausen & Neumann, 1994.
van der Linden, Harry, „Cohens sozialistische Rekonstruktion der Ethik Kants", in: *Ethischer Sozialismus, Zur politischen Philosophie des Neukantianismus*, Frankfurt: Suhrkamp, 1994, S. 146-165.
Waszek, Norbert, *G. W. F. Hegel und Hermann Cohen. Wege zur Versöhnung. Festschrift Myriam Bienenstock*, Freiburg & München, Alber, 2018.

Theodor W. Adorno
Education for Autonomy

Samir Gandesha

> Ob Autonomie sei oder nicht, hängt ab von ihrem Widersacher und Widerspruch, dem Objekt, das dem Subjekt Autonomie gewährt oder verweigert; losgelöst davon ist Autonomie fiktiv.
>
> (Theodor W. Adorno[1])

In the German context, perfectionism has been at the centre of debates between those philosophers who contend that it is the proper role of the state to foster the conditions under which its citizens can achieve the good life and therefore a condition of *eudaimonia* (flourishing), on the one hand, and those who contend that the state ought, rather, to maximize the conditions of freedom of its citizens to pursue self-directed ends, on the other. At the centre of these debates lies Kant's political philosophy. Kant marks a key departure from the paternalistic form of perfectionism that ascribes the state a pronounced role in achieving the maximization of human capacities. In his essay "In Answer to the Question What is Enlightenment?" Kant famously defines enlightenment as the "exit from self-incurred tutelage" entailing a courageous public use of reason. Enlightenment is therefore closely tied to a condition of political maturity or the capacity to speak for oneself (*Mündigkeit*) rather than reliance on another to speak on one's behalf. In other words, political maturity entails spontaneity (self-determination) and autonomy (self-legislation) as opposed to heteronomy. Kant's account of enlightenment therefore rules out a paternalistic role for the state, which is to say, an understanding of the state as in some way underwriting the happiness of its citizens as, for example, in the political philosophy of Christian Wolff.[2] By challenging the paternalism or "rational heteronomy" of these positions, Kant sought to re-establish ethics

---

* This chapter is based on a paper presented at the 13th International Sandor Ferenczi Conference "Ferenczi in Our Time," Florence, Italy, May, 2018. I would like to thank Douglas Moggach and Nadine Mooren for their incisive and helpful comments on a previous draft.
1 GS 6, 222.
2 See Moggach (2009).

on a new footing, namely, on the basis of spontaneity.³ In terms of his moral theory, spontaneity is (negative) freedom from heteronomous or external determination, and (positive) freedom to engage in rational self-legislation.

Yet Kant's own account of autonomy is a transcendental one. The moral law is determined through a critical process of reflection establishing its rationality and hence its universality. As Kant argues in *Groundwork for the Metaphysics of Morals*, in contrast to the merely instrumental, purely conditional "hypothetical imperative," which Kant saw as comprising the doctrine of consequentialism or utilitarianism, the genuinely moral or "categorical imperative" is that any rule for action must meet the following test: "Act only in accordance with that maxim through which you can at the same time will that it become a universal law."⁴ An implication of the law-like nature of the categorical imperative is that, insofar as "rational beings all stand under the law that every one of them ought to treat itself and all others never merely as means, but always at the same time as end in itself."⁵ As Kant indicates in the *Critique of Practical Reason*, his moral theory is transcendental insofar as it is premised upon the opposition between the empirical and pure (rational) will, inclination and duty, and, ultimately, the postulates of the immortality of the soul and the existence of God as the highest good. Put differently, Kant understood human beings as imperfectly rational beings comprised of both reason and sensibility. Morality, therefore, constitutes imperatives oriented towards directing sensibility under the command of reason.

Kant's moral theory comes under sustained attack by subsequent Idealists as symptomatic of the *Zerrissenheit* or dirempted nature of modern society.⁶ For example, Hegel criticizes it precisely for its formal nature.⁷ In his so-called "early theological writings", he censures Kant's opposition between duty and inclination, moral law and natural impulse, reason and passion in light of what Richard Kroner calls a "pantheism of love"⁸ which, for Hegel, transcends these narrow and artificial oppositions. This critique lodged by the young Hegel

---

3 It is an open question as to what extent Kant himself intended this shift to perfectionism, as well as whether, if he did intend it, he himself applied it to juridical relations as opposed to morality. See Guyer (2011), and in this volume Maximiliano Hernández Marcos, "Rights-Perfectionism, From Kant's *Grundlegung* to Politics. Kantian Debates".
4 Kant (2002), 37.
5 Ibid., 51.
6 See, for example, Hegel (1978).
7 See also Luca Fonnesu, "Teleology and Perfection. Law, Freedom and the Search for Unity, from Kant to the Post-Kantians," in this volume.
8 Hegel (1975), 11.

against Kant, as we shall see, returns up-dated via psychoanalytic categories in Adorno's (and Horkheimer's) thesis of the "dialectic of enlightenment."

Hegel's early theological critique will form the basis of his mature critique of *Moralität* or the "moral point of view" in his *Philosophy of Right* in which he takes Kant to task for the abstract universalism of his moral theory, one that juxtaposes a transcendental "ought," on the one side, and a historically immanent "is," on the other. Kant abstracts questions of value, Hegel claims, from an on-going commitment to, and participation in, the normative structure of a historically actual form of life.[9] Both "abstract right" and "morality," negative and positive liberty, are but dependent and subordinate "moments" or partial, one-sided aspects of the historically grounded institutions of *Sittlichkeit* or ethical life which constitute their possibility conditions.[10]

Hegel's critique, however, is itself premised upon an account of history as an explicit form of theodicy or the justification of evil in a divinely authored world. History understood as the teleological realization of the idea of Freedom embodies a secret or hidden "cunning of reason" (*List der Vernunft*) operating behind the backs of embodied, passionately striving individuals. Such a historical theodicy is expressed in the form of Hegel's infamous statement: "What is rational is actual; and what is actual is rational" ("*Was vernünftig ist, das ist wirklich; und was wirklich ist, das ist vernünftig.*").[11] While the Hegelian Right takes this as a philosophical justification of the established institutions of the state, the Hegelian Left takes it as a revolutionary injunction "to make the world philosophical."[12] This revolutionary injunction gathers particular momentum amongst republican and socialist forces in the *Vormärz* period

---

9   See Pippin (1989). Pippin and other commentators such as Terry Pinkard and Paul Redding are keen to trace the continuities rather than discontinuities between Kant and Hegel as emphasized, for example, by figures such as Taylor (1977) who emphasizes the "expressive" dimension of Hegel's thought.

10 See Hegel (1991).

11 Ibid., 20; *TWA* 7, 24.

12 As Marx writes, "When philosophy turns itself as will against the world of appearance, then the system is lowered to an abstract totality, that is, it has become one aspect of the world which opposes another one. Its relationship to the world is that of reflection. Inspired by the urge to realise itself, it enters into tension against the other. The inner self-contentment and completeness has been broken. What was inner light has become consuming flame turning outwards. The result is that as the world becomes philosophical, philosophy also becomes worldly, that its realisation is also its loss, that what it struggles against on the outside is its own inner deficiency, that in the very struggle it falls precisely into those defects which it fights as defects in the opposite camp, and that it can only overcome these defects by falling into them." (Karl Marx, "The Difference Between the Democritean and Epicurean Philosophies of Nature," (Marx/Engels (1978), 10).

that miscarries in the struggle to establish a constitutional regime in a unified Germany.

An especially important contribution to the philosophical project of defining a revolutionary programme in the *Vormärz* period, as Douglas Moggach has shown in detail, was the perfectionism of Bruno Bauer. Bauer's political philosophy is of particular interest insofar as it breaks not only with Kantian and Hegelian, but also the socialist, inflections of the doctrine. Bauer understands *Vollkommenheit* as the "active contribution to on-going historical progress" whose telos was to have been the formation of a republican constitution in the Revolution of 1848. The momentous failure of this historical event represented a profound sense of disillusionment and pessimism for him, at which point Bauer turns towards a particularly virulent form of anti-Semitism and commitment to a pre-modern model of community and an absolutist state form.[13]

This is the historico-philosophical background for Theodor W. Adorno's own contribution to the question of perfectionism understood as *autonomy*. On first glance, however, it seems quite unlikely, given the emphasis on negativity in his thought, that Adorno would have anything much to contribute to normative discussions, let alone one centered on the post-Kantian accounts of perfectionism. According to an influential interpretation, Adorno's putatively "totalizing critique" of reason entails a performative contradiction and therefore a philosophical *aporia* or dead-end. Normatively, then, Adorno's thought would seem to have little to offer.[14] Yet, in the book written contemporaneously with *Dialectic of Enlightenment*, *Minima Moralia*, Adorno suggests that his thinking is inspired by philosophy understood not as "method" but, rather, in the classical sense as the "teaching of the good life."[15] However, because life under late capitalism had come to be so dominated by the law of value, to which difference is subordinated, it must be scrutinized in its "estranged form"[16] which returns us to the question of *Zerrissenheit* introduced by the early Kantians. Accordingly, Adorno's reflections on "damaged life" are articulated as a counter-point to Aristotle's *Magna Moralia*. For this reason, Adorno's practical

---

13   See Moggach (2003).
14   See Habermas (1990) and (1984). Habermas's own discourse ethics set forth in *Moral Consciousness and Communicative Ethics* represents at attempt to address what he takes to be the normative shortcomings of the first generation of Critical Theory. He sees this contribution as a synthesis of Kant's transcendental and Hegel's immanent positions, see especially (1982), 195-216.
15   *MM*, 15.
16   Ibid.

philosophy has been read as a "negative Aristotelianism"[17] which is that we can only know the "good life" negatively, that is, on the basis of the contours of the "damaged life" (*beschädigten Leben*). There is much to recommend this argument; however, in my view, Adorno is more profoundly concerned with the fate of the "enlightenment" or the project of human freedom and emancipation from conditions of heteronomy which is most clearly outlined in *Dialectic of Enlightenment*, coauthored with Max Horkheimer.

While the Young Hegelians were increasingly aware of the new challenges posed to the prospects for human autonomy in the midst of what Hobsbawm calls the "age of revolution" (1789-1848),[18] Adorno and his Frankfurt colleagues addressed a significant portion of what Hobsbawm calls in the third volume of his trilogy the "age of extremes," in the context of the "short twentieth century" (1914-1991).[19] Adorno and Frankfurt colleagues such as Max Horkheimer, Erich Fromm, Herbert Marcuse and Leo Löwenthal, produced important psychoanalytical and social psychological accounts of the catastrophes of this century.[20] This psychoanalytical dimension, as I shall suggest below, profoundly influenced Adorno's rethinking of the concept of autonomy.

If the Young Hegelians aimed their critical reflections at the particular contradictions of German society in which bourgeois institutions and socio-economic power were particularly weak, Adorno and his colleagues were compelled to understand the trajectory that led from the failure of the revolutionary forces in 1848, through a process of socio-economic modernization "from above" under the auspices of an increasingly authoritarian Junker caste, the unification of the country under Prussian aegis through the Franco-Prussian War and its aftermath, the calamitous First World War and the ill-fated German Revolution, and the subsequent rise of Nazism, and, finally, the Holocaust. Hence, the famous opening of Adorno's magnum opus, *Negative Dialectics*,

> Philosophy, which once seemed obsolete, lives on because the moment to realize it was missed. The summary judgment that it had merely interpreted the world, that resignation in the face of reality had crippled it in itself, becomes a defeatism of reason after the attempt to change the world miscarried.[21]

17 See Freyenhagen (2003).
18 See Hobsbawm (1962).
19 See Hobsbawm (1994).
20 See, for example, Horkheimer (1982); Erich Fromm (1941) and (1950); Marcuse (1955); Löwenthal and Guterman (1970). They were, of course, building on the writings of the Freudian School, particularly *Civilization and its Discontents* (2010) and *Group Psychology and the Analysis of the Ego* (1990) as well as Ferenczi's *Bausteine zur Psychoanalyse* (1927).
21 *ND*, 3.

Adorno's statement can be understood as something of a reversal of the sequence leading from Kant and Hegel through the Left Hegelians directly to Marx's eleventh thesis on Feuerbach according to which the point was not simply to "interpret the world" but to "change it." The reversal was necessitated, in Adorno's view, because of the miscarriage of the revolutionary energies that, far from auguring human emancipation and autonomy, led to more deeply coercive and heteronomous state forms in both the West and the East. And, indeed, "theory" in the form of positivism and the Heideggerian "ontology" which opposed it was reduced to serving the imperatives of an ever more encompassing social totality. While positivism understood society in terms of increasingly abstract, law-like regularities, Heideggerian ontology answered what Adorno called the "ontological need" by proffering a form of "false concreteness" in terms of the immediacy of the "meaning of being" (*Sinn des Seins*).[22] Adorno is not, however, simply proposing a reversion to mere interpretation but suggests, rather, that subjective and objective forms are more profoundly intertwined than Marx allows, which is what makes Marx's judgment "summary." An implication of Adorno's early lecture – deeply influenced by Lukács and Walter Benjamin[23] – on the "Idea of Natural-History" is that theory entails a moment of praxis, and praxis a moment of theory; that concepts are shaped by the logic of the social and those concepts, in turn, shape social relations. The result of these developments was the nullification of what Hegel called the "the seriousness, the suffering, the patience, and the labour of the negative."[24]

For Adorno, a return to Kant's conception of autonomy was central to his development of a *negative* dialectics. It is here that we can see most clearly Adorno's contribution to a consideration of the meta-ethical and normative stakes of perfectionism. This rethinking is most startlingly articulated by Adorno's call for a "new categorical imperative" after Auschwitz. The significance of Adorno's call for such a new categorical imperative can hardly be overemphasized insofar as, like post-Kantian theories of perfectionism, Adorno is concerned with the social and historical conditions for human autonomy. So, while he draws on Kant to criticize Hegel, in line with Hegel's critique of Kant, Adorno also argues that the moral point of view must be located within its historical conditions of possibility. Yet, for Adorno, such conditions are marked by a profound caesura.

---

22 Ibid., 61-96.
23 Walter Benjamin's failed 1925 Habilitationschrift *Ursprung des deutschen Trauerspiels* is unfortunately translated by John Osborne as *Origin of German Tragic Drama* (2003).
24 Hegel (1979), 10.

To understand fully what Adorno means by a "new categorical imperative," it is necessary first to situate Adorno's programmatic statement in relation to some of the key arguments of the *Dialectic of Enlightenment* concerning the self-destruction of enlightenment. The central problem identified by this text is the "introversion" of sacrifice. (1). We will then examine specifically the meta-ethical and normative questions that arise from Adorno's call for a "new categorical imperative" (2). Central to the articulation of a new categorical imperative is a moment of "mindfulness" (*Eingedenken*) of suffering nature. In the final section of this chapter, I shall try to explicate what Adorno means by this (3).

1.   The Self-Destruction of Enlightenment

In order to be able to situate Adorno's contribution to the question of perfectionism, it is first necessary to understand it in the context of the main argument of the *Dialectic of Enlightenment*. This text bears the marks of its historical moment which is to say that it was written between 1941-44, in the midst of the Second World War. It has been read as a negative philosophy of history, one that draws a line from Odysseus to the Culture Industry and the return of anti-Semitism now in pseudo-scientific rather than theological guise.

Dialectic of Enlightenment constitutes an expansion and deepening of Adorno's development of the idea of "natural-history," presented as a lecture at the *Kant Gesellschaft* in 1932. There Adorno's aim is to show the points at which each of the two antithetical concepts "nature" and "history" cross over into one another. Adorno seeks to provide an alternative to Heidegger's attempt to dismantle the metaphysical opposition between "Being" and "time" through his "existential analytic" of Dasein. Adorno argues that history understood at its most historical reverses into its opposite, which is to say, (second) nature, while nature (inner and outer) at its most natural becomes historical. Adorno's main aim is to free up a notion of transience (*Vergänglichkeit*) which is also internal to both insofar as both nature and history entail temporal processes of passing as is most clearly manifested in the image of a ruin – so important for Benjamin's understanding of the Baroque.[25]

The crux of the argument of *Dialectic of Enlightenment* is that, like nature and history, the opposition of myth and enlightenment, respectively, are to be understood as deeply entwined. Enlightenment understood as the history of the domination of nature offers an understanding of society as a natural order

---

25   See Benjamin (2003).

governed by law-like necessity to which thought is increasingly subordinated in the form of positivism and pragmatism. In other words, it reverts to myth. On the other hand, nature is itself transformed through ever-newer forms of technologically-mediated forms of domination. What is key here is the logic of reversal which resembles Hegel's discussion of lordship and bondage.

Hegel shows in the Section of the *Phenomenology of Spirit* entitled "Self-Consciousness,"[26] the meeting of two independent consciousnesses in which a fight to the death ensues. That consciousness which values honour over life succeeds in subduing the other, which values life over honour. The first becomes the lord, the latter, the bondsman, whom the lord sets to work for him. This relation of domination and subordination, however, undergoes a reversal when it becomes clear that the lord's status is entirely dependent upon the recognition (*Anerkennung*) of the bondsman, that is, a being who has no social status, while the bondsman relies on no such recognition from the master, but is able to labour and, in the process, objectify himself in the world.

In contrast to the typical Marxist reading of the relation of lord and bondsman, Adorno sees this relation at a standstill. It does not lead to the triumph of the labouring subject, the proletariat, as what Marx termed the "grave-digger" of the bourgeoisie, rather, as in Beckett's *Endgame*, the relation between the world-historical two classes has reached a stalemate of sorts: Clov the servant of Hamm is unable to overcome him with the suggestion that their interaction during the course of the play repeats itself endlessly.[27] The dialectic, in other words, has ground to a halt.

This problem of repetition in *Endgame* points back to the arguments of both the "Idea of Natural-History" and *Dialectic of Enlightenment*. The latter text, one Adorno co-authored with his long-time friend and associate Max Horkheimer over a period of three years between 1941-44, seeks to show the intertwinement of nature and history, of "rationalized social reality" and "mastery of nature." In other words, historical progress (enlightenment) is to be understood less as moral progress than progress in the domination of nature (of external and internal nature alike), as well as social domination through enforced labour discipline and exploitation. History is depicted as none other than the repetition of blind nature. Through a virtuoso reading of Homer's *Odyssey*, the *Ur*-text of Western Civilization, they show the unity of "mythical nature and enlightened matter of nature" in the transformation of sacrifice to the Gods as a means of survival into self-renunciation or the introversion of

---

26 Hegel (1979), 111-118.
27 See Gandesha (2016).

sacrifice. Enlightenment subjectivity, they argue, is fundamentally sacrificial insofar as it entails the destruction of the possibility of human flourishing.

Horkheimer and Adorno then go on to show in a chapter on Kant, Sade and Nietzsche that the subjugation of everything natural to the sovereign subject culminates in the domination of what is blindly objective and natural. Social domination and the domination of nature is exemplified in the Sirens episode in which Odysseus has himself bound to the mast of his own ship in order to listen to their alluring song while his men have their ears stopped up with wax. Their song represents the possibility of a redemption of the past, yet a redemption which must be disavowed insofar as it threatens the ego with dissolution. The encounter with the sirens allegorizes the split between genuine art, on one side, and the culture industry, on the other:

> The fettered man listens to a concert, as immobilized as audiences later, and his enthusiastic call for liberation goes unheard as applause. In this way the enjoyment of art and manual work diverge as the primeval world is left behind.[28]

In their account of the culture industry, Horkheimer and Adorno show the way in which the former replaces what Kant called the "transcendental schema" by which the sensible manifold is related to concepts through the activity of the imagination by

> ready-made thought models, the termini technici which provide them with iron rations following the decay of language. The perceiver is no longer present in the process of perception. He or she is incapable of the active passivity of cognition, in which categorial elements are appropriately reshaped by preformed conventional schemata and vice versa, so that justice is done to the perceived object.[29]

Enlightenment, therefore, degenerates into an "idolization of the existing order." While enlightenment aims at liberating human beings and establishing them as masters of nature, because it completely elides the moment of their own "naturalness," rather than liberating them, it only more thoroughly enslaves them: "Any attempt to break the compulsion of nature by breaking nature only succumbs more deeply to that compulsion."[30]

In the service of self-preservation, the human subject seeks to disenchant nature and subject it to ever more rational forms of control and domination. Like the master, however, of the *Phenomenology*, the historical subject shows himself to be dependent upon the very nature he seeks to dominate and

---

28 Horkheimer/Adorno (2002), 27.
29 Ibid., 167.
30 Ibid., 9.

therefore undergoes a reversal and finds himself dominated. The human subject can only control and dominate nature by mimicking blind nature in order to bring it under control, just as the master must rely upon the slave's labour to transform the object world. This is the case because, as the Sirens episode shows, in which Odysseus has himself bound to the mast of his ship in order to hear their irresistible song, his men must continue to work and so have their ears blocked with wax. Self-preservation entails social domination. But it also entails the domination of internal nature as well. Odysseus is divided against himself. Indeed, in order for him to survive the threatening nature personified by the cyclops Polyphemus, Odysseus must forfeit his individuality. That is, in an exemplary demonstration of his celebrated "cunning," Odysseus tells Polyphemus that his name is "Oudeis" or "nobody", roughly homophonic with his own name. When Odysseus stabs Polyphemus in the eye, the cyclops calls out to his comrades that he has been attacked. When asked by whom, he replies, "Nobody!" leaving Odysseus and his men to escape.[31] Enlightenment, promising, above all, liberation from nature, which is to say, autonomy, culminates in its opposite: heteronomy.

Adorno will return to this problem of mastery and servitude in the "Models of Freedom" section of *Negative Dialectics*. His argument is that any historical conception of autonomy that fails to recognize its own dependence upon sensuous nature is self-subverting. Drawing implicitly on the argument of the Young Hegel, Adorno suggests that in establishing too strong a line between duty and impulse, Kantian ethics shows the subject as divided against itself and therefore *unfree*. Not only is freedom forfeited but the very life in the service of which self-preservation is itself undertaken becomes without substance, that is, lifeless. Life, therefore, becomes a living death. The aggression accumulated historically under the aegis of the civilizing process reaches a level at which it explodes in a murderous rage against the very representatives of that civilization.

2. A New Categorical Imperative

It would scarcely be an exaggeration to say that Adorno's mature philosophy can be regarded as a singular response to the challenge represented by the historical caesura of the Holocaust. This is most clearly expressed in his call in the "Meditations on Metaphysics" section of *Negative Dialectics* for a fulsome transformation of Kantian moral theory in light of the historical experience of the twentieth century. If, as we have seen, Bruno Bauer defines perfectionism

---

31   Ibid., 35.

affirmatively as the "on-going contribution to *historical progress*," then for Adorno it is defined negatively as the in terms of forestalling *historical catastrophe*. As Adorno states that,

> [a] new categorical imperative has been imposed by Hitler upon unfree mankind: to arrange their thoughts and actions so that Auschwitz will not repeat itself, so that nothing similar will happen.[32]

Yet what Adorno actually means by this statement is far from clear. How are we to understand Auschwitz? Clearly it is a proper name that refers to a complex of forty-eight concentration and extermination camps comprised of Auschwitz I, Auschwitz II (Birkenau) and Auschwitz III (Monowitz) and several sub-camps located in Oswiecim, Poland. But, it also refers, beyond that, beyond all of the actual machinery of death, to the underlying logic of genocide itself. In his lecture "The Meaning of Working Through the Past," Adorno recognizes the Armenian genocide as a key precursor to the Shoah.[33] And, indeed, recent research has shown the way in which Wilhelmine Imperial project in German South West Africa was a trial run of certain eugenicist ideas that would become manifest in the Nuremburg Laws.[34] So "Auschwitz" referred not just to the Nazis death camps as such but to the very exterminationist logic of genocide itself. For Adorno it was the end-point of the drive to forcibly reduce the "non-identical," or that which lay beyond or exceeded philosophical concepts, to identity. Rather than being a profoundly aberrant episode within the history of Western civilization, it represented the culmination of this history.[35] For the purposes of this section, the most important questions are: What are the contours of the contemporary condition of what Adorno calls *unfreedom*? And: What does it mean to arrange or, better, *re-arrange* our thoughts and actions so "nothing similar will happen"?

---

32   *ND*, 365.
33   See *MW*, 89-103.
34   See, for example, Evans (2015).
35   As the intellectual historian Enzo Traverso has argued: "The guillotine, the abattoir, the Fordist factory, and rational administration, along with racism, eugenics, the massacres of the colonial wars and those of World War I had already fashioned the social universe and the mental landscape in which the Final Solution would be conceived and set in motion. All those elements combined to create the technological, ideological, and cultural premises for that Final Solution, by constructing an anthropological context in which Auschwitz became a possibility. These elements lay at the heart of Western civilization and had been deployed in the Europe of industrial capitalism, in the age of classic liberalism." ((2003), 151).

In order to begin to make better sense of Adorno's provocative statement, it is helpful to place it within a larger constellation of statements that provide insight into Adorno's thoughts on moral philosophy. For example, in his "Reflections from Damaged Life," *Minima Moralia*, Adorno states that "*Es gibt kein richtiges Leben im falschen*" "Wrong life cannot be lived rightly."[36] This claim can be understood as identifying the limitations of the narrow confines of the kind of formal, transcendental assumptions of Kant's moral philosophy. Such limitations have to do with the divorce of such moral theory from the larger contexts of history and society or "form of life" according to an argument already made against Kant by Hegel. In his *Philosophy of Right*, Hegel argues that the Kantian moral point of view or *Moralität* presupposes a one-sided, subjective will abstracted from the mediations or relationships constitutive of the totality of "objective spirit," comprised of a constellation of social institutions of the family, civil society (*bürgerliche Gesellschaft*) and the state *senso strictu*, objective structures of recognition, which, taken together, comprise what Hegel calls *Sittlichkeit* or a meaningful ethical life. One of the enduring criticisms of Kantian philosophy as a whole is its formalism – moral reflection is abstracted from the movement of history itself. For Hegel, of course, such a movement culminates in an order in which freedom is realized in the totality of its mediations, that is, in a telos in which the "whole is true."

Yet Adorno is equally critical of this Hegelian concept of ethical life for, as he states in *Minima Moralia*, the "whole is false."[37] As already previously suggested, because it is based on a self-sacrificing logic of self-preservation and struggle for existence, the ethical life of advanced capitalism, is, itself, paradoxically *bereft* of life. As the epigram taken from Ferdinand Kürnberger to *Minima Moralia* reads: "Life does not live" (*Das Leben lebt nicht*).[38] For Hegel, it is possible to construe history as a theodicy or a philosophical justification for the existence of evil in an order created by God. Leibniz's theodicy was to be understood as the "best of all possible worlds" and was, of course, pilloried by Voltaire in *Candide*, which he wrote in response to the Lisbon earthquake. How, Voltaire asked, could we be living in the "best of all possible worlds" if God's children could be killed in Church by such a calamitous natural event? Hegel's philosophy of history was itself explicitly construed as a theodicy insofar as evil took the form of negativity – war, violence, death and destruction or what Hegel called history's "slaughter bench" – facilitates the progressive realization of freedom in the world.

---

36   *MM*, 39 and 59.
37   Ibid., 50.
38   Ibid., 20.

Adorno plays the critical moralist, Voltaire, to Hegel's rationalist Leibniz. As Adorno writes,

> The earthquake of Lisbon sufficed to cure Voltaire of the theodicy of Leibniz, and the visible disaster of the first nature was insignificant in comparison with the second, social one, which defies human imagination as it distills a real hell from human evil.[39]

The catastrophe of the Holocaust, for Adorno, is a form of evil that simply could not be negated and meaningfully incorporated into a narrative of historical progress without effacing the senseless and horrific violence visited upon the victims of the camps.[40] Auschwitz constituted a natural-historical caesura which, at the same time, because it was not simply a historical event among others but an exemplary one which crystalized the violent logic by which identity seeks to impose itself on the non-identical and forces us to see history as a whole in a different light. This did not mean that it was impossible to conceive of "Universal History." But, rather, such a history would have to be conceived in negative terms; not in terms of a history of the inexorable realization of freedom but rather in the accelerated development of the capacity for destruction not just of entire categories of people but of nature itself in the form of nuclear Armageddon (to this, of course, we can add the current climate emergency). Indeed, as an event it was qualitatively different from the Lisbon Earthquake insofar as the former unlike the latter was a historical rather than natural event, a function of human natural-historical action – secularized evil –rather than of geology and seismology. So, Adorno closes off both a metaphysical grounding of the condition for the possibility of morality in pure practical reason, on the one hand, as well as the historical grounding of reason in the actually existing institutional structures of modern ethical life which were themselves unable to forestall Auschwitz, on the other.

The tension in Adorno's thought between Kant and Hegel turns on the crucial question of the meaning of "critique" (*Kritik*) which was of course a central concept for the philosophy of the mature Kant and the young Hegel. Adorno's historico-philosophical concerns are nicely condensed in a short article simply entitled "Critique" that originated as a radio address in the series "*Politik für Nichtpolitiker*," for *Süddeutscher Rundfunk* on 26 May 1969, and appeared

---

39   *ND*, 361.
40   This is the significance of Beckett's *Endgame* for Adorno: it explores precisely the "meaning of meaninglessness." See *NL*, 241-276.

nearly one month later in *Die Zeit*.⁴¹ This was the same period in which Adorno was engaged in an important exchange of letters with Herbert Marcuse on the significance of the West German Students' Movement and was particularly concerned about the integrity of West German constitutional democracy.⁴² In myriad radio talks, interviews, newspaper articles, etc., Adorno shows himself to be deeply committed to the idea of "Education after Auschwitz"⁴³ For Adorno, such an education was necessarily an "education for autonomy" as in the discussion on educational reforms Adorno conducted with Hellmut Becker shortly before Adorno's death in August, 1969. For Adorno, education for autonomy meant, above all, an education grounded in critical sociology "for contradiction and resistance."⁴⁴ This was particularly important in the context of the *Bundesrepublik* in which democratic institutions had never really been established on as firm a footing as they were in France and the U.S. and, after the failure of the Revolution of 1848, nationalism took an increasingly authoritarian turn particularly with the formation of the German nation state under Prussian aegis.⁴⁵

Adorno's central proposition is that democracy is defined by "critique" or negativity in both the objective and subjective senses. From the outset, Adorno implicitly invokes Marx's claim against Hegel, that the truth of the State was to be located in *bürgerliche Gesellschaft*, by suggesting that politics cannot be understood as a "self-enclosed, isolated sphere (...) but rather can be conceived only in its relationship to the societal forces making up the substance of everything political and veiled by political surface phenomena."⁴⁶ Objectively, critique can be understood in relation to democracy in the form of the separation

---

41   C. The following paragraphs are drawn from a forthcoming article entitled "Crisis and Critique" for a special issue of the Spanish journal *Constelacions* on the "Horizon of the Crisis."
42   See Adorno/Marcuse (1999), 123-136.
43   *EA*, 191-204.
44   Adorno/Becker (1983), 109.
45   As one of Adorno's important interlocutors, Alfred Sohn-Rethel explains: "Unlike the bourgeois democracies which developed in England, France, Holland and Belgium, modern Germany, because its bourgeois revolution of 1848 had failed, sustained a mixed regime of feudal landed aristocracy and industrial plutocracy, the two merging by frequent intermarriage. Up to 1918, under the rule of the Kaiser, the industrial magnates, the landed aristocracy, the head of the Army and the top bureaucracy constituted the closely-knit ruling system of Germany. After the military defeat of 1918 the Weimar Republic which emerged from the collapse of the old regime appeared to inaugurate a democratic epoch, but when the Republic was hit by the disasters of the slump of the 1930s the pre-revolutionary powers reasserted themselves and, uniting with the broad masses of the Nazis, were able to create the Hitler regime." ((1987), 52).
46   *C*, 282.

of powers, from Locke and Montesquieu, which "has its lifeblood in critique"[47] insofar as each branch of government, legislative, judicial and executive, holds the others accountable, by subjecting them to critique.

Such an objective institutionalization of critique goes hand-in-glove with the subjective idea of critique which is reflected in the Kantian idea of enlightenment understood as *Mündigkeit* which means political maturity or the notion that citizens must be empowered to speak for themselves as *autonomous* subjects.[48] The citizen is able to do so, according to Adorno, "because he has thought for himself and is not merely repeating someone else; he stands free of any guardian."[49] *Mündigkeit* is vital, moreover, for the citizen's capacity to resist conformity to prevailing opinion and stands in a close relation to judgment. I want to suggest that this idea of *Mündigkeit* as *critique, resistance* and *contradiction* is central to Adorno's contribution to perfectionism.

Insofar as he identifies *Kritik's* etymological roots in the Greek verb *krino*, meaning "to decide,"[50] Adorno tacitly confirms Arendt's argument that judgment is the political faculty *par excellence*.[51] If Kant, and the Enlightenment as a whole, can be understood as seeking to pave the way for an *Ausgang* or exit from "self-incurred immaturity" and judgment, the mature Hegel ultimately undermines critique by associating it with the vanity of what he called the *Raisonneur* (literally, if rather inelegantly, according to translator Henry Pickford: carperer or argufier[52]). That is, echoing the aforementioned critique of his theodicy, Adorno argues that Hegel associated critique with the person who fails to recognize the subtle permutations of the *List der Vernunft* or the cunning of reason and is "incapable of recognizing that ultimately everything is and happens for the best."[53]

This divergence in the attitudes towards critique in Kant and Hegel points to a deep tension inherent in the historical project of the bourgeoisie as a whole: "that the logic of its own principles," Adorno argues, "could lead beyond its own sphere of interests."[54] This point cannot be emphasized enough insofar as Adorno, again drawing on Marx, emphasizes critique as a *determinate* rather than an *abstract* negation, a cancelling and preserving rather than a simple, outright rejection of bourgeois social structures, social institutions

---

47   Ibid., 282.
48   See Kant (1996), 58-64.
49   *C*, 281.
50   Ibid., 282.
51   See Gandesha (2012), 246-279.
52   *C*, 282.
53   Ibid., 283.
54   Ibid.

and thought as was then being argued on the far-Left in the *Bundesrepublik*. Adorno then turns to discuss the insufficiently developed idea of critique, paradoxically, in the insufficient nature of its bourgeois revolution. Germany, as Marx quipped, "shared the restorations of modern nations without having shared their revolutions."⁵⁵ Adorno presciently locates anti-intellectualism in the broader attempt to divest critique of its force by deeming only university professors, for example, as *legitimate* practitioners of it. Once critique is institutionalized and, in the process, co-opted in this way, it is easy, Adorno argues, effectively to disenfranchise the intellectual dissenter or non-conformist who is regarded as a "grumbler" and consequently dismissed. Therefore, in the dubious "division between responsible critique, namely, that practiced by those who bear public responsibility, and irresponsible critique, namely, that practiced by those who cannot be held accountable for the consequences, critique is already neutralized."⁵⁶ Another way critique is neutralized, in Adorno's view, is to suggest that it must be constructive or positive. As long as critique is forced to *affirm* the existing order rather than to simultaneously cancel and preserve it, it can hardly be considered critique at all. Adorno's point about dissent, as we shall see, is crucial insofar as this is what he retrieves from the Kantian inheritance which can be seen to lie at the core of his own contribution to perfectionism insofar as the *"contradiction and resistance" of the individual contributes to driving society beyond its extant limits.*

3. The "Primacy of the Object"

One way of understanding the attempted formulation of a new categorical imperative after Auschwitz is through Adorno's posthumously published essay "Subject and Object." In it, Adorno proposes a "second Copernican Revolution." In the *Critique of Pure Reason*, Kant describes his unique synthesis of rationalism and empiricism as effecting a "Copernican Revolution in metaphysics," by which he means that metaphysics cannot be grounded in the object but must be rooted in the necessary, *subjective* conditions for the possibility of experience; the idea that "It must be possible for the 'I think' to accompany all of my representations." It is this Copernican turn towards the subject that enables Kant to solve the antinomy of practical reason or that between natural causality, on the one hand, and the freedom, on the other;

---

55 Marx (1975), 176.
56 C, 284-85.

between the understanding of nature as a system of causal laws, on the one hand, and deducing the possibility of spontaneity and autonomy, on the other.

Yet, for Adorno, this is a false solution. Drawing upon the Feuerbachian critique of religion appropriated by the young Marx, Adorno argues that its falsity lies in the fact that it entails a kind of narcissistic compensation for actual human suffering. The human being is simultaneously exalted qua *rational* being and degraded qua *embodied* being. Adorno's "second Copernican Revolution" aims at establishing the primacy of the object (*Vorrang des Objekts*). In the language of *Dialectic of Enlightenment*, this entails a recuperation of a somatic impulse prior to the formation of the ego. Adorno will later refer to this as the "Addendum" which "is an impulse, the rudiment of a phase in which the dualism of extramental and intramental was not thoroughly consolidated yet, neither volitively bridgeable nor an ontological ultimate."[57] Adorno continues, "The addendum is the name for that which was eliminated in this abstraction; without it, there would be no real will at all. It is a flash of light between the poles of something long past, something grown all but unrecognizable, and that which some day might come to be."[58] Such a recuperation of the "non-identical" would, then, allow for a communicative relation between identity and the non-identical as opposed to a dominating relation between them a result of which the non-identical is sacrificed to identity.

Such a "second Copernican Revolution" would have the effect of shaking the foundations of Kantian morality in a way that I've already alluded to: 1. It challenges the priority of the individual will insofar as the object is to be understood in terms of natural-history or an order of "second nature." 2. It challenges the psychological priority of the rational ego insofar as it is decentred by the unconscious or the "objectivity," the drives, and "suffering nature" (*Leid Physis*) of the body. 3. It challenges the idealist thesis – expressed most directly by Kant's student, Fichte, that the human species can be its own ground, or can separate itself materially, from what Marx called metabolism (*Stoffwechsel*) with nature. Rather, insofar as it is itself part of nature, humanity is both subject and object. While it is possible to imagine an object without a subject, the reverse simply does not hold.

Adorno's essay "Subject and Object" can be read as a response to criticisms of *Dialectic of Enlightenment* to which the text is particularly vulnerable. This is its relentlessly negative, pessimistic and totalizing vision and rejection of enlightenment. As had previously been suggested, perhaps the most influential version of this thesis was to be later elaborated by Jürgen

---

57   ND, 228.
58   Ibid., 229.

Habermas. In the *Philosophical Discourse of Modernity*, drawing upon the work of Karl-Otto Apel, Habermas argues that, insofar as the authors of *Dialectic of Enlightenment* presuppose a critical conception of reason they then deny, they become caught in the net of a performative contradiction.[59] Earlier, in his *Theory of Communicative Action*, Habermas argues that the Weberian presentation of the process of rationalization as the spread and deepening of the reifying logic of instrumental reason is unacceptably one-sided and fails to account for a corresponding and countervailing development of a process of rationalization entailing a differentiation of separate spheres of value, each with its own specific logic. And each of the three spheres he specifies, science, morality and art, is it itself governed and unified by communicative rationality based on argumentation, the giving and taking of reasons.[60]

Dialectic of Enlightenment is to be understood less as a historical account of enlightenment centered on the problem of "instrumental reason," as conceived in the work of the later Horkheimer, for example, in *The Eclipse of Reason*, than it is to be understood in relation to the problem that will become clearer in Adorno's *Negative Dialectics*, and this is the problem of identity.[61] So, returning to my claim that insofar as "Subject and Object" is a response to *Dialectic of Enlightenment*, it represents a fleshing out of what the authors promise as a "positive conception of enlightenment which liberates it from its entanglement in blind domination."[62] "If all reification is forgetting"[63] and if the self-implosion of enlightenment culminates in this process of reification, then a transformed conception of enlightenment hinges on the nature of memory. In contrast to the conception of memory in Hegel, that is, *Erinnerung*, the re-internalization of what was externalized through a process of externalization (*Entäußerung*), a transformed conception of enlightenment entails "eingedenken der Natur im Subjeckt" ['mindfulness of nature in the subject']. Such a form of memory involves what Adorno describes as an "anamnesis of the untamed impulse that precedes the ego." Adorno's conception of autonomy is one that does not oppose subject to object, then, but emphasizes the mutual conditioning of each.

> What is decisive in the ego, its independence and autonomy, can be judged only in relation to its otherness, to the nonego. Whether or not there is autonomy depends upon its adversary and antithesis, on the object which either grants or denies autonomy to the subject. Detached from the object, autonomy is fictitious.[64]

---

59 See Habermas (1998), 106-130.
60 See Habermas (1984).
61 See Shuster, 2014.
62 Horkheimer/Adorno (2002), xviii.
63 Ibid., 191.
64 *ND*, 223.

In other words, the pure autonomy of the ego without a trace of heteronomy or other-determination is a fiction that serves, paradoxically, to further the ego's own empirical unfreedom qua apologia for "damaged life." Adorno argues

> The more freedom the subject – and the community of subjects – ascribes to itself, the greater its responsibility; and before this responsibility it must fail in a bourgeois life which in practice has never yet endowed a subject with the unabridged autonomy accorded to it in theory. Hence the subject must feel guilty.[65]

In fact, it is in the very Kantian antinomy of freedom that we find the constitution of the subject as *guilty*. This will become of vital importance for the way in which Adorno addresses Kant's treatment of the antinomy between the empirical and noumenal forms of subjectivity. That is, he argues it is the historically contingent super-ego (something that could be otherwise) rather than the transcendentally necessary principle that ensures the "factuality" of the moral law. *In other words, guilt itself is the coercive condition of freedom understood in the Kantian sense.* It is central to Adorno's argument to challenge Kant's transcendental grounding of the noumenal subject; indeed Adorno's discussion of the genesis of "character" is indebted to *Dialectic of Enlightenment* and, ultimately to psychoanalysis, which Adorno sees as running parallel to what he refers to as "the other Kant." In contrast to the transcendental Kant of the Second Critique, this is the historical Kant of "What is Enlightenment" where he defines *Mündigkeit* as an exit from "self-incurred tutelage" or a state of political immaturity. This is precisely the Kant that Adorno juxtaposes, in his account of "critique," with the mature Hegel. As Adorno suggests:

> Psychology has now concretely caught up with something which in Kant's day was not known as yet, and to which he therefore did not need to pay specific attention; with the empirical genesis of what, unanalyzed, was glorified by him as timelessly intelligible. The Freudian school in its heroic period, agreeing on this point with the *other Kant*, the Kant of the Enlightenment, used to call for a ruthless criticism of the super-ego as something truly heteronomous and alien to the ego. *The superego was recognized, then, as blindly, unconsciously internalized social coercion.*[66] (Emphasis added; S.G.)

"Social stress on freedom as existent coalesces," Adorno suggests,

> "with undiminished repression, and psychologically, with coercive traits. Kantian ethics, antagonistic in itself, has these traits in common with a criminological

---

65 Ibid., 221.
66 Ibid., 272.

practice in which the dogmatic doctrine of free will is coupled with the urge to punish harshly, irrespective of empirical conditions."[67]

A powerful reading of the problem of freedom in Adorno has recently been set forth by Martin Shuster in his book *Autonomy after Auschwitz*.[68] Shuster roots Adorno's treatment of the problem of autonomy in *Dialectic of Enlightenment* though, as he notes, the concept is not mentioned. For Shuster, this means that the implicit moral perfectionism in Adorno, that is "Adorno's own spiritual exercises" that respond to the imperative of a "transformation or re-orientation of life" in response to a moment of crisis, leads to two developments. The first has to do with the somatic dimension of thought which is what Adorno refers to as the salutary "speculative excess" of metaphysics. The second has to do with the way in which this inclusion of the somatic dimension – understood as the impulse to "express suffering" – has the effect of widening the normative "space of reasons." It means that desire and needs could, themselves, count as rational. In other words, it challenges the border so important in Kant's moral theory between the empirical and the supra-empirical subject or the idea that only action undertaken for the sake of duty could count as moral. And, finally, in the process, according to Shuster, it contributes to reconstructing a "formal model" about how we understand ourselves as agents.[69]

Shuster's is an insightful reading; however, I would suggest that if Adorno's model is about how we understand ourselves as *selves*, it must *also* be about how we *fail* to do so, and such failure must be seen, in some sense, as *necessary* insofar as somatic impulses cannot be fully captured by cognition. Psychoanalysis had systematically shown the manner in which, as Nietzsche had suggested in the *On the Genealogy of Morals*, "[...] we are necessarily strangers to ourselves, we do not comprehend ourselves, we *have* to misunderstand ourselves, for us the law 'Each is furthest from himself' applies to all eternity – we are not 'men of knowledge' with respect to ourselves."[70] As Adorno suggests in *Minima Moralia*, "True thoughts are those alone which do not understand themselves."[71]

Surprisingly, neither Freud nor psychoanalysis is mentioned in Shuster's account of "autonomy after Auschwitz," despite the fact that Adorno draws deeply upon psychoanalysis, in particular, the work of Sandor Ferenczi. In the Section on the "Models of Freedom" of *Negative Dialectics*, Adorno

---

67 Ibid., 232.
68 See Shuster (2014).
69 Ibid., 174.
70 Nietzsche (1989), 2.
71 *MM*, 192.

argues, for instance, that "What became Kant's fearfully majestic a priori is what psychoanalysts trace back to psychological conditions."[72] The reading of the *Odyssey* in *Dialectic of Enlightenment*, as the allegorical formation of the subject, shows the process whereby sacrifice is introjected as the blind, unconscious internalization of social coercion.[73]

What I want to suggest, then, is that Ferenczi's psychoanalytical insights are key to understanding Adorno's attempt to rethink the problem of perfectionism and autonomy after Auschwitz. As I have suggested elsewhere, one of the key themes of Adorno's entire corpus is the problem of the "identification with the aggressor" – an idea that originates with Ferenzci rather than, as is commonly thought, Anna Freud.[74] Indeed, the Ferenczian dimension of Adorno's thinking becomes particularly clear in Adorno's thoughts on the question of freedom. In this section of *Negative Dialectics*, Adorno engages in a psychoanalytically-informed critique of the philosophy of freedom and a speculative philosophical critique of psychoanalysis.

Adorno's diagnosis of the self-destruction of enlightenment can be understood in terms of the following proposition: because of its unstated social conditions – psychological coercion – the normative aspiration of enlightenment understood as the autonomy of the subject ultimately undermines itself. Adorno's argument is a reprise of the criticism made by the young Hegel of Kant in "The Spirit of Christianity and its Fate." Striking a rather different note from his previous critique of the "positivity" of the Christian religion in which Hegel had assimilated the latter and Kantian deontological ethics, in "The Spirit of Christianity and Its Fate," Hegel appropriates the Christian conception of love (understood as fellowship or *agape*) to challenge the antinomy between the empirical and transcendental forms of subjectivity. Hegel argues that, as in Judaism, the moral law takes the form of an "alien" imposition on natural impulse: "In the spirit of the Jews there stood between impulse and action, desire and deed, between life and trespass, trespass and pardon, an impassable gulf, an alien court of judgment."[75] Anticipating Nietzsche's criticism of the ascetic ideals in *Genealogy of Morals*, Hegel argues that such an "alien court of judgment," gave rise to an economy of debt and guilt, theft and punishment. As Kroner writes,

---

72 *ND*, 232.
73 This Ferenczian dimension has, to my mind, heretofore been largely overlooked in the secondary literature.
74 See Gandesha (2018).
75 Hegel (1975), 240.

> Kant had insisted that man as a moral agent is autonomous, that it is his own practical reason which dictates the moral law: man is-or rather, ought to be-his own master. But this is just the difficulty. Because he ought to master himself, man is not really free but is divided against himself, half-free and half-slave. At best, he is his own slave, enslaved by his master, reason. The message of Jesus overcomes this diremption and unifies man inwardly. This is the import of the remission of sin and redemption by divine love. The new ethics preached by Jesus is not rational; it is an ethics of love. And love performs what reason can never perform: it harmonizes not only man with man but man with himself.[76]

In contrast to readings of Adorno as offering a quasi-Levinasian ethics as first philosophy[77] or a negative Aristotelianism[78], J.M. Bernstein, in what is doubtless the most ambitious interpretation of Adorno's ethical theory, argues that Adorno's thought fundamentally addresses the conundrum at the heart of Kantian moral theory. This is that Kant seeks to respond to what Bernstein, following Weber, calls the "disenchantment of nature" and the "rationalization of reason." By this, Bernstein means the logic by which previous forms of mediation between subject and object – knowledge, experience and authority – are destroyed. This is the problem of *Zerrissenheit* or diremption, discussed above, which, in turn, becomes central to Hegel's philosophical project. Kant, in Bernstein's view, responds to these processes of disenchantment and rationalization, that crystallized in the doctrine of utilitarianism, only by deepening these very processes. Kant does this by dissolving the "material inferential relations among concepts into formally logical relations."[79] More precisely, the self-defeating character of enlightenment reason, as exemplified by Kant, has to do with its inability to avow "its material conditions of possibility," that is, "its being part of nature."[80] This is not, however, the nature understood as the mathematized object of physics but rather suppressed nature in which humans partake, whose very suppression is felt as an internal wound or what Adorno calls "damaged life." Remembrance of such suffering nature, in Bernstein's reading, is the very basis of genuine ethical life for Adorno.

The enlightenment aspiration to freedom, therefore results not only in unfreedom but, worse, the murderous rage against civilization that culminates in Auschwitz. Hence the need for a transformed categorical imperative. To put this differently, for Adorno, the Kantian conception of practical reason insofar

---

76 Ibid., 11.
77 See Cornell (1992).
78 See Freyenhagen (2003).
79 Bernstein (2001), 36.
80 Ibid.

as it fails to resolve the antinomy between mechanical causality and human freedom entails an opposition between an empirical and a supra-empirical subject, a subject motivated by desires and drives, on the one hand, and a subject understood as rational being motivated by duty and a concern only for obedience to the moral law, which is really a secularized version of puritanism, on the other.

If it is possible to differentiate between the two different conceptions of Enlightenment which themselves stem from the two German words for it: *Aufklärung* and *Mündigkeit*, one emphasizing the ocular and the other the aural, then it is possible to understand these as mapping on to two Kants, as Adorno suggests in *Negative Dialectics*. While the Kant of the *Critique of Practical Reason* emphasizes *Aufklärung* upon which is built the architectonic and transcendental structure of the three critiques, the Kant of "What is Enlightenment?" stresses the importance of *Mündigkeit* or the capacity to "speak truth to power." In the *Critique of Practical Reason*, the noumenal will sets itself up and against the merely empirical will, which, for Adorno, contradicts the anti-authoritarian thrust of Kant's essay on Enlightenment where Enlightenment is defined as an "*Ausgang*" or exit from self-incurred tutelage and, as we have seen in Adorno's thoughts on "Education for Autonomy," this entails "contradiction (*Widerspruch*) and resistance (*Widerstand*)." In *Negative Dialectics*, Adorno draws upon the latter to critique the former.

Adorno's view is that from a psychological perspective, the critique of practical reason sets up the moral imperative as the voice of conscience and, as such, represents the super-ego or internalized imago of father. It is here that Adorno refers, in four footnotes to Sandor Ferenczi's *Bausteine zur Psychoanalyse*, to suggest the possibility of a dissolution of the super-ego. Such a dissolution implies, as well, the dissolution of the tension between the drives and the ego insofar as in Freud's topology the role of the ego is to mediate between the drives, on the one hand, and the imperatives of law and morality on the other. Ferenczi makes the suggestion that, and, here, Adorno quotes him:

> that a real character analysis must do away temporarily, at least, with every kind of super-ego, including the analyst's. Eventually, after all, the patient must become free from all emotional ties that go beyond reason and his own libidinous tendencies. Nothing but this sort of razing of the super-ego as such can accomplish a radical cure. Successes that consist only in the substitution of one super-ego for another are still to be classified as successes of transference; they certainly do not serve the ultimate purpose of therapy, to get rid of the transference also.[81]

---

81   *ND*, 272.

Given that this for Adorno is a function of a bourgeois order and a specific division of labour between intellectual and manual labour it entails a structural identification with the aggressor. Yet, Adorno suggests, such an identification is explicitly criticized by Kant in "What Is Enlightenment?" In this essay, Kant defines enlightenment as the capacity to speak for oneself. This capacity – a capacity for "contradiction and resistance", as noted above – challenges the omnipotence of the super-ego which embodies the agency of the aggressor.

Here we arrive at some insight into what the new categorical imperative might look like. Freedom is precisely to be understood as a disavowal of identification with the aggressor: to the situation in which one is faced with considering a course of action as either an empirical, that is desiring, or a noumenal or rational subject.

> A free man would only be one who need not bow to any alternatives, and under existing circumstances there is a touch of freedom in refusing to accept the alternatives. Freedom means to *criticize and change situations*, not to confirm them by deciding within their coercive structure. Brecht, in defiance of his official creed, helped this insight along after a talk with students, when he followed up his doctrinal collectivistic piece on "Yes-sayer" with the deviating 'Naysayer.'[82] (Emphasis added; S.G.)

A transformed conception of enlightenment understood as *Mündigkeit* is not simply the capacity to engage in the activity of giving and taking of reasons but, rather, also entails the capacity to express somatic drives and suffering within, as Shuster suggests, an enlarged "space of reasons."

At the same time, while Adorno employs psychoanalysis to criticize philosophy, he also enlists philosophy to criticize psychoanalysis. Adorno praises Ferenczi for opening the question of the possibility of a complete dissolution of the super-ego in a radical form of autonomy now no longer disconnected from the body. However, Adorno suggests, because he fails to remain true to his own insights, Ferenczi remains caught within a contradiction.

> To recommend the superego on grounds of social utility or inalienability, while its own coercive mechanism strips it of the objective validity it claims in the context of effecting psychological motivations – this amounts to repeating and reinforcing, within psychology, the irrationalities which psychology braced itself to 'do away with'.[83]

---

82   Ibid., 226.
83   Ibid., 274.

In other words, in order for philosophy to be made aware of its own incapacity to identify what is non-identical, it requires psychoanalysis, at the same time, because philosophy has a speculative capacity to push beyond the *actual* to the *possible* it is able to reveal the limitations of psychoanalysis that remains a child of the very damaged life whose contours it so carefully analyzed.

With Adorno's reflection on the concept of autonomy in *Negative Dialectics* we travel a fair distance from the late-18th century debates surrounding the nature of perfectionism, spontaneity and autonomy. While it is possible to conceive an unbroken development of the notion of perfectionism stretching from Kant through Hegel and especially Bruno Bauer to Marx's famous eleventh thesis on Feuerbach, with Adorno we reach a limit and turning point. Not unlike Bauer's own profound disenchantment with the failure of the German Revolution of 1848, Adorno's thought is profoundly marked by the failure of the moment to "realize philosophy" in the early part of the 20th century. It is precisely this failure and the ensuing catastrophe, in Adorno's view, that constitutes a historical caesura. Such a caesura must be understood as issuing from what he and Horkheimer call in their thorough-going critique of the idea of historical progress the "dialectic of enlightenment." This is the idea that human self-preservation, paradoxically, manifests a tendency to destroy the very life that is to be preserved. The perfectionism that lies deeply within the tradition of German Idealism, according to Adorno, must still be pursued but, now, in a radically negative form. The fashioning of a "new categorical imperative" after Auschwitz entails a form of education directed towards a new form of *Mündigkeit*, one oriented towards contradiction without end, resistance and a steadfast refusal to "identify with the aggressor." In other words, it is a form of education oriented towards autonomy. Yet such a conception of autonomy is now conceived not in antithetical relation to both inner and outer nature but, paradoxically, in terms of its very dependence on them.

Bibliography

Adorno, Theodor W., „Negative Dialektik. Jargon der Eigentlichkeit", in: *Gesammelte Schriften*, Band 6, Frankfurt am Main: Suhrkamp, 2003. (*GS 6*)
– "Negative Dialectics", trans. by E.B. Ashton, London/New York: Continuum Books, 2007. (*ND*)
– "Critique", in: *Critical Models: Interventions and Catchwords*, transl. by Henry Pickford, New York: Columbia University Press, 1998, pp. 281-88. (*C*)
– *Minima Moralia: Reflections on Damaged Life*, London: Verso, 2005. (*MM*)

- "The Meaning of Working Through the Past," in: *Critical Models: Interventions and Catchwords*, trans. by Henry Pickford, New York: Columbia University Press, 1998, pp. 89-103. (*MW*)
- "Trying to Understand *Endgame*", in: *Notes to Literature Vol. I*, transl. by S.W. Nicholsen, New York: Columbia University Press, 1991, pp. 241-276 (*NL*)
- "Education After Auschwitz," in: *Critical Models: Interventions and Catchwords*, trans. by Henry Pickford, New York: Columbia University Press, 1998. (*EA*)

Adorno, T.W. and Marcuse, Herbert, "Correspondence on the German Students Movement", in: *New Left Review*, I/233, 1999, pp. 123-136.

Adorno, T.W. and Becker, Hellmut, "Education for Autonomy", in: *Telos*, 55, 1983, pp. 103-110.

Benjamin, Walter, *Origin of German Tragic Drama*, transl. by John Osborne, London: Verso, 2003.

Bernstein, J.M., *Adorno, Disenchantment and Ethics*, Cambridge, UK: University of Cambridge Press, 2001.

Cornell, Drucilla, *Philosophy of the Limit*, London: Routledge, 1992.

Evans, Richard J., *The Third Reich in History and Memory*, Oxford: Oxford University Press, 2015.

Ferenzci, Sandor, *Bausteine zur Psychoanalyse*, Leipzig and Wien: Internationaler Psychoanalytischer Verlag, 1927.

Freud, Sigmund, *Civilization and its Discontents*, New York: Norton, 2010.
- *Group Psychology and the Analysis of the Ego*, New York: Norton, 1990.

Freyenhagen, Fabian, *Adorno's Practical Philosophy*, Cambridge, U.K.: University of Cambridge Press, 2003.

Fromm, Erich, *Escape from Freedom*, New York: Farrar and Rinehart, 1941.
- *Psychoanalysis and Religion*, New Haven, Connecticut: Yale University Press, 1950.

Gandesha, Samir, "'In Sympathy with the Ephemeral Life: Adorno's Reading of Beckett's *Endgame*", in: *Special Issue of Discipline Filosofiche XXVI, On Theodor W. Adorno: Dialectical Thinking and the Enigma of Truth*, ed. by Giovanni Matteccui and Stefano Marino, 2, 2016.
- "Homeless Philosophy: The Philosophy of Exile and the Exile of Philosophy", in: *Arendt and Adorno: Political and Philosophical Investigations*, ed. by Samir Gandesha and Lars Rensmann, Palo Alto, CA: Stanford University Press, 2012, pp. 246-279.
- "Identifying with the Aggressor: From the 'Authoritarian' to the 'Neo-Liberal' Personality", in: *Constellations*, 25, 2018, pp. 147-164.

Guyer, Paul, "Kantian Perfectionism", in: *Perfecting Virtue. New Essays on Kantian Ethics and Virtue Ethics*, ed. by Lawrence Jost and Julian Wuerth, Cambridge: Cambridge University Press, 2011, pp. 194-213.

Habermas, Jürgen, *Philosophical Discourse of Modernity: Twelve Lectures*, trans. by F. Lawrence, Cambridge, Mass.: M.I.T. Press, 1990.

- *Moral Consciousness and Discourse Ethics*, trans. by Christian Lenhardt and S.W. Nicholsen, Cambridge, Mass.: M.I.T. Press, 1982.
- *Theory of Communicative Action Vol I: Reason and the Rationalization of Society*, trans. by Thomas McCarthy, Boston: Beacon Press, 1984.

Hegel, G.W.F., *The Difference between Fichtean and Schellingian Systems of Philosophy*, Ridgeview Publishing Co., 1978.
- *Early Theological Writings*, trans. by T.M. Knox, Pittsburgh: University of Pennsylvania Press, 1975.
- *Elements of the Philosophy of Right*, trans. by H.B. Nisbet, Cambridge, UK: Cambridge University Press, 1991.
- *Phenomenology of Spirit*, trans. by A.V. Miller, Oxford: Oxford University Press, 1979.
- *Theorie Werkausgabe*. 20 Bände, Band 7, Frankfurt/Main: Suhrkamp, 1969. (*TWA*)

Hobsbawm, Eric, *The Age of Revolution: Europe 1789-1848*, London: Weidenfeld & Nicholson, 1962.
- *The Age of Extremes: The Short Twentieth Century, 1914-1991*, London: Michael Joseph, 1994.

Horkheimer, Max, "Egoism and Freedom Movement: On the Anthropology of the Bourgeois Epoch," in: *Telos*, 54, 1982, pp. 10-60.
- Ibid. and Adorno, T.W., *Dialectic of Enlightenment*, trans. by Edmund Jephcott, Palo Alto, C.A.: Stanford University Press, 2002.

Kant, Immanuel, "An Answer to the Question: What is Enlightenment?" in: *What is Enlightenment? Eighteenth Century Answers, Twentieth Century Questions*, Berkeley: University of California Press, 1996, pp. 58-64.
- *Groundwork for the Metaphysics of Morals*, ed. and trans. by Allen Wood, New Haven: Yale University Press, 2002.

Löwenthal, Leo and Guterman, Norbert, *Prophets of Deceit: A Study of the Techniques of the American Agitator*, Pacific Book Publishers, 1970.

Marcuse, Herbert, *Eros and Civilization: A Philosophical Inquiry into Freud*, Boston: Beacon Press, 1955.

Marx, Karl, "Contribution to the Critique of Hegel's Philosophy of Law," in: *Karl Marx and Friedrich Engels, Collected Works Vol. 3: 1843-44*, New York: International Publishers, 1975, pp. 175-187.
- Ibid. and Friedrich Engels, *Marx-Engels Reader*, ed. by Robert Tucker, New York: W. W. Norton and Co. Press, 1978.

Moggach, Douglas, "Freedom and Perfection: German Debates on the State in the Eighteenth Century," in: *Canadian Journal of Political Science*, 42: 4, 2009, pp. 1003-1023.
- *The Philosophy and Politics of Bruno Bauer*, Cambridge, UK: Cambridge University Press, 2003.

Pippin, Robert, *Hegel's Idealism: The Satisfactions of Self-Consciousness*, Cambridge, U.K.: Cambridge University Press, 1989.

Shuster, Martin, *Autonomy After Auschwitz: Adorno, German Idealism and Modernity*, Chicago: University of Chicago Press, 2014.

Sohn-Rethel, Alfred, *The Economy and Class Structure of German Fascism*, trans. by Martin Sohn-Rethel, London: Free Association Books, 1987.

Taylor, Charles, *Hegel*, Cambridge: Cambridge University Press, 1977.

Traverso, Enzo, *The Origins of Nazi Violence*, New York: The New Press, 2003.

Systematischer Ausblick

Nadine Mooren & Michael Quante

Historisch betrachtet stellt der postkantische Perfektionismus eine Reaktion auf die strikt deontologische und aprioristisch verfasste Ethikkonzeption dar, die von Immanuel Kant und, in seiner Nachfolge, von Johann Gottlieb Fichte entwickelt worden ist. Seine spezifische Differenz gegenüber anderen, konsequentialistischen und perfektionistischen Konzeptionen besteht darin, dass die Autonomie als das ausschließlich zu perfektionierende Gut (oder Ziel) gilt, wobei die Vertreter dieser Position die für die Realisierung der Autonomie notwendigen Rahmenbedingungen transzendentalphilosophisch oder aber bestimmte Institutionen perfektionistisch als Manifestationen der Autonomie ausweisen. Durch diesen Zug wird die bei Kant auf moralische Selbstgesetzgebung verengte und als Ausübung absoluter rationaler Kontrolle (qua Willensfreiheit des noumenalen Ich) konzipierte Autonomie schrittweise erweitert, indem z.B. soziale Institutionen (bürgerliche Gesellschaft, Staat) und historische Prozesse mit in den Blick genommen werden. Einfach gesagt zeichnet sich der postkantische Perfektionismus durch die Berücksichtigung und Einbeziehung empirisch-sozialer Rahmenbedingungen, die für die Realisierung der Autonomie unerlässlich sind, als Weiterentwicklung der kantischen Konzeption aus.

Die von Kant entwickelte strikte Deontologie lässt sich wiederum, wie von Douglas Moggach in diesem Band ausgeführt[1], als Reaktion auf die perfektionistisch ausgelegten Ethikkonzeptionen des 18. Jahrhunderts, insbesondere der Wolff'schen Schule, aber auch des Utilitarismus englischer und französischer Provenienz, begreifen. Der deontologischen Ethik Kants liegt, dabei mit der Konzeption der Spontaneität einen Wesenszug der Leibnizschen Philosophie aufgreifend und radikalisierend, eine Konzeption der Subjektivität zugrunde, die an der praktischen Vernunft ausgerichtet ist. Dieses Primat des Praktischen ist für die Philosophie des Deutschen Idealismus, wenngleich bei einzelnen Vertretern und in unterschiedlichen Phasen auch mit Variationen, insgesamt konstitutiv.[2]

---

1 Vgl. Moggachs Beitrag „Spontaneity, Autonomy, and Perfection: Historical and Systematic Considerations" am Beginn dieses Bandes.
2 Zu Fichte und Hegel vgl. die Beiträge von Moyar und Gleeson/Ikäheimo in diesem Band.

Systematisch betrachtet stellt der postkantische Perfektionismus, darin der postkantischen Metaphysik des Deutschen Idealismus ähnlich, eine Synthese aus den Traditionslinien der perfektionistischen Ethiken des 18. Jahrhunderts einerseits und der reinen praktischen Vernunft Kants andererseits dar.[3] Weniger optimistisch könnte man den postkantischen Perfektionismus metaethisch auch als eine hybride Position analysieren, womit zweierlei im Raum steht. Auf der einen Seite lässt sich dieser Befund aus der Perspektive der strikten Konzeptionen sowohl der Deontologie als auch des konsequentialistischen Perfektionismus in einem skeptischen Sinn so deuten: Es handelt sich beim postkantischen Perfektionismus um eine instabile Mischform, in der unvereinbare Theorieelemente unter ungeklärten systematischen Voraussetzungen zusammengefügt werden.[4] Auf der anderen Seite ergeben sich, wenn man in dieser Synthese eine systematisch tragfähige und attraktive Option sieht, für eine solche optimistische Deutung Anschlussfragen. Sie lassen sich zugleich als Entwicklungsziele und Begründungslasten aktueller Ethikkonzeptionen begreifen, welche an die durch den postkantischen Perfektionismus eröffnete Theorieoption anschließen möchten.[5]

In diesem Ausblick möchten wir abschließend kurz auf vier Themenfelder hinweisen, die Fragestellungen enthalten, welche für jede Variante eines postkantischen Perfektionismus zu beantworten sind.

Der Begriff der Autonomie ist kein Bestandteil der Alltagssprache, sondern wird in seiner Bedeutung durch unterschiedliche Theoriekontexte

---

3   Zu den perfektionistischen Ethiken sind auch die utilitaristischen Konzeptionen des 18. Jahrhunderts zu zählen; außerdem kann die praktische Philosophie Fichtes (zumindest bis 1804) auch als eine solche Synthese, zumindest aber als Weiterentwicklung der kantischen Deontologie verstanden werden. Schließlich finden sich, worauf Douglas Moggach hingewiesen hat, auch schon bei Kant selbst thematische Erweiterungen der praktischen Philosophie, die in Richtung des postkantischen Perfektionismus weisen.

4   Diese Skepsis wird zum einen dadurch genährt, dass die angestrebte Synthese auf der Ebene der metaethischen Reflexion bei einzelnen Vertretern kaum, manchmal auch gar nicht vorgenommen wird. Zum anderen finden sich in der Theoriefamilie des postkantischen Perfektionismus, dies zeigen auch die Beiträge in diesem Band, Konzeptionen, in denen einer der beiden Stränge deutlich gegenüber dem anderen überwiegt (wodurch Vertreter der jeweils anderen Tradition selbstverständlich umso mehr Bedenken haben).

5   Die seit drei Jahrzehnten vor allem in der analytischen Metaethik geführte Debatte um personale Autonomie stellt einen der zentralen Bereiche dar, in denen diese Frage verhandelt wird. Einen anderen, ebenfalls zentralen Bereich, in dem es um mögliche Synthesen aus deontologischen und perfektionistischen Theorieelementen geht, kann man in der Politischen Philosophie, insbesondere in der Auseinandersetzung von (moderaten) Gerechtigkeitstheorien mit (moderaten) Vertretern von perfektionistischen Ethiken identifizieren.

und -zwecke mitbestimmt.[6] Die *erste* zentrale Aufgabe besteht deshalb darin zu explizieren, in welchem Sinne von Autonomie die Rede sein soll. Kant hat seiner Ethik einen sehr engen Begriff von Autonomie im Sinne moralischer Selbstbestimmung zugrunde gelegt, doch schon seine philosophischen Zeitgenossen, wie auch die aktuelle Philosophie, sind ihm darin nicht gefolgt. Joel Feinberg hat in einem grundlegenden Beitrag die folgenden vier Dimensionen des Autonomiebegriffs unterschieden:

- autonomy as capacity
- autonomy as condition
- autonomy as ideal
- autonomy as right[7]

Damit ist "Autonomie" als ein dichter Begriff bestimmt, denn die Dimension der "capacities" zielt auf die *deskriptiven* Bedeutungskomponenten, d.h. auf diejenigen Eigenschaften und Fähigkeiten ab, über die ein X verfügen muss, um als autonom gelten zu können. Die anderen drei Dimensionen ("condition", "ideal" und "right") stellen dagegen unterschiedliche Konzeptionen der evaluativen Bedeutungskomponente des Begriffs der Autonomie dar.[8] Unter "autonomy as ideal" fasst Feinberg die *perfektionistische* Dimension des Autonomiebegriffs, die er als "ideal of the autonomous person" definiert, genauer als dasjenige Ideal "of an authentic individual whose self-determination is as complete as is consistent with the requirement that he is, of course, a member of a community"[9]. Die *deontologische* Dimension wird in der Konzeption von "autonomy as a right" erfasst, während die *axiologische* Dimension in der Konzeption von "autonomy as a condition" eingefangen wird, wodurch Autonomie als ein nicht nur potentiell, sondern aktual vorliegender wertvoller Zustand bzw. als ein verwirklichtes Gut bestimmt wird.[10]

---

6   Wir beschränken uns hier auf die Philosophie, lassen also z.B. juristische, soziologische oder politologische Verwendungen von „Autonomie" außen vor.
7   Vgl. Feinberg (1986), Kapitel 2.
8   Wir verwenden hier „evaluativ" als Oberbegriff für „deontologisch" und „axiologisch".
9   Feinberg (1986), 47.
10 Zur Explikation der deontologischen Dimension verweist Feinberg ((1986), 47) auf den modellbildenden Fall der Selbstgesetzgebung und Souveränität politischer Gebilde; den Transfer dieser politischen Konzeption auf das sich moralisch selbst die Regeln gebende Subjekt hatte schon Kant vorgenommen. Zur Charakterisierung der axiologischen Dimension zählt Feinberg ((1986), 32-44) summarisch eine ganze Fülle denkbarer und in der Literatur auch vorfindlicher Ausgestaltungen auf: self-possession, individuality, authenticity, self-determination, self-creation, self-legislation, moral authenticity, moral independence, integrity, self-control, self-reliance, self-generation und responsibility for self.

Es ist ersichtlich, dass diese Dreiteilung der evaluativen Bedeutungskomponente der dichten Konzeption von Autonomie vor dem in diesem Band explizierten philosophiegeschichtlichen Hintergrund verständlich wird. Zudem liegt auf der Hand, dass jede ethische und metaethisch präzisierte Konzeption, die den Autonomiebegriff verwendet, an dieser Stelle Klärungsarbeit zu leisten hat.[11]

Die *zweite* zentrale Aufgabe für jede Version eines postkantischen Perfektionismus besteht darin, den metaethischen Status der evaluativen Bedeutungskomponente der zugrunde gelegten Autonomiekonzeption zu explizieren. Auf der einen Seite des möglichen Spektrums stehen primär axiologisch ausgerichtete, rein konsequentialistische Konzeptionen, in denen Autonomie (als komplexe Fähigkeit zur rationalen Selbstbestimmung) lediglich ein instrumenteller Wert zuerkannt wird, der für die Verwirklichung des (oder der) eigentlich ethisch bedeutsamen Güter benötigt wird. Auf der anderen Seite finden sich primär deontologische Konzeptionen, die in der Autonomie das Fundament für moralische Rechte des Subjekts sehen, die alle anderen Güter (im Sinne deontologischer *side-constraints*) begrenzen. Die axiologische Dimension, bei Feinberg in der Liste der autonomy-conditions expliziert, wird dann zu einer bloßen Realisierungsbedingung oder aber als ethisch nachrangig angesetzt. Innerhalb des durch diese beiden Varianten aufgespannten Spektrums finden sich dann alle Konzeptionen des postkantischen Perfektionismus, die beide evaluativen Dimensionen als intrinsisch relevant ansehen, ohne zwischen ihnen lexikalische Vorrangregeln anzusetzen. In solchen Konzeptionen ist dann eventuell kontextspezifisch, möglicherweise sogar nur in Einzelfällen die genaue Abwägung der unterschiedlichen Aspekte möglich.

Eine *dritte*, keineswegs weniger anspruchsvolle Aufgabe ergibt sich für den postkantischen Perfektionismus aus der dritten Dimension der evaluativen Bedeutungskomponente des Autonomiebegriffs, die durch die Vorstellung von Autonomie als einem *Ideal* eine perfektionistische Vorstellung ins Spiel bringt. Damit aber gehen zwei Fragen einher, die man an jede so ausgelegte Variante des postkantischen Perfektionismus anlegen kann. Die erste Frage zielt darauf zu klären, ob „Perfektion" die Erreichung eines Optimums als Zielvorgabe meint, oder ob es stattdessen um die Entfaltung von Eigenschaften und Fähigkeiten

---

11 Anders als Feinberg, der die Extension von „ist autonom" mehr oder weniger eindeutig auf menschliche Personen begrenzt, ist die Theorielandschaft auch in dieser Frage mehrdeutig. Neben menschlichen Individuen werden auch ihre Handlungen (insbesondere Entscheidungen), gelegentlich aber auch Entitäten auf der überindividuellen Ebene (Gruppen, Nationen oder auch die Gattung) als Entitäten zugelassen, denen das Prädikat „ist autonom" zugeschrieben werden kann.

geht, die notwendig sind, damit den Individuen ein je individuell selbstbestimmtes Leben ermöglicht wird.[12] Die zweite Frage lässt sich provokant so formulieren: Wie hält es der postkantische Perfektionismus mit der Geschichtsphilosophie? Diese Frage lässt sich sowohl an die primär deontologischen als auch an die primär axiologischen Konzeptionen und damit auch an alle dazwischen liegenden Versionen des postkantischen Perfektionismus richten. Die Beiträge in diesem Band zeigen nachdrücklich, auf welch unterschiedliche Weise sich die in dieser Traditionslinie stehenden Ethikkonzeptionen zu geschichtsphilosophischen Voraussetzungen und Einbettungen verhalten. Die Rede von moralischem Fortschritt oder moralischer Perfektionierung des Menschen in der Geschichte gehört jedenfalls zum expliziten oder zumindest impliziten Theoriebestand vieler ethischer Konzeptionen.[13]

Mit den gerade identifizierten Fragen geht die *vierte* zentrale Aufgabe einer jeden Version des postkantischen Perfektionismus einher. Sie lässt sich in die folgende Frage kleiden: Wie weit reicht der Paternalismus, den die jeweilige Konzeption zulässt? Unter Paternalismus verstehen wir den ethisch begründeten Eingriff in eine selbstbestimmte Handlung von X durch Y (eine andere Person oder auch eine soziale Institution wie der Staat oder das Recht), die von Y damit gerechtfertigt wird, dem Wohl von X zu dienen (also im Minimalfall, Schaden von X abzuwenden). Jede Ethikkonzeption, die nicht auf rein deontologischer Basis ein ausnahmsloses Nichteingriffsgebot als Ausdruck des Respekts vor Autonomie annimmt, wird sich der Frage stellen müssen, wie weit der Paternalismus in diesem Sinne reichen darf.[14] Auch der postkantische Perfektionismus stellt diesbezüglich keine Ausnahme dar. Es liegt auf der Hand, dass die von uns bereits identifizierten Klärungsfragen (bzw. die damit verbundenen Weichenstellungen) für diese Fragestellung relevant sind. Je weniger die Perfektionierung auf das einzelne Individuum ausgerichtet ist, sondern die Vervollkommnung der Eigenschaften und Fähigkeiten der Gattung zum Ziel hat, desto größer wird das Ausmaß paternalistischer

---

12   Moderne Tugendethiken, aber beispielsweise auch der von Amartya Sen oder Martha Nussbaum entwickelte Befähigungs- bzw. ‚Verwirklichungschancenansatz' (*capability approach*), können als Illustrationen des mit „Optimierung vs. Ermöglichung" angedeuteten Spannungsfelds dienen. Vgl. Sen (2009) und Nussbaum (2006); vgl. auch die perfektionistisch unterfütterten Überlegungen zur Tugendethik in Hurka (1987); (1993), bes. Kapitel III und (2001).

13   Vielleicht stellen, wenn wir relativistische Selbstaufgaben der philosophischen Ethik außer Betracht lassen, nur solche Ethikkonzeptionen eine Ausnahme dar, die in der rein individuellen Selbstverwirklichung des einzelnen Individuums das ausschließliche Ziel der ethischen Perfektionierung sehen.

14   Es geht hierbei nicht um die Frage, wie man nicht-autonome Menschen in ihrer Entwicklung fördern und ihnen die Entwicklung ihrer Fähigkeiten ermöglichen kann.

Handlungsweisen sein, die sich perfektionistisch begründen lassen.[15] Genauso evident ist es, dass geschichtsphilosophische Voraussetzungen, die einen Paternalismus im Hier und Jetzt mit Verheißungen zukünftigen Wohls begründen, ein hohes Maß an Paternalismus gegenüber Individuen (und deren Handlungen) zulassen können. Letztlich gilt es zu klären, wie weit eine Pflicht zur Perfektionierung als ethisch legitimierbarer Zwang etabliert werden kann, in deren Namen man in die freie Lebensführung von Individuen eingreifen darf. Jede philosophische Ethikkonzeption, die auf materiale Aspekte, die mit der Vorstellung eines individuell gelingenden und sozial konzipierten guten Lebens einhergehen, nicht gänzlich zugunsten einer rein formalistischen Ethik verzichten will, wird diese Fragen zu beantworten haben. In diesem Problemkomplex laufen, so unsere Vermutung, die metaethischen und materialen Fragen, die jeder postkantische Perfektionismus beantworten muss, unauflöslich zusammen. Zugleich handelt es sich um reale Fragen und Konflikte, die sich für alle modernen Gesellschaften unausweichlich stellen, die an der Vorstellung individueller Freiheit innerhalb funktionierender und gerechter sozialer Institutionen festhalten wollen. Der postkantische Perfektionismus bzw. Autonomieperfektionismus stellt aus unserer Sicht für diese Aufgabe ein relevantes und vielversprechendes philosophisches Angebot bereit.

Literatur

Feinberg, Joel, *Harm to Self*, New York: Oxford University Press, 1986.
Hurka, Thomas, "Why value autonomy?", in: *Social Theory and Practice*, vol. 13, Nr. 3, Herbst 1987, S. 361-382.
– *Perfectionism*, Oxford, 1993.
– *Virtue, Vice, and Value*, Oxford, 2001.
Nussbaum, Martha C., *Frontiers of Justice. Disability, Nationality, Species Membership*, Cambridge/London, 2006.
Sen, Amartya, *The Idea of Justice*, Cambridge, 2009.

---

15 Es wäre im Prinzip sogar denkbar, dass die Ausbildung und Realisierung individueller Lebenspläne gar nicht als relevanter Aspekt anerkannt wird (wenn man z.B. nur die Autonomie der Gattung perfektionieren wollte).

Zu den Autorinnen und Autoren

MYRIAM BIENENSTOCK
wurde 1990 an der Universität Lyon mit einer Arbeit über Hegel habilitiert, danach Professorin für Philosophie in Grenoble und Tours. Gastprofessuren in Frankfurt, Zürich, Münster und Berlin. Ihre Forschungsgebiete sind Hegel und der Deutsche Idealismus; die Praktische Philosophie des Deutschen Idealismus, und das Jüdische Denken im 19. bis 20. Jahrhundert, bes. Hermann Cohen, Franz Rosenzweig und Emmanuel Levinas. Sie ist die Verfasserin der Monografien *Politique du jeune Hegel* (1992) und *Cohen und Rosenzweig. Ihre Auseinandersetzung mit dem deutschen Idealismus* (2018). Zudem hat sie Hegel, Herder, Fichte, Schelling und Hermann Cohen ins Französische übersetzt. Eine vollständige Publikationsliste findet sich auf ihrer Homepage: http://mbienenstock.free.fr.

STEFANIE BUCHENAU
is Maître de conférences (HDR) in German studies at the University Paris 8 Saint-Denis. She works mainly on German Enlightenment philosophy, and is currently co-editing the volume on anthropology in the new Kant Akademieausgabe, and preparing a monograph on human dignity in 18th Century German philosophy. Her recent publications include: *The Founding of Aesthetics in the German Enlightenment, The Art of Invention and the Invention of Art* (Cambridge: University Press, April 2013, paperback edition June 2015), *Médecine et philosophie de la nature humaine, de l'Age classique aux Lumières*, co-edited with Raphaële Andrault, Claire Crignon and Anne-Lise Rey (Paris: Classiques Garnier, 2014), *Human and Animal Cognition in Early Modern Philosophy and Medicine*, co-edited with Roberto Lo Presti (Pittsburgh: University Press, 2017).

SIMON DERPMANN
is postdoctoral researcher at the University of Münster and scientific coordinator of the graduate school "Democracy, Human Rights, and Religion" funded by the Volkswagen Foundation. His research focuses on 19th century social philosophy, especially John Stuart Mill and Karl Marx, and on economic philosophy. He is currently working on a project on the philosophy of money.

LUCA FONNESU
is Full Professor of Moral Philosophy at the University of Pavia. He has held visiting appointments in Mainz, Clermont-Ferrand, Halle and St. Andrews. His

publications include the Italian edition of Fichte's *Natural Right* (Roma-Bari 1994); *Storia dell'etica contemporanea* (Roma 2006); *Per una moralità concreta* (Bologna 2010). With Lucia Ziglioli he has co-edited *System und Logik bei Hegel* (Hildesheim-New York 2016).

MARIA CRISTINA FORNARI
is Associate Professor at the University of Salento (Lecce, Italy). She collaborates to the Italian edition of Friedrich Nietzsche's *Opere* and *Epistolario* (Adelphi, Milan). Among her publications: *La morale evolutiva del gregge. Nietzsche legge Spencer e Mill* (Pisa 2006; German translation: Wiesbaden 2009); *Friedrich Nietzsche, Epistolario 1885-1889* (editor, with Giuliano Campioni) (Milan 2011); *Nietzsche y el evolucionismo. Dos ensayos* (Córdoba, Argentina 2016); *Uma aventura de mais de um século: A história das edições de Nietzsche* (São Paulo, Brazil 2019). She is a member of several international research groups, including the team *Nietzsche et son temps* of the CNRS in Paris. She is currently working on the Franco-German project *La bibliothèque de Nietzsche. Edition numérique et commentaire philosophique* (Paris-Freiburg).

ROE FREMSTEDAL
is Professor at the University of Tromsø – The Arctic University of Norway and Associate Professor at NTNU Trondheim. He is author of *Kierkegaard and Kant on Radical Evil and the Highest Good: Virtue, Happiness, and the Kingdom of God* (Palgrave Macmillan 2014) and articles in *Inquiry, International Journal for Philosophy of Religion, Journal of Value Inquiry, Journal of Religious Ethics, Kantian Review, Kierkegaard Studies Yearbook* and *Religious Studies*.

SAMIR GANDESHA
is currently Associate Professor in the Department of the Humanities and the Director of the Institute for the Humanities at Simon Fraser University. He is co-editor with Lars Rensmann of *Arendt and Adorno: Political and Philosophical Investigations* (Stanford, 2012), and co-editor with Johan Hartle of *Spell of Capital: Reification and Spectacle* (University of Amsterdam Press, 2017) and *Aesthetic Marx* (Bloomsbury Press, 2017). In the Spring of 2017, he was the Liu Boming Visiting Scholar in Philosophy at the University of Nanjing and Visiting Lecturer at Suzhou University of Science and Technology in China. In 2019, he was Visiting Fellow at the Hochschule für Gestaltung in Karlsruhe and Visiting Lecturer at Faculdade de Filosofia, Letras e Ciências Humanas – FFLCH-USP (Universidade de São Paulo). He is currently editing a book entitled *Spectres of Fascism* (Pluto Press), co-editing with Peyman Vahabzadeh *Crossing Borders: Essays in Honour of Ian Angus* (Arbeiter Ring).

LOUGHLIN GLEESON
is a PhD candidate at UNSW, Sydney. He is also currently a casual academic at Macquarie University. His research is focused primarily on Hegel and his conception of 'concrete freedom.' In addition to presenting at numerous conferences, both domestically and internationally, he has published articles and book reviews on Hegel as well as contemporary Hegelian scholars such as Axel Honneth and Robert Pippin.

MAXIMILIANO HERNÁNDEZ MARCOS
is a Tenured Professor of History of Philosophy at the University of Salamanca. He has done research stays in Frankfurt am Main, Wolfenbüttel, Mainz and Marburg. His publications include the books *La „Crítica de la razón pura" como proceso civil* (Salamanca 1994), and *Tras la luz de la ley: legislación y justicia en Prusia a finales del siglo XVIII* (Madrid 2017); the editing of the texts *Hermann Heller, El sentido de la política y otros ensayos* (Valencia 1996), and *I. Kant, „Crítica de la razón práctica"* (Madrid 2017); and the co-editing of the collective volumes *Literatura y política en la época de Weimar* (Madrid 1998), and *La primera Escuela de Salamanca (1406-1516)* (Salamanca 2012).

HEIKKI IKÄHEIMO
is Senior Lecturer at University of New South Wales in Sydney. His publications include the monographs *Self-Consciousness and Intersubjectivity* (University of Jyväskylä, 2001) and *Anerkennung* (De Gruyter, 2014), as well as the co-edited collections *Dimensions of Personhood* (Imprint Academic, 2007), *Recognition and Social Ontology* (Brill, 2011), *The Ambivalences of Recognition* (Columbia University Press, forthcoming), and *Handbuch Anerkennung* (Springer, forthcoming).

DAVID LEOPOLD
is Associate Professor of Political Theory, Department of Politics and International Relations, University of Oxford, and John Milton Fellow, Mansfield College, Oxford. His research interests include Karl Marx, left Hegelianism, and utopianism. His publications include *The Young Karl Marx: German Philosophy, the Modern State, and Human Flourishing* (Cambridge, 2007), as well as scholarly editions of Max Stirner, *The Ego and Its Own* (Cambridge, 2000), and William Morris, *News From Nowhere* (Oxford, 2003).

DOUGLAS MOGGACH
is Distinguished University Professor at the University of Ottawa, and Honorary Professor of Philosophy at the University of Sydney. He has held

visiting appointments in Beijing, Cambridge, London, Münster, and Pisa. His publications include *The Philosophy and Politics of Bruno Bauer* (Cambridge 2003), and, as editor, *De pulchri principiis. Über die Prinzipien des Schönen* (Berlin 1996; new Italian edition *Sui Principi del Bello*, Palermo 2019); *The New Hegelians* (Cambridge 2006); and *Politics, Religion and Art: Hegelian Debates* (Northwestern 2011). With Gareth Stedman Jones, he co-edited *The 1848 Revolutions and European Political Thought* (Cambridge 2018).

NADINE MOOREN

Dr. phil. ist wissenschaftliche Mitarbeiterin am Philosophischen Seminar der Westfälischen Wilhelms-Universität Münster. Zu ihren Forschungsschwerpunkten gehören die Philosophie des Deutschen Idealismus und Linkshegelianismus, Philosophische Anthropologie und Ethik. Einschlägige Veröffentlichungen (Auswahl): *Hegel und die Religion. Eine Untersuchung zum Verhältnis von Religion, Philosophie und Theologie in Hegels System* (2018); zusammen mit Michael Quante Herausgeberin des 2018 erschienenen *Kommentars zu Hegels Wissenschaft der Logik*; „Mit Hegel gegen Hegel – Feuerbachs Religionsphilosophie in *Das Wesen des Christentums*" (2015).

DEAN MOYAR

is Associate Professor in the Department of Philosophy at Johns Hopkins University. He received his B.S. from Duke University and his Ph.D. from the University of Chicago. His essays have appeared in (among others) the *Journal of Moral Philosophy* and *Hegel-Studien*. He is the co-editor (with Michael Quante) of *Hegel's Phenomenology of Spirit: A Critical Guide* (Cambridge University Press, 2007), the editor of *The Routledge Companion to Nineteenth Century Philosophy* (2010) and *The Oxford Handbook of Hegel* (2017), and the author of *Hegel's Conscience* (Oxford University Press, 2011).

MICHAEL QUANTE

ist Professor für Praktische Philosophie und principle investigator des Exzellenzclusters *Religion und Politik* an der WWU Münster. Er ist Mitherausgeber der *Hegel-Studien* und Vorsitzender des Vorstands der *Internationalen Marx-Engels-Stiftung* (IMES).

Seine Hauptarbeitsgebiete sind der Deutsche Idealismus (insbesondere Hegel und Marx), die Philosophie der Person, Handlungstheorie und Ethik. Monografien zu Marx: *Der unversöhnte Marx* (Mentis 2018) und *Studi Sulla Filosofia Di Karl Marx* (Mailand 2018); Mitherausgeber von *Die linken Hegelianer* (Fink 2015; gemeinsam mit Amir Mohseni) und des *Marx-Handbuch* (Metzler 2016, gemeinsam mit David Schweikard) sowie Herausgeber kommentierter

Studienausgaben von *Karl Marx: Ökonomisch-philosophische Manuskripte* (Suhrkamp ³2018) und von *Karl Marx: Das Kapital* (Meiner 2019).

Tim Rojek

Dr. phil. ist wissenschaftlicher Mitarbeiter an der Westfälischen Wilhelms-Universität Münster. Er studierte Philosophie, Soziologie und Klass. Literaturwissenschaften an der Universität zu Köln und promovierte zu Hegels Geschichtsphilosophie an der Universität Münster. Forschungsschwerpunkte: Klass. dt. Philosophie, Philosophie der Geistes- und Sozialwissenschaften, Geschichte des Hegelianismus und Marxismus. Seine Dissertation erschien in Buchform 2017 bei deGruyter und 2018 als Taschenbuch unter dem Titel „Hegels Begriff der Weltgeschichte. Eine wissenschaftstheoretische Studie" (Berlin/Boston 2017).

Eva Schürmann

has held the Chair for Philosophical Anthropology and Philosophy of Culture and Technology at the Otto-von-Guericke-University Magdeburg since 2011. For her book *Sehen als Praxis* (Suhrkamp 2008) she was awarded the Science Prize by the Aby-Warburg-Foundation in 2014. In the academic year 2014/15, she was Research Fellow at the Käte Hamburger Center for Advanced Study 'Law as Culture'. Since 2015 she has been Co-editor of the *Allgemeine Zeitschrift für Philosophie*. Her publications include *Vorstellen und Darstellen. Szenen einer medienanthropologischen Theorie des Geistes*. (Fink 2018) and *Seeing as practice*, Philosophical Investigation into the Relation between Sight and Insight, Palgrave Macmillan 2019.

Michael Kuur Sørensen

holds a PhD from the European University Institute, Florence. He has published mainly in the fields of European intellectual history as well as in the history of the welfare state in Europe.

Norbert Waszek

wurde 1984 (das Buch erschien 1988) an der Universität Cambridge mit einer Arbeit über Hegel und die schottische Aufklärung promoviert und 1998 unter der Leitung von Bernard Bourgeois an der Sorbonne habilitiert. Nach einer ersten Professur an der Universität Rouen, ist er seit 2003 Professor an der Universität Paris VIII (Vincennes à Saint-Denis). Im akademischen Jahr 2017/18 war er Gastprofessor am Zentrum für klassische deutsche Philosophie (Hegel-Archiv) der Ruhr-Universität-Bochum. Zentrale Forschungsgebiete sind die Aufklärung, Hegel und die Hegelsche Schule. Eine vollständige Publikationsliste findet sich auf seiner Internetseite: http://norbertwaszek.free.fr.

Personenregister

Abbt, Thomas   76, 93, 101, 111
Achenwall, Gottfried   48
Adler, Anthony Curtis   158
Adorno, Theodor W.   170, 371, 373-395
Aldermann, Harold   334
Apel, Karl-Otto   388
Aquinas, Thomas   297, 333
Aristotle (Aristoteles)   5-6, 15, 90, 97, 164-165, 272, 333, 337, 338
Augustine   297
Avineri, Shlomo   184, 193, 195-196

Baader, Franz von   75
Bauer, Bruno   14, 20, 22-23, 153, 183, 191, 203-223, 233, 236, 284, 374, 380, 395
Bauer, Edgar   191-192
Bauer, Otto   241
Baumgarten, Siegmund Jacob   92-93
Becker, Hellmut   384
Beckett, Samuel   126
Benjamin, Walter   376-377
Bentham, Jeremy   71
Berlin, Isaiah   92, 336
Bernstein, Eduard   367
Bernstein, J.M.   392
Biester, Johann Erich   64
Bilfinger, Georg Bernhard   93
Bloch, Ernst   284
Bonnet, Charles   98
Booher, Richard   92
Bosanquet, Bernard   23
Bradley, Francis Herbert   23
Brandes, Ernst   51
Brandom, Robert   165
Buffon, Georges-Louis Leclerc   96
Burke, Edmund   29, 105
Butler, Joseph   298
Byington, Steven Tracy   270, 275

Carmer, Johann Heinrich von   47
Cassirer, Ernst   3, 351-352, 354-356
Cavell, Stanley   331, 333-337, 341-343
Cicero   29, 44, 46, 48
Cieszkowski, August von   185, 232-233, 240
Cohen, Hermann   351-359, 361, 363-368

Coleridge, Samuel Taylor   125
Colli, Giorgio   332
Conant, James   333, 335, 337, 342
Conway, Daniel W.   341
Coulthard, Joseph   318

Darjes, Joachim Georg   48
Davenport, John   299, 302-303
Deleuze, Gilles   170
Descartes, René   70
Dewey, John   345
Diamond, Cora   334
Dostojewski, Fjodor Michailowitsch   126, 193

Emerson, Ralph Waldo   334-337, 342, 345
Engels, Friedrich   245, 256, 260
Ense, Karl August Varnhagen von   190
Epicur   141, 298

Feder, Johann Georg Heinrich   8
Feinberg, Joel   401-402
Ferenczi, Sandor   390-391, 393-394
Ferguson, Adam   48
Feuerbach, Ludwig   272-274, 276, 284, 287, 376, 395
Fichte, Johann Gottlieb   2, 11-12, 15, 17-19, 21-22, 76-86, 103-104, 106-108, 133-135, 139-161, 179-181, 205, 220, 230, 250, 353-356, 358-359, 361-364, 368, 387, 399
Foucault, Michel   334, 345
Frankfurt, Harry   122
Freud, Anna   391
Freud, Sigmund   390
Friedrich II.   46
Friedrich Wilhelm III.   186-188
Friedrich Wilhelm IV.   187, 219
Fromm, Erich   375

Gans, Eduard   14, 22, 183-192, 194-198, 218
Garve, Christian   29, 46-51, 61-62
Gentz, Friedrich von   51
Gerhardt, Volker   353
Gutmann, Thomas   310, 324
Guyer, Paul   14, 22

Habermas, Jürgen   170, 302, 374, 388
Hadot, Pierre   334
Hannay, Robert Alasdair   306
Hegel, Georg Wilhelm Friedrich   12-13, 18, 22, 69, 75, 84-86, 106, 124, 135, 163-181, 183-189, 192-197, 204-205, 207, 214, 216, 218, 223, 231, 235-239, 239, 252, 301, 354, 368, 372-373, 376, 378, 380, 382-385, 388-389, 391, 395
Heidegger, Martin   334, 377
Heine, Heinrich   190
Heinig, Hans Michael   194
Henrich, Dieter   187
Herder, Johann Gottfried   13, 22, 37, 76, 89-111
Heß, Moses   240
Heydenreich, Karl Heinrich   53
Hobbes, Thomas   5, 7, 15, 86, 105, 109-110, 179
Hobsbawm, Eric   375
Hölderlin, Friedrich   77, 84-85
Hollingdale, Reginald John   335
Homer   378
Honneth, Axel   168
Horkheimer, Max   373, 375, 378-379, 388, 395
Hufeland, Gottlieb   8-10, 19, 53
Humboldt, Wilhelm von   2, 9-12, 19, 21-23, 84, 156, 318-319, 321
Hume, David   48
Hurka, Thomas   89, 277, 331, 337-339

Irwin, Terrence   298
Iselin, Isaak   101

Kant, Immanuel   1-5, 7-23, 29-55, 59-66, 69-86, 91, 102-104, 109-111, 117-119, 121, 124-125, 132, 135, 139-141, 143, 145, 147-148, 152, 171, 175, 194, 204-205, 216, 228, 231-233, 236, 250, 263, 291-305, 333, 335, 338, 340-341, 351-355, 357-363, 365-367, 371-374, 376, 379-380, 382-383, 385-387, 389-395, 399-404
Kersting, Wolfgang   8
Kierkegaard, Søren   2, 23, 291-306
Kirmmse, Bruce H.   305
Klein, Ernst Ferdinand   49-50, 65
Körner, Christian Gottfried   117, 130
Kosch, Michelle   146, 148-150, 152, 154
Kreines, James   166

Kroner, Richard   372, 391
Kürnberger, Ferdinand   382

Lange, Friedrich Albert   366-368
Lassalle, Ferdinand   368
Leibniz, Gottfried Wilhelm   1, 3-5, 7-8, 10-11, 15-16, 21-22, 30, 33, 36-37, 40, 48-49, 74, 76, 102, 106, 111, 353, 356, 382-383, 399
Lessing, Gotthold Ephraim   73, 101, 103
Locke, John   6, 385
Löwenthal, Leo   375
Lübbe, Hermann   184
Ludovisi, Juno   127-128
Lukacs, Georg   376

Mackay, John Henry   280
Macor, Laura Anna   30
Marcuse, Herbert   375, 384
Marx, Karl   2, 12, 14, 17, 20, 22-23, 77, 185, 221, 234, 245-267, 270, 273, 376, 378, 384-387, 395
Mendelssohn, Moses   38, 73, 76-79, 92-95, 103
Mill, John Stuart   2, 309-329
Montesquieu, Charles de Secondat   385
Montinari, Mazzino   332
Moor, Karl   130
Morris, William   105
Möser, Justus   51-52, 54
Mozart, Wolfgang Amadeus   125
Murdoch, Iris   334

Nehamas, Alexander   334
Nietzsche, Friedrich   3, 22-23, 331-347, 379, 390-391
Nussbaum, Martha   403

Pascal, Blaise   342
Payley, William   48
Piazzesi, Chiara   342, 345
Pickford, Henry   385
Pinkard, Terry   165, 373
Pippin, Robert   165-167, 373
Plato (Platon)   94, 161, 332, 337-338, 342, 358, 364
Proudhon, Pierre-Joseph   273

Rancière, Jacques   127-128, 131-132
Rawls, John   331-336

PERSONENREGISTER 413

Raz, Joseph 23
Réaumur, René-Antoine Ferchault 98
Redding, Paul 373
Rehberg, August Wilhelm 45, 51-56, 60, 62-63, 65-66, 102
Reid, Thomas 48
Reimarus, Samuel Hermann 97
Reinhold, Karl Leonhard 9, 74-75, 77, 122, 140
Rosenkranz, Karl 184, 188
Rousseau, Jean Jacques 30-32, 46, 53, 77, 80, 85, 91-92, 97, 99, 105
Ruda, Frank 195-196
Ruge, Arnold 14, 20, 23, 190-192, 212, 227-228, 231, 233-241
Rutherford, Donald 338-339

Sade, Donatien Alphonse Francois de 379
Sandel, Michael 310
Schelling, Friedrich Wilhelm Joseph 76-77, 85-86, 125
Schiller, Friedrich 2, 9, 19, 21, 76, 82-85, 103-104, 117-135, 351, 353-355
Schlegel, Friedrich 333
Schopenhauer, Arthur 333
Schumm, George 270
Schusterman, Richard 345
Sen, Amartya 23, 403
Shakespeare, William 108
Shuster, Martin 390, 394
Smith, Adam 40, 48
Socrates (Sokrates) 100-101, 283
Sohn-Rethel, Alfred 384

Spalding, Johann Joachim 30, 32, 76, 93
Spinoza, Baruch de 70, 333
Stein, Lorenz von 193
Stirner, Max (Schmidt, Johann Kaspar) 14, 206, 233, 256, 264, 269-289
Strauß, David Friedrich 185
Svarez, Carl Gottlieb 47, 49-50
Swammerdam, Jan 98
Szondi, Peter 117

Taylor, Charles 90, 165
Taylor, Harriet 310, 325-327
Thoreau, Henry David 334
Tocqueville, Alexis de 312-313
Traverso, Enzo 381
Tucker, Benjamin R. 270

Voltaire 382-383

Wagner, Richard 333
Wannenmann, Peter 186, 189
Ware, Owen 152-153
Weitling, Wilhelm 273
Wittgenstein, Ludwig 334, 345
Wolff, Christian 1, 3, 5-12, 14, 18-19, 30-31, 33, 36-37, 46-49, 54, 72, 76, 93, 108-109, 111, 156, 228, 230-231, 353, 356, 371, 399
Wood, Allen 150-152

Yeomans, Christopher 159

Zychlinsky, Franz Zychlin von 284